The Practical
Bible
Dictionary

The Practical
Bible
Dictionary

Featuring the King James and
Barbour Simplified King James Versions

- Covers People, Places, Things, and Concepts

- Concise and Easy to Understand

- Includes Concordance of Key Words
  and Phrases

- Approximately 3,000 Entries

The
Barbour
Simplified
KJV

BARBOUR
PUBLISHING

Published by Barbour Publishing, Inc., 1810 Barbour Drive, Uhrichsville, Ohio 44683, www.barbourbooks.com

Our mission is to inspire the world with the life-changing message of the Bible.

Member of the
Evangelical Christian
Publishers Association

Printed in China.

INTRODUCTION

This book combines an up-to-date Bible dictionary and a user-friendly concordance to make your study of God's Word easier and more efficient. *The Practical Bible Dictionary* is based on the Simplified King James Version, an adaptation of the classic King James Bible. This refinement has resulted in a text that is easier to understand, while preserving the familiarity and beauty of the original KJV. In those few cases where key words differ from one version to the other—for example, *Melita* (KJV) and *Malta* (SKJV)—cross-references direct you to the appropriate words in the text.

The concordance section of the book is more than a listing of key biblical words with the passages where they occur. You will also find many important phrases such as *Body of Christ*, *Kingdom of God*, and *Right Hand of God*. In addition, many pivotal biblical events such as *Plagues Against Egypt* are included as concordance entries. These handy features should simplify your search for important facts and concepts that appear in the Bible.

To save space, the phrases "Old Testament" and "New Testament" are abbreviated as OT and NT, respectively. When you see **boldface type** in the Bible references of an entry, it indicates that these references contain the most important information on the subject.

The Practical Bible Dictionary comes to you with the prayer that it will become one of your go-to resources for exploring the riches of God's Word.

BARBOUR PUBLISHING, INC.

AARON. Elder brother of Moses and first high priest of Israel who served as Moses' spokesman. A direct descendant of Levi by both his parents, he performed several miracles during the Exodus from Egypt (Exod. 7:19). Aaron helped Hur hold up the hands of Moses during a battle with Amalek in the wilderness to bring victory to the Israelites (Exod. 17:9–12). But he yielded to idolatry when he encouraged the people to worship a golden calf (Exod. 32). In spite of this shortcoming, he was anointed and sanctified, with his sons, to minister in the priest's office (Exod. 40:12–16). Along with their sister Miriam, Aaron complained against Moses' leadership, but repented and joined Moses to pray for her recovery when she was struck with leprosy (Num. 12). His authority was affirmed by the miraculous sprouting of his staff (Num. 17:7–8). He died on Mount Hor before entering Canaan, and was succeeded as high priest by his son Eleazar (Num. 20:23–29).

Aaron is also mentioned in **Exod. 4:14; 5:1; 7:10–20; 28:1 • Lev. 8:2–27; 10:8–19 • Num. 4:19; 16:3; 17:3–10; 20:12** • 1 Chron. 6:49 • Ps. 105:26; 133:2 • Luke 1:5 • Acts 7:40 • Heb. 5:4; 7:11; 9:4.

ABANA. KJV: See *Abanah*

ABANAH. A river of Damascus, one of two which the leper Naaman preferred to go to for healing (2 Kings 5:12). The Abanah may be the same river as the Barada in modern Syria.

ABANDON [ED]
Judg. 2:12 they [Israel] *a'ed* the LORD God of their fathers
Judg. 10:13 Yet you [Israel] have *a'ed* Me and served other gods
1 Kings 19:10 children of Israel have *a'ed* Your covenant, thrown down Your altars
2 Chron. 12:1 he [Rehoboam] and all Israel with him *a'ed* the law of the LORD
2 Chron. 15:2 if you *a* Him, He will *a* you
Ezra 8:22 His [God's] power and His wrath are against all those who *a* Him

Neh. 9:31 for Your [God's] great mercies' sake... did not utterly destroy...or *a* them
Isa. 1:28 those who *a* the LORD shall be destroyed
Isa. 54:7 for a small moment I [God] have *a* you, but with great mercies I will gather
Isa. 55:7 Let the wicked *a* his way...and let him return to the LORD
Jer. 12:7 I [God] have *a'ed* My house. I have left My heritage

ABARIM. A mountain range east of the Jordan River in the territory of Moab, near the site of the ancient city of Jericho (Deut. 32:49). Its highest peak was Mount Nebo, from which Moses viewed the promised land before his death.

ABASED. KJV: See *Humbled*; *Cast Down*

ABATED. See also *Weakened*
Gen. 8:3 hundred and fifty days the waters were *a*
Judg. 8:3 their anger was *a* toward him [Gideon]

ABBA. An Aramaic word meaning "father" or "daddy." Jesus addressed the Lord with this word when praying in Gethsemane to show His close relationship to God the Father. The word is used in Mark 14:36 • Rom. 8:15 • Gal. 4:6.

ABDON. (1) A minor judge of Israel from the tribe of Ephraim who ruled for eight years (Judg. 12:13–15). He may be the same person as Bedan (1 Sam. 12:11).

(2) A messenger sent by King Josiah to ask about the Book of the Law discovered in the temple (2 Chron. 34:20–21).

ABED-NEGO. One of three young Israelites delivered miraculously from the flaming furnace of King Nebuchadnezzar of Babylon. He is mentioned in Dan. 2:49; 3:12–30. *Azariah*: Dan. 1:7.

ABEL. (1) The second son of Adam and Eve who was murdered by his brother Cain in a fit of jealousy (Gen. 4:2–25). Jesus referred to Abel as the first martyr and a righteous man (Matt.

23:35; see also Heb. 11:4). He is also mentioned in Luke 11:51 • Heb. 12:24.

(2) A fortified city where the rebel Sheba was killed when he fled from King David's army (2 Sam. 20:14, 22).

ABEL-BETH-MAACAH. A fortified town in northern Israel which was besieged by the invading armies of Syria (1 Kings 15:20), and Assyria (2 Kings 15:29).

ABEL-MEHOLAH. A town east of the Jordan River where the prophet Elisha lived and worked (1 Kings 19:16). The Midianites fled here after their defeat by the judge Gideon (Judg. 7:22).

ABEL-SHITTIM. A place in Moab where the wandering Israelites camped before entering Canaan (Num. 33:49). Also called *Shittim* (Num. 25:1).

ABEZ. A town in northern Israel allotted to the tribe of Issachar after the conquest of Canaan (Josh. 19:17–20).

ABIA. KJV: see *Abijah*

ABI-ALBON. One of David's "mighty men," an elite group of warriors known for their bravery in battle (2 Sam. 23:31).

ABIATHAR. A high priest and loyal ally of King David. Abiathar fell into disfavor when he supported a rival to Solomon as David's successor. The new king stripped him of his leadership role and banished him from Jerusalem (1 Kings 2:22–35). He is also mentioned in 1 Sam. 22:20–22; 23:6, 9; 30:7 • 2 Sam. 8:17; 15:24–35; 17:15; 19:11; 20:25 • 1 Kings 1:7–42; 4:4 • 1 Chron. 15:11; 18:16; 24:6; 27:34 • Mark 2:26.

ABIB. The first month of the Hebrew year (Exod. 23:15) when the two major festivals known as Passover and the Feast of Unleavened Bread were celebrated. This month was called *Nisan* after the Exile (Esther 3:7).

ABIDE [ING, S]. See also *Endure*; *Remain*; *Stay*

1 Kings 8:13 a house to dwell in, a settled place for You [God] to *a* in

Ps. 15:1 Lord, who shall *a* in Your tabernacle?

Ps. 91:1 shall *a* under the shadow of the Almighty

Ps. 119:90 You [God] have established the earth, and it *a's*

Luke 2:8 shepherds *a'ing* in the field, keeping watch

Luke 9:4 whatever house you enter into, *a* there

John 12:46 whoever believes in me [Jesus]...not *a* in darkness

John 14:16 another Comforter...may *a* with you forever

John 15:4 A in me [Jesus], and I in you

John 15:5 He who *a's* in me [Jesus]...brings forth much fruit

John 15:10 keep My [Jesus'] commandments...*a* in My love

1 Pet. 1:23 the word of God, which lives and *a's* for ever

1 John 2:10 He who loves his brother *a's* in the light

1 John 2:17 but he who does the will of God *a's* for ever

1 John 2:28 a in Him [Jesus]...we may have confidence...at His coming

1 John 3:14 He who does not love his brother *a's* in death

1 John 3:15 no murderer has eternal life *a'ing* in him

ABIEL. One of David's "mighty men," an elite group of warriors known for their bravery in battle (1 Chron. 11:32).

ABIEZER. One of David's "mighty men," an elite group of warriors known for their bravery in battle (2 Sam. 23:27).

ABIGAIL. Wife of Nabal, a wealthy herdsman, and later a wife of David. When Nabal insulted David's messengers, Abigail supplied David and his followers with food and appeased his anger. After Nabal died, David took Abigail as his wife (1 Sam. 25:1–39). She bore him a son, Chileab (2 Sam. 3:3). Abigail is also mentioned in 1 Sam. 27:3; 30:5 • 2 Sam. 2:2 • 1 Chron. 3:1.

ABIHAIL. Father of Queen Esther of Persia who died when Esther was young (Esther 2:15; 9:29).

ABIHU. Son of Aaron (Exod. 6:23). He was guilty, with his brother Nadab, of making a blasphemous offering to the Lord. Both were consumed by fire from heaven at God's command (Num. 3:4).

ABIJAH. Son and successor of Rehoboam as king of Judah (the Southern Kingdom) (2 Chron. 12:16). He ruled for only three years. He was succeeded by his son Asa (2 Chron. 14:1). Abijah is also mentioned in 1 Kings 14:31; 15:1–8 • 2 Chron. 11:20–22; 12:16–14:1 • Matt. 1:7.

ABIJAM. KJV: See *Abijah*

ABILENE. A Roman district in Syria in the rugged territory north of Mount Hermon. The district was governed by the tetrarch Lysanias when John the Baptist launched his ministry (Luke 3:1).

ABIMELECH. (1) A Philistine king who took Abraham's wife Sarah into his harem after Abraham told him she was his sister. He returned her after learning she was actually married to Abraham (Gen. 20:1–18). Abimelech is also mentioned in Gen. 21:22–32; 26:1–31.

(2) A son of the judge Gideon who murdered his brothers and tried to become king over all Israel (Judg. 9:1–23). He was killed while attacking the fortified city of Thebez (Judg. 9:50–54). He is also mentioned in Judg. 8:31; 10:1 • 2 Sam. 11:21.

ABINADAB. (1) A Levite who kept the ark of the covenant for a time after it was captured and then returned by the Philistines (1 Sam. 7:1).

(2) A son of King Saul killed in a battle with the Philistines at Mount Gilboa (1 Chron. 10:1–6).

ABIRAM. An ally of Korah in a rebellion against Moses in the wilderness. He was swallowed by an earthquake because of his disobedience (Num. 16:1–33). Abiram is also mentioned in Num. 26:9 • Deut. 11:6 • Ps. 106:17.

ABISHAG. A young woman who served as David's nurse in his declining years (1 Kings 1:1–15). After David died, his son Adonijah asked permission to marry her, but Solomon had him put to death (1 Kings 2:13–25).

ABISHAI. A commander of David's "mighty men," an elite group of warriors known for their bravery in battle (2 Sam. 23:18). Abishai is also mentioned in 1 Sam. 26:6–9 • 2 Sam. 2:18, 24; 3:30; 10:10–14; 16:9–11; 18:2–12; 19:21; 20:6, 10; 21:17 • 1 Chron. 2:16; 11:20; 18:12; 19:11, 15.

ABISHALOM. KJV: See *Absalom*

ABITAL. One of David's wives and mother of his son Shephatiah (2 Sam. 3:2–5).

ABLE TO DELIVER

Isa. 36:14 Hezekiah...shall not be *a-t-d* you

Ezek. 7:19 silver and their gold shall not be *a-t-d* them

Dan. 3:17 our God...is *a-t-d* us [Daniel's friends]

ABLUTION. A purification ceremony in which a person's body or clothing were washed, a ritual prescribed in the OT Law (Exod. 40:12–13).

ABNER. The commander-in-chief of King Saul's army who introduced the heroic lad David to Saul (1 Sam. 17:55–57). Abner established Saul's son Ish-bosheth as king after Saul's death (2 Sam. 2:8–30), but later shifted his loyalty to David. He persuaded all the tribes of Israel to pledge their loyalty to David as king (2 Sam. 3:17–21). After Abner was killed by David's chief military officer, the king ordered Abner buried with full honors (2 Sam. 3:32–37). He is also mentioned in 1 Sam. 14:50–51; 20:25; 26:5–15 • 2 Sam. 4:1, 12 • 1 Kings 2:5, 32 • 1 Chron. 26:28; 27:21.

ABOLISH [ED]

Isa. 2:18 He [God] shall utterly *a* the idols

Isa. 51:6 My [God's] righteousness shall not be *a'ed*

Eph. 2:15 having *a'ed* in His [Jesus'] flesh the enmity...making peace

2 Tim. 1:10 Jesus Christ, who has *a'ed* death

ABOMINATION

ABOMINATION. Something considered repulsive or detestable (Gen. 46:34). This word is applied to several different practices that God hates, including idolatry (Deut. 7:25–26), blemished animal sacrifices (Deut. 17:1), child sacrifice (Deut. 12:31), and the practice of magic in all its forms (Deut. 18:9–12). Even pretending to worship while remaining disobedient to the Lord was considered detestable (Isa. 1:13).

ABOMINATION OF DESOLATION. See also *Abomination That Makes Desolate*
Matt. 24:15 see the *a-o-d*...stand in the holy place
Mark 13:14 see the *a-o-d*...standing where it ought not

ABOMINATION THAT MAKES DESOLATE. A phrase that refers to the setting up of an idol in the temple during a future time of great tribulation (Dan. 11:31; 12:11). Some believe this prophecy was fulfilled about 165 BC when a Greek ruler, Antiochus IV (Epiphanes), committed sacrilege by sacrificing a pig on the altar in the temple in Jerusalem. Others believe this phrase refers to the beginning of the end-time when an evil being will replace God and force believers to worship him (2 Thes. 2:3–4).

ABOMINATION TO THE LORD, THINGS CONSIDERED AN
1. Engraved images (Deut. 7:25)
2. The perverse (Prov. 3:32)
3. A false balance (Prov. 11:1)
4. Lying lips (Prov. 12:22)
5. Sacrifice of the wicked (Prov. 15:8)
6. Thoughts of the wicked (Prov. 15:26)
7. Everyone who is proud in heart (Prov. 16:5)

ABOUND [ED]
Rom. 5:15 much more did the grace of God...*a* to many
Rom. 5:20 where sin *a'ed*, grace *a'ed* much more
Rom. 6:1 Shall we continue in sin, that grace may *a*?
Rom. 15:13 *a* in hope through the power of the Holy Spirit
2 Cor. 8:7 in your love...see that you also *a* in this grace

Eph. 1:8 He [God] has *a'ed* toward us in all wisdom
Phil. 4:12 I [Paul] know...how to be cast down... how to *a*
1 Thes. 3:12 increase and *a* in love toward one another

ABOVE
Gen. 1:7 God...divided the waters...*a* the firmament
Exod. 19:5 a special treasure to Me [God] *a* all people
Exod. 20:4 not make...likeness of anything... in heaven *a*
Deut. 7:6 chosen you to be a special people...*a* all people
1 Kings 8:23 no God like You in heaven *a* or on earth beneath
1 Chron. 16:25 great is the LORD...to be feared *a* all gods
1 Chron. 29:11 You [God] are exalted as head *a* all
2 Chron. 2:5 for great is our God *a* all gods
Ps. 8:1 who [God] has set Your glory *a* the heavens
Ps. 57:5 Be exalted, O God, *a* the heavens
Ps. 95:3 For the LORD is...a great King *a* all gods
Ps. 99:2 The LORD...is high *a* all the people
Prov. 31:10 a virtuous woman? For her price is far *a* rubies
Jer. 17:9 The heart is deceitful *a* all things
Dan. 6:3 Daniel was promoted *a* the...princes
Matt. 10:24 The disciple is not *a* his master
John 8:23 You are from beneath; I [Jesus] am from *a*
1 Cor. 10:13 God...will not allow you to be tempted *a* what you are able
Eph. 1:21 far *a* all principality and power
Eph. 3:20 to Him [Jesus] who is able to do...*a* all that we ask
Eph. 4:6 One God...who is *a* all and through all
Eph. 6:16 *a* all, taking the shield of faith
Phil. 2:9 given Him [Jesus] a name...*a* every name
Col. 3:1 seek those things that are *a*
Col. 3:2 Set your affection on things *a*, not on... the earth

Jas. 1:17 Every good gift and every perfect gift is from *a*

Jas. 3:17 the wisdom that is from *a* is first pure

ABRAHAM. The first great patriarch of Israel who serves as a model of faithfulness for all believers. He obeyed the Lord's call to leave his home for a land that God would reveal to him. At the same time God made a covenant with Abraham to bless all nations of the world through his descendants (Gen. 12:1–5). The Lord also promised to give the land of Canaan to the nation of Israel that would develop through Abraham's family line (Gen. 13:14–18). This must have seemed like an empty promise, since Abraham and his wife Sarah were childless.

A son named Isaac was eventually born to the couple in their old age (Gen. 21:1–4). Then, as a test of his faith, the Lord told Abraham to offer Isaac as a sacrifice (Gen. 22:1–13). Just as he raised his knife to take his son's life, God intervened to save Isaac and again promised to bless Abraham for his unwavering faith (Gen. 22:15–18). Abraham died at 175 years of age and was buried beside Sarah near Hebron (Gen. 25:7–10). His original name, Abram, was changed by the Lord to Abraham to signify that he would be the father of many nations (Gen. 17:5). Jesus is called the "son of Abraham" in Matthew's genealogy in the first verse of the NT (Matt. 1:1).

Other highlights of Abraham's life include:
1. Separated from his nephew Lot (Gen. 13:1–12)
2. Blessing by Melchizedek (Gen. 14:17–20)
3. Son Ishmael born to Hagar (Gen. 16:15–16)
4. Circumcised with his household (Gen. 17:10–27)
5. Interceded for Sodom and Gomorrah (Gen. 18:23–33)

Abraham is mentioned several times in the New Testament: Matt. 1:1–2, 17; 3:9; 8:11; 22:32 • Mark 12:26 • Luke 1:55, 73; 3:8, 34; 13:16, 28; 16:23–25, 29–30; 19:9; 20:37 • John 8:39–58 • Acts 3:13, 25; 7:2–32; 13:26 • Rom. 4:1–23; 9:7; 11:1 • 2 Cor. 11:22 • Gal. 3:6–18; 4:22 • Heb. 2:16; 6:13; 7:1–9; 11:8, 17 • Jas. 2:21–23 • 1 Pet. 3:6.

ABRAHAM'S BOSOM. A metaphor for the afterlife. In one of Jesus' parables, a beggar named Lazarus found peace and security in Abraham's bosom, while a rich man was consigned to everlasting punishment (Luke 16:19–24).

ABRAM. See *Abraham*

ABSALOM. The vain and arrogant son of King David who tried to take the kingship by force. He fell into disfavor with David when he killed his brother Amnon for molesting their sister Tamar (2 Sam. 13:20–39). Raising an army from among David's disgruntled subjects, he forced his father to flee from Jerusalem and gather his forces at Mahanaim beyond the Jordan River (2 Sam. 17:24–26). In the ensuing battle, Absalom was killed by David's commander Joab after his long hair got tangled in the branches of a tree (2 Sam. 18:9–15). David mourned grievously at his son's death (2 Sam. 18:32–33). Absalom is also mentioned in 2 Sam. 3:3; 13:1, 4; 14:1–33; **15:1–18:33;** 19:1–10; 20:6 • 1 Kings 1:6; 2:7 • 1 Chron. 3:2 • 2 Chron. 11:20–21.

ABSALOM'S PILLAR. A stone monument erected by David's son Absalom as a memorial to himself (2 Sam. 18:18). It symbolized his vanity and pride.

ABSTINENCE. To choose not to eat or drink certain things or to participate in pleasures of the flesh. The goal of this practice is to glorify God and to set an example for fellow believers (Rom. 14:21).

ABUNDANCE

1 Kings 18:41 Elijah said...there is a sound of an *a* of rain

Ps. 37:11 meek shall...delight themselves in the *a* of peace

Eccles. 5:12 a of the rich will not allow him to sleep

Matt. 12:34 the mouth speaks out of the *a* of the heart

Luke 12:15 life does not consist in the *a*...he possesses

ABUNDANT

1 Cor. 12:24 given more *a* honor to that part that lacked

2 Cor. 4:15 a grace...might overflow to the glory of God

2 Cor. 11:23 more *a* in labors, above measure in beatings

1 Tim. 1:14 grace of our Lord was exceedingly *a* with faith

1 Pet. 1:3 according to His [God's] *a* mercy has begotten us...to a lively hope

ACCAD. A fortified city built by Nimrod in the land of Shinar—an ancient kingdom between the Tigris and Euphrates rivers (Gen. 10:8–10).

ACCEPT [ED]

Job 42:9 The LORD also *a'ed* Job

Jer. 14:12 I [God] will not *a* them...consume them by the sword

Jer. 37:20 Let my supplication...be *a'ed* before you

Amos 5:22 burnt offerings...I [God] will not *a* them

Mal. 1:10 Nor will I [God] *a* an offering from your hand

Luke 4:24 no prophet is *a'ed* in his own country

Acts 10:35 he who fears Him [God]...is *a'ed* by Him

ACCEPTABLE

Ps. 19:14 meditation of my heart...*a* in Your [God's] sight

Prov. 21:3 To do justice...is more *a*...than sacrifice

Isa. 61:2 to proclaim the *a* year of the LORD

Luke 4:19 to preach the *a* year of the Lord

Rom. 12:1 bodies a living sacrifice...*a* to God

Eph. 5:10 proving what is *a* to the Lord

1 Tim. 2:3 good and *a* in the sight of God

1 Pet. 2:5 spiritual sacrifices *a* to God through Jesus Christ

ACCESS

Rom. 5:2 by whom [Jesus] we...have *a*...into this grace

Eph. 2:18 through Him [Jesus] we...have *a*...to the Father

Eph. 3:12 in whom [Jesus] we have...*a* with confidence

ACCO. A city on the Mediterranean coast near Mount Carmel (Judg. 1:31). This is the same city as Ptolemais, where the apostle Paul met with fellow believers (Acts 21:7). It is known today as Acre.

ACCOMPLISHED. See also *Ended*

Jer. 25:12 seventy years are *a*, that I [God] will punish the king of Babylon

Luke 2:6 days were *a* that she [Mary] should be delivered

Luke 12:50 how distressed I [Jesus] until it is *a*

Luke 18:31 things...concerning the Son of man shall be *a*

John 19:28 Jesus, knowing that all things were now *a*

ACCORD

Acts 1:14 All these with one *a* continued in prayer

Acts 2:1 Pentecost was...come, they were all with one *a*

Acts 2:46 one *a*...and breaking bread from house to house

Phil. 2:2 having the same love, being of one *a*

ACCOUNT [ED]. See also *Count; Consider*

Matt. 12:36 idle word that men speak, they shall give *a*

Luke 16:2 a of your stewardship...you may no longer be steward

Luke 20:35 a'ed worthy...neither marry nor are given in marriage

Rom. 14:12 every one...shall give *a* of himself to God

Gal. 3:6 Abraham believed God...*a'ed*...for righteousness

Phil. 4:17 I [Paul] desire fruit that may abound to your *a*

Philem. 18 owes you anything, put that on my [Paul's] *a*

1 Pet. 4:5 give an *a* to Him...ready to judge... the dead

ACCOUNTABILITY. A principal that humans are responsible to God and must answer to Him for their words, thoughts, and actions (Rom. 14:12).

ACCURSED
Josh. 6:18 keep yourselves from the *a* thing
Josh. 7:1 For Achan...took of the *a* things
Rom. 9:3 myself [Paul] were *a* from Christ for... countrymen
1 Cor. 12:3 no man speaking by the Spirit... calls Jesus *a*

ACCUSATION
Matt. 27:37 over His head His written *a*...JESUS THE KING OF THE JEWS
Luke 6:7 Pharisees watched Him [Jesus]...find an *a* against Him
John 18:29 Pilate...said, What *a* do you bring against this Man?

ACCUSE[D]
Matt. 12:10 "heal on the Sabbath day?"...they might *a* Him [Jesus]
Matt. 27:12 *a'd* by the chief priests...He [Jesus] answered nothing
Luke 3:14 "do not *a* anyone falsely...be content with...wages
Luke 11:54 catch something out of His [Jesus'] mouth, that they might *a* Him
Luke 23:2 *a* Him [Jesus]..."We found this fellow perverting the nation"

ACELDAMA. KJV: See *Akeldama*

ACHAIA. A province of Greece where the apostle Paul was charged with blasphemy by the Jews but released by a local official (Acts 18:12–17). Achaia is also mentioned in **Acts 19:21** • Rom. 15:26; 16:5 • 1 Cor. 16:15 • 2 Cor. 1:1; 9:2; 11:10 • 1 Thes. 1:7–8.

ACHAICUS. A Christian from the city of Corinth who visited Paul at Ephesus (1 Cor. 16:17–18).

ACHAN. A warrior under Joshua who kept some of the spoils of war taken at Jericho and hid them in his tent. God's displeasure at this act caused the Israelites to be humiliated by the defenders of the city of Ai. Achan was stoned to death for his deception (Josh. 7:16–25). He is also mentioned in Josh. 22:20 • 1 Chron. 2:7.

ACHAR. KJV: See *Achan*

ACHAZ. KJV: See *Ahaz*

ACHISH. A Philistine king of Gath to whom David fled for safety while on the run from King Saul (1 Sam. 21:10–14). Achish is also mentioned in 1 Sam. 27:2–12; 28:1–2; 29:6–10.

ACHMETHA. A Persian city where King Darius I discovered an important royal document. This decree from King Cyrus authorized the Jews to return to Jerusalem and rebuild the temple (Ezra 6:2–12).

ACKNOWLEDGE
Ps. 51:3 I *a* my transgressions...my sin is ever before me
Prov. 3:6 ways *a* Him [God], and He shall direct your paths
Jer. 3:13 *a* your iniquity, that you have transgressed against the LORD
Jer. 14:20 *a*, O LORD, our wickedness...sinned against You

ACQUAINTED
Ps. 139:3 You [God]...get *a* with all my ways
Isa. 53:3 a man of sorrows and *a* with grief

ACRE. See *Acco*

ACTS
Deut. 11:7 eyes have seen all the great *a* of the LORD
1 Sam. 12:7 reason with you...righteous *a* of the LORD
Ps. 103:7 His [God's] *a* to the children of Israel
Ps. 106:2 *a* of the LORD? Who can proclaim all His praise?
Ps. 145:4 One generation...shall declare Your [God's] mighty *a*
Ps. 150:2 Praise Him [God] for His mighty *a*

ACTS OF THE APOSTLES. A book of history in the NT which traces the expansion and development of the early church from the ascension of Jesus to Paul's imprisonment in Rome—a period of about thirty-five years. Written as a sequel to the Gospel of Luke, Acts was addressed to a man named Theophilus (Luke 1:3–4; Acts 1:1–2). The book shows how the Christian witness spread in accordance with the Great Commission of Jesus: (1) in Jerusalem (1:1–8:3), (2) throughout Judea and Samaria (8:4–12:25), and (3) to the entire world (13:1–28:31). Acts is known for its careful attention to detail and historical accuracy. It mentions ninety-five different people from thirty-two countries, fifty-four cities, and nine islands in the Mediterranean Sea.

The two major personalities of the book are the apostles Peter and Paul. In chapters 1–12, Peter takes the lead in proclaiming the gospel to nonbelievers, mostly of Jewish background, in and around Jerusalem. Paul becomes the leading witness in chapters 13–28, after his dramatic encounter with the living Christ on the road to Damascus (Acts 9:1–8). As the "apostle to the Gentiles," he traveled throughout the Mediterranean world, calling people to faith in Christ and founding churches to serve as outposts of righteousness in a pagan world.

ADALIA. A son of Haman who was executed, along with his father, when Haman's plot to destroy the Jews was exposed by Esther (Esther 9:7–10).

ADAM. The first man who was brought into being on the sixth day as the crowning achievement of God's creation (Gen. 1:26–27). Although he was created in God's image, he was fashioned from the dust of the earth. This symbolized His humble status as an earthbound being who owed his existence to the Lord. God placed Adam in a lush garden and gave him the task of working the ground (Gen. 2:15). The fruit from all the trees was his for the taking—with one exception. He was not to touch the tree of the knowledge of good and evil (Gen. 2:17).

Eve, Adam's female counterpart, yielded to temptation from Satan and ate the forbidden fruit, then encouraged Adam to do the same. This act of disobedience resulted in their expulsion from the garden and subjected them to a life of difficulties (Gen. 3:1–24). Adam's sin infected the entire human race (Rom. 3:23). But God sent another Adam—the last Adam,

Jesus Christ—to solve the problem caused by this original act of rebellion. Adam's legacy of death has been canceled by the atoning death of Jesus on the cross (1 Cor. 15:21–22).

Adam is also mentioned in Gen. **2:19–5:5** • Deut. 32:8 • 1 Chron. 1:1 • Job 31:33 • Luke 3:38 • Rom. 5:14 • 1 Cor. 15:45 • 1 Tim. 2:13–14 • Jude 14.

ADAMANT. A precious stone known for its extreme hardness. The prophet Ezekiel needed a forehead like adamant to preach to the strong-willed and rebellious Israelites of his time (Ezek. 3:9).

ADAR. The Babylonian name for the twelfth month of the Jewish year. Haman ordered the massacre of the Jews in Persia on the thirteenth day of this month (Esther 3:13).

ADBEEL. A son of Ishmael (Gen. 25:13).

ADINA. One of David's "mighty men," an elite group of warriors known for their bravery in battle (1 Chron. 11:42).

ADINO. A commander of David's "mighty men," an elite group of warriors known for their bravery in battle (2 Sam. 23:8).

ADMAH. A city near the Dead Sea destroyed with Sodom and Gomorrah (Deut. 29:23). Admah is also mentioned in Gen. 10:19; 14:2, 8 • Hos. 11:8.

ADMONISH[ING]
Rom. 15:14 you also are...also able to *a* one another
Col. 3:16 a'ing one another in psalms and hymns
2 Thes. 3:15 not...as an enemy, but *a* him as a brother

ADONI-BEZEK. A Canaanite king whose forces were defeated by the tribes of Judah and Simeon in the time of the judges (Judg. 1:3–7).

ADONIJAH. A son of David and rival of Solomon, another of David's sons, as heir to the throne (2 Sam. 3:4). Solomon won the struggle, and he seemed to harbor no animosity toward his brother. But this changed later when Adonijah asked the king's permission to marry Abishag, a member of David's harem. Solomon had Adonijah executed, apparently perceiving his request as a threat to his kingship (1 Kings 2:13–28). Adonijah is also mentioned in **1 Kings 1:5–53** • 1 Chron. 3:2.

ADONIRAM. A major official in the administration of King Solomon of Judah (1 Kings 4:6).

ADONI-ZEDEK. One of five Amorite kings who joined forces to oppose Joshua's army at Gibeon. They were defeated and put to death by Joshua (Josh. 10:1–26).

ADOPTION. An act of God's grace by which sinful people are justified by their faith in Jesus Christ and welcomed into the family of God. This concept appears several times in the writings of the apostle Paul. He probably based this idea on the practice of familial adoption among Roman families of his time. Adoptees were thought to be transformed into new persons—an apt illustration of the Christian believer's conversion (Gal. 4:4–5).

ADOPTION

Rom. 8:15 Spirit of *a*, by whom we cry, Abba, Father!
Rom. 8:23 waiting for the *a*...the redemption of our body
Gal. 4:5 that we might receive the *a* of sons
Eph. 1:5 predestined us to the *a* of children by Jesus Christ

ADORAIM. A city in southern Judah rebuilt and fortified by King Rehoboam of Judah (2 Chron. 11:5, 9).

ADRAMMELECH. (1) A pagan god worshipped by Assyrian colonists who settled in Samaria after the fall of the Northern Kingdom. Children were offered as sacrifices to this god (2 Kings 17:31).

(2) A son and assassin of Sennacherib, king of Assyria (2 Kings 19:37).

ADRAMYTTIUM. A seaport on the Mediterranean coast in the Roman province of Asia. Here the apostle Paul boarded a ship to begin his voyage to Rome (Acts 27:2).

ADRIA. KJV: See *Adriatic Sea*

ADRIATIC SEA. A name for the central part of the Mediterranean Sea due south of modern Italy. The apostle Paul was shipwrecked in these waters during his voyage to Rome (Acts 27:27).

ADULLAM. (1) A large cave in southern Israel where David hid from King Saul (1 Sam. 22:1–2).

(2) A defense city built by King Rehoboam of Judah, Solomon's son and successor (2 Chron. 11:7).

ADULTERY. Sexual intercourse with a person other than one's husband or wife, a sin specifically prohibited by the seventh of the Ten Commandments (Exod. 20:14). The adulterous relationship of King David and Bathsheba dramatizes the problems caused by this moral failure. Their encounter led to Bathsheba's pregnancy, and the king had her husband murdered to try to cover up his deed (2 Sam. 11:14–17). David confessed his wrongdoing and received God's forgiveness, but a series of disasters struck his family as a consequence of his action. Jesus expanded the concept of adultery to prohibit the cultivation of lust and desire which can lead to the actual act (Matt. 5:28).

ADULTERY

Exod. 20:14 You shall not commit *a*
Lev. 20:10 who commits *a* with another man's wife...put to death
Deut. 5:18 You shall not commit *a*
Prov. 6:32 whoever commits *a*...destroys his own soul
Jer. 7:9 Will you...commit *a*...and walk after other gods
Matt. 5:28 looks on a woman to lust...has already committed *a*
Mark 10:11 divorces his wife and marries another commits *a*
John 8:3 brought to Him [Jesus] a woman caught in *a*
Gal. 5:19 works of the flesh are...a, fornication
2 Pet. 2:14 eyes full of *a*...cannot cease from sin

ADVENT. A word meaning "arrival." In Christian usage, it refers to the arrival of God's Son in the world. Jesus left heaven and took on human flesh in order to reconcile the world to

God the Father. The season known as Advent is celebrated in many churches during the four successive Sundays before Christmas. It is a time of prayer, fasting, and quiet contemplation about the meaning and significance of Jesus' birth. The phrase "second Advent" refers to the second coming of Jesus. Just as He came to earth the first time, He will return to bring the world to its appointed end and to fulfill His promises to believers (Acts 1:10–11).

ADVERSARY. One who opposes or hinders another, an apt description of Satan (1 Pet. 5:8). Believers may draw on God's guidance to resist an adversary's power (Luke 21:15). God will eventually prevail over all His adversaries, including Satan (Rev. 20:1–10).

ADVERSARY [IES]

Deut. 32:43 He [God] will...render vengeance to His *a'ies*

1 Sam. 2:10 *a'ies* of the LORD shall be broken

1 Kings 5:4 has given me rest...there is neither *a* nor evil

Esther 7:6 The *a* and enemy is this wicked Haman

Ps. 69:19 my *a'ies* are all before You [God]

Ps. 74:10 how long shall the *a* reproach?

Ps. 109:29 Let my *a'ies* be clothed with shame

Nah. 1:2 The LORD will take vengeance on His *a'ies*

Matt. 5:25 Agree with your *a*...on the way with him

Luke 18:3 widow...came to him...Take vengeance on my *a*

Luke 21:15 wisdom, which all your *a'ies* shall not...resist

1 Cor. 16:9 great door...has opened...many *a'ies*

1 Pet. 5:8 *a* the devil...seeking whom he may devour

ADVERSITY

Ps. 35:15 in my *a* they rejoiced

Prov. 17:17 a brother is born for *a*

Prov. 24:10 faint in the day of *a*, your strength is small

Isa. 30:20 bread of *a* and the water of affliction

ADVOCATE. One who pleads the cause of another before a court of law; in modern terms, a defense attorney. This English word appears only once in the Bible, as a name or title of Christ: "If any man sins, we have an advocate with the Father, Jesus Christ the righteous" (1 John 2:1). The Greek word behind *advocate* in this verse appears four times in John's Gospel (14:16, 26; 15:26; 16:7). In these verses the word refers to the Holy Spirit, and it is translated as "Comforter" in the KJV and SKJV.

AENEAS. A lame man healed by Peter at Lydda near Joppa. His conversion influenced many people to turn to Christ (Acts 9:32–35).

AENON. A place near the Jordan River where John the Baptist was baptizing when Jesus launched His public ministry (John 3:23).

AFFECTION

Rom. 1:31 without understanding...without natural *a*

Col. 3:2 Set your *a* on things above, not...on the earth

Col. 3:5 Put to death...uncleanness, inordinate *a*, evil desire

2 Tim. 3:3 without natural *a*, truce breakers, false accusers

AFFLICT [ED]

Exod. 1:11 taskmasters...to *a* them [Israelites] with their burdens

Exod. 1:12 more they *a'ed* them [Israelites]... more they multiplied

Exod. 22:22 not *a* any widow or fatherless child

Exod. 22:23 afflict them and they cry...to Me, I will...hear their cry

Ruth 1:21 Almighty has *a'ed* me [Naomi]

1 Kings 11:39 I [God] will *a* the descendants of David for this

2 Kings 17:20 LORD rejected...Israel and *a'ed* them

Job 34:28 He [God] hears the cry of the *a'ed*

Ps. 44:2 You [God] *a'ed* the people and cast them out

Ps. 88:15 I have been *a'ed* and ready to die

Ps. 90:15 the days in which You [God] have *a'ed* us

Ps. 119:71 I have been *a'ed*, that I might learn Your statutes

Ps. 140:12 maintain the cause of the *a'ed*

Isa. 49:13 the LORD...will have mercy on His *a'ed*

Isa. 53:4 considered Him [Christ] struck... wounded...*a'ed*

Lam. 1:12 LORD has *a'ed* me in...His fierce anger

Lam. 3:33 He [God] does not willingly *a* or grieve

Nah. 1:12 Though I [God] have *a'ed* you, I will *a* you no longer

Matt. 24:9 deliver you up to be *a'ed*...for My [Jesus] name's sake

Heb. 11:37 wandered about in sheepskins...*a'ed*, tormented

Jas. 4:9 Be *a'ed* and mourn and weep

Jas. 5:13 Is anyone among you *a'ed*? Let him pray

AFFLICTION. Any condition that causes pain or suffering. Affliction may come as a result of God's judgment on sin (Rom. 2:9), or it may be God's method of purifying and perfecting the believer (2 Thes. 1:4–7). The apostle Paul described the Christian attitude toward affliction: "The sufferings of this present time are not worthy to be compared with the glory that shall be revealed in us" (Rom. 8:18).

AFFLICTION [S]

Gen. 29:32 the LORD has looked on my [Leah] *a*

Exod. 3:7 I [God] have surely seen the *a* of My people

Deut. 16:3 unleavened bread...the bread of *a*

Deut. 26:7 the LORD heard our voice and looked on our *a*

Job 30:16 days of *a* have taken hold of me

Ps. 25:18 Look on my *a* and my pain

Ps. 34:19 Many are the *a's* of the righteous

Ps. 119:153 Consider my *a*...for I do not forget Your [God's] law

Ps. 132:1 LORD, remember David and all his *a's*

Isa. 30:20 bread of adversity and the water of *a*

Lam. 1:3 Judah has gone into captivity because of *a*

2 Cor. 4:17 light *a*...is working for us...glory

Col. 1:24 fill up what is lacking in the *a's* of Christ

2 Tim. 4:5 endure *a's*...make full proof of your ministry

Jas. 1:27 visit the fatherless and widows in their *a*

AFRAID

Gen. 3:10 I [Adam] was *a*...and I hid myself

Gen. 28:17 he [Jacob] was *a*... How dreadful is this place!

Exod. 3:6 Moses...was *a* to look at God

Exod. 14:10 Egyptians marched after them. And they were greatly *a*

Num. 22:3 Moab was greatly *a* of the people [Israelites]

Deut. 7:18 You shall not be *a* of them

Deut. 31:6 Do not...be *a* of them...He [God] will not fail you

Josh. 1:9 Do not be *a*...God is with you

1 Sam. 18:12 Saul was *a* of David...the Lord was with him [David]

Esther 7:6 Haman was *a* before the king and queen

Job 3:25 what I was *a* of has come to me

Job 5:21 You shall not be *a* of destruction when it comes

Ps. 27:1 LORD...strength of my life. Of whom shall I be *a*?

Ps. 56:3 When I am *a*, I will trust in You [God]

Ps. 56:11 In God I have put my trust...I will not be *a* of what man can do to me

Ps. 91:5 You shall not be *a* of the terror by night

Isa. 12:2 God is my salvation. I will trust and not be *a*

Jer. 1:8 Do not be *a*...I [God] am with you to rescue you

Jer. 2:12 Be astonished...O heavens, and be horribly *a*...says the LORD

Jer. 42:11 Do not be *a* of the king of Babylon...I [God] am with you

Jer. 42:16 famine of which you were *a* shall follow close after you

Dan. 4:5 I saw a dream that made me [Daniel] *a*

Jon. 1:5 mariners were *a*, and every man cried to his god

Matt. 14:27 Jesus spoke...It is I; do not be *a*

Matt. 17:7 Jesus...said, Arise, and do not be *a*

Matt. 25:25 I was *a* and...hid your talent in the earth

Matt. 28:10 Do not be *a*. Go tell My [Jesus'] brothers

Mark 6:50 Be of good cheer. It is I [Jesus]. Do not be *a*

Mark 9:32 they [the disciples] did not understand...and were *a* to ask Him [Jesus]

Luke 2:9 and they [shepherds] were greatly *a*

Luke 12:4 do not be *a* of those who kill the body

John 14:27 Do not let your heart be troubled or let it be *a*

Acts 9:26 they [apostles] were all *a* of him [Paul]

Gal. 4:11 I [Paul] am *a* for you, lest I have bestowed on you labor in vain

AGABUS. A Christian prophet who warned Paul in Antioch of Syria of a worldwide famine (Acts 11:28). At Caesarea, Agabus predicted the apostle's impending arrest by binding his hands and feet with Paul's belt (Acts 21:10–11).

AGAG. (1) A king of Amalek in a prophecy of Balaam, who predicted that Israel's king would become more powerful than Agag (Num. 24:7).

(2) An Amalekite king spared by King Saul, in disobedience of God's command. This led to Saul's rejection as king of Israel by the Lord (1 Sam. 15:8–23).

AGAPE. A Greek word for selfless love, the type of love that God wants all believers to practice. Agape is primarily an act of the will rather than the emotions (Rom. 5:8). This love is the greatest of all Christian virtues. According to the apostle Paul's great discourse on agape love in 1 Corinthians 13, this love is long-suffering or patient, kind, unselfish, and generous; it is not vain or proud; it believes the best about people, giving them the benefit of the doubt when they are not on their best behavior. Such love is characteristic of God, the author of love (1 John 4:7).

AGAR. KJV: See *Hagar*

AGATE. A precious stone of the quartz family embedded in the breastplate of the high priest (Exod. 28:19).

AGREE [D]

Amos 3:3 Can two walk together unless they are *a'd*?

Matt. 5:25 A with your adversary quickly, while you are on the way with him

Matt. 20:13 Did you not *a* with me for a penny?

Mark 14:56 their testimonies did not *a* with each other

AGRIPPA. (1) Herod Agrippa I, Roman ruler over Galilee, who persecuted the Christians in Jerusalem (Acts 12:1–4).

(2) Herod Agrippa II, a Roman official before whom the apostle Paul appeared at Caesarea. He is mentioned in **Acts** 25:13–27; **26:1–32**.

AGUR. Author of Proverbs 30. He prayed that the Lord would deliver him from pride and dishonesty (Prov. 30:8–9).

AHAB. A wicked king of Israel (the Northern Kingdom) who led his people to worship the false god Baal and clashed often with the prophet Elijah. After succeeding his father, Omri, Ahab got off to a good start by building several new cities throughout the country. He also established peaceful relations with Judah, the sister nation to the south (1 Kings 22:2–4). But things took a turn for the worse when Ahab married Jezebel, daughter of a Phoenician king, and a worshipper of Baal. She influenced Ahab to encourage worship of this pagan god throughout Israel. In another binge of wrongdoing, he confiscated a man's property and had him killed to cover up the crime (1 Kings 21:1–16).

Elijah declared that God would punish the king for this wicked act (1 Kings 21:17–19). Several years later Ahab was killed in a battle with the Syrians. When his blood was flushed from his chariot, dogs lapped up the bloody water, in fulfillment of the prophet's grim prediction (1 Kings 22:38).

Ahab is also mentioned in 1 Kings 16:28–22:40 • 2 Kings 1:1; 3:1, 5; 9:7–29; 10:1–30; 21:3, 13 • 2 Chron. **18:1–34**; 21:6, 13; 22:3–8 • Mic. 6:16.

AHASUERUS. A king of Persia who selected the Jewish woman Esther as his queen. In the book of Esther, he is portrayed as a sensual pleasure-seeker who was vain, quick-tempered, and subject to manipulation by others (Esther 3:1–15). These characteristics seem to match the description of a Persian king known as Xerxes I, cited by historians. Ahasuerus deposed his first queen, Vashti, because she refused to obey his command to display her beauty to his drunken guests (Esther 1:10–12). Esther eventually succeeded her in the royal court. Esther convinced the king to allow the Jewish people to defend themselves from the death order he had issued against them (Esther 8:11–13). The king's wicked advisor Haman, who had instigated this decree, was hanged (Esther 8:7).

AHAVA. A town in Babylon situated on a canal or small stream of the same name. Here a group of exiles gathered with Ezra before beginning their journey back to Jerusalem (Ezra 8:15–31).

AHAZ. A king of Judah (the Southern Kingdom) known for his idolatrous practices. He made images of the pagan god Baal, offered children as sacrifices to the false god Molech, and worshipped at pagan high places (2 Kings 16:1–4). He paid for his wrongdoing with a series of humiliations from foreign nations, including Assyria (2 Kings 16:7–9). The one bright spot in Ahaz's reign was the message he received from the prophet Isaiah about the coming Messiah who would be known as Immanuel—God with us (Isa. 7:10–17). Ahaz is also mentioned in 2 Kings 15:38–16:20 • 2 Chron. 28:1–27 • Isa. 1:1; 7:1–12; 14:28; 38:8 • Hos. 1:1 • Mic. 1:1 • Matt. 1:9.

AHAZIAH. (1) Son and successor of Ahab as king of Israel (the Northern Kingdom). A Baal worshipper like his father (1 Kings 22:49–53), Ahaziah was injured in a fall after reigning for only two years. Rather than turning to God for help, he consulted a pagan god about his condition. He died soon thereafter in fulfillment of Elijah's prophecy (2 Kings 1:2–18). Ahaziah is also mentioned in 1 Kings 22:40 • 1 Chron. 3:11 • 2 Chron. 20:35–37.

(2) Son and successor of Jehoram as king of Judah (the Southern Kingdom). Ahaziah continued his father's evil ways by practicing idol worship. He was murdered by Jehu, a future king of Israel (the Northern Kingdom), and Ahaziah's evil mother-in-law Athaliah seized the throne for several years (2 Kings 9:27–28; 11:1–16). He is also mentioned in 2 Kings 8:24–9:29 • 2 Chron. 22:1–9.

AHIAM. One of David's "mighty men," an elite group of warriors known for their bravery in battle (2 Sam. 23:33).

AHIHUD. A leader from the tribe of Asher who helped divide the land of Canaan after the conquest (Num. 34:27).

AHIJAH. (1) One of David's "mighty men," an elite group of warriors known for their bravery in battle (1 Chron. 11:36).

(2) A prophet who told King Jeroboam I, first ruler of the breakaway Northern Kingdom, that the united kingdom of Solomon would split into two factions (1 Kings 11:29–39). Later, Ahijah foretold the death of Jeroboam's son and the elimination of his line from the kingship (1 Kings 14:1–8). Ahijah is also mentioned in 1 Kings 14:2, 18; 15:29 • 2 Chron. 9:29; 10:15.

AHIMAAZ. A spy who kept David informed about the actions of his rebellious son Absalom in Jerusalem (2 Sam. 15:27–36). When discovered, Ahimaaz fled for his life (2 Sam. 17:18–20). He is also mentioned in 2 Sam. 18:19–29 • 1 Chron. 6:8–9, 53.

AHIMELECH. (1) The high priest at the city of Nob who befriended David during his flight from Saul (1 Sam. 21:1–9). Saul ordered Ahimelech executed, along with more than eighty other priests at this location (1 Sam. 22:9–20). He is also mentioned in 1 Sam. 23:6 • 2 Sam. 8:17 • 1 Chron. 24:3, 6, 31.

(2) A Hittite who came to David's aid when he was fleeing from King Saul (1 Sam. 26:5–6).

AHINOAM. One of David's wives (1 Sam. 25:43) and mother of his firstborn son Amnon (2 Sam. 3:2).

AHITHOPHEL. An officer in King David's court who assisted Absalom in his revolt against the king (2 Sam. 15:12, 31–34). He committed suicide when he realized the plot would fail (2 Sam. 17:23). Ahithophel is also mentioned in **2 Sam. 16:15–23; 17:1–23; 23:34** • 1 Chron. 27:33–34.

AHOLIAB. A craftsman from the tribe of Dan who worked on the tabernacle in the wilderness (Exod. 31:6).

AI. A Canaanite city that turned back Joshua's assault because a warrior named Achan kept some spoils from the city of Jericho for himself. After Joshua dealt with this problem, the Israelites conquered the city (Josh. 7:2–5; 8:18–29). Ai is also mentioned in Josh. 9:3; 10:1–2; 12:9 • Ezra 2:28 • Neh. 7:32 • Jer. 49:3. *Aiath*: Isa. 10:28. *Aija*: Neh. 11:31.

AIATH. See *Ai*

AIJA. See *Ai*

AIJALON. A city west of Jerusalem where Joshua battled the five Amorite kings, during which the sun stood still (Josh. 10:12–13). In later years, King Rehoboam of Judah (the Southern Kingdom) turned this into one of his defense cities (2 Chron. 11:9).

AIJELETH SHAHAR. A musical term in the title of Psalm 22, probably indicating the melody to be sung.

AIN. Sixteenth letter of the Hebrew alphabet, used as a heading over Psalm 119:121–128. In the Hebrew language, each line of these eight verses begins with this letter.

AKELDAMA. A field near Jerusalem purchased with Judas' betrayal money, and the place where he committed suicide (Acts 1:19). The name means "field of blood."

AKKUB. A Levite after the Exile who explained the law as Ezra read it to the people (Neh. 8:7).

ALABASTER. A soft stone, similar to gypsum, which was carved into household items. Mary of Bethany anointed Jesus with fragrant oil from a flask made of alabaster (Mark 14:3).

ALAMOTH. A musical term of uncertain meaning in the title of Psalm 46, perhaps referring to a choir of women's voices.

ALARM

Jer. 4:19 the sound of the trumpet, the *a* of war

Joel 2:1 sound an *a*...for the day of the Lord is coming

ALEPH. First letter of the Hebrew alphabet, used as a heading over Psalm 119:1–8. In the Hebrew language, each line of these eight verses begins with this letter.

ALEXANDER. (1) A heretical teacher at Ephesus condemned by the apostle Paul (1 Tim. 1:19–20).

(2) Alexander the Great, Greek ruler and world conqueror. Although he is not mentioned by name in the Bible, Alexander is perhaps the "mighty king" of Daniel 11:3–4.

ALEXANDRIA. A city of Egypt on the Mediterranean coast, of which the learned Apollos was a native (Acts 18:24). Founded by Alexander the Great, it was well known for its extensive library, which drew scholars from throughout the ancient world. Citizens from Alexandria opposed Stephen, the first martyr of the church (Acts 6:9).

ALIEN. KJV: See *Foreigner*

ALIVE

Gen. 7:23 Noah only remained *a*, and those... with him

Ps. 41:2 The LORD will preserve him and keep him *a*

Ps. 71:20 You [God]...shall make me *a* again

Mark 16:11 when they heard that He [Jesus] was *a*...had been seen

Luke 15:24 my son was dead and is *a* again

Acts 1:3 He [Jesus] also showed Himself *a* after His passion

Rom. 6:11 dead indeed to sin but *a* to God through Jesus

1 Cor. 15:22 even so in Christ all shall be made *a*

Eph. 2:1 made you *a* who were dead in trespasses and sins

1 Thes. 4:17 we who are *a* and remain shall be caught up together

Rev. 1:18 I [Jesus] am *a* forevermore

Rev. 2:8 The first and the last, who was dead and is *a*

ALLIANCE. A treaty or agreement between nations or individuals (1 Kings 3:1). The prophets warned Israel against forming earthly alliances rather than depending on the Lord (Jer. 2:18).

ALLOW

Exod. 12:23 the LORD...will not *a* the destroyer to come in to your houses

Exod. 22:18 You shall not allow *a* witch to live

Judg. 16:26 A me [Samson] to feel the pillars on which the house stands

Ps. 16:10 nor will You [God] *a* Your Holy One to see corruption

Ps. 55:22 He [God] shall never *a* the righteous to be moved

Ps. 121:3 He [God] will not *a* your foot to be moved

Matt. 19:14 A little children to come to Me [Jesus]...do not forbid them

Acts 13:35 You [God] shall not *a* Your Holy One to see corruption

1 Cor. 10:13 God...will not *a* you to be tempted above what you are able

Rev. 2:20 you [church of Thyatira] *a* that woman Jezebel...to teach and to seduce

ALMIGHTY GOD. A title of God referring to His absolute power, used by the Lord Himself when talking to Abraham (Gen. 17:1).

ALMIGHTY GOD

Gen. 17:1 I am the *A-G*; walk before Me and be perfect

Rev. 19:15 He treads the winepress of the... wrath of *A-G*

ALMOND. A tree that bloomed in early spring. To the prophet Jeremiah, these blooms signaled God's coming judgment against the nation of Judah (Jer. 1:11–12).

ALMS. A KJV word for offerings of mercy made on behalf of the poor (Matt. 6:1–4; *deeds of*

charity: SKJV). Jesus declared that such giving should not be done in order to impress others. See also *Poor*.

ALOES. A spice used by Joseph of Arimathea and Nicodemus to prepare the body of Jesus for burial (John 19:38–40).

ALONE

Gen. 2:18 not good that the man should be *a*

Gen. 32:24 Jacob was left *a*...there a man wrestled with him

Exod. 24:2 Moses *a* shall come near the LORD

Num. 11:14 I [Moses] am not able to bear all these people *a*

Job 7:16 Leave me *a*, for my [Job's] days are a breath

Ps. 86:10 You are great...You are God *a*

Ps. 148:13 praise the name of the LORD...His name *a* is excellent

Eccles. 4:10 woe to him who is *a* when he falls

Isa. 2:11 the LORD *a* shall be exalted

Dan. 10:7 And I, Daniel, *a* saw the vision

Matt. 4:4 It is written, Man shall not live by bread *a*

Matt. 14:23 He [Jesus]went up...to pray...He was there *a*

Mark 1:24 Leave us *a*. What do we have we to do with You, Jesus

Mark 14:6 Leave her *a*. Why do you trouble her?

Luke 5:21 Who can forgive sins but God *a*?

John 12:24 unless a grain of wheat falls...and dies, it remains *a*

John 17:20 I [Jesus] do not ask for these *a*

Jas. 2:17 faith, if it does not have works, is dead, being *a*

ALPHA AND OMEGA. A title of Jesus that compares Him to the first and last letters of the Greek alphabet (Rev. 1:8, 11; 21:6–7). This is a poetic way of declaring that He is the beginning and the end of all things. Jesus also declared that He is the "first and the last" (Rev. 22:13). As the first, He was present with God the Father before the creation (John 1:2). As the last, He will bring the world to its appointed end in the last days.

ALPHAEUS. See *Cleophas*

ALTAR

ALTAR

ALTAR. A place where offerings or sacrifices were placed as an act of devotion to God. Some altars were probably nothing more than heaps of dirt or stones (Exod. 20:24–25). But others were more ornate and permanent, like the altar in Solomon's temple in Jerusalem (2 Chron. 4:1). Jesus eliminated the need for such physical altars when He became the once-for-all sacrifice to atone for sin (Heb. 13:10–12).

ALTAR [S]

1 Kings 1:50 Adonijah...took hold on the horns of the *a*

1 Kings 8:22 Solomon stood in front of the *a* of the Lord

Ezek. 6:4 your *a*'s shall be desolate and your images...broken

Luke 1:11 angel...standing on the right side of the *a*

Acts 17:23 an *a* with this inscription: 'To The Unknown God'

ALTARS BUILT BY OLD TESTAMENT PERSONALITIES

1. Noah (Gen. 8:20)
2. Abraham (Gen. 12:7)
3. Isaac (Gen. 26:25)
4. Jacob at Shalem (Gen. 33:20)
5. Jacob at Bethel (Gen. 35:7)
6. Moses (Exod. 17:15)
7. Joshua (Josh. 8:30)
8. Gideon (Judg. 6:24)
9. Saul (1 Sam. 14:35)
10. David (2 Sam. 24:25)

AL-TASHHETH. A word of uncertain meaning in the titles of Psalms 57, 58, 59, and 75.

ALWAYS

Gen. 6:3 My [God's] Spirit shall not *a* strive with man

1 Chron. 16:15 A be mindful of His [God's] covenant

Ps. 16:8 I have set the Lord *a* before me...I shall not be moved

Ps. 103:9 He [God] will not *a* chide: nor...keep His anger forever

Prov. 5:19 a be enraptured by her love

Mark 14:7 you *a* have the poor with you

Luke 18:1 men ought *a* to pray and not to faint

Acts 7:51 You *a* resist the Holy Spirit

Rom. 1:9 I [Paul] *a* make mention of you in my prayers

1 Cor. 1:4 I [Paul] thank my God *a* on your behalf

1 Cor. 15:58 a abounding in the work of the Lord

2 Cor. 4:10 a bearing about in the body the dying of the Lord Jesus

Eph. 5:20 giving thanks *a* for all things to God

AMALEKITES. Bitter enemies of Israel who traced their origin to Esau's son Amalek (Gen. 36:12). They launched an unprovoked attack against the Israelites in the wilderness (Exod. 17:8–16). In later years, Saul battled the Amalekites (1 Sam. 14:47–48), and they suffered a major defeat at the hands of David (1 Sam. 30:1–18). They are also mentioned in Gen. 14:7 • Num. 13:29; 14:25, 43–45 • Judg. 6:3, 33; 7:12; 10:12; 12:15 • 1 Sam. 15:6–8, 15–32; 27:8; • 2 Sam. 1:1 • 1 Chron. 4:43.

AMASA. David's nephew and commander of Absalom's rebel army (2 Sam. 19:12–13). He was forgiven by David and appointed head of his army, only to be killed later by another of David's military officers (2 Sam. 20:4–13). Amasa is also mentioned in 2 Sam. 17:25 • 1 Kings 2:5, 32 • 1 Chron. 2:17.

AMAZED

Exod. 15:15 dukes of Edom shall be *a*...inhabitants of Canaan shall melt away

Matt. 12:23 people were *a*... Isn't this the Son of David?

Matt. 19:25 disciples heard it, they were exceedingly *a*

Mark 1:27 all *a*, to such an extent that they questioned

Mark 2:12 they were all *a* and glorified God

Mark 6:51 they were greatly *a*...beyond measure

Mark 9:15 people...were greatly *a* and...greeted Him [Jesus]

Mark 10:32 Jesus went before them. And they were *a*

Luke 9:43 they were all *a* at the mighty power of God

Acts 2:7 they were all *a*...are not all these... Galileans?

Acts 2:12 they were all *a*...saying... "What does this mean?"

AMAZIAH. A king of Judah who won a decisive victory over the Edomites, then encouraged worship of their pagan gods in his homeland (2 Kings 14:1–23). A prophet asked the king: "Why have you sought after the gods of the people, which could not deliver their own people out of your hand?" (2 Chron. 25:15). After ruling for 29 years, Amaziah was assassinated by his political enemies (2 Chron. 25:25–28). He is also mentioned in 2 Kings 12:21; 13:12 • **2 Chron. 25:1–28.**

AMBASSADOR. A spokesman or representative of one nation to another. Paul reminded the Corinthian believers that all Christians, including himself, were spiritual ambassadors for Christ (2 Cor. 5:20).

AMBER. A precious stone known for its brilliance. The prophet Ezekiel compared God's glory to amber (Ezek. 1:4, 27).

AMEN. A word used to express approval (Neh. 8:6), confirm an oath (Neh. 5:13), or close a prayer (1 Cor. 14:16). The Greek term behind the word means "I tell you the truth" or "I assure you." Jesus called Himself "the Amen," implying that He spoke a truthful and binding word for the churches under His authority (Rev. 3:14).

AMETHYST. A precious stone embedded in the breastplate of the high priest (Exod. 28:19), and used in the foundation of New Jerusalem (Rev. 21:20).

AMMIEL. One of the twelve spies or scouts sent by Moses to investigate the land of Canaan. He represented the tribe of Dan (Num. 13:12).

AMMINADAB. A Levite who helped transport the ark of the covenant to Jerusalem (1 Chron. 15:10–11).

AMMONITES. A people group descended from Lot's son Ammon who evolved into enemies of the Israelites (Deut. 23:3). Their chief pagan god was Chemosh (Judg. 11:24), and the Israelites often indulged in their idolatrous practices (Ezra 9:1). The prophets of the OT often proclaimed God's judgment against the Ammonites (Jer. 49:1–2). They are also mentioned in Deut. 2:20 • 1 Sam. 11:11 • 1 Kings 11:1, 5 • 2 Chron. 20:1; 26:8; 27:5 • Neh. 4:7 • Jer. 27:3; 40:11, 14; 41:10, 15 • Ezek. 21:20, 28; 25:2–10.

AMNON. King David's oldest son whose lust drove him to rape his half-sister Tamar. Another son of David, Absalom, avenged this crime by having Amnon murdered (2 Sam. 3:2; 13:1–29).

AMON. An evil and idolatrous king of Judah (the Southern Kingdom) who reigned for only two years. Assassinated by his own officials, he was succeeded by his son Josiah (2 Kings 21:18–26). Amon is also mentioned in **2 Chron. 33:20–25** • Jer. 1:2; 25:3 • Zeph. 1:1 • Matt. 1:10.

AMORITES. A major people group that lived in Canaan when the Israelites entered the land. Joshua broke their strength with victories over the armies of Sihon and Og (Josh. 12:1–6). Remnants of the Amorites were later reduced to servitude under King Solomon (1 Kings 9:20–21). They are also mentioned in Gen. 10:16; 14:13; 15:16, 21; 48:22 • Exod. 3:8, 17; 13:5; 23:23; 33:2; 34:11 • Num. 13:29; 21:13–34; 22:2; 32:33, 39; • Deut. 1:4–44; 2:24; 3:2–9; 4:46–47; 7:1; 20:17; 31:4 • Josh. 2:10; 3:10; 5:1; 7:7; 9:1, 10; 10:5–12; 13:4, 10, 21; 24:8–18 • Judg. 1:34–36; 3:5; 6:10; 10:8, 11; 11:19–23 • 1 Sam. 7:14 • 2 Sam. 21:2 • 1 Kings 4:19; 21:26 • 2 Kings 21:11 • 1 Chron. 1:14 • 2 Chron. 8:7 • Ezra 9:1 • Neh. 9:8 • Pss. 135:11; 136:19 • Ezek. 16:3, 45 • Amos 2:9, 10.

AMOS. A prophet from a village in Judah (the Southern Kingdom) who delivered the Lord's message to the affluent classes of Israel (the Northern Kingdom). Known as the great "prophet of righteousness" of the OT, he foretold Israel's collapse and captivity by Assyria (Amos 7:17). Amos regarded himself as a simple herdsman who heeded God's call rather than a professional prophet (Amos 7:14–16).

AMOS, BOOK OF. A prophetic book of the OT written by the prophet Amos about 760 BC. His mission was to call the wayward people of the Northern Kingdom back to worship of the one true God. The prophet condemned the wealthy citizens of Israel who were cheating the poor. He also declared that the religion of the people was shallow and meaningless. Worship had degenerated into empty rituals and ceremonies that had no relationship to daily life. True religion, according to the book, demands righteous behavior. Serving the Lord is not a matter of observing rituals and feast days; it consists of following God's commands and treating others with justice. "Let judgment run down as waters," he declared, "and righteousness like a mighty stream" (Amos 5:24).

AMPHIPOLIS. A city in the province of Macedonia through which Paul and Silas passed during the second missionary journey (Acts 17:1).

AMPLIATUS. A believer at Rome greeted and commended by Paul in his epistle to the Romans (Rom. 16:8).

AMRAPHEL. A king of Shinar in Abraham's time (Gen. 14:1, 9).

ANAK. The ancestor of a tribe of giants. Anak is mentioned in **Num. 13:22–33** • Deut. 9:2 • Josh. 15:13–14; 21:11 • Judg. 1:20.

ANAKIM. A tribe of Canaanite giants, descended from Anak, that struck fear into the Israelites when Moses sent spies to investigate the land (Num. 13:33). Later they were defeated by Joshua, and their land was given to Caleb (Josh. 11:21–22; 14:12–15). The Anakim are also mentioned in Deut. 1:28; 2:10–11, 21; 9:2.

ANAMMELECH. A pagan god of the Babylonians (2 Kings 17:31).

ANANIAS. (1) A believer at Jerusalem struck dead for withholding money he had pledged to the church's common treasury and then lying about it (Acts 5:1–5).

(2) A believer at Damascus whom God used to restore Paul's sight (Acts 9:10–18). He is also mentioned in Acts 22:12–16.

(3) The Jewish high priest before whom Paul appeared after his arrest in Jerusalem (Acts 23:2).

ANATHOTH. A village near Jerusalem where the prophet Jeremiah was born (Jer. 1:1). He bought a field at Anathoth as an expression of confidence in the Lord's promise of ultimate redemption for His people (Jer. 32:7–9). Anathoth is also mentioned in Josh. 21:18 • 1 Kings 2:26 • 1 Chron. 6:60 • Ezra 2:23 • Neh. 7:27; 11:32 • Isa. 10:30 • Jer. 11:21, 23; 29:27.

ANCIENT OF DAYS. A name of God that refers to His eternal existence (Dan. 7:9, 13, 22). In contrast to localized and limited false gods, the one true God has always existed and always will. He is not bound by time or space. He alone remains the same while everything else changes. This same idea about the Lord's eternal character is expressed by the title "King of old" (Ps. 74:12).

ANDREW. A follower of John the Baptist who became a disciple of Jesus after following Him home and listening to His teachings. He also introduced his brother Simon Peter to Jesus (John 1:37–42). He continued this pattern by bringing several others to Jesus: the boy who provided a small lunch that Jesus multiplied to feed thousands of people (John 6:5–9), and certain Greek citizens who came to talk with Jesus (John 12:20–22). Andrew is also mentioned in Matt. 4:18; 10:2 • Mark 1:16, 29; 3:18; 13:3 • Luke 6:14 • John 1:44 • Acts 1:13.

ANDRONICUS. A believer greeted and commended by Paul in his letter to the Christians at Rome (Rom. 16:7).

ANGEL APPEARANCES

1. To Hagar during her pregnancy with Ishmael (Gen. 16:7–12)
2. To Lot (Gen. 19:1–22)
3. To Hagar and Ishmael in the wilderness (Gen. 21:17)

4. To Abraham (Gen. 22: 11–12, 15–18)
5. To Jacob at Haran (Gen. 28:12; 31:11–13)
6. To Jacob at Mahanaim (Gen. 32:1)
7. To Moses (Exod. 3:2)
8. To Balaam (Num. 22:22–35)
9. To Gideon (Judg. 6:11–22)
10. To Samson's mother and father (Judg. 13:3–21)
11. To Elijah (1 Kings 19:5, 7 • 2 Kings 1:3, 15)
12. To David (1 Chron. 21:16)
13. To Gad (1 Chron. 21:18)
14. To Ornan (1 Chron. 21:20, 27)
15. To Shadrach, Meshach, and Abed-nego (Dan. 3:24–28)
16. To Zechariah (Zech. 1:9–18)
17. To Joseph in Nazareth (Matt. 1:20–24)
18. To Joseph in Bethlehem (Matt. 2:13)
19. To Joseph in Egypt (Matt. 2:19–20)
20. To Zacharias (Luke 1:11–20)
21. To Mary (Luke 1:26–38)
22. To shepherds at Jesus' birth (Luke 2:9–15)
23. To Jesus in the Garden of Gethsemane (Luke 22:43)
24. To women at the tomb (Matt. 28:2–7)
25. To Mary Magdalene at the empty tomb (John 20:11–13)
26. To the apostles (Acts 5:19–20)
27. To Philip (Acts 8:26)
28. To Cornelius (Acts 10:3–7)
29. To Peter in prison (Acts 12:7–11)
30. To Paul (Acts 27:23–24)
31. To John on the isle of Patmos (Rev. 1:1)

ANGEL OF THE LORD. A messenger who spoke on God's behalf to several people in the OT, including Gideon (Judg. 6:11–13) and Elijah (1 Kings 19:5–7). There seems to be some distinction between this angel and other angelic beings, but the exact difference between them is a mystery.

ANGELS. Spiritual beings who served as God's special messengers to humankind. In addition to this function, they relieved human hunger and thirst (Gen. 21:17–19), protected God's people (Dan. 3:28), and praised the Lord (Ps. 103:20–21). Angels sometimes appeared in large groups, as when they announced the birth of Jesus Christ to shepherds (Luke 2:13–14).

ANGELS
Ps. 8:5 You [God] have made him [man] a little lower than the *a*
Ps. 148:2 Praise Him [God] all His *a*
Matt. 22:30 nor are given in marriage but are as the *a*
Matt. 24:31 He shall send His *a* with a great sound
Matt. 25:31 and all the holy *a* with Him
Luke 15:10 joy in the presence of the *a*...over one sinner who repents
Rom. 8:38 death nor life, nor *a* nor principalities
1 Cor. 13:1 tongues of men and of *a*, and have not love
Heb. 13:2 some have entertained *a* unawares

ANGER
Gen. 30:2 Jacob's *a* was kindled against Rachel
1 Sam. 11:6 his [Saul's] *a* was greatly kindled
1 Sam. 20:30 Saul's *a* was kindled against Jonathan
2 Sam. 12:5 David's *a* was greatly kindled against the man
Ps. 6:1 O LORD, do not rebuke me in Your *a*
Ps. 30:5 For His *a* endures but a moment
Ps. 78:58 provoked Him [God] to *a* with their high places
Ps. 103:8 The LORD is merciful and gracious, slow to *a*
Prov. 15:1 but harsh words stir up *a*
Prov. 16:32 He who is slow to *a* is better than the mighty
Prov. 21:14 A gift in secret pacifies *a*
Isa. 63:6 I [God] will trample the people in my *a*
Jer. 4:8 the fierce *a* of the LORD has not turned back
Lam. 4:16 the *a* of the LORD has divided them
Mic. 5:15 I [God] will carry out vengeance in *a*
Nah. 1:3 The LORD is slow to *a* and great in power
Mark 3:5 He [Jesus] looked...with *a*...for the hardness of their hearts
Eph. 4:31 Let all...*a*...and evil speaking be put away from you

Col. 3:8 put off all these: *a*, wrath, malice
Col. 3:21 Fathers, do not provoke your children to *a*

ANGER OF THE LORD

Exod. 4:14 the *a-o-t-L* was kindled against Moses
Num. 11:10 a-o-t-L was kindled...Moses was also displeased
Num. 25:3 the *a-o-t-L* was kindled against Israel
2 Sam. 6:7 the *a-o-t-L* was kindled against Uzzah
2 Sam. 24:1 the *a-o-t-L* was...against Israel...and He moved David against them
2 Kings 24:20 because of the *a-o-t-L*...Zedekiah rebelled against...Babylon
2 Chron. 25:15 the *a-o-t-L* was kindled against Amaziah
Jer. 4:8 the fierce *a-o-t-L* has not turned back from us
Jer. 12:13 be ashamed of their harvest because of the fierce *a-o-t-L*
Jer. 51:45 every man deliver his soul from the fierce *a-o-t-L*

ANGUISH

Job 15:24 Trouble and *a* shall make him afraid
Ps. 119:143 Trouble and *a* have taken hold of me
John 16:21 delivered the child, she does not remember the *a*
Rom. 2:9 a on every soul of man who does evil
2 Cor. 2:4 I [Paul] wrote to you out of much...*a* of heart

ANISE. An herb used to season food and as a healing agent. Jesus condemned the Pharisees who tithed this insignificant plant but overlooked more important matters, such as mercy and faith (Matt. 23:23).

ANNA. An aged prophetess who praised God at Jesus' presentation as an infant in the temple at Jerusalem (Luke 2:36–38).

ANNAS. A former high priest who presided at the initial trial of Jesus before the Jewish authorities. After questioning Jesus, Annas sent Him to Caiaphas, the current high priest (John 18:12–24). The apostles Peter and John also appeared before Annas (Acts 4:6–7). He is also mentioned in Luke 3:2.

ANNUNCIATION. The angel Gabriel's revelation to the virgin Mary that she would give birth to the Messiah (Luke 1:26–38). The angel of the Lord also announced Jesus' birth to Mary's espoused husband, Joseph (Matt. 1:18–25).

ANOINTING. The ritual of setting a person apart for a specific work or task. Kings, priests, and prophets were anointed by having oil poured on their heads (Exod. 29:1–7). Anointing for healing was practiced in NT times (Mark 6:13). Jesus the Messiah was anointed by God the Father for the special mission of bringing redemption to a sinful world. The Greek term *christos*, translated as "Christ," means "anointed" or "anointed one." The psalmist used this imagery when he referred to the coming Messiah as the Lord's "anointed" (Ps. 2:2). In a spiritual sense, believers are anointed by the Holy Spirit to serve as proclaimers of His love and grace in an unbelieving world (1 John 2:27).

ANOINT [ED, ING]

Exod. 30:30 a Aaron and his sons and consecrate them
Exod. 40:15 a them [Aaron's sons]...that they may minister to Me
Lev. 8:10 Moses took the *a'ing* oil and *a'ed* the tabernacle
Lev. 8:12 the *a'ing* oil on Aaron's head and *a'ed* him
Judg. 9:8 The trees went forth once to *a* a king over them
1 Sam. 15:1 The LORD sent me [Samuel] to *a* you [Saul]
1 Sam. 16:13 Samuel...*a'ed* him [David] in the midst of his brothers
2 Sam. 2:4 they *a'ed* David king over the house of Judah
1 Kings 19:15 a Hazael to be king over Syria
2 Chron. 6:42 do not turn away the face of Your *a'ed*
Ps. 20:6 the LORD saves His *a'ed*. He will hear him from...heaven
Ps. 23:5 You [God] *a* my head with oil
Isa. 45:1 This is what the LORD says to His *a'ed*, to Cyrus

Isa. 61:1 the LORD has *a'ed* me to preach good news

Mark 14:8 She has come beforehand to *a* My body for burial

Mark 16:1 bought sweet spices, that they [women] might...*a* Him

Luke 7:46 did not anoint My head...but this woman has *a'ed* My feet

John 9:6 He [Jesus] *a'ed* the eyes of the blind man

John 12:3 Mary...*a'ed* the feet of Jesus

Heb. 1:9 has *a'ed* You with the oil of gladness

Jas. 5:14 *a'ing* him with oil in the name of the LORD

ANSWER

Job 31:35 my desire is that the Almighty would *a* me [Job]

Ps. 27:7 have mercy also on me and *a* me

Ps. 86:7 I will call on You, for You will *a* me

Prov. 15:1 A soft *a* turns away wrath

Prov. 26:4 Do not *a* a fool according to his foolishness

Prov. 26:5 A *a* fool according to his foolishness

Jer. 33:3 Call to Me, and I will *a* you

Luke 21:14 not to meditate beforehand on what you shall *a*

1 Pet. 3:15 be ready to give an *a* to every man who asks you a reason

1 Pet. 3:21 the *a* of a good conscience toward God

ANT. A small insect cited as an example of hard work (Prov. 6:6–8) and wisdom (Prov. 30:25)

ANTEDILUVIANS. People who lived before the great flood. All except Noah and his family were destroyed because of their wickedness (Gen. 6:5–8).

ANTHROPOMORPHISM. A theological term for describing God with human features as an aid to understanding His mysterious nature. Biblical writers describe God as having an arm of deliverance (Exod. 6:6), eyes too pure to look upon evil (Hab. 1:13), and a nature that is provoked to anger and jealousy by idolatry (Ps. 78:58).

ANTICHRIST. A false prophet and evil being who opposes everything that Jesus Christ represents, thus his name *anti* (or "opposed to") *Christ*. The term appears only in the writings of the apostle John (1 John 2:18, 22; 4:3; 2 John 7) in the NT. Deception is the main work of the Antichrist. This is also true of Satan, another evil being who will be allied with the Antichrist in the end-time (Rev. 13:4). Before the return of Jesus, the Antichrist will make his appearance to wage war against Christ and His people (Rev. 13:6–8). But he will be defeated and cast into a lake of fire (Rev. 19:20; 20:10).

ANTIOCH OF PISIDIA. A city in the district of Asia Minor where Paul preached to Jews in the local synagogue during the first missionary journey. Their rejection of the gospel caused him to redirect his ministry to the Gentiles (Acts 13:14–51). Antioch of Pisidia is also mentioned in Acts 14:19, 21 • 2 Tim. 3:11.

ANTIOCH OF SYRIA. Capital of the Roman province of Syria, and site of a church that included many Gentiles. Barnabas ministered here by himself for a time before enlisting Paul to help him disciple these early believers. The reputation of these believers as "Christ-ones" or followers of Christ earned them a special distinction in the early church: "The disciples were first called Christians in Antioch" (Acts 11:26). This church sent Paul on two of his missionary journeys (Acts 13:1–4; 15:35–41). Antioch of Syria is also mentioned in Acts 6:5; 11:19–27; 14:26; 15:22–35; 18:22–23 • Gal. 2:11.

ANTIOCHUS IV EPIPHANES. See *Abomination That Makes Desolate*

ANTIPAS. A Christian martyr of the church at Pergamum (Rev. 2:13).

ANTIPATRIS. See *Aphek*

ANYTHING

Gen. 18:14 Is *a* too hard for the LORD?

Exod. 20:4 shall not make...likeness of *a* that is in heaven above

Exod. 20:17 shall not covet...*a* that is your neighbor's

Num. 15:30 the soul who does *a* presumptuously...shall be cut off

Ruth 1:16 May the LORD do so to me...if *a* but death parts you and me

Eccles. 9:5 the dead do not know *a*

Jer. 32:27 Is there *a* too hard for Me [God]?

Matt. 5:23 altar...there remember that your brother has *a* against you

Mark 9:29 This kind cannot come out by *a* except by prayer

Luke 19:8 If I [Zacchaeus] have taken *a* from any man...I restore him fourfold

John 13:14 If you ask *a* in My [Jesus'] name, I will do it

Rom. 13:8 Owe no man *a* but to love one another

1 Cor. 3:7 neither he who plants nor he who waters is *a*, but God who gives...increase

APE. An exotic animal imported into Israel by King Solomon (1 Kings 10:22).

APELLES. A believer at Rome commended by Paul in his letter to the Roman Christians (Rom. 16:10).

APHARSATHCHITES. Foreign colonists who settled in Samaria after the Northern Kingdom fell to Assyria (Ezra 4:9).

APHARSITES. Foreign colonists who settled in Samaria after the Northern Kingdom fell to Assyria (Ezra 4:9).

APHEK. A coastal city on the Mediterranean Sea where the Philistines captured the ark of the covenant from the Israelites (1 Sam. 4:1–11). Centuries later, Herod the Great rebuilt the city and renamed it *Antipatris* in honor of his father, Antipater. The apostle Paul passed through Antipatris when he was transported under Roman guard from Jerusalem to Caesarea (Acts 23:31).

APOCALYPTIC WRITING. A distinctive type of biblical literature that uses visions, metaphors, symbols, and numbers to communicate a message. The best example of this type of literature is the book of Revelation. These techniques were probably used by the apostle John, author of Revelation, to reveal God's message to His people while keeping it hidden from those who were persecuting early Christian believers. Other examples of apocalyptic writing are Daniel 7–12, Isaiah 24–27, Ezekiel 37–41, Zechariah 9–12, Matthew 24, and Mark 13.

APOCRYPHA. A collection of fifteen OT books included in the Bibles of some Christian groups but not considered authoritative by others. The books were written during the turbulent time between the two testaments when the Jewish people revolted against their enemies.

APOLLONIA. A town in the province of Macedonia through which Paul and Silas passed during the second missionary journey (Acts 17:1).

APOLLOS. A learned Jewish believer from Alexandria, Egypt, who ministered in the church at Ephesus. Apollos was a disciple of John the Baptist (Acts 18:24–28). After Aquila and Priscilla corrected some of his misunderstandings, he became an effective leader in the early churchy (1 Cor. 3:4–6, 22). A faction of the Corinthian church apparently favored Apollos over other church leaders (1 Cor. 1:12). He is also mentioned in Acts 19:1 • 1 Cor. 4:6; 16:12 • Titus 3:13.

APOSTASY. A falling away from the truth or renunciation of one's faith in Christ (Heb. 3:12). This is not the same as false belief or error, which are the result of ignorance. Some Christian groups view apostasy as impossible for those who have had a genuine conversion experience. They believe God's love and grace will keep believers eternally committed to Him.

APOSTLE. A person sent on a special mission with delegated authority and power. Jesus selected twelve disciples, or apostles (Mark 3:14) to learn from Him and to carry on His work after His earthly ministry was finished. But He Himself was the ultimate Apostle (Heb. 3:1). Under the authority of His Father, He came into the world on a mission of love and grace. His commitment to this purpose led Him ultimately to the cross. Paul regarded himself as an apostle because of his encounter with Christ on the Damascus Road and his personal call to missionary work (1 Cor. 15:8–10). He considered an apostle to be anyone who had received a divine call (1 Cor. 15:5–8).

APOSTLE [S]

Matt. 10:2 names of the twelve *a's* are these

Mark 6:30 *a's* gathered...and told Him [Jesus] all things

Luke 6:13 He [Jesus] chose twelve...He also named *a's*

Acts 1:26 Matthias...was numbered with the eleven *a's*

Acts 2:42 they continued steadfastly in the *a's'* doctrine

Acts 2:43 many wonders and signs were done by the *a's*

Acts 5:18 laid their hands on the *a's* and put them in...prison

Acts 8:1 they [believers] were all scattered... except the *a's*

Rom. 1:1 Paul, a servant...called to be an *a*

Rom. 11:13 I [Paul] am the *a* of the Gentiles

1 Cor. 1:1 Paul, called to be an *a* of Jesus Christ

1 Cor. 9:1 Am I [Paul] not an *a*? Am I not free?

1 Cor. 12:28 God has set some in the church, first *a's*

1 Cor. 12:29 Are all *a's*? Are all prophets? Are all teachers?

1 Cor. 15:9 I [Paul] am the least of the *a's*

2 Cor. 11:13 transforming themselves into the *a's* of Christ

2 Cor. 12:12 signs of an *a* were worked among you

Eph. 2:20 built upon the foundation of the *a's*

Eph. 4:11 And He gave some *a's*, and some prophets

Heb. 3:1 *A* and High Priest of our profession, Christ Jesus

APOTHECARY. A maker of perfumes used in worship ceremonies or for anointing bodies for burial (Exod. 30:25–35).

APPEAL. A person's right to have a decision against him heard by a higher authority. The

apostle Paul appealed a charge against him to the Roman emperor (Acts 25:11).

APPEAR [ED, ING]

Gen. 1:9 let the dry land *a*. And it was so

Gen. 12:7 the Lord *a'ed* to Abram

Gen. 35:9 God *a'ed* to Jacob...and blessed him

Exod. 3:2 angel...*a'ed* to him [Moses] in a flame of fire

Exod. 16:10 the glory of the Lord *a'ed* in the cloud

1 Sam. 3:21 the Lord *a'ed* again...revealed Himself to Samuel

1 Kings 9:2 the Lord *a'ed* to Solomon...as He had...at Gibeon

2 Kings 2:11 a chariot...*a'ed*...and Elijah went up by a whirlwind

Ps. 42:2 When shall I come and *a* before God?

Ps. 102:16 He [God] shall *a* in His glory

Song of Sol. 2:12 The flowers *a* on the earth

Mal. 3:2 who shall stand when He [God] *a's*?

Matt. 2:13 the angel of the Lord *a'd* to Joseph in a dream

Matt. 2:19 an angel of the Lord *a'd* in a dream to Joseph

Matt. 17:3 *a'ed* to them (disciples) Moses and Elijah, talking with Him

Matt. 23:27 white-washed sepulchres that indeed *a* beautiful outwardly

Matt. 24:30 then the sign of the Son of Man shall *a* in heaven

Mark 16:9 He *a'ed* first to Mary Magdalene

Mark 16:12 He [Jesus] *a'ed* in another form to two of them

Mark 16:14 He [Jesus] *a'ed* to the eleven as they sat at the table

Luke 1:11 there an angel of the Lord *a'ed* to him [Zechariah]

Luke 24:34 The Lord has risen indeed and has *a'ed* to Simon

Acts 2:3 cloven tongues like fire *a'ed* to them

2 Cor. 5:10 all *a* before the judgment seat of Christ

Col. 3:4 When Christ...*a*, then you shall also *a* with Him [Jesus]

1 Tim. 6:14 keep this commandment...until the *a'ing* of our Lord Jesus Christ

2 Tim. 1:10 revealed by the *a'ing* of our Savior

2 Tim. 4:1 judge the living and the dead at His *a'ing*

2 Tim. 4:8 to all those who love His *a'ing*

Titus 2:13 the glorious *a'ing* of the great God and our Savior

Jas. 4:14 your life...is even a vapor, that *a's* for a little time

1 Pet. 5:4 when the Chief Shepherd *a's*, you shall receive a crown of glory

APPII FORUM. KJV: See *Forum of Appias*

APPLE OF THE EYE. A phrase that refers to the pupil of the human eye, the most precious part of one of the most important organs of the body. A person or thing considered the "apple of the eye" is something highly esteemed. The imagery refers to God's deep love for Israel as His chosen people (Deut. 32:9–10).

APPOINT [ED]

Num. 1:50 **a** the Levites over the tabernacle of testimony

Josh. 20:2 **A** cities of refuge of refuge for yourselves

Job 14:5 You have *a'ed* his limits that he cannot pass

Ps. 104:19 He [God] *a'ed* the moon for seasons

Isa. 1:14 My [God's] soul hates...your *a'ed* feasts

Luke 10:1 the Lord *a'ed* seventy others also and sent them two by two

Acts 6:3 seven men...whom we may **a** over this business

1 Thes. 5:9 God *a'ed* us not to wrath, but to obtain salvation

2 Tim. 1:11 I [Paul] am *a'ed* a preacher and an apostle

Heb. 1:2 whom He [God] has *a'ed* heir [Jesus] of all things

Heb. 9:27 *a'ed* to men to die once, but after this the judgment

APPROVED

Acts 2:22 Jesus of Nazareth, a Man **a** by God... by miracles

2 Tim. 2:15 Study to show yourself **a** to God

AQUILA. A Christian believer who, with his wife Priscilla, was living at Corinth when Paul arrived there from Athens (Acts 18:1–2). They worked with the apostle in the Corinthian church and also continued his work at Ephesus (Acts 18:24–26). Aquila is also mentioned in Rom. 16:3 • 1 Cor. 16:19 • 2 Tim. 4:19.

ARABAH. The Jordan River valley (Josh. 18:18).

ARABIA. A large desert territory southeast of Israel with which Solomon and other Israelite kings established trade relations. The Arabian cities of Ophir, Raamah, and Sheba were known for their exports of gold, silver, and precious stones (1 Kings 9:28; Ezek. 27:22). The queen of Sheba brought gold and precious jewels to King Solomon from this region (1 Kings 10:1–15). The "Arabia" to which the apostle Paul retreated after his conversion was probably the territory of the Nabateans, an Arabic tribe that lived south of the city of Damascus (Gal. 1:17).

ARAD. A Canaanite city south of Hebron captured by Joshua (Josh. 12:14).

ARAM. See *Syria*

ARARAT, MOUNT. A mountainous region where Noah's ark rested when the waters of the great flood went down (Gen. 8:4). The word *Ararat* refers to an entire mountain range. But it is generally applied to a peak known as Mount Urartu, an isolated spot where the borders of Turkey, Iran, and Russia come together. Several expeditions to find evidence of the ark have been undertaken, but without success. Ararat is also mentioned in Jer. 51:27.

ARAUNAH. A Jebusite prince from whom David bought a threshing floor as a place to build an altar (2 Sam. 24:16–24). In later years, Solomon's temple was built on this site in Jerusalem. Also called *Ornan* (1 Chron. 21:15–28; 2 Chron. 3:1).

ARBITER. A mediator, umpire, or judge between contending parties. Job longed for an arbiter who could speak to God on his behalf (Job 9:33). This desire was eventually fulfilled with the coming of Jesus Christ into the world. *Daysman*: KJV.

ARCHAEOLOGY. The scientific study of people, places, and things described in the Bible. This generally involves excavation of ancient cities in modern Israel and surrounding regions. But one of the most important discoveries of modern times did not involve an archaeological dig. Several ancient scrolls, including biblical texts, were found in a cave in the hot, dry region in southern Israel. See also *Dead Sea Scrolls*.

ARCHANGEL. A chief angel, or one next in rank above a normal angelic being. Two archangels mentioned by name in the Bible are Michael (Jude 9) and Gabriel (Luke 1:19). The term *archangel* also appears in 1 Thes. 4:16.

ARCHELAUS. A son of Herod the Great; a Roman ruler in Palestine when Joseph and Mary left Egypt to settle in the territory of Galilee (Matt. 2:22).

ARCHEVITES. Foreign colonists who settled in Samaria after the Northern Kingdom fell to Assyria (Ezra 4:9).

ARCHIPPUS. A believer in the church at Colosse whom Paul encouraged (Col. 4:17).

AREOPAGUS. A rocky hill in Athens, and by association a council of Greek philosophers. Paul appeared before this group to defend his claims about Jesus and His resurrection (Acts 17:19). Although most of his audience were skeptical, several became believers (Acts 17:34).

ARETAS. A ruler whose deputy tried to capture Paul in Damascus after his conversion (2 Cor. 11:32).

ARGUMENT [S]
Job 23:4 I would order my cause before Him and fill my mouth with *a's*
Luke 9:46 arose an *a* among them [the disciples]...which of them was greatest
Rom 14:1 Receive him who is weak in the faith, but not to doubtful *a's*
Phil 2:14 Do all things without murmurings and *a's*

ARIDAI. A son of Haman who was executed, along with his father, when Haman's plot to destroy the Jews was exposed by Esther (Esther 9:7–10).

ARIDATHA. A son of Haman who was executed, along with his father, when Haman's plot to destroy the Jews was exposed by Esther (Esther 9:7–10).

ARIEL. A symbolic name for the city of Jerusalem, meaning "lion of God" (Isa. 29:1–2, 7).

ARIMATHEA. A city near Jerusalem and home of the Joseph who buried the body of Jesus in his own tomb (John 19:38). Arimathea is also mentioned in Matt. 27:57 • Mark 15:43–46 • Luke 23:51.

ARISAI. A son of Haman who was executed, along with his father, when Haman's plot to destroy the Jews was exposed by Esther (Esther 9:7–10).

ARISE
Josh. 1:2 Now therefore, *a*, go over this Jordan
Ps. 7:6 A, O LORD...because of the rage of my enemies
Ps. 82:8 A, O God, judge the earth, for You shall inherit all nations
Isa. 60:1 A! Shine! For your light has come
Jer. 18:2 A and go down to the potter's house... hear My words
Dan. 7:17 four kings who shall *a* out of the earth
Jon. 1:2 A, go to Nineveh, that great city, and cry against it
Mal. 4:2 the Sun of righteousness shall *a* with healing in His wings
Matt. 2:13 angel...appeared to Joseph... *A* and take the young Child
Matt. 24:24 false christs and false prophets shall *a*
Mark 5:41 Little girl, I [Jesus] say to you, *a*
Luke 5:24 I [Jesus] say to you, *a* and take up your bed
Luke 15:18 I will *a* and go to my father...I have sinned
Luke 17:19 He [Jesus] said... *A*, go your way. Your faith has healed you

Acts 11:7 A, Peter; slay and eat
Acts 20:30 men shall *a*, speaking perverse things

ARISTARCHUS. A believer from Thessalonica who traveled with Paul on the third missionary journey (Acts 20:4). Later he accompanied the apostle to Rome (Acts 27:2). Aristarchus is also mentioned in Acts 19:29 • Col. 4:10 • Philem. 24.

ARISTOBULUS. A believer to whose household the apostle Paul sent warm greetings in his letter to the Roman Christians (Rom. 16:10).

ARK, NOAH'S. A large wooden vessel built by Noah in which he, his family, and selected animals were saved from the great flood. Noah built the ship according to God's directions. Then he gathered others into the ark (Gen. 6:14–20). Rain fell for forty days, and water covered the earth for 150 days (Gen. 7:17–24). When the flood waters receded, the ark rested on a mountain in Ararat. After leaving the ark, Noah built an altar and offered sacrifices to God in thanksgiving for His deliverance. The Lord promised him that the earth would never be destroyed by water again (Gen. 8:18–22). To the writer of the epistle of Hebrews, the ark symbolized God's saving grace (Heb. 11:7). Noah's ark is also mentioned in **Gen. 6:12–9:18** • Matt. 24:38 • Luke 17:27 • 1 Pet. 3:20.

ARK OF GOD. See *Ark of the covenant*

ARK OF MOSES. A basket in which the infant Moses was placed (Exod. 2:3, 5).

ARK OF THE COVENANT. A portable wooden chest that symbolized God's presence to the Israelites. The ark was housed first in the tabernacle, then later in the temple in Jerusalem (1 Kings 8:1–11). It was probably carried away by King Nebuchadnezzar of Babylon along with other treasures after the fall of Jerusalem (2 Chron. 36:6, 18). This sacred object was also referred to as the "ark of God" (1 Sam. 3:3) and "ark of the testimony" (Exod. 25:22). The ark of the covenant is also mentioned in **Exod. 25:10–22** • Num. 10:33 • Deut. 10:8; 31:9, 25 • Josh. 3:3–17; 4:7–18; 6:6–13; 8:33 • Judg. 20:27–28 • 1 Sam. 4:3 • 2 Sam. 15:24–29 • 1 Kings 3:15; 6:19; 8:1–9 • 1 Chron. 15:25–29; 16:6, 37; 17:1; 22:19; 28:2, 18 • 2 Chron. 5:2–10 • Jer. 3:16. *Ark of (the) testimony*: Num. 7:89 • Josh. 4:16.

ARK OF THE LORD. See *Ark of the covenant*

ARK OF THE TESTIMONY. See *Ark of the covenant*

ARMAGEDDON. A Greek word that refers to the site of the final battle between the forces of good and evil in the end-time (Rev. 16:16). The term comes from the ancient fortress city of Megiddo which overlooked a valley known as the Plain of Jezreel in OT times. Many important battles were fought for control of this city and the adjoining territory. At the final battle of Armageddon, Satan's armies will be defeated, and he will be cast into the lake of fire (Rev. 20:1–10).

ARM OF GOD. A metaphoric reference to God's strength and power (Ps. 89:10, 13). See also *Anthropomorphism*.

ARM OF THE LORD
Isa. 51:9 O *a-o-t-L*! Awake as in the ancient days
Isa. 53:1 to whom has the *a-o-t-L* been revealed?

ARMOR-BEARER. An attendant who carried the armor and weapons of a military officer or soldier of high rank (Judg. 9:54). David served King Saul in this role for a time (1 Sam. 16:21).

ARMY. A body of soldiers armed and trained for battle. In Israel's formative years, all men twenty years old and over were subject to military duty (Num. 1:2–3). But a regular standing army did not exist until a unified government was formed during the days of Saul and David (1 Sam. 17:17–19). The prophets cautioned Israel against trusting in military might instead of relying on the Lord for strength and protection (Isa. 31:1).

ARNON RIVER. A swift stream that marked the boundary between Moab and the Amorites (Num. 21:13–28). The Arnon is also mentioned in Num. 22:36 • Deut. 2:24, 36; 3:12, 16; 4:48 • Josh. 12:1–2; 13:9, 16 • Judg. 11:13–26 • 2 Kings 10:33 • Isa. 16:2 • Jer. 48:20.

ARROW. In addition to its literal meaning, this word symbolizes calamity inflicted by God (Job 6:4) or something injurious, such as false testimony (Prov. 25:18).

ARTAXERXES I. The king of Persia in whose court Ezra and Nehemiah served (Ezra 7:1, 7). He authorized Ezra to lead a group of exiles back to Jerusalem to resettle the land (Ezra 7:1–28). About thirteen years later he allowed Nehemiah to return to rebuild the walls of Jerusalem (Neh. 2:1–10; 13:6). Artaxerxes is also mentioned in Ezra 4:7–23; 8:1 • Neh. 5:14.

ASA. A king of Judah (the Southern Kingdom) who led a religious revival in the nation. He even removed his own grandmother from her position as queen mother because she had promoted worship of a pagan goddess (1 Kings 15:8–33). Asa was also a capable military leader. After praying fervently for the Lord's guidance and protection, he won a decisive victory over an Ethiopian army (2 Chron. 14:9–15). Asa was succeeded by his son Jehoshaphat after reigning for 41 years (2 Chron. 16:12; 17:1). He is also mentioned in 1 Kings 16:8–29 • 2 Chron. 14:1–13; 15:2–19; 16:1–14 • Jer. 41:9 • Matt. 1:7–8.

ASAHEL. One of David's "mighty men," an elite group of warriors known for their bravery in battle (2 Sam. 23:24). This may have been the same man killed by Abner, commander of King Saul's army, who later supported David (2 Sam. 2:18–23). Asahel is also mentioned in 2 Sam. 2:18–32; 3:27, 30 • 1 Chron. 2:16; 11:26; 27:7.

ASAPH. A Levite choir leader (1 Chron 25:1–9) and writer or contributor of several psalms (Pss. 50; 73–83).

ASCEND [ED, ING]

Gen. 28:12 angels of God were *a'ing* and descending on it [ladder]

Josh. 10:7 Joshua *a'ed* from Gilgal, he and all the people of war

Ps. 24:3 Who shall *a* to the hill of the LORD

Ps. 68:18 You have *a'ed* on high; You have led captives

Luke 19:28 He [Jesus] went ahead, *a'ing* to Jerusalem

John 1:51 angels of God *a'ing* and descending on the Son of Man

John 6:62 see the Son of Man *a'ing* to where He was before

John 20:17 I [Jesus] have not yet *a'ed* to My Father...*a'ing* to My Father

Eph. 4:8 He [Jesus] *a'ed* on high, He led captivity captive

ASCENSION OF CHRIST. Jesus' return to His Father after His crucifixion and resurrection (Luke 24:50–51). This occurred forty days after His resurrection (Acts 1:2–11). He spent this time with His disciples, preparing them for carrying on His work. The ascension marked the beginning of Jesus' intercession at the right hand of God the Father for all believers (Rom. 8:34).

ASENATH. Joseph's Egyptian wife and mother of his two sons, Manasseh and Ephraim (Gen. 46:20). The descendants of these sons evolved into two of the twelve tribes of Israel. Asenath is also mentioned in Gen. 41:45, 50.

ASER. KJV: See *Asher*

ASHAMED

Gen. 2:25 both naked, the man and his wife, and were not *a*

Ps. 31:17 Let me not be *a*...for I have called upon You

Joel 2:26, 27 And My people shall never be *a*

Mark 8:38 shall be *a* of Me...the Son of Man shall also be *a*

Rom. 1:16 I [Paul] am not *a* of the gospel of Christ

Rom. 10:11 Whoever believes in Him shall not be *a*

2 Tim. 2:15 a workman who does not need to be *a*

1 John 2:28 not be *a* before Him at His coming

ASHDOD. A major Philistine city (Josh. 13:3) where the ark of the covenant was carried after it was captured from the Israelites. When their pagan god Dagon fell before the ark, they sent the chest to another Philistine city, and it was eventually returned to the Israelites (1 Sam. 5:1–7). Ashdod was known as Azotus in NT times. The evangelist Philip preached at Azotus and other cities on the Mediterranean coast (Acts 8:40). Ashdod is also mentioned in Josh. 11:22; 15:46–47 • 1 Sam. 6:17 • 2 Chron. 26:6 • Neh. 13:23–24 • Isa. 20:1 • Jer. 25:20 • Amos 1:8; 3:9 • Zeph. 2:4 • Zech. 9:6.

ASHER. (1) A son of Jacob through Zilpah, servant of his wife Leah (Gen. 30:12–13). He is also mentioned in Gen. 35:26; 46:17; 49:20 • Exod. 1:4 • Num. 26:46 • 1 Chron. 2:2; 7:30, 40.

(2) One of the twelve tribes of Israel that developed from Asher's descendants (Deut. 33:24). This tribe settled in northern Canaan after the conquest (Josh. 19:24, 31–34). It is also mentioned in Luke 2:36.

ASHERAH. See *Ashtaroth*

ASHES. Sitting in ashes or sprinkling them on the body symbolized extreme grief or mourning (Esther 4:3). Ashes were also used for purification (Heb. 9:13).

ASHES

Job 2:8 And he [Job] sat down among the *a*

Isa. 61:3 to give to them beauty for *a*

Jer. 25:34 Howl, you shepherds...and wallow yourselves in the *a*

ASHIMA. A pagan god worshipped by foreign colonists who settled in Samaria after the Northern Kingdom fell to Assyria (2 Kings 17:30).

ASHKELON. A major city of the Philistines where the judge Samson killed thirty of the enemy to pay off a bet he had lost (Judg. 14:19). Several OT prophets predicted that Ashkelon would be punished by the Lord, probably because of the worship of pagan gods by its citizens (Amos 1:8). Ashkelon is also mentioned in Judg. 1:18 • Jer. 25:20; 47:5, 7 • Zeph. 2:4, 7 • Zech. 9:5.

ASHTAROTH. The plural form of a pagan fertility goddess. She was often portrayed as the wife or consort of Baal, a male fertility god.

The Israelites sometimes worshipped this pagan deity (Judg. 2:11–13). Singular form: *Asherah*.

ASIA. A Roman province that included the cities of Ephesus, Smyrna, and Pergamum—the first three cities mentioned in the book of Revelation (Rev. 1:11). At first the apostle Paul was told through a vision not to enter Asia (Acts 16:6), but he later spent more than two years in and around Ephesus (Acts 19:10). Asia is also mentioned in Acts 2:9; 6:9; 19:22, 26–27, 31; 20:4, 16, 18 • 1 Cor. 16:19 • 2 Cor. 1:8 • 2 Tim. 1:15 • 1 Pet. 1:1 • Rev. 1:4.

ASK [ED, S]

Josh. 4:6 when your children *a* their fathers in the future

Judg. 1:1 the children of Israel *a'ed* the Lord, Who shall go up...for us

1 Kings 3:5 Lord appeared to Solomon in a dream... *A*. What I shall give you

Ps. 27:4 One thing I have *a'ed* of the Lord

Ps. 105:40 The people *a'ed*, and He brought quails

Jer. 37:17 king *a'ed* him [Jeremiah]...Is there any word from the Lord

Matt. 6:8 Father knows what...you...need... before you *a*

Matt. 7:7 A, and it shall be given to you

Matt. 7:9 if his son *a* for bread, will give him a stone

Matt. 18:19 two...agree concerning anything... they *a*, it shall be done

Matt. 21:22 whatever you *a* in prayer, believing, you shall receive

Mark 14:61 high priest *a'ed* Him...Are You the Christ

Mark 15:2 Pilate *a'ed* Him, Are You the King of the Jews?

Luke 11:13 your...Father give the Holy Spirit to those who *a* Him

John 14:14 If you *a* anything in My name, I will do it

John 16:24 A, and you shall receive, that your joy may be full

2 Cor. 5:20 we *a* you...be reconciled to God

Eph. 3:20 able to do exceedingly abundantly above all that we *a*

Jas. 1:5 If any of you lacks wisdom, let him *a* of God

Jas. 4:2 yet you do not have, because you do not *a*

Jas. 4:3 You *a* and do not receive because you *a* wrongly

1 John 5:14 if we *a* anything according to His will, He hears us

1 John 5:15 know He hears us, whatever we *a*, we know...we have

ASKELON. KJV: See *Ashkelon*

ASNAPPER. KJV: See *Osnapper*

ASPATHA. A son of Haman who was executed, along with his father, when Haman's plot to destroy the Jews was exposed by Esther (Esther 9:7–10).

ASSHUR. See *Assyria*

ASSUR. KJV: See *Assyria*

ASSURANCE. Total confidence in God's grace, love, and promise of eternal life. The love of believers for one another also provides assurance of God's constant presence (1 John 3:14). Obedient Christians are assured of victorious living (Rom. 8:18).

ASSYRIA. An ancient nation between the Tigris and Euphrates rivers that overran Israel (the Northern Kingdom) and carried its leading citizens into exile about 722 BC. The territory that developed into Assyria was settled by Nimrod, a descendant of Noah. Its early name was Asshur, after a son of Shem connected with their early history (Gen. 10:8–12). The Assyrians were known for their cruelty, cutting off their victims' hands and impaling them on stakes. For this violence and their pagan worship, they were condemned by the OT prophets (Isa. 10:5). Several years after conquering Israel, Assyria invaded Judah (the Southern Kingdom). But the Lord's miraculous intervention caused the death of thousands of Assyrian soldiers, and the army withdrew in defeat (2 Kings 19:35–37). The Assyrian Empire was eventually overthrown by the Babylonians.

Assyria is also mentioned in 2 Kings 18:9–37 • Ezra 4:2 • Isa. 7:17; 8:4, 7; 10:12; 14:24–25 • Hos. 10:6 • Nah. 3:18. *Asshur*: Num. 24:22–24.

ASTONISHING

Jer. 5:30 An *a* and horrible thing has been committed in the land

Dan. 11:36 the king...shall speak *a* things against the God of gods

ASTROLOGY. The study of the sun, moon, and stars in the belief that they influenced human events. This was a common practice among the pagan Babylonians (Isa. 47:1, 13).

ASYNCRITUS. A believer at Rome greeted and commended by Paul in his letter to the Roman Christians (Rom. 16:14).

ATE

Gen. 3:13 The serpent deceived me [Eve], and I *a*

Gen. 25:34 Isaac loved Esau because he **a** of his venison

Gen. 40:17 the birds *a* them out of the basket on my [baker's] head

Exod. 16:35 children of Israel *a* manna forty years

Num. 11:5 We [Israelites] remember the fish that we *a* freely in Egypt

Josh. 5:12 but they [Israelites] *a* the fruit of the land of Canaan that year

2 Sam. 9:13 he [Mephibosheth] *a* regularly at the king's [David's] table

1 Kings 19:6 And he [Elijah] *a* and drank and lay down again

2 Chron. 30:18 they [Israelites] *a* the Passover contrary to what was written

Ps. 41:9 my own familiar friend...who *a* of my bread...lifted up his heel against me

Ps. 78:25 Man *a* angels' food [manna]; He [God] sent them food to the full

Jer. 16:16 Your [God's] words were found, and I [Jeremiah] *a* them

Ezek. 3:3 I [Ezekiel] *a* it [scroll], and it was as honey for sweetness

Dan. 1:15 [Daniel and friends'] faces appeared better...than all...who *a*...king's food

Matt. 14:20 they [disciples] all *a* and were filled

ATHALIAH. The daughter of King Ahab of Israel who claimed the throne of Judah (the Southern Kingdom) by murdering all the royal heirs (2 Kings 11). But she failed to eliminate one rival named Joash, who was only one year old at the time. Athaliah was eventually deposed, and Joash took over the throne at age seven. She was the only woman and the only person who was not a descendant of David who ruled over Judah. Athaliah is also mentioned in 2 Kings 8:26 • 2 Chron. 22:2–12; 23:12–21.

ATHENS. The capital city of ancient Greece where the apostle Paul debated with learned philosophers during the second missionary journey. Athens was filled with shrines and statues devoted to pagan deities, including one to the "unknown god" (Acts 17:23). Paul used this idol as a point of departure for presenting the gospel to his audience. Athens is also mentioned in **Acts 17:15–22; 18:1** • 1 Thes. 3:1.

ATONEMENT. The process by which God restores a harmonious relationship between Himself and sinful humankind. Believers find "at-one-ment" with God, in spite of their sin, because of His grace and forgiveness. This came about in OT times through animal sacrifices that symbolized the people's repentance (Lev. 5:6). But such reconciliation with God now occurs through the sacrificial death of Jesus Christ (Rom. 5:10).

ATONEMENT
Exod. 29:36 shall offer a bull every day for a sin offering for *a*
Num. 15:25 priest shall make an *a* for all...Israel
2 Chron. 29:24 priests...presented their [animals'] blood to make an *a*

ATONEMENT, DAY OF. A holy day on which atonement was made for all Israel (Lev. 16:29–30). Preceded by special sabbaths (Lev. 23:24) and fasting, this event recognized the inability of people to make atonement for themselves (Heb. 10:1–10). On this day the Jewish high priest first made atonement for himself and then the sins of the people by sprinkling the blood of a sacrificial animal on the altar in the temple (Lev. 16:12–15).

ATTAIN [ED]
Ps. 139:6 knowledge is too wonderful...I cannot *a* it
Phil. 3:11 I [Paul] might *a* to the resurrection of the dead
Phil. 3:12 Not as though I [Paul] had already *a'ed*
Phil. 3:16 already *a'ed*, let us walk by the same rule
1 Tim. 4:6 nourished in...good doctrine that you have *a'ed*

ATTALIA. A seaport town in the province of Pamphylia from which Paul sailed back to Antioch at the end of the first missionary journey (Acts 14:25–26).

ATTEND
Ps. 17:1 O Lord; *a* to my cry. Give ear to my prayer
Ps. 86:6 O Lord...*a* to the voice of my supplications
Prov. 4:1 Hear...the instruction of a father, and *a* to know understanding

AUGUSTUS. A title of honor, meaning "his reverence," bestowed upon the emperors of the Roman Empire. The first emperor with this title was probably Octavian, the "Caesar Augustus" who ruled when Jesus was born (Luke 2:1). He is also mentioned in Acts 25:21, 25; 27:1.

AUTHORITY [IES]. See also *Dominion*
Prov. 29:2 When the righteous are in *a*, the people rejoice
Dan. 4:3 His [God's] *a* is from generation to generation
Matt. 8:9 I am a man under *a*, having soldiers under me
Matt. 20:25 those who are great exercise *a* over them
Matt. 21:23 By what *a*...? And who gave You [Jesus] this *a*
Matt. 21:27 Neither will I tell you by what *a* I [Jesus] do these things
Mark 1:22 He [Jesus] taught them as one who had *a*

Mark 1:27 For He commands even the unclean spirits with *a*

Luke 9:1 He [Jesus]...gave them power and *a* over all demons

Rom. 13:1 every soul be subject to the governing *a'ies*

1 Cor. 15:24 when He [Jesus] has put down...all *a*

1 Tim. 2:12 not allow a woman...to usurp *a* over the man

AVEN. See *On,* No. 2

AVENGER OF BLOOD. A relative who was expected to avenge the wrong committed against a member of his family. The most extreme example of this principle was taking the life of a murderer. Before formal courts of law existed, this was a type of primitive justice in OT times. To keep this practice in check, six cities of refuge were established throughout Israel. These "safe centers" sheltered people who had accidentally caused the death of another person (Num. 35:9–21). See also *Cities of Refuge.*

AVVA. An Assyrian city whose citizens settled in Samaria after the Northern Kingdom fell to Assyria (2 Kings 17:24).

AXE. A wood-cutting tool that the prophet Elisha miraculously retrieved from the Jordan River into which it had fallen (2 Kings 6:4–5).

AYIN. Sixteenth letter of the Hebrew alphabet, used as a heading over Psalm 119:121–128. In the Hebrew language, each line of these eight verses begins with this letter.

AZARIAH. (1) A prophet who encouraged King Asa of Judah to destroy all idols in the land (2 Chron. 15:1–8).

(2) A man who helped rebuild the walls of Jerusalem after the Exile (Neh. 3:23).

(3) A Levite after the Exile who explained the law as Ezra read it to the people (Neh. 8:7). See also *Abed-nego; Uzziah.*

AZEKAH. A defense city built by King Rehoboam of Judah (the Southern Kingdom), Solomon's son and successor (2 Chron 11:9).

AZMAVETH. One of David's "mighty men," an elite group of warriors known for their bravery in battle (2 Sam. 23:31).

AZZAH. KJV: See *Gaza*

BAAL. A major pagan god of the Canaanites whose immoral worship rituals were considered especially offensive by the Lord. Baal's worship involved sexual practices with temple prostitutes. These acts were thought to emulate the annual fertility cycle, supposedly controlled by Baal, that caused livestock to reproduce and crops to grow. The Israelites often blundered into idolatry by worshipping this false god (Judg. 2:13). The prophet Elijah denounced the prophets of Baal in a contest on Mount Carmel, and the God of Israel won a decisive victory (1 Kings 18:19–40). The KJV plural form of this name was *Baalim.*

Baal is also mentioned in Num. 22:41 • Judg. 6:25–32 • 1 Kings 16:31–32; 19:18; 22:53 • 2 Kings 10:18–28; 11:18; 17:16; 21:3–4 • 2 Chron. 23:17 • Jer. 2:8; 7:9; 11:13, 17; 12:16; 19:5; 23:13; 32:29, 35 • Hos. 2:8; 13:1 • Zeph. 1:4. *Baals*: 1 Sam. 12:10.

BAALAH. See *Kiriath-jearim*

BAALATH. A town built by Solomon (1 Kings 9:17–18) which became one of his storage cities (2 Chron. 8:6).

BAAL-BERITH. A name under which the Canaanite god Baal was worshipped at Shechem (Judg. 8:33; 9:4).

BAAL OF PEOR. A name under which the Canaanite god Baal was worshipped by the Moabites (Num. 25:1–9 • Deut. 4:3–4 • Ps. 106:28–29 • Hos. 9:10). *Peor*: Num. 31:16 • Josh. 22:17.

BAAL-PERAZIM. A place in central Israel where David won a decisive victory over the Philistines (2 Sam. 5:18–20).

BAAL-ZEBUB. A name under which the Canaanite god Baal was worshipped by the Philistines (2 Kings 1:2–16). *Beelzebub*: Matt. 10:25; 12:24, 27.

BAANAH. A warrior in Saul's army who assassinated Ishbosheth, Saul's son and successor. Later, David had Baanah put to death (2 Sam. 4:1–12).

BAASHA. A king of (Israel (the Northern Kingdom) who gained the throne by assassinating all the heirs of the previous king (1 Kings 15:16–30). His reign was marked by pointless wars with Judah (the Southern Kingdom). Baasha is also mentioned in 1 Kings 16:1–13 • 2 Kings 9:9 • 2 Chron. 16:1–6 • Jer. 41:9.

BABEL, TOWER OF. A tall structure symbolizing human pride and rebellion that was built in the land of Shinar after the great flood (Gen. 11:1–9). It was probably a ziggurat, a tower with terraces of diminishing size as it ascended toward the sky. God dealt with the arrogance of these builders by confusing their language so they could not communicate, then scattering them abroad.

BABY [IES]

Ps. 8:2 Out of the mouth of *b'ies* and nursing infants, You have ordained strength

Luke 1:41 when Elizabeth heard...Mary, the *b* leaped in her womb

Luke 2:16 Mary and Joseph, and the *b* lying in a manger

1 Pet. 2:2 As newborn *b'ies*, desire the sincere milk of the word

BABYLON. A powerful pagan nation in Mesopotamia that carried citizens of Judah (the Southern Kingdom) into exile about 587 BC (2 Kings 24:12–15). Spoils from their victories over Judah and other nations were used to fund the construction of their capital city, also known as Babylon. Glimpses of this pagan culture and the captive Israelites who lived there appear most notably in the book of Daniel. The prophet was apparently held in high esteem in Babylon, since he interpreted dreams for King Belshazzar. Three of his Israelite friends, Shadrach, Meshach, and Abed-nego, were selected for service at the royal court (Dan. 1:3–7).

After holding the Jewish people captive for many years, the Babylonians were defeated by the Persians about 539 BC. The Persians eventually allowed the Israelites to return to their homeland. Other names for Babylon are Sheshak (Jer. 25:26), Shinar (Isa. 11:11) and the land of the Chaldeans (Ezek. 12:13).

Most references to Babylon appear in the books of 2 Kings, Jeremiah, Ezekiel, and Daniel. In the book of Revelation, Babylon is a symbol of evil and wickedness (Rev. 14:8; 16:19; 17:5; 18:2, 10, 21).

BABYLONIA. A powerful nation that carried the Southern Kingdom of Judah into exile about 587 BC. The Babylonians were defeated by the Persians about 539 BC, fulfilling the prophecies of Isaiah and Jeremiah (**2 Chron. 36:5–21** • Isa. 14:22 • Jer. 50:9). *Land of the Chaldeans*: Ezek. 12:13. *Sheshak*: Jer. 25:26. *Shinar*: Isa. 11:11.

BABYLONISH GARMENT. A richly embroidered robe kept by Achan as part of the spoils of war after the fall of Jericho. This act of disobedience to the Lord's clear command led to Achan's death (Josh. 7:18–25).

BACK [S]

Gen. 19:26 But his [Lot's] wife looked *b*...and she became a pillar of salt

Exod. 14:21 the LORD caused the sea to go *b* by a strong east wind

Josh. 7:8 Israel turns their *b's* before their enemies

2 Sam. 12:23 Can I [David] bring him [David's child] *b*

Neh. 9:26 they [the Israelites]...threw Your law behind their *b's*

Job 39:22 He [the horse] does not turn *b* from the sword

Ps. 35:4 let those who devise my hurt be turned *b* and brought to confusion

Ps. 44:18 Our heart has not turned *b*

Prov. 10:13 a rod is for the *b* of him...void of understanding

Prov. 26:3 a bridle for the donkey, and a rod for the fool's *b*

Isa. 14:27 who can turn it [God's hand] *b*

Isa. 38:17 You [God] have cast all my sins behind Your *b*

Jer. 4:8 anger of the LORD has not turned *b* from us

Ezek. 23:35 you have...cast Me behind your *b*

Dan. 7:6 like a leopard, which had four wings of a bird upon its *b*

Matt. 24:18 Do not let him...return *b* to take his clothes

Luke 9:62 No one...who looks *b* is fit for the kingdom

John 6:66 many of His disciples went *b*

Acts 20:20 I [Paul] kept *b* nothing that was profitable to you

BACKBITE. To speak critically of fellow believers—a practice condemned by the apostle Paul (2 Cor. 12:20).

BACKSLIDE. To grow cold or negligent in one's devotion to God; to lose one's spiritual vitality. This sin may be caused by failure to cultivate the fruits of conversion (2 Pet. 1:5–9), persecution (Matt. 13:20–21), and love of material things (1 Tim. 6:10). This sin separates the offender from God's blessings, but confession and repentance bring His forgiveness. The prophet Jeremiah could be called "the backsliding preacher of the Bible"—not because he strayed from the Lord himself but because he condemned the nation of Judah for its spiritual apathy. The word appears many times throughout his book (for example, Jer. 2:19; 49:4).

BACKSLIDER

Prov. 14:14 The *b* in heart shall be filled with his own ways

BACKSLIDING [S]

Jer. 3:14 Return, O *b* children, says the Lord

Jer. 14:7 our *b's* are many; we have sinned against You

Hos. 4:16 For Israel slides back like a *b* heifer

Hos. 14:4 I [God] will heal their *b*. I will love them freely

BADGER. An animal whose skins were used as the covering for the tabernacle (Exod. 25:5).

BAHURIM. A village near Jerusalem where two of David's officials hid in a well during Absalom's rebellion (2 Sam. 17:18).

BALAAM. A practitioner of magic hired by the king of Moab to curse the Israelites to keep them out of Canaan. Balaam blessed the Israelites instead, and predicted that the Israelites were destined to defeat their enemies (Num. 22–24). Balaam is also mentioned in Deut. 23:4–5 • Josh. 13:22; 24:9–10 • Mic. 6:5 • 2 Pet. 2:15 • Jude 11 • Rev. 2:14.

BALAC. KJV: See *Balak*

BALAK. The king of Moab who hired Balaam the magician to curse the Israelites as they crossed his territory. But God led Balaam to bless them and to predict their prosperity in the land of Canaan (Num. 22–24). Balak is also mentioned in Josh. 24:9 • Judg. 11:25 • Mic. 6:5 • Rev. 2:14.

BALANCE [S]

Lev. 19:36 just *b's*, just weights, a just ephah

Job 31:6 let me be weighed in an even *b*

Prov. 11:1 A false *b* is an abomination to the LORD

Isa. 40:12 Who [God] has...weighed...the hills in a *b*

Dan. 5:27 You [Belshazzar] are weighed in the *b's* and are found lacking

Amos 8:5 falsifying the *b's* by deceit

Rev. 6:5 he who sat on it had a pair of *b's* in his hand

BALANCES. Instruments used in business transactions for measuring weight (Prov. 11:1). The use of false or dishonest balances was prohibited by the OT law (Lev. 19:36).

BALDNESS. A stigma of shame and a symbol of extreme mourning in OT times (Isa. 15:2). The pagan practice of shaving one's head may have led to the negative attitude toward this condition among the Israelites.

BALM OF [IN] GILEAD. An aromatic resin exported from Gilead and used as a medicine. To the prophet Jeremiah, this healing substance suggested that the time for healing of the idolatrous nation of Judah was past and the Lord's judgment was just around the corner (Jer. 8:22).

BAND [S]
Lev. 26:13 I [God] have broken the *b's* of your yoke
Ps. 119:61 The *b's* of the wicked have robbed me
Hos. 11:4 I [God] drew them...with *b's* of love
Matt. 27:27 the soldiers...gathered the whole *b* of soldiers to Him

BANI. (1) One of David's "mighty men," an elite group of warriors known for their bravery in battle (2 Sam. 23:36).

(2) A Levite after the Exile who explained the law as Ezra read it to the people (Neh. 8:7).

BANQUET. An elaborate meal, usually served on a special occasion. Esther exposed the plot of Haman to destroy the Jews during a banquet with the king of Persia (Esther 7:1–4). The righteous will be included in the messianic banquet in the end-time, but the wicked will be excluded (Matt. 8:11–12).

BAPTISM. A rite that signifies a believer's conversion to new life through Christ's atoning death. The practice is rooted in the ministry of John the Baptist, forerunner of Jesus. John called on people to repent and be baptized to show they had been cleansed of their sin. Even Jesus consented to baptism by John at the beginning of His public ministry (Matt. 3:13). By doing so He apparently identified with John's work and set an example for all future believers who would be baptized in His name. All Christian groups practice the ritual of baptism. But they differ widely on who should be baptized and the way in which it should be administered.

BAPTISM
Matt. 20:22 to be baptized with the *b* that I [Jesus] am baptized with
Matt. 21:25 The *b* of John—from where did it come
Mark 1:4 John...preached the *b* of repentance
Luke 12:50 I [Jesus] have a *b* to be baptized with
Rom. 6:4 we were buried with Him by *b* into death
Eph. 4:5 one Lord, one faith, one *b*
Col. 2:12 buried with Him in *b*
1 Pet. 3:21 The similar symbol to this *b*, which also now saves us

BAPTISM OF JESUS. See *Jesus Christ, Life and Ministry of*

BAPTISM OF REPENTANCE
Luke 3:3 he [John the Baptist] came...preaching the *b-o-r* for the remission of sins
Acts 13:24 John...preached...the *b-o-r* to all the people of Israel
Acts 19:4 John truly baptized with the *b-o-r*

BAPTIZE [D, ING]
Matt. 3:11 He [Jesus] shall *b* you with the Holy Spirit
Matt. 3:13 Then Jesus came...to John to be *b'd* by him
Matt. 3:14 But John forbade Him...I have need to be *b'd* by You
Matt. 3:16 when He was *b'd*, Jesus went up... out of the water
Matt. 28:19 go and teach all nations, *b'ing* them in the name of the Father
Mark 1:8 I...*b* you with water, but He shall *b* you with the Holy Ghost
Mark 16:16 He who believes and is *b'd* shall be saved
Luke 3:7 Then he [John the Baptist] said to the multitude that came forth to be *b'd*
John 1:28 beyond the Jordan, where John was *b'ing*
John 3:22 there He remained with them and *b'd*
John 3:23 John was also *b'ing*...And they came and were *b'd*
John 4:1 heard that Jesus made and *b'd* more disciples than John

John 4:2 though Jesus Himself did not *b*, but His disciples

Acts 1:5 John *b* with water, but you shall be *b'd* with the Holy Spirit

Acts 2:38 Repent, and...be *b'd* in the name of Jesus

Acts 2:41 those who gladly received his [Peter's] word were *b'd*

Acts 8:12 they [the Samaritans] were *b'd*, both men and women

Acts 8:36 what hinders me from being *b'd*

Acts 9:18 he [Paul] received sight...arose and was *b'd*

Acts 16:15 she [Lydia] and her household were *b'd*

Acts 16:33 he [Philippian jailer]...was *b'd*, he and all his household

Acts 22:16 Arise and be *b'd*, and wash away your sins

Rom. 6:3 so many of us who were *b'd* into Jesus Christ were *b'd* into His death

1 Cor. 1:13 Or were you *b'd* in the name of Paul

1 Cor. 1:17 Christ sent me [Paul] not to *b* but to preach the gospel

1 Cor. 12:13 by one Spirit we were all *b'd* into one body

1 Cor. 15:29 what shall those...*b'd* for the dead do...Why...are they *b'd*

Gal. 3:27 as many of you as have been *b'd* into Christ have put on Christ

BARABBAS. A notorious criminal chosen for release instead of Jesus when He was on trial before Pilate. It was customary for Roman authorities to grant freedom to one prisoner during the observance of the Jewish Passover (John 18:39–40). Barabbas is also mentioned in Matt. 27:16–26 • Mark 15:7–15 • Luke 23:18.

BARAK. A general who joined the female judge Deborah to win a decisive victory over the Canaanites (Judg. 4:4–24). Barak is also mentioned in Heb. 11:32.

BARBARIAN. A word used by the Greeks to designate uncouth foreigners or citizens of other nations besides Greece (Rom. 1:14 • Col. 3:11).

BAR-JESUS. A false prophet, also known as Elymas, who was struck blind when he opposed Paul and Silas during the first missionary journey (Acts 13:6–12). *Elymas:* Acts 13:8.

BAR-JONAH. A name, meaning "son of Jonah," that Jesus used for the apostle Peter (Matt. 16:17).

BARLEY. A coarse grain eaten by livestock (1 Kings 4:28) and also cooked into bread by the poor (John 6:9).

BARNABAS. A leader in the church at Antioch of Syria who enlisted Paul to help him in this ministry (Acts 11:19–26). Earlier, Barnabas had seen Paul's potential as a witness for Christ. He stood up for Paul when many Christians did not trust the former persecutor of the church (Acts 9:27–28). The church at Antioch eventually sent Barnabas and Paul to witness on the island of Cyprus and in the provinces of Asia Minor. Barnabas was the leader at first, but Paul had moved to the forefront by the time they returned. This trip eventually became known as the apostle's first missionary journey (Acts 13:1–3; 14:26–28). Barnabas is also mentioned in Acts 4:36–37; 12:25; 15:2–39 • 1 Cor. 9:6 • Gal. 2:1, 9, 13. *Joseph:* Acts 4:36.

BARREN. Unable to conceive and bear children. Barrenness was viewed as something of a curse in Bible times. Abraham and his wife, Sarah, considered it such a problem that Abraham fathered a child with Sarah's servant Hagar—with Sarah's permission (Gen. 16:1–3).

BARREN

Gen. 11:30 But Sarai was *b*; she had no child

Gen. 29:31 He [God] opened her [Leah's] womb, but Rachel was *b*

Ps. 113:9 He [God] makes the *b* woman to keep house

Luke 1:7 Elizabeth was *b*, and...well advanced in years

Luke 23:29 Blessed are the *b*, and the wombs that never bore

2 Pet. 1:8 you shall be neither *b* nor unfruitful in the knowledge of our Lord

BARTHOLOMEW. One of the twelve apostles of Jesus (Mark 3:14–19). Some scholars believe he is the same person as Nathanael (John 1:45–49). If so, he was skeptical that the Messiah could come from the humble town of Nazareth. He is known for his famous question, "Can any good thing come out of Nazareth?" (John 1:46). Bartholomew is also mentioned in Matt. 10:3 • Luke 6:14 • Acts 1:13.

BARTIMAEUS. A blind beggar healed by Jesus near the city of Jericho (Mark 10:46–52).

BARUCH. (1) A man who helped rebuild the walls of Jerusalem after the Exile (Neh. 3:20).

(2) A scribe who recorded Jeremiah's prophecies and read them at a public gathering and before the royal court (Jer. 36:4–32). He fled to Egypt, along with the prophet, after the fall of Jerusalem to the Babylonians (Jer. 43:1–7). Baruch is also mentioned in Jer. 32:12–16; 45:1–5.

BARZILLAI. An aged friend of David who brought provisions to the king and his aides when they fled to escape Absalom's rebellion (2 Sam. 17:27–29). In his final days, David asked Solomon, his son and successor, to take care of Barzillai's children (1 Kings 2:7). He is also mentioned in 2 Sam. 19:31–39.

BASHAN. A fertile plain east of the Jordan River conquered by the Israelites (Num. 21:33) and allotted to the half-tribe of Manasseh (Josh. 13:29–30). In later years, Bashan's prosperity became a symbol of arrogance and selfishness. The prophet Amos condemned the pleasure-seeking women of this region as "cows of Bashan" (Amos 4:1). Bashan is also mentioned in Num. 21:33–35 • Deut. 3:13–15; 29:7 • Josh. 13:11–12 • 2 Kings 10:32–33 • Neh. 9:22 • Ps. 22:12 • Ezek. 39:18 • Amos 4:1–13.

BASKET [S]
Gen. 40:18 Joseph answered...The three *b's* are three days
Jer. 24:2 One *b* had very good figs...the other *b* had very evil figs
Amos 8:1 behold, a *b* of summer fruit

Matt. 14:20 they took up twelve *b's* full of the fragments that remained
Mark 8:20 how many *b's* full of fragments did you take up
Acts 9:25 the disciples...let him [Paul] down... in a *b*

BATH. The standard Hebrew measure for liquids, equivalent to about six gallons (1 Kings 7:26).

BATHING. A ritualistic washing of the body to make it ceremonially clean (Lev. 15:5, 16). See also *Ceremonial Washing.*

BATHSHEBA. The woman with whom King David committed adultery and the mother of four of his sons (2 Sam. 11:1–27). She became David's wife after their adulterous affair that resulted in the birth of a son. This child died as an infant. Later she used her influence with David to assure that he chose her second son, Solomon, as his successor (1 Kings 1:28–30). Bathsheba is also mentioned in 2 Sam. 12:24 • 1 Kings 1:11, 15–31; 2:13–25. *Bath-shua:* 1 Chron. 3:5.

BATH-SHUA. See *Bathsheba*

BATTERING RAM. A heavy wooden beam used by an invading army to break down the gates and walls of a fortified city (Ezek. 4:2).

BATTLEMENTS. Heavily fortified structures on city walls to protect warriors from attack (Jer. 5:10).

BAVVAI. A man who helped rebuild the walls of Jerusalem after the Exile (Neh. 3:18).

BEAM
1 Sam. 17:7 the staff of his [Goliath's] spear was like a weaver's *b*
Matt. 7:3 why do you...not consider the *b* that is in your own eye
Luke 6:42 First cast the *b* out of your own eye

BEAR [ING, S]
Gen. 4:13 Cain said to the LORD, My punishment is greater than I can *b*
Gen. 16:11 you [Hagar]...shall *b* a son...Ishmael

Gen. 17:19 Sarah, your [Abraham's] wife, shall *b* you a son

Exod. 20:16 shall not *b* false witness against your neighbor

Exod. 37:5 he put the poles into the rings...to *b* the ark

Lev. 16:22 the goat shall *b* all their iniquities upon itself

Lev. 19:18 You shall not take vengeance or *b* any grudge

Num. 11:14 I [Moses] am not able to *b* all these people alone

Num. 14:27 How long shall I [God] *b* with this evil congregation

Deut. 5:20 You shall not *b* false witness against your neighbor

Deut. 32:11 As an eagle...*b's* them [her young] on her wings

Ps. 126:6 goes forth and weeps, *b'ing* precious seed

Prov. 25:18 A man who *b's* false witness against his neighbor is a club

Isa. 7:14 a virgin shall...*b* a son and shall call His name Immanuel

Isa. 46:4 I [God] will *b*...and will deliver you

Ezek. 4:6 you [Ezekiel] shall *b* their iniquity

Ezek. 18:19 Does the son not *b* the iniquity of the father

Ezek. 18:20 The son shall not *b*...nor shall the father *b*

Ezek. 36:7 the nations...shall *b* their shame

Mic. 7:9 I will *b* the wrath of the LORD

Matt. 3:11 whose [Jesus'] shoes I [John the Baptist] am not worthy to *b*

Mark 15:21 they compelled one Simon...to *b* His cross

Luke 13:9 if it *b's* fruit, well. And if not...cut it down

Luke 14:27 whoever does not *b* his cross... cannot be My disciple

Luke 22:10 a man shall meet you *b'ing* a pitcher

John 1:7 came as a witness, to *b* witness of the Light

John 5:31 If I *b* witness of Myself, My witness is not true

John 5:32 There is another who *b's* witness of Me [Jesus]

John 8:18 who *b's* witness of Myself, and the Father...*b's* witness of Me

John 10:25 the works that I [Jesus] do...*b* witness of Me

John 15:8 In this My Father is glorified, that you *b* much fruit

John 16:12 many things to say to you, but you cannot *b* them

John 19:17 And He, *b'ing* His cross, went out to...the place of a skull

Acts 9:15 he [Paul] is a chosen vessel...to *b* My name before the Gentiles

Rom. 8:16 The Spirit Himself *b's* witness with our spirit

Rom. 15:1 We, then, who are strong ought to *b* the weaknesses of the weak

1 Cor. 13:7 [love] *b's* all things, believes all things

2 Cor. 4:10 *b'ing* about in the body the dying of the Lord Jesus

2 Cor. 11:1 I wish that you could *b* with me... and...you do *b* with me

Gal. 6:2 *B* one another's burdens, and so fulfill the law of Christ

Gal. 6:17 I [Paul] *b* in my body the marks of the Lord Jesus

Heb. 9:28 Christ was offered once to *b* the sins of many

Heb. 13:13 Let us go forth...*b'ing* His reproach

1 John 5:6 it is the Spirit who *b's* witness because the Spirit is truth

1 John 5:7 three who *b* witness in heaven: the Father, the Word, and the Holy Spirit

1 John 5:8 three who *b* witness on earth: the Spirit, and the water, and the blood

BEAR FALSE WITNESS

Exod. 20:16 You shalt not *b-f-w* against your neighbor

Deut. 5:20 You shal not *b-f-w* against your neighbor

Matt. 19:18 You shal not steal. You shall not *b-f-w*

Rom. 13:9 you shall not *b-f-w*, you shall not covet

BEAR [S] FRUIT

Isa. 37:31 remnant...of the house of Judah shall...*b-f*

Luke 13:9 if it *b's-f*, well. And if not...cut it down

John 15:2 branch...that does not *b-f* He takes away...that *b's-f* He purges

John 15:4 branch cannot *b-f* by itself, unless it abides in the vine

BEARD. A full beard was a mark of pride to the Israelites. To shave one's beard or pull out the hair expressed deep grief and anguish (Jer. 48:37–38). David declared war against the Ammonites when they mutilated the beards of the messengers he had sent in peace (2 Sam. 10:4–6).

BEAT [ING, S]

Prov. 23:14 b him with the rod...deliver his soul from hell

Isa. 2:4 they shall *b* their swords into plowshares

Isa. 3:15 What do you mean that you *b* My people to pieces

Joel 3:10 **B** your plowshares into swords

Jon. 4:8 the sun *b* on the head of Jonah

Matt. 7:25 the winds blew and *b* on that house

Mark 4:37 the waves *b* into the ship, so that it was now full

Mark 12:5 they killed him, and many others, *b'ing* some

Acts 16:22 the magistrates...commanded them to be *b*

Acts 22:19 I [Paul] imprisoned and *b* those who believed in You

1 Cor. 9:26 So I [Paul] fight, not as one who *b's* the air

BEATITUDES, THE. The declarations of blessedness at the beginning of Jesus' Sermon on the Mount (Matt. 5:3–12). They describe the characteristics of those who commit their lives to Jesus and the rewards they receive from this commitment. See also *Sermon on the Mount.*

BEAUTIFUL

1 Sam. 16:12 he [David]...had a *b* face and was good-looking

2 Sam. 11:2 David...saw a woman...and the woman was very *b*

Eccles. 3:11 He [God] has made everything *b* in its time

Isa. 52:7 How *b* on the mountains are the feet of him who brings good news

Matt. 23:27 you [scribes and Pharisees]...indeed appear *b* outwardly

Rom. 10:15 How *b* are the feet of those who preach the gospel

BECKONED

Luke 5:7 they *b* to their partners...in the other ship

Acts 21:40 Paul...*b* with his hand to the people

Acts 24:10 after the governor had *b* to him to speak, Paul answered

BEDAN. A minor judge who apparently served between Gideon and Jephthah, two major judges of Israel. His name does not appear in the book of Judges (1 Sam. 12:11).

BEELZEBUB. A pagan god to which the Pharisees attributed the miracles of Jesus in an attempt to undermine his power and authority (Matt. 12:24). This god was worshipped in OT times by the Philistine residents of Ekron under the name of Baal-zebub (2 Kings 1:3). The name meant "lord of the fly," a god which was apparently thought to be a protector against this pest. See also *Baal-zebub.*

BEER-SHEBA. A place in southern Israel where Abraham lived for a time. It took its name from an agreement that Abraham reached with a local ruler over the rights to water his flocks from a well (Gen. 21:22–32). In later years this site developed into a city. The phrase "from Dan to Beersheba" (2 Sam. 24:15) designated the entire territory of Israel—from Dan in the north to this southernmost city. Beer-sheba is also mentioned in Gen. 26:32–33 • Judg. 20:1 • 2 Sam. 3:10 • Amos 5:5.

BEFOREHAND

Mark 13:11 do not worry *b*...about what you shall speak

1 Tim. 5:25 the good works of some also are revealed *b*

BEHAVE

BEGAN

Gen. 6:1 when men *b* to multiply on the face of the earth

2 Sam. 5:4 David was thirty years old when he *b* to reign

2 Chron. 3:1 Solomon *b* to build the house of the LORD

Jon. 3:4 Jonah *b* to enter into the city a day's journey

Matt. 4:17 Jesus *b* to preach and to say, Repent

Matt. 26:22 every one of them *b* to say to Him, Lord, is it I

Mark 6:7 He called the twelve to Himself and *b* to send them out

Mark 8:31 And He *b* to teach them that the Son of Man must suffer

Luke 14:18 they all with one consent *b* to make excuses

Luke 15:14 there arose a mighty famine...and he *b* to be in need

Luke 19:45 And He...*b* to cast out those who sold in it

John 13:5 He [Jesus]...*b* to wash the disciples' feet

BEGGAR. A person who survived on handouts from others. God instructed the Israelites to care for the poor (Deut. 15:7–10).

BEGINNING [S]

Gen. 1:1 In the *b* God created the heaven and the earth

Job 42:12 the LORD blessed the latter end of Job more than his *b*

Ps. 111:10 The fear of the LORD is the *b* of wisdom

Prov. 1:7 The fear of the LORD is the *b* of knowledge

Eccles. 7:8 The end of a thing is better than its *b*

Isa. 40:21 Has it not been told to you from the *b*

Isa. 48:3 I have declared the former things from the *b*

Matt. 19:4 He who made them at the *b* made them male and female

Matt. 20:8 give them their wages, *b* from the last to the first

Mark 13:8 famines and troubles. These are the *b's* of sorrows

Luke 24:27 b at Moses...He expounded...the things concerning Himself

John 1:1 In the *b* was the Word... and the Word was God

John 6:64 Jesus knew from the *b*...who did not believe

Col. 1:18 He [Jesus]...is the *b*, the firstborn from the dead

2 Thes. 2:13 God has from the *b* chosen you for salvation

Heb. 7:3 Melchizedek...having neither *b* of days nor end of life

2 Pet. 3:4 all things continue as they were from the *b* of creation

1 John 1:1 That which was from the *b*, which we have heard

1 John 2:13 you have known Him who is from the *b*

1 John 3:11 you heard from the *b*, that we should love one another

Rev. 1:8 I am Alpha and Omega, the *b* and the ending

Rev. 22:13 I am Alpha and Omega, the *b* and the end

BEGOTTEN. A word for Jesus, showing His distinctiveness as the only and unique—"one of a kind"—Son of His heavenly Father (John 3:16–18).

BEGOTTEN

John 1:14 we saw His glory, the glory as of the only *b* of the Father

John 1:18 the only *b* Son...He has declared Him

John 3:16 God so loved the world that He gave His only *b* Son

1 Pet. 1:3 God...has *b* us again to a living hope

BEHAVE [D]

1 Sam. 18:14 David *b'd* wisely...and the LORD was with him

Ps. 101:2 I will *b* myself wisely in a perfect way

Ps. 131:2 I have *b'd* and quieted myself, like a child

1 Cor. 13:5 [love] does not *b* improperly

2 Thes. 3:7 we ourselves did not *b* disorderly among you

45

BEHEADING. The method of execution by which John the Baptist was put to death by Herod Antipas (Matt. 14:10).

BEHEMOTH. A large animal cited by the Lord to show Job his insignificance (Job 40:15–24). The word may refer to a hippopotamus, or perhaps a mythical creature.

BEHIND

Matt. 9:20 a woman...with an issue of blood came *b* Him

Matt. 16:23 He [Jesus]...said to Peter, Get *b* Me

Phil. 3:13 forgetting those things that are *b*

Rev. 1:10 I was in the Spirit...and heard *b* me a great voice

BEHOLD

Gen. 1:31 God saw everything that He had made, and *b*, it was very good

Ps. 133:1 B, how...pleasant it is for brothers to dwell together in unity

Isa. 7:14 B, a virgin shall conceive and bear a son

Isa. 42:1 B, My Servant, whom I uphold

Isa. 59:1 B, the LORD's hand is not shortened, that it cannot save

Jer. 32:27 B, I am the LORD, the God of all flesh

Jer. 44:11 B, I [God] will set My face against you for evil

Mal. 4:5 B, I [God] will send you Elijah the prophet

Matt. 10:16 B, I [Jesus] send you forth as sheep in the midst of wolves

Matt. 12:18 B, My servant whom I have chosen

Matt. 12:49 B, My mother and My brothers

Luke 1:38 Mary said, *B* the handmaid of the Lord

John 1:36 looking at Jesus...he said, *B*, the Lamb of God

John 19:14 And he said to the Jews, *B* your King

1 Cor. 15:51 B...We shall not all sleep, but we shall all be changed

2 Cor. 5:17 b, all things have become new

1 John 3:1 B, what manner of love the Father has bestowed on us

Rev. 3:11 B, I [Jesus] come quickly. Hold fast what you have

Rev. 3:20 B, I [Jesus] stand at the door and knock

Rev. 21:5 B, I [Jesus] make all things new

BEKAH. A Hebrew weight equal to one-half shekel, or about one-quarter ounce (Exod. 38:26).

BELA. See *Zoar*

BELIAL. An OT word translated variously as "wicked," "godless," or "corrupt" (1 Kings 21:10). The apostle Paul used the term for Satan (2 Cor. 6:15).

BELIEF. An act of the will that leads people to place their trust in Jesus Christ. God responds by delivering believers from sin and shaping them into new beings who bring honor and glory to Him. In the early church, Christians were often called "believers" (Acts 5:14), an apt description for followers of Christ.

BELIEVE [D, ING, S]

Gen. 15:6 he [Abraham] *b'd* in the LORD; and He counted it to him for righteousness

Exod. 4:1 they will not *b* me [Moses] or listen to my voice

Ps. 119:66 I have *b'd* Your commandments

Jon. 3:5 the people of Nineveh *b'd* God...and put on sackcloth

Matt. 18:6 whoever causes one of these little ones who *b's* in Me

Matt. 21:22 whatever you ask in prayer, *b'ing*, you shall receive

Mark 5:36 He [Jesus] said...Do not be afraid; only *b*

Mark 9:23 If you can *b*, all things are possible

Mark 9:24 Lord, I *b*; help my unbelief

Mark 11:24 b that you have received them, and you shall have them

Luke 24:25 O fools, and slow of heart to *b*

John 3:12 earthly things and you do not *b*, how shall you *b*...heavenly things

John 3:16 whoever *b's* in Him [Jesus] should not perish

John 3:18 b's...is not condemned...does not *b* is...because he has not *b'd* in the...Son

John 3:36 He who *b's* in the Son has...life, and he who does not *b*...not see life

John 4:48 Unless you see signs and wonders, you will not *b*

John 6:29 This is the work of God, that you *b* in Him whom He has sent

John 6:35 he who *b's* in Me shall never thirst

John 6:64 some of you...do not *b*. Jesus knew... who did not *b*

John 9:36 Who is He, Lord, that I might *b* in Him

John 11:25 He who *b's* in Me, though he were dead, yet shall he live

John 11:26 whoever...*b's* in Me shall never die. Do you *b* this

John 11:27 Yes, Lord, I *b* that You are the Christ

John 12:46 whoever *b's* in Me should not abide in darkness

John 14:1 you *b* in God, *b* also in Me

John 20:25 Unless I [Thomas]...thrust my hand into His side, I will not *b*

John 20:29 have seen Me, you...*b*. Blessed are those who have not seen...yet have *b'd*

John 20:31 that you might *b*...Jesus is the Christ...*b'ing* you might have life

Acts 4:32 multitude of those who *b'd* were of one heart

Acts 8:37 If you *b*...you may. And he...said, I *b* that Jesus Christ is the Son of God

Acts 16:31 *B* in the Lord Jesus Christ, and you shall be saved

Rom. 1:16 it [the gospel] is the power of God for salvation to everyone who *b's*

Rom. 4:3 Abraham *b'd* God, and it was counted to him for righteousness

Rom. 6:8 we *b* that we shall also live with Him

Rom. 10:4 Christ is the end of the law for righteousness to everyone who *b's*

Rom. 10:9 *b* in your heart that God has raised Him from the dead, you shall be saved

Rom. 10:10 with the heart man *b's* to righteousness

Rom. 10:14 How...shall they call on Him in whom they have not *b'd*...how shall they *b*

Rom. 10:16 For Isaiah says, Who has *b'd* our report

Rom. 13:11 now our salvation is nearer than when we *b'd*

Rom. 15:13 may the God of hope fill you with all joy...in *b'ing*

1 Cor. 1:21 it pleased God by the foolishness of preaching to save those who *b*

1 Cor. 13:7 [love] bears all things, *b's* all things

2 Tim. 1:12 I [Paul] know whom I have *b'd*

Heb. 11:6 he who comes to God must *b* that He is

Jas. 2:19 You *b* that there is one God...the demons also *b*, and tremble

1 John 3:23 we should *b* in the name of His Son, Jesus

1 John 5:1 Whoever *b's* that Jesus is the Christ is born of God

1 John 5:10 He who *b's* in the Son of God has the witness in himself

BELIEVERS

Acts 5:14 And more *b* were added to the Lord

1 Tim. 4:12 be an example to the *b*, in word... in faith

BELONG [ED, S]

Ps. 3:8 Salvation *b's* to the LORD

Ps. 94:1 O LORD God, to whom vengeance *b's*

Dan. 9:9 Mercy and forgiveness *b* to the Lord our God

Luke 23:7 as soon as he [Pilate] knew that He *b'ed* to Herod's jurisdiction

1 Cor. 7:32 He who is unmarried cares for the things that *b* to the Lord

BELOVED SON

Matt. 3:17 This is My *b-S*, in whom I am well pleased

Matt. 17:5 This is My *b-S*, in whom I am well pleased. Hear Him

Mark 1:11 You are My *b-S*, in whom I am well pleased

Mark 9:7 This is My *b-S*. Hear Him

Luke 3:22 You are My *b-S*. In You I am well pleased

Luke 9:35 This is My *b-S*. Hear Him

Luke 20:13 I will send my *b-s*. Perhaps they will reverence him

2 Tim. 1:2 to Timothy, my [Paul's] dearly *b-s*: grace, mercy, and peace

BELSHAZZAR. A son or grandson of Nebuchadnezzar and the last king of the

Babylonian Empire (Dan. 5:1–2). The prophet Daniel interpreted a mysterious handwriting on the wall of Belshazzar's palace to mean that the nation would fall to another world power. That very night the king was killed when Babylon fell to the Persian army (Dan. 5:30–31). Belshazzar is also mentioned in Dan. 7:1; 8:1.

BELTESHAZZAR. See *Daniel*

BEN. A Hebrew prefix that, when placed before another word, means "son," as in Ben-Hadad, "son of Hadad."

BENAIAH. One of David's "mighty men," an elite group of warriors known for their bravery in battle (2 Sam. 23:30). He followed David's orders and helped install Solomon as David's successor (1 Kings 1:32–47). Benaiah served as a major military leader under Solomon (1 Kings 4:4). He is also mentioned in 2 Sam. 8:18; 20:23; 23:20, 22 • 1 Kings 2:25–46 • 1 Chron. 11:22–25; 18:17; 27:5–6.

BEN-AMMI. A son of Lot and ancestor of the Ammonites (Gen. 19:30–38).

BENEDICTION. A short statement, prayer, or pronouncement of God's blessing. The first benediction in the Bible was issued by the Lord. He told the living creatures, "Be fruitful and multiply, and fill the waters in the seas, and let fowl multiply in the earth" (Gen. 1:22). Other biblical benedictions include Jacob's blessing on his sons (Gen. 49), Joshua's for Caleb (Josh. 14:13), King Solomon's for the people at the dedication of the temple (2 Chron. 6:3), and Simeon's for the baby Jesus and His parents (Luke 2:34).

BENEFIT [S]

Ps. 68:19 Blessed be the Lord, who daily loads us with *b's*

Ps. 103:2 Bless the Lord, O my soul, and do not forget all His *b's*

Ps. 116:12 What shall I repay to the Lord for all His *b's*

Jer. 2:11 exchanged their glory for what does not *b*

BEN-HADAD. A general title for the kings of Damascus, Syria. Three separate Ben-hadads are mentioned in the Bible. (1) Ben-hadad I, who invaded the Northern Kingdom, in league with King Asa of Judah (1 Kings 15:18–20). He is also mentioned in 2 Chron. 16:2–4.

(2) Ben-hadad II, who waged war against King Ahab of Israel (the Northern Kingdom) (1 Kings 20:1–34). He is also mentioned in 2 Kings 6:24; 8:7–9.

(3) Ben-hadad III, who was defeated by the Assyrian army, as the prophet Amos predicted (Amos 1:4). He is also mentioned in 2 Kings 13:3, 24–25.

BENJAMIN. (1) The youngest of Jacob's twelve sons and ancestor of the tribe of Benjamin. His mother Rachel died at his birth, and named him Ben-oni, meaning "son of my pain" (Gen. 35:16–20). His father, Jacob, later gave him the name that means "son of the right hand." Benjamin was greatly loved by his full brother Joseph, who was also a son of Rachel (Gen. 43:14–30). He is also mentioned in Gen. 35:18, 24; 42:4, 36; 45:12–14, 22; 46:19, 21 • Exod. 1:3 • 1 Chron. 2:2; 7:6; 8:1.

(2) One of the twelve tribes of Israel that grew from Benjamin's descendants. This tribe settled in southern Canaan (Josh. 18:11–28). It was one of two tribes that remained loyal to the dynasty of David after the split of the united kingdom into two factions after Solomon's death (1 Kings 12:21).

(3) A man who helped rebuild the walls of Jerusalem after the Exile (Neh. 3:23).

BEREA. A city in southern Macedonia where Paul found open-minded Jews who were eager to learn. Many responded favorably to the gospel (Acts 17:10–12). After moving on, Paul left Silas and Timothy behind to disciple these new believers. Among them was Sopater, who became a missionary associate and a fellow traveler with the apostle in later years. This may be the Sosipater who joined Paul in sending greetings to the believers in Rome (Rom. 16:21).

BEREAVE [D]
Gen. 42:36 You have *b'd* me [Jacob] of my children

Jer. 15:7 I [the Lord] will *b* them of children

Jer. 18:21 let their wives be *b'd* of their children

BERITH. See *Baal-berith*

BERNICE.
A sister of Herod Agrippa II, Roman governor of Palestine before whom Paul appeared (Acts 25:13, 23; 26:1–32).

BERODACH-BALADAN.
A Babylonian king who sent ambassadors to visit King Hezekiah of Judah (the Southern Kingdom), perhaps to gain an ally against the threat from Assyria. Hezekiah foolishly showed them his riches—an act rebuked by the prophet Isaiah (2 Kings 20:12–19). *Merodach-baladan*: Isa. 39:1.

BERYL.
A precious stone, probably similar to emerald, embedded in the breastplate of the high priest (Exod. 28:20), and used in the foundation of New Jerusalem (Rev. 21:20).

BESEECH [ING]
1 Chron. 21:8 I *b* You, take away the guilt of Your servant

Jer. 38:20 I [Jeremiah] *b* you, obey the voice of the LORD

Dan. 9:16 I [Daniel] *b* You, let Your anger...be turned away

Jon. 4:3 O LORD, I [Jonah] *b* You, take my life from me

Matt. 8:5 a centurion came to Him, *b'ing* Him

Luke 7:3 he sent...to Him, *b'ing* Him that He would...heal his servant

Luke 9:38 Master, I *b* You, look at my son

Rom. 12:1 I [Paul] *b* you, brothers

1 Cor. 4:16 I [Paul] *b* you, be followers of me

2 Cor. 2:8 I [Paul] *b* you that you would confirm your love toward him

2 Cor. 5:20 we are ambassadors for Christ, as though God were *b* you by us

Eph. 4:1 I [Paul]...*b* you to walk worthy of the vocation to which you are called

Philem. 10 I [Paul] *b* you for my son Onesimus

1 Pet. 2:11 I [Peter] *b* you...abstain from fleshly lusts

BESOR.
A dry streambed near Ziklag where David battled the Amalekites (1 Sam. 30:9–21).

BEST
1 Sam. 8:14 he [the king] will take your fields... the *b* of them

Luke 15:22 Bring forth the *b* robe and put it on him

1 Cor. 12:31 But earnestly covet the *b* gifts

BESTOWED
Gal. 4:11 I [Paul] am afraid for you, lest I have *b'ed* on you labor in vain

1 John 3:1 what manner of love the Father has *b'ed* on us

BE STRONG
Deut. 31:6 *B-s* and of good courage. Do not fear

Josh. 10:25 Joshua said...*B-s* and of good courage

1 Chron. 28:10 to build a house for the sanctuary; *b-s* and do it

Isa. 35:4 *B-s*...your God will come with vengeance

Hag. 2:4 *b-s*, all you people of the land, says the LORD

1 Cor. 16:13 stand fast in the faith...*b-s*

Eph. 6:10 *b-s* in the Lord and in the power of His might

2 Tim. 2:1 *b-s* in the grace that is in Christ Jesus

BETH.
(1) Second letter of the Hebrew alphabet, used as a heading over Psalm 119:9–16. In the Hebrew language, each line of these eight verses begins with this letter.

(2) A Hebrew prefix meaning "house" and joined to many biblical place names, as in Bethel or Beth-el, "house of God."

BETHABARA. KJV: See *Bethany*, No. 2

BETHANY.
(1) A village near the Mount of Olives outside Jerusalem where Jesus raised his friend Lazarus from the grave (John 11:43–44). This was not the first time Jesus had visited Lazarus and his two sisters, Mary and Martha, in Bethany. On one occasion He gently rebuked Martha when she complained that her sister was not helping her in the kitchen. He reminded Martha that she should be listening to His teachings like her sister rather than fretting over

preparing a meal (Luke 10:38–42). Later, after His death and resurrection, Jesus ascended to heaven from Bethany (Luke 24:50–51). Bethany is also mentioned in Matt. 21:17; 26:6 • Mark 11:1, 11–12; 14:3 • Luke 19:29 • John 11:1, 18; 12:1.

(2) A place east of the Jordan River in the modern nation of Jordan where John the Baptist baptized people. He also apparently baptized Jesus at this place (John 1:28–34). This location, called "Bethany beyond the Jordan" in the SKJV, is rendered as Bethabara in the KJV.

BETHEL. A city north of Jerusalem where Jacob had a life-changing vision of angels on a staircase (Gen. 28:10–19). Later he built an altar on the site. For many years after this encounter, Bethel was revered as a sacred place. But this changed when King Jeroboam I of Israel (the Northern Kingdom) set up a calf idol at Bethel (1 Kings 12:28–33). The prophet Hosea used a play on words to show how far Bethel had fallen from its exalted position. Beth-el ("house of God") had degenerated into Beth-aven ("house of idols") (Hos. 10:5). Bethel is also mentioned in Gen. 12:8; 13:3–4; 35:1–15 • Josh. 16:2 • 1 Sam. 7:15–16; 10:3 • 2 Kings 23:4, 15–20 • Jer. 48:13 • Amos 7:10–13. *El-bethel*: Gen. 35:7. *Luz*: Gen. 28:19.

BETHESDA. A pool in Jerusalem where Jesus healed a lame man (John 5:2–8). Archaeologists have discovered an ancient pool in modern Jerusalem that featured five distinct arches with porches—a striking similarity to the description in John's Gospel.

BETH-HORON. Twin towns about eight miles from Jerusalem that served as important military outposts. They occupied opposite sides of a deep valley on the ancient road between Jerusalem and the Mediterranean Sea. Known as Upper and Lower Beth-Horon, one city sat about 800 feet higher than the other. King Solomon fortified both towns to protect Jerusalem from invading armies (2 Chron. 8:5). They are also mentioned in Josh. 10:10–14; 16:3–5 • 1 Sam. 13:18 • 1 Chron. 7:24.

BETHLEHEM. A town six miles south of Jerusalem where Jesus was born in fulfillment of OT prophecy (Mic. 5:2; Luke 2:4–7). The traditional place of His birth is visited by thousands of Holy Land pilgrims every year. In a cave beneath the ancient Church of the Nativity, they view a spot marked by a star that is reputed to be the very place where Jesus was born. Bethlehem was known as the "City of David" because King David grew up here (1 Sam. 16:1–13). The town was known in OT times as Ephrath (Gen. 35:16–19) and Ephrathah (Ruth 4:11). Bethlehem is also mentioned in Gen. 48:7 • Ruth 1:19, 22; 2:4 • 1 Sam. 17:15; 20:6, 28 • 2 Sam. 2:32; 23:14–16, 24 • 1 Chron. 11:16–26 • 2 Chron. 11:6 • Ezra 2:21 • Neh. 7:26 • Matt. 2:1–16. *Bethlehem in Judah*: Judg. 19:18.

BETH-LEHEM-JUDAH. KJV: See *Bethlehem*

BETHPHAGE. A village near Bethany and the Mount of Olives and perhaps the place from which Jesus made His triumphant entry into Jerusalem (Mark 11:1–2). This traditional site is marked by a church known as the Church of Bethphage. Inside is a painting depicting Jesus riding a donkey into Jerusalem while the crowds place palm leaves on the ground to welcome Him as a king. Bethphage is also mentioned in Matt. 21:1 • Luke 19:29.

BETHSAIDA. A fishing village near the Sea of Galilee and the home of three of Jesus' disciples: Peter, Andrew, and Philip (John 1:44). Excavations at the site have uncovered the remains of a fisherman's house, along with tools of the fishing trade. Bethsaida is also mentioned in Matt. 11:21 • Mark 6:45 • Luke 10:13 • John 12:21.

BETH-SHAN. A Philistine city where the bodies of King Saul and his sons were hung after they were killed in battle (1 Sam. 31:10–13). King David later had the bodies buried in Saul's family tomb in the territory of Benjamin (2 Sam. 21:12–14).

BETH-SHEMESH. An Israelite town where the ark of the covenant was kept for a time after it was returned by the Philistines (1 Sam. 6:11–13).

BETH-ZUR. A city in the mountains of Judah (the Southern Kingdom) fortified by King Rehoboam as a defensive outpost to protect Jerusalem (2 Chron. 11:5–7).

BETRAY [ED, S]

Matt. 17:22 Son of Man shall be *b'ed* into the hands of men

Matt. 26:2 the Son of Man will be *b'ed* to be crucified

Matt. 26:16 he [Judas] sought opportunity to *b* Him [Jesus]

Matt. 26:45 the Son of Man is being *b'ed* into the hands of sinners

Mark 14:10 Judas...went to the chief priests, to *b* Him [Jesus] to them

Mark 14:11 he sought how he might conveniently *b* Him [Jesus]

Mark 14:21 but woe to that man by whom the Son of Man is *b'ed*

Luke 22:21 the hand of him who *b's* Me [Jesus] is with Me on the table

Luke 22:48 Judas, will you *b* the Son of Man with a kiss

John 6:64 Jesus knew...who would *b* Him

1 Cor. 11:23 the Lord Jesus, the same night in which He was *b'ed*, took bread

BETROTHAL. A marriage agreement made by the parents of the bride and groom that was an integral part of the couple's union. It was considered just as binding as the actual marriage. The most notable case of betrothal in the Bible was that of Joseph and Mary to one another before Jesus was born (Matt. 1:18–19).

BETTER

1 Sam. 15:22 Behold, to obey is *b* than sacrifice

2 Kings 5:12 Are not the Abana and the Pharpar...*b* than all the waters of Israel

Ps. 37:16 A little that a righteous man has is *b* than the riches of many wicked

Ps. 84:10 a day in Your courts is *b* than a thousand

Ps. 118:8 *b* to trust in the LORD than to put confidence in man

Prov. 8:11 For wisdom is *b* than rubies

Prov. 15:16 *B* is little with the fear of the LORD than great treasure and trouble

Prov. 16:16 How much *b* is it to get wisdom than gold

Prov. 19:22 a poor man is *b* than a liar

Prov. 27:5 Open rebuke is *b* than secret love

Prov. 27:10 a neighbor who is near is *b* than a brother far away

Eccles. 4:9 Two are *b* than one, because they have a good reward for their labor

Eccles. 4:13 *B* is a poor and wise child than an old and foolish king

Eccles. 6:9 The sight of the eyes is *b* than the wandering of the desire

Eccles. 7:1 A good name is *b* than precious ointment

Eccles. 7:8 The end of a thing is *b* than its beginning

Eccles. 9:18 Wisdom is *b* than weapons of war

Song of Sol. 4:10 How much *b* is your love than wine

Dan. 1:20 found them [Daniel and his friends] ten times *b* than all the magicians

Jon. 4:8 Jonah...said, It is *b* for me to die than to live

Matt. 12:12 How much *b*, then, is a man than a sheep

Matt. 18:8 It is *b* for you to enter into life lame or maimed

1 Cor. 7:9 for it is *b* to marry than to burn

Phil. 1:23 having a desire...to be with Christ; which is far *b*

Heb. 7:22 Jesus was made a surety of a *b* covenant

BEULAH. The prophet Isaiah's name for the land of God's people after the Exile. It symbolized the nation's future prosperity and close relationship with the Lord (Isa. 62:4).

BEZALEL. A craftsman from the tribe of Judah who helped build the tabernacle in the wilderness (Exod. 31:2). *Bezaleel*: KJV.

BEZER. A fortified town east of the Jordan River designated by Moses as a city of refuge

(Josh. 20:8). Bezer is also mentioned in Deut. 4:43 • Josh. 21:36 • 1 Chron. 6:78.

BIBLE, THE. The sacred book, or collection of books, that contains guidelines for Christian belief and behavior. Its two major divisions are the OT and the NT, each containing separate books with several different types of writings. The Bible is the result of divine inspiration, being revealed by the Lord to many different writers of the past. From its original Hebrew (OT) and Greek (NT) manuscripts, it has been translated into hundreds of different languages to make God's message available to people groups around the world. The first complete English Bible translated from the original languages was the Geneva Bible, issued in 1560. The popular King James Version appeared in 1611, and numerous English versions and revisions have been published since then. The Bible is also referred to symbolically as a hammer (Jer. 23:29), a lamp (Ps. 119:105), and a sword (Eph. 6:17).

BIER. A portable frame on which a body was carried to its burial place (2 Sam. 3:31). Jesus touched the bier of a widow's son before raising him from the dead (Luke 7:14–15).

BILDAD. A friend of Job whose three speeches expressed the idea that all suffering is the direct result of sin in one's life (Job 8:1–22; 18:1–21; 25:1–6)——a doctrine that Job denied.

BILHAH. A slave girl who gave birth to two of Jacob's sons, Dan and Naphtali (Gen. 30:1–8). Bilhah is also mentioned in Gen. 29:29; 35:22, 25; 37:2; 46:25 • 1 Chron. 7:13.

BIND [ING, S]

Gen. 37:7 we [Joseph and his brothers] were *b'ing* sheaves in the field

Deut. 6:8 you shall *b* them as a sign on your hand

Ps. 147:3 He [God] heals the broken in heart and *b's* up their wounds

Prov. 3:3 b them [mercy and truth] around your neck

Isa. 61:1 the Lord...has sent me to *b* up the brokenhearted

Dan. 3:20 he [the king] commanded...men...to *b* Shadrach, Meshach, and Abednego

Matt. 12:29 how can one enter into a...man's house...except he first *b's* the...man

Matt. 16:19 whatever you *b* on earth shall be bound in heaven

Matt. 23:4 they [Pharisees] *b* heavy burdens

Mark 5:3 no man could *b* him [demon-possessed man]

Acts 22:4 I [Paul] persecuted...*b'ing* and delivering both men and women

BINNUI. A man who helped rebuild the walls of Jerusalem after the Exile (Neh. 3:24).

BIRTH

Eccles. 7:1 good name is better...the day of death than the day of one's *b*

Matt. 1:18 the *b* of Jesus Christ was in this way

John 9:1 Jesus...saw a man who was blind from his *b*

Rev. 12:2 being with child, she cried, painfully laboring in *b*

BIRTH OF JESUS. See *Jesus Christ, Life and Ministry of*

BIRTHRIGHT. A right as well as a responsibility that belonged to the firstborn son in a family. He received a double portion of his father's assets (Deut. 21:17), but he also inherited the responsibility for family leadership. In a moment of weakness, Esau traded his birthright to his younger brother Jacob for a bowl of stew (Gen. 25:28–34). In the NT, Paul called Jesus the "firstborn among many brothers," alluding to His supreme place of honor in all creation (Rom. 8:29).

BIRTHRIGHT

Gen. 25:31 Jacob said, Sell me this day your [Esau's] *b*

Heb. 12:16 Esau, who for one morsel of food sold his *b*

BISHOP. An elder, overseer, or pastor who served as leader of a local church (Titus 1:5–9). The apostle Peter referred to Jesus as the "Bishop of your souls" (1 Pet. 2:25). He is the ultimate caretaker who looks after His church and those who follow Him as Savior and Lord.

BISHOP [S]

Phil. 1:1 to all the saints...at Philippi, with the *b's*

1 Tim. 3:1 If a man desires the office of a *b*, he desires a good work

1 Tim. 3:2 A *b* then must be blameless, the husband of one wife

Titus 1:7 a *b* must be blameless as the steward of God

1 Pet. 2:25 you...are now returned to the Shepherd and *B* of your souls

BITHYNIA. A coastal province of Asia Minor which Paul and Silas were prevented from entering, through a clear message from the Holy Spirit. They were directed instead into the province of Macedonia (Acts 16:6–10).

BITTER

Exod. 1:14 they [the Egyptians] made their lives *b* with hard bondage

Exod. 12:8 they shall eat it [the Passover meal] with...*b* herbs

Exod. 15:23 could not drink of the waters of Marah...they were *b*

Isa. 24:9 Strong drink shall be *b* to those who drink it

Jer. 31:15 A voice was heard in Ramah, lamentation and *b* weeping

Hab. 1:6 I raise up the Chaldeans, that *b* and hasty nation

Jas. 3:11 Does a fountain send forth sweet water and *b*

BITTER HERBS. Herbs eaten by the Israelites during the Passover celebration as a reminder of their suffering while enslaved in Egypt (Exod. 12:8). They are also mentioned in Num. 9:11.

BITTERNESS

Job 9:18 He [God]...fills me [Job] with *b*

Job 21:25 another dies in the *b* of his soul

Acts 8:23 you are in the gall of *b* and in the bond of iniquity

Rom. 3:14 Their mouth is full of cursing and *b*

Eph. 4:31 Let all *b* and wrath...be put away from you

BLAMELESS

1 Cor. 1:8 you may be *b* on the day of our Lord Jesus

1 Tim. 3:2 A bishop then must be *b*, the husband of one wife

1 Tim. 3:10 being found *b*, let them serve in the office of a deacon

Titus 1:7 a bishop must be *b* as the steward of God

BLASPHEME [D, S]

Ps. 74:10 Shall the enemy *b* Your name forever

Ps. 74:18 the foolish people have *b'd* Your name

Mark 3:28 all sins shall be forgiven...and whatever...they *b*

Mark 3:29 he who *b's* against the Holy Ghost never has forgiveness

Rev. 13:6 he opened his mouth...to *b* His name

BLASPHEMY. Disrespectful acts such as cursing or slandering that show lack of reverence for God. In OT times, this was a capital offense, punishable by death (Lev. 24:15–16). Jesus was charged with this crime by the Jewish religious leaders for declaring that He was God's Son (Mark 14:64). To them Jesus was only as a man, although His miracles showed that He was who He claimed to be.

BLASPHEMY [IES]

Matt. 12:31 *b* shall be forgiven...but...*b* against the Holy Spirit shall not

Matt. 26:65 He [Jesus] has spoken *b*...now you have heard His *b*

Mark 2:7 Why does this man [Jesus] speak *b'ies* like this

Mark 3:28 all sins shall be forgiven...and whatever *b'ies*

Col. 3:8 put off all these: anger, wrath, malice, *b*

Rev. 13:1 I [John]...saw a beast...and on his heads the name of *b*

BLASPHEMY AGAINST THE HOLY SPIRIT.

The sin of claiming Christ's miracles were actually performed by Satan. Jesus declared that such contempt was an unforgivable sin (Matt. 12:31–32). Many interpreters believe this sin consists of rejecting the testimony of the Holy Spirit about Christ's person and work and the invitation to confess Jesus as Savior and Lord.

BLESS [ED, ING, INGS]

Gen. 1:22 God *b'ed* them, saying, Be fruitful and multiply

Gen. 2:3 God *b'ed* the seventh day and sanctified it

Gen. 9:1 And God *b'ed* Noah and his sons

Gen. 12:2 I [God] will *b* you [Abraham]...and you shall be a *b*

Gen. 22:18 in your [Abraham's] descendants shall all the nations...be *b'ed*

Gen. 27:34 Esau...said to his father, *B* me, even me also

Gen. 39:5 the Lord *b'ed* the Egyptian's house for Joseph's sake

Exod. 20:11 the Lord *b'ed* the Sabbath day and made it holy

Num. 6:24 The Lord *b* you and keep you

Num. 24:1 Balaam saw that it pleased the Lord to *b* Israel

Deut. 8:10 you shall *b* the Lord...for the good land...He has given you

Deut. 11:26 I set before you this day a *b'ing* and a curse

Deut. 11:27 a *b'ing*, if you obey the commandments of the Lord

Deut. 33:1 the *b'ing* with which Moses...*b'ed* the children of Israel

Job 1:21 The Lord gave and...has taken away. *B'ed* be...the Lord

Job 42:12 the Lord *b'ed* the latter end of Job more than his beginning

Ps. 1:1 *B'ed* is the man who does not walk in the counsel of the ungodly

Ps. 28:6 *B'ed* is the Lord because He has heard... my supplications

Ps. 29:11 The Lord will *b* His people with peace

Ps. 32:1 *B'ed* is he whose transgression is forgiven

Ps. 33:12 *B'ed* is the nation whose God is the Lord

Ps. 41:13 *B'ed* is the Lord God...from everlasting...to everlasting

Ps. 66:20 *B'ed* is God, who has not turned away my prayer or His mercy

Ps. 67:1 God...*b* us and cause His face to shine upon us

Ps. 84:4 *B'ed* are those who dwell in Your house

Ps. 94:12 *B'ed* is the man whom You chasten

Ps. 96:2 Sing to the Lord; *b* His name

Ps. 106:48 *B'ed* is the Lord God of Israel from everlasting to everlasting

Ps. 115:18 we will *b* the Lord from this time forth

Ps. 119:1 *B'ed* are those whose way is undefiled

Ps. 119:2 *B'ed* are those who keep His testimonies

Ps. 128:1 *B'ed* is everyone who fears the Lord

Ps. 145:1 I will *b* Your name forever and ever

Prov. 10:6 *B'ings* are on the head of the just

Prov. 31:28 Her children rise up and call her *b'ed*

Ezek. 34:26 I will make them...a *b'ing*...There shall be showers of *b'ing*

Matt. 5:3 *B'ed* are the poor in spirit

Matt. 5:4 *B'ed* are those who mourn

Matt. 5:5 *B'ed* are the meek

Matt. 5:6 *B'ed* are those who hunger...after righteousness

Matt. 5:7 *B'ed* are the merciful

Matt. 5:8 *B'ed* are the pure in heart

Matt. 5:9 *B'ed* are the peacemakers

Matt. 5:10 *B'ed* are those who are persecuted for righteousness' sake

Matt. 5:11 *B'ed* are you when men revile you and persecute you

Matt. 5:44 love your enemies, *b* those who curse you

Matt. 16:17 *B'ed* are you, Simon Bar-Jonah

Matt. 26:26 Jesus took bread, and *b'ed* it, and broke it

Mark 10:16 He [Jesus]...put his hands on them [the children], and *b'ed* them

Luke 1:28 You [Mary] are *b'ed* among women

Luke 11:28 Yes, rather, *b'ed* are those who hear the word of God and keep it

John 20:29 *B'ed* are those who have not seen and yet have believed

Rom. 12:14 *B* those who persecute you. *B*, and do not curse

1 Cor. 4:12 Being reviled, we *b*

1 Cor. 10:16 The cup of *b'ing* that we *b*

Gal. 3:8 the scripture...to Abraham, saying, In you all nations shall be *b'ed*

Gal. 3:9 those who are of faith are *b'ed* with faithful Abraham

Eph. 1:3 B'ed is...God...who has *b'ed* us with all spiritual *b'ings*

1 Tim. 6:15 who [Jesus] is the *b'ed* and only Potentate

Titus 2:13 that *b'ed* hope and the glorious appearing of...our Savior

Jas. 1:12 B'ed is the man who endures temptation

Jas. 3:9 With it we *b* God...and with it we curse men

Jas. 3:10 Out of the same mouth proceed *b'ing* and cursing

Rev. 1:3 B'ed is he who reads and those who hear the words of this prophecy

Rev. 5:12 Worthy is the Lamb...to receive...honor and glory and *b'ing*

Rev. 22:7 B'ed is he who keeps the sayings of the prophecy of this book

BLESSING. A declaration of God's favor upon others. In OT times, a blessing was thought to carry great power. Jacob schemed to have his father Isaac bless him instead of his older brother, Esau. Once this blessing was given, it apparently could not be changed or transferred to someone else (Gen. 27:22–35). God is the source of all blessing, and He desires to bless all people (Gen. 12:3). His most abundant blessing is granted to those who confess Christ as Savior and Lord.

BLESS THE LORD

Ps. 16:7 I will *b-t-L*, who has given me counsel

Ps. 34:1 I will *b-t-L* at all times. His praise shall continually be in my mouth

Ps. 103:1 B-t-L, O my soul, and all that is within me; bless His holy name

Ps. 103:2 B-t-L, O my soul, and do not forget all His benefits

Ps. 134:1 b-t-L, all you servants of the LORD

Ps. 134:2 Lift up your hands in the sanctuary and *b-t-L*

BLIND [ED]

Job 29:15 I was eyes to the *b* and I was feet to the lame

Ps. 146:8 The LORD opens the eyes of the *b*

Isa. 35:5 the eyes of the *b* shall be opened

Isa. 42:7 to open the *b* eyes, to bring out the prisoners

Isa. 43:8 Bring out the *b* people who have eyes

Lam. 4:14 they have wandered like *b* men in the streets

Mal. 1:8 if you offer the *b* for sacrifice, is it not evil

Matt. 11:5 the *b* receive their sight and the lame walk

Matt. 20:30 two *b* men sitting by the wayside... cried out

Matt. 23:24 You *b* guides [Pharisees], who strain out a gnat

Mark 8:22 they brought a *b* man to Him and begged Him

Mark 10:46 b Bartimaeus, the son of Timaeus, sat begging by the highway

Luke 4:18 Spirit...anointed Me to preach...recovery of sight to the *b*

Luke 6:39 Can the *b* lead the *b*

Luke 7:22 tell John...how the *b* see, the lame walk

John 9:2 who sinned, this man or his parents, that he was born *b*

John 12:40 He [God] has *b'ed* their eyes and hardened their hearts

Acts 13:11 you [Elymas the sorcerer]...shall be *b*

1 John 2:11 he who hates his brother is in darkness, and...darkness has *b'ed* his eyes

BLINDNESS. The inability to see, in a physical sense (Matt. 9:27) or to understand or comprehend, in a spiritual sense (Eph. 4:18). Jesus healed several blind people, and He harshly criticized the Pharisees for their spiritual blindness (Matt. 23:16).

BLINDNESS

Gen. 19:11 they [angels] struck the men...with *b*, both small and great

2 Kings 6:18 Strike this people...with *b*. And He struck them with *b*

Eph. 4:18 being alienated from the life of God...
because of the *b* of their heart

BLOOD. The life-sustaining fluid of the body
that serves as an apt symbol of God's atoning
grace for humankind. In the OT, the sacrifice
of an animal on an altar was a physical sign of
His forgiveness of sin (Lev. 17:11). In the NT,
the phrase "the blood of Christ" refers to His
redemptive death. He Himself declared that His
own blood would seal the new covenant with
His followers (Mark 14:24). The Lord's Supper,
or communion, memorializes this self-giving
act for believers (1 Cor. 10:16).

BLOOD

Gen. 4:10 The voice of your [Cain's] brother's
b cries to Me

Gen. 9:6 Whoever sheds man's *b*, by man shall
his *b* be shed

Exod. 7:21 there was *b* throughout all the land
of Egypt

Exod. 12:23 when He sees the *b* on the lintel...
the LORD will pass over the door

Exod. 24:8 Moses took the *b*, and sprinkled it
on the people

Lev. 7:27 Any person who eats...*b*...shall be cut
off

Lev. 15:19 if...her discharge in her body is *b*,
she shall be set apart seven days

Lev. 17:11 For the life of the body is in the *b*

Lev. 20:9 He has cursed his father or his mother.
His *b* shall be on him

Num. 35:19 The avenger of *b* himself shall slay
the murderer

1 Kings 18:28 they [priests of Baal]...cut themselves...until the *b* gushed out

1 Kings 22:38 the dogs licked up his [Ahab's] *b*

2 Kings 9:33 her [Jezebel's] *b* spattered on the
wall

1 Chron. 22:8 You [David] have shed *b* abundantly...much *b* on the earth

Ps. 30:9 What profit is there in my *b* when I go
down to the pit

Prov. 1:16 their feet...hurry to shed *b*

Prov. 1:18 they lie in wait for their own *b*

Prov. 6:17 a lying tongue, and hands that shed
innocent *b*

Isa. 1:11 I [God] do not delight in the *b* of bulls

Isa. 1:15 I [God] will not hear. Your hands are
full of *b*

Isa. 59:3 your hands are defiled with *b*, and
your fingers with iniquity

Ezek. 9:9 the land is full of *b* and the city full
of perverseness

Joel 2:31 The sun shall be turned into darkness
and the moon into *b*

Matt. 9:20 a woman... twelve years with an issue
of *b* came behind Him

Matt. 16:17 for flesh and *b* has not revealed it
to you [Peter]

Matt. 26:28 this is My *b* of the new covenant,
which is shed for many

Matt. 27:8 that field has been called the Field
of *B* to this day

Matt. 27:24 Pilate...washed his hands...I am
innocent of the *b* of this...Person

Matt. 27:25 Then all the people answered...His
[Jesus'] *b* be on us

Luke 11:50 the *b* of all the prophets...may be
required of this generation

Luke 22:44 His [Jesus'] sweat was, as it were,
great drops of *b*

John 6:53 Unless you...drink His *b*, you have
no life in you

John 19:34 one of the soldiers...pierced His
side...*b* and water came out

Acts 2:20 The sun shall be turned into darkness
and the moon into *b*

Acts 17:26 [God] has made from one *b* all
nations of men

Acts 18:6 Your *b* is on your own heads

Acts 20:28 feed the church of God, which He
has purchased with His own *b*

Rom. 5:9 having now been justified by His *b*,
we shall be saved from wrath

1 Cor. 10:16 The cup of blessing...is it not the
communion of the *b* of Christ

1 Cor. 15:50 flesh and *b* cannot inherit the kingdom of God

Eph. 2:13 you who sometimes were far off are
made near by the *b* of Christ

Eph. 6:12 we wrestle not against flesh and *b*

Col. 1:14 in whom we have redemption through His *b*

Heb. 9:12 or by the *b* of goats...but by His own *b* He entered in once

Heb. 10:4 not possible that the *b* of bulls...should take away sins

Heb. 13:12 Jesus...might sanctify the people with His own *b*

1 John 1:7 the *b* of Jesus Christ His Son cleanses us from all sin

Rev. 6:12 the sun became black...and the moon became as *b*

Rev. 7:14 These...have washed their robes and made them white in the *b* of the Lamb

Rev. 16:3 the sea...became as the *b* of a dead man

BLOT [S, TED]

Exod. 32:33 Whoever has sinned against Me, I will *b* him out of My book

Ps. 51:1 according to Your loving-kindness...*b* out my transgressions

Ps. 51:9 Hide Your face from my sins and *b* out all my iniquities

Ps. 69:28 Let them be *b'ted* out of the book of the living

Isa. 43:25 I [God]...am He who *b's* out your transgressions for My own sake

Isa. 44:22 I [God] have *b'ted* out your transgressions

Acts 3:19 Repent...that your sins may be *b'ted* out

Rev. 3:5 I [God] will not *b* out his name out of the book of life

BOANERGES. A name, meaning "sons of thunder," used by Jesus for the brothers James and John, two of His disciples (Mark 3:17). It probably reflected their boldness and fiery zeal.

BOAR. A wild hog, known for its destructive nature; cited by the psalmist as a symbol of Israel's sin and rebellion (Ps. 80:13).

BOAST. To speak of one's own accomplishments with pride and haughtiness (2 Chron. 25:19).

BOAST [ING, INGS, S]

Ps. 44:8 In God we *b* all day long

Prov. 25:14 Whoever *b's* himself of a false gift is like clouds...without rain

Prov. 27:1 Do not *b* about tomorrow

2 Cor. 9:3 lest our *b'ing* about you should be in vain

Eph. 2:9 not of works, lest any man should *b*

Jas. 3:5 the tongue is a little part and *b's* great things

Jas. 4:16 you rejoice in your *b'ings*. All such rejoicing is evil

BOAZ. A wealthy landowner of Bethlehem who was kind to Ruth, and whom she eventually married. From their union came a son named Obed, grandfather of King David of Israel (Ruth 4:21–22). Boaz is listed in the two genealogies of Jesus in the NT (Matt. 1:5; Luke 3:32). Boaz is also mentioned in Ruth 2:1–23; 3:2, 7 • 1 Chron. 2:11–12.

BODY [IES]

Num. 19:11 He who touches the dead *b*...shall be unclean

Deut. 21:23 his *b* shall not remain on the tree all night

Mic. 6:7 Shall I give...the fruit of my *b* for the sin of my soul

Matt. 6:23 if your eye is evil, your whole *b* shall be full of darkness

Matt. 26:26 Jesus took bread...Take. Eat. This is My *b*

Mark 15:43 Joseph of Arimathea...asked for the *b* of Jesus

Luke 12:22 Do not worry...for the *b*, what you shall put on

Luke 23:55 the women...saw the sepulchre and how His *b* was laid

Rom. 6:12 Do not let sin reign in your mortal *b*

Rom. 7:24 Who shall deliver me from the *b* of this death

Rom. 12:5 we, being many, are one *b* in Christ

1 Cor. 6:18 Every sin...is outside the *b*, but... fornication...against his own *b*

1 Cor. 6:19 your *b* is the temple of the Holy Spirit

1 Cor. 10:17 we, being many, are one bread and one *b*

1 Cor. 12:12 the *b* is one...and all the parts of that one *b*...are one *b*

1 Cor. 12:13 by one Spirit we were all baptized into one *b*

1 Cor. 13:3 though I [Paul] give my *b* to be burned

1 Cor. 15:44 sown a natural *b*...raised a spiritual *b*...a natural *b*...a spiritual *b*

2 Cor. 5:8 absent from the *b*...present with the Lord

Gal. 6:17 I [Paul] bear in my *b* the marks of the Lord Jesus

Phil. 1:20 Christ shall be magnified in my [Paul's] *b*

Col. 1:18 He [Christ] is the head of the *b*, the church

Jas. 3:6 the tongue among the parts of our *b*...defiles the whole *b*

1 Pet. 2:24 who Himself bore our sins in His own *b* on the tree

BODY OF CHRIST. A symbolic expression for the church used by the apostle Paul (Col. 1:24). The risen Christ is the head of His body. He assigns spiritual gifts to members of the church to accomplish His work and bring believers to maturity (Eph. 4:7–13).

BODY OF CHRIST

Rom. 7:4 you also have become dead to the law by the *b-o-C*

1 Cor. 10:16 The bread that we break, is it not the communion of the *b-o-C*

1 Cor. 12:27 you are the *b-o-C*, and members in particular

Eph. 4:12 for the work of the ministry...edifying of the *b-o-C*

BODY, SPIRITUAL. The body that believers will inhabit after they are glorified in the end-time. This body will not be subject to sickness or death. It will be like that of Christ's glorified body after His resurrection (Phil. 3:21), immortal and incorruptible (1 Cor. 15:52–53).

BOLD [LY]

Prov. 28:1 The wicked flee...the righteous are *b* as a lion

Acts 9:29 he [Paul] spoke *b'ly* in the name of the Lord Jesus

Acts 19:8 he [Paul] went into the synagogue and spoke *b'ly*

Phil. 1:14 many of the brothers...are much more *b* to speak the word without fear

Heb. 4:16 let us come *b'ly* to the throne of grace

BOLDNESS

Acts 4:13 they saw the *b* of Peter and John

Acts 4:31 they [the apostles] spoke the word of God with *b*

Eph. 3:12 in whom [Jesus] we have *b*...with confidence

Phil. 1:20 with all *b*...Christ shall be magnified in my [Paul's] body

1 John 4:17 that we may have *b* in the day of judgment

BOND [S]

Jer. 2:20 I [God] have broken your yoke and burst your *b's*

Jer. 27:2 Make yourself *b's* and yokes, and put them on your [Jeremiah's] neck

Luke 8:29 bound with chains and in fetters...he broke the *b's*

Eph. 4:3 keep the unity of the Spirit in the *b* of peace

Col. 3:14 put on charity, which is the *b* of perfectness

Philem. 10 son Onesimus, whom I [Paul] have begotten in my *b's*

BONDAGE. The state of being held against one's will by an oppressor. The Israelites were enslaved by the Egyptians before their miraculous release under the leadership of Moses. Bondage in a spiritual sense is caused by sin (Rom. 8:15).

BONDAGE

Exod. 1:14 they [the Egyptians] made...lives bitter with hard *b*

Exod. 6:6 I [God] will deliver you [the Israelites] out of their *b*

John 8:33 We are Abraham's descendants...
never in *b* to any man

Rom. 8:15 you have not received the spirit of
b again to fear

Gal. 4:9 how do you...desire again to be in *b*

Gal. 5:1 do not be entangled again with the
yoke of *b*

BOOK. Pieces of animal skin written on and
then bound together (Job 19:23). The word often
refers to a scroll, a long strip of papyrus that
was written on and then rolled up on a spool (1
Sam. 10:25). A scroll was read by being unrolled
to the appropriate passage.

BOOK OF JASHAR. An ancient collection of
poetry, now lost, which apparently described
historic events in the life of Israel (Josh. 10:13).
Book of Jasher: KJV.

BOOK OF LIFE. God's record of the names
of the saved and deeds of the righteous. The
phrase appears several times in the book of
Revelation. At the final judgment, those whose
names are not written in this book will be "cast
into the lake of fire" (Rev. 20:15). But those who
are listed there will be admitted to the heavenly
city known as New Jerusalem. This concept may
have originated with Moses. He prayed that God
would erase his name from His book instead
of wiping out the Israelites because of their
worship of the golden calf in the wilderness
(Exod. 32:32–33).

BOOK OF LIFE

Phil. 4:3 help those...fellow laborers, whose
names are in the *b-o-l*

Rev. 3:5 I will not blot out his name out of the
b-o-l

Rev. 20:12 another book was opened, which
is the *b-o-l*

Rev. 20:15 whoever was not found written in
the *b-o-l* was cast into the lake of fire

BOOK OF THE LAW. The first five books
of the OT known as the Law of Moses, or the
Pentateuch. The Israelites considered these laws
an authoritative guide for belief and behavior.
Moses wrote down these instructions from God,

then delivered them to the priests for public
reading (Deut. 31:9–11). In later years, the Book
of the Law became the basis for the religious
reforms of King Josiah of Judah when a copy
of these laws was discovered in the temple (2
Kings 22:8–23:28).

BOOTHS. Huts made of tree branches that
the Israelites lived in for seven days during
the Feast of Tabernacles. This commemorated
the temporary dwellings they lived in during
their wandering in the wilderness after they
left Egypt (Lev. 23:42).

BORE WITNESS

John 1:15 John *b-w* of Him [Jesus]

John 5:33 sent to John, and he *b-w* to the truth

John 12:17 people who were with Him...*b-w*

Acts 15:8 God, who knows the heart, *b-w* to
them

BORN

Gen. 17:17 Shall a child be *b* to him [Abraham]
who is a hundred years old

Gen. 21:5 Abraham was a hundred years old
when his son Isaac was *b*

Job 3:3 Let the day perish on which I [Job] was *b*

Job 5:7 man is *b* to trouble, as the sparks fly
upward

Job 14:1 Man who is *b* of a woman is of few days

Ps. 58:3 The wicked...go astray as soon as they
are *b*

Prov. 17:17 A friend loves at all times, and a
brother is *b* for adversity

Eccles. 3:2 a time to be *b* and a time to die

Isa. 9:6 a Child is *b* to us, a Son is given to us

Jer. 20:14 Cursed be the day on which I
[Jeremiah] was *b*

Matt. 2:1 when Jesus was *b* in Bethlehem of
Judea

Luke 1:35 the Holy One...*b* of you [Mary] shall
be called the Son of God

Luke 2:11 to you is *b* this day...a Savior

Luke 7:28 among those...*b* of women...not a
greater prophet than John the Baptist

John 9:2 who sinned, this man or his parents,
that he was *b* blind

BORN AGAIN

John 18:37 You say that I [Jesus] am a king. For this purpose I was *b*

Acts 22:28 And Paul said, But I was *b* free

1 Cor. 15:8 as by one *b* out of due time, He [Jesus] was also seen of me [Paul]

1 John 3:9 Whoever is *b* of God does not commit sin

1 John 4:7 everyone who loves is *b* of God

BORN AGAIN. See *New Birth*

BORN AGAIN

John 3:3 Jesus...said to him...unless a man is *b-a*, he cannot see the kingdom of God

John 3:7 Do not marvel that I [Jesus] said to you [Nicodemus], You must be *b-a*

1 Pet. 1:23 *b-a*, not of corruptible seed, but of incorruptible

BOSOM. A word for the human chest often used symbolically to show closeness and intimacy (Isa. 40:11). In Jesus' parable about a rich man and a poor man, "Abraham's Bosom" to which the poor man went is a metaphor for paradise, or heaven (Luke 16:22–23).

BOSOM

Exod. 4:6 The LORD said...Put...your hand into your *b*...he put his hand into his *b*

Prov. 5:20 why will you...embrace the *b* of an adulterer

Isa. 40:11 He [God] shall...carry them [lambs] in His *b*

Luke 16:22 the beggar died and was carried... into Abraham's *b*

John 1:18 The only begotten Son...in the *b* of the Father

John 13:23 one of His disciples...leaning on Jesus' *b*

BOTTLE. A word that refers to containers of animal skins in which liquids were stored (Josh. 9:4). Jesus compared the new era of grace that He instituted to new wineskins (Luke 5:37).

BOTTLE [S]

Job 32:19 my belly...is ready to burst like new *b's*

Ps. 56:8 You put my tears into Your *b*

Luke 5:37 no man puts new wine into old *b's*... will burst the *b's*...*b's* shall perish

BOTTOMLESS PIT

Rev. 9:1 to him was given the key of the *b-p*

Rev. 11:7 the beast who ascends out of the *b-p* shall make war

Rev. 20:1 I saw an angel...having the key of the *b-p*

Rev. 20:3 cast him [the devil] into the *b-p*

BOUGHT

Lev. 27:24 the field shall return to him from whom it was *b*

Jer. 32:9 I [Jeremiah] *b* the field...from Hanamel

Matt. 13:46 he [merchant]...found one pearl... sold all that he had and *b* it

Mark 11:15 Jesus...began to cast out those who sold and *b* in the temple

Luke 14:18 I have *b* a piece of ground, and I need to go and see it

1 Cor. 6:20 you were *b* with a price...glorify God

1 Cor. 7:23 You were *b* with a price; do not become the servants of men

BOUND

Gen. 22:9 Abraham...laid the wood...and *b* Isaac, his son

Judg. 16:21 the Philistines took him [Samson]... and *b* him with shackles of bronze

Dan. 3:23 Shadrach, Meshach, and Abednego, fell down *b* in the...fiery furnace

Matt. 14:3 Herod had taken hold of John and *b* him

Matt. 18:18 Whatever you bind on earth shall be *b* in heaven

Mark 5:4 he [demon-possessed man] had often been *b*

Luke 10:34 *b* up his wounds...and took care of him [wounded traveler]

John 11:44 he [Lazarus]...came out, *b* hand and foot...and his face was *b*

Acts 20:22 I [Paul] am going to Jerusalem, *b* in the Spirit

2 Tim. 2:9 but the word of God is not *b*

Rev. 20:2 he [an angel] laid hold of the dragon... and *b* him a thousand years

BOUNTIFUL [LY]

Ps. 13:6 the LORD...has dealt *b'ly* with me

Prov. 22:9 He who has a *b* eye shall be blessed

2 Cor. 9:6 he who sows *b'ly* shall also reap *b'ly*

BOW. An offensive weapon of war (Gen. 48:22). To the psalmist, the bow was a symbol of persecution by his enemies (Ps. 64:3).

BOW DOWN. To kneel and bend the head forward as an act of worship (Exod. 4:31), or to show respect toward another person. A more extreme form of bowing was falling to the knees, as Abraham did before three strangers (Gen. 18:2–3).

BOWED
Ps. 38:6 I am troubled; I am *b* down greatly
Ps. 57:6 They...prepared a net for my steps; my soul is *b* down
Isa. 2:11 the haughtiness of men shall be *b* down
John 19:30 Jesus...*b* His head and gave up His spirit

BOZRAH. The capital city of Edom that symbolized the Messiah's victory over the pagan nations (Isa. 63:1). Bozrah is also mentioned in Gen. 36:33 • 1 Chron. 1:44 • Isa. 34:6 • Jer. 49:13, 22 • Amos 1:12 • Mic. 2:12.

BRACELET. A piece of jewelry worn on the wrist (Isa. 3:19). The bracelet of King Saul was probably a military armband (2 Sam. 1:10).

BRAMBLE. A bush of thorns cited in a parable by Jotham (Judg. 9:7–15). The bush represented Abimelech, who was like a lowly shrub that wanted to rule over all the trees of the forest.

BRANCH OF RIGHTEOUSNESS. A prophetic title for the coming Messiah that refers to His godly character and sinless life. According to the prophet Jeremiah, He would be like a new branch that sprang from a dead tree trunk (Jer. 33:15). God had promised King David centuries before Jeremiah's time that a descendant of David would always rule over His people (2 Sam. 7:12–16). This promise was fulfilled in Jesus Christ. In a spiritual sense, He was the new Davidic king who came to redeem the world from bondage to sin.

BREAD. A staple food made from flour or meal and baked in loaves. The word often referred to food in general, as in Jesus' prayer, "Give us this day our daily bread" (Matt. 6:11).

BREAD OF LIFE. A name or title that Jesus used for Himself to emphasize the spiritual sustenance He provides for His people (John 6:35). As He uttered these words, He may have had in mind the manna, or bread substitute, that God provided to keep the Israelites alive in the wilderness during the Exodus (Num. 11:7–9). As spiritual bread, Jesus brings hope, joy, and eternal satisfaction to those who place their faith in Him. See also *"I Am" Statements of Jesus.*

BREAK [ING, S]
Gen. 32:24 there a man wrestled with him [Jacob] until the *b'ing* of the day
Job 9:17 For He *b's* me with a tempest
Job 19:2 How long will You...*b* me...with words
Job 34:24 He [God] shall *b* in pieces mighty men
Ps. 2:9 You shall *b* them with a rod of iron
Ps. 29:5 the LORD *b's* the cedars...the LORD *b's* the cedars of Lebanon
Ps. 46:9 He [God] *b's* the bow and cuts the spear
Ps. 48:7 You [God] *b* the ships of Tarshish
Ps. 58:6 *B* their teeth...*B* out the great teeth of the young lions, O LORD
Ps. 89:34 I [God] will not *b* My covenant
Ps. 94:5 They *b* in pieces Your people, O LORD
Eccles. 3:3 a time to *b* down and a time to build up
Isa. 14:7 The whole earth is at rest...They *b* out into singing
Isa. 42:3 A bruised reed He [God's Servant] shall not *b*
Jer. 19:11 Even so I [God] will *b* this people
Jer. 23:29 Is not My [God's] word like...a hammer that *b's* the rock
Hos. 1:5 I [God] will *b* the bow of Israel
Matt. 6:20 lay up...treasures in heaven...where thieves do not *b* in or steal
Matt. 12:20 A bruised reed He shall not *b*
Luke 24:35 He [Jesus] was known to them in the *b'ing* of bread
Acts 2:42 they [believers] continued steadfastly...in the *b'ing* of bread and in prayers

1 Cor. 10:16 The bread that we *b*, is it not the communion of the body of Christ

BREAST. Striking one's breast or chest signified extreme sorrow (Luke 23:48).

BREASTPLATE. Protective armor for the chest. The apostle Paul spoke figuratively of the "breastplate of righteousness" that all believers should wear (Eph. 6:14).

BREATH

Gen. 2:7 God formed man...and breathed into his nostrils the *b* of life

Gen. 7:22 All in whose nostrils was the *b* of life...died

Job 4:9 by the *b* of His [God's] nostrils they are consumed

Ps. 33:6 heavens were made...all the host of them by the *b* of His [God's] mouth

Ps. 94:11 LORD knows the thoughts of man... they are a *b*

Ps. 144:4 Man is like *b*; his days are like a shadow

Ps. 150:6 Let everything that has *b* praise the LORD

Ezek. 37:10 I prophesied...and the *b* came into them [dead bodies], and they lived

Acts 17:25 He [God] gives to all life and *b* and all things

BREATH OF GOD. A symbolic phrase that portrays God as the source of all life. When God created Adam from dust, He brought him to life with His own breath (Gen. 2:7). This demonstrates that God is the supreme living being who holds the power of life and death (Ps. 33:6). This is a dramatic contrast to pagan gods, who have neither life in themselves nor the power to bring life to others. In the NT, Jesus displayed this same power when He "breathed" the Holy Spirit upon His disciples (John 20:22). See also *Anthropomorphism.*

BRIBE [S]

1 Sam. 12:3 from whose hand have I received any *b*

Ps. 26:10 and their right hand is full of *b's*

Amos 5:12 they afflict the just, they take a *b*

BRIBERY. Giving gifts to others in order to win their influence or cooperation—a practice condemned often in the Bible (Amos 5:12).

BRICK. A building block made of clay and straw, and hardened in the sun or a hot furnace. The Israelite slaves were forced to make bricks in Egypt (Exod. 1:14).

BRIDE. A word used figuratively to picture the close spiritual relationship between Christ and His church, with Jesus as the groom and the church as His bride (Eph. 5:25–27).

BRIGHT AND MORNING STAR. A title that Jesus applied to Himself to emphasize the grace and forgiveness associated with His arrival on earth (Rev. 22:16). The heavenly body He referred to was the last star to disappear at dawn, and thus known to ancients as the morning star. When all the other stars disappeared in the early morning, this star twinkled on, signaling the beginning of a new day—just as Jesus' coming ushered in a new era in world history. Another title for Jesus with similar meaning is "day star" (2 Pet. 1:19).

BRIMSTONE. A mineral associated with God's judgment of evil. The cities of Sodom and Gomorrah were destroyed with burning brimstone and fire from heaven (Gen. 19:24–25).

BRONZE. A metal formed from copper mixed with zinc or tin (Num. 21:9). The word is also used as a symbol of stubbornness and rebellion toward God (Isa. 48:4).

BRONZE SEA. A large brass container in the temple court that was filled with water for purification rituals by priests (2 Kings 25:13).

BRONZE SERPENT. A metal image on a pole that Moses raised in the wilderness to heal people who had been bitten by poisonous snakes (Num. 21:9). Jesus cited this event to illustrate the healing from sin made possible by His sacrificial death (John 3:14).

BROTHERS OF JESUS. The half-brothers of Jesus; the sons of Mary and Joseph born by natural means after His birth through the action of the Holy Spirit. The four listed by name are James, Joseph, Simon, and Judas (Matt. 13:55). These four were skeptical of Jesus' claims during His earthly ministry (Matt. 13:57), but at least two apparently became believers after His resurrection. James is thought to be the author of the epistle of James, and Jude apparently wrote the epistle of Jude. Jesus also had half-sisters who are unnamed (Matt. 13:56).

BUILDER [S]

Ps. 118:22 stone that the *b's* rejected has become the head cornerstone

Mark 12:10 The stone that the *b's* rejected has become the head of the corner

Acts 4:11 This is the stone that was despised by you *b's*

Heb. 11:10 he [Abraham] looked for a city... whose *b* and maker is God

1 Pet. 2:7 the stone that the *b's* rejected...is made the head of the corner

BUILDING [S]

1 Kings 7:1 Solomon was *b* his own house for thirteen years

2 Chron. 3:3 Solomon was instructed for the *b* of the house of God

Mark 13:2 Do you see these great *b's*? Not one stone shall be left on another

1 Cor. 3:9 You are God's field; you are God's *b*

2 Cor. 5:1 we have a *b* from God, a house not made with hands, eternal

Eph. 2:21 the *b* properly framed together grows into a holy temple in the Lord

BUKKI. A leader from the tribe of Dan who helped divide the land of Canaan after the conquest (Num. 34:22).

BULL. A choice young bull offered as a sacrifice in the tabernacle and temple (Num. 15:24).

BULRUSH. A reedlike plant that grew in marshy areas. The infant Moses was hidden in a basket made from this plant (Exod. 2:3). These plants were also made into papyrus, a primitive writing material.

BURDEN [S]

Exod. 1:11 they [the Egyptians] set taskmasters over them to afflict them with their *b's*

Ps. 38:4 my iniquities...as a heavy *b*...are too heavy for me

Ps. 55:22 Cast your *b* on the Lord, and He shall sustain you

Jer. 17:22 Neither carry a *b*...on the Sabbath day

Matt. 11:30 For My yoke is easy and My *b* is light

Matt. 20:12 us who have borne the *b* and heat of the day

Matt. 23:4 they [the Pharisees] bind heavy *b's*

Gal. 6:2 Bear one another's *b's*, and so fulfill the law of Christ

Gal. 6:5 For every man shall bear his own *b*

BURIAL. Interment of the dead usually happened within a few hours because a body decomposed rapidly in the warm climate (Deut. 21:23). Bodies were often buried in natural caves or tombs hollowed out of solid rock, as in the case of Jesus (John 19:39–42).

BURIAL OF JESUS. See *Jesus Christ, Life and Ministry of*

BURN [ED, ING, S]

Exod. 3:2 the bush *b'ed* with fire, and the bush was not consumed

Exod. 30:8 when Aaron lights the lamps...he shall *b* incense

Neh. 2:17 Jerusalem lies desolate and its gates are *b'ed*

Job 30:30 my [Job's] bones are *b'ed* with heat

Job 41:19 *B'ing* lamps go out of His mouth

Ps. 79:5 Shall Your jealousy *b* like fire

Ps. 97:3 A fire goes before Him and *b's* up His enemies all around

Prov. 6:27 Can a man take fire in his bosom and his clothes not be *b'ed*

Jer. 7:9 Will you steal, murder...*b* incense to Baal

Jer. 20:9 But His word was in my [Jeremiah's] heart like a *b'ing* fire

Jer. 39:8 the Chaldeans *b'ed* the king's house

Dan. 3:17 our God...is able to deliver us from the *b'ing* fiery furnace

Luke 3:17 He [God] will *b* the chaff with unquenchable fire

Luke 24:32 Did not our hearts *b* within us

Rom. 1:27 the men...*b'ed* in their lust toward one another

1 Cor. 3:15 If any man's work is *b'ed*, he shall suffer loss

1 Cor. 7:9 for it is better to marry than to *b*

1 Cor. 13:3 though I [Paul] give my body to be *b'ed*, and do not have love

2 Pet. 3:10 the earth also and the works...in it shall be *b'ed* up

Rev. 19:20 These two were cast alive into a lake...*b'ing* with brimstone

BURNING BUSH. The flaming shrub through which God revealed Himself to Moses on Mount Sinai (Exod. 3:2–4). The mysterious plant burned but was not consumed. Theologians refer to this phenomenon as a theophany, or a visible appearance of God. The bush may have symbolized that Israel's "fiery trial" of slavery under the Egyptians was about to come to an end through God's intervention on their behalf.

BURNT OFFERING. A sacrificial animal placed on the altar and totally consumed by fire (Lev. 7:8). This complete eradication of the sacrifice may have suggested that human sin demanded radical atonement from the Lord. Instructions for burnt offerings are found in Lev. 1:1–17.

BUSYBODY. One who meddles in the affairs of others; a gossip. The apostle Peter condemned such behavior (1 Pet. 4:15).

BUY [S]

Gen. 42:3 Joseph's ten brothers went down to *b* grain in Egypt

Prov. 23:23 *B* the truth and do not sell it, also wisdom

Prov. 31:16 She considers a field and *b's* it

Amos 8:6 *b* the poor for silver and the needy for a pair of shoes

Matt. 13:44 a man...sells all that he has and *b's* that field

John 6:5 He [Jesus] said...Where shall we *b* bread, that these may eat

BUYER

Isa. 24:2 as with the *b*, so with the seller

Ezek. 7:12 Do not let the *b* rejoice or the seller mourn

BYWORD

Deut. 28:37 you shall become...a *b* among all nations

1 Kings 9:7 Israel shall be...a *b* among all people

Job 17:6 He [God] also has made me [Job] a *b*

Ps. 44:14 You [God] make us a *b* among the nations

CAESAR. A formal title for several emperors of the Roman Empire. Four separate Caesars are mentioned in the NT. (1) Augustus, who issued the decree which required Joseph to go to Bethlehem, where Jesus was born (Luke 2:1).

(2) Tiberius, who ruled during the public ministry of Jesus. He was known for his intolerance of potential rivals (John 19:12).

(3) Claudius, who expelled all the Jewish people living in Rome (Acts 18:2).

(4) Nero, the first emperor under whom the Christians were persecuted. As a Roman citizen, Paul appealed his case to Nero (Acts 25:8–12).

CAESAREA. A Roman coastal city built by Herod the Great and named for the Roman emperor Caesar Augustus. It served as the political capital of Palestine during NT times. Here is where the apostle Paul spent two years in prison before appealing his case to Rome. Caesarea is mentioned in **Acts 8:40; 9:30; 10:1, 24; 11:11; 12:19; 18:22; 21:8–16; 23:23, 33; 25:1–16**. It was often referred to as Caesarea by the Sea to distinguish it from the inland city of Caesarea Philippi.

CAESAREA PHILIPPI. A city at the foot of Mount Hermon in northern Israel where

Jesus' disciple Peter confessed Him as the Messiah (Matt. 16:13–20). This admission had a special meaning because of the city's pagan background. In OT times, it was a place where the pagan god Baal was worshipped by the Canaanites. During the time of Jesus, the city may have contained a temple devoted to worship of the Roman emperor. In contrast to these dead, impotent gods of the past, Peter declared that Jesus was the Son of the living God. He was alive and active on behalf of His people, as Jesus demonstrated through His healing and teaching ministry.

CAESAR'S HOUSEHOLD. A group of converts probably associated with the palace of the emperor in Rome. Paul sent greetings from this group to the church at Philippi (Phil. 4:22).

CAIAPHAS. The Jewish high priest who presided at the trial of Jesus before the Sanhedrin, and advised that He be put to death (John 18:12–14). After Jesus' resurrection, Caiaphas continued his opposition to Jesus. He was one of the religious leaders who questioned Peter and John about their healing of a lame man at the temple in Jerusalem (Acts 3:1–8; 4:6–7). Caiaphas is also mentioned in Matt. 26:3, 57 • Luke 3:2 • John 11:49; 18:24, 28.

CAIN. The oldest son of Adam and Eve who murdered his brother Abel. He apparently acted in a fit of jealousy because Abel's offering was accepted by the Lord while his was not. God punished Cain by sending him into exile (Gen. 4:3–17). Cain is also mentioned in Heb. 11:4 • 1 John 3:12 • Jude 11.

CAINAN. See *Kenan*

CALAMUS. A plant known for its sweet fragrance (Song of Sol. 4:14). It was used in anointing oil (Exod. 30:23).

CALEB. One of the twelve spies sent by Moses to check out the land of Canaan. Ten members of the party advised against entering the land. But Caleb—along with Joshua—declared they should place their faith in the Lord and move

into Canaan immediately (Num. 14:6–9). Caleb lived to enter the land forty years later and was given the city of Hebron for his faithfulness (Josh. 14:6–14). He is also mentioned in **Num. 13:6, 30**; 14:24, 30, 38; 26:65; 32:12; 34:19 • Deut. 1:36 • Josh. 15:13–19; 21:12 • Judg. 1:12–20 • 1 Sam. 25:3; 30:14 • 1 Chron. 4:15; 6:56.

CALF
Exod. 32:24 I [Aaron] cast it into the fire, and this *c* came out
Deut. 9:16 you had sinned...and had made yourselves a molten *c*
Ps. 106:19 They made a *c* in Horeb and worshipped the cast image
Isa. 11:6 the *c* and the young lion and the fattened *c* together
Jer. 34:18 they cut the *c* in two and passed between the parts of it
Luke 15:23 bring the fatted *c* here and kill it
Acts 7:41 they made a *c*...and offered a sacrifice to the idol

CALL [ED, S, ING]
Gen. 1:5 God *c'ed* the light Day, and the darkness...Night
Gen. 2:19 whatever Adam *c'ed* every living creature, that was its name
Gen. 12:8 he [Abraham] built an altar...and *c'ed* on the name of the LORD
Gen. 17:5 No longer shall your name be *c'ed* Abram, but...Abraham
Gen. 17:19 you [Abraham] shall *c* his name Isaac
Gen. 32:30 Jacob *c'ed* the name of the place Peniel
Gen. 35:10 Your name shall not be *c'ed* Jacob... He *c'ed* his name Israel
Gen. 49:1 Jacob *c'ed* to his sons and said, Gather one another
Exod. 2:7 Shall I...*c* for you a nurse of the Hebrew women
Exod. 2:10 she *c'ed* his name Moses...Because I drew him out of the water
Exod. 3:4 God *c'ed* to him [Moses] out of the midst of the bush
Exod. 19:20 the LORD *c'ed* Moses up to the top of the mountain

Deut. 4:26 I [Moses] *c* heaven and earth to witness against you

Deut. 28:10 all people...shall see that you are *c'ed* by the name of the LORD

Judg. 16:25 *C* for Samson, that he may entertain us

1 Sam. 3:8 the LORD *c'ed* Samuel again the third time

1 Sam. 12:18 So Samuel *c'ed* to the Lord

1 Kings 18:25 Elijah said...*c* on the name of your gods

2 Kings 5:11 I [Naaman] thought, He [Elisha] will surely...*c* on...the Lord

1 Chron. 11:7 they *c'ed* it [Jerusalem] the city of David

1 Chron. 16:8 *c* upon His name; make known His deeds

2 Chron. 7:14 if My people who are *c'ed* by My name shall...pray

Job 27:10 Will he always *c* on God

Ps. 4:1 Hear me when I *c*, O God of my righteousness

Ps. 4:3 The LORD will hear when I *c* to Him

Ps. 18:3 I will *c* on the Lord, who is worthy to be praised

Ps. 18:6 In my distress I *c'ed* on the LORD

Ps. 50:15 *c* on Me in the day of trouble

Ps. 72:17 All nations shall *c* Him blessed

Ps. 86:5 You, Lord, are...abundant in mercy to all those who *c* on You

Ps. 105:1 give thanks to the LORD; *c* on His name

Ps. 145:18 The Lord is near to all...who *c* on Him...who *c* on Him in truth

Prov. 31:28 Her children rise up and *c* her blessed

Isa. 7:14 and bear a son and shall *c* His name Immanuel

Isa. 9:6 His [Messiah's] name shall be *c'ed* Wonderful

Isa. 45:3 I, the LORD, who *c's* you by your name, am the God of Israel

Isa. 49:1 The LORD has *c'ed* Me from the womb

Isa. 55:6 *C* on Him while He is near

Isa. 62:2 you shall be *c'ed* by a new name

Isa. 62:4 But you shall be *c'ed* Hephzibah, and your land Beulah

Isa. 65:24 before they *c*, I [God] will answer

Jer. 3:17 they shall *c* Jerusalem the throne of the LORD

Jer. 33:3 *C* to Me, and I will answer you

Dan. 2:2 the king commanded to *c* the magicians

Hos. 1:6 God said to him [Hosea], *C* her name Lo-ruhamah

Hos. 11:1 I [God]...*c'ed* My son out of Egypt

Joel 1:14 Sanctify a fast. *C* a solemn assembly

Joel 2:32 whoever *c's* on the name of the Lord shall be delivered

Jon. 1:6 What do you mean, O sleeper [Jonah]? Arise, *c* on your God

Matt. 1:21 you [Joseph] shall *c* His name JESUS

Matt. 1:25 And he [Joseph] *c'ed* His name JESUS

Matt. 2:23 in a city *c'ed* Nazareth, that...He [Jesus] shall be *c'ed* a Nazarene

Matt. 5:9 the peacemakers...shall be *c'ed*...children of God

Matt. 9:13 I [Jesus] have come to *c* not the righteous but sinners to repentance

Matt. 11:16 children sitting in the markets and *c'ing* to their companions

Matt. 18:2 Jesus *c'ed* a little child to Him

Matt. 19:17 Why do you *c* Me good

Matt. 20:16 For many are *c'ed*, but few chosen

Matt. 21:13 My [God's] house shall be *c'ed* the house of prayer

Matt. 23:9 do not *c* any man on the earth your father

Matt. 27:22 What then shall I [Pilate] do with Jesus, who is *c'ed* Christ

Luke 1:13 you [Zechariah] shall *c* his name John

Luke 1:32 He [Jesus]...shall be *c'ed* theSon of the Highest

Luke 6:46 And why do you *c* Me, Lord, Lord

Luke 9:1 Then He *c'ed* His twelve disciples together and gave them power

Luke 14:13 *c* the poor, the maimed, the lame

Luke 15:21 I have sinned...and am no longer worthy to be *c'ed* your son

John 1:42 You [Peter] shall be *c'ed* Cephas...A Stone

Acts 2:21 whoever *c's* on the name of the Lord shall be saved

Acts 10:15 What God has cleansed, do not *c* that common

Acts 11:26 the disciples were first *c'ed* Christians in Antioch

Acts 13:2 Separate Barnabas and Saul...for the work to which I have *c'ed* them

Rom. 1:1 Paul, a servant...*c'ed* to be an apostle

Rom. 8:28 all things work together for good... for those who are *c'ed*

Rom. 10:12 the same Lord...is rich to all who *c* on Him

Rom. 10:13 whoever *c's* on...the Lord shall be saved

Rom. 10:14 How then shall they *c* on Him in whom they have not believed

1 Cor. 1:26 you see your *c'ing*...not many mighty, not many noble are *c'ed*

1 Cor. 7:20 Let every man remain in the same *c'ing* in which he was *c'ed*

Gal. 5:13 brothers, you have been *c'ed* to liberty

Eph. 4:1 walk worthy of the vocation to which you are *c'ed*

Phil. 3:14 I [Paul] press toward the mark for the prize of the high *c'ing* of God

1 Thes. 4:7 For God *c'ed* us not to uncleanness but to holiness

2 Tim. 2:22 follow righteousness...with those who *c* on the Lord out of a pure heart

Heb. 11:8 Abraham obeyed when he was *c'ed*

Jas. 5:14 Is anyone sick among you? Let him *c* for the elders

1 Pet. 2:9 declare the praises of Him who has *c'ed* you out of darkness

1 John 3:1 that we should be *c'ed* the sons of God

CALLING. God's appeal to people to follow Him and to serve others in His name. Some people heed His special call to vocational ministry by serving Him as full-time ministers or church workers. All people are subject to His universal call for salvation and devotion to His work in the world. As followers of Jesus, they declare the praises of Him who has called them "out of darkness into his marvelous light" (1 Pet. 2:9).

CALL ON THE LORD

2 Sam. 22:4 I will *c-o-t-L*, who is worthy to be praised

2 Tim. 2:22 follow righteousness...with those who *c-o-t-L* out of a pure heart

CALVARY. A hill just outside the city walls of Jerusalem where Jesus was crucified (Luke 23:33). The word comes from a Latin word which means "skull," thus "place of the skull." The site was first identified in 1863 by British general Charles Gordon. Popularly known as Gordon's Calvary, it has been venerated ever since by generations of evangelical Christians who visit the Holy Land. The Aramaic form of the word is *Golgotha* (Matthew 27:33; Mark 15:22; John 19:16).

CAMEL. A hardy animal ideally suited to the desert and used for riding and carrying burdens. This was Rebekah's mode of transportation when she traveled from Mesopotamia to meet her future husband, Isaac (Gen. 24:64–65).

CANAAN. (1) A son of Ham whose descendants founded several tribal peoples in and around Palestine (Gen. 9:18–27; 10: 6, 15–18 • 1 Chron. 1:8, 13).

(2) The territory between the Mediterranean Sea and the Jordan River that God promised to Abraham and his descendants (Gen. 13:15–17). Several centuries passed before this promise was fulfilled. The land had to be taken from the Canaanites, a race who had inhabited the land long before Abraham's time (Gen. 12:6). Although small in size, Canaan was strategically located between the two great civilizations of Egypt to the south and Mesopotamia to the north. Canaan is also referenced in Gen. 15:3–7 • Acts 7:11 (*Chanaan*: KJV).

CANA OF GALILEE. A village near Capernaum in the district of Galilee where Jesus performed His first miracle—the changing of water into wine at a wedding feast (John 2:1–11). The Gospel of John cites this miracle as the first of seven "signs" that Jesus performed to show His unique mission as the Son of God. Cana of Galilee is also mentioned in John 4:46–54; 21:2.

CANDACE. The title of an Ethiopian queen whose servant was baptized by Philip the evangelist (Acts 8:27).

CANDLE. A word for a small oil-burning lamp that illuminated a room. Jesus compared such light sources to the influence that believers should display in a sinful world (Matt. 5:15).

CANDLE
Ps. 18:28 For You will light my *c*
Matt. 5:15 Nor do men light a *c* and put it under a bushel
Rev. 22:5 they need no *c* or light of the sun

CANKERWORM. A locust in the early stage of its development. The prophet Joel referred to this insect as a warning of God's coming judgment (Joel 1:4).

CAPERNAUM. A city on the northwestern shore of the Sea of Galilee that served as the headquarters for Jesus during His Galilean ministry. He may have settled here for a time because five of His twelve disciples lived here. The fishermen brothers, Peter and Andrew and James and John, worked on the Sea of Galilee (Matt. 4:18–22), and Matthew was a tax collector in the town (Luke 5:27–32). Some of Jesus' most important teachings and healings occurred in or near this little town. But most of the people ignored His message. He condemned Capernaum for its unbelief, along with other nearby villages (Luke 10:15).

Capernaum is also mentioned in Matt. 4:13–17; 8:5; 11:23; 17:24 • Mark 1:21; 2:1; 9:33 • Luke 4:23, 31; 7:1 • John 2:12; 4:46; 6:17, 24, 59.

CAPH. Eleventh letter of the Hebrew alphabet, used as a heading over Psalm 119:81–88. In the Hebrew language, each line of these eight verses begins with this letter.

CAPHTOR. A region, perhaps an island, where the Philistines lived before settling in Canaan. Caphtor is mentioned in Deut. 2:23 • Jer. 47:4 • Amos 9:7.

CAPPADOCIA. A large Roman province in eastern Asia Minor. In his first epistle, the apostle Peter mentioned believers from this region (1 Pet. 1:1).

CAPTAIN OF SALVATION. A title of Jesus that emphasizes his role as the leader who sacrificed Himself to provide salvation for hopeless sinners (Heb. 2:10). In this role, He continues to guide, encourage, and inspire His followers.

CAPTIVE [S]
Ps. 68:18 You have ascended on high; You have led *c's*
Isa. 61:1 the LORD has anointed Me...to proclaim liberty to the *c's*
Jer. 13:19 Judah shall be carried away as *c's*
Jer. 39:9 Nebuzaradan...carried away *c* into Babylon the remnant of the people
Ezek. 1:1 as I [Ezekiel] was among the *c's* by the river
Luke 4:18 He [God] has anointed Me [Jesus]... to preach deliverance to the *c's*
Eph. 4:8 When He ascended...He led captivity *c*

CAPTIVITY. The deportation of the citizens of a country by a foreign power. The nation of Israel (the Northern Kingdom) was carried into captivity by the Assyrians about 722 BC (2 Kings 15:29), while Judah (the Southern Kingdom) suffered the same fate at the hand of the Babylonians in 587 BC (2 Chron. 36:6–7).

CARBUNCLE. A precious red stone embedded in the breastplate of the high priest (Exod. 28:17).

CARCHEMISH. An ancient city near the Euphrates River in Mesopotamia, where the Babylonian army defeated the Egyptians. This victory marked the beginning of Babylon's advance into the territory of Israel. Carchemish is mentioned in 2 Chron. 35:20–24 • Isa. 10:9 • Jer. 46:2 .

CARE [S]
Mark 4:19 the *c's* of this world...enter in and choke the word
Mark 4:38 Do You not *c* that we are perishing
John 10:13 he is a hired hand and does not *c* for the sheep

1 Cor. 7:33 he who is married *c's* for the things that are of the world

1 Tim. 3:5 how shall he take *c* of the church of God

1 Pet. 5:7 casting all your *c* upon Him, for He *c's* for you

CARMEL. (1) A prominent mountain in northern Israel where the prophet Elijah demonstrated the power of God in a dramatic encounter with the priests of the pagan god Baal. The reputed site of this event is marked by a monastery with an adjoining church. In the courtyard stands a statue of Elijah with upraised sword, symbolizing his victory over these idol worshippers. Mount Carmel is mentioned in Josh. 12:22; 19:26 • 1 Sam. 15:12 • 1 Kings 18:19–45 • 2 Kings 2:25; 4:25; 19:23 • 2 Chron. 26:10 • Song of Sol. 7:5 • Isa. 33:9; 35:2; 37:24 • Jer. 46:18; 50:19 • Amos 1:2; 9:3 • Mic. 7:14 • Nah. 1:4.

(2) A town in southern Judah where a wealthy sheepherder named Nabal refused to provide food for David and his hungry warriors (1 Sam. 25:2–12).

CASLUHIM. An ancient people descended from Mizraim, son of Ham (Gen. 10:14 • 1 Chron. 1:12). *Casluhim* was the Hebrew word for Egypt.

CASSIA. The bark of a tree prized for its pleasing fragrance. It was used as an ingredient of holy oil (Exod. 30:24).

CAST [ING]

Gen. 37:20 slay him [Joseph] and *c* him into some pit

Exod. 4:3 He [God] said, *C* it on the ground. And he [Moses] *c* it on the ground

Exod. 32:24 I [Aaron] *c* it into the fire, and this calf came out

Lev. 16:8 Aaron shall *c* lots on the two goats

Josh. 18:10 Joshua *c* lots for them in Shiloh

Job 8:20 God will not *c* away a perfect man

Job 30:19 He [God] has *c* me into the mire

Ps. 51:11 Do not *c* me away from Your presence

Ps. 55:22 *C* your burden on the Lord, and He shall sustain you

Jon. 1:15 they [mariners]...*c* him [Jonah] forth into the sea

Matt. 3:10 every tree that does not bring forth good fruit is...*c* into the fire

Matt. 15:26 not proper to take the children's bread and to *c* it to dogs

Matt. 21:12 Jesus...*c* out all those who sold and bought in the temple

Matt. 27:35 they...divided His garments, *c'ing* lots...for My clothing they *c* lots

Mark 1:39 He [Jesus] preached...throughout all Galilee and *c* out demons

Mark 12:43 poor widow has *c* in more than all...who have *c* into the treasury

Mark 12:44 all those *c* in out of their abundance, but she...*c* in all...she had

Luke 9:49 Master, we saw one *c'ing* out demons in Your name

John 8:7 He who is without sin...let him first *c* a stone

Rom. 13:12 let us *c* off the works of darkness

1 Pet. 5:7 *c'ing* all your care upon Him, for He cares for you

Rev. 20:15 whoever was not found...in the book of life was *c* into the lake of fire

CAST DOWN

Ps. 37:24 Though he falls, he shall not be utterly *c-d*

Ps. 42:11 Why are you *c-d*, O my soul

Matt. 27:5 And he [Judas] *c-d* the pieces of silver

Phil. 4:12 I [Paul] know both how to be *c-d* and I know how to abound

Rev. 12:9 great dragon was *c-d*...*c-d* to the earth...his angels were *c-d*

CASTLE. A fortress or defense tower. The "castle" into which Paul was taken was the quarters of the Roman soldiers at Jerusalem in the fortress of Antonia near the temple (Acts 21:34).

CASTOR AND POLLUX. Pagan gods which were considered protectors of sailors. The apostle Paul's ship to Rome featured a carving of these two gods (Acts 28:11).

CAUDA. A small island near Crete where Paul's ship anchored during a storm (Acts 27:16). *Clauda*: KJV.

CAUGHT

2 Sam. 18:9 his [Absalom's] head *c* hold of the oak

Eccles. 9:12 like the birds...*c* in a snare, so are the sons of men

Matt. 14:31 Jesus stretched out His hand and *c* him [Peter]

1 Thes. 4:17 we...shall be *c* up together...in the clouds

CAVE. A natural underground cavern used as a residence (Gen. 19:30) or as a burial place. Abraham bought a cave, known as Machpelah, where he and his family were buried (Gen. 49:29).

CEASE [D, ING]

Gen. 8:22 While the earth remains...day and night shall not *c*

Josh. 5:12 And the manna *c'd* on the next day

Neh. 6:3 Why should the work *c* while I [Nehemiah] leave it

Job 32:1 these three men *c'd* to answer Job

Ps. 37:8 *C* from anger, and forsake wrath

Ps. 85:4 O God...cause Your anger toward us to *c*

Prov. 23:4 Do not labor to be rich; *c* from your own wisdom

Eccles. 12:3 the grinders *c* because they are few

Ezek. 26:13 I will cause the noise of your songs to *c*

Jon. 1:15 they...cast him [Jonah] forth...and the sea *c'd* from her raging

Mark 4:39 the wind *c'd* and there was a great calm

Acts 5:42 they [the apostles] did not *c* to teach and preach Jesus Christ

Acts 12:5 prayer for him [Peter] was made to God without *c'ing* by the church

Rom. 1:9 without *c'ing* I [Paul] always make mention of you in my prayers

1 Cor. 13:8 whether there are tongues, they shall *c*

Col. 1:9 we also, since the day we heard it, do not *c* to pray for you

1 Thes. 5:17 Pray without *c'ing*

CEDAR. A cone-bearing evergreen tree that provided lumber used in the temple in Jerusalem (1 Kings 5:1–10).

CEDARS OF LEBANON

Judg. 9:15 let fire come out...and devour the *c-o-L*

Ps. 29:5 yes, the LORD breaks the *c-o-L*

Ps. 104:16 the trees of the LORD are full of sap, the *c-o-L*

Isa. 2:13 on all the *c-o-L* that are high and lifted up

Isa. 14:8 the fir trees rejoice over you, and the *c-o-L*

CEDRON. KJV: see *Kidron*

CENCHREA. A harbor of Corinth through which Paul passed during the second missionary journey (Acts 18:18). He later mentioned this place as the site of a church (Rom. 16:1).

CENSER. A small container in which incense was burned by a priest (Num. 16:16–39).

CENSUS. A count of the population of a country or region. A census ordered by the Roman emperor led Joseph and Mary to travel to Bethlehem, where Jesus was born (Luke 2:1–3).

CENTURION. A Roman military officer who commanded a force of one hundred soldiers (Acts 10:1, 22).

CEREMONIAL WASHING. The OT law prescribed that priests who offered sacrifices at the altar must be ritually clean (Exod. 29:4). Eventually this concern for ceremonial cleanliness included all the people. A person could be made unclean by many different actions, such as giving birth or touching a dead body. But cleanliness could be restored by going through rituals of purification. By NT times, these outward rituals had become more important than the inner spiritual reality they were meant to signify. This is why the Pharisees criticized Jesus and His disciples on one occasion for failing to perform a ritualistic washing of their hands before they ate. But Jesus declared, "There is nothing from outside a man that can defile him by entering into him. But the things that come out of him, those are what defile the man" (Mark 7:15). The sacrificial death of Jesus wiped away the need for external purification rituals.

CHAFF. The useless husks separated from kernels of grain in a threshing operation. The word is also used figuratively, as in the psalmist's comparison of the ungodly to chaff (Ps. 1:4).

CHALCEDONY. A precious stone cut from multicolored quartz and used in the foundation of the heavenly city, or New Jerusalem (Rev. 21:19).

CHALDEANS. See *Babylon*

CHAMBER. A room in a building (2 Kings 23:12). The word is also used figuratively, as in the psalmist's statement that the Lord sends rain from His chambers (Ps. 104:13).

CHANAAN. KJV: See *Canaan*, No. 2

CHANGE [D, S]
Jer. 2:11 Has a nation *c'd* its gods, which are not gods
Jer. 13:23 Can the Ethiopian *c* his skin or the leopard his spots
Dan. 2:21 He [God] *c's* the times and the seasons
Dan. 5:6 the king's face was *c'd*
Hos. 4:7 Therefore, I [God] will *c* their glory to shame
Rom. 1:23 c'd the glory of the incorruptible God
1 Cor. 15:51 We shall not all sleep, but we shall all be *c'd*
Phil. 3:21 who shall *c* our vile body...similar to His glorious body

CHARCHEMISH. KJV: See *Carchemish*

CHARGE [D]
Deut. 3:28 c Joshua and encourage him
1 Kings 2:1 David...*c'd* his son Solomon
Ps. 91:11 For He shall give His angels *c* over you
Matt. 16:20 Then He *c'd*...that they should tell no man that He was Jesus the Christ
Mark 8:15 And He *c'd* them...Be careful! Beware of the leaven of the Pharisees
Luke 8:56 He [Jesus] *c'd* them that they should tell no man what was done
Acts 7:60 Lord, do not lay this sin to their *c*

1 Tim. 6:17 C those who are rich...to trust in the living God

CHARIOT. A two-wheeled carriage drawn by horses, and used for transportation and in war (1 Kings 18:44).

CHARIOT CITIES. Cities where King Solomon kept his military chariots and chariot forces (1 Kings 9:19).

CHARIOT OF FIRE. The carriage drawn by blazing horses which came between Elijah and Elisha as Elijah was taken into heaven by a whirlwind (2 Kings 2:11).

CHARIOTS OF THE SUN. Images dedicated to the sun—a popular custom among the Persians, who worshipped this heavenly body. They believed the sun was a god who drove his chariot across the sky. All items devoted to this practice among the Israelites were burned by King Josiah of Judah (the Southern Kingdom) (2 Kings 23:11).

CHARRAN. KJV: See *Haran*

CHASTEN [ED, ING]
Ps. 38:1 O LORD, do not rebuke me...or *c* me in Your hot displeasure
Ps. 73:14 all day long I have been plagued, and *c'ed* every morning
Ps. 94:12 Blessed is the man whom You *c*, O LORD
1 Cor. 11:32 when we are judged, we are *c'ed* by the Lord
Heb. 12:6 whom the Lord loves He *c's*
Rev. 3:19 As many as I love, I rebuke and *c*

CHEBAR. A river or canal in Babylon where Jewish captives settled during the Exile. The prophet Ezekiel's visions were revealed to him at this body of water. The Chebar is mentioned in Ezek. 1:1, 3; 3:15, 23; 10:15, 20, 22; 43:3.

CHEDORLAOMER. A king of Elam who invaded Canaan and carried away Abraham's nephew Lot as a captive. Abraham launched a counterattack and rescued Lot (Gen. 14:1–16).

CHEER [FUL]
Prov. 15:13 A merry heart makes a *c'ful* face
Zech. 9:17 Grain shall make the young men *c'ful*

Matt. 9:2 Son [man with palsy], be of good *c*

John 16:33 be of good *c*: I [Jesus] have overcome the world

Acts 23:11 Be of good *c*, Paul...so you must also bear witness in Rome

2 Cor. 9:7 God loves a *c'ful* giver

CHEMOSH. Chief pagan god of the Moabites and Ammonites to which children were sacrificed (Num. 21:29 • Judg. 11:24 • 1 Kings 11:7, 33 • 2 Kings 23:13 • Jer. 48:7, 13, 46).

CHERETHIMS. See *Cherethites*

CHERETHITES. A tribe of the Philistines in southwest Palestine (1 Sam. 30:14 • Zeph. 2:5). *Cherethims*: Ezek. 25:16.

CHERITH. A brook, or perhaps a dry riverbed, east of the Jordan River where the prophet Elijah was fed by ravens while in hiding from Jezebel (1 Kings 17:3–5).

CHERUBIM. Winged creatures, perhaps an order of angels, whose function was to praise God and glorify His name. God revealed His message to the prophet Ezekiel in a series of visions in which cherubim played a prominent role (Ezek. 10:7; 11:22; 41:20). These creatures were similar to the seraphim that appeared in the prophet Isaiah's vision of God on His throne (Isa. 6:1–2).

CHETH. Eighth letter of the Hebrew alphabet, used as a heading over Psalm 119:57–64. In the Hebrew language, each line of these eight verses begins with this letter.

CHILD [HOOD]

Gen. 17:17 Shall a *c* be born to him who is a hundred years old

Exod. 22:22 You shall not afflict any widow or fatherless *c*

1 Kings 3:25 the king [Solomon] said, Divide the living *c* in two

1 Kings 17:22 the soul of the *c* came into him again, and he revived

2 Kings 5:14 his [Naaman's] skin was restored like the skin of a little *c*

Prov. 22:6 Train up a *c* in the way he should go

Eccles. 11:10 for *c'hood* and youth are vanity

Isa. 9:6 For a *C* is born to us, a Son is given to us

Jer. 1:6 Behold, I [Jeremiah] cannot speak, for I am a *c*

Hos. 11:1 When Israel was a *c*, I [God] loved him

Matt. 1:23 a virgin shall be with *c* and shall bring forth a Son

Matt. 2:13 Arise...take the young *C*...Herod will seek the young *C*

Matt. 2:14 he [Joseph] took the young *C* and His mother

Matt. 2:20 take the young *C*...into...Israel...those who sought the...*C's* life are dead

Matt. 2:21 he [Joseph]...took the young *C*...and came into the land of Israel

Matt. 18:4 whoever humbles himself like this little *c*, the same is greatest

Mark 10:15 not receive the kingdom...as a little *c*, he shall not enter

Luke 2:17 they widely made known the saying... concerning this *C*

Luke 2:40 the *C* [Jesus] grew and became strong in spirit

1 Cor. 13:11 When I was a *c*, I spoke as a *c*

2 Tim. 3:15 from *c'hood* you [Timothy] have known the holy scriptures

CHILDREN

Gen. 3:16 in sorrow you [Eve] shall bring forth *c*

Gen. 37:3 Israel loved Joseph more than all his *c*

Exod. 1:7 the *c* of Israel were fruitful and increased

Exod. 12:26 when your *c* shall say...What do you mean by this service

Exod. 20:5 visiting the iniquity of the fathers on the *c*

Num. 8:17 all the firstborn of the *c* of Israel are Mine

Deut. 24:16 fathers shall not be put to death for the *c*

Josh. 4:6 when your *c* ask their fathers...What do you mean by these stones

Josh. 18:10 Joshua divided the land for the *c* of Israel

Job 19:17 I [Job] begged for the *c's* sake

Job 19:18 Yes, young *c* despised me [Job]

Ps. 14:2 The Lord looked down...on the *c* of men

Ps. 34:11 Come, you *c*...I will teach you the fear of the LORD

Ps. 103:7 He [God] made known...His acts to the *c* of Israel

Ps. 103:13 as a father has compassion on his *c*, so the Lord...on those who fear Him

Ps. 115:14 The LORD shall increase...you and your *c*

Ps. 127:3 Behold, *c* are a heritage from the LORD

Ps. 127:4 Like arrows in the hand of a mighty man; so are *c* of the youth

Prov. 4:1 Hear, you *c*, the instruction of a father

Prov. 13:22 A good man leaves an inheritance to his children's *c*

Prov. 20:7 his *c* are blessed after him [the just man]

Prov. 31:28 Her *c* rise up and call her blessed

Isa. 54:13 all your *c* shall be taught by the LORD

Jer. 3:22 Return, you backsliding *c*...I [God] will heal

Jer. 31:15 Rachel weeping for her *c*, refusing to be comforted

Lam. 1:16 My *c* are desolate because the enemy prevailed

Hos. 2:4 I will not have mercy on her *c*, for they are the *c* of prostitution

Matt. 2:16 Herod...slew all the *c*...in Bethlehem and in all its surrounding area

Matt. 7:11 know how to give good gifts to your *c*

Matt. 18:3 Unless you...become as little *c*, you shall not enter into the kingdom

Matt. 23:37 How often I [Jesus] would have gathered your *c*

Matt. 27:25 His [Jesus'] blood be on us and on our *c*

Mark 10:13 they brought young *c* to Him

Luke 16:8 the *c* of this world are wiser...than the *c* of light

John 8:39 If you were Abraham's *c*, you would do the works of Abraham

John 12:36 that you may be the *c* of light

1 Cor. 14:20 do not be *c* in understanding...in malice be *c*

Gal. 4:28 we, brothers...are the *c* of promise

Eph. 4:14 we from now on will no longer be *c*

Eph. 6:1 C, obey your parents in the Lord

Eph. 6:4 fathers, do not provoke your *c* to wrath

1 Thes. 5:5 You are all the *c* of light and the *c* of the day

1 John 2:1 My little *c*, I write these things to you, that you may not sin

1 John 3:18 little *c*, let us love not in word... but in deed

1 John 5:21 Little *c*, keep yourselves from idols

3 John 4 no greater joy than to hear that my [John's] *c* walk in truth

CHILDREN OF GOD. The new status bestowed on believers when they accept Jesus as Lord and Savior. The classic passage on this theological truth occurs in the writings of the apostle Paul: "The Spirit Himself bears witness with our spirit that we are the children of God" (Rom. 8:16). Through the ministry of the Holy Spirit, followers of Jesus are adopted into the family of God the Father.

CHILDREN OF GOD

Matt. 5:9 Blessed are the peacemakers, for they shall be called the *c-o-G*

Gal. 3:26 you are all the *c-o-G* by faith in Christ Jesus

1 John 5:2 we know that we love the *c-o-G*: when we love God

CHILDREN WELCOMED BY JESUS. Matt. 19:13–15 • Mark 10:13–16 • Luke 18:15–17

CHILEAB. A son of David by his wife Abigail (2 Sam. 3:3).

CHINNERETH. See *Galilee, Sea of.*

CHINNEROTH, SEA OF. See *Galilee, Sea of*

CHIOS. An island passed by the apostle Paul on his way to Jerusalem after the third missionary journey (Acts 20:15).

CHISLEV. Ninth month of the Hebrew year; the month when Nehemiah was informed of the plight of the exiles who had returned to Judah (Neh. 1:1).

CHITTIM. KJV: See *Cyprus*

CHLOE. A believer in Corinth (1 Cor. 1:11).

CHOOSE [ING]

Deut. 7:7 The LORD did not...*c* you because you were more in number

Deut. 30:19 c life, that both you and your descendants may live

Josh. 24:15 c you this day whom you will serve

Phil. 1:22 Yet what I [Paul] shall *c* I do not know

Heb. 11:25 C'ing rather to suffer affliction

CHORAZIN. A city north of the Sea of Galilee where Jesus did many mighty works. He pronounced a woe on this city because of its unbelief (Matt. 11:21). He also condemned two other nearby towns, Bethsaida and Capernaum (Luke 10:13–15).

CHOSE

Deut. 10:15 He *c* their descendants after them, even you above all people

1 Sam. 17:40 he [David]...*c* five smooth stones out of the brook

1 Kings 8:16 I [God] *c* David to be over My people Israel

Neh. 9:7 You are the LORD God, who *c* Abram

Ps. 78:67–68 He [God] refused the tent of Joseph...but *c* the tribe of Judah

Luke 6:13 He [Jesus] *c* twelve of them whom He also named apostles

Acts 15:40 And Paul *c* Silas and departed, having been recommended by the brothers

CHOSEN

Deut. 7:6 God has *c* you to be a special people

Judg. 10:14 Go and cry to the gods that you have *c*

1 Chron. 16:13 you children of Jacob, His *c* ones

1 Chron. 28:5 He [God] has *c* Solomon my [David's] son to sit on the throne

Ps. 33:12 Blessed is...the people whom He has *c* for His own inheritance

Prov. 22:1 A good name is rather to be *c* than great riches

Isa. 43:10 You are...My servant whom I have *c*

Matt. 12:18 Behold, My servant whom I have *c*

Matt. 20:16 For many are called, but few *c*

Luke 10:42 Mary has *c* that good part

John 15:16 You have not *c* Me, but I have *c* you

Acts 9:15 he [Paul] is a *c* vessel for Me

1 Cor. 1:27 God has *c* the foolish things...and...*c* the weak things

2 Thes. 2:13 God has from the beginning *c* you for salvation

1 Pet. 2:9 you are a *c* generation, a royal priesthood

CHOSEN PEOPLE. A reference to the Israelites, a nation selected by the Lord to receive His special blessing. Their mission was to proclaim the virtues of the one true God to "all families of the earth" (Gen. 12:3). In the NT, the apostle Peter referred to the church founded by Jesus Christ as the new people favored by the Lord. Its mission is to glorify God through their good works and positive witness for Him (1 Pet. 2:12).

CHRIST. A title of Jesus that means "anointed one" (John 4:25). This name declares that He was God's specially chosen Messiah whom the Jewish people had been expecting for many centuries. But He came as a spiritual deliverer, not to rule over an earthly kingdom.

CHRISTIAN. A disciple or follower of Christ. The name apparently was first used of the believers in the church at Antioch of Syria (Acts 11:26). It may have been a term of derision at the time, but early believers accepted it as a badge of honor.

CHRONICLES, FIRST. A book of history in the OT that begins with a long genealogy that goes all the way back to Adam. Then the book focuses on the reign of David as king of Israel. Many scholars believe both First and Second Chronicles were written by Ezra the priest after the Jewish people returned to Jerusalem following their period of exile among the Babylonians and Persians. This was a time of great discouragement among God's people. Ezra wanted to give them hope by showing that God was with them. His promise that a descendant of David would always rule over His people had not been forgotten.

CHRONICLES, SECOND. This book picks up where 1 Chronicles ends—with Solomon's succession to the kingship following the death of his father, David, about 970 BC. After several chapters devoted to Solomon's administration, it covers the reigns of selected kings of Judah (the Southern Kingdom) after the split of the country into two nations after Solomon's death (2 Chron. 10–36). The book concludes with the fall of Judah (the Southern Kingdom) to the Babylonian army about 586 BC (2 Chron. 36:11–20).

CHRYSOLITE. A precious stone, possibly yellow topaz, used in the foundation of the heavenly city, or New Jerusalem (Rev. 21:20).

CHRYSOPRASE. A precious green stone similar to agate used in the foundation of the heavenly city, or New Jerusalem (Rev. 21:20).

CHURCH. A local body of believers assembled for Christian worship (Acts 15:4) as well as all the redeemed of the ages who belong to Christ (Gal. 1:13). Jesus commissioned the church to make disciples and teach them to continue the work He had started (Matt. 28:18–20). Christ is head of His body the church, and He is the main focus of all its activities (Col. 1:15–17).

CHURCH [ES]

Matt. 16:18 You are Peter, and on this rock I will build My *c*

Matt. 18:17 if he neglects to hear them, tell it to the *c*

Acts 2:47 the Lord added to the *c* daily such as should be saved

Acts 5:11 great fear came on all the *c*

Acts 8:3 As for Saul, he began destroying the *c*

Acts 14:23 when they [Paul and Barnabas] had ordained elders for them in every *c*

Acts 20:28 the Holy Spirit has made you overseers, to feed the *c* of God

Rom. 16:16 The *c'es* of Christ greet you

1 Cor. 14:4 he who prophesies edifies the *c*

1 Cor. 14:35 it is a shame for women to speak in the *c*

2 Cor. 11:28 come on me [Paul] daily—the care for all the *c'es*

Gal. 1:13 I [Paul] persecuted the *c* of God

Eph. 3:21 to Him be glory in the *c* by Christ Jesus

Eph. 5:25 Christ also loved the *c* and gave Himself for it

Col. 1:18 He [Christ] is the head of the body, the *c*

1 Tim. 3:5 how shall he take care of the *c* of God

1 Tim. 3:15 *c* of the living God...pillar and ground of...truth

Jas. 5:14 elders of the *c*, and let them pray over him

Rev. 1:4 John, to the seven *c'es* that are in Asia

Rev. 2:1 to the angel of the *c* of Ephesus

Rev. 2:8 to the angel of the *c* in Smyrna

Rev. 2:12 to the angel of the *c* in Pergamos

Rev. 2:18 to the angel of the *c* in Thyatira

Rev. 3:1 to the angel of the *c* in Sardis

Rev. 3:7 to the angel of the *c* in Philadelphia

Rev. 3:14 to the angel of the *c* of the Laodiceans

CHUSHAN-RISHATHAIM. A king of Mesopotamia who oppressed the Israelites during the period of the judges. He was defeated by Othniel, the first judge (Judg. 3:8–10).

CILICIA. A province of Asia Minor whose capital city was Tarsus, birthplace of the apostle Paul. He visited Cilicia soon after his conversion (Gal. 1:21) and again on his second missionary journey (Acts 15:41). It is also mentioned in Acts 6:9; 15:23; 21:39; 22:3; 23:34; 27:5.

CIRCUMCISE [D]

Gen. 17:11 you shall *c* the flesh of your foreskin

Gen. 17:24 Abraham was ninety-nine years old when he was *c'd*

Lev. 12:3 eighth day the flesh of his foreskin shall be *c'd*

Josh. 5:2 *c* the children of Israel again the second time

Jer. 4:4 *C* yourselves to the LORD, and take away the foreskins of your heart

Acts 15:1 certain men...from Judaea...said, Unless you are *c'd*...you cannot be saved

Gal. 5:2 if you are *c'd*, Christ shall profit you nothing

Phil. 3:5 *c'd* the eighth day, of the stock of Israel

CIRCUMCISION. The removal of the foreskin of the male sex organ, a ritual performed generally on the eighth day after birth (Gen. 17:9–14). This practice apparently began with

Abraham. It signified the covenant between God and His people, the nation of Israel. It eventually became a symbol of national pride to the Jewish people, who looked down on non-Jews as "the uncircumcised." But the apostle Paul declared that God made no such distinction between people, that the ritual was of no value unless accompanied by an obedient and loving spirit (1 Cor. 7:19).

CIRCUMCISION

Acts 10:45 those of the *c* who believed...were astonished

Rom. 3:1 Or what is the profit of *c*

Rom. 15:8 Christ was a minister of the *c* for the truth of God

1 Cor. 7:19 C is nothing and uncircumcision is nothing

Col. 3:11 neither Greek nor Jew, *c* nor uncircumcision

CISTERN. An underground pit for catching and storing rainwater (2 Kings 18:31). Empty cisterns were sometimes used as dungeons or prisons (Gen. 37:24).

CITIES OF REFUGE. Six Israelite cities set aside as sanctuaries for those who killed other persons by accident. These centers were Bezer, Golan, Hebron, Kedesh, Ramoth of Gilead, and Shechem. People could flee to these towns for protection from revenge by relatives of the deceased. After investigating the matter, city officials issued the final judgment on whether a person was innocent or guilty of murder. Cities of refuge are mentioned in Num. 35:11–15 • Josh. 20:2–9; 21:13, 21, 27, 32, 38 • 1 Chron. 6:57, 67.

CITIES OF THE PLAIN. Five cities in southern Canaan destroyed in Abraham's time because of the great sin of their inhabitants. These cities were Admah, Bela or Zoar, Gomorrah, Sodom, and Zeboiim (Gen. 19:22–30; Deut. 29:23).

CITIZENSHIP

Phil. 3:20 our *c* is in heaven; from where we also look for the Savior

CITY OF DAVID. See *Bethlehem.*

CLAUDA. KJV: See *Cauda*

CLAUDIUS LYSIAS. A Roman military officer who protected Paul from his enemies (Acts 21:30–35; 23:22–30).

CLEAN AND UNCLEAN ANIMALS. Lev. 11:1–47

CLEANSE [D, S]

Lev. 16:30 the priest shall make an atonement... to *c* you

Neh. 13:22 I [Nehemiah] commanded the Levites that they should *c* themselves

Ps. 51:2 Wash me thoroughly...and *c* me from my sin

Ps. 73:13 Truly I have *c'd* my heart in vain

Matt. 11:5 the lepers are *c'd* and the deaf hear

Mark 1:42 the leprosy departed...and he was *c'd*

Luke 17:17 Were there not ten *c'd*? But where are the nine

Acts 10:15 What God has *c'd*, do not call that common

2 Cor. 7:1 let us *c* ourselves from all filthiness

1 John 1:7 the blood of Jesus Christ...*c's* us from all sin

1 John 1:9 He [Jesus] is faithful and just...to *c* us from all unrighteousness

CLEAR [LY]

Gen. 44:16 how shall we *c* ourselves

Exod. 34:7 who [God] will by no means *c* the guilty

Song of Sol. 6:10 beautiful as the moon, as *c* as the sun

Amos 8:9 I [God] will darken the earth in the *c* day

Matt. 7:5 then you shall see *c'ly* to cast the speck out of

Mark 4:22 nothing hidden that shall not be made *c*

Mark 8:25 he was restored and saw every man *c'ly*

Acts 4:16 that a notable miracle has been done by them [Peter and John] is *c* to all

Rom. 1:20 the invisible things of Him [God] are *c'ly* seen

Rom. 3:21 righteousness of God without the law is *c'ly* revealed

1 John 4:9 the love of God was *c'ly* revealed toward us

Rev. 21:11 even like a jasper stone, *c* as crystal

CLEAVE

Gen. 2:24 a man shall leave his father and his mother and shall *c* to his wife

Deut. 13:4 you shall serve Him [God] and *c* to Him

CLEMENT. A fellow worker with the apostle Paul, apparently at Philippi (Phil. 4:3).

CLEOPAS. A Christian believer to whom Christ appeared on the road to Emmaus on the day of His resurrection (Luke 24:18).

CLING [S]

Deut. 10:20 you shall *c* to Him and swear by His name

Josh. 23:8 But *c* to the Lord your God

Job 19:20 My bone *c's* to my skin and to my flesh

Ps. 102:5 Because of the sound of my groaning, my bones *c* to my skin

Ps. 137:6 let my tongue *c* to the roof of my mouth—if I do not prefer Jerusalem

Mark 10:7 a man shall leave his father and mother and *c* to his wife

Rom. 12:9 Hate what is evil; *c* to what is good

CLOAK. An item of clothing, similar to a robe. The prophet Elijah placed his cloak on Elisha to bless and anoint Elisha as his successor (1 Kings 19:19). *Mantle*: KJV.

CLOPAS. The husband of Mary, one of the women who was present at the crucifixion of Jesus (John 19:25). *Alphaeus*: Matt. 10:3. *Cleophas*: KJV.

CLOTHE [D, ING]

Gen. 3:21 For Adam and...his wife...God made coats of skins and *c'd* them

2 Chron. 6:41 Let Your priests, O Lord God, be *c'd* with salvation

Job 7:5 My [Job's] flesh is *c'd* with worms

Ps. 93:1 The Lord...is *c'd* with majesty

Ps. 132:9 Let Your priests be *c'd* with righteousness

Prov. 31:25 Strength and honor are her *c'ing*

Isa. 50:3 I [God] *c* the heavens with blackness

Isa. 61:10 for He has *c'd* me with the garments of salvation

Matt. 7:15 Beware of false prophets...in sheep's *c'ing*

Matt. 25:36 naked and you *c'd* Me; I was sick and you visited Me

Mark 1:6 John was *c'd* with camel's hair

Mark 12:38 the scribes...love to go in long *c'ing*

Mark 15:17 they *c'd* Him with purple

Luke 12:28 how much more will He *c* you, O you of little faith

Luke 16:19 a certain rich man...*c'd* in purple

1 Pet. 5:5 be submissive to one another...*c'd* with humility

Rev. 19:13 And He was *c'd* with a garment dipped in blood

CLOTHES

Gen. 37:34 Jacob tore his *c* and put sackcloth on his loins

Num. 8:21 the Levites were purified, and they washed their *c*

Josh. 7:6 Joshua tore his *c* and fell to the earth

1 Kings 1:1 covered him [David] with *c*, but he could not get warm

Prov. 6:27 Can a man take fire in his bosom and his *c* not be burned

Mark 5:28 If I may but touch His *c*, I shall be healed

Acts 7:58 laid down their *c* at a young man's [Saul's] feet

CLOTHS

Exod. 39:1 they [Bezalel and Aholiab] made *c* of service...in the Holy Place

Luke 2:7 wrapped Him in swaddling *c*

John 19:40 wound it [Jesus' body] in linen *c*

CLOUD. Clouds are often associated with God's presence and protection (Exod. 16:10). They are described symbolically throughout the Bible, as in "a day of clouds," or a time of disaster (Joel 2:2). Clouds also symbolize vast armies (Jer. 4:13). At His second coming, Christ will come in "the clouds of heaven" (Matt. 24:30).

CLOUD [S]

Gen. 9:13 I [God] set My bow in the *c*

Exod. 13:21 the LORD went before them [Israel]...
in a pillar of a *c*

Exod. 40:34 a *c* covered the tent of the congregation

1 Kings 8:10 the *c* filled the house of the LORD

1 Kings 18:44 a little *c* arises out of the sea

Job 26:8 He [God] binds up the waters in His thick *c's*

Ps. 78:14 He [God] led them [Israel] with a *c*

Ps. 108:4 and Your truth reaches to the *c's*

Prov. 3:20 By His knowledge...the *c's* drop down the dew

Isa. 14:14 I will ascend above the heights of the *c's*

Isa. 19:1 the LORD rides on a swift *c*

Isa. 44:22 I [God] have blotted out your transgressions as a thick *c*

Lam. 3:44 You [God] have covered Yourself with a *c*

Joel 2:2 A day of darkness and of gloominess, a day of *c's*

Matt. 24:30 the Son of Man coming in the *c's*

Mark 9:7 a voice came out of the *c*, saying, This is My beloved Son

Luke 21:27 Son of Man coming in a *c* with power and great glory

Acts 1:9 He [Jesus] was taken up, and a *c* received Him out of their sight

1 Thes. 4:17 we...shall be caught up together with them in the *c's*

Heb. 12:1 we also are surrounded by such a great *c* of witnesses

Rev. 1:7 Behold, He comes with *c's*, and every eye shall see Him

CLUNG

Deut. 4:4 you who *c* to the LORD your God are alive this day

Ruth 1:14 kissed her mother-in-law [Naomi], but Ruth *c* to her

1 Kings 11:2 –3 Solomon *c* to these in love... seven hundred wives

Job 29:10 their tongue *c* to the roof of their mouth

Acts 17:34 some men *c* to him [Paul] and believed

COCK. KJV: see *Rooster*

COLD

Ps. 147:17 Who can stand before His *c*

Prov. 25:25 As *c* waters to a thirsty soul, so is good news

Matt. 24:12 the love of many shall grow *c*

Rev. 3:15 you [church at Laodicea] are neither *c* nor hot

COLOSSE. A city in the Roman province of Asia, situated about 100 miles east of Ephesus, and the site of a church to which Paul wrote one of his epistles (Col. 1:2).

COLOSSIANS, EPISTLE TO. A letter written by the apostle Paul to the church at Colosse that he apparently had never visited. Epaphras, one of his associates (Col. 1:7), brought word to Paul about false teachers who had infiltrated the church. To deal with this situation, the apostle sent this letter while he was imprisoned at Rome. He reminded these believers that Christ is the all-sufficient Savior, and urged them to put on the character of Christ and to express His love in their relationships with others.

COMFORT [ED, S]

Job 2:11 Job's three friends...came...to *c* him

Ps. 23:4 Your [God's] rod and Your staff, they *c* me

Isa. 40:1 *C*, *c* My people, says your God

Isa. 49:13 the LORD has *c'ed* His people

Isa. 61:2 to proclaim the acceptable year of the LORD...to *c* all who mourn

Jer. 31:15 Rachel weeping for her children, refusing to be *c'ed* for her children

Lam. 1:21 There is no one to *c* me

Matt. 5:4 Blessed are those who mourn, for they shall be *c'ed*

Luke 8:48 be of good *c*. Your faith has healed you [woman with issue of blood]

2 Cor. 1:3 Blessed be God...the Father of mercies and the God of all *c*

2 Cor. 1:4 who *c's* us in all our tribulation

Phil. 2:1 If there is therefore any consolation in Christ, if any *c* of love

1 Thes. 4:18 *c* one another with these words

COMFORTER. A title that Jesus used for the Holy Spirit when He promised to send them "another" Comforter after His resurrection and ascension (John 14:16). The Greek word behind *another* means "another of the same kind." This implies that He Himself was the first Comforter of His disciples; He was sending another like Himself to serve as His stand-in. So close and personal would be the presence of the Holy Spirit that it would seem as if He had never left.

COMFORTER
John 14:26 the *C*...shall teach you all things
John 15:26 the *C*...shall testify of Me [Jesus]
John 16:7 if I [Jesus] do not go away, the *C* will not come to you

COMMAND [ED, ING, S]
Gen. 7:5 Noah did...all that the LORD *c'ed* him
Gen. 21:4 Abraham circumcised his son Isaac... as God had *c'ed* him
Gen. 49:33 Jacob had finished *c'ing* his sons
Exod. 19:7 Moses...laid before their faces all these words that the LORD *c'ed*
Deut. 4:2 You shall not add to the word that I [God] *c* you
Deut. 5:12 Keep the Sabbath day to sanctify it, as the LORD...has *c'ed*
Josh. 1:9 Have I [God] not *c'ed* you? Be strong and of good courage
1 Sam. 13:13 You [Saul] have not kept the commandment...which He *c'ed* you
1 Chron. 16:15 the word that He *c'ed* to a thousand generations
Ps. 33:9 He [God] *c'ed*, and it stood fast
Ps. 105:8 He [God] has remembered...the word that He *c'ed*
Jer. 1:17 speak to them all that I [God] *c* you [Jeremiah]
Dan. 6:16 the king gave the *c*, and they...threw him [Daniel] into the den of lions
Matt. 28:20 observe all the things that I [Jesus] have *c'ed* you
Mark 1:27 He [Jesus] *c* even the unclean spirits with authority
Mark 6:8 [Jesus] *c'ed* them to take nothing for their journey

Luke 4:3 *c* this stone to be made bread
Luke 8:25 For He *c's* even the winds and water
John 8:5 Moses, in the Law, *c'ed* us that such should be stoned
John 15:17 These things I [Jesus] *c* you...love one another

COMMANDMENT [S]
Exod. 16:28 How long will you refuse to keep My *c's*
Exod. 34:28 he [Moses] wrote on the tablets... the Ten *C's*
Lev. 27:34 These are the *c's*...for the children of Israel on Mount Sinai
Deut. 28:9 if you keep the *c's* of the LORD your God
1 Kings 2:3 keep His statutes and His *c's*
2 Kings 17:16 they left all the *c's* of the LORD
Ps. 111:7 all His *c's* are sure
Ps. 119:10 let me not wander from Your *c's*
Ps. 119:115 I will keep the *c's* of my God
Ps. 147:15 He [God] sends forth His *c* on earth
Prov. 6:20 My son, keep your father's *c*
Prov. 10:8 The wise in heart will receive *c's*, but a talking fool shall fall
Eccles. 12:13 Fear God and keep His *c's*, for this is the whole duty of man
Amos 2:4 they have...not kept His *c's*
Matt. 15:3 Why do you [Pharisees] also transgress the *c* of God
Matt. 22:40 On these two *c's* hang all the Law and the Prophets
Mark 12:28 Which *c* is the first of all
Mark 12:29 The first of all the *c's* is...The Lord our God is one Lord
John 13:34 A new *c* I [Jesus] give to you, That you love one another
John 14:15 If you love Me, keep My *c's*
John 15:10 If you keep My *c's*, you shall abide in My love
John 15:12 This is My *c*...love one another as I have loved you
1 Cor. 7:19 Circumcision is nothing...but the keeping of the *c's* of God
Eph. 6:2 Honor your father and mother, which is the first *c* with promise
1 John 2:3 we know Him, if we keep His *c's*

2 John 6 this is love: that we walk according to His *c's*

Rev. 22:14 Blessed are those who do His *c's*

COMMANDMENT [S] OF THE LORD

Num. 9:18 At the *c-o-t-L* the children of Israel journeyed

Num. 14:41 Why now do you transgress the *c-o-t-L*

Deut. 4:2 keep the *c's-o-t-L* your God

Deut. 8:6 you shall keep the *c's-o-t-L* your God

1 Sam. 15:24 I [Saul] have transgressed the *c-o-t-L*

2 Kings 17:16 they left all the *c's-o-t-L*...and made for themselves cast images

Ps. 19:8 The *c-o-t-L* is pure, enlightening the eyes

COMMEND [ED]

Prov. 12:8 A man shall be *c'ed* according to his wisdom

Luke 16:8 the master *c'ed* the unjust steward because he had done wisely

Luke 23:46 Father, into Your hands I *c* My spirit

Rom. 16:1 I [Paul] *c* to you our sister Phoebe

COMMIT [S, TED]

Gen. 39:22 the keeper of the prison *c'ted* to Joseph's hand all the prisoners

Exod. 20:14 You shall not *c* adultery

Lev. 18:29 the souls who *c* them shall be cut off

Lev. 20:10 the man who *c's* adultery...shall surely be put to death

Josh. 22:20 Did Achan the son of Zerah not *c* a trespass

Ps. 31:5 Into Your hand I *c* My spirit

Prov. 6:32 whoever *c's* adultery with a woman lacks understanding

Prov. 16:3 *C* your works to the LORD

Jer. 2:13 For My people have *c'ted* two evils

Matt. 5:28 whoever looks on a woman to lust after her has already *c'ted* adultery

Matt. 5:32 whoever marries...divorced *c's* adultery

Mark 10:11 Whoever divorces his wife and marries another *c's* adultery

Mark 10:19 You know the commandments: Do not *c* adultery, Do not kill

John 5:22 the Father...has *c'ted* all judgment to the Son

John 8:34 whoever *c's* sin is the servant of sin

1 Cor. 6:18 he who *c's* fornication sins against his own body

1 Cor. 10:8 Nor let us *c* fornication, as some of them *c'ted*

2 Cor. 5:19 God...in Christ...has *c'ted* to us the word of reconciliation

1 Tim. 6:20 Timothy, guard what is *c'ted* to your trust

2 Tim. 1:12 He [Jesus] is able to guard what I [Paul] have *c'ted* to Him until that day

2 Tim. 2:2 the same *c* to faithful men

1 John 3:9 Whoever is born of God does not *c* sin

COMMON

Mark 12:37 the *c* people heard Him gladly

Acts 2:44 all who believed...had all things *c*

Acts 10:14 I [Peter] have never eaten anything that is *c* or unclean

1 Cor. 10:13 No temptation has taken you but such as is *c* to man

COMMUNICATION [S]

Matt. 5:37 let your *c* be Yes, yes, or No, no

Luke 24:17 What manner of *c's* are these

Eph. 4:29 Let no corrupt *c* proceed out of your mouth

COMMUNION

1 Cor. 10:16 cup of blessing that we bless, is it not the *c* of the blood of Christ

2 Cor. 6:14 what *c* does light have with darkness

2 Cor. 13:14 and the *c* of the Holy Spirit be with you all

COMPASSION [S]

Exod. 2:6 she had *c* on him [Moses] and said, This is one of the Hebrews' children

Ps. 86:15 You, O Lord, are a God full of *c*

Ps. 145:8 The LORD is gracious and full of *c*

Jer. 12:15 I [God] will return and have *c* on them

Lam. 3:22 not consumed, because His *c's* do not fail

Hos. 11:8 My heart is turned within Me. My *c's* are kindled together

Zech. 7:9 show mercy and *c* every man to his brother

Matt. 14:14 Jesus...was moved with *c* for them

Matt. 18:27 the lord of that servant was moved with *c* and released him

Mark 9:22 if You can do anything, have *c* on us

Luke 10:33 a certain Samaritan...when he saw him, he had *c* on him

Luke 15:20 his father...had *c*, and ran and fell on his neck

1 Pet. 3:8 be all of one mind, having *c* for one another

1 John 3:17 sees his brother in need and shuts up his heart of *c* from him

COMPEL [LED, S]

Matt. 5:41 whoever *c's* you to go a mile, go with him two

Mark 15:21 they *c'led* one Simon, a Cyrenian... to bear His cross

Luke 14:23 Go out into the highways and hedges, and *c* them to come in

CONANIAH. A Levite in charge of the offerings in the temple during King Hezekiah's time (2 Chron. 31:12–13).

CONCEIT. KJV: see *Eyes, Opinions*

CONCEIVE [D]

Gen. 21:2 Sarah *c'd* and bore Abraham a son

Job 3:3 Let the day perish...on which it was said, There is a male child *c'd*

Ps. 51:5 formed in iniquity, and in sin my mother *c'd* me

Isa. 7:14 a virgin shall *c* and bear a son

Matt. 1:20 what is *c'd* in her [Mary] is from the Holy Spirit

Luke 1:31 you [Mary] shall *c*...and bring forth a Son

Luke 1:36 your [Mary's] cousin Elizabeth, she has also *c'd* a son in her old age

Heb. 11:11 Sarah herself also received strength to *c*

CONCERNING

Luke 2:17 they [shepherds] widely made known the saying...*c* this Child

Luke 18:31 all things that are written...*c* the Son of Man shall be accomplished

Luke 24:27 He [Jesus] expounded...the things *c* Himself

Acts 28:22 For as *c* this sect...it is spoken against

1 Cor. 12:1 Now *c* spiritual gifts, brothers

Eph. 5:32 I [Paul] speak *c* Christ and the church

1 Thes. 5:18 this is the will of God in Christ Jesus *c* you

1 Pet. 4:12 *c* the fiery trial that is to try you

2 Pet. 3:9 The Lord is not slow *c* His promise

CONCUBINE. A female slave or mistress; a secondary or common-law wife. Concubines were common among the patriarchs of the OT (Gen. 35:22). But Jesus taught the concept of monogamy—marriage to one person only (Matt. 19:4–9).

CONDEMN [ED, S]

Job 15:6 Your own mouth *c's* you

Prov. 12:2 He will *c* a man of wicked schemes

Matt. 12:37 by your words you shall be *c'ed*

Luke 6:37 Do not *c*, and you shall not be *c'ed*

John 3:17 God did not send His Son...to *c* the world

John 8:11 Neither do I [Jesus] *c* you. Go and sin no more

CONDEMNATION

John 3:19 the *c*...men loved darkness rather than light

Rom. 8:1 no *c* to those who are in Christ Jesus

Jas. 3:1 knowing that we shall receive the greater *c*

Jas. 5:12 let your yes be yes...lest you fall into *c*

CONDUCT

Gal. 1:13 you have heard of my [Paul's] *c* in time past

Eph. 4:22 put off, concerning the former *c*, the old man

Phil. 1:27 let your *c* be as is proper for the gospel of Christ

1 Tim. 4:12 be an example to the believers in word, in *c*, in love

Heb. 13:5 Let your *c* be without covetousness

James 3:13 by good *c*, with meekness of wisdom

1 Pet. 1:15–16 be holy in all manner of *c*...it is written, Be holy, for I am holy

1 Pet. 3:16 those who falsely accuse your good *c* in Christ may be ashamed

2 Pet. 3:11 manner of persons ought you to be in all holy *c* and godliness

CONDUIT. A pipe or aqueduct through which water was channeled. King Hezekiah of Judah (the Southern Kingdom) cut a conduit through solid rock to pipe water into Jerusalem (2 Kings 20:20).

CONFESS. To admit, own up to, or take responsibility for one's sin (Josh 7:19) and to turn to God for healing and forgiveness. Such honest confession and repentance leads to salvation. The apostle Paul connected saving faith with the willingness of believers to admit publicly and boldly that Jesus was the new focus of their lives (Rom. 10:9–10).

CONFESS [ES, ING]

Ps. 32:5 I will *c* my transgressions to the LORD

Mark 1:5 baptized by him [John the Baptist]...*c'ing* their sins

Luke 12:8 the Son of Man shall also *c* him

Rom. 10:9 if you *c* with your mouth the Lord Jesus

Phil. 2:11 every tongue should *c* that Jesus Christ is Lord

Jas. 5:16 **C** your faults to one another

1 John 1:9 If we *c* our sins, He is faithful and just to forgive us

1 John 4:2 every spirit that *c's* that Jesus Christ has come in the flesh is of God

1 John 4:15 Whoever *c's* that Jesus is the Son of God, God dwells in him

Rev. 3:5 I [Jesus] will *c* his name before My Father

CONFIDENCE

Ps. 118:9 better to trust in the LORD than to put *c* in princes

Prov. 14:26 In the fear of the LORD is strong *c*

Isa. 30:15 In quietness and in *c* shall be your strength

Mic. 7:5 Do not put your *c* in a guide

Eph. 3:12 In whom [Jesus] we have...access with *c*

1 John 2:28 when He appears, we may have *c*

CONFIDENT

Prov. 14:16 but the fool rages and is *c*

2 Cor. 5:8 We are *c*...willing...to be absent from the body

Phil. 1:6 being *c*...that He who has begun a good work...will perform it

CONFIRM [ED, ING]

Deut. 27:26 Cursed is he who does not *c* all the words of this law by doing them

1 Chron. 14:2 David perceived that the LORD had *c'ed* him king

Mark 16:20 the Lord working with them and *c'ing* the word with signs

Acts 15:41 And he [Paul] went through Syria and Cilicia, *c'ing* the churches

Rom. 15:8 Jesus Christ was a minister...to *c* the promises made to the fathers

1 Cor. 1:6 as the testimony of Christ was *c'ed* in you

1 Cor. 1:8 who [Jesus] shall also *c* you to the end

2 Cor. 2:8 *c* your love toward him

CONFORMED

Rom. 8:29 He [God] also predestined to be *c* to the image of His Son

Rom. 12:2 do not be *c* to this world, but be transformed

CONIAH. See *Jehoiachin*

CONQUEST OF CANAAN BY ISRAEL.
Josh. 6–12

CONSCIENCE. A built-in or intuitive sense of right and wrong. But human history reveals that the conscience alone cannot be depended on as a moral compass for behavior. As a part of humankind's fallen sinful nature, the human conscience has been infected and hopelessly flawed by sin. A renewed conscience comes about only through the saving power of Jesus Christ (2 Cor. 5:17–18).

CONSCIENCE [S]

John 8:9 those [scribes and Pharisees]...being convicted by their own *c's*, went out

Acts 23:1 I [Paul] have lived in all good *c* before God

1 Cor. 8:12 when you...wound their weak *c*, you sin

1 Cor. 10:27 eat...asking no questions for the sake of *c*

1 Tim. 1:5 love out of a pure heart and of a good *c*

1 Tim. 3:9 holding the mystery of the faith with a pure *c*

Heb. 9:14 the blood of Christ...purge your *c* from dead works

CONSECRATION. To dedicate or set apart someone or something for God's exclusive use. In OT times, Aaron and his sons were set apart to serve as priests for the rest of the Israelites (Lev. 8:12–13). The firstborn of livestock and the first of the agricultural harvest were also dedicated to the Lord (Exod. 23:19). Jesus Christ was set apart by the heavenly Father to become the agent of salvation for a sinful world. Believers are also sanctified by Christ as His treasured possession (1 Pet. 2:9).

CONSENT [ED, ING]

Prov. 1:10 if sinners entice you, do not *c*

Luke 14:18 they all with one *c* began to make excuses

Acts 8:1 Saul *c'ed* to his [Stephen's] death

Acts 22:20 I [Paul]...was...*c'ing* to his [Stephen's] death

1 Cor. 7:5 Do not deprive one another, unless it is with *c* for a time

CONSIDER [ED, ING, S]

1 Sam. 12:24 *c* what great things He has done

Job 1:8 Have you [Satan] *c'ed* My [God's] servant Job

Job 37:14 Stand still and *c* the wondrous works of God

Ps. 8:3 When I *c* Your heavens, the work of Your fingers...the moon and...stars

Ps. 25:19 *C* my enemies, for they are many

Ps. 41:1 Blessed is he who *c's* the poor

Ps. 119:15 I will *c* Your [God's] ways

Ps. 119:153 *C* my affliction and deliver me

Ps. 144:3 the son of man that You *c* him

Prov. 6:6 Go to the ant, you sluggard! *C* her ways

Prov. 31:16 She *c's* a field and buys it

Isa. 43:18 Do not...*c* the things of old

Hag. 1:5 this is what the LORD of hosts says, *C* your ways

Matt. 6:28 *C* the lilies of the field, how they grow

Matt. 7:3 but do not *c* the beam that is in your own eye

Luke 22:24 strife among them, as to which... should be *c'ed* the greatest

Rom. 8:18 I *c* that the sufferings...not worthy to be compared

Gal. 6:1 *c'ing* yourself, lest you also be tempted

Heb. 3:1 *c* the...High Priest of our profession, Christ Jesus

CONSOLATION. A word that expresses the idea of comfort combined with encouragement. When the infant Jesus was dedicated in the temple, a godly man named Simeon recognized Him as the "consolation of Israel" (Luke 2:25). This phrase referred to the Messiah whom God had promised to send to His people.

CONSOLATION

Luke 2:25 man [Simeon] was just and devout, waiting for the *c* of Israel

Luke 6:24 But woe to you who are rich! For you have received your *c*

Acts 4:36 Barnabas...being interpreted, The son of *c*

Rom. 15:5 the God of...*c* grant you to be like-minded

Phil. 2:1 If there is therefore any *c* in Christ

CONTENT

Phil. 4:11 I [Paul] have learned in whatever state I am to be *c*

1 Tim. 6:8 having food and clothing, let us be *c* with that

Heb. 13:5 be *c* with what you have

CONTENTMENT. Freedom from worry and anxiety. This state of mind was modeled for all believers by the apostle Paul (Phil. 4:11).

CONTINUE [D, ING, S]

Luke 6:12 He [Jesus]...*c'd* all night in prayer

John 8:31 If you *c* in My word, then you are My disciples indeed

John 15:9 so have I [Jesus] loved you; *c* in My love

Acts 1:14 All these with one accord *c'd* in prayer

Acts 2:46 *c'ing* daily with one accord...they [the believers] ate their food

Acts 18:11 he [Paul] *c'd* there...teaching the word of God

Rom. 6:1 Shall we *c* in sin that grace may abound

Rom. 12:12 patient in tribulation, *c'ing* persistently in prayer

Gal. 3:10 Cursed is everyone who does not *c* in all things...in the Book of the Law

Phil. 1:25 I [Paul]...shall remain and *c* with you all for your...joy of faith

1 Tim. 4:16 Pay attention...to the doctrine. *C* in them

Heb. 13:1 Let brotherly love *c*

2 Pet. 3:4 all things *c* as they were from the beginning

1 John 2:19 they no doubt would have *c'd* with us

CONVERSATION. A word used in the King James Version that refers to one's conduct, lifestyle, or way of life. The apostle Paul cautioned young Timothy to set a good example for believers in how he lived among them (1 Tim. 4:12). See also *Citizenship, Conduct*.

CONVERSION. The general term for the process by which a person is transformed from a state of sin into a new person who desires to please the Lord. The apostle Paul was converted dramatically in his encounter with Jesus on the road to Damascus (Acts 9:1–8). But other conversions, such as that of Lydia the businesswoman, were more gradual and subdued in nature (Acts 16:14–15). See also *New Birth*.

CONVERSION

Acts 15:3 they [Paul and Barnabas] passed through...declaring the *c* of the Gentiles

CONVERSION OF PAUL. Acts 9:1–18

CONVERT [ED, ING, S]

Ps. 19:7 The law of the LORD is perfect, *c'ing* the soul

Ps. 51:13 sinners shall be *c'ed* to You

Matt. 18:3 Unless you are *c'ed* and become as little children

Acts 3:19 Repent therefore, and be *c'ed*

Jas. 5:19 if any of you strays from the truth and one *c's* him

Jas. 5:20 he who *c's* the sinner...shall save a soul

CONVICT

Job 13:10 He [God] will surely *c* you if you... show partiality

John 16:8 He [the Holy Spirit] will *c* the world of sin

CONVICTION. The process by which people become aware of their sin and their need to turn to God for forgiveness and salvation. Conviction is one of the works of the Holy Spirit (John 16:7–11).

CONVOCATION. A sacred assembly of the people of Israel for worship in connection with observance of the Sabbath or one of their major religious festivals (Lev. 23:2–8).

CORAL. A substance formed from an accumulation of tiny sea creatures (Ezek. 27:16). Coral was apparently used for making fine jewelry (Job 28:18).

CORBAN. A word denoting an offering devoted to God. Jesus condemned the Pharisees for using this practice to avoid their responsibility to take care of their parents (Mark 7:11–13).

CORE. KJV: see *Korah*

CORINTH. A major port city in Greece where the apostle Paul planted a church during his second missionary journey. Corinth was known for its secularism, diversity, immorality, corruption, and worship of pagan gods. Paul labored here for about eighteen months with assistance from several of his missionary associates, including Aquila and Priscilla. Corinth is mentioned in **Acts 18:1–18**; 19:1 • 1 Cor. 1:2 • 2 Cor. 1:1, 23 • 2 Tim. 4:20.

CORINTHIANS, FIRST. A letter written by the apostle Paul to address several different problems in the Corinthian church, including divisions, sexual immorality, and abuses of the Lord's Supper and spiritual gifts. Most of the believers at Corinth had been converted from a pagan background. They were struggling to leave their past behind and commit themselves totally to Christian ethical standards. Paul dealt decisively with these issues.

CORINTHIANS, SECOND. A follow-up letter to Paul's first epistle to the Corinthian church. Some believers were questioning his ability and authority. He defended his calling and ministry, assuring the church that his work among them was motivated by love for Christ and his concern for their welfare. He warned them to be on guard against false teachers who would undermine the gospel and cause them to falter in their commitment to Christ.

CORMORANT. A large bird cited by the prophet Isaiah as a symbol of desolation and destruction that God would bring in judgment against sinful cities (Isa. 34:11).

CORNELIUS. A Roman military officer from Caesarea who sought out the apostle Peter at Joppa and became one of the first Gentile convert to Christianity (Acts 10:1–48). This event came about through visions that God revealed to both him and Peter. Cornelius's conversion marked the beginning of the influx of Gentiles into the early church (Acts 15:7–11).

CORNERSTONE. A stone that aligned two walls and tied the building together. This phrase is also used as a title of Christ. He referred to Himself as a rejected stone who would become the "head of the corner" (Matt. 21:42). He would become the centerpiece of a new building that would include all people who accepted Him as Savior and Lord. This building would be the church, a fresh, new organism that would be born out of the ashes of the old religious order based on the OT law.

CORRUPT [ED]
Gen. 6:11 The earth also was *c* before God
Exod. 8:24 land [Egypt] was *c'ed* because of the swarm of flies
Job 17:1 My [Job's] breath is *c*. My days are extinct

Matt. 6:20 treasures in heaven, where neither moth nor rust *c's*
Luke 6:43 a good tree does not bring forth *c* fruit
2 Cor. 7:2 We have wronged no man, we have *c'ed* no man
Eph. 4:29 Let no *c* communication proceed out of your mouth
Jas. 5:2 Your riches are *c'ed*, and your garments are moth-eaten

CORRUPTION
Isa. 38:17 in love for my soul You have delivered it from the pit of *c*
Rom. 8:21 creation...shall be delivered from the bondage of *c*
1 Cor. 15:42 It [the body] is sown in *c*; it is raised in incorruption
Gal. 6:8 he who sows to his flesh shall of the flesh reap *c*

COS. A small island in the Mediterranean Sea that the apostle Paul passed on his way to Jerusalem at the close of the third missionary journey (Acts 21:1).

COUNSEL OF THE LORD
Ps. 33:11 The *c-o-t-L* stands forever
Prov. 19:21 nevertheless, the *c-o-t-L* shall stand

COUNT [ED]
Gen. 15:6 and He *c'ed* it...for righteousness
Job 31:4 Does He not see my ways and *c* all my steps
Ps. 44:22 we are *c'ed* as sheep for the slaughter
Prov. 17:28 a fool, when he remains silent, is *c'ed* wise
Luke 14:28 does not sit down first and *c* the cost
Luke 21:36 *c'ed* worthy to...stand before the Son of Man
Luke 22:37 He [Jesus] was *c'ed* among the transgressors
Acts 5:41 *c'ed* worthy to suffer shame for His name
Rom. 4:3 it was *c'ed* to him [Abraham] for righteousness
Phil. 3:7 gain to me [Paul], those I *c'ed* loss for Christ
Phil. 3:8 I [Paul] *c* all things but loss

COURAGE

Phil. 3:13 I [Paul] do not *c* myself to have apprehended

2 Thes. 1:5 that you may be *c'ed* worthy of the kingdom of God

1 Tim. 5:17 Let the elders who rule well be *c'ed* worthy

Jas. 1:2 *c* it all joy when you fall into various temptations

2 Pet. 3:9 The Lord is not slow concerning His promise, as some men *c* slowness

COURAGE

Deut. 31:6 Be strong and of good *c*. Do not fear

Ps. 31:24 Be of good *c*, and He shall strengthen your heart

Isa. 41:6 everyone said to his brother, Be of good *c*

COURIER. A person who delivered messages for a king or other high official. King Hezekiah of Judah (the Southern Kingdom) used couriers to order his subjects to observe the Passover (2 Chron. 30:6–10).

COURT OF THE GENTILES. The outermost court in the Jewish temple in Jerusalem. Non-Jewish worshippers could not go beyond this point. The splitting of the curtain between this court and the inner court at Jesus' death symbolized the Gentiles' equal access to God through His sacrifice (Matt. 27:51; Eph. 2:11–14).

COVENANT. An agreement between two people or groups, particularly that between God and His people. This agreement promised His blessings in return for their obedience and devotion (Gen. 15:1–21). The concept of covenant began in the OT, when God established such agreements with several people, including Noah, Abraham, Isaac, Jacob, and David. The prophet Jeremiah spoke of a new covenant of grace that God would establish in the future with His people (Jer. 31:31).This was accomplished with Jesus, who became the mediator of a new covenant, bringing salvation and eternal life to all who trust in Him (Heb. 10:12–17). See also *New Covenant*.

COVENANT [S]

Gen. 9:9 I [God] establish my *c* with you [Noah]

Gen. 9:13 bow in the cloud...shall be for a token of a *c*

Gen. 15:18 the LORD made a *c* with Abram

Exod. 2:24 God remembered His *c* with Abraham

Exod. 19:5 keep My *c*, then you shall be a special treasure

Exod. 34:28 he [Moses] wrote...the words of the *c*, the Ten Commandments

Deut. 4:23 Be careful, lest you forget the *c* of the LORD

Deut. 29:9 Therefore keep the words of this *c*

1 Sam. 18:3 Jonathan and David made a *c*

Jer. 11:3 Cursed is the man who does not obey... this *c*

Jer. 31:31 I [God] will make a new *c* with...Israel

Ezek. 16:62 I will establish My *c* with you

Rom. 11:27 For this is My *c*...when I shall take away their sins

Eph. 2:12 being...strangers from the *c's* of promise

Heb. 8:6 He [Jesus] is also the mediator of a better *c*

Heb. 13:20 through the blood of the everlasting *c*

COVET [ED, S]

Exod. 20:17 You shall not *c* your neighbor's house

Prov. 21:26 He greedily *c's* all the day long

Acts 20:33 I [Paul] have *c'ed* no man's silver

1 Cor. 12:31 But earnestly *c* the best gifts

1 Tim. 6:10 while some *c'ed* after, they have gone astray from the faith

COVETOUSNESS. Greed, or a strong desire for material things, a sin specifically prohibited by the Ten Commandments (Exod. 20:17). Jesus also warned against falling into this sin (Luke 12:15). To the apostle Paul, covetousness was nothing less than idolatry, or making material things more important than dedication to God (Col. 3:5).

COVETOUSNESS

Ps. 119:36 Incline my heart to Your testimonies, and not to *c*

Luke 12:15 Be careful and beware of *c*

Heb. 13:5 Let your conduct be without *c*

CREATE [D]

Gen. 1:1 In the beginning God *c'd* the heaven and the earth

Gen. 1:27 God *c'd* man in His own image

Gen. 6:7 I [God] will destroy man whom I have *c'd*

Ps. 51:10 *C* in me a clean heart, O God...renew a right spirit

Ps. 148:5 for He commanded and they were *c'd*

Isa. 45:12 I [God] have made the earth and *c'd* man on it

Isa. 65:17 I [God] *c* new heavens and a new earth

Jer. 31:22 the LORD has *c'd* a new thing in the earth

Mal. 2:10 Do we not all have one Father? Has not one God *c'd* us

1 Cor. 11:9 Nor was the man *c'd* for the woman

Eph. 2:10 we are His workmanship, *c'd* in Christ Jesus

Col. 1:16 All things were *c'd* by Him and for Him

Rev. 4:11 for You have *c'd* all things

CREATION. The actions of God through which He brought man and the physical world into existence. God existed before the world, and He produced the universe from nothing (Gen. 1:1–2). The Lord accomplished this in orderly fashion, in six successive days. The creation of the first man, Adam, was the crowning achievement of this creative process. He assigned to Adam, and all succeeding generations, the responsibility of taking care of His world.

CREATION

Mark 10:6 from the beginning of the *c* God made them male and female

Rom. 1:20 from the *c* of the world the invisible things of Him are clearly seen

Rom. 8:22 the whole *c* groans and labors in pain

CREATION OF MAN. Gen. 1:26–2:7

CREATION OF WOMAN. Gen. 2:18–25

CREATION OF THE WORLD. Gen. 1:1–25

CREATOR. A title for God which emphasizes that He is the maker of all things and the sovereign ruler of His creation (Isa. 40:28; Col.

1:15–16). He alone is eternal; the physical world owes its existence to Him.

CRETE. A large island in the Mediterranean Sea where a church was established and apparently led by Titus, Paul's missionary associate (Titus 1:4–5). Several churches may have existed on Crete, because Paul directed Titus to ordain elders, or church leaders, "in every city." In the OT, the prophet Amos identified Crete, or Caphtor, as the original home of the Philistines (Amos 9:7).

CRISPUS. Ruler of the Jewish synagogue at Corinth who became a believer (Acts 18:8) and was baptized by Paul (1 Cor. 1:14).

CROOKED

Deut. 32:5 they are a perverse and *c* generation

Eccles. 7:13 who can make straight what He has made *c*

Isa. 40:4 the *c* shall be made straight and the rough places plain

Luke 3:5 the *c* shall be made straight, and the rough ways...smooth

Phil. 2:15 sons of God...in the midst of a *c*...nation

CROSS. A wooden stake on which Jesus was put to death—a common form of capital punishment by the Roman government in NT times. The cross is a symbol of God's love, His power to save, and His continuing work of redemption through the church (1 Cor. 1:17–18).

CROSS

Matt. 27:32 They compelled him [Simon] to bear His [Jesus'] *c*

Matt. 27:42 let Him come down now from the *c*

Luke 9:23 take up his *c* daily, and follow Me

John 19:17 And He, bearing His *c*, went out to... the place of a skull

1 Cor. 1:18 the preaching of the *c* is foolishness to those who are perishing

Gal. 6:14 God forbid that I [Paul] should boast, except in the *c*

Phil. 2:8 He [Jesus]...became obedient to...death of the *c*

Heb. 12:2 who [Jesus] for the joy that was set before Him endured the *c*

CROSSING OF JORDAN RIVER INTO CANAAN. Josh. 3:1–17

CROSSING OF RED SEA. Exod. 14:21–31

CROWN.
An ornamental headdress that symbolized power and authority, especially that of kings and queens (2 Kings 11:12). The word is also used as a metaphor for righteous behavior of believers (2 Tim. 4:8), the Christian's hope in Christ (1 Thes. 2:19), and God's gift of eternal life (James 1:12).

CROWN [ED]
Ps. 8:5 You [God]...have *c'ed* him [man] with... honor

Prov. 17:6 Children's children are the *c* of old men

Mark 15:17 wove a *c* of thorns and put it around His head

Phil. 4:1 my joy and *c*, so stand fast in the Lord

2 Tim. 4:8 laid up for me [Paul] a *c* of righteousness

Heb. 2:7 You *c'ed* him with glory and honor

Heb. 2:9 But we see Jesus...*c'ed* with glory and honor

CROWN OF GLORY
Prov. 16:31 The gray head is a *c-o-g*

Isa. 28:5 the LORD of hosts shall be a *c-o-g*

Isa. 62:3 You shall...be a *c-o-g* in the hand of the LORD

1 Pet. 5:4 when the Chief Shepherd appears, you shall receive a *c-o-g*

CROWN OF LIFE
Jas. 1:12 when he is tried, he shall receive the *c-o-l*

Rev. 2:10 Be faithful to death, and I will give you a *c-o-l*

CRUCIFIXION.
The form of execution to which Jesus was sentenced by Pontius Pilate. The victim's wrists were nailed to a horizontal crossbeam; then it was raised into position and attached to a stake fixed firmly in the ground. Sometimes the feet were crossed and nailed to the stake. Without any support for the body except the nails through the feet and wrists, the victim slumped forward on the cross. This put pressure on the heart and lungs, making breathing difficult. A slow, painful death usually occurred after two or three days from a combination of shock, fatigue, suffocation, and loss of blood. But Jesus died after only six hours on the cross (John 19:30–33).

CRUCIFIXION OF JESUS.
See *Jesus Christ, Life and Ministry of*

CUBIT.
The distance from the elbow to the fingertips of an adult, the standard unit for measurement of length. It was equivalent to about eighteen inches (Gen. 6:15–16).

CUMIN.
A plant whose seeds were used as a medicine and to flavor food (Isa. 28:25–27). Jesus criticized the Pharisees for their shallow legalism by tithing the seeds from this minor plant while ignoring such major matters as mercy and faith (Matt. 23:23).

CUPBEARER.
A servant who tasted wine before it was served to the king to insure it had not been poisoned. Nehemiah served in this capacity for King Artaxerxes of Persia (Neh. 1:11).

CURSE [D, ING, S]
Gen. 3:14 you [the serpent] are *c'd* above all cattle

Gen. 12:3 I [God] will...*c* him who *c's* you [Abraham]

Lev. 20:9 everyone who *c's* his father or his mother shall...be put to death

Num. 23:11 I [Balak] took you [Balaam] to *c* my enemies

Deut. 11:26 I [Moses] set before you [Israel] this day a blessing and a *c*

Deut. 27:15 *C'd* is the man who makes any engraved or molten image

Deut. 30:19 I [Moses] have set before you life and death, blessing and *c'ing*

Josh. 6:26 *C'd* is the man...who...builds this city Jericho

Job 2:9 Do you [Job] still retain your integrity? *C* God and die

Jer. 20:14 *C'd* be the day on which I [Jeremiah] was born

Matt. 5:44 love your enemies, bless those who *c* you

Matt. 15:4 He who *c's* father or mother, let him die

Matt. 25:41 Depart from Me, you *c'd*, into everlasting fire

Mark 11:21 fig tree that You *c'd* has withered

Mark 14:71 But he [Peter] began to *c*...saying, I do not know this man [Jesus]

Acts 23:14 bound ourselves under a great *c*... eat nothing until we have slain Paul

Rom. 12:14 Bless those who persecute you. Bless, and do not *c*

Gal. 3:13 Christ has redeemed us from the *c* of the law

Jas. 3:10 Out of the same mouth proceeds blessing and *c'ing*

CUSTOM. See also *Tax*

John 18:39 a *c*, that I [Pilate] should release to you one at the Passover

Rom. 13:7 render to all their due...*c* to whom *c*

CUTH. A city from which people were sent to populate the Northern Kingdom after it fell to the Assyrians (2 Kings 17:30). *Cuthah*: 2 Kings 17:24.

CUTHAH. See *Cuth*

CYPRUS. A large island in the Mediterranean Sea which Paul and Barnabas visited during the first missionary journey. Sergius Paulus, chief official of the island, became the first convert on this evangelistic tour. Barnabas was a native of Cyprus. Cyprus is mentioned in Jer. 2:10 • Acts 4:36; 11:19–20; **13:4–13**; 15:39; 21:3, 16; 27:4.

CYRENE. A Greek city in North Africa and home of the Simon of Cyrene who carried the cross of Jesus (Matt. 27:32). Cyrene is also mentioned in Acts 2:10; 11:20; 13:1. *Cyrenian*: Mark 15:21 • Luke 23:26. *Cyrenians*: Acts 6:9.

CYRENIUS. KJV: see *Quirinius*.

CYRUS. A Persian king who defeated the Babylonians and allowed the Jewish exiles to return to their homeland about 536 BC. In contrast to the Babylonians, Cyrus treated the Jews and other subject nations with respect. He even returned the valuables from the Jewish temple that the Babylonians had claimed as spoils of war several decades before. Cyrus reasoned that kindness toward his subject nations would generate goodwill and prosperity for his government. Cyrus is mentioned in 2 Chron. 36:22–23 • **Ezra 1:1–8**; 3:7; 4:3, 5; 5:13–14, 17; 6:3, 14 • Isa. 44:28; 45:1 • Dan. 1:21; 6:28; 10:1.

D

DAGON. The chief pagan god of the Philistines, depictions of which apparently had the head and hands of a man and the tail of a fish. This idol fell before the ark of the covenant in the pagan temple at Ashdod, symbolizing the superiority of the one true God of the Israelites (1 Sam. 5:1–5). Dagon is also mentioned in Judg. 16:23 • 1 Chron. 10:10.

DALETH. Fourth letter of the Hebrew alphabet, used as a heading over Psalm 119:25–32. In the Hebrew language, each line of these eight verses begins with this letter.

DALMANUTHA. A place on the western shore of the Sea of Galilee visited by Jesus (Mark 8:10).

The parallel passage in Matthew 15:39 identifies the place as Magdala.

DALMATIA. A Roman province on the eastern coast of the Adriatic Sea to which Titus was sent by the apostle Paul (2 Tim. 4:10).

DALPHON. A son of Haman who was executed, along with his father, when Haman's plot to destroy the Jews was exposed by Esther (Esther 9:7–10).

DAMARIS. A woman of Athens converted under the apostle Paul's ministry (Acts 17:33–34).

DAMASCUS. Capital city of Syria to which the apostle Paul was traveling when converted through a vision of the living Christ (Acts 9:1–8). Several centuries before Paul's time, King David captured Damascus from the Syrians and stationed his troops in the city (2 Sam. 8:5–6). David's son and successor, Solomon, lost control over the city, and other Israelite kings battled with Syria, also known as Aram (1 Kings 15:18–20).Damascus claims to be the oldest continually inhabited city in the world. Even today, its open-air markets and ancient streets conjure up images of a biblical city. Damascus is also mentioned in Gen. 14:15 • 2 Kings 8:7–15 • 1 Chron. 18:5–6 • Isa. 8:4 • 2 Cor. 11:32–33 • Gal. 1:17.

DAMNATION. See also *Judgment*

Matt. 23:33 generation of vipers, how can you escape the *d* of hell

Mark 3:29 blasphemes against the Holy Spirit... is in danger of eternal *d*

Luke 20:47 devour widows' houses...same shall receive greater *d*

DAN. (1) A son of Jacob born to Bilhah, servant of his wife Rachel. Dan is mentioned in Gen. 30:6; 35:25; 46:23; 49:16–17 • Exod. 1:4 • Josh. 19:47–48 • 1 Chron. 2:2 • Ezek. 27:19. (2) One of the twelve tribes of Israel that grew from Dan's descendants (Gen. 30:6; Num. 1:38–39). It settled in central Palestine and along the Mediterranean Sea. The judge Samson was a member of this tribe (Judg. 13:1–2, 24).

(2) A village in the territory allotted to the tribe of Dan (Gen. 14:14 • 1 Chron. 21:2 • 2 Chron. 30:5). It was located farther north than any other city of Israel during most of the OT era. After the united kingdom split into two factions following Solomon's death, King Jeroboam of the Northern Kingdom placed a calf idol in a shrine at Dan. The phrase "from Dan to Beer-sheba" (Judg. 20:1) was a figurative way of referring to the entire country.

DANCING. Exuberant praise of the Lord through rhythmic body movements. Moses' sister Miriam and other women danced and sang to the Lord to celebrate His deliverance of the people from the pursuing Egyptian army

(Exod. 15:20). King David also "danced before the LORD with all his might" when the ark of the covenant was relocated to the city of Jerusalem (2 Sam. 6:14).

DANIEL. A prophet of the OT known for his wisdom, intelligence, and faithfulness to the one true God. After he was exiled to Babylon, he was selected as a trainee for service in the royal court. He served several kings of Babylon and Persia as an advisor and interpreter of dreams. But he refused to worship the Persian king Darius, and was thrown into a den of lions, only to emerge unharmed (Dan. 6:1–24). References to Daniel outside the book of Daniel are found in Ezek. 14:14, 20; 28:3 • Matt. 24:15 • Mark 13:14. His Babylonian name was *Belteshazzar* (Dan. 1:7).

DANIEL, BOOK OF. A book of the OT known for its images of horns and beasts, a distinction of the type of writing known as apocalyptic literature. These are similar to images that appear in the book of Revelation in the NT. The most striking prophecy in Daniel's book is his "seventy weeks" prophecy. It has been interpreted as a period of 490 years (seventy weeks, representing seventy years, multiplied by seven) from Daniel's time until the coming of the Jesus the Messiah (Dan. 9:20–27). See also *Apocalyptic Writing*.

DARIUS. Several different kings of Persia who had this title are mentioned in the Bible. But the most famous was Darius the Mede, a friend and supporter of the prophet Daniel. He is the king who was impressed by the one true God who kept the prophet safe in a den of lions (Dan. 6:1–28). Many scholars believe this king was actually Cyrus, the Persian king who allowed the Jewish exiles to return to their homeland after the Persians defeated the Babylonians (2 Chron. 36:22–23).

Other leaders named Darius include (1) Darius I or Darius the Great, who continued Cyrus's policy of restoring the Jewish people to their homeland (Ezra 6:1–12). (2) Darius II or Darius the Persian (Neh. 12:22). (3) Darius

III or Darius Codommanus, who is probably the "fourth" king of Persia mentioned by the prophet Daniel (Dan. 11:2).

DARKENED

Isa. 24:11 All joy is *d*. The joy of the land is gone
Joel 3:15 The sun and the moon shall be *d*
Mark 13:24 after that tribulation, the sun shall be *d*
Rom. 1:21 they [ungodly]...became vain...their foolish hearts were *d*

DARKNESS. A metaphor for sin, lack of spiritual understanding, and unbelief. Those who refuse to acknowledge Jesus as God's Son and accept Him in faith are stumbling in the darkness (John 12:35). Jesus condemned the Pharisees as "blind guides" (Matt. 23:24) because they were trapped in the dark themselves and led other people into the same hopeless condition.

DARKNESS

Gen. 1:2 And *d* was on the face of the deep
Exod. 10:22 a thick *d* in all the land of Egypt three days
2 Sam. 22:29 the LORD will illuminate my *d*
Job 34:22 There is no *d* or shadow of death
Ps. 18:9 He [God]...came down, and *d* was under His feet
Isa. 5:20 Woe to those who...substitute *d* for light and light for *d*
Isa. 9:2 people who walked in *d* have seen a great light
Joel 2:31 sun shall be turned into *d* and the moon into blood
Matt. 4:16 people who sat in *d* saw great light
Luke 23:44 a *d* over all the earth until the ninth hour
John 1:5 the *d* did not comprehend it [the light]
John 3:19 men loved *d* rather than light
John 12:46 whoever believes in Me should not abide in *d*
Acts 2:20 The sun shall be turned into *d*
Acts 26:18 To open their eyes and to turn them from *d* to light
2 Cor. 4:6 God, who commanded the light to shine out of *d*...shone in our hearts

Eph. 6:12 we wrestle...against the rulers of the *d* of this world
1 Pet. 2:9 who [Jesus] has called you out of *d* into His marvelous light
1 John 1:5 God is light and in Him is no *d* at all
1 John 2:11 he who hates his brother is in *d*

DATHAN. A leader from the tribe of Reuben who rebelled against Moses in the wilderness. All the rebels were destroyed when swallowed by the earth, probably by an earthquake (Num. 16:1–50).

DAUGHTER OF ZION. A symbolic expression for the city of Jerusalem and its inhabitants (Ps. 9:14).

DAVID. Second king of Israel who became the ideal monarch against whom all future rulers were judged. As a boy, he killed a Philistine giant named Goliath with his shepherd's sling (1 Sam. 17:50). This led Saul, the first king of Israel, to make David his armor bearer. But David's bravery in battle eventually turned Saul against him, and he fled into the wilderness to escape the king's wrath (1 Sam. 23:6–29).

At Saul's death, David became king over Israel's southern territory (2 Sam. 2:4). He soon united all the people under his leadership to become the undisputed king over all Israel. He ruled from Jerusalem after capturing the city and turning it into his capital (2 Sam. 5:1–9). He wrote many psalms, or worship songs, that appear in the book of Psalms. He gathered materials for the building of the temple by his successor (1 Chron. 22:1–19).

In a moment of weakness, David committed adultery with Bathsheba (2 Sam. 11:1–4). He repented (Ps. 32:1–11) and was forgiven, although the consequences of his sin remained. He suffered several family tragedies, including his son Absalom's violent death when he attempted to take the throne by force (2 Sam. 18:19–33).

God promised David that one of his descendants would always occupy the throne of Israel (2 Sam. 7:1–17). This promise was fulfilled in a material sense through his offspring who succeeded him as king. In a spiritual sense, Jesus fulfilled this promise as the Messiah from David's family line, and He was often called the "son of David" (Luke 18:38). At David's death, he was succeeded by his son Solomon (1 Kings 2:1–2).

The phrase "of David" appears in the titles of many psalms in that collection, indicating either that David wrote these psalms or that they were written in his honor: Pss. 3–9; 11–32; 34–41; 51–65; 68–70; 86; 101; 103; 108–110; 122; 124; 131; 133; 138–145.

The prophets of the Old Testament often spoke of the promised Messiah who would fulfill God's promise to David (Isa. 9:7; 55:3 • Jer. 17:25; 33:17 • Ezek. 37:24 • Zech. 12:8).

In the New Testament, Jesus was called "the Son of David" or "seed of David" or otherwise identified as a descendant of Israel's great king (Matt. 9:27; 20:31 • Luke 18:38–39 • John 7:42 • Rom. 1:3 • 2 Tim. 2:8).

DAY. A word used often in a symbolic sense, as in "the day of His wrath" (Job 20:28), referring to God's judgment.

DAY

Gen. 1:5 the evening and the morning were the first *d*

Exod. 13:3 Remember this *d* in which you came out from Egypt

Exod. 20:11 the LORD blessed the Sabbath *d* and made it holy

Deut. 4:4 you who clung to the LORD your God are alive this *d*

Deut. 11:26 Behold, I [Moses] set before you this *d* a blessing and a curse

Josh. 4:14 On that *d* the LORD magnified Joshua

Josh. 10:13 the sun stood still...and did not hasten to go down...about a whole *d*

Josh. 24:15 choose for yourselves this *d* whom you will serve

1 Kings 18:36 known this *d* that You are God in Israel

1 Chron. 16:23 proclaim His salvation from *d* to *d*

Job 3:3 Let the *d* perish on which I [Job] was born

Job 19:25 He shall stand at the latter *d* on the earth

Ps. 1:2 on His law he meditates *d* and night

Ps. 19:2 *D* to *d* utters speech

Ps. 50:15 call on Me in the *d* of trouble

Ps. 84:10 For a *d* in Your courts is better than a thousand

Ps. 86:7 In the *d* of my trouble I will call on You

Ps. 91:5 You shall not be afraid...of the arrow that flies by *d*

Ps. 118:24 This is the *d* that the LORD has made

Ps. 121:6 sun shall not strike you by *d*

Prov. 27:1 you do not know what a *d* may bring forth

Isa. 13:6 Wail, for the *d* of the Lord is at hand

Isa. 60:19 sun shall no longer be your light by *d*

Jer. 1:10 this *d* I [God] set you over the nations

Jer. 9:1 I [Jeremiah] might weep *d* and night for the slain...of my people

Jer. 20:14 Cursed be the *d* on which I [Jeremiah] was born

Joel 2:31 before...the terrible *d* of the LORD comes

Amos 5:18 Woe to you who desire the *d* of the LORD

Zech. 2:11 many nations shall be joined to the LORD on that *d*

Zech. 14:6 on that *d* that the light shall not be clear

Mal. 3:2 who may withstand the *d* of His coming

Matt. 6:11 Give us this *d* our daily bread

Matt. 7:22 Many will say to Me in that *d*, Lord, Lord

Matt. 25:13 know neither the *d* nor the hour in which the Son of Man is coming

Mark 14:25 I [Jesus] will no longer drink of the fruit of the vine until that *d*

Luke 2:11 born this *d* in the city of David a Savior

Luke 9:22 Son of Man must...be slain...raised the third *d*

Luke 19:9 This *d* salvation has come to this house

Luke 24:46 necessary for Christ to suffer...to rise from the dead the third *d*

John 9:4 I [Jesus] must work...while it is *d*

John 11:24 he [Lazarus] shall rise again...on the last *d*

1 Cor. 16:2 On the first *d* of the week, let each one of you lay aside something

2 Cor. 6:2 behold, now is the *d* of salvation

Phil. 3:5 circumcised the eighth *d*, of the stock of Israel

2 Tim. 1:12 guard what I have committed to Him until that *d*

2 Pet. 3:8 one *d* with the Lord is as a thousand years

Rev. 1:10 I [John] was in the Spirit on the Lord's *D*

Rev. 6:17 the great *d* of His wrath has come

DAY OF ATONEMENT

Lev. 23:27 a *D-o-A*. It shall be a holy convocation

Lev. 23:28 a *D-o-A*, to make an atonement... before the LORD

Lev. 25:9 On the *D-o-A* you shall make the trumpet sound

DAY OF JUDGMENT

Matt. 11:22 it shall be more tolerable for Tyre... at the *d-o-j* than for you

Matt. 12:36 every idle word...men...shall give account of it on the *d-o-j*

1 John 4:17 that we may have boldness in the *d-o-j*

DAY OF THE LORD. A phrase usually interpreted as a period in the end-time when God will bring His purpose for humankind and the world to fulfillment. This will be a day of judgment for the rebellious and sinful (Jer. 46:10) but a time of deliverance for the godly (Joel 2:28–32). Any time—whether now or in the future—when the Lord intervenes in history for the purpose of deliverance and judgment, may also be described as the day of the Lord (Isa. 13:6).

DAY OF THE LORD

Isa. 2:12 the *d-o-t-L* of hosts shall be on everyone who is arrogant

Joel 1:15 Alas...For the *d-o-t-L* is at hand

Amos 5:20 Shall not the *d-o-t-L* be darkness and not light? even very dark

Obad. 15 the *d-o-t-L* is near on all the nations

Zech. 14:1 Behold, the *d-o-t-L* is coming

Mal. 4:5 send you Elijah the prophet before the...dreadful *d-o-t-L*

Acts 2:20 sun shall be turned into darkness... before that great...*d-o-t-L* comes

1 Thes. 5:2 the *d-o-t-L* comes as a thief in the night

2 Pet. 3:10 the *d-o-t-L* will come as a thief in the night

DAY'S JOURNEY. The distance that could be traveled on foot in one day, probably about twenty-five miles (Jon. 3:3–4).

DAYSMAN. KJV: see *Arbiter*.

DAYSPRING FROM ON HIGH. A title of Jesus cited by Zacharias, father of John the Baptist (Luke 1:78). The word *dayspring* refers to the rising of the sun in the morning. Thus Zacharias thought of the Messiah as a bright light that God was preparing to send into a dark world.

DAY STAR. A star that appears just before daybreak, signaling the beginning of a new day (2 Pet. 1:19). "Bright and morning star" is a title of Jesus that picks up on this imagery (Rev. 22:16).

DEACON. A lay officer or servant in many Christian churches. Some groups claim the first deacons were the seven men of Greek background who were appointed by the church at Jerusalem to coordinate the distribution of food to the needy (Acts 6:1–7). The early church had strict qualifications for deacons (1 Tim. 3:8–13).

DEACON [S]

1 Tim. 3:10 being found blameless, let them serve in the office of a *d*

1 Tim. 3:12 Let the *d's* be the husbands of one wife

1 Tim. 3:13 who have served well in the office of a *d* obtain...good degree

DEAD

Exod. 12:30 great cry in Egypt...not a house where there was not one *d*

Josh. 1:2 Moses My servant is *d*...therefore, arise

2 Kings 4:32 when Elisha came into the house, behold, the child was *d*

Eccles. 9:5 but the *d* do not know anything

Jer. 22:10 Do not weep for the *d*; do not bemoan him

Matt. 2:19 when Herod was *d*...an angel... appeared in a dream to Joseph

Matt. 8:22 Follow Me, and let the *d* bury their *d*

Matt. 10:8 Heal the sick, cleanse the lepers, raise the *d*

Mark 6:16 It is John, whom I [Herod] beheaded. He has risen from the *d*

Mark 15:44 Pilate marveled that He was already *d*

Luke 15:24 this my son was *d* and is alive again

Luke 20:38 He is not a God of the *d* but of the living

Luke 24:46 it was necessary for Christ to suffer and to rise from the *d*

John 11:25 though he were *d*, yet shall he live

John 20:9 they did not know...that He must rise again from the *d*

Acts 17:32 when they heard of the resurrection of the *d*, some mocked

Acts 26:8 thought an incredible thing with you that God should raise the *d*

Rom. 1:4 declared to be the Son of God with power...by the resurrection from the *d*

Rom. 6:4 Christ was raised up from the *d* by... the Father

Rom. 10:9 if you...believe...that God has raised Him from the *d*

1 Cor. 15:13 no resurrection of the *d*, then Christ has not been raised

Gal. 2:19 I [Paul] through the law am *d* to the law

Eph. 2:1 He has made alive you who were *d* in trespasses and sins

Col. 1:18 who [Jesus] is...the firstborn from the *d*

1 Thes. 4:16 the *d* in Christ shall rise first

2 Tim. 2:8 Jesus Christ...was raised from the *d* according to my gospel

Jas. 2:17 Even so faith, if it does not have works, is *d*

1 Pet. 4:5 to Him who is ready to judge the living and the *d*

Rev. 1:17 when I [John] saw Him, I fell at his feet as *d*

Rev. 14:13 Blessed are the *d* who die in the Lord

DEAD SEA. See *Salt Sea*

DEAD SEA SCROLLS. The popular name for about 500 ancient manuscripts discovered in caves around the Dead Sea. Although these documents were written centuries ago, they were remarkably preserved by the dry climate of the area. Among the scrolls was a complete manuscript of the book of Isaiah, written in Hebrew.

DEAF

Isa. 35:5 the ears of the *d* shall be unstopped

Mark 7:32 they brought to Him one who was *d*

Luke 7:22 tell John...the lepers are cleansed, the *d* hear

DEATH. The end of physical life as well as the tragic spiritual condition known as separation from God. Both physical and spiritual death were the result of the sin of Adam and Eve (Gen. 2:17). Second death or eternal death is the fate of those who reject God (Rev. 21:8). But God has provided a way to avoid this form of death. He sent His Son, Jesus, as an atoning sacrifice to pay the penalty for human sin. All who accept Him as Lord and Savior will enjoy eternal fellowship with Him in the afterlife.

DEATH

Deut. 30:15 I have set before you...life and good, and *d* and evil

Deut. 33:1 Moses...blessed the children of Israel before his *d*

2 Kings 4:40 man of God, there is *d* in the pot

Job 16:16 the shadow of *d* is on my [Job's] eyelids

Ps. 13:3 Lighten my eyes, lest I sleep the sleep of *d*

Ps. 23:4 walk through the valley of the shadow of *d*

Ps. 48:14 For this God...will be our guide even to *d*

Ps. 107:14 He [God] brought them out of...the shadow of *d*

Ps. 116:15 Precious in the sight of the Lord is the *d* of His saints

Prov. 14:12 but its end are the ways of *d*

Isa. 9:2 those who dwell in...the shadow of *d*, the light has shone on them

Isa. 53:9 He [God's servant] made His grave with the...rich in His *d*

Jer. 21:8 I [God] set before you the way of life and...*d*

Matt. 4:16 to those who sat in the...shadow of *d* light has sprung up

Mark 14:34 My [Jesus'] soul is exceedingly sorrowful, to *d*

Luke 2:26 he [Simon] should not see *d* before he had seen the Lord's Christ

John 5:24 He who...believes...has passed from *d* to life

John 11:4 sickness is not to *d*, but for the glory of God

Acts 8:1 Saul consented to his [Stephen's] *d*

Rom. 5:12 so *d* passed on to all men, for all have sinned

Rom. 6:4 we were buried with Him by baptism into *d*

Rom. 6:23 the wages of sin is *d*

Rom. 7:24 Who shall deliver me [Paul] from this body of *d*

Rom. 8:38 neither *d* nor life, nor angels

1 Cor. 11:26 you declare the Lord's *d* until He comes

1 Cor. 15:26 The last enemy that shall be destroyed is *d*

1 Cor. 15:55 O *d*, where is your sting

Phil. 2:8 He [Jesus] humbled Himself...became obedient to *d*

Phil. 3:10 being made conformable to His *d*

Heb. 11:5 Enoch was taken up that he should not see *d*

1 John 3:14 we have passed from *d* to life, because we love the brothers

Rev. 1:18 I [Jesus] am alive forevermore...I have the keys of hell and of *d*

Rev. 20:14 *d* and hell were cast into the lake of fire

Rev. 21:4 there shall be no more *d* or sorrow

DEATH OF JESUS. See *Jesus Christ, Life and Ministry of*

DEBIR. A king of Eglon and one of the five Amorite kings killed by Joshua's army (Josh. 10:3–26).

DEBORAH. A brave woman who was a unique combination of judge, prophetess, and military deliverer. As a judge or mediator, she heard cases brought by members of her clan at a landmark known as the palm tree of Deborah (Judg. 4:4–5). As a prophetess and military heroine, she joined forces with Barak to defeat the Canaanite forces of Sisera (Judg. 4:6–16). She celebrated their victory in a triumphant song (Judg. 5:1–31).

DEBT [S]

Matt. 6:12 forgive us our *d's*, as we forgive our debtors

Matt. 18:27 the lord of that servant...forgave him the *d*

Rom. 4:4 to him who works, the reward is counted...by *d*

DEBTOR [S]

Rom. 1:14 I [Paul] am a *d* both to the Greeks and to the non-Greeks

Rom. 8:12 we are *d's*, not to the flesh, to live according to the flesh

DECALOGUE. See *Ten Commandments*

DECAPOLIS. A Roman province or district with a large Gentile population situated on the eastern side of the Jordan River. The name means "ten cities." Jesus performed three miracles in this area. He healed a demon-possessed man who lived among the tombs (Mark 5:2–10), restored the hearing of a deaf man with a speech impediment (Mark 7:31–37), and fed four thousand Gentiles by multiplying a few pieces of fish and bread (Mark 8:1–10).

DECEIVE [D, ING, S]

Deut. 11:16 Be careful that your heart is not *d'd*

Prov. 20:1 Wine is a mocker...and whoever is *d'd* by it is not wise

Luke 21:8 Be careful that you are not *d'd*. For many shall come in My name

Gal. 6:3 thinks himself to be something when he is nothing, he *d's* himself

Gal. 6:7 Do not be *d'd*; God is not mocked

Eph. 5:6 Do not let any man *d* you with vain words

Jas. 1:22 be doers of the word and not hearers only, *d'ing* your own selves

1 John 1:8 If we say that we have no sin, we *d* ourselves

DECEIVER[S]

Matt. 27:63 that *d* said, After three days I [Jesus] will rise again

2 John 7 many *d's* have entered into the world

DECLARE[D, ING]

1 Chron. 16:24 *D* His glory among the nations

Ps. 9:11 *D* among the people His doings

Ps. 19:1 The heavens *d* the glory of God

Ps. 66:16 I will *d* what He has done for my soul

Ps. 71:17 here I have *d'd* Your wondrous works

Ps. 96:3 *D* His glory among the nations

Isa. 48:3 I have *d'd* the former things from the beginning

John 1:18 The only begotten Son...He has *d'd* Him

Acts 15:12 *d'ing* the miracles...God had worked through them

Acts 17:23 whom you worship ignorantly, I *d* Him to you

Rom. 1:4 *d'd* to be the Son of God with power

1 Cor. 15:1 I [Paul] *d* to you the gospel...I preached

1 John 1:3 we *d* to you what we have seen and heard

1 John 1:5 the message that we...*d* to you

DECREE. An order or command issued by a government official. Mary and Joseph traveled to Bethlehem under a taxation edict issued by the Roman emperor Caesar Augustus (Luke 2:1).

DEED[S]

1 Chron. 16:8 call upon His name; make known His *d's* among the people

Luke 23:41 we receive the due reward of our *d's*

John 3:19 men loved darkness...because their *d's* were evil

Rom. 2:6 render to every man according to his *d's*

Rom. 3:28 justified by faith without the *d's* of the law

Col. 3:17 And whatever you do in word or *d*

1 John 3:18 love not in word...but in *d* and in truth

DEFILE. To make something impure or unclean. The OT Law focused on ceremonial cleanliness but had little to say about moral purity (Lev. 15:24). Jesus turned this emphasis around by teaching about the need for ethical behavior (Mark 7:1–23).

DEFILE[D, S]

Ezek. 20:7 do not *d* yourselves with the idols of Egypt

Dan. 1:8 Daniel...would not *d* himself with... the king's food

Matt. 15:20 to eat with unwashed hands does not *d* a man

Mark 7:2 saw some of His disciples eating bread with *d'd*...hands

Mark 7:18 anything from outside that enters into the man, it cannot *d* him

John 18:28 not go into the judgment hall, lest they [Pharisees]...be *d'd*

1 Cor. 3:17 If any man *d's* the temple of God

Jas. 3:6 the tongue...*d's* the whole body

DEGREES, SONG OF. A title, meaning "going up," applied to fifteen psalms of the book of Psalms (Pss. 120–134). These may have been pilgrim psalms, sung by worshippers as they were traveling to the temple at Jerusalem. The city was built on a hill. To approach it from any direction was to go "up" to Jerusalem (Matt. 20:18).

DEHAVITES. Foreign colonists who settled in Samaria after the Northern Kingdom fell to Assyria (Ezra 4:9).

DELILAH. Samson's lover who delivered him to the Philistines by revealing the secret of his strength—his long hair (Judg. 16:13–21). This signified that he was a Nazirite, a person uniquely consecrated to God (Num. 6:2–5).

DELIVER [ED, ING, S]. See also *Rescue, Save*

Exod. 18:10 Jethro said...the LORD...has *d'ed* you out of the hand of the Egyptians

Deut. 1:27 the LORD...has brought us forth...to *d* us into the hand of the Amorites

Deut. 9:10 LORD *d'ed* to me [Moses] two tablets of stone

Josh. 10:8 I [God] have *d'ed* them into your hand

Judg. 6:1 the LORD *d'ed* them into the hand of Midian

1 Sam. 17:37 He will *d* me [David] out of the hand of this Philistine

Job 16:11 God has *d'ed* me [Job] to the ungodly

Job 33:28 He [God] will *d* his [man's] soul from... the pit

Ps. 17:13 O LORD...*D* my soul from the wicked

Ps. 25:20 keep my soul, and *d* me. Let me not be ashamed

Ps. 34:4 the LORD...*d'ed* me from all my fears

Ps. 34:17 the LORD...*d's* them out of all their troubles

Ps. 41:1 The LORD will *d* him in time of trouble

Ps. 72:12 He [God] shall *d* the needy when he cries

Ps. 107:6 and He *d'ed* them out of their distresses

Ps. 116:8 You [God] have *d'ed* my soul from death

Ps. 120:2 *D* my soul, O LORD, from lying lips

Prov. 11:4 righteousness *d's* from death

Isa. 19:20 He [God] shall send them a Savior... and He shall *d* them

Isa. 46:4 I [God] will carry and will *d* you

Jer. 20:13 He [God] has *d'ed*...the poor from... evildoers

Dan. 3:17 our God...is able to *d* us from the... furnace

Dan. 6:20 is your [Daniel's] God...able to *d* you

Hos. 11:8 How shall I [God] *d* you, Israel

Joel 2:32 whoever calls on...the LORD shall be *d'ed*

Matt. 6:13 do not lead us into temptation, but *d* us from evil

Matt. 24:9 Then they shall *d* you up to be afflicted

Matt. 25:20 Lord, you *d'ed* to me five talents

Mark 10:33 Son of Man shall be *d'ed* to the chief priests

Mark 15:1 the chief priests...*d'ed* Him to Pilate

Luke 2:6 days were accomplished that she [Mary] should be *d'ed*

Luke 9:44 Son of Man shall be *d'ed* into the hands of men

Acts 22:4 I [Paul] persecuted the Way...*d'ing*... men and women into prisons

Rom. 7:24 Who shall *d* me [Paul] from...this death

Gal. 1:4 that He might *d* us from this present evil world

Col. 1:13 who [Jesus] has *d'ed* us from the power of darkness

2 Tim. 4:18 Lord shall *d* me from every evil work

2 Pet. 2:9 Lord...knows how to *d*...out of temptations

DEMAS. A coworker of the apostle Paul who eventually deserted him (2 Tim. 4:10). Demas is also mentioned in Col. 4:14 • Philem. 24.

DEMETRIUS. (1) A silversmith at Ephesus who incited a riot against the apostle Paul. His livelihood as a maker of trinkets related to the pagan goddess Diana was being threatened by Paul's preaching of the gospel (Acts 19:24–41).

(2) A believer commended by the apostle John (3 John 12).

DEMONIC POSSESSION. Invasion and control of a person by evil spirits. Demons sometimes caused physical ailments, including blindness (Matt. 12:22), deafness (Mark 9:25), and deformities of the body (Luke 13:10–17). Jesus healed several persons of this malady. Some of the Pharisees claimed they had the power to cast evil spirits out of people (Matt. 12:27). But they used magical incantations and elaborate rituals in their healing efforts. Jesus simply ordered evil spirits to come out of people. This showed His mastery over Satan and his evil forces (Mark 1:23–25).

DEMONS. Evil beings allied with Satan in opposition God and His work in the world. In the OT, King Saul was afflicted with an evil spirit that caused him to develop jealousy toward

David, and even to attempt to kill him (1 Sam. 18:10–11; 23:8). In the NT, Jesus confronted demons who had taken over people. But He proved His superiority by casting them out. Demons are also referred to as "unclean spirits" (Luke 4:36).

DEMONSTRATES

Rom. 3:5 if our unrighteousness *d* the righteousness of God

Rom. 5:8 God *d* His love toward us, in that... Christ died for us

DEN OF LIONS. A pit or enclosure where lions were kept by the kings of Persia, probably for the sport of lion hunting. The prophet Daniel was thrown into one of these pits, but he was miraculously delivered by the Lord (Dan. 6:16–24).

DENY [IED, IES, ING]

Matt. 10:33 I will also *d* him before My Father

Matt. 26:72 again he [Peter] *d'ied* with an oath, I do not know the man [Jesus]

Mark 14:30 you [Peter] shall *d* Me [Jesus] three times

Luke 9:23 let him *d* himself, and take up his cross daily

Luke 12:9 he who *d'ies* Me [Jesus] before men shall be *d'ied* before...God

1 Tim. 5:8 has *d'ied* the faith and is worse than an unbeliever

2 Tim. 2:12 If we *d* Him, He will also *d* us

Titus 2:12 *d'ing*...worldly lusts, we should live soberly

1 John 2:23 Whoever *d'ies* the Son...does not have the Father

DEPTH [S]

Ps. 106:9 so He led them through the *d's*

Ps. 130:1 Out of the *d's* I have cried to You, O Lord

Jon. 2:5 the *d* closed me [Jonah] all around

Mic. 7:19 You [God] will cast...their sins into... the *d's* of the sea

Rom. 8:39 height, nor *d*...shall be able to separate us from the love of God

Rom. 11:33 *d* of the riches both of the wisdom and knowledge of God

DERBE. A city or village in the province of Lycaonia to which Paul and Barnabas retreated after being driven from Lystra during the first missionary journey (Acts 14:6–20). Paul also visited this city on his second missionary tour (Acts 16:1). It is also mentioned in Acts 20:4.

DESCEND [ED, ING]

Gen. 28:12 behold...angels of God were ascending and *d'ing* on it [a ladder]

Prov. 30:4 Who has ascended up into heaven or *d'ed*

Matt. 7:27 the rain *d'ed*, and the floods came

Matt. 28:2 angel...*d'ed* from heaven...rolled back the stone

Mark 15:32 Let Christ...*d* now from the cross

Luke 3:22 Holy Spirit *d'ed*...like a dove

John 1:32 I [John] saw the Spirit *d'ing* from heaven like a dove

Rom. 10:7 Who shall *d* into the deep...to bring up Christ

Eph. 4:10 He [Jesus] who *d'ed*...also...ascended far above all heavens

1 Thes. 4:16 Lord Himself shall *d* from heaven with a shout

Rev. 21:10 that great city...holy Jerusalem, *d'ing* out of heaven from God

DESERT. A dry, barren, wilderness (Deut. 32:10). Jesus withdrew often to these isolated places for privacy and communion with His Father (Luke 4:42).

DESIRE [D, ING, S]

Gen. 3:16 *d* shall be for your [Eve's] husband

Deut. 5:21 You shall not *d* your neighbor's wife

Ps. 37:4 and He shall give you the *d's* of your heart

Ps. 38:9 all my *d* is before You...my groaning... not hidden from You

Ps. 73:25 none on earth that I *d* besides You

Ps. 145:16 You [God]...satisfy the *d* of every living thing

Prov. 21:25 The *d* of the slothful kills him

Song of Sol. 7:10 I am my beloved's, and his *d* is for me

Isa. 26:9 In the night I have *d'd* You with my soul

Ezek. 24:16 I take away from you the *d* of your eyes

Hos. 6:6 I [God] *d'd* mercy and not sacrifice

Amos 5:18 Woe to you who *d* the day of the LORD

Matt. 12:46 His [Jesus'] mother...stood outside, *d'ing* to speak with Him

Mark 9:35 any man *d's* to be first, the same shall be last

Mark 11:24 whatever things you *d* when you pray

Luke 22:31 Simon. Behold, Satan has *d'd* to have you

Rom. 10:1 my [Paul's] heart's *d*...for Israel is that they might be saved

2 Cor. 5:2 *d'ing* to be clothed with our house that is from heaven

Phil. 1:23 having a *d* to depart and to be with Christ

1 Tim. 3:1 *d's* the office of a bishop, he *d's* a good work

Heb. 11:16 now they *d* a better country—that is, a heavenly

1 Pet. 2:2 As newborn babies, *d* the sincere milk of the word

DESIRE OF ALL NATIONS. A title for the Messiah used by the prophet Haggai in the OT (Hag. 2:6–7). It emphasizes His universal rule and power in the end-time, when all nations will pay Him homage and recognize His universal rule throughout the earth.

DESTRUCTION [S]

Job 5:22 You shall laugh at *d* and famine

Ps. 90:3 You [God] turn man to *d*

Ps. 107:20 He [God]...delivered them from their *d's*

Prov. 16:18 Pride goes before *d*, and a haughty spirit before a fall

Isa. 13:6 day of the LORD...shall come as *d* from the Almighty

Matt. 7:13 broad is the way that leads to *d*

DETERMINE [D]

Exod. 21:22 he shall pay as the judges *d*

Ruth 1:18 she [Naomi] saw that she [Ruth] was...*d'd*...she stopped speaking

2 Chron. 2:1 Solomon *d'd* to build a house for... the LORD

Isa. 10:23 Lord GOD...shall make a destruction, a *d'd* one

Dan. 1:8 Daniel *d'd*...that he would not defile himself

Luke 22:22 Son of Man goes as it was *d'd*...woe to that man by whom...betrayed

Acts 16:37 Barnabas *d'd* to take John...with them

1 Cor. 2:2 I [Paul] *d'd* not to know anything... except Jesus Christ

DEUTERONOMY, BOOK OF. An OT book consisting mostly of speeches delivered by Moses to the Israelites as they prepared to enter Canaan. The book repeats many of the divine laws revealed to him about two generations earlier—thus its name, which means "second law." Moses cautioned the people to remain faithful to God when tempted by the pagan Canaanite culture they were about to enter. The final chapter recounts the mysterious death of Moses and the succession of Joshua as the leader of God's people. Deuteronomy's importance was recognized by NT writers, who quoted from the book more than eighty times.

DEVIL. A title for Satan which emphasizes his tactics as a liar and deceiver (Luke 4:3). The word comes from a Greek term that means "malicious accuser" or "false witness."

DEVOUT

Luke 2:25 Simeon...just and *d*, waiting for the consolation of Israel

Acts 2:5 there were Jews dwelling in Jerusalem, *d* men

DEW. Moisture which condenses during the night and collects on plants (Exod. 16:13–14). The dews during Israel's dry season brought water for growing crops (Gen. 27:28). Heavy dew provided proof to the judge Gideon that God had selected him to deliver Israel from the Midianites (Judg. 6:37–40).

DIAMOND. A precious stone, known for its hardness, embedded in the breastplate of the high priest (Exod. 28:18).

DIANA. The pagan goddess of hunting and virginity worshipped in the Roman culture of Paul's time. His preaching at Ephesus caused an uproar among craftsmen who earned their living by making images of the temple devoted to her worship (Acts 19:24–35).

DIBON. An Amorite town taken by the Israelites during their years of wandering in the wilderness (Num. 32:3).

DIE [D, S]. See also *Dying*

Gen. 2:17 when you eat of it [the forbidden tree], you shall surely *d*

Gen. 45:28 I [Jacob] will...see him [Joseph] before I *d*

Exod. 16:3 If only we had *d'd* by the hand of the LORD in the land of Egypt

Deut. 4:22 I [Moses] must *d* in this land. I must not go over the Jordan

Deut. 14:21 not eat anything that *d's* by itself

Judg. 16:30 Samson said, Let me *d* with the Philistines

Ruth 1:17 Where you [Naomi] *d*, I [Ruth] will die

2 Sam. 12:5 he [David] said...the man who has done this thing shall surely *d*

2 Chron. 25:4 every man shall *d* for his own sin

Job 2:9 Do you [Job] still retain your integrity? Curse God and *d*

Job 3:11 Why did I [Job] not *d* from the womb

Job 14:14 If a man *d's*, shall he live again

Prov. 10:21 but fools *d* for lack of wisdom

Eccles. 3:2 a time to be born and a time to *d*

Isa. 6:1 In the year that King Uzziah *d'd* I [Isaiah] also saw the Lord

Jer. 16:6 the great and the small shall *d* in this land

Jer. 31:30 everyone shall *d* for his own iniquity

Ezek. 18:32 I [God] have no pleasure in the death of him who *d's*

Jon. 4:3 it is better for me [Jonah] to *d* than to live

Matt. 26:35 Though I [Peter] should *d* with You, still I will not deny You

John 6:50 bread...from heaven, that a man may eat...and not *d*

John 11:16 Thomas...said...Let us also go that we may *d* with Him

John 11:21 Lord, if You had been here, my brother would not have *d'd*

John 11:50 it is expedient for us that one man should *d* for the people

John 12:24 if it [grain of wheat] *d's*, it brings forth much fruit

Acts 21:13 I [Paul] am ready...to *d* in Jerusalem for the name of...Jesus

Rom. 5:6 in due time Christ *d'd* for the ungodly

Rom. 5:7 For one will scarcely *d* for a righteous man

Rom. 5:8 while we were still sinners, Christ *d'd* for us

Rom. 6:9 Christ, having been raised from the dead, will never *d* again

Rom. 14:7 none of us lives to himself...no man *d's* to himself

Rom. 14:8 whether we live or *d*, we are the Lord's

1 Cor. 15:3 Christ *d'd* for our sins according to the scriptures

1 Cor. 15:22 in Adam all *d*...in Christ all shall be made alive

2 Cor. 5:14 if one *d'd* for all, then all are dead

2 Cor. 5:15 He [Jesus] *d'd* for all, that those... should...live not for themselves

Phil. 1:21 to me [Paul] to live is Christ, and to *d* is gain

Heb. 9:27 it is appointed to men to *d* once

Rev. 14:13 Blessed are the dead who *d* in the Lord

DINAH. The daughter of Jacob who was assaulted by Shechem. Her brothers avenged the crime by murdering several members of Shechem's family. Dinah is mentioned in **Gen.** 30:20–21; **34:1–31**.

DINAITES. A foreign people group that settled in Israel (the Northern Kingdom) after it fell to the Assyrians (Ezra 4:9).

DIONYSIUS. A member of the Areopagus of Athens who became a believer after hearing

Paul's testimony about Jesus the Messiah (Acts 17:34).

DIOTREPHES. A church leader condemned by the apostle John. Apparently he and other followers had rejected John's teachings (3 John 9–10).

DISCERN [ING]

1 Kings 3:9 that I [Solomon] may *d* between good and bad

Ezek. 44:23 cause them to *d* between...unclean and...clean

Matt. 16:3 you hypocrites. You can *d* the face of the sky

1 Cor. 11:29 drinks judgment to himself, not *d'ing* the Lord's body

DISCERNING OF SPIRITS. A gift of the Holy Spirit, cited by the apostle Paul, that enables believers to distinguish between true and false doctrine (1 Cor. 12:10).

DISCIPLE. A person who pledges his loyalty to another in order to learn from his teachings. From among His followers, Jesus selected twelve as His special disciples who continued His work after His ascension (Mark 3:14).

DISCIPLE

Matt. 10:24 The *d* is not above his master

Luke 14:26 If any man...does not hate his father...he cannot be My *d*

John 19:38 Joseph of Arimathea, being a *d* of Jesus

DISCIPLESHIP. The day-to-day process of following Jesus and growing in knowledge and understanding of His teachings. The term comes from the word *disciple* which means "learner" or "pupil." The first disciples of Jesus set the standard for discipleship when they answered His call to follow Him and to learn from His teachings (Matt. 4:18–21; 11:29). One metaphor for discipleship is "walking" in righteousness. Enoch in the OT was a man who "walked with God" (Gen. 5:24). The apostle Paul called on believers to "walk in the Spirit" (Gal. 5:16). Thus, to walk with the Lord as His disciple is to honor Him in the activities of everyday life.

DISCIPLES OF JESUS. The twelve followers whom Jesus selected to learn from Him and to continue His work after His earthly ministry came to an end. They are also referred to as apostles, or people sent by Jesus on a special mission. Lists of the Twelve appear in Matthew 10:2–4, Mark 3:14–19, Luke 6:13–16, and Acts 1:13–14. They are Simon Peter and his brother Andrew; the two fishermen brothers James and John; Philip; Nathanael (probably the same person as Bartholomew); Thomas (or Didymus, "the twin"); Matthew (also known as Levi); another James, the son of Alphaeus; Thaddaeus (also called Judas, son of James); Simon the Zealot; and Judas Iscariot, who betrayed Jesus to His enemies.

DISCIPLINE [S]

2 Sam. 7:9 I [God] will *d* him [Solomon] with the rod of men

Prov. 3:11 My son, do not despise the *d* of the LORD

Prov. 13:24 he who loves him [his son] *d's* him promptly

1 Cor. 9:27 but I [Paul] *d* my body and bring it into subjection

DISOBEDIENCE

Rom. 5:19 as through one man's [Adam's] *d* many were made sinners

Eph. 5:6 the wrath of God comes on the children of *d*

DISOBEDIENT

Acts 26:19 I [Paul] was not *d* to the heavenly vision

2 Tim. 3:2 boasters, proud, blasphemers, *d* to parents

Titus 1:16 they deny Him, being abominable and *d*

1 Pet. 2:7 to you who believe, He is precious, but to those who are *d*

DISPERSION. The scattering of the Jewish people among other nations. This happened on two different occasions: (1) when Israel (the Northern Kingdom) fell to the Assyrians in 722 BC, and (2) when the Babylonians overran Judah (the Southern Kingdom) in 587 BC. Leading citizens of both countries were carried into exile by these foreign nations.

DISTRESS [ED, ES]

Ps. 18:6 In my **d** I called on the Lord

Ps. 107:13 He [God] saved them out of their **d'es**

Zeph. 1:15 That day is...a day of trouble and **d**

Luke 21:23 for there shall be great **d** in the land

Rom. 8:35 shall separate us from the love of Christ? Shall tribulation, or **d**

2 Cor. 4:8 troubled on every side, yet not **d'ed**

2 Cor. 12:10 I [Paul] take pleasure...in **d'es**, for Christ's sake

1 Thes. 3:7 in all our...**d**, we were comforted... by your faith

DIVIDE [D, ING, S]

Gen. 1:6 let it [the firmament] **d** the waters from the waters

Exod. 14:16 stretch out your [Moses'] hand over the sea and **d** it

Exod. 14:21 the Lord...made the sea dry land... waters were **d'd**

Num. 33:54 you shall **d** the land by lot for an inheritance

Judg. 7:16 he [Gideon] **d'd**...men into three companies

Job 26:12 He [God] **d's** the sea with His power

Ps. 78:13 He [God] **d'd** the sea and caused them to pass through

Prov. 16:19 better to be...with the lowly than to **d** the plunder with the proud

Dan. 5:28 Your [Belshazzar's] kingdom is **d'd** and given to the Medes and Persians

Zech. 14:1 your plunder shall be **d'd** in the midst of you

Matt. 25:32 He [Jesus] shall separate them... as a shepherd **d's** his sheep from the goats

Luke 11:17 kingdom **d'd** against itself is brought to desolation

Luke 12:13 speak to my brother, that he would **d** the inheritance with me

Luke 12:53 The father shall be **d'd** against the son

Luke 15:12 And he [prodigal son's father] **d'd** his wealth between them

1 Cor. 1:13 Is Christ **d'd**? Was Paul crucified for you

2 Tim. 2:15 a workman...not...ashamed, rightly **d'ing** the word of truth

DIVINATION. The practice of foretelling the future or determining the unknown through acts of magic or reading signs (Jer. 14:14). This practice and other forms of the occult were condemned by the Lord (Deut. 18:10).

DIVISION [S]

Luke 12:51 I [Jesus] tell you, no, but rather **d**

John 9:16 How can a man...do such miracles? And there was a **d** among them

Rom. 16:17 mark those who cause **d's** and offenses

1 Cor. 3:3 there is envying and strife and **d's** among you

DIVISION OF CANAAN AMONG THE ISRAELITE TRIBES. Josh. 14:1–19:51

DIVORCE. The divine ideal is for permanence in marriage, and divorce violates the oneness which God intended from the beginning (Gen. 2:24; Matt. 19:5–6). Under the Mosaic Law, divorce was permitted in certain situations (Deut. 24:1–4), but this provision was greatly abused (Matt. 19:8). Jesus regarded adultery as the only permissible reason for divorce (Matt. 5:31–32; 19:9; Mark 10:11; Luke 16:18), and He reprimanded the Jews for their insensitive divorce practices (Matt. 19:3–9). His teaching on this subject should be compared to His love and forgiveness toward those whose marriage was less than ideal, particularly the Samaritan woman at the well (John 4:13–18) and the woman accused of adultery (John 8:1–11).

DIVORCE [D]

Lev. 21:14 a widow, or a **d'd** woman...these he [a priest] shall not take

Deut. 22:19 she shall be his wife; he may not **d** her all his days

Deut. 24:1 has found some uncleanness in her... write her a certificate of **d**

Jer. 3:8 I [God] had **d'd** her [Israel] and given her a bill of **d**

Matt. 5:32 whoever marries her who is *d'd* commits adultery

DOCTRINE.
Key principles of faith that are considered authoritative and worthy of passing on to others. Christianity's major doctrines are centered on God the Father, God the Son, and God the Holy Spirit. Other subjects that fit under these main headings include man, salvation, and the church. These insights have been revealed to human authors by the Lord and recorded in the Bible for the edification and instruction of believers. The apostle Paul impressed upon young Timothy the importance of sound doctrinal teachings (1 Tim. 4:6).

DOCTRINE [S]
Mark 11:18 the people were astonished at His [Jesus'] *d*

John 7:16 My [Jesus'] *d* is not Mine, but His who sent Me

Acts 2:42 they continued steadfastly in the apostles' *d*

Eph. 4:14 no longer be children...carried about by every wind of *d*

1 Tim. 4:13 give attendance to reading, to exhortation, to *d*

2 Tim. 3:16 All scripture is...profitable for *d*

2 Tim. 4:3 For the time will come when they will not endure sound *d*

Heb. 13:9 Do not be carried about with various and strange *d's*

2 John 9 He who abides in the *d* of Christ

DOEG.
An associate of King Saul who betrayed the high priest Ahimelech for assisting David. On Saul's orders, Doeg murdered Ahimelech and 85 priests in the city of Nob. Doeg is mentioned in **1 Sam.** 21:7; 22:9–22.

DOER [S]
Prov. 17:4 A wicked *d* listens to false lips

Rom. 2:13 the *d's* of the law shall be justified

Jas. 1:22 you be *d's* of the word and not hearers only

Jas. 1:23 if any is a hearer of the word and not a *d*

DOG.
An animal considered unclean and contemptible (Deut. 23:18). Jews referred to any people of despicable character, including Gentiles, as dogs.

DOMINION [S]
Gen. 1:28 God said...have *d* over the fish of the sea

Job 25:2 *D* and fear are with Him [God]

Ps. 8:6 You [God] made him [man] to have *d* over the works of Your hands

Ps. 72:8 He [God] shall have *d* also from sea to sea

Zech. 9:10 and His *d* shall be from sea to sea

Matt. 20:25 princes of the Gentiles exercise *d*

Rom. 6:9 Death no longer has *d* over Him [Jesus]

Col. 1:16 by Him were all things created... whether they are thrones or *d's*

1 Pet. 4:11 to whom [Jesus] be...*d* forever and ever

Jude 25 to...God, our Savior, be...*d* and power

DOMINION OF MAN.
The responsibility for ruling over the earth that God assigned to Adam after creating the world (Gen. 1:26–28). This command set humans apart from the other living creatures that He had created. Humankind alone bears the responsibility for taking care of the physical world—a duty that involves accountability to the Creator Himself.

DONKEY.
A common beast of burden (Gen. 22:3). Jesus rode a donkey into Jerusalem to symbolize His humble servanthood and the spiritual nature of His kingdom (Luke 19:30–38).

DO NOT FEAR
Gen. 15:1 *D-n-f*, Abram. I [God] am your shield

Gen. 21:17 What ails you, Hagar? *D-n-f*

Dan. 10:12 *D-n-f*, Daniel...your words were heard

Joel 2:21 *D-n-f*, O land. Be glad and rejoice

Matt. 1:20 Joseph...*d-n-f* to take to you Mary

Matt. 28:5 *D-n-f* [to the women at the tomb], for I know that you seek Jesus

Luke 1:13 *D-n-f*, Zechariah, for your prayer is heard

Luke 1:30 *D-n-f*, Mary, for you have found favor with God

Luke 2:10 **D-n-f**...I [angel] bring you [shepherds] good tidings of great joy

Luke 12:32 **D-n-f**...it is your Father's good pleasure to give you the kingdom

Acts 27:24 saying, **D-n-f**, Paul. You must be brought before Caesar

Rev. 1:17 **D-n-f**, I [Jesus] am the first and the last

DOOR. A word that Jesus used as a title for Himself in one of His "I am" statements in the Gospel of John (John 10:7–10). In a similar metaphor, He also talked about two different gates. The broad gate, representing the way of the world, was so wide that people could drift through it without any conscious thought. But the narrow gate, representing Him and His teachings, required commitment from those who wanted to follow Him (Matt. 7:13–14).

DOOR OF THE SHEEP, JESUS AS. See *"I Am" Statements of Jesus*

DORCAS. See *Tabitha*

DOTHAN. A city west of the Jordan River near Mount Gilboa. Here is where Joseph found his brothers, who sold him into slavery (Gen. 37:17–28). In later centuries during the time of the prophet Elisha, the Lord struck a unit of Syrian soldiers at Dothan with blindness (2 Kings 6:8–23).

DOUBT [ED, ING]
Matt. 14:31 you of little faith, why did you *d*
Matt. 28:17 they worshipped Him, but some *d'ed*
1 Tim. 2:8 men everywhere to pray...without wrath and *d'ing*

DOXOLOGY. A short hymn of praise to God or a declaration of His glory (1 Chron. 29:11). The word is not found in the Bible, but the concept appears frequently. One of the best known examples is the praise sung by angels after Jesus was born (Luke 2:14).

DRAGON. A mythical sea creature or winged lizard. The name is applied to Satan (Rev. 12:9) and the antichrist (Rev. 12:3).

DRAWER OF WATER. A person who carried water from a spring or well back to the household—a menial chore assigned to women, children, or slaves. This job was assigned by Joshua to the Gibeonites (Josh. 9:27).

DREAM [ED, S]
Gen. 37:5 Joseph *d'd* a *d*, and he told it to his brothers
Gen. 40:9 the chief butler told his *d* to Joseph
Gen. 41:25 Joseph said...The *d* of Pharaoh is one
Dan. 2:3 I [Nebuchadnezzar] have *d'd* a *d*, and my spirit was anxious
Joel 2:28 pour out My Spirit...old men shall *d d's*
Acts 2:17 and your old men shall *d d's*

DREAMS AND VISIONS. Mediums of revelation often used by God to make His will known. Dreams came to people in their sleep, while visions occurred during their waking hours. Joseph, Daniel, Isaiah, and Paul are among the biblical personalities who received messages from the Lord through such revelation. Joseph distinguished himself in Egypt by interpreting dreams for the pharaoh (Gen. 40–41). Daniel interpreted King Nebuchadnezzar's dream that he would fall from power (Dan. 4:18–27). Isaiah received his call as a prophet through a vision of the Lord sitting on a throne (Isa. 6:1–10). Paul's missionary thrust into Europe began with his vision of a man from Macedonia appealing for help (Acts 16:9–10).

DREAMS THROUGH WHICH GOD SPOKE TO PEOPLE
1. To Abimelech, king of Gerar (Gen. 20:3)
2. To Jacob, son of Isaac (Gen. 28:10–12)
3. To Laban, father-in-law of Jacob (Gen. 31:24)
4. To Solomon, king of Judah (1 Kings 3:5)
5. To Joseph, husband of Mary (Matt. 1:20; 2:12–13, 22)

DREGS. Worthless, bitter remnants that settle to the bottom of a wine container (Ps. 75:8). The word is also used symbolically of God's wrath and judgment (Isa. 51:17) and for laziness or indifference (Jer. 48:11; Zeph. 1:12). *Lees*: KJV.

DRINK [ING, S]
Exod. 15:24 people murmured against Moses, saying, What shall we *d*?

Job 1:13 his [Job's] sons and his daughters were eating and *d'ing* wine

Ps. 69:21 in my thirst they gave me vinegar to *d*

Ps. 78:15 He [God]...gave them *d* as out of the great depths

Prov. 5:15 *D* waters out of your own cistern

Prov. 20:1 Wine is a mocker; strong *d* is raging

Prov. 25:21 and if he [your enemy] is thirsty, give him water to *d*

Eccles. 2:24 There is nothing better for a man than that he should eat and *d*

Eccles. 9:7 *d* your wine with a merry heart

Isa. 5:11 Woe to those who rise up early...that they may pursue strong *d*

Ezek. 12:18 *d* your water with trembling

Dan. 1:12 give us [Daniel and his friends] vegetables to eat and water to *d*

Matt. 6:31 What shall we eat? or What shall we *d*

Matt. 25:42 I was thirsty and you gave Me no *d*

Mark 2:16 He [Jesus] eats and *d's* with...sinners

Mark 10:38 Can you *d* of the cup that I [Jesus] *d* of

Mark 15:23 they gave Him wine mingled with myrrh to *d*

Luke 5:30 Why do you eat and *d* with tax collectors and sinners

Luke 7:33 John the Baptist came neither eating bread nor *d'ing* wine

Luke 10:7 eating and *d'ing* such things as they give

Luke 22:18 I will not *d* of the fruit of the vine until the kingdom of God comes

John 4:7 Jesus said to her [the Samaritan woman], Give Me a *d*

John 4:14 *d's* of the water that I [Jesus] shall give him shall never thirst

John 6:53 Unless you...*d* His blood, you have no life in you

Acts 23:12 saying that they would neither eat nor *d* until they had killed Paul

Rom. 12:20 if he [your enemy] is thirsty, give him a *d*

Rom. 14:17 the kingdom of God is not eating and *d'ing*

1 Cor. 10:31 Therefore, whether you eat or *d*... do all for the glory of God

1 Cor. 11:25 as often as you *d* it, in remembrance of Me

1 Cor. 11:29 eats and *d's* judgment to himself

1 Tim. 5:23 No longer *d* water, but use a little wine

Rev. 16:6 You have given them blood to *d*

DRINK OFFERING. An offering of fine wine, usually presented in connection with another sacrifice, such as a burnt offering (Num. 29:11–18).

DROPSY. A disease that causes excessive fluid buildup in the body. Jesus healed a man with this disability (Luke 14:2–4).

DROSS. Impurities separated from ore in the process of smelting metal (Prov. 25:4). The word is used symbolically of God's judgment against the wicked (Ps. 119:119).

DROUGHT. Lack of rainfall for an extended time (Ps. 32:4). The prophet Jeremiah spoke symbolically of a spiritual drought throughout the land (Jer. 14:1–7).

DRUNKENNESS. A deranged condition caused by consuming too much wine or strong drink (1 Cor. 5:11). This vice is also spoken of symbolically to describe thoughtless people who are experiencing God's punishment (Ezek. 23:33).

DRUSILLA. The wife of Felix, Roman governor of Judea, before whom the apostle Paul appeared at Caesarea (Acts 24:24–25).

DRY BONES, EZEKIEL'S VISION OF. Ezek. 37:1–14

DUMB. KJV: see *Mute*

DUNG. A word used figuratively for something useless or worthless. The apostle Paul declared that he considered his accomplishments as nothing but dung in comparison to the joy of knowing Jesus Christ (Phil. 3:8).

DURA. A plain in Babylon where a statue of King Nebuchadnezzar was set up. Shadrach, Meshach, and Abednego were thrown into a blazing furnace for refusing to worship this image (Dan. 3:1).

DUST. Sitting in the dust dramatized a person's dejection and humiliation (Isa. 47:1). Adam was created from dust, a symbol of humankind's mortality (Gen. 3:19).

DYING. See also *Die*

2 Cor. 4:10 in the body the *d* of the Lord Jesus

Heb. 11:21 Jacob, when he was *d*, blessed both the sons of Joseph

E

EAGLE. A large bird of prey cited by the prophet Ezekiel as a symbol of God's judgment (Ezek. 17:7–10). But to the prophet Isaiah, an eagle signified the renewal of God's people (Isa. 40:31).

EARS OF GOD. A metaphor that expresses confidence in the Lord's ability to hear and respond to the needs of His people (Ps. 18:6). The psalmist contrasted this divine characteristic with the deafness of lifeless idols (Ps. 115:2–6). See also *Anthropomorphism.*

EARTH[LY]

Gen. 1:1 God created the heaven and the *e*

Gen. 6:6 it grieved the LORD that He had made man on the *e*

Gen. 9:1 Be fruitful and multiply, and replenish the *e*

Gen. 12:3 and in you [Abraham] shall all families of the *e* be blessed

Deut. 30:19 I call heaven and *e* to witness this day against you

1 Kings 10:23 Solomon exceeded all the kings of the *e*...in wisdom

Job 1:8 there is none like him [Job] on the *e*

Job 19:25 he shall stand at the latter day on the *e*

Job 38:4 Where were you [Job] when I [God] laid the foundations of the *e*

Ps. 8:1 how excellent is Your [God's] name in all the *e*

Ps. 24:1 The *e* is the LORD's, and its fullness

Ps. 37:11 But the meek shall inherit the *e*

Ps. 67:2 Your [God's] way may be known on *e*

Ps. 82:8 Arise, O God, judge the *e*...You shall inherit all nations

Ps. 96:1 O sing...a new song: sing to the LORD, all the *e*

Ps. 108:5 Be exalted, O God...and Your glory above all the *e*

Isa. 6:3 The whole *e* is full of His glory

Isa. 45:22 be saved, all the ends of the *e*

Isa. 55:9 higher than the *e*, so are My ways higher than your ways

Isa. 66:1 Heaven is My throne, and the *e* is My footstool

Joel 3:16 And the heavens and the *e* shall shake

Hab. 2:20 Let all the *e* keep silence before Him

Matt. 5:13 You are the salt of the *e*

Matt. 6:10 Your will be done on *e* as it is in heaven

Matt. 12:40 shall the Son of Man be...three nights in the heart of the *e*

Matt. 16:19 whatever you loose on *e* shall be loosed in heaven

Matt. 24:35 Heaven and *e* shall pass away, but My words shall not pass away

Matt. 28:18 All power has been given to Me in heaven and on *e*

Luke 2:14 on *e* peace, goodwill toward men

Luke 23:44 darkness over all the *e* until the ninth hour

John 3:12 I [Jesus] have told you *e'ly* things and you do not believe

John 12:32 if I [Jesus] be lifted up from the *e*

Acts 1:8 you shall be witnesses...to the farthest part of the *e*

2 Cor. 5:1 our *e'ly* house of this tabernacle is dissolved

Col. 3:2 Set your affection on things above, not on things on the *e*

Rev. 7:1 four angels standing on the four corners of the *e*

Rev. 21:1 I [John] saw a new heaven and a new *e*

EARTHQUAKE. A violent shaking of the earth (Ps. 77:18). Such frightening events were associated with God's judgment (Judg. 5:4). Jesus' death on the cross was marked by an earthquake (Matt. 27:51).

EAST SEA. See *Salt Sea*

EAST WIND. A scorching desert wind cited by Job as a symbol of God's judgment against the wicked (Job 27:21).

EAT [EN, ER, ING, S]

Gen. 2:17 the tree of...good and evil, you shall not *e*

Gen. 3:11 Have you *e'en* from the tree...you should not *e*

Lev. 11:41 every creeping thing...shall not be *e'en*

Judg. 14:14 Out of the *e'er* came forth food

Ps. 102:9 For I have *e'en* ashes like bread

Eccles. 2:24 nothing better for a man than that he should *e* and drink

Jer. 31:29 fathers have *e'en* a sour grape

Ezek. 3:1 *e* what you [Ezekiel] find. *E* this scroll

Ezek. 12:18 *e* your [Ezekiel's] bread with quaking

Matt. 6:25 do not worry for your life, what you shall *e*

Matt. 9:11 Why does your Master *e* with tax collectors and sinners

Matt. 15:20 to *e* with unwashed hands does not defile a man

Matt. 26:26 as they were *e'ing*, Jesus took bread, and blessed it

Mark 7:28 dogs under the table *e* from the children's crumbs

Mark 14:18 one of you who *e's* with Me [Jesus] shall betray Me

Luke 5:30 Why do you [disciples] *e* and drink with...sinners

Luke 7:33 John the Baptist came neither *e'ing* bread nor drinking wine

Luke 15:23 bring...the fatted calf...let us *e* and be merry

John 4:32 I [Jesus] have food to *e* that you do not know about

John 6:50 the bread...from heaven, that a man may *e*...and not die

Acts 10:13 a voice came to him, Rise, Peter; kill and *e*

1 Cor. 10:31 whether you *e* or drink...do all for the glory of God

1 Cor. 11:26 as often as you *e* this bread and drink this cup

1 Cor. 11:29 he who *e's*...unworthily *e's*...judgment to himself

2 Thes. 3:10 if any will not work, he should not *e*

Rev. 2:7 who overcomes I [Jesus] will give to *e* of the tree of life

EBAL. A mountain in Samaria where Joshua read the consequences of failing to follow the law of the Lord after the Israelites entered Canaan. Ebal is mentioned in Deut. 11:29; 27:4, 13 • **Josh. 8:30–35.**

EBED-MELECH. An Ethiopian eunuch who rescued the prophet Jeremiah from a dungeon where he had been imprisoned. The prophet declared Ebed-melech would be spared in the coming destruction of Jerusalem. He is mentioned in **Jer. 38:7–13; 39:15–18.**

EBENEZER. A site where the Philistines defeated Israel and captured the ark of the covenant (1 Sam. 5:1). Years later, Samuel erected an altar on this site and called it Ebenezer, meaning "the stone of help," to designate a victory over the Philistines (1 Sam. 7:10–12).

EBER. A great-grandson of Shem and ancestor of the Hebrew race (Gen. 10:21–25; 11:14–17 • 1 Chron. 1:18–23).

EBONY. A hard, durable wood used for decorative carvings, fine furniture, and musical instruments (Ezek. 27:15).

ECCLESIASTES, BOOK OF. A wisdom book of the OT, probably written by King Solomon. Its basic message is that that all human achievements are empty and unfulfilling when pursued as ends in themselves. He declared that wisdom, hard work, wealth, learning, fame, and pleasure do not bring happiness. Life's highest good is to "fear God and keep His commandments" (Eccles. 12:13). One of the book's most memorable passages is the poem on the proper time for all of life's events: "A time to be born and a time to die...a time to weep and a time to laugh...a time to keep silent and a time to speak" (Eccles. 3:1–7).

EDEN, GARDEN OF. The garden created by the Lord as the home for Adam and Eve, the first man and woman (Gen. 2:8). It was a place of joy and delight, containing everything they needed for a blissful life. But they rebelled against God's clear command and introduced the blight of sin into the world. The Lord banished them from the garden as part of His punishment for their disobedience (Gen. 3:22–24). The four rivers of Eden, including the Euphrates, suggest that it may have been located in Mesopotamia, the land between the Tigris and Euphrates rivers (Gen. 2:10–14). Eden is also mentioned in Gen. 4:16 • Isa. 51:3 • Ezek. 28:13; 31:9, 16–18; 36:35 • Joel 2:3.

EDIFY [IES, ING]
1 Cor. 14:4 speaks in an unknown tongue *e'ies* himself
Eph. 4:12 for the *e'ing* of the body of Christ
1 Thes. 5:11 comfort...and *e* one another

EDOM. (1) The name given to Esau, Jacob's brother, after Esau traded away his birthright (Gen. 25:30).

(2) The land where Esau's descendants settled near the Dead Sea. While traveling toward Canaan, the Israelites were denied permission to pass through Edomite territory (Num. 20:14–18). This emphasized the bad blood that had existed between these two peoples for many centuries. In later years, David conquered the Edomites (2 Sam. 8:13–14). But they apparently existed with a distinct territory and culture for several centuries (Ps. 137:7). The land of Edom is also mentioned in Gen. 36:21, 31–32, 43 • Num. 34:3 • Josh. 15:1, 21 • Judg. 11:17–18 • 2 Kings 3:8–26 • Jer. 25:21; 27:3; 40:11; 49:7–22 • Ezek.

25:12–14 • Amos 1:6–11 • Obad. 1, 8. *Idumea:* Mark 3:8. See also *Esau.*

EDREI. Capital city of the ancient kingdom of Bashan where King Og was defeated by the Israelites (Num. 21:33–35).

EGLAH. A wife of King David and mother of his son Ithream (2 Sam. 3:2–5).

EGLON. A king of Moab who oppressed Israel for eighteen years before being killed by the judge Ehud (Judg. 3:12–23).

EGYPT. The nation situated along the Nile River which enslaved the Israelites for several centuries before their miraculous deliverance by the Lord. Centuries later, King Solomon of Judah married an Egyptian princess to seal an alliance with her country. When Judah (the Southern Kingdom) fell to the Babylonians in 587 BC, several people, including the prophet Jeremiah, escaped into Egypt. Egypt also figures prominently in biblical prophecy. After Jesus was born, His parents fled into Egypt to escape a death threat from Herod the Great. When they returned to their own country, Hosea's prophecy was fulfilled: "I called My son out of Egypt" (Hos. 11:1). Egypt is also mentioned in Gen. 12:10; 37:28–36 • **Exod. 1:7–14; 12:29–36** • Isa. 19:3–25; 30:1–7; 36:6 • Jer. 46:8 • Ezek. 30:25–26 • Matt. 2:13–15.

EHUD. A judge of Israel who rallied his countrymen to defeat the Moabites after he assassinated their king (Judg. 3:15–4:1).

EKRON. One of the five chief cities of the Philistines. It was captured during the period of the judges and allotted to the tribe of Dan. Ekron is mentioned in Josh. 13:3; 15:11, 45–46; 19:43 • **Judg. 1:18** • 1 Sam. 5:10; 6:16–17; 7:14; 17:52 • 2 Kings 1:2–6, 16 • Jer. 25:20 • Amos 1:8 • Zeph. 2:4 • Zech. 9:5, 7.

ELAH. (1) A valley in Judah where David killed the Philistine giant Goliath (1 Sam. 17:1–4, 49; 21:9).

(2) A king of Israel who reigned for only two years before being assassinated and succeeded

by Zimri, one of his military officers (1 Kings 16:6–10).

ELAM. A son of Shem and ancestor of the Elamites (**Gen. 10:22** • 1 Chron. 1:17).

ELAMITES. Foreign colonists who settled in Samaria after the Northern Kingdom fell to Assyria. They are mentioned in Gen. 14:1, 9 • Ezra 4:9 • Isa. 11:11; 21:2; 22:6 • Jer. 25:25; 49:34–39 • Ezek. 32:24 • Dan. 8:2 • Acts 2:9.

EL-BETHEL. See *Bethel*

ELDAD. A leader commended by Moses for prophesying in the wilderness (Num. 11:26–29).

ELDER[S]

Matt. 15:2 Why do Your disciples transgress the tradition of the *e's*

Luke 15:25 his [father of prodigal son] *e* son was in the field

Acts 14:23 they [Paul and Barnabas] had ordained *e's* for them

Acts 20:17 he [Paul] sent to Ephesus and called the *e's*

1 Tim. 5:1 Do not rebuke an *e*, but treat him as a father

1 Tim. 5:17 Let the *e's* who rule well be counted worthy

Jas. 5:14 call for the *e's*...and let them pray over him

2 John 1 The *e*, to the elect lady and her children

Rev. 4:10 the twenty-four *e's* fall down before Him

ELDERS. (1) Leaders in OT times who governed clans, tribes, and cities (Exod. 3:18; Deut. 21:3).

(2) Leaders in the early church who may have been responsible for teaching doctrine to the congregation (Titus 1:5).

ELEAZAR. (1) A son of Aaron who succeeded his father as high priest of Israel (Num. 20:25–28). After the Israelites conquered Canaan, he helped divide the land among the twelve tribes. Eleazar is also mentioned in Exod. 6:23–25; 28:1 • Lev. 10:6–7 • Num. 3:2, 32 • Josh. 14:1; 24:33.

(2) One of David's "mighty men," an elite group of warriors known for their bravery in battle (2 Sam. 23:9).

ELECT

Isa. 42:1 My [God's] *e* in whom My soul delights

Mark 13:27 He [Jesus]...shall gather together His *e* from the four winds

Col. 3:12 Put on...as the *e* of God...hearts of mercies

1 Pet. 1:2 *e* according to the foreknowledge of God

ELECTION. God's selection of specific people on whom He confers His favor. In the OT, He chose the Israelites as His special people (Deut. 7:6–8). In the NT, the apostle Paul enlarged this concept to include all people who accept God's offer of salvation (2 Thes. 2:13).

ELECTION

Rom. 11:5 a remnant according to the *e* of grace

2 Pet. 1:10 be diligent to make your calling and *e* certain

ELECT LADY. The person, or perhaps a local church, to which the second epistle of John is addressed (2 John 1).

EL-ELOHE-ISRAEL. A name, meaning "God, the God of Israel," given by Jacob to the altar he built after he was reconciled to his brother Esau (Gen. 33:20).

ELHANAN. One of David's "mighty men," an elite group of warriors known for their bravery in battle (2 Sam. 23:24).

ELI. A high priest of Israel with whom the prophet Samuel lived during his boyhood years (1 Sam. 1:24–28). Eli's own two sons were unworthy of the priesthood (1 Sam. 2:12–25). But Eli refused to take action against their sin. He even ignored a prophet's warning and turned a deaf ear to the boy Samuel's dream about God's coming judgment (1 Sam. 3:13). The day of reckoning occurred when Eli's sons were killed during a battle with the Philistines. The news was such a shock that Eli fell and died from a broken neck (1 Sam. 4:18). He is also mentioned in 1 Kings 2:27.

ELIADA. A son of David, born in Jerusalem after he became king over all Israel (2 Sam. 5:16).

ELIAHBA. One of David's "mighty men," an elite group of warriors known for their bravery in battle (2 Sam. 23:32).

ELIAKIM. (1) An aide to King Hezekiah of Judah who mediated peace with the invading Assyrian army (2 Kings 18:18–19:2 • Isa. 22:20–25; 36:3, 11, 22; 37:2).

(2) Another name for King Jehoiakim of Judah. See *Jehoiakim.*

ELIAM. One of David's "mighty men," an elite group of warriors known for their bravery in battle (2 Sam. 23:34).

ELIAS. KJV: see *Elijah*

ELIASHIB. A high priest of Israel who helped rebuild Jerusalem's walls during Nehemiah's time (Neh. 3:1).

ELIDAD. A leader from the tribe of Benjamin who helped divide the land of Canaan after the conquest (Num. 34:21).

ELIEL. One of David's "mighty men," an elite group of warriors known for their bravery in battle (1 Chron. 11:47).

ELIEZER. Abraham's chief servant who would have been his heir if Abraham had not had a son (Gen. 15:2).

ELIHU. A friend who spoke to Job after Eliphaz, Bildad, and Zophar had failed to answer Job's questions to Elihu's satisfaction (Job 32:2–6; 34:1; 35:1; 36:1).

ELIJAH. A courageous prophet known for his dramatic encounter with the prophets of the false god Baal on Mount Carmel (1 Kings 18:17–40). Elijah opposed King Ahab and his queen, Jezebel, because of their encouragement of the worship of this false god throughout the Northern Kingdom. As Elijah's ministry wound down, he chose Elisha as his successor (1 Kings 19:16). Then Elijah was carried bodily into heaven without experiencing physical death. The prophet Malachi predicted that the Lord would send Elijah back to earth before the arrival of the Messiah (Mal. 4:5). This prophecy came to pass in a spiritual sense with the preaching of John the Baptist, forerunner of Jesus. John's lifestyle and preaching were similar to Elijah's (Matt. 17:10–13). He is also mentioned in 2 Kings 1:1–18; 2:1–11; 3:11; 9:36; 10:10, 17 • 2 Chron. 21:12 • Mal. 4:5 • Matt. 17:3–4 • Mark 9:4–13 • Luke 9:30–54 • John 1:21, 25 • Rom. 11:2 • Jas. 5:17.

ELIKA. One of David's "mighty men," an elite group of warriors known for their bravery in battle (2 Sam. 23:8, 25).

ELIMELECH. The husband of Naomi who died after moving his family to Moab to escape a famine (Ruth 1:2–3).

ELIPHAL. One of David's "mighty men," an elite group of warriors known for their bravery in battle (1 Chron. 11:35).

ELIPHAZ. (1) A son of Esau (Gen. 36:10 • 1 Chron. 1:35–36).

(2) One of the three friends who comforted Job. His speeches appear in Job 4:1–5:27; 15:1–35; 22:1–30.

ELIPHELET. (1) A son of David, born at Jerusalem after he became king over all Israel (2 Sam. 5:16).

(2) One of David's "mighty men," an elite group of warriors known for their bravery in battle (2 Sam. 23:34).

ELISABETH. KJV: see *Elizabeth*

ELISEUS. KJV: see *Elisha*

ELISHA. The prophet who succeeded Elijah as God's spokesman to Israel (the Northern Kingdom) (1 Kings 19:16–21). Elisha is known as the greatest miracle worker in the OT. Among other actions, he purified the bad waters of a spring (2 Kings 2:19–22), provided a destitute widow with a supply of oil that never ran out (2 Kings 4:1–7), provided food for one hundred prophets (2 Kings 4:42–44), and healed a Syrian military officer (2 Kings 5:1–14). Elisha is also mentioned in 2 Kings 3:11–14; 6:1–32; 7:1; 8:1–14; 9:1; 13:14–21 • Luke 4:27.

ELISHAMA. A son of David, born at Jerusalem after he became king over all Israel (1 Sam. 5:16).

ELISHUA. A son of David, born at Jerusalem after he became king over all Israel (1 Sam. 5:15).

ELIZABETH. A relative of Mary, mother of Jesus. Elizabeth was carrying the infant John the Baptist, forerunner of Jesus, in her womb when Mary paid her a visit. Elizabeth rejoiced with Mary over the coming birth of the Messiah. She is mentioned in Luke 1:5–60. *Elisabeth*: KJV.

ELIZAPHAN. A leader from the tribe of Zebulun who helped divide the land of Canaan after the conquest (Num. 34:25).

ELON. A minor judge of Israel from the tribe of Zebulun who served for ten years (Judg. 12:11–12).

ELOTH. A former Edomite city used as a port city by King Solomon (**1 Kings 9:26** • 2 Chron. 8:17; 26:2).

ELUL. Sixth month of the Hebrew year, the month in which the rebuilding of Jerusalem's wall was completed (Neh. 6:15).

ELYMAS. See *Bar-Jesus*

EMBALMING. An Egyptian burial practice that protected a body from decay. Joseph was embalmed for burial (Gen. 50:26).

EMERALD. A precious green stone used in the high priest's breastplate (Exod. 28:18) and in the foundation of the heavenly city, or New Jerusalem (Rev. 21:19).

EMERODS. KJV: see *Tumors*

EMMANUEL. See *Immanuel*

EMMAUS. A village about seven miles from Jerusalem where Jesus revealed Himself to Cleopas and another follower shortly after His resurrection (Luke 24:13–31).

EN. A Hebrew prefix that means "well" or "spring," as in En-gedi (spring of a kid), a place where David hid from King Saul (1 Sam. 23:29).

ENCHANTER. A person who used chants and rituals to drive away evil spirits (Jer. 27:9). All such practices of the occult were forbidden by the Lord (Deut. 18:10).

END [ED, S]. See also *Purpose*

Gen. 2:2 on the seventh day God *e'ed* His work

Job 42:12 the Lord blessed the latter *e* of Job

Ps. 22:27 the *e's* of the world shall...turn to the Lord

Ps. 39:4 make me to know my *e*...the measure of my days

Ps. 102:27 Your [God's] years shall have no *e*

Prov. 14:12 its *e* are the ways of death

Prov. 23:32 In the *e* it [wine] bites like a serpent

Eccles. 7:8 The *e* of a thing is better than its beginning

Eccles. 12:12 There is no *e* to making many books

Isa. 9:7 There shall be no *e* to...His government and peace

Isa. 40:2 Speak...to Jerusalem...her warfare has *e'ed*

Jer. 8:20 summer is *e'ed*, and we are not saved

Dan. 12:9 words are...sealed until the time of the *e*

Matt. 10:22 he who endures to the *e* shall be saved

Matt. 24:6 all these things must come to pass...*e* is not yet

Matt. 28:20 I [Jesus] am with you always, even to the *e* of the world

Rom. 10:4 Christ is the *e* of the law for righteousness

1 Cor. 15:24 Then the *e* comes

Eph. 3:21 be glory in the church by Christ Jesus... world without *e*

1 Pet. 4:7 But the *e* of all things is at hand

Rev. 2:26 he who overcomes and keeps My works to the *e*

Rev. 22:13 Alpha and Omega, the beginning and the *e*

END [S] OF THE EARTH

Deut. 28:49 from the *e-o-t-e*, as swift as the eagle flies

1 Sam. 2:10 The LORD shall judge the *e's-o-t-e*

Job 28:24 For He looks to the *e's-o-t-e*

Ps. 48:10 so is Your [God's] praise to the *e's-o-t-e*

Ps. 61:2 From the *e's-o-t-e* I will cry to You

Ps. 67:7 all the *e's-o-t-e* shall fear Him

Isa. 40:28 the Creator of the *e's-o-t-e*, does not lose strength

Isa. 42:10 Sing...His praise from the *e's-o-t-e*

Isa. 45:22 be saved, all the *e's-o-t-e*

Jer. 25:33 one *e-o-t-e* even to the other *e-o-t-e*

Acts 13:47 you [Paul] should be for salvation to the *e's-o-t-e*

ENDOR. A village where King Saul enlisted a medium to call up the spirit of the deceased Samuel. But Samuel's message was not what Saul wanted to hear—the king and his sons would die in a forthcoming battle with the Philistines (1 Sam. 28:7–25). It is also mentioned in Josh. 17:11 • Ps. 83:9–10.

ENDURE [D, ING, S]

Exod. 18:23 then you [Moses] shall be able to *e*

1 Chron. 16:34 for His mercy *e's* forever

Esther 8:6 how can I [Esther] *e* to see the evil that shall come

Job 8:15 He shall hold it fast, but it shall not *e*

Ps. 9:7 the LORD shall *e* forever

Ps. 19:9 The fear of the LORD is clean, *e'ing* forever

Ps. 30:5 For His anger *e's* but a moment

Ps. 89:36 His [David's] descendants shall *e* forever

Ps. 102:12 But You, O LORD, shall *e* forever

Ps. 107:1 give thanks to the LORD...His mercy *e's* forever

Ps. 145:13 Your [God's] dominion *e's* throughout all generations

Prov. 27:24 does the crown *e* to every generation

Nah. 1:6 who can *e* the fierceness of His anger?

Matt. 10:22 he who *e's* to the end shall be saved

Mark 13:13 he who *e's* to the end...shall be saved

1 Cor. 13:4 Love *e's* for a long time

1 Cor. 13:7 [love] hopes all things, *e's* all things

2 Tim. 2:3 *e* hardness as a good soldier of Jesus Christ

2 Tim. 4:3 they will not *e* sound doctrine...having itching ears

2 Tim. 4:5 watch in all things, *e* afflictions

Heb. 6:15 after he [Abraham] had patiently *e'd*

Heb. 12:2 who [Jesus] for the joy...set before Him *e'd* the cross

Jas. 1:12 Blessed is the man who *e's* temptation

Jas. 5:11 Behold, we count them happy who *e*

ENEMY [IES]

Deut. 20:4 the LORD...goes...to fight...against your *e'ies*

1 Sam. 18:29 Saul became David's *e* continually

Job 19:11 He [God] counts me...as one of His *e'ies*

Ps. 6:7 My eye...grows old because of all my *e'ies*

Ps. 9:3 When my *e'ies* turn back, they shall fall

Ps. 18:17 He [God] delivered me from my strong *e*

Ps. 23:5 You [God] prepare a table...in the presence of my *e'ies*

Ps. 27:11 lead me in a plain path, because of my *e'ies*

Ps. 61:3 You [God] have been...a strong tower from the *e*

Ps. 97:3 A fire...burns up His *e'ies* all around

Ps. 110:1 until I [God] make Your *e'ies* Your footstool

Prov. 25:21 If your *e* is hungry, give him bread

Matt. 5:44 I [Jesus] say to you, love your *e'ies*

Rom. 12:20 If your *e* is hungry, feed him

1 Cor. 15:25 He [Jesus] must reign until He [God] has put all *e'ies* under His feet

1 Cor. 15:26 The last *e* that shall be destroyed is death

Gal. 4:16 Am I [Paul]...your *e* because I tell you the truth

2 Thes. 3:15 do not count him as an *e*, but admonish him

Jas. 4:4 a friend of the world is the *e* of God

EN-GEDI. An oasis where a spring flowed into the Dead Sea, a site where David hid from King Saul in a nearby cave. It is mentioned in

Josh. 15:62 • **1 Sam. 23:29–24:1** • 2 Chron. 20:2 • Song of Sol. 1:14 • Ezek. 47:10.

ENMITY
Gen. 3:15 I [God] will put *e* between you [the serpent] and the woman

Rom. 8:7 Because the carnal mind is *e* against God

Jas. 4:4 the friendship with the world is *e* with God

ENOCH. (1) A man of great faith who "walked with God"—a reference to his steady, consistent relationship with the Lord. The father of Methuselah, Enoch was taken into God's presence without experiencing physical death (Gen. 5:21–24). He is listed among the heroes of faith in the book of Hebrews in the NT (Heb. 11:5). Enoch is also mentioned in 1 Chron. 1:3 • Luke 3:37 • Jude 14.

(2) The firstborn son of Cain and a city named for him (Gen. 4:17–18).

EN-ROGEL. A well near Jerusalem where two of King David's aides hid during the rebellion of the king's son Absalom (2 Sam. 17:17).

ENTER [ED, ING, S]
Ps. 100:4 *E* into His gates with thanksgiving

Prov. 17:10 rebuke *e's* more into a wise man than a hundred lashes into a fool

Ezek. 3:24 the Spirit *e'ed* into me [Ezekiel]

Matt. 6:6 when you pray, *e* into your closet

Matt. 7:21 Not everyone who says... Lord, Lord, shall *e*...kingdom of heaven

Mark 7:18 anything from outside that *e's* into the man, it cannot defile him

Mark 14:38 pray, lest you *e* into temptation

Luke 11:52 those who were *e'ing* in you hindered

Luke 13:24 Strive to *e* in at the narrow gate

Luke 18:25 easier for a camel...than for a rich man to *e* into the kingdom

Luke 22:3 Then Satan *e'ed* into Judas, surnamed Iscariot

John 3:4 can he *e* a second time into his mother's womb and be born

John 10:2 he who *e's* in by the door is the shepherd

Acts 11:8 nothing...unclean has *e'ed* into my [Peter's] mouth at any time

Rom. 5:12 through one man sin *e'ed* into the world

1 Cor. 2:9 nor has *e'ed* into the heart of man the things that God has prepared

Heb. 9:12 He [Jesus] *e'ed* in once into the Most Holy Place

ENVY. Resentment, jealousy, or ill feelings toward another person. Paul cautioned believers against the dangers of this sin (Rom. 13:13).

ENVY [IES, ING]
Prov. 3:31 Do not *e* the oppressor

Prov. 27:4 but who is able to stand before *e*

Mark 15:10 chief priests had delivered Him out of *e*

Rom. 13:13 Let us walk honestly...not in strife and *e'ing*

1 Cor. 13:4 love does not *e*...is not puffed up

Gal. 5:26 Let us not be boastful...*e'ing* one another

Phil. 1:15 Some...preach Christ even from *e* and strife

Titus 3:3 living in malice and *e*...hating one another

Jas. 3:16 where there is *e'ing* and strife, there is confusion

1 Pet. 2:1 laying aside all malice, and all deceit, and hypocrisies, and *e'ies*

EPAENETUS. A fellow believer at Rome greeted and commended by the apostle Paul (Rom. 16:5).

EPAPHRAS. A leader of the Colossian church (Col. 1:7–8) who visited Paul while he was imprisoned in Rome (Philem. 23).

EPAPHRODITUS. A believer from Philippi who brought a gift to Paul while he was imprisoned in Rome (Phil. 4:18). The apostle may have sent his letter to the Philippians by Epaphroditus (Phil. 2:24–29).

EPHAH. A unit of dry measure equal to about one bushel (Exod. 16:36).

EPHESIANS, EPISTLE TO. A letter of the apostle Paul to the church at Ephesus that describes the exalted Christ as Lord of the church, the world, and the entire created order. Paul declared that believers, both Jews and Gentiles, are united as one body in Christ's church to serve as agents of reconciliation to a lost world. The first three chapters focus on the redemption made possible by the atoning death of Christ. Chapters 4–6 call on the Ephesian Christians to model their lives after Christ's example and to remain faithful in turbulent times.

EPHESUS. A large and influential city of Asia Minor where Paul established a church and spent two to three years among these new believers. This is the longest time he spent at any one place during his missionary travels (Acts 18:19–21; 19:1–10). An ornate temple devoted to worship of a pagan goddess known as Diana stood in the city. Paul's teachings about Jesus began to cut into sales of images of this shrine. The silversmiths who crafted these trinkets incited a riot against the apostle. But a city official intervened on Paul's behalf, and he continued his ministry (Acts 19:35–41). The church in this city is one of the seven addressed by the apostle John in the book of Revelation (Rev. 2:1–7). Ephesus is also mentioned in Acts 20:16–17 • 1 Cor. 15:32; 16:8 • Eph. 1:1 • 1 Tim. 1:3 • 2 Tim. 1:18; 4:12 • Rev. 1:11.

EPHOD. A vest worn by the high priest while presiding at the altar (Exod. 28:4). It contained twelve precious stones engraved with the names of the twelve tribes of Israel (Exod. 28:21).

EPHPHATHA. An Aramaic word, meaning "open," spoken by Jesus when He healed a deaf man (Mark 7:34).

EPHRAIM. (1) A son born to Joseph in Egypt. He was apparently the son of Asenath, Joseph's Egyptian wife. Ephraim is mentioned in Gen. 41:52; 48:1–20 • Num. 26:28 • 1 Chron. 7:20–22.

(2) The descendants of Ephraim who developed into one of the twelve tribes of Israel (Gen. 48:8–20). This tribe settled in the northern region of Canaan after Israel conquered the land (Josh. 16:5–10).

(3) A symbolic name for the nation of Israel (Isa. 7:2–17 • Jer. 31:9–20 • Hos. 5:3–14).

(4) A city in the wilderness to which Jesus and His disciples retreated before His triumphal entry into Jerusalem (John 11:54).

(5) A forest west of the Jordan River where the forces of Absalom were defeated by David's army (2 Sam. 18:6).

EPHRATH / EPHRATHAH. Ancient names for the city of Bethlehem, cited by the prophet Micah as the birthplace of the Messiah (Mic. 5:2). See also *Bethlehem*.

EPHRON. A Hittite from whom Abraham bought a plot of ground containing a cave as a burial site for his family. Ephron is mentioned in **Gen. 23:8–20**; 25:9; 49:29–30; 50:13.

EPICUREANS. Philosophers addressed by Paul in the city of Athens (Acts 17:18). They believed the purpose of life was the pursuit of pleasure, tempered by morality and cultural refinement.

EPISTLE. A type of correspondence characterized as a formal letter. The NT contains thirteen epistles written by the apostle Paul, arranged according to length, from the longest (Romans) to the shortest (Philemon). Several other epistles from early church leaders also appear in the NT.

EQUAL
Prov. 26:7 The legs of the lame are not *e*
Ezek. 18:25 Is My way not *e*? Are not your ways unequal?
John 5:18 He [Jesus]...said that God was His Father, making Himself *e* with God
Phil. 2:6 who [Jesus]...thought it not robbery to be *e* with God
Col. 4:1 give to your servants what is just and *e*

ERASTUS. A believer who, along with Timothy, traveled from Ephesus into Macedonia under orders from the apostle Paul. He is mentioned in Acts 19:22 • 2 Tim. 4:20.

ERR [ED]
Job 6:24 understand where I [Job] have *e'ed*
Matt. 22:29 You *e*, not knowing the scriptures

ERROR

2 Sam. 6:7 God struck him [Uzzah] there for his *e*

Matt. 27:64 the last *e* shall be worse than the first

2 Pet. 3:17 being led away with the *e* of the wicked

ESAIAS. KJV: see *Isaiah*

ESAR-HADDON. A son of Sennacherib who succeeded his father as king of Assyria (2 Kings 19:37). Esar-haddon apparently was the king who resettled Samaria with foreigners after the fall of the Northern Kingdom (Ezra 4:1–2). He is also mentioned in Isa. 37:38.

ESAU. The oldest son of Isaac who traded his birthright—or his inheritance rights as the firstborn son—to his twin brother Jacob for a bowl of stew (Gen. 25:26–34). Jacob also tricked his father into blessing him rather than Esau (Gen. 27:1–41), an act for which Esau vowed to kill Jacob. But the brothers were eventually reconciled (Gen. 33:1–4). Esau was also known as *Edom* (Gen. 25:30). His descendants were the Edomites, a people group that lived in an area near the Dead Sea. Esau is also mentioned in Gen. 26:34; 28:6–9; 32:3–19; 35:1, 29; 36:1–43 • Josh. 24:4 • 1 Chron. 1:34–35 • Mal. 1:2–3 • Rom. 9:13 • Heb. 12:16. See also *Edom*.

ESCAPE [D]

1 Sam. 22:1 David...*e'd* to the cave Adullam

Job 19:20 I [Job] have *e'd* with the skin of my teeth

Ps. 71:2 cause me to *e*. Incline Your ear to me

Prov. 19:9 and he who speaks lies shall not *e*

Isa. 37:31 remnant who have *e'd* of the house of Judah

Jer. 25:35 no way to flee, nor the leader of the flock to *e*

John 10:39 but He *e'd* out of their hand

1 Cor. 10:13 God... with the temptation will also make a way of *e*

Heb. 2:3 how shall we *e* if we neglect so great a salvation

ESEK. A well abandoned by Isaac's servants after a dispute with herdsmen of the area over

the right to use it. The name means "quarrel." Isaac eventually dug another well which caused no controversy (Gen. 26:17–22).

ESH-BAAL. See *Ish-bosheth*

ESHCOL. A valley in Canaan from which the spies sent to investigate the land brought a cluster of grapes to show its fertility (**Num. 13:22–27; 32:9** • Deut. 1:24).

ESTABLISH [ED]

Gen. 9:9 I [God] *e* My covenant with you [Noah]

Ps. 7:9 *e* the just, for the righteous God tries the hearts

Ps. 78:5 He [God] *e'ed* a testimony in Jacob

Ps. 90:17 *e* the work of our hands

Prov. 3:19 The LORD...by understanding He has *e'ed* the heavens

Prov. 12:19 The lips of truth shall be *e'ed* forever

Prov. 16:3 Commit...to the LORD and your thoughts shall be *e'ed*

Ezek. 16:62 I [God] will *e* My covenant with you

Matt. 18:16 in the mouth of...witnesses every word may be *e'ed*

Acts 16:5 so the churches were *e'ed* in the faith

Rom. 10:3 going about to *e* their own righteousness

Heb. 8:6 He [Jesus] is...the mediator of a better covenant...*e'ed* on better promises

ESTHER. A young Jewish woman known for her heroism and her rags-to-riches story. After her parents died, she was raised by a relative named Mordecai. While living in Persia among other Jewish exiles, she was chosen as the new queen under King Ahasuerus (Esther 2:1–17). Through her influence with the king and the clever planning of Mordecai, she saved her countrymen from a mass extermination. Her Persian name was Hadassah.

ESTHER, BOOK OF. A historical book of the OT named for its major personality, a Jewish woman named Esther, who became queen of Persia. It recounts how an evil royal official named Haman tricked the king of the nation into issuing an order for the wholesale execution of all Jews living in the country. But

Queen Esther exposed the plot, and Haman was executed. The Lord granted the Jewish people a resounding victory over their enemies, and they celebrated with a special holiday known as the Feast of Purim.

ETAM. A defense city built by King Rehoboam of Judah (the Southern Kingdom), Solomon's son and successor (2 Chron. 11:6).

ETERNAL

Deut. 33:27 The *e* God is your refuge

Mark 3:29 blasphemes against the Holy Spirit... is in danger of *e* damnation

John 17:3 life *e*, that they might know...God

2 Cor. 4:18 things that are not seen are *e*

2 Cor. 5:1 a house not made with hands, *e* in the heavens

1 Tim. 1:17 to the King *e*, immortal, invisible

Heb. 5:9 He [Jesus] became the author of *e* salvation

Heb. 9:12 by His own blood He...obtained *e* redemption for us

ETERNAL LIFE. A new state of existence granted by God the Father to those who accept Jesus Christ as Savior and Lord. The phrase refers to the quality of life as well as its unending character. Through His resurrection, Christ became the "firstfruits" of eternal life for all believers (Rom. 8:29; 1 Cor. 15:12–58).

ETERNAL LIFE

Mark 10:17 what shall I do that I may inherit *e-l*

John 3:15 whoever believes in Him [Jesus] should not perish but have *e-l*

John 6:54 Whoever eats My [Jesus'] flesh...has *e-l*

John 6:68 You [Jesus] have the words of *e-l*

John 10:28 I [Jesus] give *e-l* to them

Rom. 6:23 the gift of God is *e-l* through Jesus Christ

1 Tim. 6:12 Fight the good fight of faith, take hold of *e-l*

1 John 2:25 promise that He [Jesus] has promised...*e-l*

1 John 3:15 no murderer has *e-l* abiding in him

1 John 5:11 God has given to us *e-l*...in His Son

Jude 21 looking for the mercy of our Lord Jesus Christ to *e-l*

ETHANIM. Seventh month of the Hebrew year; the month when the ark of the covenant was placed in the newly built temple in Jerusalem (1 Kings 8:2).

ETHIOPIA. An ancient African nation south of Egypt. During much of its history, Ethiopia was controlled by Egypt, so these two regions are often mentioned together (Ezek. 30:4). A royal official from Ethiopia was baptized by Philip the evangelist (Acts 8:36–38). Ethiopia is also mentioned in Gen. 2:13 • Job 28:19 • Ps. 68:31 • Isa. 45:14. *Ethiopians*: 2 Chron. 12:3 • Dan. 11:43 • Amos 9:7 • Acts 8:27.

EUNICE. Mother of Timothy, Paul's young missionary associate. Paul commended her for her great faith (2 Tim. 1:5).

EUNUCH. A male servant in a king's household. These servants were often emasculated if they worked among the women in the royal harem (2 Kings 9:32).

EUODIA. A Christian woman at Philippi censured by the apostle Paul for quarreling (Phil. 4:2).

EUPHRATES. A river mentioned as one of the rivers of the garden of Eden (Gen. 2:14). The Euphrates rises in modern Turkey and eventually joins the Tigris before emptying into the Persian Gulf. It is also mentioned in Gen. 15:18 • Josh. 1:4 • 2 Sam. 8:3 • 2 Kings 23:29 • 2 Chron. 35:20 • Jer. 13:4–7 • Rev. 9:14; 16:12.

EUROCLYDON. A fierce wind that struck the ship on which Paul was sailing to Rome (Acts 27:14).

EUTYCHUS. A young man from Troas who was restored to life by Paul when he fell from a window during Paul's sermon (Acts 20:9–12).

EVANGELIST. A traveling preacher of the gospel in the early church. Philip was the best example of this form of ministry (Acts 21:8).

EVANGELIST [S]

Acts 21:8 entered into the house of Philip the *e*

Eph. 4:11 He [God] gave some apostles...and some *e's*

2 Tim. 4:5 do the work of an *e*

EVE. The woman fashioned from one of Adam's ribs to serve as his helpmate and companion. Adam gave her this name, meaning "life," because she as the first woman was the mother of the human race. Eve ate fruit from the tree that God had placed off-limits, and she convinced Adam to do the same. Their disobedience resulted in the introduction of sin and death into the world. God punished the couple by driving them from the garden of Eden (Gen. 3:22–24). Eve is also mentioned in Gen. 4:1 • 2 Cor. 11:3 • 1 Tim. 2:13.

EVERLASTING

Deut. 33:27 and underneath are the *e* arms

Ps. 24:7 and be lifted up, you *e* doors

Ps. 90:2 even from *e* to *e*, You are God

Ps. 100:5 For the LORD is good; His mercy is *e*

Ps. 119:144 righteousness of Your [God's] testimonies is *e*

Isa. 9:6 His [Jesus'] name shall be called...the *e* Father

Isa. 26:4 e strength is in the LORD JEHOVAH

Isa. 40:28 the *e* God...does not lose strength, nor is weary

Isa. 60:19 the LORD shall be to you an *e* light

Jer. 31:3 I [God] have loved you with an *e* love

Dan. 7:14 His [God's] dominion is an *e* dominion

Matt. 25:41 Depart from Me [Jesus], you cursed, into *e* fire

EVERLASTING COVENANT

Gen. 9:16 the *e-c* between God and every living creature

Heb. 13:20 Jesus, that great Shepherd of the sheep, through the blood of the *e-c*

EVERLASTING LIFE

John 3:16 whoever believes in Him should not perish but have *e-l*

John 4:14 a well of water springing up into *e-l*

John 5:24 he who...believes in Him who sent Me has *e-l*

John 6:47 he who believes in Me has *e-l*

EVIDENT

Rom. 1:19 what may be known of God is *e* in them...God has shown it

1 Cor. 15:27 it is *e* that He [God] who put all things under Him [Jesus] is...exception

2 Cor. 4:10 life of Jesus might also be made *e* in our body

Gal. 5:19 works of the flesh are *e*...adultery, fornication, uncleanness

EVIL. A force that opposes God and His work in the world. The ultimate source of evil is Satan, who tries to undermine truth, honesty, and righteousness (Matt. 13:19). Sin and evil entered the world when Satan convinced Adam and Eve to disobey God by eating the forbidden fruit in the garden of Eden (Gen. 3:6). The pattern of sin and rebellion that they set in motion is behind most of the evil and suffering in the world today. In the end-time, God will triumph over evil, and Satan will be thrown into a lake of fire (Rev. 20:10).

EVIL [S]

Gen. 50:20 you thought *e* against me [Joseph], but God meant it for good

Deut. 30:15 I [Moses] have set before you... death and *e*

Josh. 24:15 if it seems *e* to you to serve the LORD

1 Sam. 16:14 an *e* spirit from the LORD troubled him [Saul]

Job 2:10 Shall we receive good at the hand of God, and...not receive *e*

Job 28:28 to depart from *e* is understanding

Ps. 23:4 valley of the shadow of death, I will not fear *e*

Ps. 34:13 Keep your tongue from *e* and your lips from...deceit

Ps. 38:20 Those...who render *e* for good are... adversaries

Ps. 51:4 Against You...have I...done this *e*

Ps. 119:101 I have restrained my feet from every *e* way

Prov. 3:7 fear the LORD and depart from *e*

Prov. 15:3 eyes of the LORD are in every place, watching the *e* and the good

Prov. 31:12 She will do him good, and not *e*

Isa. 5:20 Woe to those who call *e* good and good *e*

Jer. 1:14 Out of the north an *e* shall be unleashed

Jer. 2:13 My [God's] people have committed two *e's*

Matt. 5:11 men...say all manner of *e* against you falsely

Matt. 6:13 do not lead us into temptation... deliver us from *e*

Mark 3:4 lawful to do good on the Sabbath... or to do *e*

Luke 11:13 you then, being *e*, know how to give good gifts

John 3:19 men loved darkness...because their deeds were *e*

Rom. 7:19 I do the *e* that I [Paul] do not want

Rom. 12:9 Hate what is *e*; cling to...good

Rom. 12:21 Do not be overcome by *e*...overcome *e* with good

Eph. 5:16 redeeming the time because the days are *e*

Eph. 6:13 you may be able to withstand in the *e* day

1 Thes. 5:22 Abstain from all appearance of *e*

1 Tim. 6:10 love of money is the root of all *e*

Heb. 3:12 lest there be in any of you an *e* heart of unbelief

Jas. 3:8 the tongue...is an unruly *e*, full of deadly poison

Jas. 3:16 where there is envying...there is... every *e* work

3 John 11 Beloved, follow...not what is *e*

EVILDOER [S]

Ps. 26:5 I have hated the congregation of *e's*

Ps. 119:115 Depart from me, you *e's*

1 Pet. 4:15 let none of you suffer...as an *e*, or... busybody

EVIL-MERODACH. A son and successor of Nebuchadnezzar II as king of Babylon. He released King Jehoiachin of Judah (the Southern Kingdom), who had been imprisoned by his father for 37 years. He is mentioned in 2 **Kings** 25:27–30 • Jer. 52:31.

EXALT [ED, S]

1 Chron. 29:11 You [God] are *e'ed* as head above all

Ps. 34:3 let us *e* His [God's] name together

Ps. 46:10 I [God] will be *e'ed* among the nations

Ps. 57:11 Be *e'ed*, O God, above the heavens

Ps. 97:9 You [God] are *e'ed* far above all gods

Ps. 99:5 *E* the Lord...and worship at His footstool

Prov. 14:34 Righteousness *e's* a nation

Isa. 25:1 O Lord, You are my God. I will *e* You

Isa. 40:4 Every valley shall be *e'ed*...hill shall be made low

Luke 14:11 he who humbles himself shall be *e'ed*

Phil. 2:9 God also has highly *e'ed* Him

1 Pet. 5:6 that He may *e* you in due time

EXAMPLE

Matt. 1:19 Joseph her [Mary's] husband...not willing to make her a public *e*

John 13:15 I [Jesus] have given you an *e*

1 Tim. 4:12 be an *e* to the believers in word

EXCEEDING [LY]

Gen. 17:2 I [God]...will multiply you [Abraham] *e'ly*

Ps. 68:3 rejoice before God. Yes, let them *e'ly* rejoice

Jon. 3:3 Now Nineveh was an *e'ly* great city

Jon. 4:1 it displeased Jonah *e'ly*, and he was very angry

Matt. 2:10 they [the wise men] rejoiced with *e'ly* great joy

Matt. 5:12 be *e'ly* glad, for great is your reward in heaven

Matt. 26:38 My [Jesus'] soul is *e'ly* sorrowful, even to death

Mark 15:14 they cried out the more *e'ly*, Crucify Him [Jesus]

Eph. 2:7 He [God] might show the *e* riches of His grace

Eph. 3:20 to Him [God] who is able to do *e'ly* abundantly above all...we ask

Jude 24 Him [Jesus] who is able to...present you faultless before...His glory with *e* joy

EXCELLENT

Ps. 8:9 how *e* is Your [God's] name in all the earth

Ps. 150:2 praise Him [God] according to His *e* greatness

Isa. 12:5 for He [God] has done *e* things

Dan. 6:3 because an *e* spirit was in him [Daniel]

1 Cor. 12:31 yet, I [Paul] show you a more *e* way

Heb. 8:6 now He [Jesus] has obtained a more *e* ministry

Heb. 11:4 Abel offered...a more *e* sacrifice than Cain

EXCUSE

Luke 14:18 they all with one consent began to make *e*

Rom. 1:20 they are without *e*

EXHORT [ED, ING]

1 Thes. 2:11 we *e'ed* and comforted...every one of you

2 Tim. 4:2 e with all long-suffering and doctrine

Titus 2:9 E servants to be obedient to their own masters

Heb. 10:25 not forsaking the assembling of ourselves...but *e'ing* one another

EXODUS, BOOK OF. A book of the OT that begins where Genesis ends—with the descendants of Jacob in Egypt (Gen. 46:1–47:31). The Israelites multiplied and prospered in Egypt for several centuries but were eventually reduced to the status of slaves (Exod. 1:8–11). Exodus records how God miraculously delivered His people under the leadership of Moses, and took care of them in the wilderness while they traveled toward their new home in Canaan. During this period of about forty years, God revealed the Ten Commandments and other parts of the Law to Moses (Exod. 20–23). He also led the people to build the tabernacle as their worship center (Exod. 36–40).

EXODUS FROM EGYPT. The "going out" of the Israelites toward their new home in Canaan after more than four centuries in Egypt, much of this time as slaves. How this came about is one of the most dramatic narratives in the Bible, filled with miraculous acts by the Lord on behalf of His people. The Exodus brought to fulfillment God's promise many years before (Gen. 12:1–3) that Abraham's descendants would become His chosen people with a land of their own.

The leader of this event was Moses, a man uniquely qualified for the task. Although born an Israelite, he was reared in the court of the Egyptian king (Exod. 2:5–10). He knew how to stand before the pharaoh and plead the cause of his enslaved people. Moses also spent many years as a shepherd in the desert—the very land the Israelites had to cross while traveling to Canaan. His knowledge of life in this remote territory enhanced His skills as God's chosen leader.

The Exodus was celebrated by future generations as the defining moment of their history (Ps. 136:10–16). It was a time when a collection of powerless slaves faced off against the world's greatest superpower—and won. The Israelites always remembered it was the one true God who had set them free.

EXPEDIENT

John 11:50 e...that one man should die for the people

John 16:7 e for you that I [Jesus] go away

1 Cor. 6:12 All things are lawful...but not all things are *e*

EYE [S]

Exod. 21:24 E for *e*, tooth for tooth, hand for hand

Deut. 34:7 when he [Moses] died. His *e's* were not dim

Job 42:5 now my [Job's] *e* sees You

Ps. 6:7 My *e* is consumed because of grief

Ps. 17:8 Keep me as the apple of the *e*

Prov. 26:5 Answer a fool...lest he be wise in his own *e's*

Prov. 28:11 The rich man is wise in his own *e's*

Prov. 28:22 He who hurries to be rich has an evil *e*

Matt. 5:38 it has been said...*e* for an *e*...tooth for a tooth

Matt. 6:23 if your *e* is evil, your whole body... full of darkness

Mark 9:47 if your *e* causes you to stumble, pluck it out

Luke 6:41 the speck that is in your brother's *e*

1 Cor. 2:9 E has not seen, nor ear heard

1 Cor. 12:17 If the whole body were an *e*, where... hearing

1 Cor. 12:21 the *e* cannot say to the hand

1 Cor. 15:52 in the twinkling of an *e*, at the last trumpet

Rev. 1:7 He [Jesus] comes with clouds...every *e* shall see Him

EYES OF GOD. A symbolic expression for the Lord's awareness of everything that happens in the world and in the lives of its inhabitants. The Bible declares that He knows every act of every single day of a person's life (Job 34:21). He even sees into their innermost thoughts and the secret places of the heart (Ps. 94:11; Luke 5:22). This truth should motivate believers to make their lives an open book that is dedicated to Him and His service. See also *Anthropomorphism*.

EYE [S] OF THE LORD

Gen. 6:8 Noah found grace in the *e's-o-t-L*

1 Kings 15:5 David did...right in the *e's-o-t-L*

2 Chron. 16:9 *e's-o-t-L* run to and fro throughout the...earth

Ps. 33:18 the *e-o-t-L* is on those who fear Him

Prov. 15:3 The *e's-o-t-L* are in every place, watching the evil and the good

1 Pet. 3:12 the *e's-o-t-L* are on the righteous

EYEWITNESSES. People who give testimony to what they have actually seen and heard. The disciples of Jesus could bear such witness because they had seen Jesus at work during His earthly ministry. The apostle Peter assured early believers: "We did not follow cunningly devised fables when we made known to you the power and coming of our Lord Jesus Christ, but we were eyewitnesses of his majesty" (1 Pet. 1:16).

EYEWITNESSES

Luke 1:2 those...were *e* and ministers of the word

2 Pet. 1:16 we were *e* of His majesty

EZEKIAS. KJV: see *Hezekiah*

EZEKIEL. An OT prophet often referred to as the "prophet to the exiles." He was carried with other exiles into Babylon, where he prophesied faithfully for more than twenty years. His call came through a vision of a storm cloud in which mysterious heavenly creatures known as cherubim appeared. God spoke from a throne in the midst of the cloud, commissioning Ezekiel to his prophetic ministry (Ezek. 1:4–2:3).

EZEKIEL, BOOK OF. A prophetic book of the OT addressed to the Jewish captives in Babylon about 585 BC. The prophet painted a dark picture of the sins of the people and the losses they had suffered. But he also assured them that better days were ahead. God would lead them back to their homeland and establish His universal rule among His people through the coming Messiah (Ezek. 40–48). The book is known for its strange visions, including bones coming to life (Ezek. 37:1–7) and a strange wheel within a wheel (Ezek. 10:9–22). It is a good example of the type of writing known as apocalyptic literature. See also *Apocalyptic Writing*.

EZER. A man who helped rebuild the walls of Jerusalem after the Exile (Neh. 3:19).

EZION-GEBER. A coastal city on the Red Sea where King Solomon built a port from which he conducted extensive trade with other nations. It is mentioned in Num. 33:35–36 • Deut. 2:8 • 1 Kings 9:26–28; 22:48 • 2 Chron. 8:17–18; 20:36.

EZRA. A priest and scribe who led religious reforms in his homeland after the return of Jewish exiles from Persia (Ezra 10:1–8). Ezra wrote the book that bears his name.

EZRA, BOOK OF. An OT book that recounts events during the post-exilic period of Israel's history—the time when God's people were allowed to return to their homeland following their years of exile. Ezra is also closely related to the book of Nehemiah. Under the leadership of Ezra. a priest and scribe, the returned exiles committed themselves to God's law, put away foreign wives (Ezra 10:1–17), and confessed their sins and renewed the covenant (Neh. 9–10).

FABLE. A story in which nonliving things act like humans, as in Jotham's narrative of the trees and the bramble. It is a clever story that dramatizes Abimelech's unfit leadership (Judg. 9:1–15).

FABLES
1 Tim. 1:3–4 not to...pay attention to *f* and endless genealogies
1 Tim. 4:7 refuse profane and old wives' *f*

FACE OF GOD. A symbolic reference to God's presence, as in the psalmist's lament, "How long will You hide Your face from me?" (Ps. 13:1). The biblical writers realized that God is beyond human understanding, so they used expressions like this to communicate some sense of His character. See also *Anthropomorphism.*

FACE OF THE LORD
Ps. 34:16 The *f-o-t-L* is against those who do evil
Luke 1:76 go before the *f-o-t-L* to prepare His ways
1 Pet. 3:12 the *f-o-t-L* is against those who do evil

FAIR HAVENS. A harbor adjoining the island of Crete in the Mediterranean Sea where the apostle Paul's ship stopped on his voyage to Rome (Acts 27:8).

FAITH. A confident attitude toward God's promises, particularly His provision of salvation and eternal life for those who place their trust in Jesus Christ (John 5:24). The word also refers to the teachings of Scripture (Jude 3). Paul listed faith as one of the nine results of the Holy Spirit at work in the lives of believers (Gal. 5:22).

FAITH
Hab. 2:4 But the just shall live by his *f*
Matt. 17:20 *f* as a grain of mustard seed
Acts 6:8 Stephen, full of *f* and power, did great wonders
Rom. 1:17 righteousness of God is revealed from *f* to *f*
Rom. 3:28 justified by *f* without the deeds of the law
Rom. 5:1 justified by *f*, we have peace with God

Rom. 10:17 So then *f* comes by hearing
1 Cor. 13:13 now *f*, hope, love remain, these three
Gal. 2:20 I [Paul] live by the *f* of the Son of God
Gal. 3:24 to Christ, that we might be justified by *f*
Gal. 5:22 fruit of the Spirit is love...goodness, *f*
Eph. 2:8 by grace you are saved through *f*
Eph. 6:16 above all, taking the shield of *f*
1 Tim. 5:8 denied the *f* and is worse than an unbeliever
1 Tim. 6:12 Fight the good fight of *f*
2 Tim. 4:7 finished my course, I [Paul] have kept the *f*
Heb. 10:23 hold fast the profession of our *f*
Heb. 11:1 Now *f* is the substance of things hoped for
Heb. 12:2 Jesus, the author and finisher of our *f*
Jas. 2:17 *f*, if it does not have works, is dead, being alone
1 John 5:4 victory that overcomes the world, even our *f*
Jude 3 contend for the *f*...delivered to the saints

FAITH CHAPTER OF THE BIBLE. Heb. 11

FAITHFUL [NESS]
Ps. 31:23 for the LORD preserves the *f*
Ps. 119:90 Your [God's] *f'ness* is to all generations
Prov. 27:6 *F* are the wounds of a friend
Lam. 3:23 new every morning. Your [God's] *f'ness* is great
Matt. 25:21 Well done, good and *f* servant
Luke 16:10 *f* in what is least is also *f* in much
1 Cor. 4:2 required of stewards that a man be found *f*
1 Cor. 10:13 God is *f*, who will not allow you to be tempted
2 Thes. 3:3 the Lord is *f*, who shall establish you
1 John 1:9 He [Jesus] is *f* and just to forgive us our sins
Rev. 2:10 Be *f* to death

FAITHFULNESS. A characteristic of God that refers to His dependability and His loyalty to His people. The psalmist referred to Him as a "rock," a solid, immovable force in an unpredictable world (Ps. 62:2). Believers are also expected to be faithful in their commitment to the Lord (Rev. 2:10).

FAITHLESS

Luke 9:41 O *f* and perverse generation
John 20:27 Thomas...do not be *f*

FALL [EN, ING, S]

Ps. 116:8 You [God] have delivered...my feet from *f'ing*
Ps. 145:14 The LORD upholds all who *f*
Prov. 16:18 Pride goes before destruction... haughty spirit before a *f*
Eccles. 4:10 woe to him who is alone when he *f's*
Dan. 3:6 whoever does not *f* down and worship shall be cast...into the...furnace
Hos. 14:1 you [Israel] have *f'en* by your iniquity
Luke 2:34 this Child [Jesus] is set for the *f* and rising again of many
Luke 6:39 Shall they not both *f* into the ditch
John 12:24 grain of wheat *f's* into the ground and dies
1 Cor. 10:12 thinks he stands be careful lest he *f*
Heb. 10:31 It is a fearful thing to *f* into the hands of the living God
Jas. 1:2 joy when you *f* into various temptations
Jude 24 Now to Him who is able to keep you from *f'ing*
Rev. 14:8 Babylon is *f'en*, is *f'en*, that great city

FALL OF HUMANKIND. Adam and Eve's act of rebellion against the Lord that introduced the plague of sin into the world (Gen. 3:6). Their disobedience of God's clear command reflects the flawed condition of the entire human race. As the apostle Paul put it, "All have sinned and come short of the glory of God" (Rom. 3:23). But God has not left the world without hope. He has provided for redemption through the atoning sacrifice of His Son. Jesus is known as the Last Adam, who corrected the sin problem caused by the first Adam (1 Cor. 15:21–22).

FALLOW GROUND. See *Untilled Ground*

FALSE [LY]

Exod. 20:16 shall not bear *f* witness against your neighbor

Lev. 19:11 You shall not steal or deal *f'ly*
Prov. 11:1 A *f* balance is an abomination to the LORD
Jer. 29:9 prophesy *f'ly* to you in My name
Matt. 5:11 say all manner of evil against you *f'ly* for My [Jesus'] sake

FALSE PROPHETS. Spokesmen who deliver a misleading message while pretending to speak for the Lord. Jeremiah, a God-called prophet of the OT, was particularly angered by such messengers. He condemned Hananiah for denying the reality of God's forthcoming judgment against the sinful people of Judah (Jer. 28:1–9). In the NT, Jesus warned believers to beware of such dishonest messengers (Matt. 24:11, 24).

FALSE PROPHET [S]

Matt. 7:15 Beware of *f-p's*...in sheep's clothing
Matt. 24:11 many *f-p's* shall rise and shall deceive many
Mark 13:22 *f-p's* shall arise...show signs and wonders
Acts 13:6 a *f-p*, a Jew whose name was Bar-Jesus
2 Pet. 2:1 there were also *f-p's* among the people
1 John 4:1 many *f-p's* have gone out into the world
Rev. 19:20 the beast was taken, and with him the *f-p*

FALSE WITNESS. A person who gave false or misleading testimony about others. Several such witnesses testified in the Jewish trial against Jesus (Matt. 26:59–61). This practice is specifically prohibited by the Ten Commandments (Exod. 20:16).

FALSE WITNESS [ES]

Deut. 5:20 You shall not bear *f-w* against your neighbor
Ps. 35:11 *F-w'es*...laid to my charge things that I did not know
Prov. 6:19 A *f-w* that speaks lies
Prov. 14:5 a *f-w* will utter lies
Mark 14:56 many bore *f-w* against Him

FAMINE. A period of crop failures and food shortages due to lack of rain. Famines occurred occasionally in the hot, dry climate of Israel (Gen. 12:10).

FAST. To go without food and drink for a time in order to center one's attention on God. Jesus fasted for forty days during His time of temptation in the wilderness (Matt. 4:2).

FAST [ING]

Ps. 109:24 knees are weak through *f'ing*

Matt. 17:21 this kind does not go out but by prayer and *f'ing*

Mark 2:20 bridegroom [Jesus] shall be taken away...then they shall *f*

1 Cor. 16:13 Watch, stand *f* in the faith

Gal. 5:1 Stand *f*...by which Christ has made us free

1 Thes. 5:21 Test all things. Hold *f* what is good

Heb. 10:23 hold *f* the profession of our faith

FAN. A tool similar to a pitchfork used to toss grain into the air to separate it from the straw (Isa. 30:24). This tool is also spoken of as a symbol of God's judgment (Jer. 15:7).

FATHER

Gen. 2:24 a man shall leave his *f* and his mother

Gen. 17:5 a *f* of many nations I [God] have made you [Abraham]

Exod. 20:12 Honor your *f* and your mother

Lev. 20:9 everyone who curses his *f*...shall surely be put to death

Ps. 27:10 When my *f* and my mother forsake me...LORD will take me up

Ps. 103:13 As a *f* has compassion on his children

Prov. 4:1 Hear...the instruction of a *f*

Prov. 15:20 A wise son makes a glad *f*

Isa. 9:6 His [Jesus'] name shall be called...the everlasting *F*

Isa. 64:8 LORD, You are our *F*. We are the clay

Ezek. 18:20 nor shall the *f* bear the iniquity of the son

Mal. 2:10 Do we not all have one *F*

Matt. 5:48 even as your *F*...in heaven is perfect

Matt. 6:9 Our *F*...in heaven

Matt. 10:37 loves *f* or mother more than Me is not worthy of Me

Matt. 23:9 for One is your *F*, who is in heaven

Matt. 28:19 baptizing them in the name of the *F*

Mark 14:36 Abba, *F*, all things are possible for You

Luke 9:59 allow me first to go and bury my *f*

Luke 15:22 the *f* said to his servants, Bring... the best robe

Luke 23:34 *F*, forgive them...they do not know what they do

Luke 24:49 I [Jesus] send the promise of My *F*

John 6:44 No man can come to Me, unless the *F* who...sent Me draws him

John 10:30 My *F* and I are one

John 14:6 No man comes to the *F* except through Me

John 14:16 I [Jesus] will pray to the *F*, and He shall give you another Comforter

John 15:8 In this My *F* is glorified...bear much fruit

John 16:23 ask the *F* in My name He will give it

John 20:21 As My *F* has sent Me, even so I send you

Acts 1:7 not for you to know the times...the *F* has put in His own power

Eph. 4:6 one God and *F* of all

Phil. 2:11 confess that Jesus Christ is Lord, to the glory of God the *F*

Col. 1:19 For it pleased the *F* that in Him all fullness should dwell

Jas. 1:17 Every good gift...comes down from the *F* of lights

Jas. 2:21 Abraham our *f* justified by works

1 John 1:3 our fellowship is with the *F* and with His Son

1 John 2:1 we have an advocate with the *F*, Jesus Christ

1 John 3:1 manner of love the *F* has bestowed on us

FAULT [LESS, S]

Luke 23:4 I [Pilate] find no *f* in this man [Jesus]

Gal. 6:1 Brothers, if a man is overtaken in a *f*

Jas. 5:16 Confess your *f*'s to one another

Jude 24 present you *f'less* before the presence of His glory

Rev. 14:5 without *f* before the throne of God

FAVORITISM

Col. 3:25 for the wrong that he has done, and there is no *f*

FEAR [ED, S]

Gen. 22:12 I [God] know that you [Abraham] *f* God

Deut. 6:13 *f* the LORD your God and serve Him

Josh. 4:14 *f'ed* him [Joshua], as they *f'ed* Moses

1 Chron. 16:25 He [God] is also to be *f'ed* above all gods

Job 1:1 Job...was perfect...and one who *f'ed* God

Job 1:9 Satan answered...Does Job *f* God for nothing

Job 28:28 Behold, the *f* of the LORD—that is wisdom

Ps. 19:9 *f* of the LORD is clean, enduring forever

Ps. 23:4 I will not *f* evil, for You are with me

Ps. 27:1 The LORD is my...salvation. Whom shall I *f*

Ps. 34:11 I will teach you the *f* of the LORD

Ps. 46:2 we will not *f*, though the earth be removed

Ps. 103:13 the LORD has compassion on those who *f* Him

Ps. 111:10 *f* of the LORD is the beginning of wisdom

Ps. 112:1 Blessed is the man who *f's* the LORD

Ps. 118:6 I will not *f*. What can man do to me

Prov. 15:16 Better is little with the *f* of the LORD than great treasure with trouble

Eccles. 12:13 *F* God and keep His commandments

Mal. 4:2 to you who *f* My name, the Sun of righteousness shall arise

Matt. 28:8 they [the women] departed quickly from the sepulchre with *f*

Mark 4:41 *f'ed* exceedingly...What kind of man is this

Luke 22:2 they [chief priests and scribes] *f'ed* the people

Acts 2:43 And *f* came on every soul

Phil. 2:12 work out your own salvation with *f*

2 Tim. 1:7 God has not given us the spirit of *f*

Heb. 13:6 I will not *f* what man shall do to me

1 John 4:18 perfect love casts out *f*

Rev. 15:4 Who shall not *f* You, O Lord, and glorify Your name

FEARFUL [LY, NESS]

Ps. 55:5 *F'ness* and trembling have come on me

Ps. 139:14 I am *f'ly* and wonderfully made

Matt. 8:26 Why are you *f*, O you of little faith

Heb. 10:31 a *f* thing to fall into the hands of the living God

FEAR OF THE LORD. A phrase that refers to reverence for the one true God (Deut. 10:20). A healthy respect for the Lord is an important element of faith. It leads to worship of the Lord and obedience of His commands (Hab. 2:20).

FEAST. A major religious holiday or festival which marked some great event in Israel's history (Exod. 12:17). Several major festivals are mentioned in the Bible, including Passover, Pentecost, and Tabernacles.

FEAST OF HARVEST OR INGATHERING. See *Pentecost*

FEAST OF WEEKS. See *Pentecost*

FELIX. The governor of Judea who kept Paul in prison at Caesarea for about two years. The apostle appeared before Felix several times. He is mentioned in Acts 23:24–26; 24:3, 10–27; 25:14.

FELLOWSHIP. A feeling of oneness and cordiality among believers that grows out of their common faith in Jesus Christ (1 Cor. 1:9).

FELLOWSHIP

Acts 2:42 continued steadfastly in the apostles' doctrine and *f*

2 Cor. 6:14 what *f* does righteousness have with unrighteousness

Eph. 5:11 do not have *f* with the unfruitful works of darkness

Phil. 3:10 that I [Paul] may know Him...and the *f* of His sufferings

1 John 1:7 we have *f* with one another

FENCED CITY. KJV: see *Fortified City*

FESTUS. Successor of Felix as Roman governor of Judea before whom Paul appeared. When Paul's defense fell on deaf ears, he appealed his case to Rome. Festus is mentioned in **Acts** 24:27; 25:1–27; 26:24–32.

FIELD OF BLOOD. A burial place for poor people outside Jerusalem. It was purchased with the money Judas was paid to betray Jesus after he returned it in a spirit of remorse (Matt. 27:6–8).

FIERY SERPENTS. Deadly snakes that attacked the Israelites in the wilderness when they complained against Moses' leadership. He placed an image of a serpent on a pole as an antidote for those who were bitten (Num. 21:6–9). Jesus referred to this event to show the salvation He offers to believers (John 3:14–15).

FIG. A tree whose fruit was considered a symbol of prosperity (1 Kings 4:25). Figs were pressed into cakes and also preserved by drying (1 Sam. 25:18).

FILTHY
Ps. 14:3 they have all together become *f*
Isa. 64:6 all our righteousness is as *f* rags

FINGER OF GOD. A symbolic expression for God's power (Exod. 8:19). It also expresses His action on behalf of His people, as in the Ten Commandments being written by His finger (Exod. 31:18). See also *Anthropomorphism.*

FINGER OF GOD
Exod. 8:19 the magicians said...This is the *f-o-G*
Exod. 31:18 gave to Moses two tablets...of stone, written with the *f-o-G*
Luke 11:20 if I [Jesus] cast out demons with the *f-o-G*

FINISH [ED]
Gen. 2:1 heavens and the earth were *f'ed*
Neh. 6:15 wall was *f'ed* on the twenty-fifth day
Luke 14:28 count the cost, whether...enough to *f* it
John 4:34 My [Jesus'] food is to...*f* His [God's] work
John 17:4 *f'ed* the work that You gave Me
John 19:30 It is *f'ed.* And He...gave up His spirit
2 Tim. 4:7 I [Paul] have *f'ed* my course...kept the faith

FIRE. Flames produced from a burning substance. Fire is often associated with God's presence and power, as in God's speaking to Moses from a flaming bush (Exod. 3:2–6). Zechariah, a prophet after the Exile, described the Lord as a "wall of fire" around the city of Jerusalem (Zech. 2:5). His protection of His people was especially needed during the precarious years after their return from exile.

FIRE AND BRIMSTONE
Ps. 11:6 On the wicked He shall rain snares, *f-a-b*
Luke 17:29 the same day that Lot went out of Sodom it rained *f-a-b*
Rev. 14:10 he [worshipper of beast] shall be tormented with *f-a-b*

FIRSTBORN. The first child born into a family (Gen. 49:3). The firstborn son received a double portion of his father's property as his birthright and assumed leadership of the family. In a figurative sense, the word refers to something of supreme value, as in Paul's description of Jesus as the "firstborn among many brothers," or the exalted head of the church (Rom. 8:29).

FIRST DAY OF THE WEEK. Sunday, or the day of Christ's resurrection, which became the day of worship in the early church (Acts 20:7).

FIRSTFRUITS. The first or best of crops and livestock which were to be presented as sacrifices and offerings to the Lord (Exod. 23:19). The apostle Paul described Jesus as "the firstfruits of those who have fallen asleep" (1 Cor. 15:20). Just as the firstfruits promised the full harvest to come, the resurrection of Christ guaranteed resurrection and eternal life for all who accept Him as Savior and Lord.

FIRSTFRUITS
Exod. 23:19 first of the *f*...bring into the house of the LORD
Prov. 3:9 Honor the LORD...with the *f* of all your increase
1 Cor. 15:20 Christ has been raised...*f* of those who have fallen asleep

FLESH. A word that refers to worldly appetites or desires which can lead to sin, even after a person becomes a believer (Gal. 5:16–17). The antidote for such temptations is total reliance on the power of the Holy Spirit. The apostle Paul made this clear by contrasting the works of the flesh with the fruit of the Spirit. Yielding to the flesh results in such problems as hatred, envy, and strife, but life under the Holy Spirit's control brings love, joy, and peace (Gal. 5:19–23).

FLESH AND BLOOD

Matt. 16:17 f-a-b has not revealed it to you [Peter]

1 Cor. 15:50 f-a-b cannot inherit the kingdom of God

Eph. 6:12 wrestle not against *f-a-b* but... principalities

FLINT. A hard stone, perhaps a variety of quartz (Deut. 8:15). The word is also used symbolically to denote firmness (Ezek. 3:9).

FLOOD, GREAT. The instrument of God's judgment against a wicked world in Noah's time. This great deluge came after forty days of continuous rainfall, but Noah and his family and the animals in the ark were saved by the hand of God (Gen. 6–8).

FOLLY. Senseless and thoughtless human behavior. The book of Proverbs is filled with admonitions to avoid the pitfalls that foolish people fall into. Among other things, they refuse to listen to good advice (Prov. 12:15), fail to control their temper (Prov. 14:16), get into heated arguments (Prov. 18:6), and speak without thinking (Prov. 29:11). Foolishness is the exact opposite of wisdom—a byproduct of commitment to the Lord.

FOOLISH [LY, NESS]

Ps. 5:5 The *f* shall not stand in Your sight
Ps. 69:5 O God, You know my *f'ness*
Prov. 10:1 a *f* son is the heaviness of his mother
Prov. 12:23 the heart of fools proclaims *f'ness*
Prov. 14:17 He who is quickly angered deals *f'ly*
Prov. 15:20 a *f* man despises his mother
Eccles. 4:13 Better is...a wise child than an old and *f* king

Matt. 7:26 compared to a *f* man who built his house on the sand
Matt. 25:3 Those who were *f*...took no oil with them
1 Cor. 1:23 Christ crucified... *f'ness* to the Greeks
1 Cor. 1:27 chosen the *f* things...to confound the wise
1 Cor. 3:19 wisdom of this world is *f'ness* with God
Gal. 3:1 f Galatians, who has bewitched you
Titus 3:9 avoid *f* questions and genealogies

FOOTSTOOL. An ottoman or foot rest and a symbolic expression for submission. To treat people as a footstool was to bring them into total subjection to one's power and authority (Ps. 110:1).

FOOT-WASHING. A gesture of hospitality for guests and travelers. The ritual was generally performed by lowly domestic servants, but Jesus washed His disciples' feet to teach them a lesson in humble service (John 13:5–15).

FOREIGNER [S]

Exod. 18:3 I have been a *f* in a foreign land
Deut. 10:19 love the *f*, for you were *f's* in the land of Egypt
Job 19:15 I am a *f* in their sight
Ps. 69:8 a *f* to my mother's children
Luke 17:18 none found who returned...save this *f*

FOREKNOWLEDGE OF GOD. A characteristic of God's nature that allows Him to know events before they happen (Ps. 139:4). This ability to see into the future is a power that belongs only to Him. He warned against listening to wizards or fortune tellers who claimed to have such ability (Deut. 18:10–11).

FORERUNNER. A person who prepares the way for others to follow (Heb. 6:20). John the Baptist was the forerunner of Jesus (Mark 1:1–8).

FORGIVE [ING, S]

Num. 14:18 The LORD is longsuffering...*f'ing* iniquity

2 Chron. 7:14 then I [God] will hear...and will *f* their sin

Ps. 86:5 You, LORD, are good, and ready to *f*

Ps. 103:3 who [God] *f's* all your iniquities

Matt. 6:14 your heavenly Father will also *f* you

Matt. 18:21 how often shall my brother sin... and I [Peter] *f*

Mark 11:26 neither will your Father...*f* your trespasses

Luke 5:21 Who can *f* sins but God alone

Luke 6:37 *F*, and you shall be forgiven

Luke 23:34 *f* them, for they do not know what they do

Eph. 4:32 be kind...*f'ing* one another

1 John 1:9 He [Jesus] is faithful and just to *f* us our sins

FORGIVEN

Ps. 32:1 Blessed is he whose transgression is *f*

Matt. 12:31 blasphemy against the Holy Spirit shall not be *f*

Luke 6:37 Forgive, and you shall be *f*

Rom. 4:7 Blessed are those whose iniquities are *f*

1 John 2:12 your sins are *f* you for His name's sake

FORGIVENESS. The pardon or overlooking of the wrongful acts of others. God's pardon of human sin and rebellion is the greatest act of forgiveness in the Bible. Sin separates people from God, but He forgives this sin and reestablishes the broken relationship when they repent and turn to Him in faith (Acts 10:43). Just as God forgives believers, He expects them to practice forgiveness in their relationships with others (Matt. 5:43–48).

FORGIVENESS

Acts 26:18 that they may receive *f* of sins

Col. 1:14 in whom [Jesus] we have redemption... the *f* of sins

FORMER RAIN. The first rain of the growing season that led to the sprouting of seed and the growth of young plants (Joel 2:23).

FORNICATION. Sexual relationships outside the bonds of marriage. Paul cited fornication as a sin which believers should avoid (1 Cor. 6:18).

FORNICATION

Matt. 19:9 whoever divorces his wife, except for *f*

1 Cor. 5:1 reported that there is *f* among you

1 Cor. 6:18 commits *f* sins against his own body

Gal. 5:19 Now the works of the flesh are... adultery, *f*

1 Thes. 4:3 this is the will of God...abstain from *f*

Rev. 17:4 in her [woman on scarlet beast] hand a golden cup...of her *f*

FORTIFIED CITY. A city surrounded by a strong wall to provide protection from invaders (2 Sam. 20:6). Sometimes an army would camp around such a city for months and try to starve its inhabitants into submission. *Fenced city*: KJV. See also *Siege*.

FORTUNATUS. A believer from the city of Corinth who encouraged the apostle Paul in his work at Ephesus (1 Cor. 16:17).

FORUM OF APPIAS. A place on the Roman road known as the Appian Way where the apostle Paul's friends met him as he approached Rome. It was about forty miles south of the city (Acts 28:15). *Appii forum*: KJV.

FOUNDATION [S]

Job 38:4 Where were you [Job] when I [God] laid the *f's* of the earth

Isa. 28:16 I [God] lay in Zion a stone for a *f*

Matt. 25:34 inherit the kingdom prepared for you from the *f* of the world

1 Cor. 3:11 no man can lay a *f* other than... Jesus Christ

Eph. 2:20 built upon the *f* of the apostles

Heb. 1:10 You, Lord...have laid the *f* of the earth

Heb. 11:10 city that has *f's*, whose builder and maker is God

Rev. 21:14 And the wall of the city had twelve *f's*

FOUNTAIN. A source of water such as a well or spring (Deut. 8:7). The prophet Jeremiah spoke symbolically of God's blessings upon His people as a fountain (Jer. 2:13).

FOX. An animal of the dog family known for its cunning (Luke 13:32). The judge Samson used a fox to destroy the crops of the Philistines (Judg. 15:4).

FRANKINCENSE. A gum from a tree which gave off a pungent odor when burned in sacrificial ceremonies (Neh. 13:9). Frankincense was one of the gifts presented to the infant Jesus by the wise men (Matt. 2:11).

FREE [LY]

Gen. 2:16 Of every tree of the garden you may *f'ly* eat

Ps. 51:12 uphold me with Your *f* Spirit

Matt. 10:8 *F'ly* you have received; *f'ly* give

John 8:32 and the truth shall make you *f*

Rom. 3:24 justified *f'ly* by His grace through... Christ Jesus

Rom. 6:18 *f* from sin...you became the servants of righteousness

Rom. 8:2 Jesus has made me [Paul] *f* from the law of sin

1 Cor. 9:19 though I [Paul] am *f* from all men

Gal. 3:28 there is neither slave nor *f*

Gal. 5:1 in the liberty by which Christ has made us *f*

Col. 3:11 neither Greek nor Jew...slave nor *f*

Rev. 22:17 let him take the water of life *f'ly*

FREE WILL. The right and ability of humans to decide whether to obey God's commands or to ignore His instructions. The exercise of this free choice is an essential element in the process of salvation. God wants everyone to follow Him, but only those who choose to accept Him through the exercise of their faith—their own free will—will become citizens of His kingdom (Eph. 2:8).

FRIEND OF TAX COLLECTORS AND SINNERS. This description of Jesus by the Pharisees was intended as a criticism, but Jesus considered it a compliment. He willingly associated with the outcasts of society because He came into the world as the Savior of people like them (Matt. 11:19). On another occasion he told the Pharisees, "Those who are well have no need of the physician, but those who are sick. I came to call not the righteous but sinners to repentance" (Mark 2:17).

FRONTLET. A small leather case containing passages of scripture, worn upon the forehead as a literal obedience of Deuteronomy 6:6–8.

FRUIT OF THE SPIRIT. Nine attitudes and actions, cited by the apostle Paul in Galatians 5:22–23. They characterize those who live under the control of the Holy Spirit. Heading the list is love, an unselfish quality that places the needs of others ahead of one's own. Joy and peace produce a quiet sense of contentment, no matter the circumstances of life. Longsuffering, or patience, is the ability to remain faithful to the Lord and to others across a lifetime. Temperance, or moderation, declares that life is a blend of many different elements rather than a single-minded devotion to one or two. The qualities of gentleness, goodness, and meekness—in combination with deep faith— produce believers who are effective witnesses for the Lord. Unbelievers are naturally curious about the light that spirit-led Christians radiate in a dark world.

FURLONG. A Greek measure of length, equal to about 650 feet or one-eighth of a mile (Luke 24:13).

G

GAASH, MOUNT. A mountain in the hill country of Ephraim where Joshua was buried. Mount Gaash was known for its brooks. It is mentioned in Josh. 24:29–30 • Judg. 2:9 • 2 Sam. 23:30 • 1 Chron. 11:32.

GABRIEL. An archangel, or chief angel, who appeared to Daniel (Dan. 8:16), Zechariah (Luke 1:18–19), and the virgin Mary (Luke 1:26–27). All these appearances were connected with God's promise about the coming Messiah.

GAD. (1) A son of Jacob, born to Zilpah. He is mentioned in Gen. 30:11; 35:26; 46:16; 49:19 • Exod. 1:4 • 1 Chron. 5:11.

(2) One of the twelve tribes of Israel that developed from Gad's descendants. After the conquest of Canaan, this tribe settled east of the Jordan River in the area known as Gilead. It is mentioned in **Num. 32:1–36** • Josh. 13:24–28; 22:9–34.

(3) A prophet who instructed King David to buy a site on which the temple in Jerusalem was built in later years (1 Chron. 21:18–22).

GADARA. A Greek city in the territory east of the Jordan River known as the Decapolis. Jesus healed a demon-possessed man at Gadara (Mark 5:1–20).

GADARENES. People from the area of Gadara in Perea where Jesus healed a demon-possessed man (Mark 5:1–20 • Luke 8:26, 37). *Gergesenes*: Matt. 8:28.

GADDI. One of the twelve spies or scouts sent by Moses to investigate the land of Canaan. He represented the tribe of Manasseh (Num. 13:1–2, 11).

GADDIEL. One of the twelve spies or scouts sent by Moses to investigate the land of Canaan. He represented the tribe of Zebulun (Num. 13:1–2, 10).

GAIN [ED, S]
Matt. 18:15 If he hears you...have *g'ed* your brother
Mark 8:36 profit a man if he *g's* the whole world
Luke 19:16 your pound has *g'ed* ten pounds
1 Cor. 9:20 I [Paul] became as a Jew, that I might *g* the Jews
Phil. 1:21 to me [Paul] to live is Christ, and to die is *g*
1 Tim. 6:6 godliness with contentment is great *g*

GAIUS. A traveling companion of the apostle Paul who was caught up in the riot incited against the apostle in Ephesus (Acts 19:29).

GALATIA. A territory of central Asia Minor which contained several cities visited by the apostle Paul during the first missionary journey—Antioch of Pisidia, Derbe, Iconium, and Lystra (Acts 13–14)—all located in southern Galatia. Paul's letter to the Galatians (Gal. 1:1–2) was apparently addressed to churches in and around these cities. It is also mentioned in **Acts 16:6; 18:23** • 1 Cor. 16:1 • 2 Tim. 4:10 • 1 Pet. 1:1.

GALATIANS, EPISTLE TO. A short epistle of the apostle Paul to the churches of Galatia on the themes of Christian liberty and justification by faith alone. The apostle was saddened to learn that some members of the church were being led astray. A group of false teachers known as the Judaizers had convinced them that faith in the grace of Christ was not sufficient for salvation. They taught that it was also necessary to submit to circumcision and observe Jewish holy days. Paul condemned these false teachers and informed the Galatians that they were foolish indeed if they returned to the bondage of the law from which the grace of Christ had set them free (3:1; 5:1).

GALBANUM. A gum from a plant used to produce incense, which was burned by a priest at the altar (Exod. 30:34).

GALILEE. The northernmost province of Israel during NT times and the area where Jesus spent most of His earthly ministry (Mark 3:7). This was the home territory of several of His disciples. Galilee had a mixed population of Jews and Gentiles. Important towns in this territory included Cana, Bethsaida, Capernaum, Nazareth, Magdala, and Tiberias. The city of Capernaum served as His headquarters during His Galilean ministry (Matt. 4:13). The prophet Isaiah referred to the area as "Galilee of the Gentiles" (Isa. 9:1). It is also mentioned in Mark 1:9–28 • Luke 23:6–55 • John 4:3–54.

GALILEE, SEA OF. A fresh-water lake about fourteen miles long and seven miles wide which took its name from the surrounding Roman province. Fed by the Jordan River, it provided the livelihood for many commercial fishermen, including several disciples of Jesus: the brothers James and John and the brothers Peter and Andrew. Jesus called these brothers to leave their vocation on the lake and become His disciples (Mark 1:16–20). Later, Jesus calmed the waters of Galilee after He and His disciples were caught in a boat in a storm (Mark 4:35–41). The body of water was also referred to as the Sea of Chinnereth (Josh. 12:3), the lake of Gennesaret (Luke 5:1), and the Sea of Tiberias (John 21:1).

GALLIO. A Roman ruler of Achaia who refused to get involved in the dispute between Paul and the Jewish leaders in Corinth (Acts 18:12–17).

GALLOWS. A platform on which people were executed. Haman was hanged on the very gallows he had prepared for Mordecai (Esther 5:14; 7:10).

GAMALIEL. A member of the Jewish Sanhedrin who stepped forward in defense of the apostles in Jerusalem. If the Jesus whom they were preaching was a false prophet, Gamaliel reasoned, the Christian movement would soon fade away. But if they were preaching the truth, it could not be stopped by human opposition. Convinced by this reasoning, the Sanhedrin released the apostles (Acts 5:34–41). Gamaliel is probably the same learned rabbi under whom the apostle Paul studied in his early years (Acts 22:3).

GARDEN OF EDEN. Gen. 2:8–3:24

GAREB. One of David's "mighty men," an elite group of warriors known for their bravery in battle (2 Sam. 23:8, 38).

GASHMU. An influential Samaritan leader who opposed Nehemiah's rebuilding of the wall of Jerusalem after the Exile (Neh. 6:6).

GATH. Home of the Philistine giant Goliath, whom the boy David defeated (1 Sam. 17:4). After he became king, David captured the city (1 Chron. 18:1). Later, King Rehoboam of Judah (the Southern Kingdom) fortified Gath to shore up the nation's defenses (2 Chron. 11:5, 8). It is also mentioned in Josh. 11:22 • 1 Sam. 5:8; 6:17; 21:10–15; 27:3–12 • 2 Kings 12:17 • Amos 6:1–2• Mic. 1:10.

GATH-HEPHER. A city near Nazareth; hometown of the prophet Jonah (2 Kings 14:25).

GAVE UP

Gen. 25:8 Then Abraham *g-u* his spirit and died
Matt. 27:50 Jesus, when He had cried again...*g-u* His spirit
Luke 23:46 having said this, He [Jesus] *g-u* His spirit
Rev. 20:13 the sea *g-u* the dead who were in it

GAZA. A Philistine city where the judge Samson killed many of his enemies by destroying one of their pagan temples (Judg. 16:21–30). In the NT, the evangelist Philip baptized an Ethiopian eunuch along the road leading to this city (Acts 8:26–38). It is also mentioned in Josh. 10:41; 11:22; 15:47 • Jer. 25:20 • Amos 1:6–7.

GAZER. KJV: see *Gezer*

GEDALIAH. A governor of Judah (the Southern Kingdom) appointed by King Nebuchadnezzar of Babylon. Gedaliah was assassinated after ruling for only two months. He is mentioned in 2 Kings 25:22–25 • **Jer.** 39:14; **40:5–16**; 41:1–18; 43:6.

GEDEON. KJV: see *Gideon*

GEHAZI. A servant of Elisha who claimed a reward from Naaman after Naaman was healed by the prophet. Gehazi was struck with leprosy because of his dishonesty and greed. He is mentioned in **2 Kings** 4:12–36; **5:20–27**; 8:4–6.

GENEALOGIES OF JESUS. Two different lists of the ancestors of Jesus that appear in the Gospels of Matthew (1:1–17) and Luke (3:23–38). Matthew's record goes back to Abraham, while Luke's list begins with Adam. The purpose of both genealogies was apparently to show that Jesus was the legitimate heir, in a spiritual sense, to the throne of David.

GENEALOGY. A record of the descendants of a person or family (1 Chron. 5:1–7). It was similar to a family tree of modern times. These records documented inheritance rights and a person's right of succession as a clan leader, king, or high priest.

GENERAL EPISTLES. The name for eight epistles of the NT: Hebrews; James; 1 and 2 Peter; 1, 2, and 3 John; and Jude. This designation suggests that they were addressed to broad, general problems rather than to local, specific issues.

GENERATION [S]

Gen. 2:4 the *g's* of the heavens and of the earth

Num. 32:13 all the *g* that had done evil...was consumed

Ps. 24:6 This is the *g* of those who seek Him

Ps. 33:11 thoughts of His heart to all *g's*

Ps. 71:18 I have declared Your strength to this *g*

Ps. 85:5 draw out Your anger to all *g's*

Ps. 90:1 You [God] have been our dwelling place in all *g's*

Ps. 100:5 His [God's] truth endures to all *g's*

Prov. 27:24 does the crown endure to every *g*

Eccles. 1:4 One *g* passes away, and another *g* comes

Dan. 4:3 and His authority is from *g* to *g*

Matt. 24:34 *g* shall not pass until all these things are fulfilled

Luke 3:7 *g* of vipers, who has warned you

Luke 16:8 wiser in their *g* than the children of light

Col. 1:26 mystery...has been hidden from ages and from *g's*

1 Pet. 2:9 But you are a chosen *g*, a royal priesthood

GENESIS, BOOK OF. The first book of the OT known as "the book of beginnings" because of its accounts of the creation of the world and the early history of the Israelites. Major events and subjects covered in the book include: (1) God's creation of the physical world and Adam and Eve's sin in the Garden of Eden (chaps. 1–3); (2) Noah and the great flood (chaps. 4–9); (3) the tower of Babel and the scattering of humankind (chap. 11); and (4) the life stories of the patriarchs: Abraham and Isaac (chaps. 12–27), Jacob (chaps. 25–35), and Joseph (chaps. 37–50).

GENNESARET. See *Galilee, Sea of*

GENTILE [S]

Isa. 42:6 a covenant to the people, as a light to the *G's*

Isa. 60:3 *G's* shall come to your light

Jer. 16:19 *G's* shall come to You from the ends of the earth

Mal. 1:11 My [God's] name shall be great among the *G's*

Matt. 12:18 Behold, My servant...He shall show judgment to the *G's*

Mark 10:42 to rule over the *G's* exercise lordship

Luke 2:32 A light to lighten the *G's*...glory of... Israel

Acts 9:15 for he [Paul] is a chosen vessel...to bear My [God's] name before the *G's*

Acts 13:46 we [Paul and Barnabas] are turning to the *G's*

Acts 14:27 He [God]...opened the door of faith to the *G's*

Acts 18:6 From hereafter I [Paul] will go to the *G's*

Rom. 2:9 of the Jew first and also of the *G*

Rom. 3:29 Is He the God of the Jews only...Is He not also of the *G's*

1 Cor. 12:13 baptized into one body, whether... Jews or *G's*

Eph. 3:6 *G's* should be...partakers of His [God's] promise

GENTLENESS. A kind and benevolent attitude toward others. The prophet Isaiah declared that the coming Messiah would reflect such an attitude. He would be like a shepherd who tended the most vulnerable sheep among his flock with special care (Isa. 40:11). This prophecy was fulfilled when Jesus exercised His power in a spirit of compassion to heal the sick (Matt. 20:34).

GERAR. A place in southern Canaan where Abraham was reprimanded by Abimelech, a local king, for lying about his wife Sarah's identity (Gen. 20:1–18).

GERGESENES. See *Gadarenes*

GERIZIM, MOUNT. A mountain in central Canaan where Joshua pronounced God's blessings for keeping God's laws (Josh. 8:33–35). In later years, this mountain was considered a sacred worship place by the Samaritans (John 4:1–21). Mount Gerizim is also mentioned in Deut. 11:29; 27:12 • Judg. 9:7.

GESHEM. An Arabian who opposed Nehemiah's rebuilding of Jerusalem's defensive wall after the Exile (Neh. 2:19; 6:2).

GETHSEMANE. A garden on the Mount of Olives outside Jerusalem where Jesus prayed on the night of His betrayal and arrest. Here he faced the temptation to reject His divine mission and to avoid the suffering of the cross. But He was strengthened through prayer to declare, "Not My will, but Yours be done" (Luke 22:42). A church known as the Church of All Nations occupies the site today. In a small garden in the church courtyard, ancient olive trees with twisted trunks remind visitors of the agony that Jesus endured on this fateful night before His trial and crucifixion. Gethsemane is also mentioned in Matt. 26:36–56 • Mark 14:32.

GEUEL. One of the twelve spies or scouts sent by Moses to investigate the land of Canaan. Geuel represented the tribe of Gad (Num. 13:1–2, 15).

GEZER. A Canaanite city captured by Joshua and allotted to the Levites (Josh. 21:20–21). In later years, Solomon turned Gezer into an important military outpost (1 Kings 9:15–16). It is also mentioned in **Josh. 10:33**; 12:12; 16:3, 10 • Judg. 1:29 • 2 Sam. 5:25 • 1 Chron. 6:67; 7:28; 14:16; 20:4.

GIANTS. People of larger-than-normal size and strength such as the Philistine Goliath, whom David killed (2 Sam. 21:20–22). Races of giants mentioned in the Bible are the Anakim (Deut. 2:11), Emim (Deut. 2:10), and Zamzummim (Deut. 2:20).

GIBBETHON. A Canaanite town captured by Joshua and allotted to the Levites (Josh. 21:20, 23).

GIBEAH. Hometown of Saul, the first king of Israel, and capital of his kingdom (1 Sam. 14:16;

15:34). Before Saul's time, many residents of the city were killed during a civil war between the tribe of Benjamin and the other tribes of the nation (Judg. 20:21). It is also mentioned in Judg. 19:12–16; 20:4–43 • **1 Sam. 10:26** • Hos. 9:9; 10:9. *Gibeath*: Josh. 18:28.

GIBEON. A royal Canaanite city whose inhabitants tricked Joshua into forming an alliance with them to avoid the fate of other cities of Canaan. Excavations at Gibeon have uncovered a huge well that descends through solid rock to a depth of eighty-two feet. Gibeon is mentioned in **Josh. 9:3–21**; 10:1–41 • 2 Sam. 21:1–9.

GIDEON. A judge of Israel who defeated a large Midianite army with just a few men by using an unusual battle strategy. Armed with pitchers, torches, and trumpets, Gideon and his warriors crept into the enemy camp at night. At his signal, they blew their trumpets and broke the pitchers that masked their torches inside. This flooded the camp with noise and light, creating panic. In their confusion, the Midianites actually killed some of their own comrades (Judg. 6–8). Gideon is listed in the NT as one of the heroes of the faith (Heb. 11:32). *Jerubbaal*: Judg. 6:25–32.

GIFT [S]

Prov. 19:6 every man is a friend to him who gives *g's*

Matt. 2:11 they [wise men] presented *g's* to Him [Jesus]

Matt. 5:24 reconciled to your brother, and then come and offer your *g*

Luke 11:13 If you…being evil, know how to give good *g's* to your children

John 4:10 If you knew the *g* of God

Rom. 1:11 I [Paul] may impart some spiritual *g* to you

Rom. 12:6 differing *g's* according to the grace that is given to us

1 Cor. 12:4 diversities of *g's*, but the same Spirit

1 Cor. 12:31 But earnestly covet the best *g's*

1 Cor. 13:2 though I [Paul] have the *g* of prophecy

2 Cor. 9:15 Thanks be to God for His unspeakable *g*

1 Tim. 4:14 Do not neglect the *g* that is in you [Timothy]

Jas. 1:17 Every good *g* and every perfect *g* is from above

GIFT OF GOD

Eccles. 3:13 enjoy the good of all his labor, it is the *g-o-G*

Acts 8:20 you [Simon the magician] thought... the *g-o-G* could be purchased

Rom. 6:23 g-o-G is eternal life through Jesus Christ

Eph. 2:8 saved through faith...not of yourselves; it is the *g-o-G*

2 Tim. 1:6 stir up the *g-o-G*

GIHON. (1) One of the four rivers of the garden of Eden (Gen. 2:13).

(2) A place near Jerusalem where Solomon was anointed king as his father David's successor (1 Kings 1:33–34).

GILBOA, MOUNT. A mountain range in northern Israel where King Saul and his sons were killed in a battle with the Philistines. David, who succeeded Saul, mourned their deaths in a sad song. Mount Gilboa is mentioned in 1 Sam. 31:1–8 • 2 Sam. 1:6, 21 • **1 Chron. 10:1–8.**

GILEAD. (1) A fertile, flat tableland east of the Jordan River settled by the tribes of Gad, Reuben, and Manasseh (**Deut. 3:12–17** • 2 Sam. 17:26 • 1 Kings 17:1). Gilead was known for its spices and perfumes that it exported to other countries (Jer. 8:22).

(2) A hill where Gideon divided his army for battle against the Midianites (Judg. 7:1–7).

GILGAL. A site near the Jordan River where the Israelites erected memorial stones before beginning the campaign to conquer Canaan. These stones commemorated God's faithfulness in leading them to this land He had promised to give them (Josh. 4:19–20). In later years, Saul was crowned as Israel's first king at Gilgal (1 Sam. 11:15). It is also mentioned in Josh. 10:1–43 • 1 Sam. 13:4–15 • Amos 4:4–5.

GIMEL. Third letter of the Hebrew alphabet, used as a heading over Ps. 119:17–24. In the Hebrew language, the first line of each of these eight verses begins with this letter.

GIRGASHITES. An ancient tribe which inhabited Canaan (Gen. 10:15–16 • Deut. 7:1).

GIVE [S]

Gen. 12:7 To your [Abraham's] descendants I [God] will *g* this land

Exod. 20:12 that your days may be long on the land that the Lord...*g's* you

Num. 6:26 The Lord lift up His countenance... *g* you peace

Deut. 16:17 Every man shall *g* as he is able

Josh. 21:43 the Lord gave...all the land that He swore to *g* to their fathers

1 Kings 3:9 Therefore *g* Your servant [Solomon] an understanding heart

1 Chron. 16:34 g thanks to the Lord, for He is good

Ps. 5:1 G ear to my words, O Lord; consider my meditation

Ps. 29:2 G to the Lord the glory due to His name

Ps. 29:11 Lord will *g* strength to His people

Ps. 37:4 He [God] shall *g* you the desires of your heart

Ps. 85:12 Lord shall *g* what is good

Ps. 91:11 He [God] shall *g* His angels charge over you

Ps. 107:1 g thanks to the Lord, for He is good

Ps. 119:125 I am Your servant; *g* me understanding

Ps. 119:130 The entrance of Your words *g's* light

Prov. 2:6 For the Lord *g's* wisdom

Prov. 22:9 he *g's* of his bread to the poor

Prov. 25:21 If your enemy is hungry, *g* him bread

Isa. 7:14 the Lord...shall *g* you a sign...a virgin shall conceive...bear a son

Isa. 49:6 I [God] will also *g* You [Messiah] as a light to the Gentiles

Mic. 6:7 Shall I *g* my firstborn for my transgression

Matt. 5:15 a candle...*g's* light to all...in the house

Matt. 6:11 G us this day our daily bread

Matt. 10:8 Freely you have received; freely *g*

Matt. 11:28 Come to Me...I will *g* you rest

Matt. 16:19 g to you the keys of the kingdom

Matt. 20:28 even as the Son of man came...to *g* His life as a ransom for many

Mark 8:37 what shall a man *g* in exchange for his soul

Mark 10:40 sit on My [Jesus'] right hand...is not Mine to *g*

Luke 12:32 for it is your Father's good pleasure to *g* you the kingdom

Luke 15:12 g me the portion of goods that falls to me

Luke 20:22 Is it lawful for us to *g* taxes to Caesar

John 4:14 water that I [Jesus] shall *g* him shall never thirst

John 10:11 good shepherd *g's* His [Jesus'] life for the sheep

John 13:34 new commandment I [Jesus] *g* to you

John 14:16 and He [God] shall *g* you another Comforter

John 16:23 Whatever you ask...in My [Jesus'] name He [God] will *g* it you

Acts 6:4 g ourselves continually to prayer

Rom. 14:12 every one...shall *g* account...to God

1 Cor. 3:7 nor he who waters, but God who *g's* the increase

1 Cor. 13:3 though I [Paul] *g* my body to be burned

1 Cor. 15:57 thanks be to God, who *g's* us the victory

2 Cor. 3:6 the Spirit *g's* life

2 Cor. 9:7 let every man *g*...not grudgingly or of necessity

1 Thes. 5:18 G thanks in everything, for this is the will of God

Jas. 4:6 God...*g's* grace to the humble

1 Pet. 3:15 always be ready to *g* an answer

Rev. 2:10 and I [Jesus] will *g* you a crown of life

GIVING, PRINCIPLES OF. 2 Cor. 8:1–24; 9:6–8

GLAD [LY, NESS]

1 Chron. 16:31 heavens be *g*, and let the earth rejoice

Ps. 9:2 I will be *g* and rejoice in You [God]

Ps. 30:11 You [God] have...girded me with *g'ness*

Ps. 46:4 the streams...make *g* the city of God

Ps. 68:3 let the righteous be *g*

Ps. 100:2 Serve the LORD with *g'ness*

Ps. 118:24 the day...the LORD has made...rejoice and be *g* in it

Ps. 122:1 g when they said to me, Let us go into the house of the LORD

Prov. 15:20 A wise son makes a *g* father

Joel 2:21 Be *g* and rejoice, for the LORD will do great things

Matt. 5:12 be exceedingly *g*, for great is your reward

Mark 12:37 common people heard Him [Jesus] *g'ly*

Luke 15:32 fitting that we should make merry and be *g*

John 20:20 the disciples were *g* when they saw the Lord

Acts 13:48 when the Gentiles heard this, they were *g*

Rom. 10:15 beautiful are the feet of those who... bring *g* tidings

2 Cor. 12:15 I [Paul] will very *g'ly* spend and be spent

GLORIFY [IED, ING]

Ps. 86:12 g Your name forevermore

Isa. 49:3 are My [God's] servant...in whom I will be *g'ied*

Matt. 5:16 see your good works and *g* your Father

Matt. 9:8 multitudes...marveled and *g'ied* God

Luke 2:20 shepherds returned, *g'ing* and praising God

Luke 7:16 came a fear on all, and they [crowd] *g'ied* God

Luke 23:47 centurion saw what was done, he *g'ied* God

John 12:23 hour has come...Son of Man should be *g'ied*

John 14:13 that the Father may be *g'ied* in the Son

John 17:1 that Your Son may also *g* You

John 17:4 I [Jesus] have *g'ied* You [God] on the earth

Rom. 8:30 those whom He [Jesus] justified, He also *g'ied*

Rom. 15:6 with one mind and one mouth you may *g* God

1 Cor. 6:20 *g* God in your body

2 Thes. 1:12 name of our Lord...may be *g'ied* in you

1 Pet. 4:16 but let him *g* God in this matter

GLORY

1 Sam. 4:21 named the child Ichabod...The *g* has departed

1 Chron. 16:24 Declare His [God's] *g* among the nations

1 Chron. 29:11 Yours, O LORD, is the greatness... and the *g*

Ps. 24:7 and the King of *g* shall come in

Ps. 29:2 Give to the LORD the *g* due to His name

Ps. 57:5 let Your [God's] *g* be above all the earth

Ps. 72:19 let the whole earth be filled with His [God's] *g*

Ps. 84:11 The LORD will give grace and *g*

Ps. 96:3 Declare His [God's] *g* among the nations

Ps. 113:4 LORD is high above all nations, and His *g* above the heavens

Prov. 17:6 the *g* of children are their fathers

Isa. 6:3 The whole earth is full of His [God's] *g*

Isa. 66:18 all nations and tongues...shall come and see My [God's] *g*

Jer. 13:16 Give *g* to the LORD your God

Hag. 2:9 *g* of this latter house [temple] shall be greater

Matt. 6:13 kingdom and the power and the *g*

Matt. 6:29 Solomon in all his *g* was not arrayed

Mark 10:37 sit, one on Your [Jesus'] right hand... in Your *g*

Luke 21:27 the Son of Man coming in a cloud with power and great *g*

John 1:14 we saw His [Jesus'] *g*...full of grace

Rom. 5:3 we also *g* in tribulations

Rom. 8:18 sufferings...are not worthy to be compared with the *g*...revealed

1 Tim. 1:17 to the King eternal...be...*g* forever

Heb. 2:7 You [God] crowned Him [Jesus]with *g*...honor

1 Pet. 4:13 when His [Jesus'] *g* shall be revealed

1 Pet. 5:4 you shall receive a crown of *g* that does not fade away

Rev. 4:11 You are worthy, O Lord, to receive *g*

GLORY OF GOD. A phrase that refers to the Lord's splendor, honor, and moral perfection. His glory overwhelmed the shepherds on the night of Jesus' birth (Luke 2:9). God's glory continued to abide with Jesus throughout His earthly ministry. At His transfiguration, God's glory was so intense that His face and clothes glowed with God's presence (Luke 9:29–32). In the end-time, all believers will share in God's glory (Col. 3:4).

GLORY OF GOD

Ps. 19:1 The heavens declare the *g-o-G*

John 11:4 sickness is not to death, but for the *g-o-G*

Rom. 3:23 all have sinned...come short of the *g-o-G*

1 Cor. 10:31 whatever you do, do all for the *g-o-G*

Phil. 2:11 Jesus Christ is Lord, to the *g-o-G* the Father

GLORY OF THE LORD

Exod. 24:16 the *g-o-t-L* abided on Mount Sinai

Ps. 104:31 The *g-o-t-L* shall endure forever

Isa. 40:5 the *g-o-t-L* shall be revealed...all flesh shall see it

Isa. 60:1 the *g-o-t-L* has risen on you

Ezek. 11:23 the *g-o-t-L* went up from the midst of the city

Hab. 2:14 knowledge of the *g-o-t-L*, as the waters cover the sea

Luke 2:9 *g-o-t-L* shone around them [shepherds]

GNASHING OF TEETH

Matt. 8:12 There shall be weeping and *g-o-t*

Matt. 22:13 cast him into outer darkness. There shall be weeping and *g-o-t*

Luke 13:28 weeping and *g-o-t*, when you shall see...yourselves thrust out

GNOSTICISM. A heretical movement of NT times which taught that salvation came through superior knowledge. While Gnosticism is not mentioned by name in scripture, it was probably what the apostle Paul condemned when he declared that true knowledge comes from God and does not consist of idle speculation (Col. 2:8).

GODHEAD. A term referring to God that has essentially the same meaning as "godhood" (Rom. 1:20). Just as manhood is that quality that makes a man a man, so godhead or godhood refers to those qualities that make God, God. These characteristics are referred to as the attributes of God. He has always existed, and He always will. He is holy, morally pure, and totally separate from humankind in His essential character. He is all-powerful as well as all-knowing and all-seeing. He is just and merciful in His dealings with humankind. He is the sovereign ruler of the universe who demands unquestioning loyalty and fervent praise.

GODLINESS. Righteous behavior of people who are devoted to God. Godliness also leads to love for others (1 Tim. 4:7–8).

GODLY [INESS]

2 Cor. 7:10 g sorrow produces repentance
1 Tim. 4:8 g'iness is profitable for all things
1 Tim. 6:6 g'iness with contentment is great gain
2 Tim. 3:5 a form of *g'iness* but denying its power
2 Tim. 3:12 all who will live *g* in Christ Jesus shall suffer persecution
Titus 2:12 live soberly, righteously, and *g*

GOD-MAN. A word often used of Jesus because of His unique nature. He was the divine Son of God. But He came to earth as a man born in the flesh. He experienced all the things that are common to the human race (Heb. 4:15). He was both fully human and fully divine.

GOD WHO SEES. A name for God used by Hagar, Sarah's servant, when the angel of the Lord appeared to her in the wilderness ("You, God, See Me," Gen. 16:13). After she conceived a child by Abraham, Hagar was driven away by Sarah, Abraham's wife. The Lord assured Hagar that He was aware of her plight, and He would bless her and others through the life of her unborn child. After she gave birth to a son, she named him Ishmael, meaning "God hears."

GOG. The leader of a confederacy of armies pitted against Israel. The prophet Ezekiel declared that they would be destroyed (Ezek. 38:2–4). In the book of Revelation, Gog represents the forces of evil which oppose God and His people (Rev. 20:7–8). He is also mentioned in Ezek. 38:2–18; 39:1–11.

GOLAN. A city in the territory of Manasseh designated as one of the six cities of refuge. It is mentioned in Deut. 4:41–43 • Josh. 20:8–9; 21:27.

GOLD. A precious mineral used in Solomon's temple (1 Kings 7:48–50). Gold also symbolized the splendor of the heavenly city, or new Jerusalem (Rev. 21:16–18).

GOLDEN CALF. An idol built and worshipped by the Israelites in the wilderness as they waited for Moses to come down from Mount Sinai (Exod. 32:1–4). It was probably an image of Apis, a sacred bull worshipped by the Egyptians. In later years, King Jeroboam of Israel (the Northern Kingdom) set up pagan golden calves at Dan and Bethel (1 Kings 12:26–30).

GOLGOTHA. See *Calvary*

GOLIATH. A Philistine giant from the city of Gath who defied the entire army of King Saul. He may have been a descendant of Anak, ancestor of a race of giants (Num. 13:33). Goliath was killed by David with a single stone from his sling (1 Sam. 17:4–54). He is also mentioned in 1 Sam. 21:9; 22:10 • 2 Sam. 21:19 • 1 Chron. 20:5.

GOMER. A prostitute whom the prophet Hosea took as his wife (Hos. 1:2–3). She eventually left Hosea and was sold into slavery, but the prophet restored her as his wife at God's command (Hos. 3:1–5). The prophet's devotion to Gomer represented God's unconditional love for His wayward people.

GOMORRAH. One of the five "cities of the plain" destroyed with earthquake and fire because of its evil inhabitants (Gen. 19:23–29). The other four were Admah, Sodom, Zeboiim, and Zoar (Gen. 14:2–3). Gomorrah and Sodom were cited in later years as examples of God's judgment against evil, as in Deut. 29:23; 32:32 • Isa. 1:9–10; 13:19 • Jer. 23:14; 49:18; 50:40 • Amos 4:11 • Zeph. 2:9 • Matt. 10:15 • 2 Pet. 2:6.

GOODNESS. Moral excellence or righteousness; a fruit of the Spirit cited by the apostle Paul (Gal. 5:22). True goodness comes from God, who is holy, righteous, merciful, and loving (Rom. 15:14).

GOODNESS

Ps. 23:6 Surely *g* and mercy shall follow me

Ps. 33:5 The earth is full of the *g* of the LORD

Ps. 107:8 that men would praise the LORD for His *g*

Prov. 20:6 Most men will each proclaim his own *g*

Gal. 5:22 fruit of the Spirit is...gentleness, *g*, faith

GOOD SHEPHERD. A name that Jesus used for Himself that emphasizes His commitment to His followers. In an extended discourse in John 10, He declared several truths about Himself in relationship to His sheep. He knows each one personally and calls them by name (John 10:3); He guides them by showing the way (John 10:4); He offers shelter and safety (John 10:9); and unlike hired shepherds, He is willing to give His life for His sheep (John 10:12–15).

GOOD WORKS. Acts and deeds of believers done in the Lord's service and for His glory. Good works flow naturally from a life that has been transformed by God's grace. As the apostle Paul declared, "We are His workmanship, created in Christ Jesus for good works" (Eph. 2:10). Christ was an example in good works through His healing and teaching ministry (John 10:32). Believers show through their service to others that God is alive and active in their lives.

GOOD WORKS

Matt. 5:16 see your *g-w* and glorify your Father

Acts 9:36 Dorcas...was full of *g-w* and charitable deeds

Eph. 2:10 we are His [God's] workmanship... for *g-w*

2 Tim. 3:17 man of God may be...furnished for all *g-w*

GOPHER WOOD. The wood used for Noah's ark, probably cut from an evergreen tree known as cypress (Gen. 6:14).

GOSHEN. An Egyptian district north of the delta region of the Nile River where the Israelites settled and lived during their years in Egypt. It is mentioned in Gen. 45:10; 46:28–29, 34; 47:1–27; 50:8 • Exod. 8:22; 9:26.

GOSPEL. The joyous "good news" of salvation that God has provided through the atoning death of His Son (Mark 1:1, 15). The word is also used of the teachings of Jesus and the apostles (Col. 1:5).

GOSPEL

Matt. 24:14 g of the kingdom...preached in all the world

Mark 16:15 preach the *g* to every creature

Luke 4:18 He [God] has anointed Me [Jesus] to preach the *g* to the poor

Rom. 1:16 I [Paul] am not ashamed of the *g* of Christ

Rom. 10:15 beautiful are the feet of those who preach the *g* of peace

1 Cor. 9:14 those who preach the *g* should live by the *g*

Gal. 1:7 some who...would pervert the *g* of Christ

Gal. 4:13 I [Paul] preached the *g* to you at the first

Eph. 6:15 feet fitted with the preparation of the *g* of peace

Phil. 1:12 things...have occurred rather for the furtherance of the *g*

Phil. 1:27 conduct be as is proper for the *g* of Christ

2 Tim. 1:8 partaker of the afflictions of the *g*

2 Tim. 2:8 Jesus...was raised from the dead according to my [Paul's] *g*

1 Pet. 4:17 result for those who do not obey the *g* of God

GOSPELS, FOUR. The books of Matthew, Mark, Luke, and John at the beginning of the NT. They contain accounts of the life and ministry of Jesus. Each Gospel writer approached his subject from a little different perspective. Matthew showed how Jesus was the fulfillment of OT prophecy. Mark described Jesus as a person of action who identified with people through the human side of His divine-human nature. Luke focused on Jesus as the universal Savior for all mankind, including the Gentiles. John wrote his Gospel from a theological perspective, explaining the meaning behind Jesus' words and deeds. These gospels together render a fuller picture of Him than would be possible from a single narrative. See also *Synoptic Gospels*.

GOSSIP. Idle talk or baseless rumors. The apostle Paul referred to people who spread such tales as "tattlers and busybodies" (1 Tim. 5:13).

GOVERNOR. A ruler over a nation or a territory, and a name applied to Jesus in a prophecy about his birth (Matt. 2:6). Jesus was not a governor of a political territory. He was sent as a spiritual ruler to guide and direct His people in the ways of the Lord. His rule was by love and not by force. Earthly governors come and go, but His rulership lasts forever (Isa. 9:7).

GOZAN. A district or river of Mesopotamia to which the people of Israel (the Northern Kingdom) were deported after the fall of Samaria to the Assyrians (2 Kings 18:11).

GRACE. God's unmerited favor and love by which He grants salvation to believers through the exercise of their faith in Jesus Christ (Acts 15:11; Titus 2:11). The apostle Paul declared that this acceptance into the kingdom of God cannot be earned; it is a gift of His grace (Eph. 2:8).

GRACE

Gen. 6:8 Noah found *g* in the eyes of the LORD

Ps. 84:11 The LORD will give *g* and glory

John 1:14 saw His [Jesus'] glory...full of *g* and truth

John 1:17 g and truth came by Jesus Christ

Rom. 3:24 justified freely by His [God's] *g*

Rom. 5:20 sin abounded, *g* abounded much more

Rom. 6:1 Shall we continue in sin that *g* may abound

2 Cor. 8:9 you know the *g* of our Lord Jesus Christ

2 Cor. 9:8 God is able to make all *g* abound

2 Cor. 12:9 My [God's] *g* is sufficient for you

Eph. 1:7 forgiveness of sins, according to the riches of His [God's] *g*

Eph. 2:8 by *g* you are saved through faith

Eph. 4:7 g according to the measure of the gift of Christ

Col. 4:6 speech always be with *g*, seasoned with salt

1 Tim. 1:14 g of our Lord was exceedingly abundant

Titus 3:7 justified by His [God's] *g*, we should be made heirs...of eternal life

Heb. 4:16 let us come boldly to the throne of *g*

Jas. 4:6 God...gives *g* to the humble

2 Pet. 3:18 grow in *g* and in the knowledge of...Jesus

Rev. 22:21 g of our Lord Jesus Christ be with you all

GRACE OF GOD

Luke 2:40 the Child [Jesus] grew...*g-o-G* was on Him

1 Cor. 15:10 by the *g-o-G* I [Paul] am what I am

Eph. 3:7 I [Paul] was made a minister, according to the gift of the *g-o-G*

Titus 2:11 the *g-o-G* that brings salvation

Heb. 2:9 that He [Jesus], by the *g-o-G*, should taste death for every man

1 Pet. 4:10 as good stewards of the manifold *g-o-G*

GRACIOUS [LY]

Num. 6:25 The LORD...be *g* to you

Ps. 77:9 Has God forgotten to be *g*

Ps. 103:8 LORD is merciful and *g*, slow to anger

Ps. 119:29 g'ly grant me Your [God's] law

Isa. 33:2 O LORD, be *g* to us

Amos 5:15 God...will be *g* to the remnant of Joseph

Luke 4:22 bore Him [Jesus] witness and wondered at the *g* words

GRAPE. A luscious fruit, eaten fresh or dried, or made into wine. The soil of Israel was ideally suited for the cultivation of this crop. The scouts sent to investigate Canaan returned with a huge cluster of grapes (Num. 13:23).

GRASS. A plant eaten by livestock. Grass is also cited as symbol of insignificance and the brevity of life. The prophet Isaiah declared, "All flesh is grass, and all its loveliness is like the flower of the field" (Isa. 40:6).

GRASSHOPPER. A flying insect cited as a symbol of insignificance (Isa. 40:22). The scouts sent to investigate Canaan thought of themselves as grasshoppers in comparison to the inhabitants of the land (Num. 13:33).

GRAVE [S]

Job 17:1 The *g's* are ready for me [Job]

Job 21:13 in a moment [the wicked] go down to the *g*

Ps. 30:3 You [God] have brought up my soul from the *g*

Ps. 88:3 my life draws near to the *g*

Eccles. 9:10 no work...or wisdom in the *g*

Isa. 53:9 He [God's servant] made His *g* with the wicked

Matt. 27:52 *g's* were opened...bodies of the saints...arose

John 5:28 all who are in the *g's* shall hear His voice

John 11:17 he [Lazarus] had already been lying in the *g* four days

1 Cor. 15:55 O *g*, where is your victory

1 Tim. 3:8 the deacons must be *g*, not double-tongued

GRAVEN IMAGE. An image of a false god made from wood or stone and set up in a prominent place as an object of worship (Exod. 20:4). The prophets warned God's people against such false worship (Isa. 44:9–10; Hos. 11:2). The psalmist declared that confusion reigned in the minds of "those who serve engraved images, who boast in their idols" (Ps. 97:7).

GREAT [ER]

Gen. 1:16 two *g* lights: the *g'er* light to rule the day

Gen. 12:2 I [God] will make of you [Abraham] a *g* nation

1 Sam. 12:24 what *g* things He [God] has done for you

1 Chron. 11:9 So David grew *g'er* and *g'er*

1 Chron. 16:25 *g* is the Lord, and greatly to be praised

Job 32:9 *G* men are not always wise

Ps. 31:19 Oh how *g* is Your [God's] goodness

Ps. 47:2 the Lord...is a *g* King over all the earth

Ps. 48:1 *G* is the Lord, and greatly to be praised

Ps. 77:13 Who is so *g* a God as our God

Ps. 95:3 Lord is a *g* God and a *g* King above all gods

Ps. 119:156 *G* are Your tender mercies, O Lord

Ps. 126:3 The Lord has done *g* things for us

Prov. 22:1 good name is rather to be chosen than *g* riches

Isa. 9:2 people who walked in darkness have seen a *g* light

Jer. 10:6 You [God] are *g*, and Your name is *g* in might

Jer. 32:17 You [God]...made the...earth by Your *g* power

Dan. 7:17 These *g* beasts, which are four, are four kings

Joel 2:31 sun shall be turned into darkness... before the *g*...day of the Lord

Jon. 1:2 go to Nineveh, that *g* city, and cry against it

Hag. 2:9 The glory of this latter house [temple] shall be *g'er*

Matt. 4:16 people...in darkness saw *g* light

Matt. 5:12 Rejoice...for *g* is your reward in heaven

Matt. 11:11 least...is *g'er* than he [John the Baptist]

Matt. 19:22 he [rich young ruler] went away sorrowful, for he had *g* possessions

Matt. 20:26 *g* among you, let him be your minister

Mark 12:31 no other commandment *g'er* than these

Mark 13:26 Son of Man coming...with *g* power

Luke 1:32 He [Jesus] shall be *g*...the Son of the Highest

Luke 2:5 Mary, his [Joseph's] betrothed wife, being *g* with child

Luke 10:2 harvest is truly *g*, but the laborers are few

Luke 22:44 His [Jesus'] sweat was, as it were, *g* drops of blood

John 13:16 servant is not *g'er* than his master

John 15:13 No man has *g'er* love than this

Acts 16:26 a *g* earthquake...the foundations of the prison were shaken

Eph. 5:32 a *g* mystery...concerning Christ and the church

Heb. 2:3 escape, if we neglect so *g* a salvation

Heb. 4:14 Since then we have a *g* high priest [Jesus]

Heb. 12:1 surrounded by such a *g* cloud of witnesses

Jas. 3:5 Even so the tongue...boasts *g* things

1 John 4:4 *g'er* is He [God]...in you

3 John 4 no *g'er* joy than to hear...my [John's] children walk in truth

Rev. 6:17 the *g* day of His [God's] wrath has come

GREAT COMMISSION. Jesus' charge to His disciples to continue His work after He ascended to God the Father (Matt. 28:19–20). This involved stepping outside their familiar surroundings ("go"), witnessing to total strangers ("all nations"), bringing people into God's kingdom ("baptizing"), and nurturing them into effective followers of the Savior ("teaching them to observe all the things that I have commanded you"). This directive is a brief summary of the mission of the church. The book of Acts shows how the church accepted this mission and penetrated the known world with the good news of the gospel.

GREAT FLOOD. Gen. 7:1–8:22

GREAT HIGH PRIEST. A name of Jesus that emphasizes His superiority to the sacrificial system of the OT. He stands above all earthly priests—even the exalted high priest of Israel—because He laid down His own life as the perfect sacrifice for sin (Heb. 4:14).

GREAT SEA. See *Mediterranean Sea*

GREAT TRIBULATION. A period of suffering and distress in the end-time (Rev. 7:14). This event was first predicted by the prophet Daniel. Jesus declared that it would be a time of evil caused by false Christs and false prophets when natural disasters strike the earth (Mark 13:22).

GREECE. An ancient world power which reached its greatest strength in the time between the testaments, about 400 BC to AD 1. The apostle Paul ministered in this region (Acts 20:2–3). He also witnessed to philosophers in Athens, the cultural center of Greece (Acts 17:16–31). Greece is referred to in the OT as *Javan* (Isa. 66:19).

GREED. Excessive desire for material things; a sin distinctly prohibited by the Ten Commandments (Exod. 20:17). Jesus also warned against the insatiable desire for possessions by affirming that "a man's life does not consist in the abundance of the things that he possesses" (Luke 12:15).

GREEKS. Non-Jewish people who were heavily influenced by Greek culture and traditions. Shortly before Jesus' trial and crucifixion, a group of Greeks sought an audience with Him in Jerusalem (John 12:20–21).

GRIEF

Job 2:13 they saw that his [Job's] *g* was very great

Ps. 6:7 My eye is consumed because of *g*

Prov. 17:25 A foolish son is a *g* to his father

Isa. 53:3 a man of sorrows [God's servant] and acquainted with *g*

Jer. 45:3 LORD has added *g* to my [Jeremiah's] sorrow

GRIEVE [D]

Gen. 6:6 it *g'd* the LORD that He had made man... it *g'd* Him in His heart

Ps. 78:40 often they...*g* Him [God] in the desert

Ps. 95:10 Forty years long I [God] was *g'd* with this generation

Mark 3:5 He [Jesus]...*g'd* for the hardness of their hearts

Mark 10:22 he [rich young ruler]...went away *g'd*...he had great possessions

John 21:17 Peter was *g'd* because He [Jesus] said... Do you love Me

Eph. 4:30 do not *g* the Holy Spirit

GROW [S]

Ps. 104:14 He [God] causes the grass to *g* for the cattle

Matt. 6:28 Consider the lilies of the field, how they *g*

Eph. 2:21 the building...*g's* into a holy temple

1 Pet. 2:2 sincere milk of the word, that you may *g* by it

2 Pet. 3:18 *g* in grace and in...our Lord and Savior

GUARD

Ps. 91:11 He [God] shall...*g* you in all your ways

Phil. 4:7 peace of God...*g* your hearts...through Christ

2 Tim. 1:12 He is able to *g* what...I have committed

GUIDE [S]

Ps. 48:14 this God...will be our *g* even to death

Isa. 58:11 the LORD shall *g* you continually

Matt. 23:24 You blind *g's*, who strain out a gnat

John 16:13 He [Holy Spirit] will *g* you into all truth

Acts 8:31 How can I [Ethiopian eunuch], unless some man should *g* me

GUILT [Y]

Deut. 19:13 put away the *g* of innocent blood from Israel

Ezra 9:15 we are before You [God] in our *g*

Isa. 6:7 your [Isaiah's] *g* is taken away, and your sin purged

Isa. 40:2 her [Jerusalem's] *g* has been removed

Matt. 26:66 They...said, He [Jesus] is *g'y* of death

1 Cor. 11:27 eats...drinks...unworthily shall be *g'y* of the...blood of the Lord

Jas. 2:10 yet offends in one point, he is *g'y* of all

HABAKKUK. A prophet of Judah (the Southern Kingdom) who was probably a contemporary of Jeremiah and author of the book which bears his name (Hab. 1:1; 3:1).

HABAKKUK, BOOK OF. A short prophetic book of the OT which questions the coming suffering and humiliation of God's people at the hands of the pagan Babylonians (Hab. 1:1–4; 1:12–2:1). Since the prophet Habakkuk had the audacity to question the ways of God, his book bears some similarities to the book of Job. God's response to Habakkuk's questions made it clear that He was using the Babylonians as an instrument of judgment against His wayward people (Hab. 1:5–11; 2:2–20). After this assurance, Habakkuk closed his inquiry with a psalm of praise to God for His mercy and salvation (Hab. 3:3–19).

HABOR. A district of the Assyrian Empire where captives from Israel (the Northern Kingdom) were settled during the Exile (2 Kings 17:6).

HADAD. An Edomite ruler who opposed King Solomon (1 Kings 11:14–22).

HADADEZER. A king of Zobah in Syria who was defeated by David's army (2 Sam. 8:3–7; 10:6–19).

HADASSAH. See *Esther*

HADES. The Greek word behind the English word *hell* in Jesus' parable of the rich man and Lazarus. Jesus described the rich man as "in torment in hell" (Luke 16:23), the fate of all nonbelievers.

HAGAR. Sarah's Egyptian slave who became the mother of Ishmael by Abraham (Gen. 16:1–4). She was driven into the wilderness with her son because of conflict with Sarah, but God intervened to save them (Gen. 21:9–21). In the NT, the apostle Paul used Hagar's experience as an allegory of the freedom of the gospel. As a slave-wife, Hagar represented bondage to the OT law. But Sarah was a freeborn wife who eventually gave birth to Isaac, the child through whom God's covenant with Abraham was passed on. Thus, Sarah and Isaac symbolized the new covenant instituted by Jesus Christ and the freedom of the gospel (Gal. 4:22–31).

HAGGAI. A prophet after the Babylonian Exile, and author of the OT book which bears his name (Hag. 1:1). He was a contemporary of the prophet Zechariah, and is also mentioned in Ezra 5:1; 6:14.

HAGGAI, BOOK OF. A short prophetic book of the OT written to lift the spirits of Israelites who had returned to their homeland after the Exile. The people were encouraged to finish the task of rebuilding the temple because of its central role in their faith (Hag. 1:1–2:9). But the prophet also reminded them that the physical temple could not serve as a substitute for commitment to the Lord. Obeying His commands was more important than temple sacrifices (Hag. 2:10–19).

HAGGITH. A wife of David and mother of his son Adonijah (2 Sam. 3:4).

HAI. KJV: see *Ai*

HAIL. Frozen precipitation. Moses called down a plague in the form of falling ice on Pharaoh's Egypt (Exod. 9:23). Hail is also cited as a symbol of God's judgment in the end-time (Rev. 8:7).

HALAH. A district of the Assyrian Empire where captives from Israel (the Northern Kingdom) were settled during the Exile. It is mentioned in 2 Kings 17:6; 18:11 • 1 Chron. 5:26.

HALF-SHEKEL TAX. A tax which all adult males were required to pay for support of the temple (Exod. 30:13–14). Jesus miraculously produced a coin to pay this tax for Himself and Peter (Matt. 17:24–27).

HALF-TRIBE OF MANASSEH. The portion of the tribe of Manasseh that settled on the eastern side of the Jordan River (Num. 32:31–33). The rest of this tribe lived on the western side in the land previously known as Canaan. It is mentioned in Deut. 29:8 • Josh. 22:10 • 1 Chron. 6:61, 71.

HALLELUJAH. A Hebrew word rendered as "praise the LORD" in several psalms in the book of Psalms (Ps. 104:35). It was probably uttered as a formal call to worship in the temple.

HALLOW. To consecrate or set something apart for holy use. In His model prayer, Jesus prayed that the name of God the Father would be hallowed, or treated with honor and respect (Luke 11:2).

HAM. The youngest of Noah's three sons (Gen. 5:32; 6:10; 7:13; 9:18, 22 • 1 Chron. 1:4, 8). Ham had four sons of his own: Cush, Mizraim, Put, and Canaan. Mizraim's descendants settled in Egypt, while the tribes of Cush and Put apparently lived in other African territories. Canaan's descendants evolved into the people who inhabited Canaan before being displaced by the Israelites (Gen. 10:6–20).

HAMAN. The villain of the book of Esther. Haman was an influential aide to the king of Persia who plotted to destroy the Jewish people throughout the empire. But Queen Esther exposed the plan, and Haman was hanged for his crime (Esther 7:10).

HAMATH-ZOBAH. A city of Syria captured by King Solomon (2 Chron. 8:3).

HAMMER. A driving tool used by carpenters. It was cited by the prophet Jeremiah as a symbol of the power of God's Word (Jer. 23:29).

HAMMOTH-DOR. A city of refuge in the territory of Naphtali (Josh. 21:32).

HANAMEEL. KJV: see *Hanamel*

HANAMEL. A cousin of Jeremiah from whom the prophet bought a field, in spite of the Babylonian threat to overrun Jerusalem. This signified his hope for the future of God's people (Jer. 32:7–12).

HANAN. A Levite after the Exile who explained the law as Ezra read it to the people (Neh. 8:5–7).

HANANI. (1) A prophet who condemned King Asa of Judah (the Southern Kingdom) for paying protection money to the king of Syria (2 Chron. 16:7).

(2) A brother of Nehemiah who brought news about the suffering citizens of Jerusalem (Neh. 1:2–3). Hanani later became governor of Jerusalem (Neh. 7:2).

HANANIAH. A man who helped rebuild the walls of Jerusalem after the Exile (Neh. 3:8, 30).

HANDBREADTH. A measure of length based on the width of an adult hand, or about four inches (Exod. 25:25). The word also symbolized the brevity of life (Ps. 39:5).

HAND OF GOD. A symbolic expression for the Lord's unlimited power and His mighty acts on behalf of His people. It refers frequently to His work of creation, as in the declaration of the psalmist, "The heavens are the work of Your hands" (Ps. 102:25). See also *Anthropomorphism*.

HAND OF GOD

Job 2:10 receive good at the *h-o-G*, and...not receive evil

Eccles. 9:1 the wise, and their works are in the *h-o-G*

Acts 7:56 I [Stephen] see...the Son of Man standing at the right *h-o-G*

Col. 3:1 things that are above, where Christ sits on the right *h-o-G*

1 Pet. 3:22 who [Jesus]...is at the right *h-o-G*

HANDWRITING ON THE WALL. Dan. 5:5–28

HANGING. A form of capital punishment used for Haman, who died on the gallows he had prepared for Mordecai (Esther 7:9–10).

HANNAH. Mother of the prophet Samuel who prayed earnestly for his birth when she was unable to conceive (1 Sam. 1:9–11). After her prayer was answered, she devoted Samuel to God's service (1 Sam. 1:24–28) and offered a prayer of thanksgiving for God's blessings (1 Sam. 2:1–10).

HANUN. (1) An Ammonite king whom King David defeated because he insulted David's messengers of good will (2 Sam. 10:2–14). (2) A

man who helped rebuild the walls of Jerusalem after the Exile (Neh. 3:13).

HARA. A site in Assyria where some of the captives from Israel (the Northern Kingdom) were settled after the fall of their nation (1 Chron. 5:26).

HARAN. A city of Mesopotamia where Abraham lived with his father for a time before obeying God's command to move into Canaan (Gen. 12:4–5). Later, Jacob also lived in Haran, where he married the sisters Leah and Rachel (Gen. 28:10; 29:4–5). It is also mentioned in **Gen. 11:31–32; 27:43 • 2 Kings 19:12 • Isa. 37:12 • Ezek. 27:23 • Acts 7:2, 4.**

HARDNESS OF HEART. An attitude of stubborn opposition to the will and purpose of God (Heb. 3:15). The pharaoh of Egypt hardened his heart because he resisted God's command to release the Israelites from slavery (Exod. 7:14).

HARLOTRY. Sexual favors provided by a prostitute. The prophets of the OT often used the term symbolically to condemn worship of false gods among the Israelites (Isa. 1:21).

HAROD. A well near the mountains of Gilboa where Gideon and his army camped before going into battle against the Midianites (Judg. 7:1).

HARP. A stringed musical instrument often associated with worship in OT times (Ps. 147:7). The harp is an ancient instrument (Gen. 4:21). The biblical harp was similar to the modern harp with its many strings. The boy David calmed King Saul by playing a harp (1 Sam. 16:23).

HARVEST. The gathering of crops after the growing season. The Israelites celebrated the harvest with thanksgiving and a festival known as Pentecost (Exod. 23:16; Isa. 9:3). Jesus referred to a spiritual harvest that was needed to bring people into the kingdom of God (Matt. 9:37).

HASHABIAH. A Levite who helped rebuild the walls of Jerusalem after the Exile (Neh. 3:17).

HASSHUB. A man who helped rebuild the walls of Jerusalem after the Exile (Neh. 3:11).

HATE. Strong feelings of contempt or animosity toward another person. Jesus taught His followers not to hate their enemies but to repay their slights with love (Luke 6:27–31).

HATE [D, S]

Lev. 19:17 You shall not *h* your brother in your heart

Ps. 5:5 You [God] *h* all workers of iniquity

Ps. 41:7 All who *h* me whisper...against me

Ps. 69:4 Those who *h* me without reason...more than the hairs of my head

Ps. 119:163 I *h*...lying, but I love Your law

Prov. 8:13 The fear of the LORD is to *h* evil

Prov. 13:24 He who spares his rod *h's* his son

Prov. 14:20 poor is *h'd* even by his own neighbor

Eccles. 3:8 a time to love and a time to *h*

Isa. 1:14 My [God's] soul *h's* your New Moons

Amos 5:21 I [God] *h*, I despise, your feast days

Matt. 5:44 I [Jesus] say to you...do good to those who *h* you

Matt. 6:24 he will *h* the one and love the other

Mark 13:13 *h'd* by all men for My name's sake

Luke 14:26 and does not *h* his father, and mother

John 12:25 he who *h's* his life...shall keep it

John 15:18 it [the world] *h'd* Me before it *h'd* you

John 15:23 He who *h's* Me [Jesus] also *h's* My Father

1 John 2:9 says he is in the light and *h's* his brother is in darkness

1 John 4:20 man says I love God and *h's* his brother, he is a liar

HATTUSH. A man who helped rebuild the walls of Jerusalem after the Exile (Neh. 3:10).

HAZAEL. A leader who was anointed king of Syria by the prophet Elijah at God's command (1 Kings 19:15). He murdered the reigning monarch, Ben-hadad, in order to take the throne (2 Kings 8:7–15). King Jehoash of Judah (the Southern Kingdom) paid off Hazael with treasures from the temple to prevent an attack against Jerusalem (2 Kings 12:17–18). He is also

mentioned in 2 Kings 9:14–15; 10:32; 12:17–18; 13:3, 22–25 • 2 Chron. 22:5–6 • Amos 1:4.

HAZOR. A city about ten miles north of the Sea of Galilee destroyed by Joshua during the conquest of Canaan (Josh. 11:1–13). Later, the Canaanites rebuilt the city. But again they were defeated—this time by the judges Deborah and Barak (Judges 4:1–16). In later centuries, King Solomon built Hazor into a heavily fortified military outpost to protect his kingdom from attack from the north (1 Kings 9:15). Excavations at Hazor have uncovered the remains of a massive city gate from Solomon's time. It is also mentioned in Josh. 12:19; 19:36 • 1 Sam. 12:9 • 2 Kings 15:29.

HE. Fifth letter of the Hebrew alphabet, used as a heading over Ps. 119:33–40. In the Hebrew language, the first line of each of these eight verses begins with this letter.

HEAD [S]

Gen. 3:15 He [God's Servant] shall bruise your [the serpent's] *h*

1 Sam. 17:51 David...slew him [Goliath], and cut off his *h*

2 Sam. 14:25 to the crown of his *h* there was no blemish on him [Absalom]

1 Chron. 29:11 You [God] are exalted as *h* above all

Job 1:20 Job arose...and shaved his *h*

Ps. 3:3 You, O LORD, are...the lifter up of my *h*

Ps. 23:5 You [God] anoint my *h* with oil

Ps. 24:7 Lift up your *h's*, O you gates

Ps. 118:22 The stone...has become the *h* cornerstone

Ps. 140:7 You [God] have covered my *h* in the day of battle

Jer. 9:1 Oh that my [Jeremiah's] *h* were waters

Dan. 7:6 beast also had four *h's*

Matt. 10:30 hairs of your *h* are all numbered

Matt. 21:42 The stone that the builders rejected... has become the *h* of the corner

Matt. 27:39 those...reviled Him, wagging their *h's*

Mark 6:28 brought his [John the Baptist's] *h* on a platter

Mark 14:3 a woman... broke the box and poured it [ointment] on His *h*

Mark 15:17 wove a crown of thorns and put it around His *h*

Luke 9:58 Son of Man does not have anywhere to lay His *h*

John 19:30 He bowed His *h* and gave up His spirit

Acts 18:6 Your blood is on your own *h's*

Rom. 12:20 heap coals of fire on his [your enemy's] *h*

1 Cor. 11:3 the man is the *h* of the woman

1 Cor. 12:21 eye cannot say to the hand...or...the *h* to the feet, I have no need of you

Col. 1:18 He [Jesus] is the *h* of the body, the church

Rev. 1:14 His *h* and His hair were white like wool

Rev. 17:3 I [John] saw a woman...having seven *h's* and ten horns

HEAD OF ALL PRINCIPALITY AND POWER. A title of Jesus used by the apostle Paul that emphasizes His exalted status over all creation (Col. 2:9–10). This is a distinction that He shares with God the Father. Paul also referred to Jesus' supreme authority by calling Him the "head of the body, the church" (Col. 1:18) and the "head over all things" (Eph. 1:22).

HEAL [ING]

2 Chron. 7:14 I [God] will hear from heaven... forgive their sin...*h* their land

Ps. 41:4 LORD, be merciful to me. *H* my soul

Eccles. 3:3 a time to kill and a time to *h*

Jer. 3:22 I [God] will *h* your backslidings

Mal. 4:2 Sun of righteousness shall arise with *h'ing* in His wings

Matt. 4:23 Jesus went about...*h'ing* all manner of sickness

Matt. 10:8 *H* the sick, cleanse the lepers, raise the dead

Luke 4:18 He [God] has sent Me [Jesus] to *h* the brokenhearted

Luke 9:2 He [Jesus] sent them [disciples]...to *h* the sick

1 Cor. 12:30 Do all have the gifts of *h'ing*...Do all interpret

HEAR [ING, S]

Deut. 6:4 H, O Israel: The LORD our God is one

1 Sam. 3:9 Speak, LORD, for Your servant [Samuel] *h's*

Job 35:13 Surely God will not *h* vanity

Job 42:5 I [Job] have heard of You by the *h'ing* of the ear

Ps. 4:3 The LORD will *h* when I call to Him

Ps. 17:6 Incline Your ear...and *h* my speech

Ps. 55:17 and He shall *h* my voice

Ps. 65:2 O You who *h's* prayer

Ps. 69:33 For the LORD *h's* the poor

Ps. 86:1 Bow down Your ear, O LORD; *h* me

Ps. 115:6 They have ears, but they do not *h*

Prov. 4:1 H, you children, the instruction of a father

Prov. 13:1 wise son *h's* his father's instruction

Prov. 18:13 answers a matter before he *h's* it, it is folly

Prov. 19:20 H counsel and receive instruction

Eccles. 7:5 better to *h* the rebuke of the wise than...to *h* the song of fools

Isa. 1:2 H, O heavens, and give ear, O earth

Isa. 59:1 LORD's hand is not shortened...nor is His ear heavy, that it cannot *h*

Isa. 65:24 while they are still speaking, I [God] will *h*

Jer. 22:29 O earth...*h* the word of the LORD

Ezek. 37:4 dry bones, *h* the word of the LORD

Matt. 7:24 h's these sayings of Mine and does them

Matt. 13:9 Who has ears to *h*, let him *h*

Matt. 13:13 h'ing they do not *h*, nor do they understand

Matt. 13:16 blessed are...your ears, for they *h*

Matt. 17:5 This is My beloved Son...*H* Him

Mark 7:37 He [Jesus] makes...the deaf to *h*

Luke 2:46 found Him...sitting in the midst of the teachers...*h'ing* them

Luke 8:21 My [Jesus'] brothers are these who *h* the word of God and do it

Luke 11:28 Yes...blessed are those who *h* the word of God and keep it

John 3:8 wind blows...you *h* the sound of it

John 10:27 My sheep *h* My voice...I know them

Acts 2:8 how do we *h* every man in our own tongue

Acts 9:7 the men...stood speechless, *h'ing* a voice but seeing no man

Acts 17:21 Athenians...spent their time in nothing...but...*h'ing* something new

Acts 28:28 salvation...has been sent to the Gentiles...that they will *h* it

Rom. 10:14 how shall they *h* without a preacher

1 Cor. 12:17 whole body were an eye, where would the *h'ing* be

Jas. 1:19 let every man be swift to *h*, slow to speak

1 John 5:14 if we ask anything according to His will, he *h's* us

Rev. 2:7 *h* what the Spirit says to the churches

Rev. 3:20 any man *h's* My voice and opens the door

Rev. 22:17 let him who *h's* say, Come

HEARD

Gen. 3:8 they [Adam and Eve] *h* the voice of the LORD God

Exod. 3:7 I [God] have surely...*h* their [Israel's] cry

Job 42:5 I [Job] have *h* of You by the hearing of the ear

Ps. 28:6 the LORD...has *h* the voice of my supplications

Ps. 34:4 I sought the Lord, and He *h* me...delivered me

Ps. 40:1 He [God] inclined to me and *h* my cry

Ps. 116:1 I love the LORD because He has *h* my voice

Ps. 119:26 I have declared my ways, and You *h* me

Isa. 6:8 *h* the voice of the Lord, saying, Whom shall I send

Isa. 40:28 Have you not *h*...God...does not lose strength

Isa. 42:2 He [God's servant] shall not...make His voice *h* in the street

Jer. 31:15 A voice was *h* in Ramah...bitter weeping

Matt. 6:7 the heathen...think that they shall be *h* for their many words

Mark 12:37 the common people *h* Him gladly

Luke 2:20 shepherds returned...praising God for all...they had *h* and seen

Luke 12:3 spoken in darkness shall be *h* in the light

Acts 4:20 speak the things that we have seen and *h*

Acts 9:4 *h* a voice saying...Saul, Saul

Acts 11:1 apostles...*h* that the Gentiles had also received the word of God

Acts 17:32 *h* of the resurrection...some mocked

Rom. 10:14 how shall they believe in Him of whom they have not *h*

1 Cor. 2:9 Eye has not seen, nor ear *h*

Phil. 4:9 things that you have...*h* and seen...do

1 John 1:3 we declare to you what we have seen and *h*

1 John 3:11 the message that you *h* from the beginning

Rev. 1:10 I [John] was in the Spirit...and *h* behind me a great voice

HEART. The internal organ that pumps blood throughout the human body. To the Israelites, the heart was the center of existence. It was the source of a person's emotions (Gen. 42:28) and wisdom or skill (Exod. 35:35). God did not judge a person by his outer appearance but by his heart, or inner motives and secret thoughts (1 Sam. 16:7). Jesus declared that people act and speak from the heart, so they should treat it with caution and great respect (Matt. 15:18–19).

HEART [S]

Exod. 7:14 the LORD said...Pharaoh's *h* is hardened

Deut. 6:5 love the LORD your God with all your *h*

Deut. 10:16 Therefore circumcise the foreskin of your *h*

1 Sam. 12:24 serve Him in truth with all your *h*

Ps. 7:10 God...saves the upright in *h*

Ps. 13:5 my *h* shall rejoice in Your salvation

Ps. 19:8 statutes of the LORD are right, rejoicing the *h*

Ps. 19:14 Let the...meditation of my *h* be acceptable

Ps. 24:4 He who has clean hands and a pure *h*

Ps. 37:4 He [God] shall give you the desires of your *h*

Ps. 40:8 Your [God's] law is within my *h*

Ps. 51:10 Create in me a clean *h*, O God

Ps. 53:1 fool has said in his *h*, There is no God

Ps. 66:18 regard iniquity in my *h*, the Lord will not hear me

Ps. 90:12 teach us to number our days, that we may apply our *h's* to wisdom

Ps. 119:11 Your [God's] word have I hidden in my *h*

Ps. 139:23 Search me, O God, and know my *h*

Ps. 147:3 He [God] heals the broken in *h*

Prov. 2:2 apply your *h* to understanding

Prov. 3:5 Trust in the LORD with all your *h*

Prov. 15:13 merry *h* makes a cheerful face

Prov. 16:5 Everyone who is proud in *h* is an abomination

Prov. 17:22 A merry *h* does good like a medicine

Prov. 21:2 but the LORD ponders the *h's*

Eccles. 9:7 and drink your wine with a merry *h*

Jer. 17:9 The *h* is deceitful above all things

Jer. 29:13 you shall...find Me, when you search... with all your *h*

Jer. 31:33 I [God] will put My law within them and write it on their *h's*

Ezek. 11:19 I [God] will give them one *h*...a *h* of flesh

Ezek. 36:26 I [God] will also give you a new *h*...a new spirit inside you

Matt. 5:8 Blessed are the pure in *h*...they shall see God

Matt. 6:21 where your treasure is, there your *h* will be also

Matt. 11:29 I [Jesus] am meek and lowly in *h*

Matt. 15:8 honors Me with their lips, but their *h* is far from Me

Mark 12:30 love the Lord your God with all your *h*

Luke 2:19 Mary kept all these things... pondered...in her *h*

John 14:1 Do not let your *h's* be troubled

Acts 4:32 those who believed were of one *h*

Rom. 1:24 God also gave them up...through the lusts of their own *h's*

Rom. 5:5 love of God has been poured out in our *h's*

Rom. 10:9 believe in your *h* that God has raised Him from the dead

2 Cor. 3:2 You are our letter, written in our *h's*

2 Cor. 4:6 God...has shone in our *h's*

2 Cor. 9:7 so let every man give as he purposes in his *h*,

Phil. 4:7 peace of God...shall guard your *h's* and minds through Christ

2 Thes. 3:5 Lord direct your *h's* into the love of God

Heb. 3:12 lest there be in any of you an evil *h* of unbelief

Heb. 3:15 do not harden your *h's* as in the rebellion

Heb. 4:12 word of God is living...a discerner... of the *h*

Jas. 4:8 purify your *h's*, you double minded

HEAVEN. The place where believers will enjoy eternal life with God the Father and Jesus, His Son. Since words cannot describe the glories of heaven, biblical writers reverted to symbolic language to show what it is like. Heaven is a place where believers will enjoy everlasting fellowship with God. While the surroundings will be beautiful, the greatest joy will come from being in the Lord's presence (Rev. 21:3). Existence in heaven will take on the qualities or attributes of God's nature: holiness (Rev. 21:27), love (1 Cor. 13:13), joy (Rev. 19:6–7), and moral perfection (1 John 3:2). The Bible also declares that believers will not be idle in heaven. God's people will serve Him in this wonderful place (Rev. 22:3).

HEAVEN [S]

Gen. 1:1 God created the *h* and the earth

Deut. 1:10 you are this day like the stars of *h*

Deut. 4:39 that the LORD, He is God in *h* above

2 Sam. 22:14 The LORD thundered from *h*

1 Kings 8:23 no God like You in *h* above or on earth beneath

2 Kings 2:11 Elijah went up by a whirlwind into *h*

1 Chron. 16:26 gods of the people are idols... Lord made the *h's*

2 Chron. 7:14 I [God] will hear from *h*...forgive their sin

Job 28:24 For He...sees under the whole *h*

Ps. 8:3 consider Your *h's*, the work of Your fingers

Ps. 11:4 Lord's throne is in *h*

Ps. 19:1 The *h's* declare the glory of God

Ps. 57:5 Be exalted, O God, above the *h's*

Ps. 89:6 who in the *h* can be compared to the Lord

Ps. 103:11 For as the *h* is high above the earth, so great is His mercy

Ps. 108:5 Be exalted, O God, above the *h's*

Ps. 121:2 help comes from the Lord, who made *h* and earth

Ps. 136:26 thanks to the God of *h*...mercy endures forever

Ps. 139:8 If I ascend up into *h*, You are there

Eccles. 3:1 a time for every purpose under *h*

Isa. 55:9 *h's* are higher than the earth, so are My ways higher than your ways

Jer. 23:24 Do I not fill *h* and earth? says the Lord

Jer. 32:17 You [God] have made the *h's* and the earth by Your great power

Jer. 51:15 He [God]...has stretched out the *h's* by His understanding

Mal. 3:10 test Me...if I will not open for you the windows of *h*

Matt. 4:17 Jesus began to preach...Repent, for the kingdom of *h* is at hand

Matt. 5:3 poor in spirit, for theirs is the kingdom of *h*

Matt. 5:12 Rejoice...for great is your reward in *h*

Matt. 5:34 do not swear at all; neither by *h*

Matt. 5:48 even as your Father who is in *h* is perfect

Matt. 6:9 Father who is in *h*, hallowed be Your name

Matt. 6:20 lay up for yourselves treasures in *h*

Matt. 7:21 Not everyone...shall enter...kingdom of *h*

Matt. 16:19 give to you [Peter] the keys of the kingdom of *h*

Matt. 18:3 become as little children, you shall not enter into the kingdom of *h*

Matt. 19:14 of such [little children] is the kingdom of *h*

Matt. 26:64 you shall see the Son of Man... coming in the clouds of *h*

Matt. 28:18 All power has been given to Me in *h* and on earth

Mark 1:10 He [Jesus] saw the *h's* opened and the Spirit...descending on Him

Mark 13:32 But no man knows of that day...no, not even the angels who are in *h*

Luke 3:22 voice came from *h* that said...In You [Jesus] I [God] am well pleased

Luke 16:17 easier for *h* and earth to pass than for one tittle of the law to fail

Luke 24:51 He [Jesus] was parted...carried up into *h*

John 3:27 receive nothing except what is given him from *h*

John 6:38 I [Jesus] came down from *h*, not to do My own will, but...Him who sent me

Acts 1:11 Men of Galilee, why do you stand gazing up into *h*

Acts 4:12 no other name under *h* given among men in which we must be saved

2 Cor. 5:1 house not made with hands, eternal in the *h's*

Phil. 2:10 every knee should bow, of things in *h*

1 Thes. 4:16 Lord himself shall descend from *h* with a shout

Jas. 5:12 do not swear, neither by *h*...let your yes be yes

2 Pet. 3:13 we...look for new *h's* and a new earth

Rev. 5:3 no man in *h*...was able to open the book

Rev. 20:1 angel come down from *h*, having the key of the bottomless pit

Rev. 21:1 And I [John] saw a new *h* and a new earth

HEAVEN AND EARTH

Gen. 14:19 Blessed be Abram...possessor of *h-a-e*

Exod. 20:11 in six days the Lord made *h-a-e*

Ps. 69:34 Let the *h-a-e* praise Him, the seas

Ps. 124:8 Our help is in...the Lord, who made *h-a-e*

Matt. 5:18 until *h-a-e* pass, one jot...shall in no way pass

Matt. 24:35 H-a-e shall pass away, but My words shall not pass away

Acts 17:24 Lord of *h-a-e*, does not dwell in temples made with hands

HEAVENLY

Matt. 6:14 your *h* Father will also forgive you

Luke 2:13 with the angel there was a multitude of the *h* host

John 3:12 how shall you believe if I [Jesus] tell you of *h* things

Acts 26:19 I [Paul] was not disobedient to the *h* vision

HEAVENLY CITY. The future city built by God as a dwelling place for those who belong to Him (Heb. 11:10–16). It will be known as "new Jerusalem," the place where God dwells among the redeemed (Rev. 21:2–10).

HEAVE OFFERING. An offering consisting of the firstfruits of the harvest (Num. 15:19–21). It was presented to God before being given to the priests. It was also known as a peace offering (Josh. 22:23).

HEBREWS, EPISTLE TO. An epistle of the NT, author unknown, written to believers of Jewish background. These Christians were wavering in their commitment and were even considering returning to their former Jewish customs and beliefs. The book emphasized that Jesus Christ had replaced Judaism as God's perfect revelation and that they should not stumble in their loyalty to Him. The author declared that Jesus is superior to angels (Heb. 1:1–2:18) and Moses (Heb. 3:1–16) and that He is the great high priest who offered Himself—rather than a sacrificial animal—as an atoning sacrifice for sin (Heb. 4–10). The book closes with an appeal for believers to remember the great heroes of the faith (Heb. 11) and to strand firm in their Christian beliefs (Heb. 12–13).

HEBRON. An ancient town in Canaan where Abraham bought a plot of ground with a cave as a burial place for himself and his family (Gen.

23:13–17). Known as the cave of Machpelah, it was the final resting place for his wife Sarah, his son Isaac and Isaac's wife Rebekah, and Abraham's grandson Jacob and Jacob's wife Leah (Gen. 49:29–31). After the conquest of Canaan, Hebron was designated one of the six cities of refuge (Josh. 20:7). Caleb received Hebron as part of his share of the land of Canaan (Josh 14:13–14). David made this his capital city for the first seven and one-half years of his reign. Here all the tribal leaders met and proclaimed David king of all Israel (2 Sam. 5:1–3). In later years, King Rehoboam of Judah turned Hebron into one of his defense cities (2 Chron. 11:5–10). Also called Kiriath-arba (Gen. 23:2 • Josh. 14:15).

HEIR [S]

Mark 12:7 This is the *h*. Come, let us kill him

Gal. 3:29 Abraham's descendants and *h's* according to the promise

Gal. 4:7 if a son, then an *h* of God through Christ

Titus 3:7 justified by His grace...be made *h's*

Heb. 1:2 whom He [God] has appointed *h* [Jesus] of all things

Heb. 11:9 Isaac and Jacob, the *h's* with him [Abraham] of the same promise

HEIR OF ALL THINGS. A title of Jesus that shows the supreme authority granted to Him by God the Father (Heb. 1:1–2). This heirship involved participating with God in the creation of the physical world (John 1:3). He sets the terms by which people are held accountable for their sins. Then He Himself, through His atoning death, became the means by which believers are made righteous in God's sight (1 Cor. 1:30).

HELAM. A place where David won a decisive victory over the Syrians (2 Sam. 10:16–19).

HELEB. One of David's "mighty men," an elite group of warriors known for their bravery in battle (2 Sam. 23:8, 29).

HELEZ. One of David's "mighty men," an elite group of warriors known for their bravery in battle (2 Sam. 23:8, 26).

HELL. The place of eternal torment reserved for unbelievers. Some people think of hell in a figurative sense—as separation from God in a state of meaningless existence. But Jesus warned that the body (a physical reality) as well as the soul (a spiritual entity) can be cast into hell (Matt. 5:29). This seems to argue that hell is more than a spiritual metaphor. The Bible portrays hell as a "lake of fire" (Rev. 19:20), "everlasting destruction" (2 Thes. 1:9), and the "second death" (Rev. 20:14). Whether defined literally or figuratively, hell should be avoided at all costs. Those who accept Jesus Christ as Savior and Lord don't have to worry about their eternal destiny.

HELL [FIRE]

Job 26:6 H is naked before Him [God]...destruction has no covering

Ps. 18:5 sorrows of *h* surrounded me

Ps. 139:8 make my bed in *h*, behold, You [God] are there

Prov. 27:20 H and destruction are never full

Jon. 2:2 Out of the belly of *h* I [Jonah] cried

Matt. 5:22 says, You fool, shall be in danger of *h'fire*

Matt. 10:28 fear Him [God]...able to destroy... soul and body in *h*

Matt. 16:18 gates of *h* shall not prevail against it [the church]

Luke 10:15 Capernaum...shall be thrust down to *h*

Rev. 1:18 I [Jesus] have the keys of *h* and of death

Rev. 20:14 death and *h* were cast into the lake of fire

HELMET. An armored head covering worn by soldiers. Paul spoke figuratively of the "helmet of salvation" which protects believers in the battle against Satan (Eph. 6:17).

HELPER. A title growing out of the apostle Paul's description of the Holy Spirit's role as comforter and intercessor on behalf of believers (Rom. 8:26).

HEM. A decorative fringe on an item of clothing which served as a visible reminder of God's commandments (Exod. 28:33–34).

HENNA. A plant that produced a red dye, used as a cosmetic by women (Song of Sol. 4:13).

HENOCH. See *Enoch*, No. 2

HEPHER. One of David's "mighty men," an elite group of warriors known for their bravery in battle (1 Chron. 11:11, 36).

HEPHZIBAH. A symbolic name used by the prophet Isaiah to describe Jerusalem's restoration to God's favor (Isa. 62:4). The word means "My delight is in her."

HERALD. A messenger who delivered a formal proclamation or announced good news (Dan. 3:4)

HERESY. False teachings that deny essential doctrines of the Christian faith. Jesus warned against false teachers who would mislead His followers. He characterized them as people who dressed in "sheep's clothing" but were actually "ravenous wolves" (Matt. 7:15). They would fool believers with their subtle approach, lead them into error, and plant seeds of discord.

HERMES. A Christian in Rome to whom the apostle Paul sent greetings (Rom. 16:14). *Hermas*: KJV.

HERMOGENES. A believer from the province of Asia who deserted Paul at Ephesus (2 Tim. 1:15).

HERMON, MOUNT. The highest and most prominent mountain on Israel's northern border, visible on a clear day from more than one hundred miles away. Biblical writers wrote eloquently of Hermon's beauty and the heavy dew it produced to water the nation's crops (Ps. 133:3). This may have been the mountain on which Jesus was transfigured before His disciples (Mark 9:2–8). But another claimant to this honor is Mount Tabor near the Sea of Galilee (Jer. 46:18). Mount Hermon is also mentioned in **Josh 11:3**, 17; 12:1, 5 • Pss 89:12; 133:3. *Senir*: Ezek. 27:5. *Senir, Sirion*: Deut. 3:9.

HEROD. The name or title of several Roman rulers in Israel during NT times:

(1) Herod the Great, who was in power when Jesus was born. He is mentioned in **Matt. 2:1–22** • Luke 1:5.

(2) Herod Archelaus, son and successor of Herod the Great and ruler in Judea soon after the birth of Jesus (Matt. 2:22).

(3) Herod Antipas, who had John the Baptist executed. He is mentioned in **Matt. 14:1–12** • Mark 6:14–22; 8:15 • Luke 3:1, 19; 9:7, 9; 13:31; 23:7–12 • Acts 4:27; 13:1.

(4) Herod Philip, ruler in extreme northern Galilee when Jesus began His public ministry (Luke 3:1, 19–20).

(5) Herod Agrippa I, who executed James, leader of the Jerusalem church (Acts 12:1–19).

(6) Herod Agrippa II, before whom Paul made his defense at Caesarea (Acts 25:13–26:32).

HERODIANS. An influential Jewish group that supported Roman rule and Greek customs in NT times. While they were natural enemies of the Pharisees, they joined forces with this group against Jesus on two occasions (Mark 3:6; 12:13–14). The Herodians are also mentioned in Matt. 22:16.

HERODIAS. The wife of Herod Antipas who requested the execution of John the Baptist. She was angry at John because he had condemned her immorality and unlawful marriage (**Matt. 14:1–11** • Mark 6:17).

HERODION. A believer at Rome greeted and commended by Paul, who called him "my countryman" (Rom. 16:11).

HEZEKIAH. A godly king of Judah (the Southern Kingdom) who reversed the trend toward idolatry that infected his country. He destroyed pagan images and altars, reopened the temple in Jerusalem that his father had closed, and renewed the celebration of religious festivals. Hezekiah even destroyed the bronze serpent that Moses had erected in the wilderness centuries earlier because it had become an object of worship. In response to a threat from Assyria, he strengthened Jerusalem's defenses and built a tunnel to tap a water source outside the city wall. Hezekiah suffered a serious illness toward the end of his reign. But the Lord answered his prayer for healing and granted him fifteen additional years of life (Isa. 38:1–5). He is also mentioned in 2 Kings 18:1–8; 19:1–37; 20:1–21 • **2 Chron. 29:1–36; 31:1–21** • Isa. 38:9–22 • Matt. 1:9–10.

HEZRO. One of David's "mighty men," an elite group of warriors noted for their bravery in battle (2 Sam. 23:8, 35).

HIDDAI. One of David's "mighty men," an elite group of warriors known for their bravery in battle (2 Sam. 23:8, 30).

HID [DEN]
Gen. 3:8 Adam and his wife *h* themselves from... the LORD
Exod. 3:6 Moses *h* his face, for he was afraid to look at God
Ps. 38:9 my groaning is not *h'den* from You
Ps. 51:6 in the *h'den* part You shall make me to know wisdom
Ps. 119:11 Your [God's] word have I *h'den* in my heart
Isa. 53:3 we *h*...our faces from Him [God's servant]
Matt. 5:14 A city that is set on a hill cannot be *h'den*
Matt. 11:25 You [God] have *h'den* these things from the wise
Luke 13:21 It [kingdom of God] is like leaven, which a woman took and *h*
1 Cor. 2:7 the *h'den* wisdom that God ordained before the world
Heb. 11:23 Moses...was *h'den* three months by his parents

HIDDEKEL. See *Tigris River*

HIDE [ING, S]
Job 14:13 You [God] would *h* me in the grave
Ps. 10:1 Why do You *h* Yourself in times of trouble
Ps. 13:1 How long will You [God] *h* Your face from me
Ps. 17:8 *H* me under the shadow of Your wings
Ps. 51:9 *H* Your face from my sins
Ps. 69:17 Do not *h* Your face from Your servant

Ps. 119:114 You [God] are my **h'ing** place and my shield

Prov. 19:24 A slothful man **h's** his hand in his bosom

Isa. 45:15 You are a God who **h's** Yourself

Jer. 23:24 Can anyone **h** himself in secret places that I [God] shall not see

Rev. 6:16 **h** us from the face of Him who sits on the throne

HIERAPOLIS. A city in Asia Minor mentioned by Paul (Col. 4:13).

HIGH [ER, EST, LY]

Gen. 14:18 Melchizedek...was the priest of the Most **H** God

Deut. 28:1 God will set you on **h** above all nations

Ps. 7:17 I will...sing praise to the name of the Lord Most **H**

Ps. 47:2 the Lord Most **H** is awesome...a great King

Ps. 61:2 lead me to the rock that is **h'er** than I

Ps. 69:29 let Your salvation, O God, set me up on **h**

Ps. 91:1 He who dwells in the secret place of the Most **H**

Ps. 93:4 Lord on **h** is mightier than...many waters

Ps. 97:9 You, Lord, are **h** above all the earth

Ps. 99:2 The Lord...is **h** above all the people

Ps. 103:11 as the heaven is **h** above the earth, so great is His mercy

Ps. 113:4 The Lord is **h** above all nations

Isa. 6:1 I [Isaiah] also saw the Lord...**h** and lifted up

Isa. 33:5 The Lord is exalted, for He dwells on **h**

Isa. 52:13 My [God's] Servant shall be exalted... be very **h**

Isa. 55:9 heavens are **h'er** than the earth, so are My ways **h'er** than your ways

Matt. 4:8 the devil took Him up on an exceedingly **h** mountain

Luke 1:28 Rejoice, you [Mary] who are **h'ly** favored

Luke 1:32 He [Jesus]...shall be called the Son of the **H'est**

Luke 2:14 Glory to God in the **h'est**, and on earth peace

Luke 24:49 remain...until...endued with power from on **h**

Eph. 4:8 ascended on **h**, He led captivity captive

Eph. 6:12 wrestle...against spiritual wickedness in **h** places

Phil. 2:9 God also has **h'ly** exalted Him

Phil. 3:14 the prize of the **h** calling of God in Christ Jesus

HIGH PLACE. A hilltop or elevated site where false gods were worshipped (2 Kings 12:3). These shrines were condemned by the Lord (Ps. 78:58).

HIGH PRIEST. The chief priest or head of the priesthood, an office that traced its lineage back to Aaron, Israel's first high priest (Exod. 28:1–3). Aaron was set apart from his fellow priests by his special clothes, his unique duties, and the responsibilities he inherited as the spiritual leader of the nation of Israel. The most important duty of the high priest was to conduct the ritual known as the Day of Atonement. On this sacred day, He alone entered the most sacred part of the temple, made atonement for his own sins, and then sprinkled blood on the altar to offer atonement for the sins of all the people (Lev. 16:11–15). The author of Hebrews described Jesus as the great high priest who laid down His own life as a living sacrifice on behalf of sinners (Heb. 4:14–16).

HIGH PRIEST [S]

Matt. 26:65 **h-p** tore his clothes, saying, He [Jesus] has spoken blasphemy

John 18:19 **h-p** then asked Jesus about His... doctrine

Heb. 3:1 Apostle and **H-P** of our profession, Christ Jesus

Heb. 4:15 we do not have a **h-p** who cannot be concerned with...our weaknesses

Heb. 6:20 even Jesus, made a **h-p** forever

Heb. 7:27 who [Jesus] does not need, as those **h-p's**, to offer up daily sacrifices

HIGH PRIESTLY PRAYER. A long prayer of Jesus in which he prayed for Himself, His disciples, and all future believers (John 17).

He reviewed His life and ministry, rejoiced in His experiences with His followers, and looked forward to the unity and love that God and the redeemed will share in eternity.

HILKIAH. A high priest during the reign of King Josiah of Judah (the Southern Kingdom) who found the lost Book of the Law (2 Kings 22:8). It became a catalyst for religious reforms that swept the nation (2 Kings 23:1–15). Hilkiah is also mentioned in 2 Chron. 34:9–22.

HIN. A unit of measure, equal to about one and one-half gallons (Exod. 29:40).

HINNOM VALLEY. A deep ravine near Jerusalem where child sacrifice was practiced by Ahaz, a wicked king of Judah (the Southern Kingdom) (2 Chron. 28:1–33). Because of this despicable practice, the valley became an image of hell, the place of eternal punishment for the wicked. The Greek word for Hinnom is *Gehenna*, the word Jesus used when He declared that the scribes and Pharisees would not escape "the damnation of hell" (Matt. 23:33). Hinnom Valley is also mentioned in Josh. 15:8; 18:16 • 2 Kings 23:10 • 2 Chron. 33:6 • Neh. 11:30 • Jer. 7:31–32; **19:2–6**.

HIRAM. A king of Tyre who assisted David and Solomon with their building projects in Jerusalem by sending materials and skilled workmen (1 Kings 5:7–11). Hiram also provided ships for Solomon's trading agreements with other nations (1 Kings 10:22). He is also mentioned in **2 Sam. 5:11** • 1 Kings 9:11–27; 10:11 • 1 Chron. 14:1. *Huram*: 2 Chron. 2:3–12.

HITTITES. An ancient people who occupied Canaan before the Israelites conquered the land (Exod. 3:17). Remnants of this race lived on in Israel for a time, since Uriah, a warrior in David's army, was a Hittite (2 Sam. 11:6). They are also mentioned in Gen. 23:10–20 • 1 Kings 15:5.

HIVITES. Descendants of Canaan (Gen. 10:15–17) who lived in Canaan before and after the Israelites occupied their territory (Deut. 7:1).

HOBAB. See *Jethro*

HODIAH. A Levite after the Exile who explained the law as Ezra read it to the people (Neh. 8:7).

HOLD [ING]

Exod. 20:7 Lord will not *h* him guiltless who takes His name in vain

Job 6:24 Teach me, and I will *h* my tongue

Ps. 83:1 Do not keep silent, O God. Do not *h* Your peace

Ps. 139:10 Your [God's] right hand shall *h* me

Jer. 2:13 they have...carved out...cisterns that can *h* no water

Luke 16:13 he will *h* to the one and despise the other

Phil. 2:16 *h'ing* forth the word of life...I [Paul] may rejoice

1 Thes. 5:21 Test all things. *H* fast what is good

1 Tim. 3:9 *h'ing* the mystery of the faith

Heb. 4:14 we have a great high priest...Jesus... let us *h* fast our profession

Heb. 10:23 *h* fast the profession of our faith

Rev. 3:11 *H* fast what you have...that no man takes your crown

HOLINESS. An attribute of God that refers to His moral excellence. The Hebrew word behind holiness means "separation" or "setting apart." Thus, God's holiness indicates that He is totally unlike humans or any other part of His creation. As the very essence of goodness, He is incapable of any wrongdoing. He is on a different plane than anything that is impure, sinful, or morally imperfect. Jesus was the perfect example of holiness. As the "Holy One of God" (Mark 1:24), He emphasized God's demand for righteous behavior among His followers (Matt. 5:20).

HOLY [INESS]

Exod. 3:5 place on which you [Moses] stand is *h* ground

Exod. 15:11 Who is like You [God], glorious in *h'iness*

Exod. 20:8 Remember the Sabbath day, to keep it *h*

Lev. 11:44 you shall be *h*, for I [God] am *h*

Lev. 20:7 be *h*, for I am the Lord your God

Ps. 11:4 The Lord is in His *h* temple

Ps. 24:3 who shall stand in His [God's] *h* place

Ps. 29:2 Worship the LORD in the beauty of *h'iness*

Ps. 51:11 do not take Your *H* Spirit from me

Ps. 89:18 and the *H* One of Israel is our King

Ps. 96:9 worship the LORD in the beauty of *h'iness*

Ps. 99:5 worship at His footstool, for He is *h*

Ps. 103:1 all that is within me; bless His *h* name

Ps. 145:21 let all flesh bless His *h* name forever

Isa. 6:3 one [seraphim] cried...*H, h, h*, is the LORD of hosts

Hab. 2:20 the LORD is in His *h* temple...earth keep silence

Rom. 12:1 bodies as a living sacrifice, *h*, acceptable to God

Rom. 16:16 Greet one another with a *h* kiss

1 Cor. 3:17 temple of God is *h*; you are that temple

Eph. 5:27 it [the church] should be *h* and without blemish

1 Thes. 4:7 God called us...to *h'iness*

1 Tim. 2:8 men everywhere to pray, lifting up *h* hands

2 Tim. 3:15 from childhood you [Timothy] have known the *h* scriptures

1 Pet. 1:16 it is written, Be *h*, for I [God] am *h*

1 Pet. 2:5 you also...are built up as...a *h* priesthood

1 Pet. 2:9 you are a chosen generation...a *h* nation

Rev. 21:2 I, John, saw the *h* city, new Jerusalem

HOLY GHOST. KJV: see *Holy Spirit*

HOLY PLACE. The sacred innermost sanctuary of the temple and tabernacle which only the high priest could enter (Exod. 28:29). Even he could go in only one day a year—on the Day of Atonement—when he made a special sacrifice for himself and the sins of the people. See also *Atonement, Day of.*

HOLY SPIRIT. The third person of the trinity. The OT contains glimpses and promises of the Holy Spirit (Gen. 1:2, 6:3; Zech. 4:6), but a full picture of His character emerges in the NT. The Spirit rested on Jesus from His birth (Luke 1:35). He promised to send the Holy Spirit as a comforter and advocate in His absence (John 14:16). The full display of the Spirit's power occurred at Pentecost after Jesus' resurrection and ascension (Acts 2:1–21). The Spirit's role is to glorify the Son (John 16:14), empower believers (John 14:12–27), and convict unbelievers of sin and coming judgment (John 16:8–11). Several different names are applied to the Holy Spirit, including Comforter (John 14:16), Spirit of adoption (Rom. 8:15), and Spirit of truth (John 16:13).

HOLY SPIRIT

Matt. 1:18 she [Mary] was found with child from the *H-S*

Matt. 3:11 He [Jesus] shall baptize you with the *H-S*

Matt. 12:31 blasphemy against the *H-S* shall not be forgiven

Matt. 28:19 baptizing them in the name of the...*H-S*

Luke 1:35 The *H-S* shall come on you [Mary]

Luke 1:67 his father, Zechariah, was filled with the *H-S*

Luke 2:25 the *H-S* was on him [Simeon]

Luke 3:22 *H-S* descended on Him...like a dove

John 14:26 the *H-S*...shall teach you all things

Acts 1:8 receive power after the *H-S* has come on you

Acts 6:3 choose from among you seven men... full of the *H-S*

Acts 13:2 *H-S* said, Separate Barnabas and Saul for me

Rom. 14:17 kingdom of God is...joy in the *H-S*

1 Cor. 12:3 no man can say that Jesus is the Lord but by the *H-S*

2 Pet. 1:21 holy men of God spoke...by the *H-S*

HOLY WEEK. The week of the Christian year between Palm Sunday and Easter Sunday when believers commemorate the death and resurrection of Jesus. This week is also called Passion Week, referring to His suffering.

HOMER. A unit of dry measure, equal to about six bushels (Ezek. 45:11).

HONEST [LY, Y]

Rom. 13:13 Let us walk *h'ly*...not in rioting

Phil. 4:8 things are *h*, whatever things are just

1 Tim. 2:2 lead a quiet...life in all godliness and *h'y*

HONESTY. Uprightness and fairness in dealing with others; a characteristic of believers (2 Cor. 8:21).

HONOR [ED, S]

Exod. 20:12 *H* your father and your mother

1 Chron. 16:27 Glory and *h* are in His presence

Ps. 8:5 You [God]...have crowned him [man] with glory and *h*

Prov. 3:9 *H* the LORD with your possessions... and...firstfruits

Prov. 22:4 By...the fear of the Lord are riches and *h*

Matt. 13:57 Jesus said...prophet is not without *h* except in his own country

Mark 7:6 people *h's* Me [God] with their lips... heart is far from Me

John 5:23 He who does not *h* the Son does not *h* the Father

John 12:26 If any man serves Me [Jesus], my Father will *h* him

Rom. 12:10 kindly affectionate to one another... preferring one another in *h*

1 Cor. 12:26 if one part is *h'ed*, all the parts rejoice

Rev. 4:11 You are worthy, O Lord, to receive glory and *h*

HOPE. To look forward to the fulfillment of God's promises with confident expectation. The apostle Paul called Jesus the "hope of glory" (Col. 1:27). To know Christ as Savior and Lord is to be assured of life everlasting and eternal fellowship with Him.

HOPE [D]

Job 7:6 My [Job's] days...are spent without *h*

Ps. 38:15 in You, O LORD, I *h*. You will hear

Ps. 71:5 You are my *h*, O Lord GOD

Ps. 119:114 You [God] are... my shield; I *h* in Your word

Ps. 146:5 Happy is he...whose *h* is in the LORD

Jer. 17:7 Blessed is the man...whose *h* is the LORD

Lam. 3:24 LORD is my portion...Therefore I will *h* in Him

Rom. 12:12 rejoicing in *h*, patient in tribulation

Rom. 15:13 the God of *h* fill you with all joy

1 Cor. 13:13 now faith, *h*, love remain, these three

Col. 1:27 which is Christ in you, the *h* of glory

1 Thes. 4:13 lest you sorrow as others who have no *h*

Heb. 11:1 faith is the substance of things *h'd* for

1 Pet. 3:15 every man who asks you a reason for the *h* that is in you

HOPHNI. A son of Eli the high priest whose lust and greed made him unworthy of the priesthood (1 Sam. 2:22–25, 34). Along with his brother Phinehas, he was killed by the Philistines (1 Sam. 4:10–11).

HOR, MOUNT. (1) A mountain in the territory of the Edomites where Aaron died and was buried. It is mentioned in **Num. 20:22–29; 21:4; 33:37–41 • Deut. 32:50.**

(2) A mountain in northern Israel (Num. 34:7–8).

HORN OF SALVATION. A title for both God and Jesus which signifies their saving power. In OT times, the horn of an animal was a symbol of strength. To lift one's horn in arrogance like an ox was to show power (Ps. 75:4–5). Thus, David declared that God had been a horn of salvation by delivering him from his enemies (Ps. 18:2). This imagery from the OT was picked up and applied to Jesus in a spiritual sense. Zechariah, father of John the Baptist, declared that God through His Son had "raised up a horn of salvation for us in the house of His servant David" (Luke 1:69).

HOSANNA. A triumphal shout by the crowds as Jesus entered Jerusalem a few days before His crucifixion (Matt. 21:9). The expression means "save us now." Just a few days later, the crowds were shouting "crucify Him" (Luke 23:21) because He refused to become the military deliverer they wanted Him to be.

HOSEA. A prophet who delivered God's message of judgment to Israel (the Northern Kingdom) during its final chaotic years before it fell to the Assyrians. His name, meaning "deliverance," sent a message about the nation's precarious situation as it teetered on the brink of destruction. Hosea recorded his prophecies in the OT book that bears his name. He is also mentioned in Rom. 9:25.

HOSEA, BOOK OF. A prophetic book of the OT which compares the spiritual idolatry of God's people with the physical adultery of the prophet's wife, Gomer (Hos. 1:2; 2:2–5). Just as Hosea redeemed her from slavery and restored her as his mate, God promised that He would eventually restore His people as His own after punishment by their enemies. This book is a treatise on the nature of God, emphasizing His demand for righteousness, the punishment He would inflict, and His steadfast love.

HOSHEA. The last king of Israel (the Northern Kingdom) who served as a puppet ruler under King Shalmaneser of Assyria. After Hoshea quit paying protection money to Assyria, he was taken to Assyria as a captive. He is mentioned in 2 **Kings** 15:30; 17:1–6; 18:1–10.

(2) Another name for Joshua (Num. 13:16). See *Joshua*.

HOSPITALITY. The gracious provision of food and lodging to strangers. Kindness toward travelers and strangers was encouraged in both OT and NT times (Lev. 19:33–34; 1 Pet. 4:9).

HOSPITALITY

1 Tim. 3:2 A bishop then must be...given to *h*, able to teach

1 Pet. 4:9 Show *h* to one another without complaining

HOUR [S]

Matt. 10:19 that same *h* it shall be given you what you shall speak

Matt. 24:42 you do not know what *h* your Lord will come

Matt. 26:40 could you [Peter] not watch with Me one *h*

Mark 13:32 no man knows of that day and that *h*

Luke 12:40 Son of Man is coming at an *h* when you do not think

John 11:9 Are there not twelve *h's* in the day

John 12:23 *h* has come...Son of Man should be glorified

HOUSE [S]

Gen. 12:1 Get out of your [Abraham's] country... from your father's *h*

Gen. 28:17 he [Jacob]...said...This is none other than the *h* of God

Gen. 39:4 he [Potiphar] made him [Joseph] overseer over his *h*

Exod. 12:7 blood...strike it...on the upper door-post of the *h's*

Exod. 20:2 I am...God, who brought you...out of the *h* of bondage

Exod. 20:17 You shall not covet your neighbor's *h*

Deut. 6:7 talk of them when you sit in your *h*

Deut. 25:14 not have in your *h* differing measures

Josh. 24:15 But as for me [Joshua] and my *h*, we will serve the LORD

2 Sam. 12:10 sword shall never depart from your [David's] *h*

1 Kings 12:19 Israel has rebelled against the *h* of David

1 Chron. 17:1 I [David] dwell in a *h* of cedar

1 Chron. 22:6 Then he [David]...charged him [Solomon] to build a *h* for the LORD

2 Chron. 2:1 Solomon determined to build a *h* for the...LORD

2 Chron. 7:16 sanctified this *h*, that My [God's] name may be there forever

2 Chron. 21:7 LORD would not destroy the *h* of David

Job 17:13 If I [Job] wait, the grave is my *h*

Job 22:18 Yet He filled their *h's* with good things

Ps. 66:13 I will go into Your *h* with...offerings

Ps. 69:9 the zeal of Your *h* has eaten me up

Ps. 84:4 Blessed are those who dwell in Your *h*

Ps. 84:10 rather be a doorkeeper in the *h* of my God

Ps. 127:1 Unless the LORD builds the *h*

Prov. 12:7 the *h* of the righteous shall stand

Prov. 15:25 The LORD will destroy the *h* of the proud

Isa. 2:5 *h* of Jacob...let us walk in the light of the LORD

Jer. 18:3 Then I [Jeremiah] went down to the potter's *h*

Jer. 29:28 build *h's* and dwell in them

Ezek. 43:5 the glory of the LORD filled the *h*

Amos 3:15 great *h's* shall come to an end, says the Lord

Hag. 2:9 glory of this latter *h*...greater than of the former

Mal. 3:10 that there may be food in My *h*

Matt. 2:11 when they [wise men] had come into the *h*, they saw the young Child

Matt. 7:24 a wise man who built his *h* on a rock

Matt. 10:6 go rather to the lost sheep of the *h* of Israel

Matt. 13:57 Jesus said...A prophet is not without honor except...in his own *h*

Matt. 15:24 I [Jesus] was sent only to the lost sheep of the *h* of Israel

Matt. 23:14 you [scribes and Pharisees] devour widows' *h's*

Mark 3:25 if a *h* is divided against itself

Mark 11:17 My [God's] *h* shall be called...the *h* of prayer

Luke 14:23 compel them to come in, that my *h* may be filled

Luke 19:9 This day salvation has come to this *h*

John 14:2 In My Father's *h* are many mansions

Acts 16:31 and you shall be saved, and your *h*

Acts 28:30 Paul dwelled two...years in his own hired *h*

1 Cor. 16:19 Aquila and Priscilla greet you...with the church...in their *h*

2 Cor. 5:1 a building from God, a *h* not made with hands

1 Tim. 3:5 if a man does not know how to rule his own *h*

1 Tim. 3:12 deacons...ruling...their own *h's* well

1 Tim. 5:8 for those of his own *h*, he has denied the faith

1 Pet. 2:5 you also...are built up as a spiritual *h*

1 Pet. 4:17 judgment must begin at the *h* of God

HOUSEHOLD

Matt. 10:36 a man's enemies shall be those of his own *h*

Gal. 6:10 do good...to those who are of the *h* of faith

Eph. 2:19 fellow citizens with the saints and of the *h* of God

HOUSE OF THE LORD

Deut. 23:18 You shall not bring...the price of a dog into the *h-o-t-L*

1 Sam. 3:15 Samuel...opened the doors of the *h-o-t-L*

1 Kings 6:1 he [Solomon] began to build the *h-o-t-L*

1 Kings 8:11 glory of the LORD had filled the *h-o-t-L*

1 Kings 8:63 the king [Solomon] and all the children of Israel dedicated the *h-o-t-L*

1 Kings 14:26 And he [Shishak] took away the treasures of the *h-o-t-L*

2 Kings 22:8 I [Hilkiah] have found the Book of the Law in the *h-o-t-L*

2 Kings 25:9 he [Nebuzaradan] burned the *h-o-t-L*

2 Chron. 36:7 Nebuchadnezzar...carried off... vessels of the *h-o-t-L*

Ps. 23:6 I will dwell in the *h-o-t-L* forever

Ps. 27:4 I may dwell in the *h-o-t-L* all the days

Ps. 122:1 glad when they said... Let us go into the *h-o-t-L*

HULDAH. A female prophet who foretold the collapse of Jerusalem when consulted by King Josiah of Judah (the Southern Kingdom) (2 Kings 22:14–20). Other female prophets mentioned in the Bible are Miriam (Exod. 15:20), Deborah (Judg. 4:4), Noadiah (Neh. 6:14), and the unnamed wife of the prophet Isaiah (Isa. 8:3).

HUMAN SACRIFICE. The practice of sacrificing children to a pagan god (2 Kings 3:26–27). This was common among pagan worshippers, but it was specifically prohibited by the Lord (Deut. 18:10). King Manasseh of Judah (the Southern Kingdom) sacrificed his own son to the pagan god Molech (2 Kings 21:1, 6).

HUMBLE [D, S]

Ps. 10:12 O God, lift up Your hand; do not forget the *h*

Ps. 35:13 clothing was sackcloth. I *h'd* my soul

Isa. 5:15 and the mighty man shall be *h'd*

Ezek. 21:26 Exalt him who is low, and *h* him who is high

Matt. 18:4 whoever *h's* himself like this little child...is greatest

Luke 18:14 he who *h's* himself shall be exalted

Phil. 2:8 He [Jesus] *h'd* Himself...became obedient to death

Jas. 4:10 H yourselves...and He shall lift you up

HUMILITY. A meek and unselfish spirit; a recognition that all good gifts come from the Lord in spite of human unworthiness (Rom. 12:3; 1 Pet. 5:5). The prophet Micah declared that God prefers a spirit of humility in worshippers more than material sacrifices they bring to Him (Mic. 6:8). The best example of humility is the life of Jesus (Matt. 11:29). He urged believers to practice this Christian grace in all their relationships (Matt. 23:12).

HUMILITY

Acts 20:19 serving the Lord with all *h* of mind

1 Pet. 5:5 be clothed with *h*, for God resists the proud

HUR. A man who helped Aaron hold up the arms of Moses to give the Israelites victory over the Amalekites (**Exod. 17:8–13**; 24:14).

HURAI. One of David's "mighty men," an elite group of warriors known for their bravery in battle (1 Chron. 11:11, 32).

HURAM. See *Hiram*

HUSBAND [S]

Gen. 3:16 your [Eve's] desire shall be for your *h*

Prov. 12:4 A virtuous woman is a crown to her *h*

Isa. 54:5 For Your Maker is your *h*; the LORD of hosts is His name

Matt. 1:19 Joseph, her [Mary's] *h*, being a just man

Mark 10:12 if a woman divorces her *h*...she commits adultery

1 Cor. 7:3 the *h* render due benevolence to the wife

1 Cor. 7:14 unbelieving *h* is sanctified by the wife

Eph. 5:25 H's, love your wives...as Christ...loved the church

Col. 3:19 H's, love your wives and do not be bitter against them

1 Tim. 3:2 A bishop...must be blameless, the *h* of one wife

1 Tim. 3:12 Let the deacons be the *h's* of one wife

1 Pet. 3:1 wives, be in submission to your own *h's*

Rev. 21:2 John, saw...new Jerusalem...prepared as a bride adorned for her *h*

HUSHAI. A loyal advisor of King David (2 Sam. 15:32–37) who became a spy for him in Jerusalem during Absalom's revolt (2 Sam. 17:1–16). Hushai is also mentioned in 2 Sam. 16:16–19 • 1 Kings 4:16 • 1 Chron. 27:33.

HYMENAEUS. A believer condemned by the apostle Paul for his false teachings (1 Tim. 1:19–20; 2 Tim. 2:16–17).

HYPOCRISY

Isa. 32:6 the vile person will speak wickedness, and his heart will work iniquity, to practice *h*

Matt. 23:28 inside you [Pharisees] are full of *h*

Mark 12:15 He [Jesus], knowing their [Pharisees'] *h*, said...Bring Me a penny

Luke 12:1 Beware of the leaven of the Pharisees, which is *h*

HYPOCRITE [S]

Job 20:5 and the joy of the *h* but for a moment

Matt. 6:2 do not sound a trumpet...as the *h's* do

Matt. 6:16 do not be like the *h's*, with a sad face

Matt. 7:5 You *h*. First cast the beam out of your own eye

Matt. 23:13 Woe to you, scribes and Pharisees, *h's*

HYPOCRITES. People who pretend to be something they are not. Jesus cautioned people against pointing out the faults of others while ignoring their own (Matt. 7:1–5). He condemned the Pharisees for their hypocritical behavior. They made a big show of doing good deeds to gain the praise of others. They pretended to be godly and righteous but were actually blind and insensitive to God's truth (Matt. 23:16). The opposite of hypocrisy is sincerity and purity of motive.

HYSSOP. A plant used in purification ceremonies (Lev. 14:6). It was also symbolic of spiritual cleansing (Ps. 51:7).

I AM GOD
Ps. 46:10 Be still and know that *I-a-G*
Isa. 45:22 be saved, all the ends of the earth. For *I-a-G*
Hos. 11:9 I-a-G, and not man

"I AM" STATEMENTS OF JESUS IN JOHN'S GOSPEL
1. Bread of life (John 6:35)
2. Light of the world (John 8:12)
3. Door of the sheep (John 10:7)
4. Good shepherd (John 10:11, 14)
5. Resurrection and the life (John 11:25)
6. Way, the truth, and the life (John 14:6)
7. True vine (John 15:1)

I AM THAT I AM. A name by which God identified Himself to Moses at the burning bush (Exod. 3:14). It is a form of the verb "to be" in the Hebrew language. The name expresses God's self-existence and the unchangeableness of His character, implying that He transcends the past, the present, and the future—He has always been, He is, and He will always be. The Lord went on to declare that He would be a source of strength for Moses as he led the Israelites out of slavery in Egypt. In the NT, Jesus used the phrase "I Am" to show that He was of the same divine essence as God the Father (John 8:58).

IBHAR. A son of David, born at Jerusalem after David became king of all Israel (1 Chron. 3:5–6).

IBZAN. A minor judge of Israel who ruled for seven years. He had thirty sons and thirty daughters (Judg. 12:8–10).

ICHABOD. A grandson of Eli who was given this symbolic name, meaning "inglorious," when his mother learned that Eli and Phinehas were dead (1 Sam. 4:19–22).

ICONIUM. Capital of the province of Lycaonia in Asia Minor; a city visited by Paul and Barnabas on the first missionary journey. It is mentioned in **Acts 13:51; 14:1, 19–22; 16:1–7 •** 2 Tim. 3:11.

IDLE [NESS]
Prov. 19:15 and an *i* soul shall suffer hunger
Prov. 31:27 She...does not eat the bread of *i'ness*
Eccles. 10:18 and through *i'ness* of the hands the house leaks
Matt. 12:36 every *i* word that men speak, they shall give account
Luke 24:11 words seemed to them [the disciples] as *i* tales

IDOL [S]
Lev. 19:4 Do not turn to *i's*
1 Chron. 16:26 all the gods of the people are *i's*
Ps. 135:15 The *i's* of the nations are silver and gold
Ezek. 14:6 Repent and turn...from your *i's*
Acts 7:41 they [Israelites] made a calf...offered a sacrifice to the *i*
1 Cor. 8:4 we know that an *i* is nothing in the world
2 Cor. 6:16 what agreement does the temple of God have with *i's*
1 John 5:21 Little children, keep yourselves from *i's*

IDOLATRY. Worship of false gods, a practice prohibited by the first two of the Ten Commandments (Exod. 20:3–4). Prominent idols mentioned in the Bible are the golden calves of Aaron (Exod. 32:4) and King Rehoboam of Israel (the Northern Kingdom) (2 Chron. 11:15), the fertility god Baal (Judg. 2:13), and the grain god of the Philistines known as Dagon (Judg. 16:23). The prophet Isaiah is noted for his descriptions of the folly of idolatry (Isa. 44:9–20). A more common form of idolatry in modern times is placing a higher value on things than devotion to the Lord.

IDUMEA. See *Edom*, No. 2

IGAL. (1) One of the twelve spies or scouts sent by Moses to investigate the land of Canaan. Igal represented the tribe of Issachar (Num. 13:1–2, 7).

(2) One of David's "mighty men," an elite group of warriors known for their bravery in battle (2 Sam. 23:8, 36).

IGNORANCE. Lack of knowledge or understanding. In a spiritual sense, ignorance is callous rejection of the truth—refusing to acknowledge God and the evidence about Himself that He has planted in nature and revealed through His word. The apostle Paul described people in this condition as darkened by their deliberate blindness (Eph. 4:18).

IGNORANCE

Num. 15:27 And if any soul sins through *i*

Acts 17:30 And God winked at the times of this *i*

1 Pet. 2:15 you may put to silence the *i* of foolish men

IGNORANT [LY]

Acts 4:13 they [the Sanhedrin]...perceived that they [Peter and John] were...*i* men

Acts 17:23 whom you worship *i'ly*, I [Paul] declare Him to you

1 Cor. 12:1 concerning spiritual gifts...I [Paul] would not have you *i*

1 Thes. 4:13 do not want you to be *i*, brothers, concerning those who are asleep

2 Pet. 3:8 do not be *i* of this...one day with the Lord is as a thousand years

ILAI. One of David's "mighty men," an elite group of warriors noted for their bravery in battle (1 Chron. 11:11, 29).

ILLYRICUM. A district on the eastern coast of the Adriatic Sea. The apostle Paul mentioned Illyricum as the furthermost point to which he had traveled (Rom. 15:19).

IMAGE [S]

Gen. 31:19 Rachel had stolen the *i's* that were her father's

Exod. 20:4 You shall not make for yourself any graven *i*

Deut. 7:25 You shall burn the engraved *i's* of their gods with fire

2 Kings 17:10 they set up for themselves *i's*

Ps. 97:7 Confounded are all those who serve engraved *i's*

Ps. 106:19 They made a calf...and worshipped the cast *i*

Isa. 21:9 He [God] has broken all the carved *i's* of her [Babylon's] gods

Isa. 42:8 I [God] will not give My glory...or My praise to carved *i's*

Mic. 1:7 all its carved *i's* shall be beaten to pieces

Mark 12:16 And He [Jesus] said...Whose *i* and inscription is this

Rom. 1:23 changed the glory of...God into an *i* made similar to corruptible man

Rom. 8:29 to be conformed to the *i* of His Son

1 Cor. 15:49 we shall also bear the *i* of the heavenly

2 Cor. 3:18 we all...are being changed into the same *i* from glory to glory

Col. 1:15 He [Jesus] is the *i* of the invisible God

IMAGE OF GOD

Gen. 1:27 God created man...in the *i-o-G*

Gen. 9:6 for in the *i-o-G* He made man

2 Cor. 4:4 the glorious gospel of Christ, who is the *i-o-G*

IMAGE OF GOD IN MAN. A phrase that probably refers to humankind's unique ability to have a relationship with God (Gen. 1:27). People have the ability to reason, think, plan, and make decisions—elements of personhood that make humans a unique species. Humans best express the divine image in which they were created when they are in right relation with the Creator and serve as responsible stewards of His physical world (Gen. 1:28).

IMAGINATION [S]

Gen. 6:5 God saw...every *i* of the thoughts of his [man's] heart was...evil

Luke 1:51 He [God]...has scattered the proud in the *i* of their hearts

Rom. 1:21 they did not glorify Him as God...but became vain in their *i's*

IMMANUEL. A name, meaning "God with us," given to Jesus even before He was born by an angel who appeared to Joseph (Matt. 1:23). Centuries before Jesus was born, the prophet Isaiah had also used this title for the coming Messiah (Isa. 7:14). The promise of God's presence with His people is a familiar biblical theme. For example, Moses was assured that the Lord would be with him when God called him to return to Egypt to free His people from slavery (Exod. 3:12). King David declared that God's presence would follow him wherever he went (Ps. 139:9–10). *Emmanuel:* KJV.

IMMORTALITY

1 Cor. 15:53 For...this mortal must put on *i*

2 Tim. 1:10 Jesus...has brought life and *i* to light through the gospel

IMMUTABILITY. A term that refers to God's unchangeable nature (Mal. 3:6). He does not "mutate" from one type of being into another. He is constant and dependable—the same yesterday, today, and forever (James 1:17). As God's Son, Jesus Christ assures believers that God's mercy is unwavering (Heb. 13:8). He is an anchor of hope for all who place their faith in Him (Heb. 6:17–19).

IMPOSSIBLE

Matt. 17:20 and nothing shall be *i* for you

Mark 10:27 With men it is *i*, but not with God

Luke 18:27 things...*i* with men are possible with God

Heb. 11:6 without faith it is *i* to please Him [God]

IMPUTATION. The process of transferring something to another person. Through His death on the cross, Jesus paid the penalty for sin. When believers accept Jesus as Lord and Savior, He "imputes" or transfers His righteousness to them, thus bridging the gap that separates people from God. The apostle Paul explained it like this: God "made him who knew no sin to be sin for us, that we might be made the righteousness of God in Him" (2 Cor. 5:21).

IMPUTE [D, ING]

Ps. 32:2 Blessed is the man to whom the LORD does not *i* iniquity

Rom. 4:8 Blessed is the man to whom the Lord will not *i* sin

Rom. 4:22 it was *i'd* to him [Abraham] for righteousness

2 Cor. 5:19 God was in Christ...not *i'ing* their trespasses to them

Jas. 2:23 it was *i'd* to him [Abraham] for righteousness

INCARNATION. A word for the birth and existence of Christ in human form. It comes from a Latin word meaning "taking flesh." When Jesus was born into the world, He was described as "the Word...made flesh" (John 1:14). While He was the divine Son of God, He was also fully human. The Gospel of Mark attests to the reality of the incarnation. Like any normal person, Jesus grew tired (Mark 4:38) and expressed a wide range of human emotions, including amazement (Mark 6:6), disappointment (Mark 8:12), and sorrow (Mark 14:34).

INCENSE. A sweet-smelling substance that was burned at the altar by a priest (Exod. 30:7–8). This symbolized their connection to God. They thought of their prayers as a pleasant aroma offered to the Lord (Lev. 1:9). The gift of frankincense presented to the baby Jesus by the wise men was probably a form of incense (Matt. 2:11).

IN CHRIST

Rom. 8:1 no condemnation for those who are *i-C*

Rom. 12:5 we, being many, are one body *i-C*

1 Cor. 4:10 fools for Christ's sake, but you are wise *i-C*

1 Cor. 15:19 if we have hope *i-C* only in this life

1 Cor. 15:22 as in Adam all die, even so *i-C* all shall be made alive

2 Cor. 2:14 to God, who...causes us to triumph *i-C*

INCLINE

2 Cor. 5:17 if any man is *i-C*, he is a new creature
2 Cor. 5:19 namely, that God was *i-C*, reconciling the world to Himself
Eph. 1:10 He [God] might gather...in one all things *i-C*
Phil. 2:1 If there is therefore any consolation *i-C*
Phil. 2:5 Let this mind be in you, which was also *i-C*
Phil. 3:14 the prize of the high calling of God *i-C*
1 Thes. 4:16 the dead *i-C* shall rise first

INCLINE [D, S]

Ps. 17:6 i Your [God's] ear to me and hear my speech
Ps. 40:1 I waited patiently...and He [God] *i'd* to me and heard my cry
Prov. 2:18 her [the strange woman's] house *i's* to death
Prov. 4:20 My son...*i* your ear to my sayings

INCORRUPTIBLE

1 Cor. 9:25 those do it to obtain a corruptible crown...we, an *i*
1 Cor. 15:52 dead shall be raised *i*, and we shall be changed

INCREASE [D, ING, S]

Gen. 7:18 the waters...were *i'd* greatly on the earth
Exod. 1:7 the children of Israel...*i'd* abundantly
Lev. 26:4 and the land shall yield its *i*
Job 1:10 his [Job's] possessions have *i'd* in the land
Ps. 3:1 how those are *i'd* who trouble me [David]
Ps. 67:6 Then the earth shall yield her *i*
Ps. 73:12 these are the ungodly...they *i* in riches
Ps. 105:24 And He [God] *i'd* His people greatly
Prov. 1:5 A wise man will hear and will *i* learning
Prov. 24:5 a man of knowledge *i's* strength
Eccles. 1:18 he who *i's* knowledge *i's* sorrow
Eccles. 5:10 not...satisfied with silver, nor he who loves abundance with *i*
Isa. 9:7 no end to the *i* of His [Messiah's] government and peace
Luke 2:52 Jesus *i'd* in wisdom and stature
Luke 17:5 apostles said to the Lord, *I* our faith
John 3:30 He [Jesus] must *i*, but I [John the Baptist] must decrease

Acts 6:7 word of God *i'd*; and the...disciples multiplied
1 Cor. 3:7 neither he who plants...is anything, but God who gives the *i*
Col. 1:10 being fruitful in every good work and *i'ing* in the knowledge of God
1 Thes. 3:12 the Lord make you *i* and abound in love

INDIA. A region that served as the eastern limit of the Persian Empire (Esther 1:1; 8:9).

INFIRMITY [IES]. See also *Sickness, Weakness*

Matt. 8:17 He [Messiah] Himself took our *i'ies*...bore our sicknesses
Rom. 8:26 the Spirit also helps our *i'ies*
Gal. 4:13 through *i* of the flesh I [Paul] preached the gospel

INHERIT [ED]

Josh. 14:1 countries that the children of Israel *i'ed*
Ps. 37:9 those who wait on the LORD...shall *i* the earth
Ps. 37:29 The righteous shall *i* the land
Prov. 11:29 He who troubles his own house shall *i* the wind
Matt. 5:5 Blessed are the meek, for they shall *i* the earth
Matt. 25:34 Come...*i* the kingdom prepared for you
Luke 18:18 Master, what shall I [rich young ruler] do to *i* eternal life
1 Cor. 6:10 nor extortioners shall *i* the kingdom of God
Gal. 5:21 those who do such things shall not *i* the kingdom of God
Rev. 21:7 He who overcomes shall *i* all things

INHERITANCE. A gift of property or rights passed from one generation to another. In spiritual terms, believers have an inheritance that comes directly from the Lord (Eph. 1:13–14). As God's one and only Son, Jesus Christ became the heir of His heavenly Father. He shares this inheritance with all believers—salvation through His atoning death as well as the joy of eternal fellowship with Him.

INHERITANCE

Num. 18:23 among the children of Israel they [Levites] have no *i*

Num. 27:8 a man dies and has no son...cause his *i* to pass to his daughter

Deut. 32:9 Jacob is the lot of His [God's] *i*

Josh. 11:23 Joshua gave it [Canaan] for an *i* to Israel

Ps. 2:8 I [God] shall give you the nations as your *i*

Ps. 33:12 Blessed is...the people whom He [God] has chosen for His own *i*

Ps. 94:14 nor will He [God] forsake His *i*

Prov. 20:21 An *i* may be gotten hastily at the beginning

Mark 12:7 kill him [the heir], and the *i* shall be ours

Eph. 1:11 In Him [Jesus] we also have obtained an *i*

Eph. 5:5 no...idolater, has any *i* in the kingdom of Christ

Heb. 11:8 Abraham...called...into a place...he would later receive as an *i*

INIQUITY [IES]. See also *Guilt*

Exod. 20:5 jealous God, visiting the *i* of the fathers on the children

Num. 14:18 The LORD is longsuffering... forgiving *i*

Job 13:23 How many are my *i'ies* and sins

Job 15:16 filthy is man, who drinks *i* like water

Job 34:22 There is no darkness...where the workers of *i* may hide

Ps. 5:5 You [God] hate all workers of *i*

Ps. 25:11 O LORD, pardon my *i*, for it is great

Ps. 31:10 My strength fails because of my *i*

Ps. 51:2 Wash me thoroughly from my *i*

Ps. 51:5 I was formed in *i*, and in sin my mother conceived me

Ps. 51:9 blot out all my *i'ies*

Ps. 85:2 You [God] have forgiven the *i* of Your people

Ps. 103:10 He [God] has not dealt with us...or rewarded us according to our *i'ies*

Prov. 10:29 destruction shall come to the workers of *i*

Isa. 53:5 He [God's servant] was bruised for our *i'ies*

Isa. 53:6 LORD...laid the *i* of us all on Him [God's servant]

Isa. 59:2 your *i'ies* have separated you from your God

Isa. 64:6 our *i'ies*, like the wind, have taken us away

Jer. 14:20 We acknowledge, O LORD...the *i* of our fathers

Jer. 31:30 everyone shall die for his own *i*

Lam. 5:7 we have borne their [our fathers'] *i'ies*

Matt. 23:28 you [Pharisees] are full of hypocrisy and *i*

Luke 13:27 Depart from Me, all you workers of *i*

Rom. 4:7 Blessed are those whose *i'ies* are forgiven

1 Cor. 13:6 [love] does not rejoice in *i*, but... in the truth

2 Tim. 2:19 everyone who names the name of Christ depart from *i*

Heb. 10:17 I [God] will remember their sins and *i'ies* no more

Jas. 3:6 the tongue is a fire, a world of *i*

INN.
A lodging place for travelers. The inns of Bible times were generally crude shelters that offered little comfort. Jesus was born in the adjoining stable of such an inn (Luke 2:7).

INSPIRATION.
God's influence or direction in human affairs. His inspiration is the source of human understanding (Job 32:8). He inspired the human authors of the Bible to record His commands as a trustworthy guide for His people (2 Tim. 3:16). Divine inspiration has occurred in many forms, including His audible voice (Rev. 1:10–11), dreams (Gen. 20:3), and visions (Ezek. 11:24–25).

INSTRUCT [ED]

Job 40:2 Shall he who contends with the Almighty *i* Him

Ps. 32:8 I [God] will *i* you and teach you...guide you

Prov. 21:11 when the wise is *i'ed*, he receives knowledge

Luke 1:4 certainty of those things in which you have been *i'ed*

1 Cor. 2:16 who has known the mind of the Lord, that he may *i* Him

Phil. 4:12 I [Paul] am *i'ed* both to be full and to be hungry

INTEGRITY

Job 2:9 Do you [Job] still retain your *i*

Job 31:6 Let me [Job] be weighed...that God may know my *i*

Ps. 25:21 Let *i* and uprightness preserve me

Prov. 19:1 Better is the poor who walks in his *i* than...perverse

Prov. 20:7 The just man walks in his *i*

INTERCESSION. Prayer offered on behalf of others. To pray like this is to intercede—or stand between—them and the Lord on their behalf. Abraham prayed for God to spare the city of Sodom (Gen. 18:20–32). Jesus prayed to God the Father to protect His disciples after His ascension. He also prayed for all future believers (John 17:20–25). Then, in the most unselfish petition imaginable, Jesus prayed for those who were putting Him to death (Luke 23:34). Now in heaven, He continues His intercessory work for all believers (Rom. 8:34).

INTERCESSION [S]

Rom. 8:26 the Spirit Himself makes *i*...with groanings

Rom. 8:34 who [Jesus] also makes *i* for us

1 Tim. 2:1 that...prayers, *i's*, and giving of thanks be made for all men

Heb. 7:25 He [Jesus] always lives to make *i* for them

IN THE BEGINNING

Gen. 1:1 *I-t-b* God created the heaven and the earth

John 1:1 *I-t-b* was the Word, and the Word was with God

Heb. 1:10 You, Lord, *i-t-b* have laid the foundation of the earth

IN THE SIGHT OF GOD

Prov. 3:4 find favor and good understanding *i-t-s-o-G*

Luke 16:15 what is highly esteemed among men is an abomination *i-t-s-o-G*

Gal. 3:11 no man is justified by the law *i-t-s-o-G*

IN THE SPIRIT

Ezek. 37:1 The hand of the Lord...carried me [Ezekiel] out *i-t-S* of the Lord

John 11:33 when Jesus saw her [Mary] weeping...He groaned *i-t-s*

Acts 19:21 Paul purposed *i-t-S* to go to Jerusalem

Acts 20:22 I [Paul] am going to Jerusalem, bound *i-t-S*

Rom. 8:9 But you are not in the flesh but *i-t-S*

Gal. 5:16 walk *i-t-S*...not fulfill the lust of the flesh

Gal. 5:25 If we live *i-t-S*, let us also walk *i-t-S*

Rev. 1:10 I [John] was *i-t-S* on the Lord's Day

Rev. 21:10 he [an angel] carried me [John] away *i-t-S* to a great...mountain

INVISIBLE

Rom. 1:20 *i* things of Him [God] are clearly seen

Col. 1:15 He [Jesus] is the image of the *i* God

1 Tim. 1:17 to the King eternal, immortal, *i*...be honor and glory

IRA. One of David's "mighty men," an elite group of warriors known for their bravery in battle (2 Sam. 23:8, 38).

IRIJAH. A guard who arrested the prophet Jeremiah while Jerusalem was under attack by the Babylonian army (Jer. 37:11–14).

ISAAC. The son born to Abraham and Sarah in their old age, in fulfillment of God's promise (Genesis 21:3–12). When Isaac was young, the Lord tested Abraham's faith by directing him to offer Isaac as a sacrifice. But just as Abraham raised a knife to take his son's life, God stopped him and provided a ram as a substitute offering. This proved that Isaac was destined to become heir to the covenant that God had established with Abraham. Isaac lived a life of quiet faith and devotion to God. He also had a son, Jacob, whose twelve sons developed into the twelve tribes of Israel. Isaac is also mentioned in **Gen. 17:19, 21; 22:2–14; 24:4–67; 25:5–28; 26:1–35; 27:1–46 • Heb. 11:9, 20.**

ISAIAH. A major prophet of the OT best known for his prophecies about the coming Messiah in the book that bears his name. Isaiah was called to his ministry in a dramatic vision of God. He answered this divine call with enthusiasm and determination when he declared, "Here I am. Send me" (Isa. 6:8). Preaching in the capital city of Jerusalem, he warned that the nation of Judah (the Southern Kingdom) would be overrun by a foreign power, but a righteous remnant of God's people would be preserved (Isa. 1:2–9; 11:11). Isaiah is also mentioned in 2 Kings 19:2–20; 20:1–19 • 2 Chron. 26:22; 32:20, 32 • Matt. 4:14.

ISAIAH, BOOK OF. The best-known prophetic book of the OT because of its theme of salvation and redemption of God's people. Jesus began His public ministry by identifying with the book's promise of comfort and healing (Isa. 61:1; Luke 4:18–19). Because of this anticipation of the good news preached by Jesus, the book is sometimes called the "fifth Gospel." In the early part of the prophet's ministry, Judah's sister nation, the Northern Kingdom, fell to the Assyrians (2 Kings 17:5, 23). Isaiah declared that the same thing would happen to Judah (the Southern Kingdom) unless the people turned from their idolatry and followed the one true God. The book is also known for several passages known as servant songs (Isa. 42:1–4; 49:1–6; 50:4–9; 52:13–53:12). The Israelites had failed to follow God's call to act as His messengers to the world, so this task would be passed on to His ultimate Servant, Jesus the Messiah.

ISCARIOT, JUDAS. The disciple who betrayed Jesus. He is mentioned in Matt. 10:4; 26:14, 25, 47; 27:3 • Mark 3:19; 14:10, 43 • Luke 22:3, 47–48 • John 6:71; 12:4; 13:2, 26, 29; 18:2–5 • Acts 1:16, 25.

ISH-BOSHETH. The youngest son of King Saul who succeeded his father as king of Israel for a brief time. Ish-Bosheth was eventually assassinated by two of his own military officers, clearing the way for David to become the undisputed king (2 Sam. 4:8–12; 5:3–4). He is also mentioned in 2 Sam. 2:8–15; 3:7–15. *Esh-baal*: 1 Chron. 8:33.

ISHMAEL. A son of Abraham born to Hagar, a servant of his wife Sarah (Gen. 16:1–11). After Ishmael was born, God told Abraham that Ishmael was not the fulfillment of God's promise to make Abraham's descendants into a great nation. This would come about through a son named Isaac, who would be born soon to Abraham and his wife, Sarah (Gen. 17:15–21). Ishmael's descendants eventually settled in northern Arabia. Modern-day Arabs claim him as their distant ancestor. He is also mentioned in Gen. 21:9–21; 25:9–18 • 1 Chron. 1:28–31.

ISRAEL. (1) Another name for Jacob, meaning "prince of God," given to him after he wrestled with an angel (Gen. 32:28; 35:10). The nation that developed from the descendants of Jacob's twelve sons eventually became known as Israel. See *Jacob*.

(2) A name for ten northern tribes (the Northern Kingdom) that split into a separate nation after the death of Solomon (1 Kings 12:1–33). Two southern tribes, Benjamin and Judah, remained loyal to David's dynasty and were known as the nation of Judah (the Southern Kingdom).

(3) A general name for the entire nation of the Jewish people (Num. 1:2).

ISRAELITES. The people whom the Lord selected to receive His special blessing. They are often referred to as the "children of Israel" or God's "chosen people." Their mission was to proclaim the truths about the one true God to the rest of the world. God promised to bless the Israelites and make their name great. But they in turn were to be a blessing to "all families of the earth" (Gen. 12:3).

ISSACHAR. (1) A son of Jacob by his wife Leah (Gen. 30:17–18).

(2) One of the twelve tribes of Israel that developed from Issachar's descendants (1 Chron. 12:32). After the death of Saul, Israel's first king, members of the tribe switched their allegiance from Saul's family to David as the new ruler.

ITALIAN COHORT. A unit of the Roman army to which the centurion Cornelius was attached. He was baptized by the apostle Peter as one of the first Gentile converts to Christianity (Acts 10:1). *Italian band*: KJV.

ITALY. A country whose capital city, Rome, was the seat of the Roman Empire in NT times (Acts 18:2). The apostle Paul appealed his case to Rome and sailed there as a prisoner (Acts 27:1–6).

ITHAMAR. Youngest son of Aaron who oversaw the tabernacle during the wilderness wanderings (Exod. 6:23; 28:1; **38:21** • Lev. 10:6–16 • 1 Chron. 24:1–6).

ITTAI. One of David's "mighty men," an elite group of warriors known for their bravery in battle (2 Sam. 23:8, 29).

ITUREA. A small Roman province in northern Israel ruled by Herod Philip when John the Baptist began his ministry (Luke 3:1).

J

JAASIEL. One of David's "mighty men," an elite group of warriors known for their bravery in battle (1 Chron. 11:11, 47).

JABBOK RIVER. A small stream in a deep canyon which runs into the Jordan River north of the Dead Sea. Jacob wrestled with an angel at a point on this river later called Peniel (Gen. 32:24–31). It is also mentioned in Num. 21:24 • Deut. 2:37; 3:16 • Josh. 12:2 • Judg. 11:13, 22.

JABESH-GILEAD. A city of Gilead south of the Sea of Galilee that King Saul defended against an attack by the Ammonites (1 Sam. 11:1–11). The men of this city gave Saul and his sons a decent burial after their bodies were desecrated by the Philistines (1 Sam. 31:11–13). Also called *Jabesh* (1 Chron. 10:12).

JABIN. A king of Hazor who was defeated by the judges Deborah and Barak at the Kishon River (Judg. 4:2).

JACHIN AND BOAZ. Two ornamental pillars which stood in front of Solomon's temple at Jerusalem. They are mentioned in 1 Kings 7:13–22 • 2 Chron. 3:17.

JACINTH. A precious stone used in the foundation of new Jerusalem (Rev. 21:20).

JACOB. A son of Isaac and twin brother of Esau (Gen. 25:21–26). Jacob's twin brother was the firstborn son and thus entitled to inherit most of his father's property. But Jacob convinced Esau to swap his birthright for a pot of stew (Gen. 25:30–33). With his mother Rebekah's help, Jacob deceived his father and received his blessing as well (Gen. 27:25–32). While fleeing Esau's wrath, Jacob struggled with an angel and was given the name *Israel*, meaning "prince with God" (Gen. 32:22–30). In later years, Jacob mourned his favorite son, Joseph, whom he presumed dead. But his joy was restored when Joseph was discovered alive and well in Egypt. Jacob and his large family moved to Egypt at Joseph's initiative to escape a famine in Canaan. Jacob died in Egypt after blessing Joseph and his sons (Gen. 48:1–22), as well as Jacob's other sons. They were destined to become the founders of the tribes from which the nation of Israel would emerge (Gen. 49:1–28).

Other highlights of Jacob's life include
1. Worked seven years for Leah (Gen. 29:16–25)
2. Worked seven years for Rachel (Gen. 29:26–30)
3. Birth of his sons (Gen. 29:31–30:24)
4. Name changed from Jacob to *Israel* (Gen. 32:28; 35:10)
5. Reconciled with Esau (Gen. 33:1–16)
6. Died in Egypt (Gen. 49:29–33)
7. Buried in Canaan (Gen. 50:1–14)

Jacob is also mentioned in Exod. 1:1, 5 • Lev. 26:42 • Josh. 24:4 • 1 Sam. 12:8 • Mal. 1:2 • Matt. 1:2; 8:11 • Luke 1:33; 13:28 • John 4:5, 12 • Acts 3:13; 7:8–46 • Rom. 9:13; 11:26 • Heb. 11:9, 20–21.

JACOB'S WELL. The site where Jesus talked with a Samaritan woman and offered her "living water" (John 4:3–6). This well was apparently associated with the patriarch Jacob, although it is not mentioned in the OT.

JADON. A man who helped rebuild the walls of Jerusalem after the Exile (Neh. 3:7).

JAEL. A woman who killed Sisera, a commander in a Canaanite army. This led to a decisive victory for the Israelites. Jael is mentioned in Judg. 4:17–22; 5:6, 24.

JAH. See *Yah*

JAIR. A minor judge of Israel who led the nation for twenty-two years (Judg. 10:3–5).

JAIRUS. An official of a synagogue near Capernaum whose daughter was brought back to life by Jesus. Jairus is mentioned in Mark 5:22–23, 36–43 • Luke 8:41–42, 49–56.

JAMBRES AND JANNES. Two Egyptian magicians who opposed Moses and resisted divine truth, according to the apostle Paul (2 Tim. 3:8). They are not mentioned by name in the OT.

JAMES. (1) A son of Zebedee and brother of Jesus' disciple John. James and his brother left their trade as fishermen to follow Jesus (Matt. 4:21–22). Jesus called them "sons of thunder," probably because of their fiery temperament (Mark 3:17). This James is also mentioned in Matt. 10:2; 17:1 • Mark 1:19, 29; 5:37; 9:2; 10:35, 41; 13:3; 14:33 • Luke 5:10; 6:14; 8:51; 9:28, 54 • Acts 1:13; 12:2.

(2) Another disciple of Jesus, who is called the son of Alphaeus to distinguish him from James the son of Zebedee. He is mentioned in Matt. 10:3 • Mark 3:18 • Luke 6:15 • Acts 1:13.

(3) The half-brother of Jesus who became a leader in the church at Jerusalem, in spite of his earlier skepticism about Jesus (Acts 21:17–18; Gal. 1:19). This James was probably the author of the epistle of James in the NT. He is also mentioned in Matt. 13:55; 27:56 • Mark 6:3; 15:40; 16:1 • Acts 12:17; 15:13 • 1 Cor. 15:7 • Gal. 2:9, 12 • Jas. 1:1 • Jude 1.

JAMES, EPISTLE OF. A short NT epistle—written probably by James, the half brother of Jesus—known for its plain language and practical application of the gospel to the believer's daily life. According to James, the true test of Christianity is in the living and doing of its truth rather than in speaking, hearing, and even believing its doctrines (Jas. 1:22–27). Authentic faith results in acts of ministry to others (Jas. 2:17). Other emphases in James are equality of all people before God (Jas. 2:1–9) and the ability of spoken words to bless or curse (Jas. 3:3–10).

JAMIN. A Levite after the Exile who explained the law as Ezra read it to the people (Neh. 8:7).

JANNES. See *Jambres and Jannes*

JAPHETH. A son of Noah who survived the great flood (Gen. 5:32). His descendants populated several nations of the ancient world (Gen. 10:2–5). Japheth is also mentioned in **Gen.** 6:10; 7:13; **9:18–27** • 1 Chron. 1:4–5.

JAPHIA. A king of Lachish and one of five Amorite kings captured and executed by Joshua's army (Josh. 10:3–27).

JAPHO. KJV: see *Joppa*

JARMUTH. A royal Canaanite city captured by Joshua (Josh. 10:1–27). Centuries later, Jarmuth was resettled by the Israelites after the Exile (Neh. 11:4, 29).

JASHAR. See *Book of Jashar*

JASHOBEAM. A commander of David's "mighty men," an elite group of warriors known for their bravery in battle (1 Chron. 11:10–11). He is also mentioned in 1 Chron. 27:2.

JASON. A believer in Thessalonica who was grabbed by an angry mob because he provided lodging for Paul and Silas (Acts 17:5–9). This may be the same Jason whom Paul referred to as among "my countrymen" (Rom. 16:21).

JASPER. A precious stone embedded in the breastplate of the high priest (Exod. 28:20) and used in the foundation of new Jerusalem (Rev. 21:19).

JAVAN. (1) A grandson of Noah and father of the ancient nation of Greece (Gen. 10:2; Isa. 66:19).

(2) A name for ancient Greece (Isa. 66:19).

JAVELIN. A short spear or dart used in hand-to-hand combat (1 Sam. 19:9–10).

JAZER. A city east of the Jordan River occupied by the conquering Israelites. It was noted for its fertile grazing lands (Josh. 13:24–25).

JEALOUSY. A feeling of ill will or resentment toward others because of their good fortune or favored position. Joseph's brothers were jealous of him because he was their father's favorite son (Gen. 37:10–11).

JEBUS. See *Jerusalem*

JEBUSITES. Enemies of the Israelites who descended from Canaan (Gen. 10:15–16). They controlled a city known as Jebus (later called Jerusalem) before David captured it and turned it into his capital (2 Sam. 5:6–7). The Jebusites are also mentioned in Gen. 15:21 • Josh. 15:63 • Judg. 1:21; 3:5; 19:11 • 1 Kings 9:20 • 1 Chron. 11:4–6 • 2 Chron. 8:7 • Ezra 9:1 • Neh. 9:8.

JECONIAH. See *Jehoiachin*

JEDAIAH. A man who helped rebuild the wall of Jerusalem after the Exile (Neh. 3:10).

JEHOAHAZ. (1) The son and successor of Jehu as king of Israel (the Northern Kingdom) (2 Kings 10:35). Jehoahaz led Israel into sin and idolatry (2 Kings 13:1–2). He is also mentioned in 2 Chron. 25:17, 25.

(2) The son and successor of Josiah as king of Judah (the Southern Kingdom). A sinful king, he reigned only three months before being deposed by the pharaoh of Egypt (2 Kings 23:31–34 • 2 Chron. 36:2, 4). Also called *Shallum* (1 Chron. 3:15 • Jer. 22:11).

JEHOASH. A king who succeeded his father Jehoahaz as ruler of Israel (the Northern Kingdom) (2 Kings 14:8–14). (2) Another

name for Joash, a king of Judah (the Southern Kingdom) (2 Kings 11:21).

JEHOIACHIN. Son and successor of Jehoiakim as king of Judah (the Southern Kingdom). Evil like his father, Jehoiachin was king when the nation was defeated by Nebuchadnezzar and the people were deported to Babylon (2 Kings 24:8–16). He was eventually released from prison and treated with respect by his enemies (Jer. 52:31–34). Also called *Coniah* (Jer. 22:24; 37:1) and *Jeconiah* (1 Chron. 3:16–17).

JEHOIADA. A priest who kept the boy Joash in hiding until he could be crowned king of Judah (the Southern Kingdom). Joash replaced the wicked Athaliah, who had killed all the other royal heirs and taken the throne (2 Chron. 22:10–12).

JEHOIAKIM. Son and successor of Josiah as king of Judah (the Southern Kingdom). An evil ruler who exploited the people and led them into idolatry, Jehoiakim was taken into captivity by the Babylonian army (2 Chron. 36:5–6). He is best known as the king who burned the scroll on which the prophet Jeremiah had recorded his prediction about the fall of Jerusalem and Jehoiakim's defeat (Jer. 36:20–23). He is also mentioned in 2 Kings 24:1–6 • 1 Chron. 3:15–16 • Jer. 26:1–23 • Dan. 1:1–2. Also called *Eliakim* (2 Kings 23:34).

JEHORAM. (1) A wicked king of Judah (the Southern Kingdom) who murdered his own brothers in order to succeed his father Jehoshaphat. He died in disgrace from a mysterious disease. Jehoram is mentioned in 1 Kings 22:50 • **2 Chron. 21:1–20.** *Joram*: 2 Kings 8:21.

(2) Son and successor of Ahaziah as king of Israel (the Northern Kingdom). He was assassinated by his successor, Jehu. He is mentioned in 2 Kings 1:17; 3:1, 6; 9:24. *Joram*: 2 Kings 8:16.

JEHOSHAPHAT. Son and successor of Asa as king of Judah (the Southern Kingdom) (1 Kings 15:24). A reformer like his father, Jehoshaphat discouraged idolatry and sent teachers to help people understand God's law (2 Chron. 17:3–9).

He was rebuked by the prophet Jehu for forming an alliance with Ahab, the wicked king of Israel (the Northern Kingdom) (2 Chron. 19:1–3). Jehoshaphat is also mentioned in 1 Kings 22:2–50 • **2 Chron. 17:1–12; 18:1–21:1** • Matt. 1:8.

JEHOSHUAH. KJV: see *Joshua*

JEHOVAH. A translation of *Yahweh*, a Hebrew word for God which indicates his eternity and self-existence. Yahweh is rendered as "Lord," printed with a capital L followed by small capital letters, in most English versions of the Bible, although some translations render the word as Yahweh or Jehovah. The name can be found in Exod. 6:3 • Ps. 83:18 • Isa. 12:2; 26:4. *YAH* is an abbreviated form of this name (Ps. 68:4; *JAH*: KJV).

JEHOVAH-JIREH. A name for God meaning "the Lord will provide." It was used by Abraham to commemorate God's provision of a ram in place of his son Isaac as a sacrifice (Gen. 22:14).

JEHOVAH-NISSI. A name for God meaning "the Lord is my banner." Moses used this name to show that God led the Israelites to victory over the Amalekites (Exod. 17:15–16).

JEHOVAH-SHALOM. The name of an altar built by the judge Gideon, meaning "the Lord is peace" (Judg. 6:24).

JEHU. A king of Israel (the Northern Kingdom) known for his elimination of all possible threats to his authority. He was anointed by a messenger of the prophet Elisha (2 Kings 9:1–13) to end the dynasty of the wicked King Ahab. Jehu promptly seized the throne by assassinating all of Ahab's sons, his wife Jezebel, and Ahab's court officials and close friends. He also murdered the king of Judah (the Southern Kingdom) and members of the royal family—well beyond what was necessary to establish Jehu's authority (2 Kings 9:14–37). The one bright spot in Jehu's reign was the elimination of Baal worship throughout Israel (2 Kings 10:18–28). (2) A prophet who rebuked King Jehoshaphat of Judah (the Southern Kingdom) for forming an alliance with Ahab, the wicked king of Israel (the Northern Kingdom) (2 Chron. 19:1–2).

JEIEL. One of David's "mighty men," an elite group of warriors known for their bravery in battle (1 Chron. 11:11, 44). *Jehiel*: KJV.

JEMIMA. A daughter of Job born after his recovery from affliction (Job 42:14).

JEPHTHAE. KJV: see *Jephthah*

JEPHTHAH. A judge of Israel who delivered Israel from the Ammonites. He is known for his rash vow to the Lord that resulted in the loss of his only child. Jephthah is mentioned in **Judg. 11:1–40; 12:1–7** • Heb. 11:32.

JEREMIAH. A major prophet of the OT who preached one uncompromising message for more than forty years—that Judah (the Southern Kingdom) was headed for disaster unless the people turned from their idolatry and renewed their commitment to the Lord. Jeremiah was called to this daunting task even before he was born (Jer. 1:4–10). He is often called the "weeping prophet" because he wept openly over the sins of Judah (Jer. 9:1). His messages are recorded in the book that bears his name. He is mentioned outside the book of Jeremiah in 2 Chron. 35:25; 36:12, 21–22 • Ezra 1:1 • Dan. 9:2 • Matt. 2:17; 16:14; 27:9.

JEREMIAH, BOOK OF. A major prophetic book of the OT noted for its stern warnings about the consequences of Judah's (the Southern Kingdom's) sin and rebellion. The prophet declared that the nation was destined to fall to the Babylonians unless the people repented and turned back to God. But the book also offered glimmers of hope. While the people of Judah would be brutalized and carried into captivity, they would eventually return to their homeland and renew their commitment to the Lord (Jer. 30:3). The book is also known for its concept of a new covenant (Jer. 31:31–34). This new agreement between God and His people would be based on grace and forgiveness. It would replace the old covenant of law that had failed to keep the people devoted to the Lord.

Jeremiah's prophecies of disaster were fulfilled during his lifetime. The Babylonian army sacked Jerusalem, tore down its temple and defensive wall, and carried the leading citizens of Judah into captivity (Jer. 52:4–16).

JEREMIAS. KJV: see *Jeremiah*

JEREMY. KJV: see *Jeremiah*

JERIBAI. One of David's "mighty men," an elite group of warriors known for their bravery in battle (1 Chron. 11:11, 46).

JERICHO. (1) Jericho of the OT. A fortified city near the Jordan River; the first Canaanite stronghold to fall to the invading Israelites (Josh. 6:1–27). Archaeological evidence shows that this city dated back to about 7000 BC, at least 5,600 years before Joshua's time. Joshua placed a curse on the city (Josh. 6:26), and it was never rebuilt. Old Testament Jericho is also mentioned in Num. 22:1; 31:12 • Deut. 34:3 • 2 Kings 2:4–18.

(2). Jericho of the NT. A city built on a site about two miles from the ruins of OT Jericho. This is where Jesus healed blind Bartimaeus (Mark 10:46–52) and confronted the tax collector Zacchaeus (Luke 19:1–9).

JEROBOAM. (1) Jeroboam I, the first king of Israel (the Northern Kingdom) after the united nation split into two factions following the death of King Solomon. An official in Solomon's administration, Jeroboam led the ten northern tribes to rebel when Solomon's son Rehoboam succeeded him as king (1 Kings 12:19–20). Jeroboam established idol worship in the cities of Bethel and Dan (1 Kings 12:26–30) and was ultimately defeated by King Abijah of Judah (the Southern Kingdom) and struck down by the Lord (2 Chron. 13:19–20).

(2) Jeroboam II, a wicked king of Israel (the Northern Kingdom) who succeeded his father Joash (2 Kings14:23–29). Jeroboam was denounced by the prophet Amos for his wickedness and his encouragement of idol worship (Amos 7:7–9).

JERUBBAAL. A name given to the judge Gideon by his father after Gideon destroyed the altar of Baal at Ophrah (Judg. 6:32). The name probably means "let Baal contend."

JERUSALEM. The religious and political capital of Israel, still revered today as the "Holy City." Situated about fifty miles from the Mediterranean Sea and about twenty miles west of the Jordan River, Jerusalem was known as Salem in Abraham's time (Gen. 14:18). King David captured the city (then called Jebus) from the Jebusites about 1000 BC and turned it into his capital (1 Chron. 11:4–5). His son Solomon built the temple in Jerusalem as the center of worship for his people about 950 BC (1 Kings 5:5–8). About five centuries later, the city fell to the Babylonians, and its leading citizens were taken into exile (Jer. 39:1–8). These exiles eventually returned to their homeland and rebuilt Jerusalem (Ezra 1:1–4 • Neh. 12:27–47). In NT times, Jesus wept over the city because of its spiritual indifference (Matt. 23:37). He entered Jerusalem as a victorious spiritual leader (Matt. 21:9–10), and was crucified on a hill just outside the city wall (Luke 9:31; 23:33). After Jesus ascended into heaven, the church was launched in Jerusalem (Acts 2:1–47). The apostle John described the future heavenly city as "new Jerusalem" (Rev. 21:2).

JERUSALEM COUNCIL. A meeting held during the early days of Christianity to determine how non-Jews would be accepted into the church. The issue was whether Gentiles first had to identify with Judaism by being circumcised before they could be baptized (Acts 15:1–6). The council concluded that circumcision was unnecessary (Acts 15:8–19), paving the way for rapid growth of the Christian movement among Gentiles throughout the Roman world. See also *Judaizers*.

JESHUA. A Levite after the Exile who explained the law as Ezra read it to the people (Neh. 8:7). See also *Joshua*.

JESHURUN. A poetic term for the nation of Israel, meaning "beloved one" (Isa. 44:2), and referring to the divine favor under which it existed. *Jesurun*: KJV.

JESSE. Father of King David and an ancestor of the Messiah. The prophet Isaiah referred to this future ruler of God's people as "a Rod... from the stump of Jesse" (Isa. 11:1) and "a Root of Jesse" (Isa. 11:10). This prophecy was fulfilled in a spiritual sense through Jesus Christ, who emerged through Jesse's family line (Matt. 1:5–6; Luke 3:32). He is also mentioned in **Ruth 4:17, 22** • 1 Sam. 16:1–22 • 1 Chron. 2:13–15 • Acts 13:22 • Rom. 15:12.

JESUS CHRIST. Son of God and Savior of the world. The Jewish people had been expecting a Messiah for many centuries. It finally happened when Jesus was born in a stable in Bethlehem during the reign of Herod the Great, Roman ruler over Palestine (Matt. 2:1–2). Although Jesus was conceived by the Holy Spirit and born to the virgin Mary, He grew up like any Jewish boy. He grew physically and mentally (Luke 2:51–52). Yet He had a consciousness of His divine mission at an early age (Luke 2:49).

After launching His public ministry, Jesus was baptized by John the Baptist, who had been divinely appointed to pave the way for Jesus' coming (Matt. 3:1–6). He was immediately tempted by Satan to take the easy way out and avoid the suffering that loomed in His future. But Jesus refused to compromise and proceeded to pursue the mission to which God had called Him (Matt. 4:1–11).

Jesus preached and healed (Mark 1:38–42), taught the people about the kingdom of God (Luke 12:31–32), and sought the lost (Luke 19:10). He ministered first in Judea in southern Israel. Then He moved into the region of Galilee in the north and chose the city of Capernaum on the Sea of Galilee as His home base. Jesus taught that faith in a loving Father is more important than blind obedience to the law (Matt. 6:10, 33). He even healed people on the Sabbath (Mark 2:27–28) and ignored other rituals that the Pharisees considered essential for right standing with God.

As Jesus' three-year ministry drew to a close, He disappointed many of His followers by making a triumphal entry into Jerusalem on a donkey. This symbolized His humility and His commitment to the spiritual kingdom He had come to establish. They were expecting Him to be a military deliverer who would overthrow the Roman government and return the Jewish nation to its glory days (Luke 24:19–21).

After eating the Passover meal with His disciples, Jesus was betrayed into the hands of the Sanhedrin. The members of this Jewish court declared Him guilty of blasphemy, then took him to Pilate, the Roman governor. Pilate sentenced Jesus to death by crucifixion on a charge of treason against the Roman government. But the grave did not have the final word. As Jesus had predicted, He arose from the dead, conquering sin and death for all believers (1 Cor. 15:57).

After spending forty days with His followers to prove He was alive, Jesus ascended to His Father in heaven. There He intercedes for all believers (Heb. 7:25), awaiting the time of His victorious return when all people of the earth will confess that "Jesus Christ is Lord, to the glory of God the Father" (Phil. 2:11).

JESUS CHRIST, APPEARANCES OF, AFTER HIS RESURRECTION

1. To Mary Magdalene at the empty tomb (Mark 16:9 • John 20:11–18)
2. To another woman at the empty tomb (Matt. 28:1–10)
3. To two followers on their way to Emmaus (Mark 16:12–13 • Luke 24:13–32)
4. To Peter, apparently in Jerusalem (Luke 24:33–35)
5. To ten of His disciples in Jerusalem, Thomas absent (Luke 24:36–43 • John 20:19–25)
6. To the eleven disciples in Jerusalem, Thomas present (John 20:26–29)
7. To His disciples at the Sea of Galilee (John 21:1–14)
8. To His disciples at His ascension near Jerusalem (Mark 16:19–20 • Luke 24:44–53)
9. To five hundred followers (1 Cor. 15:6)
10. To James and all the apostles (1 Cor. 15:7)
11. To the apostle Paul (1 Cor. 15:8)

JESUS CHRIST, LIFE AND MINISTRY OF

1. Genealogies of (Matt. 1:1–17 • Luke 3:23–38)
2. Birth in Bethlehem (Luke 2:1–20)
3. Flight into Egypt and settlement in Nazareth (Matt. 2:13–23 • Luke 2:39–40)
4. Found among esteemed teachers in Jerusalem (Luke 2:41–52)
5. Baptized by John the Baptist (Matt. 3:13–17 • Mark 1:9–11)
6. Tempted in the wilderness (Matt. 4:1–11 • Mark 1:12–13 • Luke 4:1–13)
7. Centered His early ministry around Capernaum in Galilee (Matt. 4:13–16 • Luke 4:22–31)
8. Selected twelve disciples for special training (Matt. 10:2–4 • Mark 3:13–19 • Luke 6:12–16)
9. Sermon on the Mount (Matt. 5:1–7:29 • Luke 6:17–49)
10. Sent disciples out to preach and heal (Matt. 10:1, 5–42 • Mark 6:7–13 • Luke 9:1–6)
11. Predicted His death, resurrection, and return (Luke 12:35–59)
12. Transfiguration (Matt. 17:1–8 • Mark 9:2–8 • Luke 9:28–36)
13. Triumphal entry into Jerusalem (Matt. 21:1–11 • Mark 11:1–11 • Luke 19:28–40 • John 12:12–19)
14. Instituted the memorial supper (Matt. 26:26–30 • Mark 14:22–26 • Luke 22:14–20)
15. Agonized in prayer in Gethsemane (Matt. 26:36–46 • Mark 14:26, 32–42 • Luke 22:39–46)
16. Betrayed by Judas Iscariot and arrested (Matt. 26:47–56 • Mark 14:43–52 • Luke 22:47–53 • John 18:1–12)
17. Trial before the Jewish authorities (Matt. 26:57–68; 27:1–2 • Mark 14:53–65; 15:1 • Luke 22:54–23:1 • John 18:24)
18. Trial before Pilate (Matt. 27:2–26 • Mark 15:1–15 • Luke 23:2–25 • John 18:28–19:16)
19. Crucifixion by Roman soldiers (Matt. 27:33–37 • Mark 15:22–26 • Luke 23:32–34 • John 19:17–24)
20. Death (Matt. 27:45–54 • Mark 15:33–39 • Luke 23:44–48 • John 19:28–30)
21. Burial in Joseph's tomb (Matt. 27:57–60 • Mark 15:42–46 • Luke 23:50–54 • John 19:38–42)
22. Resurrection (Matt. 28:2–4 • 1 Cor. 15:1–19)
23. Appearances to His followers (see *Jesus, Appearances of, After His Resurrection*)
24. Great Commission to His followers (Matt. 28:16–20 • Mark 16:15–18 • Acts 1:7–8)
25. Ascension to His Father (Mark 16:19 • Luke 24:50–51 • Acts 1:9–11)

JESUS CHRIST, MIRACLES OF

1. Blind Bartimaeus healed (Matt. 20:29–34 • Mark 10:46–52 • Luke 18:35–43)
2. Blind man at Bethsaida healed (Mark 8:22–26)
3. Centurion's servant healed (Matt. 8:5–13 • Luke 7:1–10)
4. Daughter of a Canaanite woman healed (Matt. 15:21–28 • Mark 7:24–30)
5. Deaf man healed (Mark 7:31–37)
6. Demon-possessed blind man healed (Matt. 12:22–24)
7. Demon-possessed boy healed (Matt. 17:14–21 • Mark 9:14–29 • Luke 9:37–42)
8. Demon-possessed mute man healed (Matt. 9:32–34)
9. Demon-possessed man healed at Capernaum (Mark 1:21–26 • Luke 4:31–35)
10. Ear of Malchus healed (Luke 22:50–51 • John 18:10)
11. Feeding of the five thousand (Matt. 14:13–21 • Mark 6:30–44 • Luke 9:10–17 • John 6:1–15)
12. Feeding of the four thousand (Matt. 15:29–38 • Mark 8:1–10)
13. First miraculous catch of fish on the Sea of Galilee (Luke 5:4–10)
14. Jairus's daughter healed (Matt. 9:23–26 • Mark 5:35–42 • Luke 8:49–56)
15. Lame man healed on the sabbath (John 5:1–15)
16. Lazarus raised from the dead (John 11:1–44)
17. A leper healed (Matt. 8:1–4 • Mark 1:40–45 • Luke 5:12–16)
18. Man blind from birth healed (John 9:1–41)
19. Man with a paralyzed hand healed on the Sabbath (Matt. 12:9–14 • Mark 3:1–6 • Luke 6:6–11)

20. Man with the dropsy healed (Luke 14:1–6)
21. Paralyzed man healed (Matt. 9:1–8 • Mark 2:1–12 • Luke 5:17–26)
22. Peter's mother-in-law healed (Matt. 8:14–15 • Mark 1:29–31 • Luke 4:38–39)
23. Production of a coin to pay the temple tax (Matt. 17:24–27)
24. Royal official's son healed (John 4:46–54)
25. Second miraculous catch of fish at the Sea of Galilee (John 21:1–14)
26. Stilling of the storm (Matt. 8:18, 23–27 • Mark 4:35–41 • Luke 8:22–25)
27. Ten lepers healed (Luke 17:11–19)
28. Transfiguration before His disciples (Matt. 17:1–8 • Mark 9:2–8 • Luke 9:28–36)
29. Two blind men healed (Matt. 9:27–31)
30. Walking on the water (Matt. 14:24–36 • Mark 6:45–56 • John 6:16–21)
31. Water turned into wine (John 2:1–11)
32. Widow's son raised from the dead (Luke 7:11–17)
33. Wild man among the tombs healed (Matt. 8:28–34 • Mark 5:1–20 • Luke 8:26–39)
34. Withering of a fig tree (Matt. 21:19–22 • Mark 11:20–26)
35. Woman with a crooked back healed (Luke 13:10–17)
36. Woman with a hemorrhage healed (Matt. 9:20–22 • Mark 5:24–34 • Luke 8:43–48)

JESUS CHRIST, PARABLES OF

1. Barren fig tree (Luke 13:1–9)
2. Buried treasure (Matt. 13:44)
3. Candle on a candlestick (Mark 4:21–25 • Luke 8:16–18)
4. Fishing net (Matt. 13:47–51)
5. Good Samaritan (Luke 10:25–37)
6. Great banquet (Luke 14:15–24)
7. House built on a rock (Matt. 7:24–29)
8. Landowner (Matt. 13:52)
9. Leaven in dough (Matt. 13:33–35 • Luke 13:20–21)
10. Lost coin (Luke 15:8–10)
11. Lost sheep (Matt. 18:12–14 • Luke 15:1–7)
12. Minas or pounds (Luke 19:11–27)
13. Mustard seed (Matt. 13:31–32 • Mark 4:30–32 • Luke 13:18–19)
14. Persistent widow (Luke 18:1–8)
15. Precious pearl (Matt. 13:45–46)
16. Prodigal son (Luke 15:11–32)
17. Proud Pharisee (Luke 18:9–14)
18. Rich fool (Luke 12:13–21)
19. Rich man and Lazarus (Luke 16:19–31)
20. Seed growing unseen (Mark 4:26–29)
21. Sheep and goats (Matt. 25:31–46)
22. Shrewd manager (Luke 16:1–13)
23. Sower and soils (Matt. 13:1–9 • Mark 4:1–9 • Luke 8:4–8)
24. Talents (Matt. 25:14–30)
25. Ten virgins (Matt. 25:1–13)
26. Two sons and a vineyard (Matt. 21:28–32)
27. Unforgiving servant (Matt. 18:21–35)
28. Wedding banquet (Matt. 22:1–14)
29. Wheat and weeds (Matt. 13:24–43)
30. Wicked tenants in a vineyard (Matt. 21:33–46 • Mark 12:1–12 • Luke 20:9–19)
31. Workers hired for a vineyard (Matt. 20:1–16)

JESUS CHRIST, PROPHECIES ABOUT.
See *Messianic Prophecies*

JETHRO. Father-in-law of Moses who advised Moses to appoint leaders to share his leadership responsibility during the Exodus from Egypt (Exod. 18:13–25). Moses married Jethro's daughter Zipporah (Exod. 2:16–22; 4:18). Moses invited Jethro to accompany the Israelites to Canaan, but he chose to stay with his own people (Num. 10:29–30). Also called *Reuel* (Exod. 2:18) and *Hobab* (Judg. 4:11).

JEZEBEL. The scheming wife of King Ahab who influenced him to promote worship of the pagan god Baal throughout Israel (the Northern Kingdom) (1 Kings 16:31–32). She also had an innocent man killed so Ahab could confiscate his property (1 Kings 21:7–16). After Ahab was killed, she died a gruesome death at the hands of Jehu, Ahab's successor (2 Kings 9:30–37). Jezebel is also mentioned in 1 Kings 18:4, 13; 19:1–2 • Rev. 2:20.

JEZREEL. (1) A fortified city where a palace of King Ahab of Israel (the Northern Kingdom) was located (1 Kings 21:1). Here Jezebel and Ahab's sons and associates were assassinated by the forces of the new king, Jehu (2 Kings 10:1–10).

(2) A symbolic name, meaning "God scatters," given by the prophet Hosea to his son, signifying God's judgment against Jehu for his violent actions (Hos. 1:4).

JOAB. Chief commander of King David's army during most of his reign (1 Kings 11:14–16). Joab led the army to victories in several decisive battles during David's administration (2 Sam. 10:6–14). On orders from David, he sent Uriah the Hittite to his death to cover up the king's adulterous affair with Uriah's wife, Bathsheba (2 Sam. 11:14–17). Joab supported Adonijah rather than Solomon as David's successor. At David's orders, Solomon had Joab executed (1 Kings 2:5–6, 28–34). He is also mentioned in 1 Sam. 26:6 • 2 Sam. 2:13–32; 3:22–31; 14:1–33; 18:2–29; 20:9–23 • 1 Chron. 11:6–39; 19:8–15; 21:2–6; 27:7, 24, 34.

JOANNA. A follower of Jesus who prepared spices for His burial and proclaimed His resurrection to His disciples. Joanna is mentioned in **Luke** 8:1–3; 23:55–56; **24:1–10**.

JOASH. A king of Judah (the Southern Kingdom) who succeeded his father Ahaziah at age seven. He was hidden from the wicked queen Athaliah to prevent his assassination (2 Kings 11:1–21). Joash brought religious reforms to Judah by repairing the temple (2 Kings 12:4–5) and banning worship of the pagan god Baal (2 Kings 11:18–20). But Joash grew lax in his commitment to the Lord in the final years of his reign (2 Chron. 24:17–19). He was forced to pay protection money to the nation of Syria by stripping the temple and his royal palace of their treasures (2 Kings 12:17–18). After reigning for forty years, Joash was assassinated by his own officials, and succeeded by his son Amaziah (2 Chron. 24:24–25; 2 Chron. 25:1). Also called *Jehoash* (2 Kings 11:21).

JOATHAM. KJV: see *Jotham*

JOB. A godly man of the OT whose faith sustained him through great pain and suffering.

The book that bears his name is filled with long discussions about the meaning behind his misfortunes. Job eventually came to a greater understanding of God and the human circumstances through which He works (Job 42:3–6). In the NT, the author of the epistle of James praised Job for his faith (James 5:11). He is also mentioned in Ezek. 14:14, 20.

JOB, BOOK OF. A wisdom book of the OT that addresses the issue of human suffering, particularly the question of why the righteous suffer. The book is written in the form of a poetic drama revolving around the discussion of this problem by Job and three "friends." After Job lost his children and earthly possessions (Job 1:1–2:13), these people arrived to offer comfort and speculation about the reason for his suffering. Back-and-forth discussions between them and Job take up most of the book (Job 3:1–37:24). Finally, Job heard from God, who identified Himself as the sovereign Lord of the universe who did not have to defend His actions to any mere mortal (Job 38:1–41:34). Armed with this new understanding (Job 42:5), Job was rewarded by the Lord with the restoration of his family and possessions (Job 42:10–15).

JOCHEBED. Mother of Moses, Aaron, and Miriam (Exod. 6:20). She is alluded to in the NT as one of the heroes of the faith (Heb. 11:23).

JOD. Tenth letter of the Hebrew alphabet, used as a heading over Ps. 119:73–80. In the Hebrew language, the first line of each of these eight verses begins with this letter.

JOEL. (1) One of David's "mighty men," an elite group or warriors known for their bravery in battle (1 Chron. 11:11, 38).

(2) A son of Samuel and a corrupt judge of Israel. His dishonesty, along with that of his brother Abiah, was one factor that led the people to ask Samuel to appoint a king to rule Israel (1 Sam. 8:1–5).

(3) A prophet of Judah (the Southern Kingdom) who used the devastation of a plague of locusts to call the people back to worship of the one true God. His prophecies appear in the

OT book that bears his name. He is mentioned in Joel 1:1 • Acts 2:16.

JOEL, BOOK OF. A brief prophetic book of the OT which paints a disturbing picture of the coming judgment of God against His people because of their sin. It was written during the dark days before the nation of Judah (the Southern Kingdom) fell to the Babylonians. The prophet predicted the outpouring of God's spirit (Joel 2:28–32), an event which happened on the day of Pentecost in NT times (Acts 2:16–21), The book also proclaimed salvation through Christ (Joel 2:32) and pictured the eternal age with blessings for God's people (Joel 3:17–21).

JOHANAN. A supporter of Gedaliah, governor of Judah (the Southern Kingdom) (2 Kings 25:22–23). Johanan took refugees to Egypt after the fall of Jerusalem to the Babylonian army (Jer. 43:4–6).

JOHN, APOSTLE. A fisherman and brother of James, among the first disciples called by Jesus (John 1:35–39). In the Gospel that John wrote, he is apparently the member of the Twelve whom he refers to as "that disciple whom Jesus loved" (John 21:7). John was apparently the disciple whom Jesus asked to take care of His mother while He was dying on the cross (John 19:26–27). After Jesus ascended to His Father, John worked with the apostle Peter in Jerusalem to call people to faith in Christ (Acts 4:13; 8:14–15). Later, John wrote a significant part of the NT—the Gospel that bears his name as well as First, Second, and Third John and the book of Revelation. He is also mentioned in Matt. 4:21; 10:2; 17:1 • Mark 1:19, 29; 3:17; 5:37; 9:2, 38; 10:35, 41; 13:3; 14:33 • Luke 5:10; 6:14; 8:51; 9:28, 49, 54; 22:8 • Acts 1:13; 3:1–11; 4:19; 12:2 • Gal. 2:9 • Rev. 1:1, 4, 9; 21:2.

JOHN, EPISTLES OF. Three short epistles of the NT written by John, one of the twelve disciples of Jesus. First John focuses on the incarnation of Christ (1 John 1:1–5), Christian discipleship (1 John 1:6–10), false teachings about Christ (1 John 2:1–8), and the meaning of love and fellowship (1 John 2:15–5:3). Second

John calls on believers to abide in the commandments of God (2 John 1–6) and reject false teachers (2 John 7–13). Third John commends the believers Gaius (3 John 1–8) and Demetrius (3 John 12), while condemning Diotrephes (3 John 9–11). The apostle John probably wrote all three of these epistles from Ephesus about AD 95.

JOHN, GOSPEL OF. One of the four Gospels of the NT, written by the apostle John with a definite purpose—to show that "Jesus is the Christ, the Son of God" (John 20:31). John focused on the theological meaning of the events in Jesus' life rather than the events themselves. For example, many of Jesus' miracles are interpreted as "signs" of His divine power and unique relationship to the Father (John 20:30). Jesus' "I am" sayings, in which He revealed selected attributes or characteristics of His divine nature, are also unique to this Gospel. John included little of the teachings of Jesus that appear in the other Gospel accounts. Instead, He portrays Jesus giving long, extended monologues about His reason for coming into the world and His inevitable return to the Father. A full five chapters (13:1–17:26) are devoted to Jesus' farewell discourses to His disciples. These reveal the inner mind of Jesus and His conception of His divine mission in the world.

JOHN THE BAPTIST. The prophet whose role as forerunner prepared the way for the coming of Jesus Christ. John preached repentance and baptized converts in the Jordan River (Matt. 3:1–6), reluctantly agreeing to baptize Jesus after proclaiming Him as the "Lamb of God" (John 1:29). John apparently continued his preaching for a time after Jesus launched His public ministry (John 3:22–24). Some of Jesus' first disciples had also been followers of John (John 1:35–37). John denounced the hypocrisy of the Pharisees and the immorality in the household of Herod Antipas—a declaration for which he was put to death (Matt. 14:3–12). John magnified Jesus rather than himself (John 3:23–30), and Jesus commended him for his faithfulness

(Luke 7:24–28). He is also mentioned in Matt. 3:1–14; 4:12; 9:14; 11:2–18; 16:14; 17:13; 21:25–32 • Mark 1:4–14; 2:18; 6:14–29; 8:28; 11:30–32 • Luke 1:13–63; 3:2–20; 5:33; 7:18–33; 9:7–9; 11:1; 16:16; 20:4, 6 • John 1:6–40; 4:1; 5:33–36; 10:40–41 • Acts 1:5, 22; 10:37; 11:16; 13:24–25; 19:4.

JOIADA. A man who helped rebuild the wall of Jerusalem after the Exile (Neh. 3:6).

JONAH. An OT prophet who was swallowed by a "great fish" while fleeing from God's call to preach to the pagan Assyrians (Jon. 1:17). After God delivered Jonah from the fish, he did as directed, and many people turned to the Lord (Jon. 3:5–10). Jonah's story appears in the book that bears his name. He is also mentioned in 2 Kings 14:25 • Luke 11:30.

JONAH, BOOK OF. A short prophetic book of the OT which shows that God can use a negative example to teach a positive lesson. The negative example was Jonah, who was called to preach to the people of Nineveh, capital of Assyria. This nation was a powerful enemy of Israel (Jon. 1:2). The pagan Assyrians were known for their cruelty in warfare. The Israelites tended to believe that they had an exclusive claim on God's love because of their status as God's chosen people. But this view was proven false when the Assyrians turned to the Lord at the prophet's grudging message (Jon. 3:5). Thus the positive message from Jonah's book: God is concerned for all nations of the world, not just the Israelites of the prophet's native land (Jon. 4:1–11).

JONAS. KJV: see *Jonah*

JONATHAN. King Saul's oldest son, who formed a legendary friendship with David, even while his father was trying to kill David (1 Sam. 20:1–42). David never forgot his loyal friend, even after Jonathan was killed in a battle with the Philistines. When David became king, he provided food and lodging for Jonathan's handicapped son, Mephibosheth, at his palace in Jerusalem (2 Sam. 9:1–13). Jonathan is also mentioned in 1 Sam. 13:2–22; 14:1–49; 18:1–4;

19:1–7; 23:16–18; 31:2 • 2 Sam. 1:4–26; 4:4; 21:7–14 • 1 Chron. 8:33–34; 9:39–40; 10:2.

JOPPA. A coastal city near the Mediterranean Sea where the apostle Peter had a revolutionary vision that changed the course of the early church. The Lord revealed that the Jewish food laws Peter had always observed were no longer in effect. This meant that Gentiles were not second-class citizens, as the Jews believed, but people whom God loved and accepted. A few days later, Peter baptized a Gentile named Cornelius and several members of his household (Acts 10:44–48). This event paved the way for aggressive preaching of the gospel to Gentiles throughout the Roman world. Joppa is also mentioned in Josh. 19:46 • 2 Chron. 2:16 • Ezra 3:7 • Jon. 1:3 • **Acts** 9:36–43; **10:5–32**; 11:5, 13.

JORAM. See *Jehoram*

JORDAN RIVER. Israel's largest and most important river; the stream in which Jesus was baptized by John the Baptist (Matt. 3:13–17). Th Jordan runs across the entire length of Israel, descending to the lowest point on earth where it empties into the Dead Sea. This sharp fall has given the river its name, which means "the descender." The Jordan played a central role in the entrance of God's people into Canaan. God miraculously stopped the river's flow, and the Israelites crossed safely into the land that God had promised to Abraham and his descendants (Josh. 3:14–16). The Jordan River is also mentioned in Gen. 13:8–13; 32:10 • Num. 34:12 • Deut. 3:27 • Josh. 4:1–24 • 2 Sam. 17:22–24 • 2 Kings 2:5–14; 5:10–14.

JOSAPHAT. KJV: see *Jehoshaphat*

JOSEPH. (1) The son of Jacob by Rachel who was sold to a band of traders by his jealous brothers. Enslaved and imprisoned in Egypt, Joseph became an important official under the pharaoh. He was eventually reunited with his father and brothers when they came to Egypt to buy grain. Joseph considered the circumstances that brought him to Egypt a series of divine actions that saved the lives of Jacob's family (Gen. 45:4–8). He made arrangements for his father and all his descendants to settle in Egypt to escape a famine (Gen. 47:1–4). He is mentioned in **Gen. 37, 39–50** • Exod. 1:5–8; 13:19 • Num. 27:1; 32:33; 34:23; 36:12 • Deut. 27:12 • Josh. 14:4; 16:1, 4; 17:1–16; 24:32 • Ps. 105:17 • John 4:5 • Acts 7:9–18 • Heb. 11:21–22.

(2) The husband of Mary, Jesus' mother. A descendant of King David (Matt. 1:20), he was known as a righteous man. Joseph took Mary as his wife after an angel explained the circumstances of Mary's pregnancy (Matt. 1:19–25). Joseph was with Mary when Jesus was born in Bethlehem (Luke 2:16). He took Mary and Jesus to Egypt to escape Herod's attempt to kill the young child (Matt. 2:13). Later, he brought the family to Nazareth, where Jesus grew up and probably worked with Joseph in his trade as a carpenter (Matt. 13:55). He is also mentioned in Matt. 1:16–24; 2:13–23 • Luke 1:27; 2:4–43; 3:23 • John 1:45; 6:42.

(3) A man of Arimathea, a member of the Jewish Sanhedrin who claimed the body of Jesus, prepared it for burial, and laid it in his own new tomb (Mark 15:43–46 • Luke 23:50–53 • John 19:38).

(4) A half-brother of Jesus (Matt. 13:55). *Joses*: KJV.

JOSES. KJV: see *Barnabas*

JOSHUA. Moses' successor who led the Israelites to victory over the Canaanites after they entered the promised land. Several years before, he was one of the twelve scouts sent by Moses to investigate Canaan (Num. 13:1–2, 8). After leading the Israelites to displace the Canaanites, Joshua supervised the assignment of land allotments to each of the twelve tribes (Josh.13–17). He is also mentioned in Exod. 17:9–14; 24: 13; 32:17; 33:11 • Num. 11:28; 14:6–38; 26:65; 27:18–23; 32:12, 28; 34:17 • Deut. 1:38; 3:21, 28; 31:3–23; 32:44; 34:9 • **Josh. 1:1–24:31** • Judg. 2:6–23 • 1 Kings 16:34 • 1 Chron. 7:27 • Neh. 8:17. *Hoshea*: Num. 13:8.

JOSHUA, BOOK OF. A historical book of the OT which records the conquest and settlement of the land of Canaan by the Israelites. It takes its name from its major figure, Joshua, who succeeded Moses as leader of the Israelites. Included in the book are accounts of the major battles for the land, the division of the conquered territories (Josh. 13–17), and Joshua's stirring farewell address to the people before his death. He cautioned the people against worshipping the gods of the pagan Canaanites whom they had defeated (Josh. 24:1–23).

JOSIAH. A godly king of Judah (the Southern Kingdom) who was only eight years old when he took the throne (2 Kings 22:1). At first the young king probably had trusted advisors to help him govern the country. Josiah launched a campaign to destroy pagan altars, purify the temple, and make needed temple repairs (2 Chron. 34:1–9). During the construction project, workmen found a copy of the Book of the Law, probably a portion of the book of Deuteronomy. After listening to passages from the book, the king was shocked at how far the nation had drifted from God's commands. He used the document to reinforce the reform movement already in progress. Later, he led the people in a public renewal of their commitment to the Lord (2 Chron. 34:29–32). Josiah is also mentioned in **2 Kings 23:3–25** • Matt. 1:10–11.

JOSIAS. KJV: see *Josiah*

JOT. The English word for the *jod*, the smallest letter in the Hebrew alphabet (Matt. 5:18). Jesus cited this letter figuratively for a matter of minor importance. The *jod* is used as a heading over Psalm 119:73–80. In the Hebrew language, the first line of each of these eight verses begins with this letter.

JOTHAM. The son and successor of Uzziah as king of Judah (the Southern Kingdom). A contemporary of several OT prophets (Isa. 1:1; Mic. 1:1), Jotham was a good king but failed to destroy pagan worship sites (2 Kings 15:32–35). He improved the temple, strengthened Jerusalem's defensive wall, and fortified buildings throughout Judah (2 Chron. 27:1–4). Jotham is also mentioned in 2 Kings 15:5–38; 16:1 •

1 Chron. 3:12; 5:17 • 2 Chron. 26:21, 23 • Isa. 7:1 • Hos. 1:1 • Matt. 1:9.

JOURNEY [ED, ING, S]

Gen. 12:9 Abram *j'ed*, going on still toward the south

Exod. 3:18 let us [Israelites] go three days' *j*...that we may sacrifice to the LORD

Jon. 3:3 Nineveh was...great city of three days' *j*

Luke 9:3 Take nothing for your *j*, neither staffs

Luke 10:33 Samaritan, as he *j'ed*, came where he [the wounded traveler] was

Luke 13:22 He [Jesus] went through the cities...teaching and *j'ing* toward Jerusalem

Luke 15:13 younger son...took his *j* into a far country

Acts 9:3 as he [Paul] *j'ed*, he came near Damascus

2 Cor. 11:26 on *j's* often, in perils from waters

JOY. A feeling of delight or well-being that is based on confidence in God's presence and never-failing promises. Joy in the Lord is a persistent theme in the writings of the apostle Paul (Phil. 4:4).

JOY

Ps. 16:11 In Your presence is fulness of *j*

Ps. 30:5 Weeping may endure for a night, but *j* comes in the morning

Ps. 43:4 Then will I go...to God my exceeding *j*

Ps. 51:12 Restore...the *j* of Your salvation

Ps. 126:5 Those who sow in tears shall reap in *j*

Prov. 15:21 Foolishness is *j* to him who is destitute of wisdom

Isa. 12:3 draw water out of the wells of salvation with *j*

Isa. 52:9 Break forth into *j*...you desolate places of Jerusalem

Lam. 5:15 j of our heart has ceased; our dance has turned into mourning

Matt. 2:10 they [wise men]...rejoiced with...great *j*

Matt. 28:8 And they [the women] departed quickly...with fear and great *j*

Luke 2:10 bring you [shepherds] good tidings of great *j*

Luke 15:10 j...over one sinner who repents

John 16:20 your sorrow shall be turned into *j*

Acts 20:24 I [Paul] might finish my course with *j*

Rom. 14:17 kingdom of God is...peace and *j*

Gal. 5:22 fruit of the Spirit is love, *j*, peace

Heb. 12:2 who [Jesus] for the *j* that was set before Him endured the cross

Jas. 1:2 count it all *j* when you fall into various temptations

3 John 4 no greater *j*...children walk in truth

JOYFUL [LY, NESS]

Ps. 35:9 my soul shall be *j* in the LORD

Ps. 66:1 Make a *j* noise to God, all you lands

Ps. 95:1 make a *j* noise to the rock of our salvation

Ps. 149:5 Let the saints be *j* in glory...sing aloud

Eccles. 9:9 Live *j'ly* with the wife whom you love

Isa. 49:13 Sing, O heavens. And be *j*, O earth

Luke 19:6 he [Zacchaeus]...received Him [Jesus] *j'ly*

Col. 1:11 Strengthened...to all patience...with *j'ness*

JOZABAD. A Levite after the Exile who explained the law as Ezra read it to the people (Neh. 8:7).

JUBAL. A descendant of Cain who was a skilled musician. Jubal was regarded as the ancestor of the people who play the harp and the flute (Gen. 4:21).

JUBILEE. A year of celebration set aside to promote justice and liberty throughout Israel. Occurring every fiftieth year, it had a leveling effect by giving people a chance for a new start. During this year, those serving as indentured servants were released from their debts and set free. All properties forfeited because of indebtedness since the last jubilee year were restored to the original owners. Even cropland was included in the jubilee celebration; it was allowed to go unplanted as a conservation measure (Lev. 25:8–55).

JUDAEA. KJV: see *Judea*

JUDAH. (1) A son of Jacob who became one of the most prominent of his twelve sons. It was Judah who convinced his brothers to sell their younger brother Joseph into slavery rather than kill him (Gen. 37:26–27). Years later, Judah offered himself as a ransom for his brother Benjamin before Joseph in Egypt (Gen. 43:8–9; 44:16–34). When Jacob blessed his sons near the end of his life, he bestowed his favor on Judah rather than his three older sons. Jacob predicted that Judah's descendants would become the dominant tribe of Israel (Gen. 49:8–11). He is also mentioned in Gen. 29:35; 38:1–26; 43:3, 8; 44:14–18; 46:12, 28 • Exod. 1:2 • Num. 26:19 • Ruth 4:12 • 1 Chron. 2:1–10; 4:1, 21, 27; 5:2; 9:4 • Neh. 11:24.

(2) The tribe of Judah that grew from Judah's descendants (Josh. 15:1–12). This tribe became the messianic line through which Jesus' ancestry was traced by two Gospel writers (Matt. 1:2–3; Luke 3:30).

(3) The Southern Kingdom, or nation of Judah. Founded after Solomon's death, the Southern Kingdom was composed largely of the tribes of Judah and Benjamin, while the rebellious ten northern tribes retained the name of Israel. Solomon's son Rehoboam was the first king of Judah, with the capital at Jerusalem (1 Kings 14:21). The nation eventually drifted into idolatry, turning a deaf ear to great prophets such as Isaiah and Jeremiah, who tried to bring them back to worship of the one true God. Judah was overrun and taken into exile by the Babylonians about 587 BC (2 Chron. 36:4–20). A remnant returned to rebuild Jerusalem several decades later (2 Chron. 36:20–23).

JUDAIZERS. A group of zealous believers in the early church who taught that Gentiles had to be circumcised before they could become Christians (Acts 15:1). The Judaizers were denounced by the apostle Paul, who insisted that faith alone was the path to salvation (Acts 15:12; Gal. 6:15). The Judaizers were also opposed by Peter and James at the Jerusalem Council (Acts 15:8–19). See also *Jerusalem Council*.

JUDAS. (1) Judas, brother of James, one of the twelve disciples of Jesus (Luke 6:13–16). His identification as the brother of James distinguishes him from the Judas who betrayed Jesus. This Judas is possibly the same disciple called *Lebbaeus* (Matt. 10:3) and *Thaddaeus* (Mark 3:18).

(2) Judas Iscariot, the disciple who betrayed Jesus for thirty pieces of silver (Matt. 26:15; John 13:2, 26). The word *Iscariot* identified Judas as a citizen of Kerioth, a city in southern Judah (Josh. 15:25). Judas Iscariot was the only member of the group who was not a native of the region of Galilee. After realizing the gravity of his act of betrayal, he committed suicide (Matt. 27:3–5).

JUDE. The half-brother of Jesus who is thought to be the author of the NT epistle which bears his name. Jude (rendered "Judas" in Matthew 13:55) was skeptical of Jesus' claims during His earthly ministry (John 7:5), but he apparently became a believer after His resurrection (Acts 1:14).

JUDE, EPISTLE OF. A short NT epistle that addresses the problem of false teachers within the church. Jude called on believers to base their faith on the true doctrine taught by the apostles (Jude 17) as well as the love of Christ (Jude 21). Jude identified himself as a "brother of James" (Jude 1). This was probably another half-brother of Jesus who wrote the epistle of James.

JUDEA. The southernmost province of the three Roman districts into which Israel was divided in NT times. The other two were Samaria and Galilee. The name *Judea* was derived from "Jewish," a word describing those who returned to the nation of Judah (the Southern Kingdom) after the Exile. In His "great commission," Jesus declared that the proclamation of the gospel should begin at Judea but eventually extend into the entire world (Acts 1:8). It is also mentioned in Matt. 2:1, 5, 22 • Mark 1:5; 3:7 • Luke 6:17 • John 4:3, 47, 54 • Acts 10:37 • Rom. 15:31 • 2 Cor. 1:16 • Gal. 1:22 • 1 Thes. 2:14.

JUDGE [D, S]
Gen. 18:25 Shall not the *J* of all the earth do right
Exod. 18:13 the next day...Moses sat to *j* the people
Judg. 2:16 the LORD raised up *j's*

1 Sam. 2:10 the LORD shall *j* the ends of the earth

1 Sam. 8:6 Now give us a king to *j* us

1 Kings 3:9 Give...Your servant [Solomon] an understanding heart to *j* Your people

Job 22:13 Can He [God] *j* through the dark cloud?

Ps. 7:8 *J* me, O LORD, according to my righteousness

Ps. 7:11 God *j's* the righteous

Ps. 43:1 *J* me, O God, and plead my cause

Ps. 72:2 He [God] shall *j* Your people with righteousness

Ps. 75:7 God is the *J*...puts down one...sets up another

Prov. 31:9 *j* righteously, and plead the cause of the poor

Lam. 3:59 LORD, You have seen my wrong. *J* my cause

Matt. 7:1 Do not *j*, that you not be *j'd*

John 7:24 Do not *j* according to the appearance

John 12:48 word that I [Jesus] have spoken... shall *j* him in the last day

Rom. 14:10 But why do you *j* your brother?

2 Tim. 4:1 Jesus Christ, who shall *j* the living and the dead

2 Tim. 4:8 crown...the righteous *J*, shall give me [Paul] on that day

Jas. 2:4 you...have become *j's* with evil thoughts

Jas. 4:12 Who are you who *j's* another?

Rev. 19:11 in righteousness He [Jesus] *j's* and makes war

JUDGE OF ALL THE EARTH. A name of God that emphasizes His role as the ultimate dispenser of justice in the world. Abraham used this name when he talked with the Lord about His decision to destroy the wicked city of Sodom (Gen. 18:25). Abraham reasoned that the God of justice would not destroy the righteous people who lived there along with the wicked. So God sent an angel to warn the righteous Lot and his family to flee before His judgment fell (Gen. 19:1, 15–17).

JUDGES, BOOK OF. A historical book of the OT that covers about three hundred years in the history of the Israelites. This was a dark time following the conquest of Canaan when the people sinned against the Lord. As punishment, God would send enemy oppressors against the nation. They would repent and pray for deliverance, and God would raise up a judge, or military champion, to defeat their enemies. But then the cycle of sin-oppression-repentance-deliverance would start all over again.

JUDGES OF ISRAEL. Military leaders or deliverers who led Israel between the time of Joshua's death and the beginning of the kingship under Saul. Israel's judges served in times of disunity and spiritual decline among the twelve tribes (Judg. 17:6; 21:25) as well as times when all the tribes were oppressed by their enemies. Notable victories of the judges include Deborah and Barak's defeat of the Canaanite king Jabin (Judg. 4:4–24), Gideon's 300 warriors who subdued the Midianites (Judg. 7:1–8:21), and Samson's massacre of the Philistines (Judg. 15:14–16).

Judges are mentioned in the book of Judges and in 1 Samuel:

1. Othniel (Judg. 3:9–11)
2. Ehud (Judg. 3:15–30)
3. Shamgar (Judg. 3:31)
4. Deborah and Barak (Judg. 4:4–24)
5. Gideon (Judg. 6:11–8:32)
7. Abimelech (Judg. 9:1–54)
8. Tola (Judg. 10:1–2)
9. Jair (Judg. 10:3–5)
10. Jephthah (Judg. 11:1–12:7)
11. Ibzan (Judg. 12:8–10)
12. Elon (Judg. 12:11–12)
13. Abdon (Judg. 12:13–15)
14. Samson (Judg. 14:1–16:31)
15. Eli (1 Sam. 4:15–18)
16. Samuel (1 Sam. 7:15)
17. Samuel's sons (1 Sam. 8:1–3).

JUDGMENT. The ability to discern between good and bad by applying a universal standard. God alone has the wisdom and power to judge with righteousness and truth. He has delegated this right and authority to His Son, Jesus (John

5:22). Divine judgment is an expression of God's chastening love for believers (Heb. 12:5–6).

JUDGMENT

Exod. 12:12 I [God] will execute *j* against...gods of Egypt

1 Chron. 18:14 David reigned...and carried out *j*

Job 8:3 Does God pervert *j*?

Job 32:9 Nor do the aged understand *j*

Ps. 1:5 the ungodly shall not stand in the *j*

Ps. 72:2 He [God] shall judge...Your poor with *j*

Ps. 101:1 I will sing of mercy and *j*: to You, O LORD

Ps. 119:66 Teach me good *j* and knowledge

Prov. 21:3 To do justice and *j* is more acceptable to the LORD than sacrifice

Prov. 29:26 every man's *j* comes from the LORD

Eccles. 12:14 God shall bring every work into *j*

Isa. 42:1 He [God's servant] shall bring forth *j* to the Gentiles

Jer. 33:15 He [Messiah] shall execute *j* and righteousness

Amos 5:24 But let *j* run down like waters

Matt. 5:22 whosoever is angry with his brother... shall be in danger of the *j*

John 5:29 those who have done evil, to the resurrection of *j*

John 5:30 As I [Jesus] hear, I judge. And My *j* is just

John 9:39 For *j* I [Jesus] have come into this world

Rom. 14:10 we shall all stand before the *j* seat of Christ

1 Cor. 11:29 he...eats and drinks *j* to himself

2 Cor. 5:10 we must all appear before the *j* seat of Christ

Heb. 9:27 appointed to men to die once, but after this the *j*

1 Pet. 4:17 *j* must begin at the house of God

1 John 4:17 we may have boldness in the day of *j*

Rev. 14:7 Fear God...for the hour of His *j* has come

JUDGMENT OF GOD

Rom. 2:3 do you think...that you shall escape the *j-o-G*

2 Thes. 1:5 evidence of the righteous *j-o-G*

JULIA. A believer at Rome to whom the apostle Paul sent greetings (Rom. 16:15).

JUNIA. A believer at Rome greeted and commended by Paul (Rom. 16:7).

JUPITER. chief god of Roman mythology and a name applied to Barnabas by the citizens of Lystra (Acts 14:12).

JUST

Gen. 6:9 Noah was a *j* man

Job 4:17 Shall mortal man be more *j* than God?

Ps. 37:12 The wicked plots against the *j*

Prov. 4:18 path of the *j* is like the shining light

Prov. 11:1 a *j* weight is His [God's] delight

Prov. 20:7 The *j* man walks in his integrity

Eccles. 7:20 not a *j* man upon earth who...does not sin

Isa. 45:21 no other God besides Me, a *j* God and a Savior

Hab. 2:4 But the *j* shall live by his faith

Matt. 1:19 Joseph, her [Mary's] husband, being a *j* man

Luke 2:25 Simeon...was *j* and devout

Rom. 1:17 as it is written, The *j* shall live by faith

Col. 4:1 give to your servants what is *j*

1 Pet. 3:18 For Christ also has once suffered for sins, the *j* for the unjust

1 John 1:9 He [Jesus] is faithful and *j* to forgive us our sins

JUSTICE. Fairness and impartiality in the treatment of all people. This sense of justice is rooted in the divine nature. The Lord is a God of truth who always does what is just and fair (Ps. 89:14). In OT times, He was particularly concerned about just treatment of the poor and oppressed, including widows, orphans, and strangers and foreigners in the land (Ps. 82:3–4; Jer. 49:11). Because God is just, He demands that His people practice justice in all human relationships. The prophet Micah declared that to "do justice" was more important than offering sacrifices and performing other religious rituals (Mic. 6:7–8).

JUSTICE

Job 8:3 Or does the Almighty pervert *j*?

Ps. 82:3 do *j* to the afflicted and needy

Prov. 21:3 To do *j*...is more acceptable...than sacrifice

Jer. 9:24 I am the LORD who exercises... *j*

Jer. 23:5 a King [Jesus] shall...carry out judgment and *j*

Mic. 6:8 what does the LORD require...but to do *j*

JUSTIFICATION. The divine process through which God makes a person just, and therefore acceptable to Him (Rom. 5:9). Jesus fulfilled God's demand for such righteousness among believers. Through His atoning death, God the Father charged the sin of humans to Christ and credited the godliness of His Son to hopeless sinners. To be justified is to have peace with God and hope for eternal life (Titus 3:5–7).

JUSTIFICATION

Rom. 4:25 who [Jesus] was...raised again for our *j*

Rom. 5:18 the free gift came on all men to *j* of life

JUSTIFY [IED, IES]

Job 9:20 If I *j* myself, my own mouth...condemn me

Job 25:4 How then can man be *j'ied* with God?

Matt. 12:37 by your words you shall be *j'ied*

Rom. 3:24 *j'ied* freely by His [God's] grace through...Christ Jesus

Rom. 3:28 *j'ied* by faith without the deeds of the law

Rom. 5:1 having been *j'ied* by faith, we have peace with God

Rom. 8:33 It is God who *j'ies*

1 Cor. 6:11 you were *j'ied* in the name of the Lord

Gal. 2:16 a man is *j'ied* not by the works of the law

Titus 3:7 *j'ied* by His [God's] grace, we should be made heirs...of eternal life

Jas. 2:21 Was not Abraham our father *j'ied* by works

JUSTUS. A friend and believer at Corinth who provided lodging for the apostle Paul (Acts 18:7).

KAB. A dry measure of about three pints (2 Kings 6:25). *Cab*: KJV.

KADESH. A wilderness area south of the Dead Sea where Moses sent scouts to investigate the land of Canaan (Num. 13:1–16, 26). They reported that the territory was fertile enough to support the people. But it was inhabited by powerful tribes entrenched behind walled cities (Num. 13:28–29). At this news the people cried out against the Lord and Moses for leading them to what they perceived to be a dead end. God punished them for their disobedience by forcing them to wander in the wilderness for forty years until all the doubters were dead (Num.14:31–34). Kadesh is mentioned in Gen. 14:7; 16:14; 20:1 • **Num.** 20:1, 14, 16–22; **33:36–37** • Deut. 1:46 • Judg. 11:16–17 • Ps. 29:8. Also called *Kadesh-barnea* (**Num.** 32:8 • Josh. 14:7).

KANAH. A stream between the territories of Ephraim and Manasseh (Josh. 16:8–9; 17:9).

KAPH. See *Caph*

KARKOR. A place east of the Jordan River where the judge Gideon's forces defeated the remnants of the fleeing Midianite army (Judg. 8:10–12, 21).

KEDAR. A son of Ishmael, grandson of Abraham, and founder of an Arabic tribe. The people who descended from Kedar lived in the desert between Arabia and Babylon. Kedar is mentioned in Gen. 25:12–13 • Isa. 21:17 • Jer. 49:28–29.

KEDESH. A city of refuge situated in the territory of Naphtali in northern Israel. Kedesh is mentioned in Josh. 20:1–7 • Judg. 4:10–11 • 1 Chron. 6:76.

KEEP [ING, S]

Exod. 12:14 **k** it [the Passover] as a feast to the LORD

Exod. 19:5 **k** My covenant, then you shall be a special treasure

Exod. 20:8 Remember the Sabbath day, to **k** it holy

Exod. 31:14 **k** the Sabbath...it is holy to you

Deut. 5:10 showing mercy to...those who...**k** My commandments

Ps. 17:8 **K** me as the apple of the eye. Hide me

Ps. 34:13 **K** your tongue from evil...your lips from...deceit

Ps. 119:4 You have commanded us to **k** Your precepts

Ps. 119:34 Give me understanding, and I shall **k** Your law

Ps. 119:146 save me...I shall **k** Your testimonies

Ps. 121:4 He who **k's** Israel...neither slumber nor sleep

Ps. 127:1 Unless the LORD **k's** the city, the watchman wakes in vain

Prov. 3:1 let your heart **k** my commandments

Prov. 4:23 **K** your heart with all diligence

Prov. 13:3 He who **k's** his mouth **k's** his life

Prov. 21:23 **k's** his...tongue **k's** his soul from troubles

Prov. 29:11 fool utters all his mind...wise man **k's** it in

Eccles. 3:7 time to **k** silent and a time to speak

Isa. 26:3 will **k** him whose mind is steadfast on You

Ezek. 20:19 walk in My statutes, and **k** My judgments

Hab. 2:20 Let all the earth **k** silence before Him

Mark 7:9 reject the commandment...that you [Pharisees] may **k** your own tradition

Luke 2:8 shepherds...**k'ing** watch over their flock

Luke 11:28 Yes, rather, blessed are those who hear the word of God and **k** it

John 9:16 This man [Jesus] is not from God, because he does not **k** the sabbath

John 14:15 If you love Me, **k** my commandments

John 15:10 If you **k** My commandments, you shall abide in My love

1 Cor. 7:19 Circumcision is nothing...but the **k'ing** of the commandments

1 Cor. 14:28 no interpreter, let him **k** silent in the church

Eph. 4:3 **k** the unity of the Spirit in the bond of peace

2 Thes. 3:3 Lord...shall establish you...**k** you from evil

Jas. 1:27 undefiled religion...is this...to **k** himself unblemished

Jas. 2:10 **k's** the whole law, and yet offends in one point, he is guilty of all

1 John 5:3 this is the love of God...**k** His commandments

1 John 5:21 Little children, **k** yourselves from idols

Jude 24 unto Him who is able to **k** you from falling

Rev. 2:26 he who...**k's** My works...to him I will give power

KEEP HIS COMMANDMENTS

Deut. 13:4 You shall walk after the LORD...and **k-H-c**

Ps. 78:7 That they might...not forget the works of God but **k-H-c**

Eccles. 12:13 **k-H-c**, for this is the whole duty of man

1 John 2:3 we do know that we know Him, if we **k-H-c**

KEILAH. A fortified city in southern Israel defended against the Philistines by David's army (1 Sam. 23:1–5).

KELITA. A Levite after the Exile who explained the law as Ezra read it to the people (Neh. 8:7).

KENAN. A son of Enoch who lived before the great flood (1 Chron. 1:1–2). Also called *Cainan* (Gen. 5:9).

KENITES. A nomadic tribe that inhabited the desert regions near the Dead Sea. They may have been associated with the Midianites, since Moses' father-in-law Jethro is called a Midianite (Exod. 18:1) as well as a Kenite (Judg. 1:16). They are mentioned in Gen. 15:19 • Num.

24:20–22 • Judg. 4:11, 17–22 • 1 Sam. 15:6; 30:29 • 1 Chron. 2:55.

KENIZZITES. A Canaanite tribe whose land was promised to Abraham's descendants (Gen. 15:18–19).

KENOSIS. A theological term that refers to the humanity and humility of Christ. The term comes from a Greek word that means "to make empty." The apostle Paul declared, "He [Jesus] made himself of no reputation" (Phil. 2:7). Some translations render this phrase as "He emptied himself." Paul went on to say that Jesus "took on Himself the form of a servant, and was made in the likeness of men." This refers to His willingness to become flesh so He could identify fully with human beings.

KEPT

Exod. 3:1 Moses *k* the flock of Jethro

Ps. 18:21 For I have *k* the ways of the LORD

Ps. 32:3 When I *k* silent, my bones grew old

Ps. 78:56 they...provoked...God...did not *k* His testimonies

Ps. 119:55 I have remembered Your name...and have *k* Your law

Matt. 19:20 these things I have *k* from my youth

Luke 2:19 But Mary *k* all these things...in her heart

John 17:12 I [Jesus] *k* them [the disciples] in Your name...none...is lost

Gal. 3:23 before faith came, we were *k* under the law

2 Tim. 4:7 I [Paul] have fought a good fight...*k* the faith

1 Pet. 1:5 *k* by the power of God through faith

KERIOTH. A fortified city of Moab marked for destruction, according to the prophet Amos (Amos 2:2; *Kirioth*: KJV). This may be the same place as the hometown of Judas Iscariot, the disciple who betrayed Jesus. The word *Iscariot* means "man of Kerioth."

KETURAH. A wife of Abraham whom he apparently married after the death of Sarah. Keturah gave birth to six sons, who became the ancestors of six Arabian tribes (Gen. 25:1–6

• 1 Chron. 1:32–33). One of Keturah's sons was Midian, apparently the ancestor of the tribe known as the Midianites. Jethro, Moses' father-in-law, was from Midian (Exod. 3:1).

KEY. A tool for locking and unlocking a door; a word used figuratively to symbolize authority, privilege, or power (Isa. 22:22; Rev. 1:18). Jesus told His disciple Peter that He would give him "the keys of the kingdom of heaven" (Matt. 16:19), implying Peter's future leadership of the church.

KEY [S]

Judg. 3:25 they took a *k* and opened...their lord had fallen down dead

Matt. 16:19 give to you the *k's* of the kingdom

Luke 11:52 you [lawyers] have taken away the *k* of knowledge

Rev. 9:1 to him [angel] was given the *k* of the bottomless pit

KID. A young goat used as a sacrificial offering (Gen. 27:9) or served as a meal on special occasions (Luke 15:29).

KIDRON BROOK. A small stream just outside Jerusalem that ran through a deep valley of the same name. Its name means "gloomy" or "dusky place," perhaps because of the many burial sites in the area. David crossed the brook while fleeing from the rebellion of his son Absalom (2 Sam. 15:23–30). It is also mentioned in 2 Kings 23:4–6, 12 • 2 Chron. 15:16; 29:16; 30:14 • Jer. 31:40 • John 18:1.

KILL [ED, S]

Gen. 37:31 they [Joseph's brothers]...*k'ed* a young goat

Exod. 2:14 intend [Moses] to *k* me [Hebrew slave], as you *k'd* the Egyptian?

Exod. 20:13 You shall not *k*

Num. 35:15 everyone who *k's* any person unintentionally may flee

Deut. 5:17 You shall not *k*

1 Sam. 2:6 The LORD *k's*, and makes alive

2 Sam. 12:9 You [David] have *k'ed* Uriah the Hittite

Ps. 44:22 for Your sake we are *k'ed* all day long

Prov. 21:25 The desire of the slothful *k's* him

Eccles. 3:3 a time to *k* and a time to heal

Matt. 5:21 whoever *k's*...in danger of the judgment

Matt. 23:37 O Jerusalem...you who *k* the prophets

Mark 3:4 Is it lawful...on the Sabbath...to save life or to *k*?

Mark 8:31 Son of man must suffer...and be *k'ed*

Mark 9:31 after He has been *k'ed*, He shall rise

Mark 12:7 let us *k* him [the heir]...inheritance shall be ours

Luke 12:4 do not be afraid of those who *k* the body

Luke 12:5 after He has *k'ed*, has power to cast into hell

Luke 15:23 bring the fatted calf here and *k* it

Luke 22:2 chief priests and scribes sought how they might *k* Him

John 10:10 thief does not come except to *k* and to destroy

John 16:2 whoever *k's* you will think that he is serving God

Acts 10:13 Peter; *k*, and eat

Acts 12:2 he [Herod] *k'ed* James the brother of John

Rom. 8:36 For Your sake we are *k'ed* all day long

2 Cor. 3:6 letter *k's*, but the Spirit gives life

Jas. 4:2 You *k* and desire to have and cannot obtain

Rev. 11:7 beast...shall overcome them [two witnesses], and *k* them

KINDNESS. Treating others with respect; a characteristic of God that He desires in His followers (Col. 3:12). The OT often uses two words, love and kindness, joined together—or lovingkindness—to express this divine quality (Ps. 40:11). The NT word *grace* best expresses this idea of God's divine love and favor. The ultimate expression of God's kindness was His gift of Jesus to the world.

KING. The monarch or supreme ruler over a nation. Beginning with the first king, Saul (1 Sam. 10:1), both Judah (the Southern Kingdom) and Israel (the Northern Kingdom) had a succession of kings across several centuries until both nations were overrun by foreign powers. The books of 1 and 2 Samuel, 1 and 2 Kings, and 1 and 2 Chronicles report on the reigns of many of these kings. A few in Judah were godly rulers who honored God and followed His law, but most of the kings of the northern territory were evil and corrupt. They led God's people into sin and idolatry. In the NT, the name "King of kings" is applied to Jesus implying that His sovereignty has no limits. When He returns in the end-time, His supreme rule over all the earth will be prominently displayed for everyone to see (Rev. 19:16).

KINGDOM [S]

Exod. 19:6 to Me a *k* of priests and a holy nation

1 Sam. 15:28 The LORD has torn the *k* of Israel from you [Saul] this day

2 Sam. 7:16 your [David's] house and your *k* shall be established forever

1 Kings 4:21 And Solomon reigned over all *k's*

1 Chron. 29:11 Yours is the *k*, O LORD...You are exalted

Ps. 22:28 the *k* is the LORD's

Ps. 68:32 Sing to God, you *k's* of the earth

Ps. 145:13 Your *k* is an everlasting *k*

Dan. 2:39 another *k*...shall arise after you

Dan. 4:3 His *k* is an everlasting *k*

Dan. 4:31 the *k* has departed from you [Nebuchadnezzar]

Dan. 5:28 Your [Belshazzar's] *k* is divided...given to the Medes

Matt. 6:10 Your *k* come. Your will be done

Matt. 8:12 children of the *k*...cast into outer darkness

Matt. 24:7 nation shall rise against nation...*k* against *k*

Mark 3:24 *k* is divided against itself, that *k* cannot stand

Luke 1:33 of His *k* there shall be no end

Luke 4:5 the devil...showed to Him all the *k's* of the world

Luke 12:32 your Father's good pleasure to give you the *k*

Luke 23:42 remember me [thief] when You [Jesus] come into Your *k*

John 18:36 My **k** is not of this world

1 Thes. 2:12 God, who has called you to His **k**

Rev. 11:15 **k's** of this world have become the **k's** of our Lord

KINGDOM OF GOD. The spiritual reign of God in the hearts of believers (Luke 17:20–21). Jesus preached the "gospel of the kingdom of God" (Mark 1:14) and taught His disciples to seek His kingdom (Matt. 6:33) and to pray for its arrival on earth (Matt. 6:10). In one of His parables, He compared the kingdom to seed scattered on the ground. Some seed would sprout and grow in good soil. But other seed would fall on rocky ground and fail to take root. This shows that the kingdom will flourish in the hearts of some people but will be rejected by others (Matt. 13:3–8). This kingdom is also referred to as the kingdom of heaven (Matt. 4:17) and "the kingdom of [God's] dear Son" (Col. 1:13).

KINGDOM OF GOD

Matt. 6:33 seek first the **k-o-G** and His righteousness

Mark 1:15 time is fulfilled, and the **k-o-G** is at hand

Mark 9:47 better...to enter into the **k-o-G** with one eye

Mark 10:14 do not forbid them [children]... such is the **k-o-G**

Mark 10:25 eye of a needle than for a rich man to enter into the **k-o-G**

Luke 9:2 He sent them [the disciples]...to preach the **k-o-G**

Luke 9:62 No man who...looks back is fit for the **k-o-G**

John 3:3 unless a man is born again...cannot see the **k-o-G**

Rom. 14:17 **k-o-G** is not eating and drinking, but righteousness

1 Cor. 6:9 the unrighteous shall not inherit the **k-o-G**

1 Cor. 15:50 flesh and blood cannot inherit the **k-o-G**

KINGDOM OF HEAVEN

Matt. 5:10 Blessed are those who are persecuted...theirs is the **k-o-h**

Matt. 5:20 you shall in no circumstance enter into the **k-o-h**

Matt. 7:21 Not everyone who says to Me, 'Lord, Lord,' shall enter into the **k-o-h**

Matt. 16:19 I [Jesus] will give to you...keys of the **k-o-h**

Matt. 18:4 humbles himself like this little child, the same is greatest in the **k-o-h**

Matt. 23:13 you [scribes and Pharisees]...shut up the **k-o-h** against men

KING'S HIGHWAY. An important road linking Damascus and Egypt that ran through Israel (Num. 20:17–21).

KING'S VALLEY. A valley east of Jerusalem where Abraham met the king of Sodom as well as the mysterious Melchizedek, king of Salem (Gen. 14:17–18). *King's dale*: KJV.

KINGS, FIRST. A historical book of the OT that traces the reigns of several Israelite kings, beginning with David and Solomon. But the pivotal event in the book is the split of their united kingdom into two rival factions—Judah (the Southern Kingdom) and Israel (the Northern Kingdom)—after Solomon's death. Several kings of both nations are mentioned in the book. But major attention is focused on Ahab of Israel and his evil wife, Jezebel. They promoted worship of the pagan god Baal throughout their nation. God raised up the prophet Elijah to condemn their idolatry and predict that God would punish their evil deeds. This prophecy was fulfilled in the final chapter of the book when Ahab was killed during a battle with the Syrians (1 Kings 22:34–40).

KINGS, SECOND. A historical book of the OT that picks up where 1 Kings leaves off. It continues the accounts of the reigns of various kings of Judah (the Southern Kingdom) and Israel the Northern Kingdom). Many of Israel's kings supported worship of pagan gods. God's punishment fell in 722 BC, when the Assyrians overran the nation and carried away many of its citizens as captives and slaves (2 Kings 17:5–23). The kings of Judah, since they were descendants of the great king David, were generally a better lot than the kings of Israel. But Judah also had its share of evil kings, including Manasseh (2 Kings 21:1–6). About 135 years after Israel fell to a foreign power, God sent the same punishment upon Judah. The leading citizens of the nation were carried into exile when Jerusalem fell to the Babylonians in 587 BC. The book of 2 Kings ends with Jerusalem in shambles and the beautiful temple destroyed and looted by a pagan army (2 Kings 25:21)—a far cry from the glory days of David and Solomon.

KINSMAN. A close relative who had the right to buy back the freedom or property that had been lost by members of the clan (Lev. 25:48–49). Boaz, a kinsman of Naomi, acted as a redeemer for Naomi when he married Ruth, Naomi's daughter-in-law (Ruth 4). In a spiritual sense, God is the kinsman or redeemer of His people (2 Sam. 7:23).

KIRIATH-ARBA. See *Hebron*

KIRIATH-JEARIM. A fortified city of the Gibeonites where the ark of the covenant was kept for a time. It rested safely in the care of Abinadab and his son Eleazar (1 Sam. 7:1) before King David moved it to Jerusalem (2 Sam. 6:1–15). Kiriath-jearim is also mentioned in Josh. 9:17; 15:60; 18:28 • **1 Chron. 13–16.** *Baalah*: Josh. 15:9.

KISHON RIVER. A river in northern Israel where the judges Deborah and Barak defeated the forces of the Canaanite king Sisera (Judg. 4:7). The prophet Elijah also killed the prophets of Baal in this vicinity (1 Kings 18:40). It is also mentioned in Judg. 4:13 • Ps. 83:9.

KISON. KJV: see *Kishon*

KISS. A sign of affection often used symbolically, as in the psalmist's description of righteousness and peace kissing each other (Ps. 85:10). Jesus was betrayed by Judas with the infamous "Judas kiss" (Matt. 26:49).

KISS [ED]
Gen. 50:1 Joseph...wept on him [Jacob] and *k'ed* him

Ps. 85:10 righteousness and peace have *k'ed* each other
Matt. 26:49 he [Judas]...said, Hail, Master, and *k'ed* Him
Luke 15:20 his [prodigal son's] father...fell on his neck and *k'ed* him
Luke 22:48 Judas, will you betray the Son of Man with a *k*?
2 Cor. 13:12 Greet one another with a holy *k*
1 Pet. 5:14 Greet one another with a *k* of loss

KITTIM. See *Cyprus*

KNEELING. Like bowing, kneeling was a symbol of respect (Ps. 95:6) or subjection to another person (2 Kings 1:13). Kneeling was also a stance in prayer which showed reverence for God (Luke 22:41).

KNOCK [ED]
Luke 11:9 k, and it shall be opened to you
Acts 12:13 as Peter *k'ed* at the door...Rhoda came
Rev. 3:20 I [Jesus] stand at the door and *k*

KNOWLEDGE. Information, facts, and insights gained through study and experience. Lack of basic knowledge about God can lead to sin and idolatry (Isa. 5:13). Moral knowledge comes from study of the Bible, communion with God through prayer, and directing one's life in accordance with the divine will.

KNOWLEDGE
Gen. 2:17 tree of the *k* of good and evil, you shall not eat
1 Sam. 2:3 for the LORD is a God of *k*, and by Him actions are weighed
Job 21:22 Shall anyone teach God *k*, since He judges
Job 35:16 He [Job] multiplies words without *k*
Ps. 19:2 night to night reveals *k*
Ps. 139:6 Such *k* is too wonderful for me
Prov. 1:7 fear of the LORD is the beginning of *k*
Prov. 10:14 Wise men lay up *k*, but the mouth of the foolish...destruction
Prov. 20:15 the lips of *k* are a precious jewel
Prov. 24:5 a man of *k* increases strength
Eccles. 1:18 he who increases *k* increases sorrow

Hos. 6:6 I [God] desired...*k* of God more than... offerings

Hab. 2:14 earth...filled with the *k* of the glory of the LORD

Rom. 11:33 depth of the riches...wisdom and *k* of God

1 Cor. 12:8 to one is given...word of wisdom... to another...word of *k*

1 Cor. 13:2 though I [Paul]...understand...all *k*

Eph. 3:19 know the love of Christ, which surpasses *k*

Phil. 1:9 love may abound...in *k* and in all judgment

1 Tim. 2:4 all men...to come unto the *k* of the truth

2 Tim. 3:7 never able to come to the *k* of the truth

2 Pet. 1:5 add to your faith, virtue; and to virtue, *k*

2 Pet. 3:18 grow in grace and in the *k* of our Lord

KNOW THAT I AM THE LORD

Exod. 7:5 Egyptians shall *k-t-I-a-t-L*, when I stretch out My hand on Egypt

Ezek. 6:7 slain shall fall...and you shall *k-t-I-a-t-L*

Ezek. 16:62 I will establish My covenant with you...you shall *k-t-I-a-t-L*

Ezek. 30:19 will carry out judgments in Egypt, and they shall *k-t-I-a-t-L*

KNOW THE LORD

Jer. 31:34 no longer...teach...*K-t-L*, for they shall all know Me

Heb. 8:11 not teach...his brother, saying, *K-t-L*, for all shall know Me

KOHATH. Second son of Levi (Gen. 46:11) and founder of the Kohathites. They cared for the ark of the covenant and other items associated with the tabernacle while the Israelites journeyed in the wilderness (Num. 3:30–31). Kohath is also mentioned in Exod. 6:18–19.

KOPH. Nineteenth letter of the Hebrew alphabet, used as a heading over Ps. 119:145–152. In the Hebrew language, the first line of each of these eight verses begins with this letter.

KOR. A unit for measuring liquids, possibly equivalent to fifty or more gallons (Ezek. 45:14).

KORAH. A Levite who incited a rebellion against the leadership of Moses and Aaron in the wilderness. Korah apparently was resentful of Aaron's position as high priest. As punishment for their sin, Korah and all his followers were swallowed by the earth. He is mentioned in Exod. 6:21, 24 • Num. 16:30–33 • Jude 11.

LABAN. A resident of Mesopotamia who was involved in the marriages of two of the famous patriarchs of the Bible, Isaac and Jacob. Laban gave permission for his sister Rebekah to marry Isaac (Gen. 24:55–67). In later years, he provided sanctuary for his sister's son Jacob, who eventually married two of Laban's daughters. Jacob worked seven years for Laban for the privilege of marrying Rachel, only to be tricked into marrying her older sister Leah instead. Then Jacob worked another seven years for Rachel (Gen. 29:5–30). Laban is also mentioned in Gen. 24:29, 50; 30:25–40; 31:2–55.

LABOR [ED, S]

Exod. 20:9 Six days you shall *l* and do all your work

Ps. 104:23 Man goes out...to his *l* until the evening

Ps. 127:1 Unless the LORD builds the house, those who build it *l* in vain

Prov. 23:4 Do not *l* to be rich

Eccles. 3:9 What profit does he...have from that in which he *l*'s

Eccles. 3:13 man should...enjoy the good of all his *l*

Matt. 11:28 Come to Me, all you who *l* and are heavy-laden

1 Cor. 3:8 his own reward according to his own *l*

1 Cor. 15:58 your *l* is not in vain in the Lord

2 Cor. 11:23 more abundant in *l's*, above measure in beatings

Phil. 2:16 I [Paul] have not...*l'ed* in vain

Heb. 4:11 Therefore let us *l* to enter into that rest

LABORER [S]

Matt. 9:37 The harvest...is plentiful, but the *l's* are few

Luke 10:7 for the *l* is worthy of his hire

1 Cor. 3:9 For we are *l's* together with God

LACHISH. An Amorite city in southern Canaan captured by Joshua (Josh. 10:3–35). In later years, King Solomon's son and successor Rehoboam turned the city into a defensive outpost to protect Judah (the Southern Kingdom) from Egypt (2 Chron. 11:5–12). Lachish was reoccupied by the Israelites after the Exile (Neh. 11:25–30). It is also mentioned in Josh. 12:11; 15:39 • 2 Kings 14:19; 18:14–17 • 2 Chron. 25:27 • Isa. 36:1–2 • Jer. 34:1, 7.

LACK [S]

Gen. 18:28 Will You [God] destroy all the city for *l* of five?

Hos. 4:6 people are destroyed for *l* of knowledge

Matt. 19:20 these things I have kept...what do I still *l*

Luke 18:22 Yet you *l* one thing. Sell all...distribute to the poor

Luke 22:35 When I [Jesus] sent you [the disciples] without purse...did you *l* anything?

Jas. 1:5 any of you *l's* wisdom, let him ask of God

LAISH. A Canaanite city captured by the tribe of Dan. They changed its name from Laish to Dan (Judg. 18:29).

LAKE OF FIRE. A word picture for hell, the eternal destiny of unbelievers. Filled with burning brimstone (Rev. 19:20), this place is described as the "second death" (Rev. 20:14). Those consigned to the lake of fire include Satan (Rev. 20:10), people whose names do not appear in the book of life (Rev. 20:15), and unbelieving sinners (Rev. 21:8).

LAMB OF GOD. A name or title for Jesus used by John the Baptist when he saw Jesus approaching at the beginning of His ministry (John 1:29, 35–36). Lambs were choice young sheep used as sacrificial animals in Jewish worship rituals (Lev. 14:12–13; 1 Sam. 7:9). Thus, John recognized the redemptive role that Jesus was destined to fill. Centuries before Jesus was born into the world, the prophet Isaiah recognized that the Messiah would come on a mission of redemptive suffering for hopeless sinners (Isa. 53:7). On the night before His crucifixion, Jesus gathered with His disciples to eat a meal that was part of the observance of the Jewish Passover. Just as the blood of the first Passover lamb had been an agent of deliverance for the Israelites in Egypt, so His shed blood would provide spiritual deliverance for sinful people. As Jesus passed the cup among His disciples, He told them, "This is My blood of the new covenant, which is shed for many for the remission of sins" (Matt. 26:28).

LAMB OF GOD

John 1:29 the **L-o-G** who takes away the sin of the world

John 1:36 he [John the Baptist] said, Behold the **L-o-G**

LAME

Prov. 26:7 The legs of the *l* are not equal

Luke 7:22 tell John...how the blind see, the *l* walk

Luke 14:13 call the poor...the *l*, the blind

LAMECH. A son of Methuselah and the father of Noah (Gen. 5:25–31 • 1 Chron. 1:3). Lamech is listed in Luke's genealogy of Jesus (Luke 3:36).

LAMED. Twelfth letter of the Hebrew alphabet, used as a heading over Psalm 119:89–96. In the Hebrew language, the first line of each of these eight verses begins with this letter.

LAMENTATIONS OF JEREMIAH. A short OT book that expresses the prophet's despair at the destruction of Jerusalem by the pagan Babylonians. Jeremiah loved the city and his native land, although he was compelled by the Lord to deliver a harsh message of judgment against his fellow citizens. When the inevitable finally happened, he was overcome with grief and despair over this tragic event. Jeremiah spoke of throwing dust on one's head (Lam. 2:10), a sign of mourning. He described people as hissing and shaking their heads to show their contempt for the fallen city (Lam. 2:15–16). The phrase "the crown has fallen from our head" (Lam. 5:16) expresses the loss of the position of honor that once belonged to Judah (the Southern Kingdom).

LAMP [S]

Judg. 7:20 broke the pitchers...held the *l*'s in their...hands

2 Sam. 22:29 For You are my *l*, O LORD

Job 41:19 Burning *l*'s go out of his [Leviathan's] mouth

Ps. 119:105 Your [God's] word is a *l* to my feet

Matt. 25:3 foolish took their *l*'s and took no oil with them

LANDMARK. A property line indicated by a pile of stones or some other object. Moving such a marker to take another's property was forbidden by the OT law (Deut. 19:14).

LAND OF PROMISE. A description of Canaan, or the territory eventually inhabited by the Israelites. This land was promised by God to Abraham's descendants (Gen. 12:1–7). Several centuries after Abraham's time, the promise was fulfilled when Joshua led the Israelites to take the land from the Canaanites (Josh. 10–12).

LAODICEA. A major city in Asia Minor where one of the seven churches addressed in the book of Revelation was located. This church was rebuked because of its complacency (Rev. 3:14–18). It is also mentioned in Col. 2:1; 4:13–16.

LASCIVIOUSNESS. KJV: see *Lewdness*

LASEA. A seaport on the island of Crete by which Paul's ship passed on his way to Rome (Acts 27:7–8).

LASHES

Deut. 25:3 He [judge] may give him [wicked man] forty *l*, and not exceed

Prov. 17:10 rebuke enters more into a wise man than a hundred *l* into a fool

Isa. 53:5 and with His [Jesus'] *l* we are healed

Luke 12:47 that servant...shall be beaten with many *l*

2 Cor. 11:24 Five times I [Paul] received from the Jews forty *l* less one

LAST

Isa. 2:2 in the *l* days...LORD's house shall be established

Isa. 44:6 I [God] am the first and I am the *l*

Matt. 20:8 give them [the laborers] their wages... from the *l* to the first

Mark 9:35 desires to be first, the same shall be *l* of all

Mark 10:31 many who are first shall be *l*

1 Cor. 15:26 The *l* enemy that shall be destroyed is death

1 Cor. 15:45 The *l* Adam was made a reviving spirit

2 Tim. 3:1 in the *l* days perilous times shall come

Heb. 1:2 has in these *l* days spoken...by His [God's] Son

Rev. 1:11 I [Jesus] am Alpha and Omega, the first and the *l*

Rev. 22:13 I [Jesus] am...the first and the *l*

LAST JUDGMENT. A time in the future when God will intervene in history to judge the wicked, reward the righteous, and bring the universe to its appointed conclusion. This final judgment is sometimes referred to as the "great white throne" judgment. This term comes from the book of Revelation, where God is depicted as judging the earth while seated on a great white throne (Rev. 20:11). The last judgment will be universal in scope. All people and nations of the earth will be judged. Unbelievers will be condemned to eternal punishment, while believers will enter into eternal life. Only God the Father knows when this will happen. Jesus declared that even He did not know the exact time that this would occur (Matt. 24:36).

LAST SUPPER. See *Lord's Supper*

LATTER RAIN. Rain that fell late in the growing season, allowing crops to reach full maturity before the harvest (Jer. 3:3).

LAVER. A basin or bowl in which a priest purified himself by washing his hands while officiating at the altar (Exod. 30:18–21).

LAWFUL [LY]

Matt. 12:2 Your [Jesus'] disciples are doing what is not *l*...on the Sabbath day

Matt. 19:3 Is it *l* for a man to divorce his wife for any reason?

Mark 3:4 Is it *l* to do good on the Sabbath...or to do evil

Mark 12:14 Is it *l* to give taxes to Caesar or not?

1 Cor. 6:12 All things are *l* to me [Paul], but not all things are expedient

1 Tim. 1:8 the law is good if a man uses it *l'ly*

LAWGIVER. A title of God that emphasizes His role as the sovereign Lord of creation (Isa. 33:22). He is the source of truth, righteousness, and holiness. He has the right to make the laws and set the standards by which people should live.

LAWLESS

1 Tim. 1:9 law is made...for the *l* and disobedient

LAW OF MOSES. The authoritative rule of conduct spelled out in the Ten Commandments and the Pentateuch—the books of Genesis, Exodus, Leviticus, Numbers, and Deuteronomy. This code was revealed to Moses by the Lord on Mount Sinai (Exod. 20:1–17; Deut. 5:1–2). The most important of these laws is the command to worship God alone and not to bow down to false gods—the demand of the first commandment. God's moral law also specifies that people should honor God's name, show respect to parents, observe the Sabbath appropriately, refrain from adulterous relationships, deal honestly with people, avoid excessive desire for material things that leads to greed, practice honesty in business, and show kindness and generosity toward the poor.

The Pentateuch also contains many laws of a ceremonial and civil nature, many of which are not applicable to modern times. Ceremonial laws dealt with the distinctive worship rituals of ancient Israel, including regulations about the priesthood, religious holidays or festivals, foods that could or could not be eaten, and purification rituals. Civil laws dealt with such matters as compensation for personal injuries and damaged property, how slaves were to be treated, and the circumstances that exempted certain people from going to war.

LAY [ING, S]

Prov. 10:14 Wise men *l* up knowledge

Isa. 28:16 I [God] *l* in Zion a stone for a foundation

Jer. 6:21 Behold, I [God] will *l* stumbling blocks before this people

Ezek. 25:17 know that I am the LORD, when I *l* My vengeance on them

Matt. 6:20 *l* up for yourselves treasures in heaven

Matt. 28:6 Come, see the place where the Lord *l*

Luke 9:58 Son of Man does not have anywhere to *l* His head

Luke 12:21 he who *l's* up treasure...not rich toward God

Luke 21:12 *l* their hands on you [the disciples] and persecute you

John 10:15 I [Jesus] *l* down My life for the sheep

John 13:37 Peter said...Lord...I will *l* down my life for Your sake

John 15:13 that a man *l* down his life for his friends

1 Cor. 3:11 no man can *l* a foundation other than...Jesus Christ

1 Cor. 16:2 *l* aside something to store, as God has prospered

1 Tim. 4:14 with the *l'ing* on of the hands of the council of elders

1 Tim. 5:22 Do not *l* hands on any man suddenly

Heb. 12:1 *l* aside...the sin that so easily besets us

1 Pet. 2:1 *l'ing* aside all malice, and all deceit

LAYING ON OF HANDS. A ritual by which a person was blessed or set apart for service. On the Day of Atonement, the high priest placed his hands on the scapegoat to symbolize the transfer of the sins of the people to the animal (Lev. 16:21). The patriarch Jacob placed his hands on his sons and grandsons to convey his special blessing (Gen. 48:14, 18). In the NT, the members of the church at Antioch of Syria laid their hands on Paul and Barnabas to confirm their calling as missionaries and to set them apart for this service (Acts 13:2–3). See also *Ordination*.

LAZARUS. A brother of Mary and Martha and a friend of Jesus whom He raised from the dead. According to the Gospel of John, this miracle was the last performed by Jesus before His crucifixion (John 11:43–44). Because it was so spectacular and so close to Jerusalem, the Jewish Sanhedrin stepped up its plans to arrest Jesus and have Him executed (John 11:45–57). Their death plans even included Lazarus because his miraculous emergence from the grave caused many people to believe in Jesus (John 12:10).

LEAD [S]

Exod. 13:21 LORD went before them [Israelites]... to *l* them

Ps. 23:2 He [God] *l's* me beside the still waters

Ps. 25:5 L me in Your [God's] truth, and teach me

Ps. 61:2 *l* me to the rock that is higher than I

Ps. 139:10 even there Your [God's] hand shall *l* me

Isa. 11:6 And a little child shall *l* them

Isa. 40:11 He [God]...shall gently *l* those who are with young

Matt. 6:13 do not *l* us into temptation...deliver us from evil

Matt. 7:14 the way is narrow that *l's* to life

Luke 6:39 He [Jesus] spoke a parable...Can the blind *l* the blind?

Rev. 7:17 Lamb...shall *l* them to living fountains of waters

LEAH. The oldest daughter of Laban whom Jacob was tricked into taking as his first wife (Gen. 29:16–35). Jacob worked for Laban for seven years for the privilege of marrying his younger daughter, Rachel, only to discover that Leah had been substituted for Rachel. Then Jacob worked for Laban for seven more years in order to marry Rachel. But Jacob's marriage to Leah turned out to be a blessing in disguise. She bore six of his sons—Reuben, Simeon, Levi, Judah, Issachar, and Zebulun (Gen. 29:16–35;

30:9–20). The descendants of these sons developed into six of the twelve tribes of the nation of Israel. Leah is also mentioned in Gen. 31:4, 14; 33:1–7; 34:1; 35:23; 46:15, 18; 49:31.

LEARN [ED, ING]

Ps. 119:73 that I may *l* Your [God's] commandments

Prov. 1:5 A wise man...will increase *l'ing*

Isa. 1:17 L to do well...relieve the oppressed

Jer. 10:2 This what the LORD says: Do not *l* not the way of the nations

Dan. 1:17 God gave them [Daniel and his friends]...skill in all *l'ing* and wisdom

Matt. 11:29 Take My [Jesus'] yoke...and *l* from Me

Phil. 4:11 I [Paul] have *l'ed* in whatever state I am to be content with it

2 Tim. 3:7 ever *l'ing* and never able to come to the...truth

Heb. 5:8 though He [Jesus] was a Son, He *l'ed* obedience

LEAST

Matt. 2:6 Bethlehem, in the land of Judah, are not the *l* among the princes of Judah

Matt. 25:40 you have done it to one of the *l* of these My [Jesus'] brothers

Luke 7:28 he who is *l* in the kingdom...is greater than he [John the Baptist]

Luke 9:48 who is *l* among you all, the same shall be great

Eph. 3:8 To me [Paul], who am less than the *l* of all saints

LEAVEN. An ingredient added to bread to make it rise (Exod. 12:15–20). The Israelites left Egypt in such a hurry that they didn't have time to add leaven to the bread they were baking (Exod. 12:39). This led to their later practice of baking bread without leaven in a ritual known as the Feast of Unleavened Bread. This observance occurred in association with the yearly Passover. In one of His parables, Jesus compared the kingdom of God with leaven in dough, suggesting that His spiritual kingdom had a power out of all proportion to its size that caused it to permeate and influence all of society (Luke 13:20–21).

LEAVEN [S]

Matt. 13:33 kingdom of heaven is similar to *l*

Luke 12:1 beware of the *l* of the Pharisees

1 Cor. 5:6 know that a little *l l's* the whole lump

LEBANON. A rugged mountainous region along the northern border of Israel. King Solomon used lumber from cedar trees that grew in Lebanon in the construction of the temple and other buildings in Jerusalem. It is mentioned in Deut. 1:7; 3:25 • Josh. 11:16–17; 12:7; 13:5–7 • Judg. 3:1–3 • 1 Kings 5:5–18 • Isa. 29:17; 37:24 • Ezek. 17:3 • Hos. 14:5–7.

LEBBAEUS. See *Judas*, No. 1

LED

Ps. 68:18 You have ascended on high; You have *l* captives

Prov. 4:11 I have taught you...I have *l* you in right paths

Isa. 55:12 go out with joy, and be *l* out with peace

Luke 4:1 Jesus...was *l* by the Spirit into the wilderness

Luke 24:50 He [Jesus] *l* them out as far as to Bethany

Acts 8:32 He [Jesus] was *l* as a sheep to the slaughter

Acts 9:8 l him [Paul] by the hand...into Damascus

Rom. 8:14 as are *l* by the Spirit of God...are the sons of God

Gal. 5:18 if you are *l* by the Spirit, you are not under the law

2 Pet. 3:17 lest you also...being *l* away with the error of the wicked

LEEK. A vegetable of the onion family that the Israelites longed for while they wandered in the wilderness (Num. 11:5).

LEHI. A site where the judge Samson killed one thousand Philistines with an unusual weapon, the jawbone of a donkey (Judg. 15:14–15).

LEMUEL. An unknown king who apparently wrote several sayings in the book of Proverbs (Prov. 31:1).

LENTIL. A vegetable similar to the pea used in the stew for which Esau traded his birthright (Gen. 25:29–34).

LEPER [S]

2 Kings 5:1 Naaman...was also a mighty man... but he was a *l*

2 Kings 15:5 the king [Azariah]...was a *l* to the day of his death

Matt. 8:2 a *l* came and worshipped Him [Jesus]

Matt. 11:5 l's are cleansed and the deaf hear

Mark 14:3 in the house of Simon the *l*, as He [Jesus] sat at the table

Luke 17:12 ten men who were *l's*...met Him [Jesus]

LEPROSY. A general word for a variety of dreaded skin diseases. The Mosaic Law required a person with this disability to live in isolation from others (Lev. 13:45–46). Jesus once healed ten lepers and sent them to the priest for verification and purification (Luke 17:11–14).

LEVI. (1) A son of Jacob and Leah (Gen. 29:34). His three sons were ancestors of the three major branches of the Levitical priesthood: Kohathites, Gershonites, and Merarites. As members of the priestly tribe of Levi, they were responsible for assisting the priests of Israel in their spiritual ministry to the rest of the nation. Levi and his descendants are mentioned Gen. 34:25, 30; 35:23; 49:5 • Exod. 1:2; 6:16 • Num. 3:17; 16:1; 26:59 • 1 Chron. 6:38, 43, 47 • Ezra 8:18.

(2) Another name for Matthew, the tax collector who became a disciple of Jesus (Luke 5:27).

LEVIATHAN. A monster mentioned by Job as a force that only the Lord could tame (Job 41:1). The word is also used figuratively of an enemy of Israel, probably Egypt (Isa. 27:1).

LEVIRATE MARRIAGE. The term *levirate* means "husband's brother." It refers to a form of marriage in which a man was encouraged to marry his brother's widow if his brother had died with no male heirs. The purpose of this custom was to provide an heir and an estate for the deceased relative and to care for widows

(Deut. 25:5–10). The union of Boaz and Ruth was a levirate marriage (Ruth 3–4).

LEVITES. Members of one of the twelve tribes of Israel who were descendants of Levi, third son of Jacob and Leah (Gen. 29:34). The Levites were responsible for taking care of the tabernacle and assisting the priests in their ceremonial duties (Num. 3:5–10). When Canaan was divided, the Levites were assigned forty-eight towns in areas occupied by other tribes rather than a specific part of the land (Josh. 21:1–8). These were known as Levitical cities.

LEVITICUS, BOOK OF. An OT book devoted mainly to rituals known as ceremonial law, or worship instructions for the people of ancient Israel. The book describes the establishment of the priesthood, at God's command, through Aaron, his sons, and their successors (Lev. 8:6–12). The priests were to preside at the altar in the tabernacle—later the temple—when people presented their offerings to God. Various types of offerings are described in Leviticus—burnt offerings, grain offerings, peace offerings, sin offerings, and guilt or trespass offerings. But the most significant offering in terms of its symbolism for modern believers was the blood offering—presenting the blood of a sacrificial animal to God. New Testament believers taught that Jesus was the ultimate blood sacrifice. He gave His life by shedding His own blood to make atonement for sin (Heb. 10:10).

LEWDNESS. Unbridled lust, a serious sin to be avoided by believers (1 Pet. 4:3). Paul declared that victory over this sin requires repentance (2 Cor. 12:21) and living in the spirit of Christ (Gal. 5:22–25). *Lasciviousness*: KJV.

LEWDNESS

Judg. 20:6 they have committed *l* and reckless-ness in Israel

Jer. 13:27 have seen your [Jerusalem's] adulter-ies...the *l* of your prostitution

Mark 7:21–22 out of the heart of men, proceed... wickedness, deceit, *l*

Gal. 5:19 works of the flesh are...adultery, for-nication, uncleanness, *l*

Eph. 4:19 being past feeling, have given them-selves over to *l*

Jude 4 certain men...turning the grace of our God into *l*

LIAR[S]

Ps. 116:11 I said in my haste, All men are *l's*

Prov. 19:22 a poor man is better than a *l*

Rom. 3:4 let God be true but every man a *l*

Titus 1:12 The Cretans are always *l's*, evil beasts

1 John 1:10 say that we have not sinned...make Him [God] a *l*

1 John 4:20 man says, I love God and hates his brother, he is a *l*

LIBERTINES. A name for members of the Jerusalem synagogue who opposed the martyr Stephen (Acts 6:9). They were probably Jews who had been imprisoned by the Roman authorities, then released.

LIBERTY

Lev. 25:10 consecrate the fiftieth year and pro-claim *l*

Ps. 119:45 walk at *l*, for I seek Your [God's] precepts

Isa. 61:1 sent me [God's servant]...to proclaim *l* to the captives

Luke 4:18 to set at *l* those who are bruised

Acts 26:32 This man [Paul] might have been set at *l*

1 Cor. 8:9 lest this *l* of yours...becomes a stum-bling block

2 Cor. 3:17 where the Spirit of the Lord is, there is *l*

Gal. 5:1 Stand fast, therefore, in the *l* by which Christ has made us free

2 Pet. 2:19 While they promise them *l*, they... are the servants of corruption

LIBYA. A region of northern Africa from which pilgrims came to Jerusalem on the day of Pentecost (Acts 2:10). The Simon who carried Jesus' cross was from Cyrene, Libya's chief city (Matt. 27:32). In the OT, Libya is mentioned in Ezek. 30:5; 38:5. It was also called *Put* (Ezek. 27:10) and *Lubim* (Nah. 3:9).

LICE. Small biting insects which made up the third plague sent by the Lord against the Egyptians (Exod. 8:16–18).

LIE [S]

Lev. 19:11 not steal...or *l* to one another

Num. 23:19 God is not a man, that He should *l*

Job 13:4 forgers of *l's*...physicians of no value

Ps. 23:2 He [God] makes me to *l* down in green pastures

Ps. 58:3 the wicked...go astray...speaking *l's*

Ps. 62:9 men of high degree are a *l*; to be laid in the balance

Prov. 3:24 When you *l* down, you shall not be afraid

Prov. 14:5 A faithful witness will not *l*

Prov. 14:25 a deceitful witness speaks *l's*

Isa. 11:6 and the leopard shall *l* down with the young goat

Ezek. 34:15 I [God] will feed my flock...cause them to *l* down

Nah. 3:1 Woe to the bloody city! It is all full of *l's* and robbery

Zeph. 3:13 remnant of Israel shall not...speak *l's*

Mark 5:23 My [Jairus's]...daughter *l's* at the point of death

Acts 5:3 Ananias, why has Satan filled your heart to *l*

Rom. 1:25 exchanged the truth of God into a *l*

Rom. 12:18 as much as it *l's* in you, live peaceably

1 John 1:6 say...we have fellowship with Him [God]...walk in darkness, we *l*

LIE IN WAIT

Ps. 59:3 behold, they *l-i-w* for my soul; the mighty are gathered against me

Ps. 71:10 those who *l-i-w* for my soul take counsel

Prov.. 1:11 they [sinners] say, Come with us; let us *l-i-w* for blood

Mic. 7:2 They all *l-i-w* for blood. Every man hunts his brother

Eph. 4:14 by which they [false teachers] *l-i-w* to deceive

LIFE. Physical life began with God, who placed this animating force in Adam, the first man (Gen. 2:7). Moses exhorted the Israelites in the wilderness to "choose life" to be assured of a future in the land of promise (Deut. 30:19). Continuing fellowship with the Lord was essential for their well-being. This concept of life in harmony with God's purpose reached its fulfillment in Jesus. He restored sick people to wholeness and brought salvation to sinners whose lives were mired in sin. Life in eternal fellowship with Him is Jesus' gift to those who accept Him as Savior and Lord (John 10:10).

LIFE

Gen. 2:7 LORD God...breathed into his [man's] nostrils the breath of *l*

Deut. 19:21 shall give *l* for *l*, eye for eye, tooth for tooth

Josh. 1:5 No man...stand before you [Joshua] all the days of your *l*

Job 2:6 he [Job] is in your [Satan's] hand. But spare his *l*

Job 36:6 He [God] does not preserve the *l* of the wicked

Ps. 23:6 mercy shall follow me all the days of my *l*

Ps. 27:1 LORD is the strength of my *l*. Of whom shall I be afraid?

Ps. 31:10 my *l* is spent with grief and my years with sighing

Ps. 38:12 Those...who seek after my *l* lay snares for me

Prov. 4:23 Keep your heart...for out of it are the springs of *l*

Prov. 8:35 For whoever finds me finds *l*

Prov. 18:21 Death and *l* are in the...tongue

Jer. 21:8 I [God] set before you the way of *l* and...death

Matt. 6:25 do not worry for your *l*, what you shall eat

Matt. 19:16 what good thing shall I do...have eternal *l*

Matt. 20:28 Son of Man came...to give His *l* a ransom for many

Mark 8:35 whoever will save his *l* shall lose it

Luke 12:15 *l* does not consist in the abundance of the things...he possesses

John 1:4 In Him [Jesus] was *l*...the light of men

John 3:15 whoever believes in Him [Jesus]... have eternal *l*

John 3:36 He who believes in the Son has everlasting *l*

John 5:21 the Son gives *l* to whom He will

John 6:35 I [Jesus] am the bread of *l*

John 6:47 he who believes in Me [Jesus] has everlasting *l*

John 6:63 It is the Spirit who gives *l*...flesh profits nothing

John 10:10 I [Jesus] have come that they might have *l*

John 10:15 and I [Jesus] lay down My *l* for the sheep

John 11:25 I [Jesus] am the resurrection and the *l*

John 14:6 I [Jesus] am the way, the truth, and the *l*

John 15:13 that a man lay down his *l* for his friends

Rom. 6:23 gift of God is eternal *l* through Jesus Christ

Rom. 8:38 neither death nor *l*, nor angels nor principalities

1 Cor. 15:19 hope...only in this *l*, we are of all men most miserable

Phil. 2:16 holding forth the word of *l*

Jas. 4:14 what is your *l*? It is even a vapor, that... vanishes away

1 John 2:25 this is the promise...even eternal *l*

1 John 3:14 passed from death to *l*...we love the brothers

1 John 5:12 He who has the Son has *l*

Rev. 20:15 not found written in the book of *l* was cast into the lake of fire

Rev. 22:17 let him take the water of *l* freely

LIGHT. The opposite of darkness; a metaphor for many important ideas in the Bible. Light is often cited as an image of God's presence (Ps. 27:1). It also represents truth and goodness and God's redemptive work (Ps. 119:105). The prophet Isaiah compared the promised Messiah to a great light who would bring salvation to people trapped in the darkness of sin (Isa. 9:2). Jesus fulfilled this prophecy when He declared

He had been sent on a redemptive mission by God the Father as the "light of the world" (John 8:12). In His Sermon on the Mount, Jesus referred to believers as "the light of the world" (Matt. 5:14). His followers should reflect His light to others.

LIGHT [S]

Gen. 1:3 God said, Let there be *l*, and there was *l*

Gen. 1:16 two great *l's*: the greater *l* to rule the day

Ps. 27:1 The LORD is my *l* and my salvation

Ps. 119:105 Your [God's] word is...a *l* to my path

Prov. 4:18 path of the just is like the shining *l*

Isa. 2:5 Come...and let us walk in the *l* of the LORD

Isa. 9:2 people...in darkness have seen a great *l*

Isa. 60:1 Arise! Shine! For your *l* has come

Isa. 60:3 Gentiles shall come to your *l*

Amos 5:18 day of the LORD is darkness and not *l*

Matt. 5:14 You are the *l* of the world

Matt. 11:30 My [Jesus'] yoke is easy and My burden is *l*

Luke 2:32 A *l* to lighten the Gentiles...glory of... Israel

Luke 16:8 children of this world are wiser... than the children of *l*

John 1:4 In Him [Jesus] was life...life was the *l* of men

John 1:9 That was the true *L* [Jesus]

John 8:12 I [Jesus] am the *l* of the world

Acts 9:3 a *l* from heaven shone all around him [Paul]

Acts 13:47 set you [Paul] to be a *l* to the Gentiles

Acts 26:18 turn them from darkness to *l*

Rom. 13:12 and let us put on the armor of *l*

Phil. 2:15 midst of...perverse nation...you shine as *l's*

Jas. 1:17 Every good gift...is...from the Father of *l's*

1 Pet. 2:9 who [Jesus] has called you...into His marvelous *l*

1 John 1:5 God is *l* and in Him is no darkness

1 John 2:10 He who loves his brother abides in the *l*

LIGHT OF THE WORLD, JESUS AS. See *"I Am" Statements of Jesus*

LIGURE. A precious stone in the breastplate of the high priest (Exod. 28:19).

LIKENESS

Gen. 1:26 make man in Our image, according to Our *l*

Ezek. 10:10 four had one *l*, as if a wheel...in the midst of a wheel

Phil. 2:7 took on Himself [Jesus]...form of a servant...in the *l* of men

LINE. A tool similar to a tape measure used for measuring distance. The prophet Amos told Amaziah, a priest, that the Lord's punishment would include division of Amaziah's property by line (Amos 7:17).

LINEN. Cloth made from flax. The rich wore "fine linen" (1 Chron. 15:27), while the poor wore clothes of unbleached flax. Linen was also used for curtains and veils in the tabernacle (Exod. 26:1).

LINTEL. A horizontal beam that supported the wall above a door. In Egypt, the Israelites placed blood from a sacrificial lamb on the lintels of their doors to avoid the destroyer (Exod. 12:22–23).

LINUS. A Christian at Rome who joined the apostle Paul in sending greetings to Timothy (2 Tim. 4:21).

LION OF THE TRIBE OF JUDAH. A name of Jesus in the book of Revelation (Rev. 5:5) that probably arose from the prophecy of Jacob in the book of Genesis. He declared that his son Judah was destined to become the greatest among all his twelve sons. He referred to Judah symbolically as a lion, or a fearless ruler, who would lead God's people (Gen. 49:8–12). This prophecy was fulfilled dramatically throughout the Bible. The tribe of Judah, composed of Judah's descendants, took the lead on the Israelites' trek through the wilderness after they left Egypt (Num. 10:14). Moses' census of the people in the wilderness revealed that the tribe

of Judah was the most numerous (Num. 1:27; 26:22). King David, the popular ruler of Israel, was a member of this tribe (2 Sam. 5:5). Most significantly of all, Jesus the Messiah sprang from the line of Judah. The genealogy of Jesus in the Gospel of Matthew traces His lineage back to Judah (Matt. 1:2–3; *Judas*: KJV). Thus Jesus is the Lion of the tribe of Judah who rules among His people as supreme Savior and Lord.

LIPS. This part of the body is often used metaphorically, as in Moses' description of his poor speaking skills as "uncircumcised lips" (Exod. 6:12, 30). Covering of the lips was a gesture of shame or mourning (Mic. 3:7). Speech that honors God comes from "righteous lips" (Prov. 16:13).

LITTER. A portable chair on poles upon which a royal official was carried. A covering provided protection from the sun and rain (Isa. 66:20).

LIVE [ING, S]

Gen. 2:7 and man became a *l'ing* soul

Gen. 45:7 God sent me [Joseph]...to save your *l's*

Deut. 8:3 that man does not *l* by bread alone

Job 14:14 If a man dies, shall he *l* again?

Job 19:25 I [Job] know that my Redeemer *l's*

Ps. 63:4 Thus will I bless You [God] while I *l*

Ps. 142:5 You [God] are my refuge...in the land of the *l'ing*

Jer. 2:13 abandoned Me [God] the fountain of *l'ing* waters

Ezek. 37:3 Son of man, can these bones *l*?

Dan. 6:26 tremble and fear before the God of Daniel...the *l'ing* God

Jon. 4:3 better for me [Jonah] to die than to *l*

Hab. 2:4 But the just shall *l* by his faith

Matt. 4:4 Man shall not *l* by bread alone

Mark 12:27 not the God of the dead but...of the *l'ing*

Mark 12:44 she [a widow]...cast in...all her *l'ing*

Luke 9:56 Son of Man came not to destroy men's *l's* but to save them

Luke 15:13 younger son...wasted his substance with wasteful *l'ing*

Luke 24:5 Why do you seek...the *l'ing* among the dead?

John 4:10 He [Jesus] would have given...*l'ing* water

John 6:51 I [Jesus] am the *l'ing* bread

John 11:25 believes in Me [Jesus], though he were dead, yet shall he *l*

John 11:26 whoever *l's*...in Me [Jesus] shall never die

Acts 10:42 He [Jesus]...was ordained...Judge of *l'ing* and dead

Acts 17:28 in Him [Jesus] we *l* and move and have our being

Rom. 12:1 present your bodies as a *l'ing* sacrifice

Rom. 12:18 If it is possible...*l* peaceably with all men

Rom. 14:7 none of us *l's* to himself...no man dies to himself

Rom. 14:8 whether we *l* or die, we are the Lord's

1 Cor. 9:14 preach the gospel should *l* by the gospel

Gal. 2:14 why do you [Peter] compel the Gentiles to *l* as the Jews do

Gal. 2:19 I [Paul]...am dead to the law that I might *l* for God

Gal. 2:20 I [Paul] *l*; yet not I, but Christ *l's* in me

Gal. 5:25 *l* in the Spirit, let us also walk in the Spirit

Phil. 1:21 to me [Paul] to *l* is Christ, and to die is gain

2 Tim. 4:1 Jesus Christ...shall judge the *l'ing* and the dead

Heb. 4:12 For the word of God is *l'ing* and powerful

1 Pet. 1:3 a *l'ing* hope through the resurrection of Jesus Christ

1 Pet. 2:5 You also, as *l'ing* stones, are built up as a spiritual house

1 John 3:16 we ought to lay down our *l's* for the brothers

1 John 4:9 God sent His...Son...that we might *l* through Him

Rev. 1:18 I am He [Jesus] who *l's*, and was dead

LIVELY

Exod. 1:19 they [Hebrew women] are *l* and have delivered

Ps. 38:19 my enemies are *l* and they are strong

LIVING GOD

Josh. 3:10 you shall know that the *l-G* is among you

Ps. 42:2 My soul thirsts for God, for the *l-G*

Jer. 10:10 He [God] is the *l-G* and an everlasting King

Dan. 6:20 O Daniel, servant of the *l-G*

Matt. 16:16 Peter...said, You are the Christ, the Son of the *l-G*

John 6:69 we [disciples] believe...You are...the Son of the *l-G*

2 Cor. 6:16 For you are the temple of the *l-G*

1 Tim. 3:15 church of the *l-G*, the pillar and ground of the truth

Heb. 10:31 a fearful thing to fall into the hands of the *l-G*

LO-AMMI. A symbolic name given by the prophet Hosea to his second son to signify God's rejection of rebellious Israel (the Northern Kingdom) (Hos. 1:8–9). The name means "not my people."

LOCUST. A plant-eating insect similar to the grasshopper. God sent swarms of locusts as a plague on the Egyptians to convince the pharaoh to free the Israelite slaves (Exod. 10:1–4). The prophet Joel cited the devastation of a plague of locusts to call the people back to worship of the one true God (Joel 1:4–6).

LOD. See *Lydda*

LOFT. The upper story or upper room built on the flat roof of a house (1 Kings 17:19).

LOGOS. A Greek term, meaning "the Word," that John the apostle used for Jesus in the prologue to his Gospel (John 1:1–18). By describing Jesus in this fashion, John compared Jesus to the powerful spoken word of God that brought the world into being (Gen. 1:6).

LOIS. The grandmother of Timothy who instructed him in the moral principles of the OT. Paul commended her for her faith (2 Tim. 1:5).

LONG-SUFFERING

Ps. 86:15 But You, O Lord, are...gracious, *l*

Gal. 5:22 fruit of the Spirit is love...*l*, gentleness

2 Pet. 3:9 Lord is...*l* toward us, not willing that any should perish

LONG-SUFFERING OF GOD. A concept which means that God is patient with sinners. The Lord was patient in His dealings with His people, the Israelites. Although they often rebelled against Him, He worked patiently to bring them back into His will (Exod. 34:6). He longs to see people repent and turn to Him for forgiveness and salvation (Rom. 2:4). Other words often used for this divine attribute are *forbearance, perseverance, restraint,* and *steadfastness.* Believers should imitate God's long-suffering in their service for Him and their dealings with others. The apostle Paul expressed it like this: "Be steadfast, immovable, always abounding in the work of the Lord" (1 Cor. 15:58).

LORD IS GOOD

Ps. 34:8 O taste and see that the *L-i-g*

Ps. 100:5 the *L-i-g*; His mercy is everlasting

Lam. 3:25 The *L-i-g* to those who wait for Him

Nah. 1:7 The *L-i-g*, a stronghold in the day of trouble

LORD OF HOSTS. A name of God expressing His supremacy that appears many times throughout the OT (for example, Ps. 24:10). The compound Hebrew word behind the name is *Yahweh-sabaoth.* Sabaoth means "armies" or "hosts." Thus, one meaning of the name is that God is superior to any human army, no matter its number. The Lord often led His people, the Israelites, to victory over a superior military force (Judg. 7:12–25). Another possible meaning is that God exercises control over all the hosts of heaven—or the heavenly bodies—including the sun, moon, and stars. The psalmist declared, "Praise Him, all His hosts. Praise Him, sun and moon; praise Him, all you stars of light" (Ps. 148:2–3).

LORD OF LORDS. A name or title of Jesus that emphasizes His supreme authority in the end-time when He will return to earth in victory over His enemies (Rev. 19:16). As Lord of Lords, He will be superior in power and authority to all the rulers of the earth. Some monarchs of the ancient world were worshipped as divine by their subjects. But only Jesus is worthy of worship and total commitment.

LORD'S DAY. Sunday, the first day of the week, and the day of worship observed by most Christian groups (Rev. 1:10). The Jewish day of rest and worship fell on Saturday, the last day of the week. But after Christ's resurrection on the first day, Christians adopted Sunday as their normal day of worship (Acts 20:7).

LORD'S PRAYER. Jesus' model prayer that He taught to His disciples in response to their request, "Lord, teach us to pray" (Luke 11:1). The prayer teaches believers to approach God reverently (Matt. 6:9–10), to ask Him to meet their physical needs on a daily basis (Matt. 6:11), and to seek His forgiveness and protection (Matt. 6:12–13). The conclusion of the prayer acknowledges that God alone is all powerful and worthy of honor and praise.

LORD'S SUPPER. Jesus' final meal with His disciples on the night before He was arrested and crucified. It is also known as the Memorial Supper. He and His disciples were in Jerusalem to celebrate the Jewish Passover. During this religious holiday, the Jewish people ate a special meal to symbolize God's deliverance of His people from Egyptian slavery. Jesus turned this meal into a supper of remembrance to signify His approaching death. He made it clear to His disciples that the bread and wine they ate and drank together symbolized His broken and bleeding body. He also charged them to remember His sacrificial death whenever they celebrated this memorial meal in the future (Luke 22:14–20). The Lord's Supper is still observed by church groups all over the world, although in different forms ranging from very informal to highly ritualistic. Some other names by which it is known are Communion; Holy Communion; the Mass, the Eucharist, and the Lord's Table. The event is often called the Last Supper, and referred to in Matt. 26:26–30 • Mark 14:22–26 • 1 Cor. 11:17–34.

LORD WAS WITH HIM

Gen. 39:3 his [Joseph's] master saw that the *L-w-w-h*

1 Sam. 3:19 Samuel grew, and the *L-w-w-h*

1 Sam. 18:12 Saul was afraid of David because the *L-w-w-h*

1 Sam. 18:14 David behaved wisely...and the *L-w-w-h*

2 Kings 18:7 the *L-w-w-h*, and he [Hezekiah] prospered

1 Chron. 9:20 Phinehas...was the ruler...and the *L-w-w-h*

Luke 1:66 hand of the *L-w-w-h* [John the Baptist]

LO-RUHAMAH. A symbolic name for the prophet Hosea's daughter, meaning "not pitied." It expressed God's rejection of the rebellious people of Israel (the Northern Kingdom) (Hos. 1:6). But the prophet referred to the faithful remnant of the nation as *Ruhamah*, meaning just the opposite, or "pitied" (Hos. 2:1, 23).

LOSE [S]

Eccles. 3:6 a time to get and a time to *l*

Matt. 10:39 *l's* his life for My [Jesus'] sake shall find it

Mark 8:36 gains the whole world and *l's* his own soul

Luke 17:33 Whosoever seeks to save his life shall *l* it

LOSS

Acts 27:22 no *l* of any man's life...but only of the ship

1 Cor. 3:15 man's work is burned, he shall suffer *l*

Phil. 3:7 what things were gain to me [Paul]...I counted *l*

LOST

Ps. 119:176 I have gone astray like a *l* sheep

Matt. 15:24 I [Jesus] was sent only to the *l* sheep of the house of Israel

Luke 15:6 I have found my sheep that was *l*

Luke 19:10 Son of man has come to seek and to save what was *l*

John 17:12 I [Jesus] have kept those...none of them [the disciples] is *l*

LOT. Abraham's nephew who accompanied Abraham to Canaan and traveled with him to Egypt to escape a famine (Gen. 12:5; 13:1). Later, back in Canaan, Abraham and Lot accumulated herds of livestock that competed for the same pasturelands. Given first choice of the available land, Lot chose the fertile plains in the Jordan River valley. He failed to consider the consequences of living close to the pagan cities of Sodom and Gomorrah (Gen. 13:6–12). When God destroyed these two cities because of their wickedness, He sent two angels to rescue Lot and his family. But his wife was turned to a pillar of salt when she looked back at the burning city of Sodom (Gen. 19:26). Lot was an ancestor of the Moabites and the Ammonites, people groups which became enemies of the Israelites in later centuries (Gen. 19:37–38). He is also mentioned in **Gen.** 11:27, 31; 12:4–5; 14:12–16; **19:1–29** • Deut. 2:9, 19 • Ps. 83:8 • Luke 17:28–29 • 2 Pet. 2:7.

LOTS, CASTING OF. A way of making decisions by casting small stones out of a container (Josh. 18:6). People believed that God made His will known through this method (Prov. 16:33). The apostles used the casting of lots to select Matthias as the successor to Judas Iscariot (Acts 1:26).

LOT'S WIFE. The woman turned into a pillar of salt when she looked back on the burning city of Sodom (Gen. 19:26). Jesus used her as an example of the dangers of delay and disobedience (Luke 17:30–32).

LOVE. See *Agape*

LOVE [D, ING, LY, S]

Gen. 29:20 to him [Jacob] but a few days, for the *l* he had for her [Rachel]

Gen. 37:3 Israel *l'd* Joseph more than all his children

Lev. 19:18 *l* your neighbor as yourself. I am the LORD

Deut. 6:5 *l* the LORD your God with all your heart

Josh. 23:11 be careful that you *l* the LORD your God

Job 19:19 those whom I [Job] *l'd* have turned against me

Ps. 87:2 The LORD *l's* the gates of Zion

Ps. 116:1 I *l* the LORD, because He has heard my voice

Ps. 119:97 O how *l* I Your [God's] law

Prov. 3:12 those whom the LORD *l's*, He corrects

Prov. 7:18 take our fill of *l* until the morning

Prov. 10:12 Hatred stirs up strife, but *l* covers all sins

Prov. 17:17 A friend *l's* at all times

Prov. 22:1 to be chosen than great riches...*l'ing* favor rather than silver

Eccles. 3:8 A time to *l* and a time to hate

Eccles. 9:9 Live joyfully with the wife whom you *l*

Song of Sol. 2:4 his [bridegroom's] banner over me was *l*

Song of Sol. 8:7 Many waters cannot quench *l*

Jer. 31:3 I [God] have *l'd* you with an everlasting *l*

Hos. 11:4 I [God] drew them with...bands of *l*

Mic. 6:8 what does the LORD require...but to...*l* mercy

Matt. 5:44 *l* your enemies, bless those who curse you

Matt. 10:37 *l's* father or mother more than Me [Jesus] is not worthy of Me

Matt. 22:39 You shall *l* your neighbor as yourself

Luke 16:13 he will hate the one and *l* the other

John 3:16 God so *l'd* the world...gave His only begotten Son

John 13:34 *l* one another; as I [Jesus] have *l'd* you

John 14:15 If you *l* Me [Jesus], keep My commandments

John 15:9 Father has *l'd* Me [Jesus], so have I *l'd* you

John 21:15 Simon...do you *l* Me [Jesus] more than these

Rom. 5:8 God demonstrates His *l* toward us

Rom. 8:28 all things work together for good for those who *l* God

Rom. 8:37 we are more than conquerors through Him [Jesus] who *l'd* us

1 Cor. 2:9 things that God has prepared for those who *l* Him

2 Cor. 5:14 the *l* of Christ compels us

2 Cor. 9:7 for God *l's* a cheerful giver

Gal. 2:20 live by the faith of the Son of God, who *l'd* me [Paul]

Gal. 5:22 But the fruit of the Spirit is *l*, joy, peace

Eph. 3:19 *l* of Christ, which surpasses knowledge

Eph. 4:15 speaking the truth in *l*...grow up... into Him [Jesus]

Eph. 5:2 walk in *l*, as Christ has also *l'd* us

Eph. 5:25 Husbands, *l* your wives, even as Christ also *l'd* the church

Phil. 1:9 that your *l* may abound yet more and more

Phil. 4:8 whatever things are *l'ly*...of good report

1 Tim. 6:10 *l* of money is the root of all evil

2 Tim. 1:7 God has not given us the spirit of fear, but of...*l*

Heb. 12:6 whom the Lord *l's* He chastens

Jas. 1:12 receive the crown of life...promised to those who *l* Him [Jesus]

1 John 2:10 He who *l's* his brother abides in the light

1 John 2:15 any man *l's* the world, the *l* of the Father is not in him

1 John 3:14 He who does not *l* his brother abides in death

1 John 4:7 everyone who *l's* is born of God

1 John 4:10 not that we *l'd* God, but that He *l'd* us

1 John 4:16 he who dwells in *l* dwells in God

1 John 4:19 We *l* Him [Jesus], because He first *l'd* us

1 John 4:20 how can he...*l* God, whom he has not seen

1 John 5:3 this is the *l* of God, that we keep His commandments

Rev. 2:4 you [the church at Ephesus] have left your first *l*

LOVE CHAPTER OF THE BIBLE. 1 Cor. 13

LOVE FEAST. A meal eaten by early believers when they met for fellowship and to observe the Lord's Supper (Acts 2:42, 46). Paul condemned some of the Corinthian Christians for their sinful behavior and selfish indulgence at these events (1 Cor. 11:20–22).

LOVE OF GOD

Rom. 5:5 the *l-o-G* has been poured out in our hearts

Rom. 8:39 height nor depth...shall...separate us from the *l-o-G*...in Christ

1 John 3:16 perceive the *l-o-G*, because He [Jesus] laid down His life for us

1 John 4:9 In this [God's Son] the *l-o-G* was clearly revealed toward us

LOVE ONE ANOTHER

John 13:34 that you *l-o-a*; as I [Jesus] have loved you

Rom. 13:8 Owe no man anything but to *l-o-a*

1 John 3:11 the message...you heard...we should *l-o-a*

1 John 4:7 Beloved, let us *l-o-a*, for love is of God

LOVE YOUR NEIGHBOR

Matt. 5:43 it has been said, You shall *l-y-n*, and hate your enemy

Matt. 19:19 you shall *l-y-n* as yourself

Matt. 22:39 second is like it: You shall *l-y-n* as yourself

Mark 12:31 *l-y-n* as yourself. There is no other commandment greater

Rom. 13:9 any other commandment...namely, You shall *l-y-n* as yourself

Gal. 5:14 all the law is fulfilled in one word... *l-y-n* as yourself

Jas. 2:8 fulfill the royal law... You shall *l-y-n* as yourself

LOVING-KINDNESS. A distinct term for the concept of God's love and grace in the OT. Two words are joined together to show the depth of God's love and kindness toward His people. The term appears many times throughout the Psalms, as in the psalmist's declaration, "O continue Your loving-kindness to those who know You, and Your righteousness to the upright in heart" (Ps. 36:10).

LOVING-KINDNESS

Ps. 36:7 How excellent is Your *l*, O God!

Ps. 63:3 Your [God's] *l* is better than life, my lips...praise You

Ps. 92:2 to declare Your [God's] *l* in the morning

Jer. 9:24 I am the Lord who exercises *l*, justice

LUBIM. See *Libya*

LUCAS. KJV: see *Luke*

LUCIFER. A word of uncertain meaning that appears in the book of Isaiah: "How you have fallen from heaven, O Lucifer" (Isa. 14:12). The word means "light-bringer." Most interpreters believe the prophet was referring to the fall from power of the king of Babylon, the most powerful ruler of Isaiah's time. But some believe that Lucifer refers to Satan. According to an ancient Jewish myth, Lucifer was once an angel. He led other angels in heaven to rebel against the Lord, and they were cast out of heaven. These are the "fallen angels" that Jewish scholars cited to explain the origin of evil in the world. But the Bible gives no simple explanation for evil and how it came to be. The only certainty is that evil exists, and that God will triumph over all the forces of evil in the end-time (Rev. 19:17–20).

LUCIUS. A teacher in the church at Antioch of Syria who laid hands on Paul and Barnabas, sending them out on the first missionary journey (Acts 13:1).

LUDIM. A people descended from Mizraim, a son of Ham (Gen. 10:13 • 1 Chron. 1:11).

LUKE. A believer of Gentile descent who was a traveling companion and missionary associate of the apostle Paul (Acts 16:10; 20:5). Luke is believed to have written the Gospel that bears his name, as well as the book of Acts. He is probably the person behind the "we" passages in the book of Acts (Acts 27:1–28:16). Luke apparently accompanied Paul on his trip to Rome, and remained with the apostle while he was in prison (2 Tim. 4:11). His Gospel and the book of Acts together make up about one-fourth of the NT. Luke addressed both books to a person named Theophilus (Luke 1:1–3; Acts 1:1). Luke is also mentioned in Col. 4:14 • Philem. 24.

LUKE, GOSPEL OF. One of the four Gospels of the NT, known for its portrayal of Jesus as the Savior of all people, Gentiles as well as Jews. Luke did not identify himself as the author, but early church tradition ascribed this writing to him. He was not an eyewitness of the ministry of Jesus. But he revealed that he had access to information from actual eyewitnesses which he included in his account (Luke 1:1–4). Of the four Gospels, Luke gives the most complete picture of the life of Jesus. It is the only Gospel that records the facts about His birth (Luke 2:1–12). Many of Jesus' most beloved parables appear only in the Gospel of Luke—for example, the lost coin and the lost son, also known as the prodigal son (Luke 15:1–32). Luke is also the most inclusive of all the Gospels. He portrays Jesus associating with people of all classes—poor, outcasts, sinners, women, and tax collectors. The hero of one of Jesus' parables is even a compassionate Samaritan—a member of a race of half-breeds whom the Jewish people despised (Luke 10:25–37). See also *Synoptic Gospels*.

LUKEWARM. A term for weak faith or shallow spirituality. Members of the church at Laodicea, one of the seven churches of Asia Minor, were criticized for this problem (Rev. 3:16).

LUST. Excessive sexual craving or desire for the forbidden. Unbridled lust leads to sin and produces death (James 1:14–15). Believers are enabled to resist lust through the power of the Holy Spirit (Titus 2:12).

LUST [S]
Matt. 5:28 whoever look on a woman to *l* after her
Mark 4:19 the *l's*...enter in and choke the word

Rom. 1:24 God...gave them up to uncleanness through the *l's* of...own hearts
Gal. 5:16 walk in the Spirit...not fulfill the *l* of the flesh
Jas. 4:3 that you may spend it on your *l's*
1 John 2:16 the *l* of the eyes, and the pride of life

LUZ. See *Bethel*

LYCAONIA. A Roman province in southern Asia Minor where the apostle Paul preached in its three major cities—Derbe, Lystra, and Iconium—during the first missionary journey (Acts 14:1–6).

LYCIA. A mountainous province of Asia Minor (Acts 27:5). Paul made stops in Patara (Acts 21:1) and Myra, Lycia's major cities, during one of his missionary journeys.

LYDDA. A town near Joppa where the apostle Peter healed a lame man (Acts 9:32–35). The healing amazed the people of the area, and many turned to the Lord. The city was known as Lod in OT times (1 Chron. 8:12 • Ezra 2:33 • Neh. 7:37; 11:35).

LYDIA. A businesswoman from the city of Thyatira who became a believer under the apostle Paul's ministry at Philippi. She may have been the first convert to Christianity in this city, and thus a member of the church that Paul founded here. Members of her household followed her in placing their faith in Jesus (Acts 16:13–15, 40).

LYSANIAS. The governor of Abilene, a region in Syria, when John the Baptist began his ministry (Luke 3:1).

LYSIAS, CLAUDIUS. A Roman military officer who rescued the apostle Paul from an angry mob at Jerusalem (Acts 23:23–30).

LYSTRA. A city in central Asia Minor where Paul healed a lame man and was stoned by unbelieving Jews (Acts 14:6–20). He stopped in Lystra again at the end of his first missionary tour. Here he met a young man named Timothy, who eventually became one of his most beloved missionary associates (Acts 16:1–2 • 2 Tim. 3:11).

MAACAH. (1) A wife of David and mother of his son Absalom (2 Sam. 3:3).

(2) Mother of King Abijah of Judah (the Southern Kingdom). She was deposed from her position as queen mother because she made an image of the pagan goddess Asherah (1 Kings 15:13).

MAASEIAH. A Levite after the Exile who explained the law as Ezra read it to the people (Neh. 8:7).

MACCABEES. A family of Jewish zealots who revolted against their enemies during the period between the testaments. The most notable leader of the revolt was Judas Maccabeus, who led his forces to victory over the Greek despot Antiochus IV (Epiphanes). See also *Abomination That Makes Desolate.*

MACEDONIA. A Roman province north of Greece where the apostle Paul had a vision that changed his travel plans (Acts 16:9–12). During the second missionary journey, he and Silas traveled through several territories where they planned to preach the gospel. But at each place, the Holy Spirit told them to keep moving. Finally, Paul had a vision of a man from Macedonia urging them to visit their territory. They obeyed and visited several Macedonian cities that were responsive to the gospel. This marked the beginning of Christianity in the territory now known as Europe. Macedonia is also mentioned in Acts 18:5; 19:21–29; 20:1–3; 27:2 • Rom. 15:26 • 1 Cor. 16:5 • 2 Cor. 1:16; 2:13; 7:5; 8:1; 9:2–4; 11:9 • Phil. 4:15 • 1 Thes. 1:7–8; 4:10 • 1 Tim. 1:3.

MACHIR. (1) A son of Manasseh and ancestor of the Machirites (Gen. 50:23 • Num. 26:29; 32:39–40 • Judg. 5:14).

(2) A friend of David who brought provisions to the king and his aides when they fled to escape Absalom's rebellion (2 Sam. 17:27–29).

MACHPELAH. A field with a cave which Abraham bought as a burial ground for his wife

Sarah (Gen. 23:8–18). He was also eventually buried here, along with other members of his family (Gen. 25:9–10; 49:29–33). The cave today is revered as a sacred Muslim site.

MAD [NESS]
1 Sam. 21:13 he [David]...pretended to be *m* in their hands

Eccles. 2:2 I said of laughter, It is *m'ness*

Eccles. 9:3 and *m'ness* is in their heart while they live

John 10:20 He [Jesus] has a demon and is *m*

Acts 26:24 Much learning is driving you [Paul] *m*

MADE KNOWN
Ps. 98:2 The LORD has *m-k* His salvation

Dan. 2:45 God has *m-k* to the king what shall happen

Luke 2:17 they widely *m-k* the saying that was told them

John 15:15 things...heard from My [Jesus'] Father I have *m-k* to you

Eph. 1:9 having *m-k* to us the mystery of His [God's] will

Phil. 4:6 let your requests be *m-k* to God

1 John 1:1 the life [of Jesus] was *m-k*, and we have seen it

1 John 3:8 For this purpose the Son of God was *m-k*

MADE PLAIN
1 Cor. 3:13 every man's work shall be made *m-p*

Prov. 15:19 the way of the righteous is *m-p*

Rom. 10:20 I was *m-p* to those who did not ask after Me

1 Cor. 3:13 every man's work shall be made *m-p*

MADIAN. KJV: see *Midian*

MAGDALA. A fishing village near the Sea of Galilee and the home of Mary Magdalene, a follower of Jesus (Matt. 15:39; 27:56). On display in a museum near what is believed to be the site of Magdala is a vessel dubbed the "Jesus Boat." This wooden craft was pulled from the mud not far from the shore of the Sea of Galilee in

1986. Scientific testing has dated it to the first century AD, the time when Jesus taught and healed along the shores of this lake.

MAGI. See *Wise Men*

MAGIC. Practices of the occult such as witchcraft and fortune-telling (Lev. 19:31). These practices were considered an abomination to God because they were a form of idolatry. Practitioners of black magic attempt to manipulate the so-called "spirit world" to their advantage. But only one supreme power exists—and He is not subject to human control.

MAGNIFICAT. The virgin Mary's song of praise upon being greeted by her relative Elizabeth a few months before Jesus was born (Luke 1:46–55). In Latin this song begins with the word *magnificat*, meaning "magnify." Mary began her song by declaring, "My soul magnifies the Lord." She went on to praise the Lord for keeping His promise to bless Abraham and his descendants.

MAGNIFY [IED, IES]
Josh. 4:14 LORD *m'ied* Joshua in the sight of all Israel
Job 7:17 What is man, that You [God] should *m* him
Ps. 34:3 O *m* the LORD with me
Ps. 40:16 say continually, The LORD is *m'ied*
Ps. 69:30 I will...*m* Him [God] with thanksgiving
Luke 1:46 Mary said, My soul *m'ies* the Lord
Phil. 1:20 Christ shall be *m'ied* in my [Paul's] body

MAGOR-MISSABIB. A symbolic name, meaning "fear on every side," given by the prophet Jeremiah to Pashhur, an official of the temple in Jerusalem (Jer. 20:3). The name implied that Pashhur and his family would be taken captive when the city fell to the Babylonians.

MAHALATH / MAHALATH LEANNOTH. Phrases in the titles of Psalms 53 and 88 which probably refer to a musical instrument or a tune to be used in worship.

MAHANAIM. The name which Jacob gave to a site near the Jabbok River where he was visited by angels while waiting for his estranged brother Esau (Gen. 32:1–2). The name means "two armies" or "two camps," apparently referring to Jacob's party of wives and servants, as well as this host of angels. To Jacob's relief, Esau welcomed him and assured him that all had been forgiven (Gen. 33:1–4). In later centuries this site developed into a city. Mahanaim was the place from which King Saul's son Ishbosheth reigned for two years as king over parts of northern Israel, while David ruled in the south (2 Sam. 2:8–11). It is also mentioned in Josh. 13:26–30; 21:38 • 2 Sam. 17:24, 27 • 1 Kings 4:14 • 1 Chron. 6:80.

MAHARAI. One of David's "mighty men," an elite group of warriors known for their bravery in battle (2 Sam. 23:28).

MAHER-SHALAL-HASH-BAZ. The symbolic name, meaning "hasten the booty," given by the prophet Isaiah to his second son (Isa. 8:1–4). It signified the destruction of Syria and Israel (the Northern Kingdom), nations that were threatening Jerusalem and the Southern Kingdom.

MAHLON. A son of Naomi who died about ten years after he married Ruth (Ruth 1:5).

MAJESTY ON HIGH. A title of God that refers to His glory and splendor. After Jesus ascended into heaven, He "sat down at the right hand of the Majesty on high" (Heb. 1:3). The phrase declares that God is incomparable in His magnificence and power.

MAJOR PROPHETS. The five prophetic book—Isaiah, Jeremiah, Lamentations, Ezekiel, and Daniel—which appear first in the OT. The term refers to their greater length, not their importance. The short book of Lamentations is associated with this group because it was written by the prophet Jeremiah. All the other shorter prophetic writings that follow these books are known as the Minor Prophets.

MALACHI. An OT prophet who delivered God's message to the people of Judah (the Southern Kingdom) after their return from exile (Mal.

1:1). His name means "messenger of the Lord." Malachi's writings appear in the book that bears his name.

MALACHI, BOOK OF. A short prophetic book of the OT directed against the shallow and meaningless worship practices of God's people after the Exile. Their initial excitement after they returned to their homeland soon cooled and turned to indifference. They began to withhold tithes and offerings and to offer defective animals as sacrifices. Even the priests became negligent in their duties. Malachi addressed these abuses and called the people to renew their faith in the Lord (Mal. 2:1–8; 3:8–10). The prophet closed his book with a word of hope about the future Messiah. God would send a messenger similar to the prophet Elijah, who would announce the arrival of the day of the Lord (Mal. 4:5–6). Many interpreters see this as a reference to John the Baptist, forerunner of Jesus.

MALCHI-SHUA. A son of King Saul who was killed by the Philistines in a battle on Mount Gilboa (1 Sam. 14:49; 31:8 • 1 Chron. 10:2).

MALCHUS. A servant of the high priest whose ear was severed by Peter on the night of Jesus' arrest. Jesus rebuked Peter and restored the ear (John 18:10–11).

MALE
Gen. 1:27 m and female He [God] created them
Mark 10:6 from the beginning of...creation God
    made them *m* and female
Luke 2:23 Every *m*...shall be called holy to the
    Lord
Gal. 3:28 neither *m* nor female...all one in Christ
    Jesus

MALICE. A feeling similar to hate; ill will toward another, or an intense desire to cause harm to others. Paul instructed believers to rid their lives of this sin (Eph. 4:31).

MALICE
Eph. 4:31 wrath and anger...be put away from
    you, with all *m*
Titus 3:3 living in *m* and envy

1 Pet. 2:1 laying aside all *m*, and all deceit

MALTA. An island in the Mediterranean Sea where the apostle Paul escaped to shore when his ship was wrecked while on his voyage to Rome. He and the other passengers remained on Malta for three months until another ship arrived to take them on to Rome. The apostle made good use of the time by healing several people, including the father of Publius, the local island official (Acts 28:1–11). *Melita:* KJV.

MAMRE. (1) A town or district near Hebron where Abraham lived for a time (Gen. 13:18; 18:1–4; 23:17–19; 25:9; 35:27; 49:30; 50:13).

(2) An Amorite chief and supporter of Abraham who gave his name to the plain where Abraham lived (Gen. 14:13, 24).

MANAEN. A prophet and teacher in the church at Antioch of Syria. He was among those who laid hands on Paul and Barnabas, endorsing their call to missionary service (Acts 13:1–3).

MANASSEH. (1) Joseph's firstborn son who was born to his Egyptian wife, Asenath (Gen. 41:50–51). Although Manasseh was not a full-blooded Israelite, he was accepted by his grandfather Jacob and given the same status as his own sons (Gen. 48:20). Manasseh is also mentioned in Gen. 41:51; 46:20; 48:1–20; 50:23 • Num. 26:28–29; 27:1; 32:39–41; 36:1 • Deut. 3:12–15 • Josh. 13:31; 17:1–3 • 1 Kings 4:13 • 1 Chron. 7:14, 17.

(2) The descendants of Manasseh who developed into one of the twelve tribes of Israel. This tribe occupied both sides of the Jordan River (Josh. 16:4–9 • Rev. 7:6).

(3) A wicked king of Judah (the Southern Kingdom) who encouraged pagan worship among his subjects during his long reign of fifty-five years—longer than any other king of the nation. In addition to worshiping the sun, moon, and stars, he committed sacrilege by sacrificing his own son to the pagan Ammonite god Molech (2 Kings 21:1–6). When Judah (the Southern Kingdom) fell to the Babylonians, Manasseh was taken into captivity. He later

repented and was allowed to return to Jerusalem (2 Chron. 33:10–20).

MANASSES. KJV: see *Manasseh*

MANDRAKE. A plant whose fruit was thought to generate fertility. Jacob's wife Leah apparently ate a mandrake before her fifth son, Issachar, was born (Gen. 30:14–18).

MANEH. KJV: see *Mina*

MANGER. A feeding trough for farm animals in which the baby Jesus was laid after His birth in Bethlehem (Luke 2:7).

MANKIND

Lev. 18:22 You shall not lie with *m* as with womankind; it is abomination

1 Cor. 6:9 unrighteous shall not inherit...nor abusers of themselves with *m*

Jas. 3:7 every kind of beast...has been tamed by *m*

MANNA. A bread substitute that God miraculously provided for the Israelites in the wilderness (Num. 11:7–9). The word comes from a Hebrew term meaning "what," showing the mysterious nature of the substance (Exod. 16:15). It appeared on the ground each day with the morning dew, but it spoiled before the next day, when a fresh supply appeared. Manna was provided for forty years until the Israelites reached the land of Canaan (Exod. 16:35).

MANTLE. KJV: see *Cloak*

MARA. A name, meaning "bitter," which Naomi called herself to express her sorrow at the death of her husband and sons (Ruth 1:20).

MARANATHA. An Aramaic phrase, meaning "come, O Lord," used by the apostle Paul (1 Cor. 16:22). It may have been a popular declaration of the imminent return of Jesus Christ used by early believers.

MARCUS. KJV: see *Mark, John*

MARESHAH. A town of Judah (the Southern Kingdom) built for defensive purposes by King Rehoboam (2 Chron. 11:5, 8).

MARKETPLACE. A large open area in a city where trade was conducted (Acts 16:19–20). Jesus referred to this area where children often played (Luke 7:32).

MARK, GOSPEL OF. The shortest and most concise of the Gospels of the NT and probably the first of the four to be written. Mark portrays Jesus as a person of action. He uses the word *immediately* to show that Jesus was on an important mission for God and had no time to waste (Mark 1:12; 2:8; 8:10). While Mark makes it clear that Jesus was the Son of God (Mark 15:39), he also emphasizes the humanity of Jesus more than the other Gospel writers. He included incidents from Jesus' ministry incidents which show His anger (Mark 11:15–17), disappointment (Mark 8:12), sorrow (Mark14:33–34), and fatigue (Mark 4:38). The Gospels of Matthew and Luke were written after Mark. They apparently included material from Mark as well as additional accounts of Jesus' life from other sources. A careful study of these three Gospels shows that all but a few verses from Mark appear in Matthew and Luke. See also *Synoptic Gospels*.

MARK, JOHN. A relative of Barnabas who accompanied Paul and Barnabas on the first missionary journey. Mark left midway through the trip and returned to Jerusalem (Acts 13:13). Because of this, Paul refused to take Mark on his second journey. So Barnabas took Mark and set off in a different direction (Acts 15:37–39). In later years, Paul spoke of Mark with warmth and affection (Col. 4:10). He is recognized by most scholars as the author of the Gospel that bears his name. He is also mentioned in Acts 12:12 • 2 Tim. 4:11 • 1 Pet. 5:13.

MARRIAGE. The voluntary commitment of a man and a woman to each other as husband and wife—a union described by Jesus as a "one flesh" relationship (Matt. 19:5). Marriage was sanctioned by the Lord Himself when he brought Adam and Eve together in the garden of Eden (Gen. 2:18). Love for and submission to one's mate were enjoined by the apostle Paul (Eph. 5:22–29). The commitment of a husband

and wife to each other is a fitting symbol of Christ's love for His church (Eph. 5:23–25).

MARRIAGE

Matt. 22:2 a certain king who made a *m* for his son

Mark 12:25 neither marry nor are given in *m*

Heb. 13:4 *M* is honorable in all...the bed undefiled

Rev. 19:9 called to the *m* supper of the Lamb

MARRY [IED, IES]

Jer. 3:14 Return...for I [God] am *m'ied* to you

Matt. 5:32 whoever *m'ies* her who is divorced commits adultery

Mark 10:11 Whoever divorces his wife and *m'ies* another commits adultery

Luke 14:20 *m'ied* a wife, and therefore I cannot come

Luke 16:18 divorces his wife and *m'ies* another commits adultery

1 Cor. 7:9 let them *m*, for it is better to *m* than to burn

1 Cor. 7:33 he who is *m'ied* cares for the things... of the world

1 Tim. 5:14 the younger women to *m*, bear children, guide the house

MARS' HILL. See *Areopagus*

MARTHA. A woman rebuked by Jesus for her unnecessary worry after she welcomed Him into her home (Luke 10:38–42). Martha was frustrated because her sister Mary was not helping to prepare a meal for their special guest. Jesus pointed out that Martha was busy with secondary matters while Mary was doing what was most important—spending time listening to Him. Martha and Mary were sisters of Jesus' friend Lazarus, whom He raised from the dead (John 11:43–44). She is also mentioned in John 12:2.

MARVEL [ED]

Matt. 8:10 He [Jesus] *m'ed*...I have not found such great faith

Matt. 8:27 *m'ed*, saying, What manner of man [Jesus] is this

Matt. 21:20 they [the disciples] *m'ed*, saying, How soon the fig tree has withered

Mark 6:6 He [Jesus] *m'ed* because of their unbelief

Mark 15:44 Pilate *m'ed* that He [Jesus] was already dead

Luke 2:33 Joseph and His mother *m'ed* at those things...spoken of Him [Jesus]

John 3:7 Do not *m* that I [Jesus] said... You [Nicodemus] must be born again

John 7:15 Jews *m'ed*... How does this man [Jesus] know letters

Acts 4:13 they [religious leaders] *m'ed*...they [Peter and John] had been with Jesus

Gal. 1:6 I [Paul] *m* that you are...removed from Him [Jesus] who called you

1 John 3:13 Do not *m*, my brothers, if the world hates you

MARVELLOUS. KJV: see *Marvelous, Astonishing*

MARVELOUS

1 Chron. 16:24 Declare His [God's] glory...his *m* works among all nations

Ps. 31:21 He [God] has shown me His *m* kindness

Ps. 98:1 for He [God] has done *m* things

Ps. 139:14 I will praise You [God]...*M* are Your works

1 Pet. 2:9 Him [Jesus] who has called you out of darkness into His *m* light

Rev. 15:3 Great and *m* are Your works, Lord God Almighty

MARY. (1) A peasant girl firm from the village of Nazareth who became the mother of Jesus (Matt. 1:16). While engaged to Joseph and still a virgin she was told by an angel that she would give birth to the Messiah (Luke 1:28–33). Later, she traveled with Joseph to Bethlehem (Luke 2:4–7) and gave birth to Jesus in fulfillment of OT prophecy (Isa. 7:14). After Jesus was born, she fled to Egypt with Joseph to escape Herod's slaughter of innocent children (Matt. 2:13–18). Mary was present when Jesus turned water into wine at a wedding feast (John 2:3–11). She also looked on as He was crucified. While dying on the cross, Jesus commended His mother to

the care of His disciple John (John 19:26–27). Mary was present with a group of believers in the upper room after the ascension of Jesus (Acts 1:14).

(2) Mary Magdalene, who became a follower of Jesus after He healed her of possession by demons (Luke 8:1–3). She was one of the women who looked on as Jesus was crucified (Mark 15:40). She came to His tomb on resurrection morning to finish anointing His body, only to find that the tomb was empty (Mark 16:1–8). According to John's Gospel, Mary was the first person to whom Jesus appeared after He rose from the dead. She reported to His disciples that she had seen Him alive. To prove that Mary's report was true, Jesus appeared to them in His resurrection body that same day (John 20:11–20).

(3) Mary, sister of Martha and Lazarus. According to the Gospel of John, she was the woman who poured an expensive ointment on His feet and wiped them with her hair (John 12:3). This is the Mary whom Jesus commended for sitting at His feet and listening to His teachings (Luke 10:39–42).

MASKIL. A Hebrew word in the titles of several psalms, including Psalms 32 and 142. It may have referred to carefully crafted psalms to be sung at annual festivals.

MASSAH AND MERIBAH. A site in the wilderness near Mount Sinai where the Israelites complained against Moses and Aaron because of lack of water. Moses stuck a rock with his staff to produce water (Exod. 17:4–7).

MATHUSALA. KJV: see *Methuselah*

MATTANIAH. See *Zedekiah*

MATTHEW. A person whom Jesus called away from his duties as a tax collector to become one of the twelve disciples (Matt. 9:9–13). Also known as Levi (Mark 2:14), Matthew invited many of his friends and associates to meet Jesus. This angered the Pharisees, who criticized Jesus for associating with people whom they considered unworthy sinners (Luke 5:30–32).

As an eyewitness of Jesus' ministry of healing and teaching, Matthew wrote the Gospel that bears his name. He is also mentioned in Matt. 10:3 • Mark 3:18 • Luke 6:15 • Acts 1:13. *Levi*: Luke 5:27–32.

MATTHEW, GOSPEL OF. The first Gospel of the NT that serves as a bridge between the two grand divisions of the Bible, the OT and the NT. For many centuries the Jewish people had looked forward to the coming of the Messiah. Matthew affirmed that Jesus was this long-awaited Savior and King. Matthew quoted extensively from the OT to show that Jesus fulfilled the Scriptures (Matt. 1:22; 4:14; 12:17; 21:4; 27:35). He traced Jesus' ancestry to two of the greatest personalities in Israelite history—Abraham (Matt. 1:2) and David (Matt. 1:6). Another characteristic of this Gospel is its emphasis on the teaching ministry of Jesus. The Sermon on the Mount (5:1–7:29) summarizes the ethical standards that Jesus established for those who belong to the kingdom of God. See also *Synoptic Gospels*.

MATTHIAS. A follower of Jesus whom the disciples chose to replace Judas (Acts 1:23–26).

MAZZAROTH. A constellation of stars, or perhaps the changing of the seasons, cited in the book of Job as evidence of God's power (Job 38:31–33).

MEASURE [D, ING, S]

Deut. 25:14 not have...differing *m's*, a great and a small

Deut. 25:15 you shall have a perfect and just *m*

Job 38:5 Who has laid its *m's*, if you know?

Ps. 39:4 LORD, make me to know...the *m* of my days

Isa. 40:12 Who [God] has *m'd* the waters... hollow of His hand

Ezek. 40:3 a man...with a line of flax...and a *m'ing* rod

Hos. 1:10 Israel shall be like the sand of the sea...cannot be *m'd*

Mark 4:24 with what *m* you *m*, it shall be *m'd* to you

Luke 13:21 like leaven, which a woman took and hid in three *m's* of flour

2 Cor. 11:23 above *m* in beatings, more frequent in prisons

Gal. 1:13 beyond *m* I [Paul] persecuted the church

Eph. 4:7 grace according to the *m* of the gift of Christ

Eph. 4:13 all come...to the *m*...of the fullness of Christ

Rev. 6:6 I [John] heard a voice... A *m* of wheat for a penny

MEBUNNAI. One of David's "mighty men," an elite group of warriors known for their bravery in battle (2 Sam. 23:27).

MEDAD. An Israelite in the wilderness who, along with Eldad, prophesied after being filled with God's Spirit (Num. 11:26–29). Both were commended by Moses.

MEDEBA. An ancient Moabite town near the Dead Sea taken by the Israelites and assigned to the tribe of Reuben (Josh. 13:8–16).

MEDES. Descendants of Japheth who founded an ancient kingdom between the Tigris River and the Caspian Sea (Gen. 10:2 • 2 Kings 17:6 • Esther 1:3, 19 • Isa. 13:17 • Dan. 5:30–31; 6:1–28 • Acts 2:9).

MEDIA. A territory in Mesopotamia to which citizens of Judah (the Southern Kingdom) were deported during the Exile (2 Kings 17:6; 18:11).

MEDIATOR

1 Tim. 2:5 one God and one *m* between God and men

Heb. 8:6 He [Jesus] is also the *m* of a better covenant

Heb. 9:15 He [Jesus] is the *m* of the new covenant

MEDIATOR OF THE NEW COVENANT. A title of Jesus that emphasizes His sacrificial death as the event that reconciles sinful human-kind to God the Father (Heb. 9:15; *mediator of the new testament*: KJV). God had promised through the prophet Jeremiah that He would establish a new covenant with His people. This would be a spiritual covenant written on their hearts rather than a covenant of law (Jer. 31:31–34). On the night before His crucifixion, Jesus declared that He was implementing this new covenant that had been promised by His Father. This covenant would be based on His blood that would be shed to provide redemption and forgiveness of sin for believers (Matt. 26:28).

MEDITATE [S]

Ps. 1:2 on His [God's] law he *m's* day and night

Ps. 119:15 I will *m* on Your [God's] precepts

Ps. 143:5 I *m* on all Your [God's] works

Luke 21:14 not to *m* beforehand on what you shall answer

1 Tim. 4:15 M upon these things. Give yourself... to them

MEDITATION. Deep reflection on spiritual truths in the Bible (Ps. 119:148), a practice that brings understanding (Ps. 49:3) and a sense of well-being (Ps. 63:5–6).

MEDITERRANEAN SEA. The ocean that served as the western boundary of the nation of Israel. In OT times, King Solomon traded goods with other nations across these waters through an alliance with Hiram, king of Tyre (1 Kings 10:22). Later, in the NT, the apostle Paul visited many places in the territory around this body of water. While sailing toward Rome, his ship was wrecked in a storm. But he survived and went on to share his faith with others in this Roman capital city. The Mediterranean is referred to in the King James and Simplified King James Versions as the *Great Sea* (Num. 34:6), *sea of Joppa* (Ezra 3:7), and *sea of the Philistines* (Exod. 23:31).

MEDIUM. A person who claimed to be able to summon the spirit of a person from the dead to deliver a message to the living. King Saul consulted a medium to call up the spirit of Samuel (1 Sam. 28:3–20). Such sorcery was considered an abomination by the Lord (Deut. 18:9–11).

MEEK [NESS]

Num. 12:3 the man Moses was very *m*, above all the men...on...earth

Ps. 37:11 But the *m* shall inherit the earth

Ps. 147:6 LORD lifts up the *m*; He casts the wicked down

Isa. 61:1 to preach good news to the *m*

Matt. 5:5 Blessed are the *m*...they shall inherit the earth

Matt. 11:29 I [Jesus] am *m* and lowly in heart

Gal. 5:23 faith, *m'ness*, self-control. Against such there is no law

Gal. 6:1 restore...in the spirit of *m'ness*...lest you...be tempted

Col. 3:12 Put on...kindness...*m'ness*, long-suffering

1 Pet. 3:15 always be ready to give an answer... with *m'ness* and fear

MEEKNESS. A spirit of kindness, gentleness, and humility. This attitude was commended by Jesus in His Sermon on the Mount (Matt. 5:5). He modeled this spirit during His earthly ministry (Matt. 11:29) and taught His followers that true greatness consisted of serving others rather than being served (Matt. 20:26–28). The apostle Paul cited meekness as one of the fruits of the spirit (Gal. 5:22–23).

MEGIDDO. A fortified city west of the Jordan River (Judges 1:27) that is associated with the great battle in the end-time. A major trade route linking Egypt in the south to Syria in the north passed through the valley near this city. Thus, the country that occupied Megiddo had a distinct commercial and military advantage over other nations of the ancient world. Many important battles have been fought for control of this city and the territory through which this ancient highway passed. Megiddo is mentioned in Josh. 12:21; 17:11 • Judg. 1:27–28; 5:19–21 • 1 Kings 4:12; 9:15–27 • 2 Kings 23:29–30 • Zech. 12:11. See also *Armageddon*: Rev. 16:16.

MEGIDDON. KJV: see *Megiddo*

MELATIAH. A man who helped rebuild the walls of Jerusalem after the Exile (Neh. 3:7).

MELCHISEDEC. KJV: see *Melchizedek*

MELCHI-SHUA. KJV: see *Malchi-shua*

MELCHIZEDEK. The mysterious priest and king who received tithes from Abraham (Gen. 14:18–20). Centuries later, the writer of Hebrews in the NT declared that the priesthood of Jesus was far superior to that of Melchizedek, even though he seemed supernatural in origin (Heb. 7:1–17). The Messiah was also described as a priest "according to the order of Melchizedek" (Ps. 110:4).

MELITA. KJV: see *Malta*

MEM. Thirteenth letter of the Hebrew alphabet, used as a heading over Psalm 119:97–104. In the Hebrew language, each line of these eight verses begins with this letter.

MEMBER[S]
Rom. 12:5 so we...are one body in Christ, and each one is a *m*

1 Cor. 6:15 your bodies are the *m's* of Christ

1 Cor. 12:27 you are the body of Christ, and *m's* in particular

Eph. 4:25 speak truth every man...for we are *m's* of one another

MEMORIAL SUPPER. See *Jesus Christ, Life and Ministry of*; *Lord's Supper*

MEMPHIS. An ancient Egyptian city on the west bank of the Nile River. Many of the pyramids are located near the site of this ancient city. Memphis is mentioned in Isa. 19:13 • Jer. 2:16; 44:1; 46:14, 19 • Ezek. 30:13, 16. *Noph*: KJV.

MENAHEM. A king of Israel (the Northern Kingdom) who murdered Shallum in order to assume the throne. He continued the killing spree that began when Shallum assassinated his predecessor to become Israel's monarch. Menahem paid tribute to Tiglath-pileser III, king of Assyria, in order to maintain his power (2 Kings 15:14–22).

MEPHIBOSHETH. The crippled son of Jonathan, whom King David summoned to his palace and took care of for the rest of his life (2 Sam. 9:1–13). This showed the high esteem that David had for his friend Jonathan, who was killed in a battle with the Philistines (1 Sam. 31:2). Mephibosheth is also mentioned in 2 Sam. 4:4; 16:1–4; 19:24–30; 21:7. *Merib-baal*: 1 Chron. 8:34.

MERCIFUL

Deut. 21:8 Be *m*, O LORD, to Your people Israel
Ps. 41:4 I said, LORD, be *m* to me. Heal my soul
Ps. 67:1 God be *m* to us and bless us
Ps. 103:8 LORD is *m* and gracious, slow to anger
Matt. 5:7 Blessed are the *m*, for they shall obtain mercy

MERCURIUS. The Roman name for the pagan god Mercury, the god of commerce. The people of the city of Lystra called the apostle Paul by this name after he healed a crippled man (Acts 14:12).

MERCY. An attribute or characteristic of God similar to His grace. This part of His nature is mentioned often in the Psalms (Pss. 31:9; 109:26). The apostle Paul described God as "the Father of mercies" (2 Cor. 1:3). Since God is merciful, He expects believers to show mercy to others (Matt. 5:7).

MERCY [IES]

Gen. 39:21 LORD was with Joseph and showed him *m*
Exod. 20:6 showing *m* to...those who love Me [God]
1 Chron. 16:34 He [God] is good, for His *m* endures forever
Ps. 6:2 Have *m* on me, O LORD, for I am weak
Ps. 13:5 But I have trusted in Your [God's] *m*
Ps. 23:6 *m* shall follow me all the days of my life
Ps. 25:6 Remember, O LORD, Your tender *m'ies*
Ps. 40:11 Do not withhold Your [God's] tender *m'ies*
Ps. 85:7 Show us Your *m*, O LORD...grant us Your salvation
Ps. 94:18 My foot slips, Your *m*, O LORD, held me up
Ps. 103:8 LORD is...slow to anger and abundant in *m*
Ps. 103:17 *m* of the LORD is from everlasting
Ps. 119:77 Let Your [God's] tender *m'ies* come to me
Ps. 136:1 give thanks to the LORD...His *m* endures for ever
Isa. 49:13 the LORD...will have *m* on His afflicted
Hos. 6:6 For I [God] desired *m* and not sacrifice

Mic. 6:8 LORD require of you, but to...love *m*
Matt. 23:23 you [Pharisees]...have omitted the weightier matters...*m*, and faith
Luke 16:24 Father Abraham, have *m*...and send Lazarus
Rom. 12:1 *m'ies* of God...present your bodies a living sacrifice
2 Cor. 1:3 Father of *m'ies*, and the God of all comfort
Eph. 2:4 God, who is rich in *m*...loved us
Col. 3:12 Put on...hearts of *m'ies*, kindness
Titus 3:5 according to His [God's] *m* He saved us
Heb. 4:16 obtain *m* and find grace to help
1 Pet. 2:10 had not obtained *m* but now have obtained *m*
Jude 21 *m* of our Lord Jesus Christ to eternal life

MERCY SEAT. The golden cover on the ark of the covenant (Exod. 25:21–22). On the Day of Atonement, the high priest sprinkled blood of sacrificial animals on the mercy seat to atone for the sins of the people (Lev. 16:11–16).

MEREMOTH. A Levite who helped rebuild the walls of Jerusalem after the Exile (Neh. 3:21).

MERIBAH. See *Massah and Meribah*

MERIB-BAAL. See *Mephibosheth*

MERODACH. A pagan Babylonian god of war (Jer. 50:2).

MERODACH-BALADAN. See *Berodach-baladan*

MERRY

Prov. 15:13 A *m* heart makes a cheerful face
Prov. 17:22 A *m* heart does good like a medicine
Luke 15:23 bring the fatted calf...let us eat and be *m*
Jas. 5:13 Is anyone *m*? Let him sing psalms

MESHA. A king of Moab who led an unsuccessful invasion of Israel (the Northern Kingdom). He offered his son as a sacrifice to the pagan god Chemosh (2 Kings 3:4, 26–27).

MESHACH. A friend of the prophet Daniel who was thrown into a fiery furnace for refusing to worship a pagan image (Dan. 1:7). He was saved through God's miraculous intervention (Dan. 3:28).

MESHULLAM. A priest who helped rebuild the walls of Jerusalem after the Exile (Neh. 3:6).

MESOPOTAMIA. The territory between the Tigris and Euphrates rivers where Abraham and his family settled for a time. Later, Abraham sent his servant to the city of Nahor in Mesopotamia to find a bride for his son Isaac (Gen. 24:10). The Babylonian Empire flourished in this general vicinity during OT times. Citizens of Mesopotamia were present in Jerusalem on the day of Pentecost (Acts 2:9). It is also mentioned in Deut. 23:4 • Judg. 3:8, 10 • 1 Chron. 19:6 • Acts 7:2. Also called *Padan-aram* (Gen. 25:20).

MESSENGER
Prov. 13:17 A wicked *m* falls into trouble
Mal. 3:1 I [God] will send My *m*...he shall prepare the way
Luke 7:27 I send My [God's] *m* before Your face

MESSIAH. The name given by the Jewish people to a heroic leader of the future. They expected this person to be a military deliverer who would throw off the yoke of Rome and restore the fortunes of the nation. The Greek term *christos*, rendered as "Christ," means "anointed" or "anointed one," referring to the Messiah or God's chosen one. Jesus fulfilled this longing of the people of Israel but in an unexpected way. He became a spiritual Savior who delivered believers from their bondage to sin (Rom. 6:1–9). During His ministry He actually discouraged people from identifying Him by this name because it would feed their unrealistic expectations (Matt. 16:20).

MESSIANIC PROPHECIES. Prophecies about the coming of the Messiah recorded in the OT and fulfilled in the NT. Scores of these prophecies have been identified, but here is a list of the major ones:
1. Star out of Jacob (Num. 24:17 • Luke 3:34)
2. Of the house of David (Isa. 11:1–10 • Matt. 1:1)
3. Son of man (Dan. 7:13 • Mark 8:38)
4. Named Immanuel (Isa. 7:14 • Matt. 1:22–23)

5. Chief cornerstone (Ps. 118:22 • 1 Pet. 2:4, 7)
6. A prophet like Moses (Deut. 18:15–19 • Mark 6:14–15)
7. Bring in the new covenant (Jer. 31:31–34 • Heb. 12:24)
8. Call the Gentiles (Isa. 11:10 • Rom. 15:9–12)
9. Die for mankind's sin (Isa. 53:4–6 • 1 Pet. 1:18–20)
10. Born of a virgin (Isa. 7:14 • Matt. 1:18–25)
11. Born at Bethlehem (Mic. 5:2 • Luke 2:4–7)
12. Flight into Egypt (Hos. 11:1 • Matt. 2:13–15)
13. Preceded by a forerunner (Mal. 3:1–2 • Mark 1:1–8)
14. Ministry of miracles (Isa. 35:5–6 • Matt. 11:4–5)
15. Meek and gentle (Isa. 42:1–4 • Matt. 12:15–21)
16. Full of wisdom and power (Isa. 11:2 • Matt. 3:16–17)
17. Anointed to preach God's good news (Isa. 61:2–3 • Luke 4:43)
18. Triumphal entry into Jerusalem (Zech. 9:9–10 • Matt. 21:1–11)
19. Betrayed for thirty pieces of silver (Zech. 11:12–13 • Matt. 26:14–15)
20. Rejected by His own people (Isa. 53:3 • John 1:11)
21. Crucified with criminals (Isa. 53:12 • Matt. 27:38)
22. Silent before His accusers (Isa. 53:7 • Mark 15:4–5)
23. Mocked on the cross (Ps. 22:6–8 • Matt. 27:39–44)
24. No bones broken (Ps. 34:20 • John 19:32–33, 36)
25. Died for others (Isa. 53: 1–12 • 1 Pet. 3:18)
26. Buried with the rich (Isa. 53:9 • Matt. 27:57–60)
27. Ascended to His Father (Ps. 68:18 • Eph. 4:8–10)
28. Makes intercession for believers (Zech. 6:13 • Rom. 8:34)
29. Serves as a heavenly high priest (Zech. 6:12–13 • Heb. 8:1–2)
30. Exalted above all (Ps. 2:6–12 • Phil. 2:9–11)

METHUSELAH. A son of Enoch and the grandfather of Noah. Methuselah lived to the age of 969 to become the oldest person recorded in the Bible. He is mentioned in **Gen. 5:21–27** • 1 Chron. 1:3 • Luke 3:37.

MICAH. A minor prophet of the OT known for his prediction that Jesus the Messiah would be born in Bethlehem Ephrathah, an ancient name for the city of Bethlehem (Mic. 5:2). His writings appear in the OT book that bears his name, and he is also mentioned in Jer. 26:18.

MICAH, BOOK OF. A short OT book addressed to the citizens of both Judah (the Southern Kingdom) and Israel (the Northern Kingdom). Micah mentions three kings of Judah: Jotham, Ahaz, and Hezekiah (1:1)—a period that stretched from about 750 to 687 BC. The prophet declared that the people would be punished by the Lord for their sin and rebellion. But in the future, God would restore His people through a remnant of those who would remain faithful to Him (Mic. 2:12).

MICAIAH. A prophet who predicted that King Ahab of Israel (the Northern Kingdom) would be killed in a forthcoming battle. This was a dramatic contrast to that of false prophets, who assured the king he would be victorious (1 Kings 22:8–28). Micaiah was imprisoned for his negative message, but his prediction was fulfilled (1 Kings 22:29–39). He is also mentioned in 2 Chron. 18:7–27.

MICHAEL. An archangel, or an angel of high rank, who was thought to serve as a guardian of the nation of Israel. He is mentioned in Dan. 10:13, 21; 12:1 • Jude 9 • Rev. 12:7.

MICHAL. A wife of David who criticized the king for his joyous dancing as the ark of the covenant was moved to Jerusalem. The daughter of King Saul, she died without bearing children as the result of her critical attitude. She is mentioned in 1 Sam. 14:49; 18:20–28; 19:9–17; 25:44 • 2 Sam. 3:13–16; 6:16–23.

MICHMASH. A town near Jerusalem where Saul's son Jonathan won an impressive victory over the Philistines (1 Sam. 14:1–18).

MICHTAM. A word in the titles of Ps. 16 and Pss. 56–60, perhaps designating a particular type of psalm.

MIDDLE WALL OF PARTITION. A barrier which kept Gentiles from entering the most sacred area of the Jewish temple in Jerusalem. Christ's atoning death broke this partition and brought reconciliation to people of all races (Eph. 2:14–18).

MIDIAN. (1) A son of Abraham and founder of the Midianites (Gen. 25:1–4 • 1 Chron. 1:32–33).

(2) A region in the Arabian desert occupied by the Midianites (Exod. 2:15 • Judg. 7:8–25; 8:3–28 • Acts 7:29).

MIDIANITES. Residents of the land of Midian, a desert region east and south of the Dead Sea. A band of Midianites bought Joseph and sold him as a slave in Egypt (Gen. 37:28). In later years Moses, after fleeing Egypt, spent several years as a sheepherder in the territory of Midian and married a Midianite woman (Exod. 3:1; 18:1–4). During the period of the judges, Midianites invaded Israel, stealing crops and livestock. They were defeated by the judge Gideon (Judg. 7:25). The Midianites are also mentioned in Gen. 37:36 • Num. 31:2–7 • Judg. 6:2–33 • Ps. 83:9.

MIDNIGHT

Exod. 12:29 at *m* the Lord struck all the firstborn...of Egypt

Ps. 119:62 At *m* I will rise to give thanks to You [God]

Mark 13:35 do not know when the master...is coming...at *m*

Acts 16:25 at *m* Paul and Silas were praying and singing praises

MIDWIFE. A Hebrew woman who assisted other women in giving birth. Many midwives refused the Egyptian pharaoh's orders to kill the male babies born to Israelite women (Exod. 1:15–17).

MIGDOL. A place in Egypt where citizens of Judah (the Southern Kingdom) fled after their nation fell to the Babylonians (Jer. 44:1; 46:14).

MIGHT

Deut. 6:5 love the LORD your God...with all your *m*

2 Sam. 6:14 David danced...with all his *m*

2 Chron. 20:6 in Your [God's] hand is...power and *m*

Job 23:3 Oh, that I knew where I *m* find Him [God]

Ps. 119:11 Your [God's] word have I hidden in mine heart...I *m* not sin

Ps. 145:6 the *m* of Your [God's] awesome acts

Eccles. 9:10 hand finds to do, do it with all your *m*

Jer. 9:1 I [Jeremiah] *m* weep day and night for... my people

Jer. 9:23 nor let the mighty man boast in his *m*

Zech. 4:6 Not by *m*...but by My [God's] Spirit

Mark 14:35 if...possible, the hour *m* pass from Him [Jesus]

John 3:17 the world *m* be saved through Him [Jesus]

John 10:10 I [Jesus] have come that they *m* have life

John 20:31 that you *m* believe that Jesus is the Christ

Rom. 10:1 my [Paul's]...prayer...for Israel is that they *m* be saved

1 Cor. 9:22 all things to all men...I [Paul] *m* save some

2 Cor. 4:10 life of Jesus *m*...be made evident in our body

2 Cor. 8:9 He [Jesus] became poor, that you through His poverty *m* be rich

Gal. 4:5 we *m* receive the adoption of sons

Eph. 6:10 be strong in the Lord and in the power of His *m*

1 John 4:9 God sent His...Son...that we *m* live through Him

MIGHTY

Exod. 1:7 children of Israel...became exceedingly *m*

Deut. 6:21 LORD brought us [Israelites] out...*m* hand

2 Sam. 1:27 How the *m* have fallen

1 Chron. 11:11 number of the *m* men whom David had

Job 12:19 He [God]...overthrows the *m*

Job 34:24 He [God] shall break in pieces *m* men

Job 36:5 Behold, God...is *m* in strength and wisdom

Ps. 24:8 LORD strong and *m*, the LORD *m* in battle

Ps. 50:1 The *m* God, even the LORD, has spoken

Ps. 89:6 who among the...*m* can be like the LORD

Ps. 150:2 Praise Him [God] for His *m* acts... excellent greatness

Isa. 9:6 His [Jesus'] name shall be called...the *M* God

Ezek. 20:34 I [God]...will gather you...with a *m* hand

Amos 5:24 judgment run down like waters and righteousness like a *m* stream

Matt. 13:58 He [Jesus] did not do many *m* works...because of their unbelief

Acts 2:2 from heaven a sound like a *m* rushing wind

1 Cor. 1:26 not many *m*, not many noble are called

1 Cor. 1:27 foolish things of the world to confound the...*m*

1 Pet. 5:6 Humble yourselves...under the *m* hand of God

MIGHTY MEN. An elite group of brave warriors who supported David before and after he became king (2 Sam. 23:8–39). Joshua also led courageous soldiers known as "mighty men of valor" (Josh. 1:14; 10:7).

MILCOM. Supreme god of the Ammonites (1 Kings 11:5). Solomon built a sanctuary for worship of this pagan god, but it was destroyed during King Josiah's reforms (2 Kings 23:12–13). Also called *Molech* (Lev. 20:2) and *Moloch* (Acts 7:43).

MILETUM. KJV: see *Miletus*

MILETUS. A coastal city of Asia Minor where the apostle Paul gave a moving farewell address to the leaders of the church at Ephesus (Acts 20:15–38). It is also mentioned in 2 Tim. 4:20.

MILLENNIUM. The one-thousand-year period in the end-time during which Satan will be bound (Rev. 20:1–2). This period is the subject of much speculation. Premillennialists expect a literal reign of one thousand years by Christ on earth after His return. Postmillennialists believe that one thousand years of peace will precede Christ's second coming, during which time much of the world will be converted. Amillennialists teach that the language about this period is symbolic—a round number for a long and undetermined period.

MILLO. A defensive fortress tower built by David near Jerusalem (2 Sam. 5:9). Later, it was strengthened by King Solomon in anticipation of a siege by the Assyrian army (1 Kings 9:15). Millo is also mentioned in 1 Kings 9:24; 11:27 • 2 Kings 12:20 • 1 Chron. 11:8 • 2 Chron. 32:5.

MINA. A Hebrew weight equal to fifty shekels, or about two pounds (Ezek. 45:12).

MIND [S]
Neh. 4:6 the people had a *m* to work
Prov. 29:11 A fool utters all his *m*
Isa. 26:3 keep him whose *m* is steadfast on You in perfect peace
Mark 12:30 love the Lord...with all your *m*
Luke 8:35 the man [demoniac]...clothed and in his right *m*
Rom. 1:28 God gave them over to a reprobate *m*
Rom. 11:34 who has known the *m* of the Lord
Rom. 12:2 transformed by the renewing of your *m*
Eph. 4:17 do not walk as other Gentiles...vanity of their *m*
Phil. 2:2 the same love, being of one accord, of one *m*
Phil. 2:3 in lowliness of *m* let each esteem others better than themselves
Phil. 2:5 this *m* be in you, which was also in Christ Jesus
Phil. 4:7 peace of God...shall guard your hearts and *m's*
2 Tim. 1:7 God has not given us the spirit of fear, but...of a sound *m*
Heb. 8:10 I [God] will put My laws into their *m's*
1 Pet. 1:13 Therefore prepare your *m* for action

MINDFUL
1 Chron. 16:15 Always be *m* of His [God's] covenant
Ps. 8:4 what is man, that You [God] are *m* of him
Ps. 115:12 Lord has been *m* of us; He will bless us

MINISTER [ED, S]
Ps. 9:8 He [God] shall *m* judgment to the people
Ps. 103:21 Bless the Lord...you *m's* of His
Matt. 20:28 Son of man came not to be *m'ed* to but to *m*
Mark 10:43 great among you shall be your *m*
Rom. 15:16 I [Paul] should be the *m* of Jesus... to the Gentiles
1 Cor. 3:5 Who then is Paul...Apollos, but *m's* through whom you believed
2 Cor. 11:23 Are they *m's* of Christ...I [Paul] am more
Eph. 3:7 I [Paul] was made a *m*, according to... grace
1 Pet. 4:10 even so *m* the same to one another

MINISTRY. A term for the biblical concept of sacrificial service. The idea originated with Abraham, whom God promised to make into a great nation, the Israelites. But they in turn were expected to serve as His witnesses to the other peoples and nations of the world (Gen. 12:2). Ministry demands a spirit of sacrificial service after the example of Christ (Matt. 20:26–28). All believers are called to be ambassadors for Christ in the work of serving others (2 Cor. 5:18–20).

MINISTRY
Acts 6:4 we [apostles] will give ourselves continually...to the *m* of the word
2 Cor. 5:18 God...has given to us the *m* of reconciliation
Eph. 4:12 perfecting of the saints, for the work of the *m*
2 Tim. 4:5 work of an evangelist, make full proof of your *m*
Heb. 8:6 now He [Jesus] has obtained a more excellent *m*

MINOR PROPHETS. The twelve prophets of the OT whose books were placed last in the prophetic writings because of their shorter length—Hosea, Joel, Amos, Obadiah, Jonah, Micah, Nahum, Habakkuk, Zephaniah, Haggai, Zechariah, and Malachi. Their brevity contrasts with the longer length of the "major" prophets: Isaiah, Jeremiah, Ezekiel, and Daniel. Lamentations is a shorter book, but it appears after the book of Jeremiah because it was written by this major prophet.

MIRACLE. An event contrary to natural law that is performed by the Lord through His unlimited power. Most miracles in the Bible occurred during the period of the Exodus, the ministries of Elijah and Elisha, the period of the Exile, the ministry of Jesus, and the work of the apostles during the early period of Christian history. Jesus did not perform His miracles to dazzle the crowds or showcase His power. His miracles declared that the kingdom of God had arrived, and it was being fulfilled in His mission of compassion and redemption. Jesus also demonstrated through His mighty works that He was Lord over nature and death (Mark 4:39 • John 11:43–45). Other words that mean essentially the same thing as miracles are "signs" (Exod. 7:3), "wonders" (Josh. 3:5), and "marvelous works" (Ps. 105:5).

MIRACLE [S]

Mark 6:52 they [the disciples] did not consider the *m* of the loaves

John 2:11 This beginning of *m's* Jesus did in Cana

John 3:2 can do these *m's* that You [Jesus] do unless God is with him

John 9:16 How can a man who is a sinner do such *m's*

John 12:37 though He [Jesus] had done so many *m's*...they still did not believe

Acts 6:8 Stephen...did great wonders and *m's*

1 Cor. 12:10 to another the working of *m's*

MIRACLES OF JESUS. See *Jesus Christ, Miracles of*

MIRIAM. A sister of Aaron and Moses who led a triumphant song of praise to God after the Israelites were delivered from the pursuing Egyptian army at the Red Sea (Exod. 15:2–21). In the wilderness she and Aaron rebelled against Moses' leadership. She was struck with a mysterious skin disease but healed after Moses' fervent prayer for her recovery (Num. 12:1–16). Miriam died and was buried in the wilderness at Kadesh (Num. 20:1). She is also mentioned in **Exod.** 2:4–10 • Num. 26:59 • Deut. 24:9 • 1 Chron. 6:3 • Mic. 6:4.

MISSIONS. The process of carrying out Jesus' Great Commission to disciple and teach all peoples. Jesus declared that this was one of the purposes of the church (Matt. 28:19–20). Even in the OT, Abraham was called to be a blessing to all nations (Gen. 12:1–3), and the prophet Jonah was sent by the Lord to preach to the pagan citizens of Nineveh (Jon. 1:2).

MIZPAH. (1) A place where Jacob and his father-in-law Laban made a covenant and agreed to a friendly separation. They marked the site with a pile of stones (Gen. 31:44–53).

(2) A city in the territory of the tribe of Benjamin where Saul was presented as the first king of Israel (1 Sam. 10:17).

MIZRAIM. A son of Ham whose descendants settled in Egypt (Gen. 10:6, 13 • 1 Chron. 1:8, 11). See also *Egypt*.

MNASON. A Christian from the island of Cyprus who accompanied Paul on his last visit to Jerusalem (Acts 21:16).

MOAB. (1) A son of Lot and an ancestor of the Moabites. Moab is mentioned in Gen. 19:33–37 • Num. 21:11–29 • Judg. 11:15–25 • Ruth 1:1–22 • Jer. 48:1–47.

(2) The country of the Moabites, a tribal group that opposed Israel. Moab inhabited the territory east of the Jordan River and the Dead Sea and south of the Arnon River (Deut. 1:5–7). The strength of the Moabites varied across several centuries of Israel's history. The tribes of Reuben and Gad settled in northern Moab before the conquest of Canaan (Num. 32:1–37). Ehud won a significant victory over their forces during the period of the judges (Judg. 3:15–30). David also fought and conquered the Moabites (2 Sam. 8:2).

They are also mentioned in Gen. 19:37 • Num. 22:4 • Deut. 2:9, 11, 29 • 1 Kings 11:1, 33 • 2 Kings 3:18, 21–24; 23:13; 24:2 • 1 Chron. 18:2 • Ezra 9:1.

MOCK [ED, ING, S]

1 Kings 18:27 Elijah *m'ed* them [prophets of Baal]... Cry...he is a god

Job 12:4 I [Job] am like one *m'ed* by his neighbor

Prov. 14:9 Fools *m* at sin

Prov. 17:5 Whoever *m's* the poor taunts his Maker

Jer. 20:7 object of ridicule daily—everyone *m's* me

Mark 10:34 they shall *m* Him [Jesus] and scourge Him

Mark 15:31 chief priests also, *m'ing*...said... He [Jesus] cannot save Himself

Luke 18:32 He [Jesus] shall be delivered to the Gentiles, and shall be *m'ed*

Luke 23:36 the soldiers also *m'ed* Him [Jesus]

Acts 2:13 *m'ing* said, These men [converts at Pentecost] are full of new wine

Gal. 6:7 Do not be deceived; God is not *m'ed*

MODEL PRAYER OF JESUS. See *Lord's Prayer*

MOLECH. See *Milcom*

MOLOCH. See *Milcom*

MONEY

Gen. 42:25 Joseph commanded...to restore every man's *m* into his sack

Exod. 22:25 lend *m* to any of My [God's] people... you shall not be to him as a usurer

Judg. 17:18 the Philistines came up to her [Delilah] and brought *m* in their hand

2 Chron. 24:5 gather *m* from all Israel to repair the house of...God from year to year

Eccles. 7:12 m is a defense, but...wisdom gives life

Isa. 55:1 come, buy wine and milk without *m* and without price

Matt. 17:27 when you have opened its [fish's] mouth, you shall find a piece of *m*

Matt. 21:19 Show Me [Jesus] the tax *m*. And they brought to Him a penny

Mark 11:15 Jesus went into the temple...and overthrew the tables of the *m* changers

1 Tim. 3:8 deacons must be grave...not greedy for *m*

1 Tim. 6:10 the love of *m* is the root of all evil

MONEY CHANGERS.
People driven out of the temple by Jesus because they had turned this holy place into a commercial site. They were converting foreign coins into local currency, perhaps charging excessive fees for this service. Jesus overturned their tables and drove them out of the temple (Matt. 21:12).

MONOGAMY.
The marriage of one man to one woman—the pattern established by the Lord in the first book of the Bible (Gen. 2:18–24). In spite of this principle, many of the OT patriarchs, such as Jacob, had more than one wife (Gen. 29:16–35).

MONOTHEISM.
The belief in one supreme God, in contrast to polytheism, or the worship of several gods. This concept was first revealed by the Lord to the Israelites. One of their oldest confessions of faith, known as the Shema, declared, "Hear, O Israel: The LORD our God is one LORD" (Deut. 6:4). This principle was eventually adopted by two other world religions—Christianity and Islam. See also *Polytheism*.

MOON.
The heavenly body referred to as the "lesser light" in the account of God's creation of the universe (Gen. 1:16). The Jewish calendar was based on the cycles of the moon. Each new moon marked the beginning of a new month, and its arrival was celebrated with special sacrifices (Num. 28:11–15; Ps. 81:3). The moon was worshipped under various names by pagan peoples of the ancient world, but God forbade this practice by the Israelites (Deut. 4:19).

MORDECAI.
A Jewish exile and a minor official in the court of the king of Persia. Mordecai refused to bow down and honor a man named Haman, the king's second in command. Enraged, Haman persuaded the king to issue a decree for the slaughter of all Jewish people throughout

Persia (Esther 3:8–12). With the help of his cousin, Queen Esther, Mordecai thwarted the plot (Esther 4:13–17) and was honored and promoted by the king (Esther 6:10–11; 8:1–2).

MORE

Gen. 3:1 Now the serpent was *m* subtle than any beast of the field

Gen. 29:30 he [Jacob] also loved Rachel *m* than Leah

Gen. 37:3 Now Israel loved Joseph *m* than all his children

Exod. 1:9 children of Israel are *m* and mightier than we [Egyptians]

Exod. 9:34 he [Pharaoh] sinned even *m* and hardened his heart

Esther 2:17 the king loved Esther *m* than all the women

Isa. 52:14 His [God's Servant's] appearance was marred *m* than any man

Matt. 7:25 Isn't life *m* than food and the body *m* than clothing?

Luke 12:7 do not fear. You are of *m* value than many sparrows

Acts 17:11 These [Bereans] were *m* noble… they…searched the scriptures daily

MOREH.
A place near Shechem where Abraham built an altar soon after settling in Canaan (**Gen. 12:6–7** • Deut. 11:30).

MORESHETH-GATH.
Birthplace of the prophet Micah (Mic. 1:14).

MORIAH.
A mountainous area to which Abraham traveled at the Lord's command to sacrifice his son Isaac (Gen. 22:1–13). After an animal sacrifice was provided, Abraham renamed the site Jehovah-jireh, meaning "the Lord will provide" (see Gen. 22:14). Centuries later, King Solomon built God's temple on this site (2 Chron. 3:1).

MORNING STAR.
See *Bright and Morning Star*

MORTALITY.
The certainty of physical death, the common lot of all human beings. The Bible compares the fragile nature of human life to water spilled on the ground (2 Sam. 14:14), a broken pot (Eccles. 12:6), a flower that blooms for just a short time (Isa. 40:6), a fog at dawn that disappears with the rising sun (Hos. 13:3), and a passing breeze (Ps. 78:39). But that is not the end of the story, according to the apostle Paul, who declared, "The gift of God is eternal life through Jesus Christ our Lord" (Rom. 6:23). Jesus has replaced the certainty of death with a promise of eternal life for those who claim Him as Lord and Savior.

MOSERAH.
A place in the wilderness where Moses' brother Aaron died and was buried (Deut. 10:6). Also called *Moseroth* (Num. 33:30–31).

MOSES.
The great lawgiver and prophet of Israel who led the Israelites out of slavery in Egypt and brought them to the border of the promised land. He is the undisputed central character in the narratives in the books of Exodus, Leviticus, Numbers, and Deuteronomy. As an infant, Moses was adopted by an Egyptian princess (Exod. 2:10). After killing an Egyptian slave overseer, he fled into the land of Midian, where he became a shepherd (Exod. 3:1), married the daughter of a priest, and fathered two sons (Exod. 18:3–4). He reluctantly answered the call to lead God's people out of slavery (Exod. 3:11–4:9), and returned to Egypt, where he enlisted his brother Aaron as his helper and spokesman (Exod. 4:27–31). After ten plagues sent by the Lord upon the Egyptians, the pharaoh finally released the Israelites, who entered the wilderness area in the Sinai Peninsula under Moses' leadership.

In the wilderness Moses received the Ten Commandments (Exod. 20:1–17) and other parts of the Mosaic Law, exhorted the people to remain faithful to God, built the tabernacle at God's command (Exod. 36–40), and sent scouts to investigate Canaan (Num. 13). He impatiently struck a rock for water at Kadesh, a sin which the Lord punished by forbidding him from entering the promised land (Num. 20:1–13). The people were often resentful of Moses' authority. But he refused to allow their stubborn attitude to turn him away from the task that God had called him to do. When the time came for him to step aside, he handed the reins of leadership to his young associate, Joshua, whom he had trained for the job (Deut. 34:9). After getting just a glimpse of Canaan from a high peak along its border, he died at the age of 120 (Deut. 34:7). In the NT, Moses is listed as one of the great heroes of the faith (Heb. 11:23–26).

Moses is also mentioned in Josh. 1:1–17; 8:31–35; 11:12–23; 13:8–33; 14:2–11; 22:4–9 • 2 Kings 18:4–12 • 1 Chron. 23:13–15 • Ps. 106:16–32 • Isa. 63:11–12 • Dan. 9:11, 13 • Matt. 17:3–4 • Mark 9:4–5 • Luke 16:29–31 • John 7:19–23 • Acts 7:20–44 • Rom. 10:5, 19 • Heb. 3:2–16 • Rev. 15:3

MOST HIGH. A name for God, signifying His majesty, which appears especially in the book of Psalms (Pss. 9:2; 73:11; 107:11). The prophet Daniel also used this name (Dan. 4:24; 7:18). In his long speech in the NT, the martyr Stephen declared that "the Most High does not dwell in temples made with hands" (Acts 7:48).

MOURN [ING, S]

Job 2:11 Job's three friends...came...to *m* with him

Ps. 38:6 I am troubled...I go *m'ing* all day long

Ps. 88:9 Mine eye *m's* because of affliction

Eccles. 3:4 a time to *m* and a time to dance

Isa. 60:20 the days of your *m'ing* shall be ended

Isa. 61:2 to comfort all who *m*

Amos 8:10 And I [God] will turn your feasts into *m'ing*

Matt. 5:4 Blessed are those who *m*...shall be comforted

Matt. 9:15 children...*m* as long as the bridegroom [Jesus] is with them

Jas. 4:9 Be afflicted and *m* and weep

MOURNING. The expression of grief or sorrow at a great loss. The usual mourning period was seven days, but this was extended to thirty days for Moses and Aaron (Num. 20:29 • Deut. 34:8). Jesus demonstrated the human side of His nature when He mourned at the death of His friend Lazarus (John 11:33–36).

MOVE [D, ING, S]

Gen. 1:2 Spirit of God *m'd* on the...waters

Gen. 9:3 Every *m'ing* thing that lives shall be food

Ps. 16:8 He [God] is at my right hand, I shall not be *m'd*

Ps. 46:5 God is in the midst of her [Jerusalem]... not be *m'd*

Ps. 62:2 He [God]...is my defense; I shall not be greatly *m'd*

Ps. 69:34 praise Him [God], the seas, and everything that *m's*

Ps. 96:10 the LORD reigns. The world...shall not be *m'd*

Isa. 6:4 posts of the door *m'd* at the voice of him who cried out

Mark 6:34 Jesus...was *m'd* with compassion for them [the crowds]

John 5:3 multitude...waiting for the *m'ing* of the water

Acts 17:28 in Him [God] we live and *m* and have our being

Heb. 12:28 a kingdom that cannot be *m'd*

2 Pet. 1:21 men...spoke as they were *m'd* by the Holy Spirit

MULTITUDE [S]

Gen. 32:12 your [Jacob's] descendants...cannot be numbered for *m*

Exod. 12:38 mixed *m* also went up with them [Israelites]

Ps. 69:13 O God, in the *m* of Your mercy, hear me

Ps. 109:30 I will praise him [God] among the *m*

Joel 3:14 *M's*, *m's* in the valley of decision

Matt. 5:1 seeing the *m's*, He [Jesus] went up on a mountain

Matt. 15:33 should we get...bread...as to feed so great a *m*

Matt. 22:33 when the *m* heard this, they were astonished

Mark 4:1 whole *m* was on the land by the sea

Mark 5:31 the *m* thronging You [Jesus]...yet You say... Who touched Me?

Luke 2:13 with the angel there was a *m* of the heavenly host

Luke 23:1 whole *m*...arose and led Him [Jesus] to Pilate

John 6:2 great *m* followed Him [Jesus] because they saw His miracles

1 Pet. 4:8 for love covers the *m* of sins

Rev. 7:9 a great *m*—which no man could number

MURDER. The unlawful taking of a human life by another person, a crime prohibited by the Ten Commandments (Exod. 20:13). The death penalty was enforced in cases of willful homicide (Lev. 24:17), but cities of refuge were provided as sanctuaries for persons guilty of manslaughter, or accidental killing (Num. 35:11). Jesus warned of intense anger that could lead to murder (Matt. 5:20–22). See also *Cities of Refuge.*

MURMUR [ED, ING, INGS]

Exod. 15:24 the people *m'ed* against Moses

Num. 14:27 I [God] have heard...*m'ings* of the children of Israel

Luke 5:30 Pharisees *m'ed* against His [Jesus'] disciples

John 6:41 *m'ed*...because He [Jesus] said, I am the bread...from heaven

John 7:12 was much *m'ing* among the people concerning Him [Jesus]

Phil. 2:14 Do all things without *m'ings* and arguments

MUSIC. Performance of rhythmic sounds through singing and musical instruments as a form of worship. After the Lord delivered the Israelites from the Egyptian army at the Red Sea, the sister of Moses led the women to give joyful thanks with timbrels and dancing (Exod. 15:20–21). The early Christians also worshipped with music (Eph. 5:19). Fragments of some early Christian hymns even made their way into the NT (1 Tim. 3:16).

MUSTARD SEED. A tiny seed from a common herb that Jesus cited to illustrate the power of faith (Luke 17:6).

MUTE

Isa. 53:7 as a sheep before its shearers is *m*

Mark 7:37 He [Jesus] makes both the deaf to hear and the *m* to speak

Luke 1:20 you [Zechariah] shall be *m*...not able to speak

1 Cor. 12:2 You know that you were Gentiles, carried away to these *m* idols

MUTH-LABBEN. A musical term in the title of Ps. 9, perhaps referring to the tune for the psalm.

MYRA. A coastal town in Asia Minor where Paul changed ships during his voyage to Rome (Acts 27:5–6).

MYRRH. An aromatic gum resin used in perfume, and one of the gifts presented by the wise men to the infant Jesus (Matt. 2:11).

MYRTLE. A common evergreen shrub which symbolized God's provision for His people (Isa. 41:19).

MYSIA. A province in Asia Minor through which Paul and Silas passed on the second missionary journey (Acts 16:7–10).

MYSTERY. A word that the apostle Paul used for the gospel, implying it was shown to humankind only through divine revelation (Rom. 16:25–26).

MYSTERY [IES]

Mark 4:11 To you [the disciples] it has been given to know the *m* of the kingdom

Luke 8:10 it is given to know the *m'ies* of the kingdom...to others...in parables

1 Cor. 2:7 we speak the wisdom of God in a *m*

1 Cor. 4:1 ministers of Christ and stewards of the *m'ies* of God

1 Cor. 13:2 though I [Paul]...understand all *m'ies* and all knowledge

1 Cor. 15:51 I tell you a *m*: We shall not all sleep

Eph. 5:32 a great *m*, but I [Paul] speak concerning Christ

1 Tim. 3:9 holding the *m* of the faith with a pure conscience

NAAMAN. An officer in the Syrian army who was healed of leprosy by the prophet Elisha. At first Naaman refused to immerse himself in the Jordan River for healing, as commanded by the prophet. The proud military man declared that the rivers of his home country were better than all the rivers of Israel. But he finally obeyed, was healed, and praised the God of Israel (2 Kings 5:1–15). Naaman is also mentioned in Luke 4:27.

NAARAI. One of David's "mighty men," an elite group of warriors noted for their bravery in battle (1 Chron. 11:37).

NABAL. A wealthy and ill-tempered herdsman who refused to help David and his army while he was on the run from King Saul. Nabal's wife Abigail brought food to the desperate men. Later, after Nabal died, David took Abigail as his wife (**1 Sam. 25:2–42 • 2 Sam. 3:3**).

NABOTH. A landowner whose death was planned by Jezebel so her husband, King Ahab of Israel (the Northern Kingdom), could take possession of his prime piece of property (1 Kings 21:1–23). The prophet Elijah announced God's judgment against Ahab for this crime. The king was eventually killed in a battle. Dogs lapped up the water when his blood was flushed from his chariot (1 Kings 22:34–38).

NADAB. (1) The oldest son of Aaron who was killed, along with his brother Abihu, for presenting an offering that God deemed unworthy (Exod. 24:1, 9–12; 28:1 • **Lev. 10:1–7**).

(2) A king of Israel (the Northern Kingdom), who was assassinated by Baasha, his successor (1 Kings 14:20; 15:25–31).

NAHARAI. One of David's "mighty men," an elite group of warriors known for their bravery in battle (2 Sam. 23:37).

NAHASH. A king of Ammon who befriended David (2 Sam. 10:1–2).

NAHBI. One of the twelve spies or scouts sent by Moses to investigate the land of Canaan. He represented the tribe of Naphtali (Num. 13:14).

NAHUM. (1) A prophet of Judah (the Southern Kingdom) who announced God's forthcoming judgment against the pagan city of Nineveh (Nah. 1:1). His prophecies appear in the OT book that bears his name.

(2) An ancestor of Jesus in Joseph's line (Luke 3:25).

NAHUM, BOOK OF. A short prophetic book of the OT that predicted the downfall of the pagan nation of Assyria (Nah. 3:7–19) because of the atrocities which it had committed against God's people. This happened in 612 BC when the Assyrians were defeated by the Babylonians. The book portrays God as the sovereign Lord of history who has the final word in the conflict between good and evil (Nah. 1:1–15).

NAIN. A village south of Nazareth near the Sea of Galilee where Jesus raised a widow's son from the dead (Luke 7:11–17). A small church on the site of this village commemorates the event. Two paintings inside the church depict the miracle of Jesus.

NAIOTH. A place where Samuel lived and conducted his school for prophets, and a place to which David fled from King Saul (1 Sam. 19:18–23; 20:1).

NAOMI. A woman from Bethlehem who moved to Moab with her husband and two sons to escape a famine (Ruth 1:1–2). One of her sons married Ruth, a native of Moab. When Naomi's husband and sons died, she returned to Bethlehem along with Ruth (Ruth 1:6–16). Later, she worked behind the scenes to arrange Ruth's marriage to Boaz (Ruth 3:1–5).

NAPHTALI. (1) A son of Jacob by Bilhah, Rachel's maid. He is mentioned in Gen. 30:8; 35:25; 46:24; 49:21 • Exod. 1:4 • 1 Chron. 2:2; 7:13 • Ezek. 48:34.

(2) One of the twelve tribes of Israel that developed from Naphtali's descendants (Num. 1:42). This tribe was assigned the fertile, mountainous territory in northern Israel, which included the cities of Hazor, Kedesh, and Ramah (Josh. 19:32–38; 20:7). The prophet Isaiah predicted that Naphtali in "Galilee of the Gentiles" would see a great light (Isa. 9:1–7). This was fulfilled in Jesus' ministry in the region of Galilee (Matt. 4:12–16).

NAPHTUHIM. Inhabitants of central Egypt who were descendants of Mizraim, son of Ham (Gen. 10:13).

NARCISSUS. A Christian in Rome whose household was greeted by the apostle Paul (Rom. 16:11).

NATHAN. (1) A courageous prophet who condemned King David for his infamous double sin—his adulterous affair with Bathsheba and the murder of her husband, Uriah. Nathan told the king a clever story about a rich man who had many flocks of sheep. But to provide a meal for a guest in his house, the wealthy man took the one little lamb that a poor man owned. Outraged at this selfish act, David declared that the rich man should be put to death. Then Nathan pointed out that he, the king, was actually the man in the story (2 Sam. 12:1–25). Nathan also assisted David when his son Adonijah attempted to seize the throne and wrote histories of David's and Solomon's administrations. He is also mentioned in 2 Sam. 7:2–17 • 1 Kings 1:8–45 • 1 Chron. 17:1–15; 29:29 • 2 Chron. 9:29; 29:25 • Ps. 51:1.

(2) A son of David by Bathsheba, born after David became king of all Israel (1 Chron. 3:1–5).

NATHANAEL. See *Bartholomew*

NATION [S]

Gen. 12:2 I [God] will make of you [Abraham] a great *n*

Gen. 17:5 a father of many *n's* have I [God] made you [Abraham]

Gen. 25:23 Two *n's* are in your [Rebekah's] womb

Exod. 19:6 you [Israel] shall be to Me [God]...a holy *n*

Deut. 9:1 possess *n's* greater and mightier than yourself

Deut. 28:1 God will set you...above all *n's* of the earth

1 Sam. 8:5 give us a king to judge us like all the *n's*

2 Sam. 7:23 what one *n*...is like Your [God's] people Israel

1 Chron. 16:24 Declare...His [God's] marvelous works among all *n's*

Ps. 22:28 and He [God] is the ruler among the *n's*

Ps. 33:12 Blessed is the *n* whose God is the LORD

Ps. 67:2 Your [God's] way may be known...saving health among all *n's*

Ps. 72:11 all kings...all *n's* shall serve Him [God]

Ps. 82:8 judge the earth...You [God] shall inherit all *n's*

Ps. 96:5 For all the gods of the *n's* are idols

Ps. 113:4 The LORD is high above all *n's*

Prov. 14:34 Righteousness exalts a *n*

Isa. 2:4 N shall not lift up a sword against *n*

Isa. 40:15 Behold, the *n's* are like a drop in a bucket

Isa. 52:10 LORD has made bare His...arm in...all the *n's*

Isa. 60:12 *n*...that will not serve you shall perish

Jer. 1:5 ordained you [Jeremiah] as a prophet to the *n's*

Jer. 2:11 Has a *n* changed its gods

Jer. 50:41 a people shall come from the north, and a great *n*

Ezek. 12:15 when I [God] scatter them among the *n's*

Mic. 4:3 N shall not lift up a sword against *n*

Zeph. 3:6 I [God] have cut off the *n's*...towers are desolate

Hag. 2:7 and the desire of all *n's* shall come

Zech. 8:22 strong *n's* shall come to seek the LORD

Mal. 3:9 you have robbed Me [God], even this whole *n*

Matt. 24:7 *n* shall rise against *n*...kingdom against kingdom

Matt. 24:14 gospel of the kingdom...preached...to all *n's*

Matt. 25:32 all *n's* shall be gathered before Him [Jesus]

Matt. 28:19 teach all *n's*, baptizing them

Luke 24:47 repentance...preached...among all *n's*

John 11:50 one man should die...that the whole *n* should not perish

Acts 2:5 devout men from every *n* under heaven

Acts 10:35 in every *n* he who fears Him [God]... is accepted by Him

Acts 17:26 And [God] has made of one blood all *n's*

Phil. 2:15 in the midst of a crooked and perverse *n*

1 Pet. 2:9 you are a chosen generation...a holy *n*

Rev. 7:9 multitude—which no man could number, of all *n's*

NATURAL

Rom. 1:26 even their women exchanged the *n* use

1 Cor. 2:14 *n* man does not receive the things of the Spirit

1 Cor. 15:44 It is sown a *n* body...raised a spiritual body

2 Tim. 3:3 without *n* affection, truce breakers

NATURE. A word which refers to the inner essence of humankind. Adam and Eve's disobedience in the garden of Eden introduced sin into the world and corrupted human nature (Gen. 3:12–19). The cure for this sinful condition is redemption through the atoning death of Jesus Christ (Rom. 6:23).

NATURE

Rom. 1:26 women exchanged the natural use into what is against *n*

Rom. 2:14 Gentiles...by *n* do the things contained in the law

2 Pet. 1:4 you might be partakers of the divine *n*

NAUM. KJV: see *Nahum*, No. 2

NAZARENE. A native or inhabitant of the city of Nazareth. Since this is where Jesus grew up, He was called a "Nazarene" (Matt. 2:23).

NAZARETH. The boyhood home of Jesus (Mark 1:24); an obscure town in the region of Galilee. An angel announced to the virgin Mary in this city that she would give birth to the Messiah (Luke 1:26–38). The boy Jesus and His parents returned to Nazareth after their flight into Egypt (Matt. 2:19–23). Nazareth is where Jesus grew up—from the time when He was a child (Luke 2:39–40) until the age of about thirty, when He launched His public ministry (Luke 3:23). Jesus tried to explain His mission as the Messiah to His friends in the town. But they refused to believe that one of their own could be the Messiah (Luke 4:14–30). In modern times, Nazareth has grown into a thriving Arabic population center. Its main attraction is the Basilica of the Annunciation, a church built over the reputed site of the angel's announcement to Mary that she would give birth to the Son of God.

NAZARITE. A person who made a vow to dedicate himself exclusively to God for some special service (Num. 6:1–21). While under such a vow, A Nazarite was not to shave, cut his hair, drink wine, or defile himself by touching a dead body. Nazarites mentioned in the Bible are Samson (Judg. 13:4–7), Samuel (1 Sam. 1:11, 28), and John the Baptist (Luke 1:15). Nazarites are also mentioned in Lam. 4:7 • Amos 2:11–12.

NEAPOLIS. A seaport at Philippi where the apostle Paul landed on the second missionary journey (Acts 16:11).

NEBO. (1) The highest point of Mount Pisgah near Jericho where Moses died after viewing the promised land and where he was buried (Deut. 32:49; 34:1–6). This peak, in a region known as Moab, was near the northern end of the Dead Sea on the eastern side of the Jordan River. A church on Mount Nebo, known as the Memorial Church of Moses, pays tribute to this great leader.

(2) The Babylonian god of science and knowledge condemned by the prophet Isaiah (Isa. 46:1).

NEBUCHADNEZZAR. The king of Babylon who overran Jerusalem and carried many of the residents of Judah into exile about 587 BC

(2 Kings 25:1–26). During the Exile, Daniel predicted trouble for the king because of the prophet's strange dream about a fallen tree. About a year later Nebuchadnezzar was driven from office. He apparently went mad and lived for a time among animals, eating grass like an ox (Dan. 4:33). Nebuchadnezzar eventually recovered his sanity and served as a witness to God's power and authority. He praised the Lord and declared, "He is able to humble those who walk in pride" (Dan. 4:37). Nebuchadnezzar is also mentioned in 2 Chron. 36:7–13 • Jer. 28:11–14; 51:34 .

NEBUCHADREZZAR. KJV: see *Nebuchadnezzar*

NEBUZARADAN. An officer in King Nebuchadnezzar's army during the Babylonian siege of Jerusalem (2 Kings 25:8–20). He treated the prophet Jeremiah with kindness, giving him the choice of fleeing to Egypt or remaining in Jerusalem after the city fell (Jer. 39:11–14; 40:1–5).

NECHO. KJV: see *Neco*

NECO. A pharaoh of Egypt who defeated King Josiah of Judah (the Southern Kingdom) in a battle in the valley of Megiddo (2 Chron. 35:22–25). *Necho*: KJV.

NEED [ED, S]
Matt. 3:14 I [John the Baptist] have *n* to be baptized by You [Jesus]
Matt. 6:8 Father knows what things you have *n* of
Luke 5:31 Those who are healthy do not *n* a physician
Luke 15:7 joy...over one sinner...than...righteous people who *n* no repentance
John 4:4 He [Jesus] *n'ed* to go through Samaria
Acts 2:45 sold their possessions...and divided them...as every man had *n*
Acts 17:25 as though He [God] *n'ed* anything... He gives to all life
1 Cor. 12:21 eye cannot say to the hand, I have no *n* of you
Phil. 4:19 But my God shall supply all your *n*

2 Tim. 2:15 a workman who does not *n* to be ashamed
Heb. 4:16 and find grace to help in time of *n*
Heb. 7:27 who [Jesus] does not *n*...to offer... sacrifices, first for His own sins

NEEDLE. A small tool used in sewing. Jesus compared the difficulty of the wealthy reaching heaven with putting a camel through the eye of a needle (Matt. 19:24).

NEEDY
Deut. 15:11 open your hand...to your *n*, in your land
Job 24:14 The murderer...kills the poor and *n*
Ps. 37:14 The wicked have...bent their bow to cast down the poor and *n*
Ps. 40:17 I am poor and *n*; yet the Lord thinks of me
Ps. 82:3 do justice to the afflicted and *n*
Ps. 86:1 O Lord; hear me, for I am poor and *n*
Prov. 31:9 and plead the cause of the poor and *n*
Amos 8:6 buy the poor for silver...*n* for a pair of shoes

NEGINAH. A term in the titles of Psalm 61 which may refer to stringed instruments such as harps or lyres.

NEGINOTH. A term in the titles of several psalms which may refer to stringed instruments such as harps or lyres (Pss. 4, 6, 54, 55, 67, 76).

NEGLECT [ED, S]
Matt. 18:17 if he *n's* to hear them, tell it to the church
Acts 6:1 widows were *n'ed* in the daily ministry
1 Tim. 4:14 Do not *n* the gift that is in you [Timothy]
Heb. 2:3 how shall we escape if we *n* so great a salvation

NEHEMIAH. An official under King Artaxerxes of Persia who rallied the citizens of Jerusalem to rebuild the city wall after the Exile (Neh. 1:1–2:20). The account of this construction project and other religious reforms he implemented appear in the OT book that bears his name.

NEHEMIAH, BOOK OF. A historical book of the OT which records the rebuilding of

Jerusalem's defensive wall after the Exile under the leadership of Nehemiah. The book is a good case study in effective leadership. Nehemiah sought God's guidance and prayed for the people of Judah. He did a careful analysis of the work to be done and organized the laborers for maximum effectiveness, completing the project in just fifty-two days (Neh. 6:15–19). The book also recounts the religious reforms undertaken by Nehemiah and his colleague Ezra. They led the people to recommit themselves to the Lord (Neh. 8:1–13:31).

NEHILOTH. A musical term in the title of Psalm 5, probably denoting a wind instrument such as the flute.

NEIGHBOR [S]

Exod. 20:16 not bear false witness against your *n*
Lev. 19:13 not defraud your *n* or rob him
Lev. 19:18 but you shalt love your *n* as yourself
Ps. 79:4 We have become a reproach to our *n's*
Prov. 11:12 He who is void of wisdom despises his *n*
Prov. 14:20 The poor is hated even by his own *n*...rich has many friends
Prov. 24:28 Do not be a witness against your *n* without cause
Prov. 27:10 a *n* who is near is better than a brother far away
Jer. 31:34 no longer shall every man teach his *n*
Zech. 8:17 let none of you plan evil...against his *n*
Matt. 22:39 You shall love your *n* as yourself
Luke 10:36 Which of these three...was *n* to him who fell among the thieves
Luke 15:6 he calls...*n's*, saying... Rejoice with me...I have found my sheep
Rom. 13:10 Love works no ill to his *n*
Gal. 5:14 You shall love your *n* as yourself
Eph. 4:25 speak truth every man with his *n*
Jas. 2:8 fulfill the royal law... love your *n* as yourself

NEPHEG. A son of David, born in Jerusalem after David became king over all Israel (2 Sam. 5:13–15).

NEREUS. A Christian at Rome to whom the apostle Paul sent greetings (Rom. 16:15).

NERGAL. A Babylonian god of war (2 Kings 17:30).

NERGAL-SHAREZER. A Babylonian prince who released Jeremiah from prison (Jer. 39:3–14).

NERO. The fifth emperor of the Roman Empire known for his persecution of Christians. Although he is not mentioned by name in the Bible, he is probably the emperor under whom Paul and Peter were martyred. Some interpreters claim that the mysterious beast from the sea in the book of Revelation refers to Nero (Rev. 13:3, 12).

NETHINIM. People of non-Jewish background who served as assistants to the Levites. They did such menial tasks as cleaning the temple and carrying wood and water to the altar. Many of the Nethinim were slaves or captives of war assigned to the Levites (Ezra 8:17–20).

NEW

Exod. 1:8 there arose a *n* king...who did not know Joseph
Ps. 40:3 And He [God] has put a *n* song in my mouth
Ps. 96:1 sing to the LORD a *n* song...all the earth
Eccles. 1:9 there is nothing *n* under the sun
Isa. 1:14 My [God's] soul hates your *N* Moons
Isa. 42:10 Sing to the LORD a *n* song
Isa. 65:17 I [God] create *n* heavens and a new earth
Lam. 3:23 They [God's mercies] are *n* every morning
Ezek. 36:26 I [God] will put a *n* spirit inside you
Amos 8:5 will the *N* Moon be gone, that we may sell grain
Matt. 27:60 laid it [Jesus' body] in his [Joseph's] own *n* tomb
Mark 2:22 no man puts *n* wine into old bottles
Luke 22:20 cup is the *n* covenant in My [Jesus'] blood
John 13:34 A *n* commandment I [Jesus] give to you
Acts 2:13 men [converts at Pentecost] are full of *n* wine

1 Cor. 5:7 Purge out the old leaven...may be a *n* lump

2 Cor. 3:6 who [Jesus]...made us able ministers of the *n* covenant

2 Cor. 5:17 if any man is in Christ, he is a *n* creature

Eph. 4:24 put on the *n* man

2 Pet. 3:13 we...look for *n* heavens and a *n* earth

Rev. 21:1 I [John] saw a *n* heaven and a *n* earth

Rev. 21:5 Behold, I [Jesus] make all things *n*

NEW BIRTH. A state of regeneration or resurrection from spiritual death (Romans 6:4–8). The phrase comes from Jesus's words to Nicodemus, "You must be born again" (John 3:7). The Holy Spirit brings regeneration and produces a changed person. This comes about by God's grace through faith in Christ rather than through one's own efforts or good works (Eph. 2:8–9).

NEW COVENANT. God's final covenant with His people through which His grace is expressed to all believers. Foretold by the prophet Jeremiah (Jer. 31:31–34), the new covenant was symbolized by Jesus when He ate the last supper with His disciples. He called the cup the "new covenant in My blood" (Luke 22:20). Christ, the mediator of a new and better covenant, assures the believer's eternal inheritance (Heb. 8:6). See also *Mediator of the New Covenant.*

NEW COVENANT

Jer. 31:31 I [God] will make a *n-c* with the house of Israel

Matt. 26:28 this is My blood of the *n-c*...shed for many

Luke 22:20 cup is the *n-c* in My blood, which is shed for you

2 Cor. 3:6 who [God] also made us able ministers of the *n-c*

Heb. 8:8 I [God] will make a *n-c* with the house of Israel

Heb. 8:13 In that He [God] says, A *n-c*, He has made the first old

Heb. 12:24 and to Jesus the mediator of the *n-c*

NEW HEAVENS AND NEW EARTH. A phrase that refers to the perfected universe that will occur in the end-time. The concept comes from the writings of the apostle Peter. At the second coming of Christ, Peter declared, the present evil age will be replaced by the age to come. The entire universe (heavens and earth) will be remade by the power of God (2 Pet. 3:10–13). A new heavens and new earth are necessary because the old universe has been hopelessly marred by human sin. The physical world must be purified and re-created as a fitting and final dwelling place for the righteous (Rom. 8:19–21).

NEW JERUSALEM. The heavenly city of the end-time (Rev. 21:2–22:5) that stands in contrast to the sinful city known as "Babylon the great." The apostle John identified this holy, eternal city as the church, which he referred to as the wife of the lamb. The lamb is Jesus Christ, the founder and sustainer of the church (Rev. 21:9). John declared that this new Jerusalem will not be a human creation. It was made possible by God Himself through the atoning death of His Son, Jesus.

NEW JERUSALEM

Rev. 3:12 the city of my God, which is *n-J*

Rev. 21:2 I, John, saw the holy city, *n-J*, coming down...from God

NEWNESS

Rom. 6:4 even so we also should walk in *n* of life

Rom. 7:6 serve in *n* of the Spirit...not in the oldness of the letter

NEW TESTAMENT. The second major division of the Bible, composed of twenty-seven books. It is also known as the "new covenant" to magnify the coming of the Messiah and His redemptive ministry of grace (Jer. 31:31–34 • Heb. 9:15). The theme of this section of God's Word is the life and ministry of Jesus Christ and the growth and development of the early church. See also *Old Testament.*

NIBHAZ. An idol worshipped by the Avvites, who settled in Samaria (2 Kings 17:31).

NICANOR. One of the seven men set apart for special service in the church at Jerusalem. Their role was to take care of the Greek-speaking widows who had been neglected in the church's food distribution ministry (Acts 6:1–5).

NICODEMUS. An influential Pharisee who came to talk with Jesus out of curiosity over His teachings. Jesus impressed upon Nicodemus the necessity of being born again (John 3:1–21). Nicodemus was a member of the Jewish high court known as the Sanhedrin. Later, he cautioned his fellow Jewish officials not to prejudge Jesus (John 7:50–51). After Jesus was crucified, Nicodemus and Joseph of Arimathea claimed His body and helped prepare it for burial (John 19:38–40). Nicodemus may have been an undeclared or secret follower of Jesus.

NICOLAITANS. An early sect whose heretical beliefs were compared to those of the wizard Balaam in the OT. The church at Pergamum was rebuked for its openness to their teachings (Rev. 2:6, 14–15).

NICOLAS. One of the seven men set apart for special service in the church at Jerusalem. Their role was to take care of the Greek-speaking widows who had been neglected in the church's food distribution ministry (Acts 6:1–5).

NICOPOLIS. A city on the coast of the Adriatic Sea where the apostle Paul spent the winter (Titus 3:12).

NILE RIVER. The great river of Egypt which begins in Africa and runs for more than 3,500 miles across Africa and Egypt, emptying finally into the Mediterranean Sea. Its annual overflow built up rich soil ideal for growing grain. The Nile was so essential to the livelihood of the Egyptians that they revered it as a god. So when God plagued Egypt by making the Nile's waters run red with blood, He proved His superiority to the pagan religious system of this ancient nation (Exod. 7:17). The baby Moses was hidden in the tall grass at the edge of the Nile (Exod. 2:3). The name *Nile* is not found in the King James or Simplified King James Versions, where it is called "the river of Egypt" (Gen. 15:18 • 2 Kings 24:7).

NIMROD. A descendant of Noah who became a powerful king in Shinar, an ancient name for Mesopotamia (Gen. 10:8–12 • 1 Chron. 1:8–10). Nimrod is also associated with the nation of Assyria (Mic. 5:6).

NINEVE. KJV: see *Nineveh*

NINEVEH. The capital of Assyria on the Tigris River where the prophet Jonah preached God's message of judgment.

Many residents of Nineveh repented and turned to the Lord (Jon. 3:5–9). Excavations have revealed that Nineveh was, indeed, the "great city" described in the book of Jonah (Jon. 3:2). Its massive defensive wall stretched for eight miles around the city. Archaeologists also uncovered the ornate palace of King Sennacherib that covered about five acres. Nineveh is also mentioned in Gen. 10:11–12 • 2 Kings 19:36 • Isa. 37:37 • Nah. 1:1; 2:8; 3:7 • Zeph. 2:13 • Matt. 12:41 • Luke 11:32.

NISAN. See *Abib*

NISROCH. A false god worshipped by King Sennacherib of Assyria (2 Kings 19:36–37 • Isa. 37:38).

NO. KJV: see *Thebes*

NOADIAH. A prophetess who tried to persuade Nehemiah to halt the rebuilding of the wall of Jerusalem (Neh. 6:14).

NOAH. A righteous man who built a large boat to escape the great flood. The Lord revealed to Noah that He intended to destroy all living things with a catastrophic deluge. But Noah and his sons and their families would be spared in a giant ark in which they could escape (Gen. 6:11–18). After building the ark, he entered with his family and selected animals (Gen. 7:1–24). After the flood was over, Noah built an altar and offered a sacrifice of thanksgiving to the Lord (Gen. 8:20–21). Then God promised Noah that He would never judge the world again with floodwaters. The Lord sealed this promise by placing a rainbow in the sky (Gen. 9:8–17). Jesus compared the great flood of Noah's time to His own second coming. Just like those who did not expect judgment by water in OT times, many people will be unprepared for the Lord's return (Luke 17:22–27). Noah is also mentioned in Gen. 10:1, 32 • 1 Chron. 1:4 • Isa. 54:9 • Ezek. 14:14, 20 • Heb. 11:7 • 1 Pet. 3:20 • 2 Pet. 2:5.

NOB. A city near Jerusalem where David fled to escape King Saul's wrath (1 Sam. 21:1–9). Ahimelech, a local priest, provided food for David and his hungry warriors. When Saul discovered this, he ordered Ahimelech's death and the slaughter of eighty-five other priests who lived at Nob (1 Sam. 22:13–19). It is also mentioned in Neh. 11:32 • Isa. 10:32.

NOBLEMAN. A unnamed person of high rank whose son was healed by Jesus (John 4:46–54).

NOD. A territory east of the garden of Eden where Cain fled after murdering his brother Abel (Gen. 4:16–17).

NOE. KJV: see *Noah*

NOGAH. A son of David who was born in Jerusalem after David became king over all Israel (1 Chron. 3:7; 14:6).

NOPH. KJV: see *Memphis*

NORTHERN KINGDOM (ISRAEL) FALLS TO ASSYRIA. 2 Kings 17

NORTHERN TRIBES OF ISRAEL REVOLT AGAINST SOLOMON'S SON REHOBOAM. 1 Kings 12:6–24

NOTHING
Deut. 2:7 God has been with you...forty years; you have lacked *n*
Josh. 11:15 He [Joshua] left *n* undone of all that the LORD commanded Moses
2 Sam. 12:3 poor man had *n* except one little ewe lamb
Job 8:9 we...know *n*, because our days on earth are a shadow
Ps. 49:17 when he dies he shall carry *n* away
Prov. 13:7 There is one who makes himself rich, yet has *n*
Eccles. 2:24 *n* better for a man than that...his soul enjoy good in his labor
Isa. 40:17 All nations are as *n* before Him [God]

Isa. 41:29 they are all *n*. Their works are *n*
Isa. 44:10 cast an image that is profitable for *n*
Jer. 32:17 there is *n* too hard for You [God]
Matt. 5:13 salt...is thereafter good for *n* but to be cast out
Matt. 17:20 *n* shall be impossible for you
Mark 6:8 commanded them [the disciples]... take *n* for their journey
Mark 7:15 *n* from outside a man...can defile him
Luke 5:5 toiled all the night, and have taken *n*
Luke 23:9 but He [Jesus] answered him [Pilate] *n*
John 3:27 receive *n* except what is given him from heaven
John 5:19 The Son [Jesus] can do *n* of Himself
John 15:5 For without Me [Jesus] you can do *n*
Acts 11:8 *n* common or unclean...entered into my [Peter's] mouth
Rom. 14:14 I [Paul] know...there is *n* unclean by itself
1 Cor. 1:19 I [God]...will bring to *n* the understanding of the prudent
1 Cor. 7:19 Circumcision is *n* and uncircumcision is *n*
1 Cor. 13:2 though I [Paul]...have not love, I am *n*
Phil. 2:3 Let *n* be done through strife or boastfulness
1 Tim. 6:7 For we brought *n* into this world
Heb. 7:19 For the law made *n* perfect

NOTICE
2 Sam. 3:36 all the people took *n* of it
Ps. 144:3 what is man, that You *n* him
Isa. 58:3 afflicted our soul, and You do not *n*

NUMBERS, BOOK OF. An OT book which traces the wanderings of the Israelites in the wilderness as God was preparing them to enter the land of Canaan. Its name comes from the two "numberings" (censuses) of the Israelites that were commanded by the Lord in chapters 1 and 26. During this period of about forty years, the people showed their rebellious spirit and lack of faith. They complained about Moses and his leadership and about their food and water supply (Num. 20:1–5). They grumbled against God and accused Him of abandoning them in the wilderness, even though He provided miraculously for their needs time after time (Num. 14:1–4). Some of the Israelite men even worshipped the false gods of the Moabites (Num. 25:1–18). Finally, even Moses lost his patience with the people when he struck a rock to produce water rather than speaking to it as the Lord directed. God punished Moses by declaring that he would not be allowed to enter the land of Canaan (Num. 20:1–13).

NUN. (1) The fourteenth letter of the Hebrew alphabet, which appears as a heading over Psalm 119:105-112. In the original Hebrew language, each of these eight verses begins with this letter, forming an acrostic poem.

(2) The father of Moses' aide and successor, Joshua (Exod. 33:11).

NYMPHAS. A Christian of Laodicea to whom the apostle Paul sent greetings (Col. 4:15).

O

OATH. A solemn promise to God to attest that a statement was true or to affirm a covenant (2 Sam. 21:7). A good example is the promise Ruth made to her mother-in-law Naomi: "May the LORD do so to me, and more also, if anything but death parts you and me" (Ruth 1:17). If a person used the Lord's name in an oath, it was considered a sacred promise with serious consequences if the vow was broken (Judg. 11:30–36). Jesus declared that a simple "yes" or "no" rather than assent to an oath was appropriate for members of the kingdom of God (Matt. 5:34–37).

OATH [S]

Matt. 5:33 perform your *o*'s to the Lord

Matt. 26:72 he [Peter] denied with an *o*, I do not know the man [Jesus]

Heb. 7:20 He [Jesus] was not made priest without an *o*

Jas. 5:12 nor by any other *o*. But let your yes be yes

OBADIAH. (1) A prophet of Judah (the Southern Kingdom) who condemned the Edomites for their mockery of Jerusalem. His prophecies appear in the OT book which bears his name (Obad. 1).

(2) A godly servant of King Ahab who hid one hundred prophets of the Lord to escape Queen Jezebel's wrath (1 Kings 18:3–4).

OBADIAH, BOOK OF. The shortest book in the OT, a prophecy containing only twenty-one verses. The book pronounces God's judgment against the Edomites, the descendants of Esau, because they had participated in the destruction of the city of Jerusalem when it fell to the Babylonian army (Obad. 10–14).

OBED. One of David's "mighty men," an elite group of warriors known for their bravery in battle (1 Chron. 11:47).

OBED-EDOM. A servant of David in whose house the ark of the covenant was kept for a time before being moved to Jerusalem (2 Sam. 6:10–12 • **1 Chron. 13:13–14**; 15:24–25).

OBEDIENCE. An idea closely related to the concept of hearing. To really hear God's commands is to obey what He commands. Jesus was perfectly obedient to the Father, and He requires obedience of His followers (Heb. 5:8–9).

OBEDIENCE

Rom. 5:19 so through the *o* of One [Jesus] many shall be made righteous

2 Cor. 10:5 bringing into captivity every thought to the *o* of Christ

Heb. 5:8 Though He [Jesus] was a Son, He learned *o*

OBEDIENT

Isa. 1:19 willing and *o*, you shall eat the good of the land

Acts 6:7 company of the priests were *o* to the faith

Phil. 2:8 He [Jesus] humbled Himself and became *o* to death

1 Pet. 1:14 As *o* children, not...according to the former lusts

OBEY [ED, ING, S]

Gen. 22:18 you [Abraham] have *o'ed* My [God's] voice

Exod. 5:2 Who is the LORD, that I [Pharaoh] should *o* His voice

Deut. 27:10 you shall *o* the voice of the LORD your God

Josh. 24:24 We will serve the LORD our God... we will *o* His voice

1 Sam. 15:22 Behold, to *o* is better than sacrifice

Jer. 11:3 Cursed is the man who does not *o*... this covenant

Jer. 26:13 amend your ways...and *o* the voice of the LORD

Mark 4:41 even the wind and the sea *o* Him [Jesus]

Acts 5:29 We [the apostles] ought to *o* God rather than men

Gal. 3:1 bewitched you [Galatians]...not *o* the truth

Eph. 6:1 Children, *o* your parents in the Lord

Col. 3:20 Children, *o* your parents in all things

Heb. 5:9 He [Jesus] became the author of...salvation to all those who *o* Him

Heb. 11:8 Abraham *o'ed*...not knowing where he went

Jas. 3:3 bits in the horses' mouths, that they may *o* us

1 Pet. 1:22 purified your souls in *o'ing* the truth

OBSERVER OF TIMES.
A practitioner of black magic who was thought to be able to foretell the future through reading signs (Deut. 18:10–14).

ODED.
A prophet who urged that captives from Judah (the Southern Kingdom) be treated with kindness after they were taken into Israel

(the Northern Kingdom). His intervention led to their release and return to their homeland (2 Chron. 28:9–15).

OFFER [ED, ING, INGS, S]

Gen. 4:4 LORD had respect for Abel and for his *o'ing*

Gen. 22:2 *o* him [Isaac] there for a burnt *o'ing*

Lev. 10:1 Nadab and Abihu...*o'ed* strange fire before the LORD

Ps. 50:23 whoever *o's* praise glorifies Me [God]

Ps. 51:16 You [God] do not delight burnt *o'ing*

Ps. 96:8 bring an *o'ing*, and come into His [God's] courts

Ps. 119:108 Accept...the freewill *o'ings* of my mouth

Hos. 6:6 I [God] desired...the knowledge of God more than burnt *o'ings*

Amos 5:22 Nor will I [God] regard the peace *o'ings*

Mal. 3:8 How have we robbed You [God]? In tithes and *o'ings*

Matt. 5:24 be reconciled to your brother, and then...*o* your gift

Mark 12:33 to love Him [God] with all the heart...is more than...*o'ings*

Luke 6:29 strikes you on the one cheek *o* the other also

Luke 11:12 if he asks for an egg, will he *o* him a scorpion

Luke 21:4 these have cast in to the *o'ings* of God out of...abundance

Luke 23:36 the soldiers also mocked Him [Jesus]...*o'ing* Him vinegar

1 Cor. 8:1 Now concerning things *o'ed* to idols

Eph. 5:2 Christ...has given Himself for us, an *o'ing*

2 Tim. 4:6 I [Paul] am now ready to be *o'ed*

Heb. 7:27 He [Jesus] did this once when He *o'ed* up Himself

Heb. 9:28 Christ was *o'ed* once to bear the sins of many

Heb. 10:10 sanctified through the *o'ing*...of Jesus Christ

Heb. 10:12 He [Jesus] had *o'ed* one sacrifice for sins forever

Heb. 11:4 Abel *o'ed* to God a more excellent sacrifice

Heb. 11:17 Abraham, when he was tested, *o'ed* up Isaac

Heb. 13:15 let us continually *o* the sacrifice of praise to God

Jas. 2:21 Was not Abraham our father justified... when he had *o'ed* Isaac

OFFERING. Something presented to God as an act of worship. Offerings brought to the Lord in OT times were placed on the altar by officiating priests. These items included sacrificial animals, fine wine, grain, or in some cases a complete meal. The people believed these sacrifices would atone for their sins and restore fellowship with God. With the coming of Jesus Christ, the need for such sacrifices no longer exists. He Himself is the perfect offering that atones for sin and reconciles sinners to God the Father (Heb. 7:26–27).

OFFICES OF CHRIST. The three major roles—prophet, priest, and king—that Jesus filled in His ministry of redemption. As prophet, He is the last in a long line of prophets whom God sent to reveal His divine character and His will for the human race (Matt. 21:11). His priestly work was accomplished through His atoning death when He became the once-for-all sacrifice for sin (Heb. 9:12). As king, Jesus is "the prince of the kings of the earth" (Rev. 1:5). In the end-time, every knee will bow and every tongue will confess "that Jesus Christ is Lord, to the glory of God the Father" (Phil. 2:11).

OFFSPRING

Job 5:25 descendants...great and your [Job's] *o* like the grass

Acts 17:28 For we are also His [God's] *o*

Acts 17:29 we are the *o* of God

Rev. 22:16 I [Jesus] am the root and the *o* of David

OG. An Amorite king defeated by Moses and the Israelites. His territory east of the Jordan River was settled by the tribe of Manasseh. He is mentioned in **Num. 21:32–35** • Deut. 3:1, 8, 10–13 • Josh. 12:4 • Ps. 135:11.

OHOLAH AND OHOLIBAH. Symbolic names used by the prophet Ezekiel for the city of Jerusalem and the nation of Judah (the Southern Kingdom). He portrayed the people as these two prostitute sisters who were lusting after the pagan practices of the surrounding nations (Ezek. 23:1–11). *Aholah and Aholibah*: KJV.

OIL. A liquid extracted from olives. It was used as a fuel for lamps as well as for anointing (Ps. 23:5), in food preparation (1 Kings 17:12), and as medicine (Luke 10:34). In a parable of Jesus, five women who attended a wedding feast were caught unprepared because they ran out of oil for their lamps (Matt. 25:1–13).

OINTMENT. A perfumed oil made of olive oil and spices and used in anointing ceremonies and for preparing bodies for burial. A woman anointed Jesus with this expensive substance, and He accepted it as an anointing of His body before His forthcoming death (Mark 14:3).

OLD MAN / NEW MAN. Eph. 4:17–29

OLD TESTAMENT. The first of the two major sections into which the Bible is divided. The OT contains thirty-nine individual books, including writings on the law, history, wisdom literature, and prophetic books. This section of the Bible is also known as the "old covenant" because it points to the coming of the new covenant in Jesus Christ. See also *New Testament*.

OLIVES, MOUNT OF. A hill in eastern Jerusalem where Jesus was betrayed by Judas on the night before His crucifixion (Matt. 26:30, 47). It took its name from the olive trees that grew on the site. From this location Jesus sent two of His disciples into the Holy City to locate a room where they could observe the Passover meal together. He turned this meal into a memorial supper of His approaching death, now referred to as the Last Supper or the Lord's Supper. The garden of Gethsemane, where Jesus agonized in prayer on the night of His arrest, was also located on the Mount of Olives. After His death and resurrection, He ascended to God the Father, apparently from a site on the Mount of Olives. It is also mentioned in 2 Sam. 15:30 • Zech. 14:4 • Matt. 21:1; 24:3 • Mark 11:1; 13:3; 14:26 • Luke 19:29, 37; 21:37; 22:39 • John 8:1. *Mountain called Olivet*: Acts 1:12.

OLIVET DISCOURSE. Jesus' long monologue with His disciples on the Mount of Olives about future events. Signs of the end-time mentioned by Him include the appearance of false messiahs, chaos in the heavens, widespread wars, and the return of Jesus Himself (Matt. 24–25).

OLYMPAS. A Christian in Rome greeted by the apostle Paul (Rom. 16:15).

OMER. A dry measure of two to three quarts (Exod. 16:16).

OMNIPOTENCE. A characteristic of God's nature which refers to His unlimited and infinite power. The term is derived from two Latin words, *omni* ("all") and *potens* ("power"). Many examples of God's unlimited power occur throughout the Bible. He created the universe from nothing by the power of His word (Gen. 1:1–3). He struck Egypt with ten plagues to convince the pharaoh to release the Israelite slaves (Exod. 7–12). He divided the waters of the Jordan River to allow the Israelites to cross into Canaan (Josh. 3:14–17). The prophet Jeremiah was familiar with all these mighty acts. "Ah, Lord GOD!" he declared, "There is nothing too hard for You" (Jer. 32:17).

OMNIPRESENCE. A characteristic of God's nature that refers to His universal presence and His ability to be everywhere at the same time. Since He exists as eternal Spirit, He is not limited by time and space. God fills heaven and earth and everything in between (Jer. 23:23). Believers can rest in the confidence that He is always with them, no matter where they happen to be. Through every circumstance of life, His presence is as near as the air they breathe.

OMNISCIENCE. A characteristic of God that refers to His perfect and pervasive knowledge. The term comes from two Latin words, *omni* ("all") and *sciere* ("to know"). Thus, He knows everything about the world and its inhabitants.

God requires no outside source of enlightenment or knowledge (Isa. 40:14). His Son, Jesus, is the key who opens all the hidden treasures of the Father's wisdom and knowledge (Col. 2:2–3).

OMRI. A king of Israel (the Northern Kingdom) who built Samaria as the capital city of his nation. He was a wicked ruler who led the nation into idolatry (1 Kings 16:23–28). Omri was the father of the wicked king Ahab, his successor (1 Kings 16:29). He is also mentioned in 2 Kings 8:26 • 2 Chron. 22:2 • Mic. 6:16.

ON. (1) A leader who joined Korah and others in the rebellion against Moses and Aaron in the wilderness (Num. 16:1–14).

(2) A city of lower Egypt known as a center of sun worship. Joseph's wife Asenath was the daughter of a priest from this city (Gen. 41:45, 50). *Aven*: Amos 1:5.

ONAN. A son of Judah who failed to consummate a marriage union with Tamar (**Gen. 38:8–10**; 46:12 • Num. 26:19 • 1 Chron. 2:3).

ONESIMUS. A runaway slave who was converted under the ministry of the apostle Paul in Rome (Philem. 10). The apostle eventually sent Onesimus back to his master, Philemon, a wealthy believer in the city of Colosse. Onesimus carried a letter from Paul which is now known as his epistle to Philemon.

ONESIPHORUS. A Christian from Ephesus who befriended Paul while he was a prisoner in Rome. Paul commended him for his service (2 Tim. 1:16–18; 4:19).

ONLY BEGOTTEN SON. A name for Jesus that describes His special relationship with God the Father. He is unique—the one and only of His kind who has ever existed. Jesus used this name for Himself in His discussion with Nicodemus about the meaning of the new birth (John 3:1–21). One verse from that discussion, John 3:16, is probably the best known passage in the entire Bible. It has been called "the gospel in a nutshell" because it declares so clearly why Jesus came into the world. This name of Jesus appears only in the writings of the apostle John

(John 1:18; 3:18 • 1 John 4:9). John also referred to Jesus as the "only begotten of the Father" (John 1:14).

ONYCHA. An ingredient in sacred incense which Moses was instructed to prepare (Exod. 30:34). It may have been a gum resin derived from a plant.

ONYX. A precious stone in the breastplate of the high priest (Exod. 28:20). Onyx was one of the items that King David collected to decorate the temple in Jerusalem (1 Chron. 29:2). Job declared that wisdom from God was more desirable than this prized gem (Job 28:16).

OPEN [ED, S]

Gen. 3:7 eyes of them [Adam and Eve] both were *o'ed*

Job 11:5 that God would...*o* His lips against you

Ps. 51:15 O Lord, You *o* my lips

Ps. 119:131 I *o'ed* my mouth and panted...for Your [God's] commandments

Ps. 145:16 You [God] *o* Your hand and satisfy the desire of every living thing

Ps. 146:8 The LORD *o's* the eyes of the blind

Prov. 13:3 he who *o's* his lips wide shall have destruction

Prov. 27:5 O rebuke is better than secret love

Isa. 35:5 Then the eyes of the blind shall be *o'ed*

Isa. 42:7 to *o* the blind eyes, to bring out the prisoners

Isa. 53:7 He [God's servant] did not *o* His mouth

Lam. 3:46 enemies have *o'ed* their mouths against us

Ezek. 3:2 I [Ezekiel] *o'ed* my mouth, and He [God] caused me to eat that scroll

Mal. 3:10 test Me [God]...if I will not *o* the windows of heaven for you

Matt. 3:16 heavens were *o'ed* to Him [Jesus]

Matt. 7:7 Knock, and it shall be *o'ed* to you

Matt. 27:52 graves were *o'ed*. And many bodies...arose

Mark 7:34 He [Jesus]...said... Ephphatha (that is, Be *o'ed*)

Luke 24:31 eyes were *o'ed* and they [Emmaus travelers] knew Him [Jesus]

John 9:30 do not know where He [Jesus] is from...yet He has *o'ed* my eyes

John 10:21 Can a demon *o* the eyes of the blind?

Acts 9:8 when his [Saul's] eyes were *o'ed*, he saw no man

Acts 14:27 He [God] had *o'ed* the door of faith to the Gentiles

Acts 26:18 to *o* their eyes and to turn them from darkness to light

Rom. 3:13 Their throat is an *o* sepulchre

1 Cor. 16:9 a great...door has *o'ed* to me [Paul]

1 Pet. 3:12 His [God's] ears are *o* to their [the righteous'] prayers

Rev. 3:7 He [Jesus] who *o's* and no man shuts

Rev. 3:8 I [Jesus] have set before you an *o* door

Rev. 3:20 any man...*o's* the door, I [Jesus] will come in

Rev. 4:1 a door was *o'ed* in heaven

Rev. 5:9 worthy to take the book and to *o* its seals

OPENLY

Matt. 6:4 Father who sees in secret shall...reward you *o*

Mark 8:32 He [Jesus] spoke that saying [about his death] *o*

John 11:54 Jesus no longer walked *o* among the Jews·

OPHIR. A famous gold-producing region visited by the ships of King Solomon and his Phoenician neighbors. It is mentioned in **1 Kings 9:26–28; 10:11; 22:48 • 1 Chron. 29:4 • 2 Chron. 8:18; 9:10 • Job 22:24; 28:16 • Ps. 45:9 • Isa. 13:12.**

OPHRAH. Hometown of the judge Gideon where an angel assured him of divine guidance in his forthcoming battle with the Midianites (**Judg. 6:11–14, 24; 8:27, 32; 9:5**).

OPINIONS

1 Kings 18:21 How long will you halt between two *o*?

Rom. 11:25 lest you should be wise in your own *o*

Rom. 12:16 Do not be wise in your own *o*

ORDAIN [ED]

1 Chron. 17:9 I [God] will *o* a place for My people Israel

Ps. 8:3 the moon and the stars, which You [God] have *o'ed*

Jer. 1:5 I [God]...*o'ed* you [Jeremiah] as a prophet to the nations

Mark 3:14 He [Jesus] *o'ed* twelve, that they should be with Him

John 15:16 I [Jesus] have chosen you and *o'ed* you

Rom. 13:1 authorities that exist are *o'ed* by God

1 Cor. 9:14 Lord has *o'ed*...those who preach... should live by the gospel

ORDINANCE [S]

Exod. 12:43 LORD said... This is the *o* of the Passover

Lev. 18:4 You shall...keep My [God's] *o's*

1 Pet. 2:13 Submit yourselves to every *o* of man

ORDINANCES. A word for baptism and the Lord's Supper, rituals intended to commemorate the great events of redemption. The Lord's Supper memorializes the shed blood and broken body of Christ (1 Cor. 11:23–26). Baptism symbolizes the death, burial, and resurrection of Jesus and the believer's victory over sin and death (Rom. 6:3–6).

ORDINATION. A rite by which a person is set apart for special service to the Lord and His people. In OT times, kings were commissioned to their office by having oil poured on their heads. When Jesus began His public ministry, "He ordained twelve, that they should be with Him and that He might send them out to preach" (Mark 3:14). Jesus Himself was sent into the world by God the Father on a special mission. So He is sometimes described as one ordained for ministry by the Lord (Acts 17:31). Ordination is still practiced by many church groups. Pastors and other leaders are set apart for special service to the church through a ceremony of ordination. See also *Laying On of Hands.*

OREB. One of two Midianite princes killed by the judge Gideon and his army near the Jordan River (Judg. 7:25). Oreb's name was applied to a prominent rock in that area (Isa. 10:26).

ORGAN. A wind instrument that produced a distinctive high sound (Gen. 4:21). It was probably similar to a modern flute.

ORIGINAL SIN. A phrase that refers to the first recorded sin committed in the Bible—Adam and Eve's disobedience of God's command. Both ate a fruit from a tree in the garden of Eden that God had declared off-limits (Gen. 2:17; 3:6). According to the apostle Paul, this sin of rebellion against God's authority infected the entire human race from that point on (Rom. 5:12–19). The only cure for this sin problem is the declaration of one's faith in Jesus Christ, who offers forgiveness of sin through His sacrificial death (Rom. 6:23).

ORION. A constellation of innumerable stars that gives evidence of God's power and majesty (Job 9:9).

ORNAN. See *Araunah*

ORPAH. A Moabite woman who married a son of Naomi and Elimelech. Orpah remained in her own country after Naomi and Ruth moved to Bethlehem when tragedy struck the family (Ruth 1:4–15).

ORPHANS. Children who have lost their parents. Kindness toward such children was commanded by the Mosaic law (Deut. 24:17). Jesus told believers He would not leave them as orphans when He ascended to the Father; He would send the Holy Spirit, who would serve as their guardian and guide (John 14:18). Caring for orphans and widows is a mark of true religion (Jas. 1:27).

OSEE. KJV: see *Hosea*

OSHEA. See *Joshua*

OSNAPPER. The last of the great kings of Assyria (Ezra 4:10). This is probably the same king as the Ashurbanipal of Assyrian history. *Asnapper*: KJV.

OSTRICH. A large, flightless bird noted for its running speed and strange nesting habits (Job 39:13–18).

OTHNIEL. The first judge of Israel who defeated a king of Mesopotamia (Judg. 3:9–11).

OUGHT

Luke 11:42 You [Pharisees] *o* to have done these

Luke 12:12 Holy Spirit shall teach you...what you *o* to say

Luke 18:1 men *o* always to pray and not to faint

John 13:14 you also *o* to wash one another's feet

John 19:7 and by our law He [Jesus] *o* to die

Acts 5:29 We [the apostles] *o* to obey God rather than men

Rom. 12:3 not to think of himself more highly than he *o* to think

Rom. 15:1 strong *o* to bear the weaknesses of the weak

Eph. 5:28 men *o* to love their wives as their own bodies

Col. 4:6 you may know how you *o* to answer every man

Heb. 2:1 we *o* to pay more earnest attention... things that we have heard

Jas. 3:10 My brothers, these things *o* not to be so

2 Pet. 3:11 what manner of persons *o* you to be

1 John 4:11 Beloved...we also *o* to love one another

OUR PASSOVER. A title of Jesus cited by the apostle Paul to emphasize that He shed His blood to bring redemption to humankind (1 Cor. 5:7). The apostle compared Jesus' atoning death to the time when the Lord "passed over" the houses of the Israelites but struck the firstborn of Egyptian households. This was the climactic plague against the Egyptians that led to their release from slavery. This event was commemorated by the annual Passover festival, one of the most important Jewish holidays. It was during this annual celebration in Jerusalem that Jesus was crucified (Matt. 26:2).

OVEN. A large earthenware container filled with hot coals and ashes. Utensils with food were placed over the opening for cooking (Hos. 7:7).

OVERCOME [S]

Num. 13:30 for we are well able to *o* it [Canaan]

John 16:33 be of good cheer: I [Jesus] have *o* the world

Rom. 12:21 Do not be *o* by evil, but *o* evil with good

1 John 2:13 young men...you have *o* the wicked one

1 John 5:4 this is the victory that *o's* the world... our faith

Rev. 17:14 Lamb shall *o* them, for He is Lord of lords

Rev. 21:7 He who *o's* shall inherit all things

OVERSEER. An elder, bishop, or presbyter who provided spiritual leadership for a group of believers (Acts 20:28).

OWE [S]

Matt. 18:28 he [servant] laid hands on him... saying, Pay me what you *o*

Luke 16:5 How much do you *o* to my master?

Rom. 13:8 *O* no man anything but to love one another

Philem. 18 If he [Onesimus]...*o's* you anything, put that on my [Paul's] account

OXGOAD. A spike used to control oxen before a plow. The judge Shamgar killed six hundred Philistines with an oxgoad (Judg. 3:31; 5:6).

OZIAS. KJV: see *Uzziah*

P

PAARAI. One of King David's thirty-seven "mighty men," an elite group of warriors recognized for their bravery in battle (2 Sam. 23:35).

PACE. A biblical measure of length. The pace was based on the typical stride of an adult male (2 Sam. 6:13).

PADAN-ARAM. See *Mesopotamia*

PAID

2 Kings 12:11 they [king's officials] *p*...the carpenters and builders

Prov. 7:14 This day I have *p* my vows

Lam. 5:4 We have *p* to drink our water; our wood has been sold to us

Jon. 1:3 he [Jonah] *p* the fare...to go...to Tarshish

Luke 12:59 you shall not depart...until you have *p* the very last mite

Heb. 7:9 Levi also...*p* tithes through Abraham

PALAL. A priest who helped rebuild the walls of Jerusalem after the Exile (Neh. 3:25).

PALESTINA. KJV: see *Philistia*

PALESTINE. The region, also known as Canaan, which became the land inhabited by the Israelites. The name referred originally to the territory of the Philistines, especially the coastal plain south of Mount Carmel (Joel 3:4).

PALM. A tree whose branches were scattered before Jesus by the crowd when He made His triumphal entry into Jerusalem (John 12:13). People holding palm branches symbolize the victory of the Jesus the Lamb in the end-time (Rev. 7:9).

PALMERWORM. A locust in the larval stage of its development (Joel 1:4). This insect was sent as a plague on rebellious Israel (Amos 4:9).

PALTI. One of the twelve spies or scouts sent by Moses to investigate the land of Canaan. He represented the tribe of Benjamin (Num. 13:9).

PALTIEL. A leader from the tribe of Issachar who helped divide the land of Canaan after the conquest (Num. 34:26).

PAMPHYLIA. A Roman province in southern Asia Minor visited by the apostle Paul and his missionary associates Barnabas and John Mark on the first missionary journey. It was at Perga, Pamphylia's capital city, that Mark left the group and returned to Jerusalem. It is mentioned in Acts 2:10; **13:13; 14:24–25; 15:38; 27:5.**

PANTHEISM. The belief that God does not exist as a separate being from the universe, that He is actually identical with the physical world. The term comes from two Greek words, *pan*, meaning "all," and *theos*, meaning "God." Thus, pantheists believe that the natural world does not reflect God; it *is* God. But the Bible declares that God created the universe separate and apart from Himself (Gen. 1:1). He exists apart from, in addition to, and above the world (Ps. 8:1).

PANTHEON. A collection of the numerous gods that existed in the pagan religious systems of many nations of the ancient world. For example, the Greek and Roman pantheons consisted of gods devoted to war, commerce, science, literature, hunting, and fertility. By contrast, the Bible declares that only one supreme God exists, and He expresses Himself in three divine dimensions, as Father, Son, and Holy Spirit.

PAPER. An English word for papyrus, an ancient writing material made from reeds which grew in swampy areas (2 John 12).

PAPHOS. A city on the island of Cyprus where Paul blinded a pagan magician during the first missionary journey. This led to the conversion of Sergius Paulus, Roman governor of the island (Acts 13:6–13).

PARABLE. A short story or illustration based on daily life that presents an important spiritual truth. The word comes from a term that means "comparison" or "a casting alongside." In the OT, the prophet Nathan told a parable to convict King David of his sin of adultery (2 Sam. 12:1–7). Jesus used parables to present truth to His receptive hearers and to conceal the lesson from those who were critical or unreceptive (Matt. 13:10–16). Not all His parables were extended stories. He also used short parabolic sayings or "one-liners" such as "salt of the earth" (Matt. 5:13) and "casting pearls before swine" (Matt. 7:6) to communicate spiritual realities.

PARABLES OF JESUS. See *Jesus Christ, Parables of*

PARACLETE. A Greek word for the Holy Spirit that expresses the idea of a helper called to one's side. It is translated as "Comforter" (John 14:16) and "advocate" (1 John 2:1).

PARADISE. A word for heaven that Jesus used to comfort the dying thief who placed his hope in the Lord (Luke 23:43).

PARADOX. A paradox exists when two statements or propositions are placed side by side and, though both true, seem to contradict each other. This was one of the favorite teaching devices of Jesus. To be great, He declared, believers must become servants (Matt. 20:20–26); to save their lives, they must lose them (Luke 9:24–26); to be exalted, they must become humble (Matt. 23:12); to find rest, they must carry His yoke (Matt. 11:28–30).

PARAN. A wilderness region into which Hagar fled with her son Ishmael when driven away from Abraham's household (Gen. 21:21). In later years, Moses sent scouts from Paran to explore the land of Canaan (Num. 13:3). The prophet Habakkuk mentioned a "Mount Paran," perhaps a distinct mountain peak in this desolate region (Hab. 3:3). Also called *El-paran* (Gen.14:6).

PARAPET. A protective railing around a flat-roofed house to prevent falls (Deut. 22:8). *Battlement*: KJV.

PARCHMENT. Writing material made from the skin of animals. Paul asked Timothy to bring parchments to him in prison (2 Tim. 4:13).

PARDON. A word for divine forgiveness. God will pardon those who repent and turn to Him (Isa. 55:7). The loving father in Jesus' parable had compassion on his repentant son, extended pardon, and celebrated his return (Luke 15:18–24).

PARDON [ED, S]

1 Sam. 15:25 p my [Saul's] sin, and return with me
Neh. 9:17 a God ready to *p*, gracious and merciful
Ps. 25:11 O LORD, *p* my iniquity, for it is great
Jer. 33:8 I [God] will *p* all their iniquities

Mic. 7:18 Who is a God like You, who *p's* guilt

PARENTHOOD. The duty of parents is to train and correct their children (Deut. 4:9). God promised to bless parents who teach their children to obey the Lord (Prov. 22:6 • Eph. 6:4).

PARMASHTA. A son of Haman who was executed, along with his father, when Haman's plot to destroy the Jews was exposed by Esther (Esther 9:7–10).

PARMENAS. One of the seven persons of Greek background who were appointed by the church at Jerusalem to coordinate the distribution of food to needy widows (Acts 6:1–7).

PARSHANDATHA. A son of Haman who was executed, along with his father, when Haman's plot to destroy the Jews was exposed by Esther (Esther 9:7–10).

PARTHIANS. Inhabitants of Parthia who were in Jerusalem on the day of Pentecost (Acts 2:1, 9). Parthia was a country north of Media and Persia.

PARTIALITY. To show favoritism or preference toward some people over others. God's grace and wisdom are available to everyone and free of favoritism or hypocrisy (James 3:17). Since God loves all people, believers should follow His example in their treatment of others. The apostle Paul encouraged Timothy to practice all the things he had taught him, "doing nothing with partiality" (1 Tim. 5:21).

PARTIALITY

Prov. 24:23 it is not good to show *p* in judgment
Rom. 2:11 For there is no *p* with God
Eph. 6:9 there is no *p* with Him [Jesus]
1 Pet. 1:17 who [God] without *p* judges...every man's work

PARVAIM. A city or region from which Solomon brought gold to decorate the temple (2 Chron. 3:6). It may have been the same place as Ophir (1 Kings 9:28).

PASHHUR. A priest who had Jeremiah imprisoned because the prophet predicted the destruction of Jerusalem. Jeremiah declared that Pashhur and his household would die as captives in Babylon (Jer. 20:1–6; 38:1).

PASHUR. KJV: see *Pashhur*

PASSION WEEK. See *Holy Week*

PASSOVER AND FEAST OF UNLEAVENED BREAD. A Jewish festival which commemorated the Exodus of the Israelites from Egypt (Josh. 5:10–12). It celebrated how God "passed over" the Israelite houses in Egypt that were sprinkled with blood while killing the firstborn of all Egyptian households. The seven-day Feast of Unleavened Bread recalled the haste with which the slaves left Egypt (Exod. 12:33–34). The Passover eventually developed into a pilgrimage festival. The Israelites were encouraged to travel to Jerusalem to observe this annual holiday. Jesus and His disciples were in the city for this event when He turned the Passover meal that they ate together into a memorial of His approaching death (Luke 22:14–20). Just as the blood of a sacrificial lamb saved the Israelites from destruction, so Jesus' blood was an agent of deliverance. He was the ultimate Passover sacrifice that delivers humankind from bondage to sin (1 Cor. 5:7). Passover is also mentioned in Num. 9:2–14 • 2 Chron. 30:1–18; 35:1–19 • Matt. 26:2–19 • Mark 14:1–16 • Heb. 11:28.

PASTOR. The chief spiritual leader of a congregation of God's people (Eph. 4:11–13). Pastors are called of God to guide and instruct believers and to build up the body of Christ. See also *Shepherd.*

PASTORAL EPISTLES. The three letters of the apostle Paul—1 and 2 Tim. othy and Titus—which deal with practical matters involving the work of a local church. He instructed Timothy and Titus to appoint qualified church leaders and to deal with threats to church unity and the truths of the gospel (1 Tim. 3:1–13 • Titus 1:5–11).

PATARA. A port city in Asia Minor where the apostle Paul changed ships on his third missionary journey (Acts 21:1–2).

PATHROS. The region of upper Egypt where Israelites practiced pagan worship rituals. The prophet Jeremiah condemned them for their refusal to turn to the Lord (Jer. 44:1–19). Pathros is also mentioned in Isa. 11:11 • Ezek. 29:14; 30:14.

PATIENCE. The ability to stay faithful to the Lord under trying circumstances. The apostle Paul cited patience, or long-suffering, as one of the nine fruits of the Holy Spirit in the life of believers (Gal. 5:22). The author of Hebrews compared the life of faith to a marathon that requires a steady, consistent pace. Completing this race successfully demands that believers keep their eyes on Jesus, "the author and finisher of our faith" (Heb. 12:2).

PATIENCE

Rom. 5:3 knowing that tribulation works *p*

Rom. 15:5 the God of *p*...grant you to be like-minded

1 Thes. 1:3 Remembering...your work of faith... and *p* of hope

1 Tim. 6:11 follow after...faith, love, *p*, meekness

Heb. 12:1 run with *p* the race that is set before us

Jas. 1:3 knowing that the trying of your faith works *p*

Jas. 5:7 farmer waits for the...fruit of the earth and has long *p* for it

PATIENT [LY]

Ps. 40:1 I waited *p'ly* for the LORD, and He inclined to me

Eccles. 7:8 the *p* in spirit is better than the proud in spirit

Rom. 12:12 rejoicing in hope, *p* in tribulation

1 Thes. 5:14 support the weak, be *p* toward all men

Heb. 6:15 after he [Abraham] had *p'ly* endured, he obtained the promise

Jas. 5:7 Be *p* therefore, brothers, until the coming of the Lord

PATMOS. A desolate island where the apostle John was imprisoned by the Roman government and where he wrote the book of Revelation (Rev. 1:9). Patmos was only about ten miles long and six miles wide. The Romans often sent prisoners to isolated islands like this in the Mediterranean Sea. John's imprisonment probably occurred during the reign of the emperor Domitian about AD 90. God used this place and time to give John a series of visions that told about the future—the end of the present age and the arrival of the kingdom of God in its fullness.

PATRIARCHS. The founding fathers of the nation of Israel. The word is derived from a combination of the Latin term *pater* ("father") with the Greek work *archo* ("to rule"). Thus, a patriarch was a father who ruled over a family or clan. Fifteen people in the OT are considered the patriarchs of the Israelites: Abraham; his son Isaac; Isaac's son Jacob; and Jacob's twelve sons whose descendants developed into the twelve tribes of Israel.

PATROBAS. A fellow believer at Rome greeted and commended by the apostle Paul (Rom. 16:14).

PAUL THE APOSTLE. The great missionary known for his faithful preaching of the gospel throughout the Roman world during the early years of Christianity. Formerly known as Saul, he was a strict Pharisee who developed a hatred for the Christian movement in its early years in Jerusalem. He looked on while Jewish religious leaders stoned Stephen to death (Acts 7:59–60; 8:1). Later, Paul traveled to Damascus north of Jerusalem to persecute believers in that city. He was converted to Christianity in his famous encounter with Jesus known as his "Damascus road" experience (Acts 9:1–8). From then on he was a loyal follower of Jesus who became known as the apostle to the Gentiles (see Acts 9:15).

Paul eventually worked with the believers in Jerusalem. But he was forced to flee to his hometown, Tarsus, when fanatical Jews threatened to kill him (Acts 9:27–30). Several years later he was on the move again, this time to Antioch of Syria to help Barnabas minister to converts from a Gentile background in the city of Antioch of Syria (Acts 11:25–26). Under the sponsorship of this church, Paul traveled

with various missionary partners throughout the Roman world for the next several years. He founded churches in several major cities of the Roman Empire, including Philippi, Thessalonica, Corinth, and Ephesus. His witness for Christ came to an end in the city of Rome, where he was detained by the Roman authorities (Acts 28:30–31). Most scholars believe he was eventually released but finally executed during a second Roman imprisonment.

During his ministry, Paul wrote thirteen letters, or epistles, to encourage the churches he founded as well as individuals associated with him in his missionary work. These letters—Romans, 1 and 2 Corinthians, Galatians, Ephesians, Philippians, Colossians, 1 and 2 Thessalonians, 1 and 2 Tim. othy, Titus, and Philemon—make up about one-fourth of the New Testament.

PAULUS, SERGIUS. The Roman governor of Cyprus who became a believer during Paul's visit to that island on the first missionary journey (Acts 13:4–12).

PAVEMENT, THE. A paved area in Pilate's courtroom where Jesus was sentenced to crucifixion and turned over to the mob (John 19:13–16). Also called *Gabbatha*.

PAVILION. A word used figuratively by the psalmist for the place where God dwells and where the righteous find shelter (Ps. 27:5).

PAY [ING]

Ps. 66:13 I will *p* You [God] my vows

Eccles. 5:4 you make a vow to God, do not put off *p'ing* it

Matt. 18:34 his lord...delivered him to the tormentors until he should *p* all

Matt. 23:23 you [scribes and Pharisees] *p* tithe of mint and anise and cumin

Rom. 13:6 for this reason you also *p* taxes...they are God's ministers

PE. Seventeenth letter of the Hebrew alphabet, used as a heading over Psalm 119:129–136. In the Hebrew language, the first line of each of these eight verses begins with this letter.

PEACE. Inner tranquility and a feeling of well-being that results from a right relationship with God and other people. After His resurrection, Jesus stood among His disciples and declared, "Peace be to you" (John 20:19). These words were the common greeting used by the Jewish people of that day—a wish for their wholeness and contentment. Peace is one of the nine fruits of the Spirit cited by the apostle Paul (Gal. 5:22). Just as believers are assured of God's peace, they are urged to pursue peace and to live peaceably with all people (2 Tim. 2:22).

PEACE

Ps. 4:8 I will both lay me down in *p* and sleep

Ps. 34:14 Seek *p*, and pursue it

Ps. 55:18 He [God] has delivered my soul in *p*

Ps. 83:1 Do not hold Your *p*, and do not be still, O God

Ps. 119:165 Those who love Your [God's] law have great *p*

Ps. 122:7 *P* be within your [Jerusalem's] walls

Eccles. 3:8 a time of war and a time of *p*

Isa. 9:6 His [Messiah's] name shall be called... Prince of *P*

Isa. 26:3 keep him in perfect *p*...mind is steadfast on You [God]

Isa. 48:22 There is no *p*...for the wicked

Isa. 52:7 beautiful...the feet of him...who proclaims *p*

Isa. 53:5 chastisement of our *p* was on Him [God's servant]

Jer. 29:7 seek the *p* of the city...in its *p* you shall have *p*

Matt. 10:34 I [Jesus] came to send not *p* but a sword

Mark 4:39 He [Jesus]...said to the sea, *P*, be still

Luke 2:14 Glory to God...on earth *p*, goodwill toward men

Luke 10:5 whatever house you enter... say, *P* be to this house

John 14:27 I [Jesus] give to you My *p*

John 16:33 that in Me [Jesus] you might have *p*

Rom. 2:10 honor, and *p* to every man who works good

Rom. 5:1 we have *p* with God through...Jesus Christ

Rom. 10:15 beautiful are the feet of those who preach the gospel of *p*

Rom. 14:19 follow after the things that make for *p*

1 Cor. 14:33 God is the author not of confusion but of *p*

Gal. 5:22 fruit of the Spirit is love, joy, *p*, long-suffering

Eph. 2:14 He [Jesus] is our *p*, who has made both one

Eph. 4:3 unity of the Spirit in the bond of *p*

Phil. 4:7 the *p* of God, which passes all understanding

Col. 3:15 let the *p* of God rule in your hearts

2 Thes. 3:16 may the Lord of *p* Himself give you *p*

PEACE OFFERING. See *Heave Offering*

PEARL. A gem to which Jesus compared the kingdom of heaven (Matt. 13:45–46).

PECULIAR. KJV: see *Special*

PEDAHEL. A leader from the tribe of Naphtali who helped divide the land of Canaan after the conquest (Num. 34:28).

PEDAIAH. A man who helped rebuild the walls of Jerusalem after the Exile (Neh. 3:25).

PEKAH. A king of Israel (the Northern Kingdom) who gained the throne during the dark days when Assyria was threatening an invasion. Pekah was eventually assassinated and succeeded by Hoshea (**2 Kings 15:23–31 •** 2 Chron. 28:6 • Isa. 7:1–9).

PEKAHIAH. An evil king of Israel (the Northern Kingdom) who reigned for only two years before being murdered and succeeded by Pekah, one of own his military officers (2 Kings 15:23–26).

PELAIAH. A Levite after the Exile who explained the law as Ezra read it to the people (Neh. 8:7).

PELETHITES. A select unit of soldiers who provided protection for King David, especially during the rebellions of Absalom and Sheba. They are mentioned in 2 Sam. 8:18; 15:14–18; 20:7, 23 • 1 Kings 1:38, 44 • 1 Chron. 18:17.

PELICAN. A large bird cited as a symbol of loneliness and desolation (Ps. 102:6–7).

PEN. A writing instrument. Job longed for an iron pen to write his words of complaint in rock so they would be preserved forever (Job 19:24).

PENIEL. A place east of the Jordan River where Jacob wrestled with an angel. The angel knocked Jacob's hip out of joint and changed his name from Jacob to *Israel*, meaning "prince of God" (Gen. 32:24–32). This event signified that the covenant between God and His special people, the Israelites, would be continued through Jacob. From that point on, the nation that sprang from the twelve sons of Jacob was known as Israel. In later centuries, Peniel developed into a city that served as an important defense outpost for the nation of Israel (the Northern Kingdom). Also called *Penuel* (Judg. 8:8).

PENKNIFE. A knife used to sharpen a pen made from a reed. This instrument was used to destroy Jeremiah's prophecies as they were read to King Jehoiakim of Judah (the Southern Kingdom (Jer. 36:23).

PENNY. An English word for the denarius, a silver coin that was paid as the daily wage of an unskilled worker (Matt. 20:2–13).

PENTATEUCH. The Greek name for the first five books of the OT: Genesis, Exodus, Leviticus, Numbers, and Deuteronomy. It was called the Torah or the "law of Moses" by the Israelites (Ezra 7:6). Authorship of the Pentateuch has been ascribed to Moses, who led God's people out of slavery in Egypt. Jesus recognized the value of the law and came to fulfill its spiritual requirements (Matt. 5:17–18).

PENTECOST. An annual Jewish feast that commemorated the end of the harvest. The name comes from a Greek word that means "fiftieth day" because it was observed on the fiftieth day after the Passover celebration. Pentecost was an occasion when the people expressed thanks to God for the crops He had provided. It was sometimes referred to as the "day of the firstfruits" (Num. 28:26) because the first loaves of bread made from the wheat harvest were offered to the Lord on that day. Pentecost was the holiday being observed in Jerusalem when the Holy Spirit came in power upon the early Christian believers (Acts 2). This event had been foretold by the prophet Joel (Joel 2:28–32). Pentecost is also mentioned in Acts 20:16 • 1 Cor. 16:8. *Feast of Harvest* or *Feast of Ingathering*: Exod. 23:16. *Feast of Weeks*: Exod. 34:22.

PENUEL. See *Peniel*

PEOPLE OF GOD. A phrase for the Israelites, God's chosen people (see Deut. 14:2), as well as all people who have accepted Jesus as Lord and Savior (1 Pet. 2:10). Redeemed believers are members of God's "special people" (Titus 2:14).

PEOPLE OF GOD
Judg. 20:2 leaders...presented themselves in the assembly of the *p-o-G*
Heb. 4:9 There remains a rest for the *p-o-G*
Heb. 11:25 choosing...to suffer affliction with the *p-o-G*
1 Pet. 2:10 in time past were not a people...are now the *p-o-G*

PEOR. A mountain from which Balak, king of Moab, encouraged the wizard Balaam to curse the Israelites. Through God's intervention, Balaam blessed them instead (Num. 23:28; 24:1–2). See also *Baal of Peor*.

PERCEIVE [D, ING, S]
Job 33:14 God speaks...twice—yet man does not *p* it
Job 38:18 Have you [Job] *p'd* the breadth of the earth?
Isa. 6:9 see indeed, but do not *p*
Mark 7:18 Do you not *p* that anything from outside...cannot defile
Luke 6:41 do not *p* the beam that is in your own eye
Luke 8:46 I [Jesus] *p* that virtue is gone out from Me
Luke 9:47 Jesus, *p'ing*...their heart, took a child
Acts 4:13 they [the Sanhedrin]...*p'd* that they [Peter and John] were unlearned...men

Acts 10:34 I [Peter] *p* that God shows no partiality

1 John 3:16 we *p* the love of God, because He [Jesus] laid down His life

PERDITION. The state of unbelievers who reject Jesus Christ. Jesus called Judas the "son of perdition" because of his act of betrayal (John 17:12). Perdition, or eternal damnation, is the final destiny of the Antichrist (Rev. 17:8–11).

PEREZ-UZZAH. A name that David gave to the site where Uzzah was struck dead for touching the ark of the covenant (2 Sam. 6:6–8).

PERFECT. A word that generally refers to the state of maturity to which believers should strive as followers of Jesus (Matt. 5:48). While perfection in this life will never be reached, the apostle Paul urged believers to keep striving to become like Jesus Christ (Phil. 3:12–15).

PERFECT [ED, ING, LY]

Gen. 6:9 Noah was a just man and *p* in his generations

Job 1:1 that man [Job] was *p* and upright

Ps. 18:30 His [God's] way is *p*. The word of the LORD is tried

Ps. 18:32 It is God who...makes my way *p*

Ps. 19:7 law of the LORD is *p*, converting the soul

Prov. 4:18 path of the just...shines...until the *p* day

Matt. 5:48 even as your Father who is in heaven is *p*

Rom. 12:2 prove what is that good...and *p* will of God

1 Cor. 1:10 *p'ly* joined together in the same mind

1 Cor. 13:10 But when what is *p* has come

2 Cor. 12:9 My [Jesus'] grace is sufficient... strength is made *p* in weakness

Eph. 4:12 the *p'ing* of the saints, for the work of the ministry

2 Tim. 3:17 that the man of God may be *p*

Heb. 5:9 being made *p*, He [Jesus] became the author of eternal salvation

Heb. 10:14 He [Jesus] has *p'ed*...those who are sanctified

Jas. 1:17 good gift and every *p* gift is from above

1 John 4:12 If we love one another...His [God's] love is *p'ed* in us

1 John 4:18 no fear in love, but *p* love casts out fear

PERFECTION

Ps. 50:2 Out of Zion, the *p* of beauty, God has shone

2 Cor. 13:9 also this we pray for, even your *p*

Heb. 6:1 let us go on to *p*

Heb. 7:11 if *p* were through the Levitical priesthood...what further need

PERGA. The capital of the province of Pamphylia visited by the apostle Paul and Barnabas on the first missionary journey (Acts 13:13–14; 14:25).

PERGAMOS. KJV: see *Pergamum*

PERGAMUM. A city where one of the seven churches of Asia Minor cited by the apostle John in the book of Revelation was located. The church was rebuked for its toleration of sexual immorality and false teachings. John described the city as the place of "Satan's seat" (Rev. 2:13), a possible reference to the practice of emperor worship. Remains of a temple devoted to worship of the Roman emperor Trajan have been uncovered here. Some members of the church at Pergamum had succumbed to the false doctrine of a group known as the Nicolaitans. (Rev. 2:15). *Pergamos*: KJV.

PERISH [ED, ES, ING]

2 Sam. 1:27 the mighty have fallen and the weapons of war *p'ed*

Job 3:3 Let the day *p* on which I [Job] was born

Job 33:18 He keeps...his life from *p'ing* by the sword

Job 34:15 all flesh shall *p* together...man shall turn again to dust

Ps. 1:6 but the way of the ungodly shall *p*

Ps. 68:2 the wicked *p* in the presence of God

Prov. 29:18 Where there is no vision, the people *p*

Matt. 18:14 that one of these little ones should *p*

Mark 4:38 Master [Jesus], do You not care that we [the disciples] are *p'ing*

Luke 15:17 servants have enough bread...and I [prodigal son] *p* with hunger

John 3:16 whoever believes in Him [Jesus] should not *p*

John 6:27 Labor not for the food that *p'es*

1 Cor. 1:18 preaching of the cross is foolishness to those who are *p'ing*

2 Cor. 4:16 outward man is *p'ing*, yet the inner man is...renewed

2 Pet. 3:9 Lord...is long-suffering toward us, not willing that any should *p*

PERIZZITES. A tribal group defeated by Joshua's forces during the conquest of Canaan (Josh. 17:15). Later, the Perizzites were forced into service as laborers on King Solomon's construction projects (1 Kings 9:20–21). They are also mentioned in Gen. 15:20; 34:30 • Exod. 3:8, 17; 23:23 • Deut. 7:1; 20:17 • **Josh. 3:10**; 12:8; 24:11 • Judg. 1:4–5; 3:5 • 2 Chron. 8:7 • Ezra 9:1 • Neh. 9:8.

PERSECUTE [D, ING, S]

Ps. 7:1 Save me from all those who *p* me

Ps. 31:15 Deliver me...from those who *p* me

Ps. 119:161 Princes have *p'd* me without cause

Matt. 5:10 Blessed are those...*p'd* for righteousness' sake

Matt. 5:11 Blessed are you when men revile you and *p* you

Matt. 5:44 Love your enemies...pray for those who...*p* you

John 15:20 If they have *p'd* Me [Jesus], they will also *p* you

Acts 9:4 Saul, Saul, why are you *p'ing* Me [Jesus]

Rom. 12:14 Bless those who *p* you. Bless, and do not curse

1 Cor. 15:9 I [Paul] *p'd* the church of God

2 Cor. 4:9 *p'd*, but not forsaken; thrown down, but not destroyed

Phil. 3:6 concerning zeal, *p'ing* the church

PERSECUTION. Oppression and discrimination against those who are committed to the Lord. Godly people have been subjected to such practices since OT times. The prophet Jeremiah was imprisoned by his own people for preaching that their country was headed for destruction unless they turned to the Lord (Jer. 32:2). Jesus taught that His followers would face persecution by an unbelieving world. But those who remain faithful to Him in spite of these troubles will inherit the kingdom of God (Matt. 5:10–12).

PERSECUTION

Lam. 5:5 Our necks are under *p*. We...have no rest

Acts 8:1 there was a great *p* against the church... at Jerusalem

Rom. 8:35 Who shall separate us from the love of Christ? Shall...distress, or *p*

2 Tim. 3:12 all who will live godly in Christ Jesus shall suffer *p*

PERSEVERANCE. Persistence, or endurance through difficult circumstances. The apostle Paul encouraged believers at Corinth to keep on doing the Lord's work because labor for Him is never in vain (1 Cor. 15:58). Steadfastness in doing good works shows that a believer's faith is genuine (James 2:14–26). The model of perseverance is Jesus Himself. Though hounded by His enemies, tempted by Satan, and misunderstood by His disciples, He completed His redemptive mission with His declaration from the cross: "It is finished" (John 19:30). The author of Hebrews urged his readers to finish the race of Christian discipleship by following Jesus' example (Heb. 12:1–2).

PERSIA. An ancient world empire that conquered the Babylonians, paving the way for Jewish exiles to return to their homeland in Judah (the Southern Kingdom). King Cyrus of Persia authorized this return (2 Chron. 36:22–23). Several other Persian kings are mentioned in the OT. Darius the Great ordered the work on the temple in Jerusalem to continue after it had been stopped for several years (Ezra 4:21; 6:1–3). Another king, Ahasuerus, also known as Xerxes, selected a Jewish girl named Esther as his queen (Esther 2:16–17). The Persian king Artaxerxes authorized other groups of Jewish exiles to return to Jerusalem. He even sent materials with Nehemiah, one of his officials, to be used in construction of Jerusalem's defensive wall (Neh. 2:1–8). Persia's capital city was Susa, where the prophet Daniel had visions of great world empires and the future Messiah (Dan. 8:2; *Shushan*: KJV). Persia is also mentioned in Ezra 1:1–8; 3:7; 7:1; 9:9 • Esther 1:3–18; 10:2 • Ezek. 27:10; 38:5 • Dan. 10:1–20; 11:2.

PERSIS. A fellow believer at Rome greeted and commended by the apostle Paul (Rom. 16:12).

PERSUADE [D, S]

Luke 16:31 they will not be *p'd* if one rises from the dead

Acts 18:13 fellow [Paul] *p's* men to worship God contrary to the law

Acts 26:28 You [Paul] almost *p* me [Agrippa] to become a Christian

Rom. 8:38 I [Paul] am *p'd*, that neither death nor life

Rom. 14:14 I [Paul]...am *p'd*...that there is nothing unclean by itself

2 Cor. 5:11 knowing the terror of the Lord, we *p* men

2 Tim. 1:12 know whom I [Paul] have believed and am *p'd* that He [Jesus] is able

PETER THE APOSTLE. The most prominent of Jesus' disciples and the one who became the main leader of the church after Jesus' ascension (Acts 2:14–40). Peter was the first disciple to recognize Jesus as the Messiah—God's Son who had been sent into the world to redeem sinful humankind. Jesus told Peter that His church would be established through believers who accepted the same truth about Him and His mission that Peter had declared (Matt. 16:13–19).

Peter swore he would always be faithful to his Master. But he denied Jesus three times on the night He was arrested (Matt. 26:74–75). After being forgiven and restored by Jesus, Peter went on to become a bold Christian witness in the early years of the church. On the day of Pentecost, he preached the famous sermon that led three thousand people to declare their faith in Jesus (Acts 2:14–41).

Peter also played a key role in one of the turning points of early Christianity. Through a vision of clean and unclean animals, he realized that God included all people, not just Jews, in His invitation to salvation. This insight opened the door for acceptance of Gentiles into the church (Acts 10:9–15).

Other details and highlights of Peter's life include:

1. A fisherman and brother of Andrew (Matt. 4:18)
2. Called by Jesus (Matt. 4:18–22)
3. Included among Jesus' twelve apostles (Matt. 10:2–4)
4. Walked on the water to meet Jesus (Matt. 14:28–33)
5. Confessed Jesus as the Son of God (Matt. 16:13–19)
6. Condemned by Jesus for refusing to believe that Jesus would die (Matt. 16:21–23)
7. Witnessed the transfiguration of Jesus (Matt. 17:1–8 • 2 Pet. 1:16–18)
8. With Jesus in the Garden of Gethsemane (Mark 14:32–42)
10. Cut off the ear of a servant when Jesus was arrested (John 18:10–11)
11. Ran to inspect the empty tomb after Jesus was resurrected (John 20:1–8)
12. Reinstated by Jesus and challenged to continue His work (John 21:15–22)

In later years, Peter wrote the epistles of 1 and 2 Peter in the NT. Peter was also called *Simon* or *Simon Peter* (Matt. 16:16).

PETER, FIRST EPISTLE OF. A short epistle written by the apostle Peter to encourage believers who were being persecuted because of their faith in Jesus. He addressed the letter to believers who had been "scattered throughout Pontus, Galatia, Cappadocia, Asia, and Bithynia" (1 Pet. 1:1). Perhaps harassment from Roman officials had forced Christians to flee to these distant territories. Peter encouraged them to follow the example of Christ, whose persecution, death and resurrection provided assurance and hope for the future (1 Pet. 4:1–6).

PETER, SECOND EPISTLE OF. A brief epistle of only three chapters written by the apostle Peter to address troubling problems within the church. False teachers were leading people astray with their views of the nature of Christ and His second coming. Peter corrected these false views and advised the leaders of the church to deal firmly with heretical teachers. He was particularly forceful in response to scoffers who doubted the second coming of Christ (2 Pet. 3:1–9).

PETHOR. A town near the Euphrates River. It was home of the wizard Balaam, who was hired by the king of Moab to curse the Israelites (Num. 22:5–7).

PETITION. A prayer in the form of an earnest request for a personal need. The apostle Paul prayed for the removal of an affliction that he referred to as his "thorn in the flesh." But this didn't happen, apparently because the Lord was using this problem to show the adequacy of His grace in the apostle's life (2 Cor. 12:7–9).

PHARAOH. A title for several kings of Egypt:
(1) The unnamed ruler who refused to release the Israelites from slavery until the Lord killed the Egyptian firstborn (Exod. 12:29).
(2) Shishak, who attacked Jerusalem and plundered the temple (1 Kings 14:25–26).
(3) So, who made an alliance with King Hoshea of Israel (the Northern Kingdom) (2 Kings 17:4).
(4) Neco, whose archers mortally wounded King Josiah of Judah (the Southern Kingdom) at Megiddo (2 Kings 23:29).
(5) Hophra, whom God declared would fall to his enemies (Jer. 44:30).

PHARISEES. Members of a Jewish sect who insisted on keeping all the oral traditions that had grown up around the Jewish law. The word means "separated ones," indicating that they separated themselves from the common people and concentrated on the study and interpretation of the law. To them, the traditional interpretations of the law of Moses that had been added over several centuries were more important than the original law itself. Jesus criticized them for ignoring the commands of God while emphasizing "the tradition of men" (Mark 7:8). Jesus criticized the Pharisees for their hypocrisy. They pretended to be more zealous in their commitment to the law than any other group in Israel. But Jesus declared that this was nothing but a cover-up for their inner corruption and lack of compassion (Matt. 23:25–27). The Pharisees are also mentioned in Matt. 12:14–34; 15:12–14; 16:1; 19:3; 22:15 • Luke 7:36–50; 11:53–54 • Acts 5:34; 15:5; 23:5–8; 26:5 • Phil. 3:5.

PHARPAR. A river of Damascus, one of two which the leper Naaman preferred to go to for healing (2 Kings 5:12). He was offended when told by the prophet Elisha to bathe in the Jordan River rather than the rivers of Damascus (2 Kings 5:9–12). See also *Abanah*.

PHEBE. KJV: see *Phoebe*

PHENICE. KJV: see *Phoenicia*

PHENICIA. KJV: see *Phoenicia*

PHILADELPHIA. A city in Asia Minor and site of one of the seven churches addressed in the book of Revelation (Rev. 1:11). The name means "city of brotherly love," and the church in this city had lived up to its name by doing unselfish works of service to others. Jesus commended these believers for taking advantage of the opportunity He had given them (Rev. 3:8). Jesus reminded these believers of the certainty of His second coming. Keeping their eyes on this promise would enable them to remain faithful until they received the crown of eternal life (Rev. 3:11).

PHILEMON. A wealthy believer in the church at Colossae to whom the apostle Paul appealed on behalf of a runaway slave (Philem. 1).

PHILEMON, EPISTLE TO. Paul's shortest NT letter, written to help a runaway slave named Onesimus, who was converted under the apostle's ministry. Paul encouraged Philemon, the owner of Onesimus and a fellow believer, to welcome his slave back as a Christian brother

(Philem. 16). Paul also hinted that Onesimus should be given his freedom in the spirit of Christian love (Philem. 21). This little letter demonstrates the warm side of Paul's personality, showing that Jesus Christ has the power to transform all human relationships.

PHILETUS. A teacher condemned by Paul for his false teachings about the resurrection (2 Tim. 2:17–18).

PHILIP. (1) One of the twelve disciples of Jesus. He responded to Jesus' invitation to discipleship and brought another disciple, Nathanael, to meet Jesus (John 1:43–51). Later, during the final days of Jesus' earthly ministry, he also brought a group of Gentiles to see Jesus (John 12:21–22). He is also mentioned in Matt. 10:3 • Mark 3:18 • Luke 6:14 • John 6:5–7; 14:8–12 • Acts 1:13.

(2) One of the seven men of Greek background chosen to distribute food to needy widows in the church at Jerusalem (Acts 6:5–6). He is often referred to as "the evangelist" (Acts 21:8) because of his zealous preaching of the gospel. Philip preached to the Samaritans (Acts 8:5) and also led an official from Ethiopia to Christ (Acts 8:26–38).

(3) A Roman official in northern Israel at the time when John the Baptist began his ministry (Luke 3:1). See also *Herod*, No. 4.

PHILIPPI. A city of Macedonia visited by Paul and Silas during the second missionary journey. Here they were imprisoned but miraculously rescued by God when the prison was shaken by an earthquake (Acts 16:12–34). This was the first city in Greece to receive the gospel, and a businesswoman named Lydia became the first convert (Acts 16:12–15). Later, while imprisoned in Rome, Paul wrote a letter to the Christians in this city that became known as his epistle to the Philippians (Phil. 1:1). Philippi is also mentioned in Acts 20:6 • 1 Thes. 2:2.

PHILIPPIANS, EPISTLE TO. A short NT epistle written by the apostle Paul to the church at Philippi that is best characterized as a "friendship letter." Unlike most of his other letters, this epistle was not written to deal with a church problem. The apostle expressed warm thoughts toward these believers and assured them of his appreciation for their support of his ministry (Phil. 1:3–11; 4:10–23). Philippians has been called Paul's "epistle of joy" because of his exhortation, "Rejoice in the Lord always, and again I say, rejoice" (Phil. 4:4).

PHILISTIA. A coastal region about forty miles long beside the Mediterranean Sea which served as the land of the Philistines (Gen. 21:32–34). The major cities of Philistia were Ashdod, Askelon, Ekron, Gath, and Gaza (Jer. 25:20). It is also mentioned in Exod. 15:14 • Ps. 60:8; 87:4; 108:9 • Isa. 14:29, 31. *Land of the Philistines*: Gen. 21:32–34 • Exod. 13:17 • 1 Sam. 27:1.

PHILISTIM. KJV: see *Philistines*

PHILISTINES. The people of Philistia who became formidable enemies of the Israelites during OT times. The Philistines are first mentioned in connection with the patriarch Abraham. He grazed his herds in the region of Gerar, where he dealt with the local Philistine leader Abimelech (Gen. 20:15; 21:34). In later centuries, the Philistines tried to extend their territory into the region occupied by Israel. Saul, Israel's first king, had the misfortune of serving as leader of Israel during this period of Philistine aggression. Their monopoly on making and sharpening iron weapons put Saul and his army at a distinct disadvantage (1 Sam. 13:19–20). He and his sons were eventually killed in a battle with the Philistines (1 Sam. 31:1–9). Not until the time of David, Israel's popular warrior-king, were the Philistines finally defeated (2 Sam. 8:1). They are also mentioned in Gen. 10:14; 26:1–18 • Exod. 13:17 • Josh. 13:2–3 • Judg. 14:1–4; 15:3–20; 16:5–31 • 1 Sam. 17:8–57 • 2 Sam. 21:15–19 • 1 Chron. 10:1–12 • Jer. 47:1–4 • Amos 6:2; 9:7.

PHILISTINES, SEA OF THE. See *Great Sea*

PHILOLOGUS. A Christian at Rome to whom the apostle Paul sent greetings (Rom. 16:15).

PHINEHAS. (1) Aaron's grandson who became the third high priest of Israel (Num. 25:11–13).

At God's command Phinehas killed an Israelite man named Zimri for contributing to Israel's corruption with idolatry (Num. 25:6–15).

(2) A priest judged for his immorality and corrupt leadership (1 Sam. 2:22–24). Phinehas and his brother Hophni died in battle with the Philistines, as foretold by a prophet (1 Sam. 2:27, 34; 4:10–11).

PHLEGON. A fellow believer at Rome greeted and commended by Paul (Rom. 16:14).

PHOEBE. A servant of the church at Cenchrea near Corinth whom Paul commended for her loyal support of him and other believers (Rom. 16:1–2). *Phebe*: KJV.

PHOENICIA. A long, narrow country on the coast of the Mediterranean Sea just north of Israel. The inhabitants of Phoenicia were a seafaring people who descended from the Canaanites. King Hiram of the Phoenician city of Tyre furnished cedar timber and craftsmen for the construction of Solomon's temple in Jerusalem (1 Kings 5:1–10). Jesus visited this region (Matt. 15:21), and the apostle Paul also traveled through Phoenicia (Acts 11:19; 15:3; 21:2–3).

PHOENIX. A haven of Crete (Acts 27:12).

PHRYGIA. A region of central Asia Minor visited by the apostle Paul (Acts 16:6). Jews from Phrygia were in Jerusalem on the day of Pentecost (Acts 2:10).

PHUT. See *Libya*

PHYGELUS. A believer condemned by Paul because he deserted the apostle (2 Tim. 1:15). *Phygellus*: KJV.

PHYLACTERY. A tiny leather box containing strips of parchment on which portions of the OT law were written. The Pharisees wore these boxes as a literal obedience of God's command, "Bind them [God's laws] as a sign on your hand, and they shall be as frontlets between your eyes" (Deut. 6:8). Jesus denounced such outward displays of piety as hypocritical (Matt. 23:5).

PHYSICIAN. A title that Jesus applied to Himself to emphasize His concern for the outcasts of society. The scribes and Pharisees were horrified that Jesus and His disciples would associate with such sinful people. But Jesus replied to their criticisms, "Those who are healthy do not need a physician; but those who are sick do" (Luke 5:31). He had been sent to people such as these. They needed a Savior and deliverer. He was the physician who could heal them of their desperate sickness known as sin. See also *Friend of Tax Collectors and Sinners*.

PHYSICIAN [S]

Gen. 50:2 Joseph commanded...the *p's* to embalm his father

2 Chron. 16:12 in his disease he [Asa] did not seek the LORD but sought the *p's*

Jer. 8:22 Is there no balm in Gilead...no *p* there

Matt. 9:12 healthy do not need a *p*, but those who are sick

Mark 5:26 [a certain woman] had suffered many things of many *p's*

Luke 4:12 say this proverb to Me [Jesus], *P*, heal Yourself

Col. 4:14 Luke, the beloved *p*, and Demas greet you

PIERCE [D, ING, INGS]

Job 30:17 My [Job's] bones are *p'd*...in the night season

Prov. 12:18 There is one who speaks like the *p'ings* of a sword

Zech. 12:10 they shall look at Me [the Messiah] whom they have *p'd*

Luke 2:35 sword shall *p* through your [Mary's] soul

John 19:34 one of the soldiers...*p'd* His [Jesus'] side

Heb. 4:12 word of God is...sharper...two-edged sword, *p'ing*...soul and spirit

Rev. 1:7 He [Jesus] comes...every eye shall see Him...also those who *p'd* Him

PIGEON. A bird offered as a sacrifice by Mary and Joseph when Jesus as an infant was dedicated in the temple (Luke 2:24). This humble offering was often presented by the poor who could not afford a larger animal (Lev. 5:7).

PILATE, PONTIUS. The procurator or Roman governor of Judea who presided at Jesus' trial and sentenced Him to death by crucifixion. After questioning Jesus, Pilate sensed that He was innocent. He tried to dodge responsibility for Jesus' fate by sending Him to Herod at the next judicial level (Luke 23:6–11). When this ploy failed, Pilate proposed that Jesus be set free to satisfy the Roman custom of releasing one Jewish prisoner during the Passover festival. But the crowd refused, crying out instead for the freedom of a notorious criminal named Barabbas (John 18:39–40). Pilate finally bowed to public pressure and sentenced Jesus to death. He washed his hands to claim that he was "innocent of the blood of this just Person" (Matt. 27:24). Pilate is also mentioned in Matt. 27:2–65 • Mark 15:1–44 • Luke 3:1; 13:1 • John 18:29–38; 19:1–38 • Acts 3:13; 4:27; 13:28 • 1 Tim. 6:13.

PILLAR OF FIRE AND CLOUD. A visible sign of God's presence that guided the Israelites in the wilderness after they left Egypt (Exod. 14:24). This phenomenon apparently existed as a cloud during the day and took the form of a fire at night to protect the people and serve as a guiding light. Both clouds and fire are associated with God's power and presence (Exod. 13:21). Jesus identified Himself as the "light of the world" (John 8:12). With this metaphor, He challenged the people to pay allegiance to Him just as they had followed this mysterious light in the wilderness.

PINNACLE. A high point of the temple in Jerusalem that gave a panoramic view of the surrounding area. Satan tempted Jesus to impress the people by jumping from this high place (Matt. 4:5–7).

PIRAM. One of five Amorite kings who formed an alliance to resist the Israelites when they invaded Canaan (Josh. 10:3). They were defeated and executed by Joshua's forces.

PISGAH, MOUNT. A mountain range in Moab from which Moses viewed the land of Canaan before his death. It is mentioned in **Num.** 21:20; 23:14 • Deut. 3:27; **34:1–6**. See also *Nebo*.

PISHON. A river which flowed from the garden of Eden (Gen. 2:10–14). *Pison*: KJV.

PISIDIA. A rugged province in central Asia Minor visited by Paul and Barnabas on the first missionary journey. When the Jews in this region rejected Paul's message, he declared that he would direct his preaching to Gentiles (Acts 13:14–16, 41).

PISON. KJV: see *Pishon*

PIT. In the OT, "the pit" is often used synonymously for sheol, an underground place where departed spirits lived (Ps. 30:3). In the NT, the "bottomless pit" is the place into which Satan will be cast in the end-time (Rev. 20:1–3).

PITCH. A substance used on Noah's ark, probably as a sealant (Gen. 6:14). It may have been asphalt or bitumen, a mineral found in the Dead Sea area.

PITHOM. A supply city in lower Egypt built by Israelite slaves (Exod. 1:11).

PLAGUES AGAINST EGYPT. Ten calamities sent upon the Egyptians for their failure to release the Israelite slaves:
1. Water turned into blood (Exod. 7:20–25)
2. Frogs (Exod. 8:1–7)
3. Lice (Exod. 8:16–19)
4. Flies (Exod. 8:20–24)
5. Diseased livestock (Exod. 9:3–7)
6. Boils (Exod. 9:8–12)
7. Hail (Exod. 9:13–25)
8. Locusts (Exod. 10:1–15)
9. Darkness (Exod. 10:21–23)
10. Death of Egyptian firstborn (Exod. 12:1–36)

PLAIN, SEA OF THE. See *Salt Sea*

PLATTER. A dish or utensil on which food was served. Jesus used the word figuratively to condemn the hypocrisy of the scribes and Pharisees (Matt. 23:25–26).

PLEASE [D, ING]

1 Sam. 12:22 it has *p'd* the LORD to make you His people

Ps. 40:13 Be *p'd*, O LORD, to deliver me

Ps. 69:31 This also shall *p* the LORD better than an ox

Isa. 53:10 it *p'd* the LORD to bruise Him [God's servant]

Mic. 6:7 Will the LORD be *p'd* with thousands of rams

Matt. 17:5 My [God's] beloved Son, in whom I am well *p'd*

Luke 3:22 My [God's] beloved Son. In You [Jesus] I am well *p'd*

John 8:29 I [Jesus] always do those things that *p* Him [God]

Rom. 8:8 those who are in the flesh cannot *p* God

1 Cor. 1:21 it *p'd* God by the foolishness of preaching to save

Col. 1:19 it *p'd* the Father that in Him [Jesus] all fullness should dwell

Col. 3:20 obey your parents...this is well *p'ing* to the Lord

Heb. 11:6 without faith it is impossible to *p* Him [God]

1 John 3:22 do those things that are *p'ing* in His [God's] sight

PLEASURE [S]

Job 22:3 any *p* to the Almighty that you are righteous

Job 36:11 obey...Him [God], they shall spend their...years in *p's*

Ps. 147:11 The LORD takes *p* in those who fear Him

Ps. 149:4 For the LORD takes *p* in His people

Prov. 21:17 He who loves *p* shall be a poor man

Isa. 44:28 he [Cyrus]...shall perform all My [God's] *p*

Ezek. 33:11 I [God] have no *p* in the death of the wicked

Mal. 1:10 I have no *p* in you, says the LORD of hosts

Luke 12:32 your Father's good *p* to give you the kingdom

Eph. 1:9 His [Jesus'] good *p*...He has purposed in Himself

2 Tim. 3:4 lovers of *p's* more than lovers of God

Heb. 11:25 choosing...to suffer affliction...than to enjoy the *p's* of sin

Rev. 4:11 You [God] have created all things...for Your *p* they...were created

PLEDGE. Something given to a lender to guarantee repayment of a debt. The prophet Amos condemned using the pledge as a tool to oppress the poor (Amos 2:8).

PLEIADES. A brilliant cluster of stars cited by Job as evidence of God's dominion in the universe (Job 9:9).

PLOWSHARE. An agricultural tool cited by the prophet Isaiah as a symbol of the coming era of peace under the Messiah (Isa. 2:4).

PLUMB LINE. A construction tool used to establish proper alignment of a wall. The term is also used figuratively of God's test for the uprightness of His people (Amos 7:7–9).

POETIC WRITINGS. The five books of the OT which are written almost entirely in poetic form—Job, Psalms, Proverbs, the Song of Solomon, and Lamentations—as well as those sections of other books which use this form. Sections of several of the prophetic books, for example, appear in poetry. In many of these writings, a unique literary form known as parallelism rather than rhyming or alliteration is used to express ideas. In parallelism, one line of poetry is advanced, contrasted, or repeated by the next line to convey thought. For example, "Have mercy on me, O LORD; for I am weak. / O LORD, heal me; for my bones are vexed" (Ps. 6:2).

POLYGAMY. A family system under which a man is married to more than one wife at the same time. Abraham took Hagar, his wife Sarah's female servant, as his wife when Sarah was unable to bear children (Gen. 16:1–3). His grandson Jacob repeated this practice of multiple wives in later years (Gen. 29:15–30:13). But polygamy was contrary to God's original plan and divine ideal of marriage—a union between one man and one woman (Gen. 2:18–24 • Matt. 19:4–6). See also *Monogamy*.

POLYTHEISM. The practice of worshipping many gods, in contrast to monotheism, which emphasized devotion to the one and only true God. The nations surrounding Israel worshipped multiple gods, a practice which led to immorality (Num. 25:1–9), prostitution, and child sacrifice (Jer. 7:29–34). The first two of the Ten Commandments declare that devotion to the one and only supreme God was not to be mixed with worship of any other false, pagan god (Exod. 20:3–5). See also *Monotheism.*

POMEGRANATE. A small tree which bore apple-shaped fruit with many edible seeds. The scouts who explored Canaan discovered this tree (Deut. 8:7–8). In later centuries, King Solomon decorated the temple with drawings of this tree and its fruit (1 Kings 7:18).

PONTUS. A coastal region along the Black Sea in northern Asia Minor; the birthplace of Aquila, an associate of the apostle Paul (Acts 18:2). People from Pontus were in Jerusalem on the day of Pentecost (Acts 2:9). It is also mentioned in 1 Pet. 1:1.

POOL. A reservoir which held water for cities (John 5:2). King Hezekiah of Judah (the Southern Kingdom) built a pool with an adjoining tunnel to bring water into Jerusalem (2 Kings 20:20).

POOR. A class of people in need of financial aid, including widows, orphans, the handicapped, and strangers and aliens in the land. God had a special concern for people like this, and He directed the Israelites to take care of them (Deut. 15:11). Jesus also demonstrated God's concern for the poor (Luke 6:20). He had compassion on people with physical disabilities and restored several of them to health (Mark 8:22–23).

POOR

Lev. 19:10 You shall leave them [grapes] for the *p*

Deut. 15:11 the *p* shall never cease being in the land

2 Sam. 12:3 the *p* man had nothing except one little ewe lamb

Job 5:15 He [God] saves the *p* from the sword

Job 30:25 Was my [Job's] soul not grieved for the *p*?

Job 36:6 He [God]...gives justice to the *p*

Ps. 34:6 This *p* man cried, and the LORD heard him

Ps. 40:17 I am *p* and needy; yet the Lord thinks of me

Ps. 72:13 He [God] shall spare the *p* and needy

Ps. 109:22 I am *p* and needy, and my heart is wounded

Prov. 14:20 The *p* is hated even by his own neighbor

Prov. 21:17 He who loves pleasure shall be a *p* man

Prov. 22:2 rich and *p*...the LORD is the Maker of them all

Prov. 22:22 Do not rob the *p* because he is *p*

Eccles. 4:13 Better is a *p* and wise child than an old and foolish king

Isa. 25:4 You [God] have been a strength to the *p*

Amos 2:6 they [Israel] sold...the *p* for a pair of shoes

Matt. 5:3 Blessed are the *p* in spirit

Mark 10:21 sell whatever you [rich young ruler] have, and give to the *p*

Mark 14:7 For you always have the *p* with you

Luke 4:18 anointed Me [Jesus] to preach the gospel to the *p*

Luke 14:13 make a feast, call the *p*, the maimed

Luke 19:8 Lord, half of my [Zacchaeus's] goods I give to the *p*

1 Cor. 13:3 though I [Paul] give all my goods to feed the *p*

2 Cor. 8:9 He [Jesus] was rich, yet for your sake He became *p*

Jas. 2:5 Has not God chosen the *p* of this world to be rich in faith

PORATHA. A son of Haman who was executed, along with his father, when Haman's plot to destroy the Jews was exposed by Esther (Esther 9:7–10).

PORTION. A word usually used of inheritance rights (Gen. 31:14). The psalmist called God "my portion" (Ps. 119:57). He thought of the Lord as his spiritual heritage, passed down to him by godly people of past generations. But unlike an earthly inheritance that could be squandered, this was a legacy that would last forever.

POSSESSION [S]

Gen. 17:8 I [God] will give...Canaan, for an everlasting *p*

Gen. 47:27 they [Israel] had *p's* in it [in Egypt] and grew and multiplied

Ps. 2:8 I [God] shall give You [His Son]...farthest parts of the earth for Your *p*

Mark 10:22 he [rich young ruler]...went away grieved, for he had great *p's*

Acts 5:1 Ananias, with Sapphira his wife, sold a *p*

POSSIBLE

Matt. 19:26 but with God all things are *p*

Matt. 26:39 if it is *p*, let this cup pass from Me [Jesus]

Mark 9:23 all things are *p* to him who believes

Luke 18:27 things that are impossible with men are *p* with God

Rom. 12:18 If it is *p*...live peaceably with all men

Heb. 10:4 it is not *p* that the blood of bulls... should take away sins

POST. KJV: see *Courier*

POSTERITY. A word for a person's children and grandchildren. The prophet Jehu told King Baasha of Israel (the Northern Kingdom) that his misguided leadership would destroy him and his posterity (1 Kings 16:2–4).

POTENTATE. A title of God used by the apostle Paul ("the blessed and only Potentate," 1 Tim. 6:15) that refers to His unlimited authority and right to rule over the universe.

POTIPHAR. A high Egyptian officer to whom Joseph was sold as a slave when he arrived in Egypt. Potiphar had Joseph imprisoned when his wife falsely accused Joseph of trying to seduce her (**Gen.** 37:36; **39:1–20**).

POTI-PHERAH. An Egyptian priest whose daughter Asenath married Joseph (Gen. 41:45).

POTTER. A craftsman who made bowls and pots from clay on a revolving wheel (Jer. 18:3).

God as the master potter is a graphic biblical image. While the prophet Jeremiah looked on, a potter ruined a vase he was working on and had to start over again with the same lump of clay. Jeremiah compared the nation of Judah (the Southern Kingdom) to this pottery remaking process. Give up your sinful ways, he declared, or you will be reshaped by the Lord's discipline (Jer. 18:1–9).

POUND. A dry measure of uncertain volume. Mary of Bethany anointed Jesus with a pound of costly ointment (John 12:3).

POWER [S]

Exod. 15:6 Your right hand, O LORD, has become glorious in *p*

1 Chron. 29:11 Yours, O LORD, is the greatness and the *p*

Job 37:23 He [God] is excellent in *p* and in judgment

Ps. 49:15 redeem my soul from the *p* of the grave

Ps. 68:35 He [God]...gives strength and *p* to His people

Ps. 111:6 He [God] has shown...the *p* of His works

Prov. 18:21 Death and life are in the *p* of the tongue

Jer. 32:17 You [God] have made...the earth by Your great *p*

Nah. 1:3 The LORD is slow to anger and great in *p*

Zech. 4:6 Not by might, nor by *p*, but by My [God's] Spirit

Matt. 6:13 Yours [God's] is the kingdom and the *p*

Matt. 24:30 Son of Man coming in the clouds... with *p*

Matt. 28:18 All *p* has been given to Me [Jesus]

Mark 5:30 Jesus, knowing...that *p* had gone out of Him

Mark 13:25 the *p's* that are in heaven shall be shaken

Luke 4:32 His [Jesus'] word was with *p*

Luke 9:1 He [Jesus]...gave them [disciples] *p*... over all demons

Luke 24:49 remain in the city of Jerusalem until you [disciples] are endued with *p*

John 1:12 He [Jesus] gave *p* to become the sons of God

John 19:11 no *p* at all against Me [Jesus] unless it were given you [Pilate] from above

Acts 6:8 Stephen, full of faith and *p*, did great wonders

Rom. 8:38 neither death nor life...nor principalities nor *p's*

1 Cor. 4:20 kingdom of God is not in words but in *p*

Eph. 6:10 be strong in the Lord, and in the *p* of His might

Eph. 6:12 we wrestle...against principalities, against *p's*

2 Tim. 1:7 God has not given us the spirit of fear, but of *p*

Rev. 4:11 You [God] are worthy...to receive glory and honor and *p*

POWERFUL

Ps. 29:4 voice of the LORD is *p*

Song of Sol. 8:6 jealousy...coals of fire that have a very *p* flame

Heb. 4:12 For the word of God is living and *p*

POWER OF GOD

Matt. 22:29 not knowing the scriptures or the *p-o-G*

Luke 22:69 Son of Man shall sit on the right hand of the *p-o-G*

Rom. 1:16 it [the gospel] is the *p-o-G* for salvation

1 Cor. 1:18 the preaching of the cross...is the *p-o-G*

1 Cor. 2:5 your faith should stand in the *p-o-G*

PRAETORIUM. The official residence of Pontius Pilate, Roman governor of Jerusalem. After being beaten on orders from Pilate, Jesus was taken to the governor's residence, where he was mocked by soldiers (Mark 15:16).

PRAISE. An act of worship in which God is exalted for who He is and the blessings He bestows on His people (Ps. 21:13). The entire book of Psalms might be called "the praise book of the Bible." It is filled with expressions of praise to God for His goodness, mercy, truth, justice, righteousness, and protection, as well as His instructions for daily living through His written word, the Bible. The book ends with this dramatic exclamation: "Let everything that has breath praise the LORD. Praise the LORD" (Psalm 150:6).

PRAISE [D, ING, S]

1 Chron. 16:25 great is the LORD, and greatly to be *p'd*

1 Chron. 29:13 we thank You [God] and *p* Your glorious name

Ps. 18:3 call on the LORD, who is worthy to be *p'd*

Ps. 21:13 so will we sing and *p* Your [God's] power

Ps. 44:8 In God we boast...and *p* Your name forever

Ps. 47:7 sing *p's* with understanding

Ps. 51:15 my mouth shall declare Your [God's] *p*

Ps. 67:3 Let the people *p* You, O God; let all the *p* You

Ps. 79:13 declare Your [God's] *p* to all generations

Ps. 84:4 they will still be *p'ing* You [God]

Ps. 92:1 a good thing...to sing *p's* to Your [God's] name

Ps. 100:4 Enter into His [God's]...courts with *p*

Ps. 145:3 Great is the LORD, and greatly to be *p'd*

Isa. 42:10 Sing to the LORD...His *p* from the ends of the earth

Luke 2:20 shepherds returned, glorifying and *p'ing* God

John 12:43 loved the *p* of men more than the *p* of God

Acts 16:25 Paul and Silas were...singing *p's* to God

1 Pet. 2:9 declare the *p's* of Him [God] who has called you out of darkness

Rev. 19:5 *P* our God, all you His servants...you who fear Him

PRAISE THE LORD

Gen. 29:35 she [Leah] said, Now I will *p-t-L*

Ps. 7:17 I will *p-t-L* according to His righteousness

Ps. 107:15 Oh that men would *p-t-L* for His goodness

Ps. 117:1 O *p-t-L*, all you nations...all you people

Ps. 150:6 Let everything that has breath *p-t-L*

PRAY [ING, S]

2 Chron. 7:14 My [God's] people...humble themselves and *p*

Ps. 5:2 to You [God] I will *p*

Ps. 55:17 Evening and morning and at noon I will *p*

Jer. 14:11 LORD said to me [Jeremiah], Do not *p* for this people, for their good

Dan. 6:11 these men...found Daniel *p'ing*... before his God

Matt. 6:6 when you *p*, enter into your closet

Matt. 6:9 p according to this manner: Our Father who is in heaven

Mark 6:46 He [Jesus] departed to a mountain to *p*

Mark 11:25 when you stand *p'ing*, forgive

Mark 13:33 Watch and *p*. For you do not know when the time is

Luke 6:28 p for those who spitefully use you

Luke 11:1 Lord, teach us [the disciples] to *p*

John 14:16 I [Jesus] will *p* to the Father...He shall give you another Comforter

John 17:9 I [Jesus] *p* for them [the disciples]... whom You [God] have given Me

Acts 10:9 Peter went up on the housetop...to *p*

Rom. 8:26 we do not know what we should *p* for as we ought

1 Cor. 14:14 if I [Paul] *p* in an unknown tongue, my spirit *p's*

1 Thes. 5:17 P without ceasing

Jas. 5:13 Is any among you afflicted? Let him *p*

Jas. 5:16 p one for another, that you may be healed

PRAYER. Communion with God the Father. This spiritual exercise is based on the conviction that people are totally dependent on Him for their existence. Elements of sincere prayer are adoration of God and His nature (Matt. 6:9–10), confession of one's sins and unworthiness (1 John 1:9), supplication for one's own needs (1 Tim. 2:1–3), intercession on behalf of others (Jas. 5:15), and thanksgiving to God for His love and grace (Phil. 4:6). Jesus was a model of prayer for His followers. He arose early in the morning to pray (Mark 1:35), prayed all night before choosing His twelve disciples (Luke 6:12–13), prayed in Gethsemane on the night of His betrayal (Luke 22:44), and prayed on the cross for His enemies (Luke 23:34). He also gave His disciples a model prayer to follow in their communion with the Father (Matt. 6:9–13). But Jesus also warned against hypocritical prayer— sentiments mouthed just to impress people and mindless repetition of words that did not come from the heart (Matt. 6:7). See also *Lord's Prayer*.

PRAYER

2 Chron. 7:12 I [God] have heard your [Solomon's] *p*

Ps. 6:9 the LORD will receive my *p*

Ps. 66:20 God...has not turned away my *p*

Ps. 102:17 He [God] will regard the *p* of the destitute

Prov. 15:29 The LORD...hears the *p* of the righteous

Matt. 21:22 whatever you shall ask in *p*, believing, you shall receive

Luke 19:46 My [God's] house is the house of *p*

Acts 6:4 we [the apostles] will give ourselves continually to *p*

Rom. 10:1 my [Paul's]...*p* to God for Israel is that they might be saved

Jas. 5:15 the *p* of faith shall save the sick

Jas. 5:16 fervent *p* of a righteous man avails much

PREACH [ED, ING]

Isa. 61:1 the LORD has anointed me [God's servant] to *p* good news

Matt. 3:1 John the Baptist came *p'ing* in the wilderness

Matt. 4:17 Jesus began to *p* and to say, Repent

Matt. 24:14 this gospel...shall be *p'ed* in all the world

Mark 1:4 John baptized...and *p'ed*...repentance

Mark 3:14 that He [Jesus] might send them [the disciples] out to *p*

Luke 24:47 remission of sins should be *p'ed* in His [Jesus'] name

Acts 5:42 they [the apostles] did not cease to...*p* Jesus Christ

Acts 8:4 those [believers]...went everywhere *p'ing* the word

Acts 8:5 Philip went down to...Samaria and *p'ed* Christ

1 Cor. 1:18 *p'ing* of the cross is foolishness to those who are perishing

1 Cor. 1:21 it pleased God by the foolishness of *p'ing* to save those who believe

1 Cor. 1:23 but we *p* Christ crucified

1 Cor. 9:27 lest...when I [Paul] have *p'ed* to others, I myself should be disqualified

1 Cor. 15:14 if Christ has not been raised, then our *p'ing* is useless

2 Cor. 4:5 we do not *p* ourselves, but Christ Jesus the Lord

Eph. 3:8 I [Paul] should *p* among the Gentiles

Phil. 1:18 Christ is *p'ed*, and in it I [Paul] do rejoice

2 Tim. 4:2 *P* the word. Be ready in season

1 Pet. 3:19 He [Jesus] also went and *p'ed* to the spirits in prison

PREACHER

Eccles. 1:2 Vanity of vanities, says the *P*

Rom. 10:14 and how shall they hear without a *p*

2 Tim. 1:11 I [Paul] am appointed a *p*...of the Gentiles

PREACHING. The practice of proclaiming the truths of the gospel to a congregation or a group of listeners. The prophets of the OT were called by God to preach about God's judgment as well as good tidings of His deliverance (Isa. 61:1–2). In the Great Commission, Jesus urged His disciples to preach the gospel to all people (Mark 16:15). The preaching of the apostles and other Christ-followers in the NT was generally a fervent call for people to accept Jesus as Lord and Savior (Acts 2:38).

PREACH THE GOSPEL

Mark 16:15 Go into all the world and *p-t-g* to every creature

Luke 4:18 He [God] has anointed Me [Jesus] to *p-t-g* to the poor

Rom. 1:15 I [Paul] am ready to *p-t-g* to you also who are at Rome

Rom. 10:15 How beautiful are the feet of those who *p-t-g*

1 Cor. 1:17 Christ sent me [Paul] not to baptize but to *p-t-g*

1 Cor. 9:14 those who *p-t-g* should live by the gospel

PRECEPT [S]

Ps. 119:27 Make me to understand the way of Your [God's] *p's*

Ps. 119:100 I understand...because I keep Your [God's] *p's*

Isa. 28:10 *p* on *p*, line on line...here a little and there a little

Dan. 9:5 we have sinned...even by departing from Your [God's] *p's*

Mark 10:5 He [Moses] wrote you this *p* because of the hardness of your heart

PRECIOUS

Ps. 116:15 *P* in the sight of the LORD is the death of His saints

Ps. 139:17 How *p* also are Your thoughts to me, O God

Prov. 17:8 A gift is like a *p* stone in the eyes of him who has it

Eccles. 7:1 A good name is better than *p* ointment

Isa. 28:16 a tested stone, a *p* cornerstone

Matt. 26:7 a woman came...having an alabaster box of very *p* ointment

1 Cor. 3:12 if any man builds on this foundation gold, silver, *p* stones

Rev. 21:19 foundations...were garnished with...*p* stones

PREDESTINATION. A theological concept that refers to God's advance knowledge of human events. The term comes from a Latin word that means "to decide upon beforehand." Since God is all-knowing (omniscient), He knows all things, even our choices long before we make them. So He knows who will become believers and become part of His kingdom. But God's foreknowledge of what will happen does not mean that He will predestinate some people to be saved and others to be eternally lost. Because of Adam and Eve's fall in the garden of Eden, people sin by their own free choice. No person deserves salvation, but God's love for sinners applies to everyone. The apostle Paul expressed it like this: "The gospel of Christ...is the power of God for salvation to everyone who believes" (Rom. 1:16).

PREDESTINE [D]

Rom. 8:29 whom He [God] foreknew, He also *p'd*

Eph. 1:5 having *p'd* us to the adoption of children by Jesus Christ

Eph. 1:11 *p'd* according to the purpose of Him [God] who works all

PREPARATION DAY. The day before the Jewish Sabbath or the celebration of a religious festival (Matt. 27:62). Preparation for the Passover celebration involved cooking the Passover meal, baking unleavened bread, and choosing appropriate clothing for the occasion.

PRESENCE OF THE LORD

Gen. 3:8 Adam and his wife hid...from the *p-o-t-L*

Ps. 114:7 Tremble, earth, at the *p-o-t-L*

Jon. 1:3 Jonah rose up to flee...from the *p-o-t-L*

2 Thes. 1:9 punished with...destruction from the *p-o-t-L*

PRICE

1 Chron. 21:24 I [David] will truly buy it [threshing floor] for the full *p*

Job 28:18 the *p* of wisdom is above rubies

Prov. 31:10 find a virtuous woman? For her *p*... above rubies

Isa. 55:1 buy wine and milk without money and without *p*

Matt. 13:46 when he had found one pearl of great *p*

Acts 5:2 [Ananias] kept back part of the *p*

1 Cor. 6:20 you were bought with a *p*. Therefore glorify God

PRIDE. A feeling of arrogance because of one's accomplishments or status in life. Pride is the very opposite of humility, or putting others before oneself. Excessive pride is a serious sin because it attributes to oneself the glory and honor that belong to God alone. Jesus told a parable about a self-righteous Pharisee and a penitent tax collector to emphasize the problem of pride. The proud Pharisee thanked God that he was not a sinner like other people. But the humble tax collector prayed for God to show mercy toward him as a sinner (Luke 18:13). Jesus declared that this humble man "went down to his house justified rather than the other" (Luke 18:14).

PRIDE

Lev. 26:19 I [God] will break the *p* of your power

Ps. 10:2 wicked in his *p* persecutes the poor

Ps. 73:6 *p* surrounds them around as a chain

Prov. 8:13 The fear of the LORD is to hate...*p*

Prov. 16:18 *P* goes before destruction

1 John 2:16 the lust of the eyes, and the *p* of life

PRIEST. A religious leader who made sacrificial offerings on behalf of the people. The priesthood originated with Aaron, and his descendants succeeded him in that office (Exod. 29:9, 44). According to the author of the book of Hebrews, earthly priests die and are succeeded by others who serve only for a limited time. But Jesus has a permanent priesthood because He lives to guide His followers and to intercede on their behalf before God the Father (Heb. 7:24–25).

PRIESTHOOD OF BELIEVERS. A doctrine which declares that believers have direct access to God because of the atoning sacrifice of Christ. In OT times, only the high priest was allowed to enter the most sacred place in the temple in Jerusalem. But when Jesus died on the cross, the curtain that stood before this sacred space was split from top to bottom. This showed that all people now had equal access to God's presence (Matt. 27:50–51). This doctrine also emphasizes the ministry responsibility of all followers of Jesus. As priests of God, believers are commissioned to reach out to others in a spirit of love (2 Cor. 5:20).

PRIESTHOOD OF CHRIST. One of Christ's offices as the Son of God, emphasizing His offering of His own blood to obtain redemption for believers (Heb. 9:11–12). See also *Offices of Christ*.

PRINCE OF PEACE. A title for the coming Messiah used by the prophet Isaiah (Isa. 9:6).

Jesus would be God's anointed ruler who would bring peace and tranquility by reconciling humankind to God the Father. The apostle Peter also referred to Jesus as the "Prince of life" (Acts 3:15).

PRINCIPALITY. A powerful class of angels and demons. The apostle Paul declared that Christ is superior to such beings (Eph. 1:20–21).

PRINCIPALITY [IES]

Rom. 8:38 neither death nor life, nor angels nor *p'ies*

Eph. 1:21 far above all *p* and power, might and dominion

Eph. 6:12 we wrestle...against *p'ies*, against powers

Col. 1:16 by Him [Jesus] all things were created...*p'ies* or powers

PRISCILLA. A believer who, with her husband, Aquila, was a fellow laborer with the apostle Paul. The couple was associated with the apostle in his work at Ephesus. After he left the city, they stayed on and instructed an eloquent preacher named Apollos more thoroughly in the Christian faith (Acts 18:18–28). They also apparently worked with Paul at Corinth. He lived with them here for a time, and they practiced their mutual craft of tent-making while presenting the gospel to citizens of the area (Acts 18:1–3).

PRISON. A place where prisoners were housed. These places were little more than crude dungeons, empty cisterns, or holes in the ground, particularly in OT times (Jer. 52:11). The prophet Jeremiah was thrown into such a place for declaring that the nation of Judah (the Southern Kingdom) was headed for disaster unless it turned to the Lord (Jer. 37:15–16). The apostle Paul was imprisoned several times, and he referred to himself as a "prisoner of the Lord" (Eph. 4:1). He wrote several of his letters from a Roman prison.

PROCHORUS. One of the seven men set apart for special service in the church at Jerusalem. Their role was to take care of the Greek-speaking widows who had been neglected in the church's food distribution ministry (Acts 6:1–5).

PROCLAIM [ED]

Lev. 23:4 holy convocations that you shall *p*

Prov. 20:6 Most men will each *p* his own goodness

Isa. 61:1 the LORD...has sent me [God's servant]... to *p* liberty to the captives

Jon. 3:5 people of Nineveh believed God, and *p'ed* a fast

Luke 12:3 whispered in closets shall be *p'ed* on the housetops

PRODIGAL. A word meaning "foolish" or "reckless." It is applied to the main character in a parable of Jesus—the son who spent his inheritance foolishly, fell into poverty, and finally returned to his father to ask forgiveness and reinstatement as a servant. His father, representing the love and forgiveness of God, welcomed the young man back as a son (Luke 15:11–32).

PROFANE [D]

Ezek. 23:38 they have *p'd* my [God's] Sabbaths

Ezek. 44:23 teach...the difference between the holy and *p*

Mal. 2:11 Judah has *p'd* the holiness of the LORD

1 Tim. 4:7 refuse *p* and old wives' fables

2 Tim. 2:16 shun *p* and vain babblings

PROFESS [ING]

Matt. 7:23 then I [Jesus] will *p*... I never knew you

Rom. 1:22 *P'ing* themselves to be wise, they became fools

Titus 1:16 They *p* that they know God, but in works they deny Him

PROFESSION

1 Tim. 6:12 you...have professed a good *p*

Heb. 3:1 consider the...High Priest of our *p*, Christ Jesus

Heb. 10:23 Let us hold fast the *p* of our faith

PROFIT [S]

Ps. 30:9 What *p* is there in my blood when I go down to the pit?

Eccles. 1:3 What *p* does a man have from all his labor

Mark 8:36 p a man if he gains the whole world and loses his own soul

John 6:63 the Spirit who gives life; the flesh *p's* nothing

Rom. 3:1 What is the *p* of circumcision?

1 Cor. 13:3 and do not have love, it *p's* me nothing

Jas. 2:14 What does it *p*...though a man...have not works

PROMISE. A solemn pledge to perform a specific action or to grant a certain blessing, particularly the promises made by God to His people (2 Pet. 3:9).

PROMISE [D, S]

Josh. 23:10 He [God]...fights for you, as He has *p'd* you

2 Chron. 1:9 let Your [God's] *p* to my father, David, be established

Jer. 33:14 I [God] will perform that good thing that I have *p'd*

Luke 24:49 behold, I [Jesus] send the *p* of My Father

Rom. 15:8 Jesus Christ was a minister...for truth of God, to confirm the *p's* made

Gal. 3:21 Is the law then against the *p's* of God?

Gal. 3:29 Abraham's descendants and heirs according to the *p*

Gal. 4:28 we, brothers...are the children of *p*

Eph. 3:6 Gentiles should be...partakers of His [God's] *p*

Eph. 6:2 Honor your father and mother...first commandment with *p*

Titus 1:2 eternal life, which God, who cannot lie, *p'd*

Heb. 11:9 he [Abraham] sojourned in the land of *p*

Jas. 1:12 crown of life that the Lord has *p'd*

2 Pet. 3:4 Where is the *p* of His [Jesus'] coming?

1 John 2:25 the *p* that He [Jesus] has *p'd* us: even eternal life

PROPHECIES ABOUT JESUS. See *Messianic Prophecies*

PROPHECY. Messages from God delivered by His righteous spokesmen through the inspiration and power of the Holy Spirit. Sometimes these divine messages were communicated through actions rather than words. For example, the prophet Isaiah walked around without his outer robe (Isa. 20:2). This was a warning for the people to turn from their sinful ways or they would be stripped by their enemies. Isaiah also gave his sons symbolic names that predicted God's judgment (Isa. 7:3–4; 8:1–4).

PROPHECY [IES]

1 Cor. 12:10 to another *p*, to another discerning of spirits

1 Cor. 13:2 though I [Paul] have the gift of *p*

1 Cor. 13:8 whether there are *p'ies*, they shall fail

2 Pet. 1:20 no *p* of the scripture is of any private interpretation

PROPHESY [IED, IES]

Ezek. 37:4 He [God] said to me, *P* to these bones...hear the word

Joel 2:28 your sons and your daughters shall *p*

Amos 7:15 Lᴏʀᴅ said to me, Go, *p* to My people Israel

Matt. 7:22 have we not *p'ied* in Your [Jesus'] name

Mark 7:6 Isaiah *p'ied* well of you hypocrites

Acts 2:18 pour out My [God's] Spirit...and they shall *p*

Rom. 12:6 let us *p* according to the proportion of faith

1 Cor. 13:9 we know in part and we *p* in part

1 Cor. 14:5 he who *p'ies* is greater than he who speaks with tongues

PROPHET. An inspired messenger called by God to declare His will, who spoke by divine authority. Prophets emphasized that they spoke for the Lord by declaring, "This is what the Lᴏʀᴅ says" (Jer. 28:16). Jesus was the last in a long line of prophets whom God sent to His people across many centuries. He Himself claimed to be a prophet (Luke 13:33). He was the ultimate spokesman for the Lord, since He came into the world as God's own Son (John 3:16).

PROPHETESS. A female prophet or the wife of a prophet. Noted prophetesses include Miriam (Exod. 15:20), Deborah (Judg. 4:4), Huldah (2 Kings 22:14), and Anna (Luke 2:36). In the NT, four daughters of the evangelist Philip were said to prophesy (Acts 21:8–9).

PROPITIATION. A word that refers to one of the classical theories of the atoning death of Jesus Christ (1 John 4:10). It comes from an old English word meaning "to appease" or "to satisfy." According to this view, God is a holy God who cannot tolerate sin. He is also a just God who must punish sin wherever He finds it. So sin separates people from God and makes them liable to His punishment. But God loved the world too much to allow it to continue in this hopeless situation. He sent His Son, Jesus, to die to pay the penalty that He demanded from human beings because of our sin. Jesus was the sacrifice that covered over or atoned for our sin and restored the broken relationship between a holy God and sinful people.

Another NT term that means basically the same as propitiation is *ransom*. In the OT, this described the price that was paid to purchase a person's freedom from slavery or punishment. In the NT, Jesus applied this word to Himself when he declared, "The Son of Man did not come to be ministered to, but to minister, and to give his life as a ransom for many" (Mark 10:45).

PROPITIATION

Rom. 3:25 whom [Jesus] God has set forth to be a *p*...through faith

1 John 2:2 He [Jesus] is the *p* for our sins...not for ours only

1 John 4:10 God...sent His Son to be the *p* for our sins

PROSTITUTION. See *Harlotry*

PROUD

Job 40:12 Look at everyone who is *p* and bring him low

Ps. 94:2 Render a reward to the *p*

Ps. 119:69 The *p* have forged a lie against me

Prov. 6:17 a *p* look, a lying tongue

Prov. 16:5 Everyone who is *p* in heart is an abomination

Eccles. 7:8 the patient in spirit is better than the *p* in spirit

2 Tim. 3:2 men shall be...covetous, boasters, *p*

Jas. 4:6 God resists the *p*, but gives grace to the humble

PROVE [D]. See also *Test*

1 Kings 2:2 be strong, and *p* yourself a man

Eccles. 7:23 All this I have *p'd* by wisdom

Rom. 3:9 we have *p'd*...both Jews and Gentiles are all under sin

Rom. 12:2 you may *p* what is that good and... perfect will of God

Gal. 6:4 But let every man *p* his own work

PROVERBS, BOOK OF. A book of wisdom in the OT filled with short, pithy sayings on how to live with maturity and integrity under the watchful eye of God—the source of all wisdom. Proverbs declares that true wisdom consists of respect for God and living in harmony with His commands (Prov. 15:33). The very first verse of Proverbs identifies its author as King Solomon (Prov. 1:1), who was noted for his great wisdom (1 Kings 4:29–34). But some sections in the book are attributed to other writers, including Agur (Prov. 30:1) and King Lemuel (Prov. 31:1). Solomon probably wrote the basic core of Proverbs but added some writings from other sources and gave proper credit to their writers. The book reads like a manual of instructions for daily living, with occasional humor to make a point: "Even a fool, when he remains silent, is counted wise, and he who shuts his lips is esteemed a man of understanding" (Prov. 17:28).

PROVIDENCE. God's guidance of human acts or historical events to bring about His purpose. One of the best biblical examples of providence is the account of Joseph and his brothers in the book of Genesis. In a fit of jealousy, his brothers sold him into slavery in Egypt. But God, through a series of timely events, brought good out of this bad situation. Finally reunited with his brothers, Joseph forgave them and declared, "God sent me before you to preserve you a posterity in the earth and to save your lives by a great deliverance" (Gen. 45:7).

PROVINCE. A district or section of a nation, often the outlying area of an extended world power such as the Persian and the Roman empires (Esther 3:12). In the NT, this word refers to districts conquered and controlled by the Romans (Acts 25:1).

PROVOKE [D, ING]

Deut. 32:16 They **p'd** Him [God]...with foreign gods

Ps. 78:17 sinned...against Him [God] by **p'ing** the Most High

Ps. 78:58 **p'd** Him [God] to anger with their high places

1 Cor. 10:22 Do we **p** the Lord to jealousy?

1 Cor. 13:5 [love] is not easily **p'd**, does not think evil

Gal. 5:26 Let us not be boastful, **p'ing** one another

Eph. 6:4 fathers, do not **p** your children to wrath

Heb. 10:24 consider one another to **p** to love and to good works

PRUDENCE. Discernment or understanding (Matt. 11:25). The prudent person foresees evil (Prov. 22:3) and is crowned with knowledge (Prov. 14:18).

PRUNING HOOK. A tool for cutting shrubs and vines. To beat pruning hooks into spears was a sign of war (Joel 3:10). To do the opposite was a sign of peace (Isa. 2:4).

PSALMS, BOOK OF. A poetic book of the OT filled with hymns of praise and prayers of thanksgiving to God. Several things about the Psalms make it unique among the books of scripture: It is the longest book of the Bible; it was written by many different authors across a period of several centuries; and parts of the book were used as a hymnal in the worship services of ancient Israel. Its title is derived from a Greek word which implies that these psalms were to be sung to the accompaniment of musical instruments. King David wrote many of these psalms (see titles of Pss. 54, 59, 65). But

many other unknown writers contributed to this book. Many of the psalms were written in a poetic form known as parallelism—a literary technique in which the first phrase is followed by a second that repeats, adds to, or contrasts with the first phrase, as in this example: "For the LORD knows the way of the righteous, / but the way of the ungodly shall perish" (Ps. 1:6).

Several musical terms appear throughout the Psalms, particularly in the titles of individual psalms. The word *michtam* in the title of Psalm 16 probably indicated that this psalm was to be sung to a particular cadence or tune. The word *selah* (Ps. 44:8) may have marked the place for a pause in the singing. *Sheminith* (Ps. 12 title) probably indicated the instrument to be used when this particular hymn was sung. Generations of believers have found the psalms to be a rich source of devotional inspiration, with their emphasis on the goodness, stability, power, and faithfulness of God.

PTOLEMAIS. See *Acco*

PUAH. A brave midwife, who along with Shiphrah, refused to enforce the Egyptian pharaoh's order to kill all babies born to Israelite women (Exod. 1:15).

PUBLICAN. See *Tax Collector*

PUBLIUS. A Roman official who entertained the apostle Paul on the island of Malta after a shipwreck. Paul healed his father of a fever (Acts 28:7–8).

PUDENS. A believer at Rome who joined Paul in sending greetings to Timothy (2 Tim. 4:21).

PUL. See *Tiglath-pileser*

PUNISH [ED, MENT, MENTS]

Gen. 4:13 My [Cain's] **p'ment** is greater than I can bear

Lev. 26:18 you will not yet listen...I [God] will **p** you seven times more

Ezra 9:13 You our God have **p'ed** us less than our iniquities deserve

Ps. 59:5 God of Israel, awake to **p** all the nations

Ps. 149:7 to execute vengeance on the nations... **p'ments** on the people

Prov. 17:26 to *p* the just is not good

Isa. 13:11 And I [God] will *p* the world for its evil

Jer. 21:14 I [God] will *p* you according to...your actions

Jer. 50:18 Behold, I [God] will *p* the king of Babylon

Lam. 3:39 Why does a living man complain... for the *p'ment* of his sins

Matt. 25:46 shall go away into everlasting *p'ment*...righteous into eternal life

2 Thes. 1:9 *p'ed* with everlasting destruction from the presence of the Lord

Heb. 10:29 much more severe *p'ment*...who... scorned the Spirit of grace

PUNISHMENT. A penalty for wrongdoing. The OT law designated specific punishments for crimes committed against others. The general rule was repayment in kind for any loss suffered, or "eye for eye" (Exod. 21:24). Jesus' teachings on forgiveness and redemption took center stage in the NT, making punishment a secondary concern. But the concept of eternal punishment for those who refuse to accept Christ as Savior emerged in the writings of the apostle Paul. He declared that unbelievers will be "punished with everlasting destruction" in the final judgment (2 Thes. 1:8–9).

PURIFICATION. Ceremonial or spiritual cleansing. The OT law prescribed purification rites for people who had been ceremonially defiled by touching a corpse, by contact with bodily discharges, by childbirth, and by leprosy (Lev. 14–15). In Jesus' day, the Pharisees and other Jewish leaders emphasized such rules to the detriment of people's relationship with God, a practice that Jesus had no patience with. Real purity, He declared, was not a matter of keeping external rules but aligning one's heart

and actions with the will and purpose of God (Matt. 15:11).

PURIFY [IED, IES]

Lev. 8:15 Moses...*p'ied* the altar

Neh. 12:30 priests and the Levites *p'ied* themselves and *p'ied* the people

Ps. 12:6 words of the Lord are pure...*p'ied* seven times

Ps. 51:7 *P* me with hyssop, and I shall be clean

Titus 2:14 that He [Jesus] might...*p*...a special people

Jas. 4:8 and *p* your hearts, you double-minded

1 Pet. 1:22 *p'ied* your souls in obeying the truth

1 John 3:3 every man who has this hope...*p'ies* himself

PURIM, FEAST OF. A religious festival which celebrated the delivery of the Jews from Haman's oppression in Queen Esther's time (Esther 9:21–32).

PURPLE. The color preferred by kings and other royal officials; a bright dye made from shellfish. Lydia, a convert under Paul's ministry, was a businesswoman who sold purple cloth (Acts 16:14).

PURPOSE [D, S]

Eccles. 3:1 a time for every *p* under the heaven

John 18:37 I [Jesus] am a king. For this *p* I was born

Rom. 8:28 for those who are the called according to His [God's] *p*

2 Cor. 9:7 let every man give as he *p's* in his heart

Eph. 3:11 eternal *p* that He [God] *p'd* in Christ Jesus

1 John 3:8 For this *p* the Son of God was made known

PUT. See *Libya*

PUTEOLI. A city on the coast of southern Italy visited by the apostle Paul (Acts 28:13–14).

Q

QUAIL. Small birds which God provided miraculously as food for the Israelites in the wilderness during the Exodus from Egypt (Exod. 16:12–13).

QUARREL [LED, S]

Gen. 26:20 herdsmen of Gerar *q'led* with Isaac's herdsmen

Isa. 45:9 Woe to him who *q's* with his Maker!

Col. 3:13 forgiving one another if any man has a *q* against any

2 Tim. 2:24 the servant of the Lord must not *q*

QUARTUS. A believer at Corinth from whom Paul sent greetings to the church at Rome (Rom. 16:23).

QUATERNION. A company of four soldiers, four of which guarded the apostle Peter in prison, only to have him escape when summoned by an angel (Acts 12:4).

QUEEN. A woman who, along with the king, ruled over a country, or the wife or mother of a king. Queen Esther used her influence as the wife of King Ahasuerus of Persia to save her people from disaster (Esther 5:2).

QUEEN OF HEAVEN. A fertility goddess worshipped by the citizens of Jerusalem during the idolatrous days before the fall of the nation of Judah (the Southern Kingdom) (Jer. 7:18; 44:17). This may have been the goddess Asherah.

QUEEN OF SHEBA. The wealthy ruler of ancient Sheba in Arabia who visited King Solomon. She was impressed with the king's wealth, influence, and wisdom (1 Kings 10:1–9).

QUENCH [ED]

2 Chron. 34:25 My [God's] wrath...shall not be *q'ed*

Song of Sol. 8:7 Many waters cannot *q* love

Jer. 7:20 My [God's] anger...shall not be *q'ed*

Matt. 12:20 reed He [God's servant] shall not break...smoking flax He shall not *q*

Mark 9:44 their worm does not die...the fire is not *q'ed*

Eph. 6:16 you shall...*q* all the fiery darts of the wicked

1 Thes. 5:19 Do not *q* the Spirit

QUICK [LY]. See also *Alive; Live; Revive*

Gen. 27:19 How is it that you have found it so *q'ly*

Exod. 32:8 They [Israelites] have *q'ly* turned aside...way I commanded them

Josh. 23:16 you [Israelites] shall perish *q'ly* from off the good land

Ps. 81:14 I [God] would have *q'ly* subdued their enemies

Prov. 14:17 He who is *q'ly* angered deals foolishly

Eccles. 4:12 a three-stranded cord is not *q'ly* broken

Isa. 11:3 make Him [God's servant] of *q* understanding

Matt. 5:25 Agree with your adversary *q'ly*

John 13:27 Jesus said to him [Judas], What you do, do *q'ly*

Titus 1:7 a bishop must be...not *q'ly* angered

Rev. 2:16 Repent, or else I will come to you *q'ly* and will fight

Rev. 22:12 behold, I come *q'ly*, and My reward is with Me

QUICKSANDS. Sandbars and shifting sands off the African coast in the Mediterranean Sea which posed a hazard for ships (Acts 27:17).

QUIRINIUS. Roman governor of Syria at the time when Jesus was born (Luke 2:1–4). *Cyrenius*: KJV.

QUIVER. A sheath for arrows carried by foot soldiers or hung on the sides of chariots (Lam. 3:13). The word is also used figuratively for the blessing of children (Ps. 127:4–5).

QUMRAN, KHIRBET. A site near the Dead Sea where the Dead Sea Scrolls were discovered. See also *Dead Sea Scrolls*.

R

RAAMSES. A supply city in the Nile River delta of Egypt, built by Israelite slaves at the command of the pitiless pharaoh (Exodus 1:11).

RABBAH. Capital city of the Ammonites, first mentioned as the place where the giant bedstead of King Og of Bashan was located in

Joshua's time (Deut. 3:11; *Rabbath*: KJV). Later, Rabbah was captured by David's army (2 Sam. 12:26–31). Several OT prophets predicted the destruction of the city (Amos 1:14). Rabbah is also mentioned in 1 Chron. 20:1 • Jer. 49:2–3 • Ezek. 21:20; 25:5.

RABBATH. KJV: see *Rabbah*

RABBI. A title of honor and respect meaning "master" or "teacher." Nicodemus addressed Jesus with this title when he sought to learn more about Him and His teachings (John 3:2). Its Aramaic form is *rabboni* (John 20:16).

RAB-SHAKEH, THE. The title of a military officer under King Sennacherib of Assyria who demanded the surrender of Jerusalem from King Hezekiah of Judah (the Southern Kingdom) (2 Kings 18:17).

RACA. A term of contempt, meaning "worthless" or "good for nothing." Jesus cautioned against using this word for a fellow human being, emphasizing that it would lead to God's judgment and condemnation (Matt. 5:21–22).

RACE. A contest of speed such as running, a feature of the popular Greek games of NT times. The word is used as a symbol of the goal of Christlikeness to be pursued by all believers (Heb. 12:1).

RACE

Eccles. 9:11 I...saw...that the *r* is not to the swift
1 Cor. 9:24 in a *r* all run, but one receives the prize
Heb. 12:1 run with patience the *r* that is set before us

RACHAB. KJV: see *Rahab*

RACHEL. A wife of Jacob, who was tricked into marring Rachel's older sister Leah instead. Then Jacob worked seven additional years to take Rachel as his wife (Gen. 29:6–31). For many years Rachel was not able to bear children. She finally gave birth to two sons, Joseph and Benjamin, but died at Benjamin's birth and was buried near Bethlehem (Gen. 35:16–24).

This tomb was still visible several centuries later during the period of the judges (1 Sam. 10:2). Rachel is also mentioned in Gen. 30:1–25; 31:4–34; 33:1–7; 46:19–25; 48:7 • Ruth 4:11 • Jer. 31:15–17 • Matt. 2:18.

RAGE

2 Kings 5:12 So he [Naaman] turned and went away in a *r*
Ps. 2:1 Why do the nations *r* and the people plot a vain thing?
Ps. 7:6 lift up Yourself [God] because of the *r* of my enemies
Prov. 6:34 For jealousy is the *r* of a man
Dan. 3:13 Nebuchadnezzar in his *r* and fury gave the command
Luke 6:11 they [scribes and Pharisees] were filled with *r*

RAHAB. (1) A prostitute in Jericho who hid the spies sent by Joshua to scout the city (Josh. 2:1–6). Later she and her family were spared when Jericho fell to the invading Israelites (Josh. 6:22–25). After Jericho fell, Rahab and her family apparently joined the Israelite community as people of faith in the one true God (Josh. 6:25). From her family line emerged King David, and eventually the long-awaited Messiah. Rahab is listed in Matthew's genealogy of Jesus (Matt. 1:5; *Rachab*: KJV), and also cited for her great faith by the writer of the book of Hebrews (Heb. 11:30–31). She is also mentioned in the book of James (Jas. 2:25).

(2) A symbolic name for the forces of evil overcome by the Lord (Isa. 51:9).

RAHEL. KJV: see *Rachel*

RAIN. Moisture from the sky that sustains life on earth. Rain was sometimes withheld because of the sin of God's people (Deut. 11:17). Rain is also cited as a symbol of the truth of God's word and His abundant righteousness (Hos. 10:12).

RAINBOW. An arch of colors in the sky after the great flood, given by God as a sign of His covenant with Noah. The rainbow signified that He would never again destroy the world with water (Gen. 9:9–17).

RAISE [D, S]

Judg. 2:16 Nevertheless, the LORD *r'd* up judges

Ps. 41:10 LORD, be merciful to me and *r* me up

Ps. 113:7 He [God] *r's* up the poor out of the dust

Jer. 23:5 I [God] will *r* to David a righteous Branch

Amos 9:11 On that day I [God] will *r* up the tabernacle of David

Hab. 1:6 I [God] *r* up the Chaldeans, that bitter...nation

Matt. 10:8 Heal the sick, cleanse the lepers, *r* the dead

Matt. 16:21 He [Jesus] must...be killed, and be *r'd* again

John 2:19 Destroy this temple, and in three days I [Jesus] will *r* it up

John 5:21 as the Father *r's* up the dead and gives them life

Acts 10:40 God *r'd* Him [Jesus] up the third day

Rom. 6:4 as Christ was *r'd*...we also should walk in newness of life

Rom. 10:9 believe...God has *r'd* Him [Jesus] from the dead

1 Cor. 6:14 God...will also *r* us up

1 Cor. 15:16 if the dead are not raised, then Christ has not been *r'd*

2 Tim. 2:8 Jesus Christ...was *r'd* from the dead

Heb. 11:19 considering that God was able to *r* him [Isaac] up

RAM. A male sheep offered as a sacrifice by priests at the altar (Num. 15:6).

RAMAH. A town in the territory of Ephraim where the prophet Samuel was born (1 Sam. 1:19-20). Here the elders of Israel asked him to appoint a king to rule the nation (1 Sam. 8:4-5). Samuel was buried at Ramah (1 Sam. 28:3).

RAMATH-LEHI. A place in southern Israel where the judge Samson killed one thousand Philistine warriors with the jawbone of a donkey (Judg. 15:17).

RAMESES. A district of Egypt where Jacob and his descendants settled (**Gen. 47:11** • Exod. 12:37 • Num. 33:3, 5).

RAMOTH-GILEAD. A city in northern Israel where King Ahab of Israel (the Northern Kingdom) was killed in a battle with the Syrians (1 Kings 22:29-38). The city was located in Gilead, a territory of fertile pastureland on the eastern side of the Jordan River. It was originally an Amorite city that became one of Israel's six cities of refuge. *Ramoth-in-Gilead* (Deut. 4:43 • Josh. 20:8 • 1 Chron. 6:80). *Ramah*: 2 Kings 8:29. *Ramoth*: 1 Kings 22:3

RAMPART. A low wall or embankment built as a defensive barrier for a walled city (Lam. 2:8).

RAM'S HORN. An instrument fashioned from the horn of a male sheep. It was blown like a trumpet to summon worshippers as well as warriors (Josh. 6:4–13).

RAN

Gen. 18:2 when he [Abraham] saw them [three visitors], he *r* to meet them

Gen. 33:4 Esau *r* to meet him [Jacob] and embraced him

Exod. 9:23 LORD sent thunder and hail, and the fire *r* along on the ground

Matt. 28:8 they [the women] departed...and *r* to bring His [Jesus'] disciples word

Mark 5:6 when he [the demoniac] saw Jesus far off, he *r* and worshipped Him

Luke 8:33 the herd [of pigs] *r* violently down a steep place into the lake

Gal. 5:7 You *r* well. Who hindered you

RANSOM. See *Redeemer*

RANSOM

Prov. 13:8 The *r* of a man's life are his riches

Hos. 13:14 I [God] will *r* them from the power of the grave

Mark 10:45 the Son of Man...to give His life as a *r* for many

1 Tim. 2:6 Who [Jesus] gave Himself as a *r* for all

RAPTURE. A doctrine which deals with the transformation of believers into a glorified state at Christ's return (Phil. 3:20–21). The doctrine is based on the apostle Paul's description of this event: "The dead in Christ shall rise first. Then we who are alive and remain shall be caught up together with them in the clouds to meet the Lord in the air" (1 Thes. 4:16–17). Bible interpreters disagree on the exact timing of the rapture. Some believe it will occur before the second coming of Christ and the great tribulation that will strike the earth. Others believe it will happen at the same time as His return.

READY

Exod. 17:4 They are almost *r* to stone me [Moses]

Job 17:1 My [Job's] days are extinct. The graves are *r* for me

Ps. 86:5 You, Lord, are good, and *r* to forgive

Luke 12:40 you also be *r*...the Son of Man is coming

Luke 22:33 Lord, I [Peter] am *r* to go with You... to death

Rom. 1:15 I [Paul] am *r* to preach the gospel... at Rome

2 Tim. 4:6 For I [Paul] am now *r* to be offered

1 Pet. 3:15 always be *r* to give an answer to every man

REAP [ING, S]

Lev. 19:9 you shall not wholly *r* the corners of your field

Job 4:8 those who...sow wickedness *r* the same

Ps. 126:5 Those who sow in tears shall *r* in joy

Prov. 22:8 He who sows iniquity shall *r* vanity

Hos. 8:7 they have sown the wind...*r* the whirlwind

Matt. 25:24 a hard man, *r'ing* where you have not sown

Luke 12:24 Consider the ravens, for they neither sow nor *r*

John 4:37 One sows and and another *r's*

2 Cor. 9:6 he who sows bountifully shall also *r* bountifully

Gal. 6:7 whatever a man sows, that he shall also *r*

Gal. 6:9 we shall *r*, if we do not faint

REAPING. The practice of harvesting grain at the end of the growing season. The reapers often left some stalks of grain to be gathered by poor people (Ruth 2:3, 14).

REASON

1 Sam. 12:7 stand still, that I [Samuel] may *r* with you before the Lord

Job 13:3 I desire to *r* with God

Isa. 1:18 Come now, and let us *r* together, says the LORD

Dan. 4:36 At the same time my *r* returned to me [Nebuchadnezzar]

Matt. 16:8 O you of little faith, why do you *r* among yourselves

James 3:17 wisdom that is from above is...easy to *r* with

1 Pet. 3:15 answer...every man who ask you a *r* for the hope that is in you

REBA. One of five Midianite princes killed by Joshua's army in the plains of Moab (Josh. 13:21).

REBECCA. KJV: see *Rebekah*

REBEKAH. The wife of Isaac and the mother of his twin sons, Jacob and Esau. She showed favoritism toward Jacob (Gen. 25:28), even conspiring with him to fool Isaac into blessing Jacob rather than the oldest son, Esau. When Esau threatened to kill Jacob, Rebekah sent Jacob to live with her brother Laban in Haran (Gen. 27:41–45). After Rebekah died, she was buried in the family tomb at Machpelah (Gen. 49:30–31). She is also mentioned in Gen. 22:23; 24:15–67; 26:7–8, 35; 28:5 • Rom. 9:10.

REBUKE [D, S]

Ps. 6:1 O LORD, do not *r* me in Your anger

Ps. 50:8 I [God] will not *r* you for your sacrifices

Ps. 119:21 You [God] have *r'd* the proud who are cursed

Prov. 9:7 He who *r's* a scorner gets shame for himself

Prov. 27:5 Open *r* is better than secret love

Eccles. 7:5 It is better to hear the *r* of the wise

Ezek. 25:17 I [God] will execute...vengeance... with furious *r's*

Nah. 1:4 He [God] *r's* the sea and makes it dry

Matt. 16:22 Peter took Him [Jesus] and began to *r* Him

Mark 8:33 He [Jesus] *r'd* Peter, saying, Get behind me, Satan!

Luke 8:24 Then He [Jesus] arose and *r'd* the wind

Titus 2:15 These things speak...and *r* with all authority

Rev. 3:19 As many as I [Jesus] love, I *r* and chasten

RECEIVE [D, ING, S]

Job 2:10 r good at the hand of God, and...not *r* evil

Prov. 19:20 Hear counsel and *r* instruction

Isa. 40:2 Jerusalem...has *r'd* double from the LORD's hand

Mal. 3:10 there will not be enough room to *r* it [God's blessing]

Matt. 7:8 For everyone who asks *r's*

Matt. 10:8 Freely you have *r'd*; freely give

Matt. 11:5 blind *r* their sight and the lame walk

Matt. 18:5 whoever *r's* one such little child...*r's* Me [Jesus]

Matt. 21:22 whatever you ask in prayer, believing, you shall *r*

Mark 10:15 whoever shall not *r* the kingdom of God as a little child

Luke 23:41 we [two thieves] *r* the due reward of our deeds

John 1:11 He [Jesus] came to His own...His own did not *r* Him

John 3:27 man can *r* nothing except what is given him from heaven

John 14:3 I [Jesus] will come again and *r* you to Myself

John 20:22 He [Jesus] breathed on them [the disciples] and said... *R* the Holy Spirit

Acts 1:8 you [the apostles] shall *r* power after... Holy Spirit has come

Acts 8:17 they [the Samaritans] *r'd* the Holy Spirit

Acts 17:11 they [the Bereans] *r'd* the word with all readiness of mind

Acts 20:35 It is more blessed to give than to *r*

Rom. 8:15 you have *r'd* the Spirit of adoption

1 Cor. 2:14 natural man does not *r* not the things of the Spirit

1 Cor. 3:14 If any man's work...remains, he shall *r* a reward

Heb. 11:8 a place that he [Abraham] would later *r* as an inheritance

Heb. 11:13 died in faith, not having *r'd* the promises

Jas. 1:12 man who endures temptation...shall *r* the crown of life

Jas. 4:3 You ask and do not *r* because you ask wrongly

1 Pet. 1:9 r'ing the result of your faith, even... salvation

1 Pet. 5:4 you shall *r* a crown of glory that does not fade away

Rev. 4:11 You are worthy, O Lord, to *r* glory and honor

RECHAB. Father of Jehonadab and ancestor of the Rechabites (2 Kings 10:15–23 • Jer. 35:6–19).

RECHABITES. A tribal group that lived in tents as nomads and abstained from drinking wine. The prophet Jeremiah pointed to them as a model of sacrifice and commitment, in contrast to the waywardness of the people of Judah (the Southern Kingdom) (Jer. 35:1–19).

RECKON. KJV: see *Consider*; *Count*; *Settle*

RECONCILE [D, ING]

Matt. 5:24 be *r'd* to your brother...then...offer your gift

2 Cor. 5:19 God was in Christ, *r'ing* the world to Himself

2 Cor. 5:20 ask you on Christ's behalf, be *r'd* to God

Eph. 2:16 He [Jesus] might *r* both to God...by the cross

RECONCILIATION. The process by which humankind's separation from God is replaced by a relationship of peace and fellowship. Sin barred people from fellowship with a holy God. But His Son's atoning death paid the penalty demanded for human sin, allowing hopeless sinners into God's presence (2 Cor. 5:18).

RECONCILIATION

2 Cor. 5:18 God...has given to us the ministry of *r*

Heb. 2:17 He [Jesus] might...make *r* for the sins of the people

RECORDER. An official who kept records of a king's administration and served as a counselor or advisor (2 Kings 18:18, 37).

REDEEM [ED, ING, S]

Ps. 26:11 R me, and be merciful to me

Ps. 34:22 The LORD *r's* the soul of His servants

Ps. 49:15 But God will *r* my soul from...the grave

Ps. 77:15 You [God] have...*r'ed* Your people

Ps. 107:2 Let the *r'ed* of the LORD say so

Isa. 43:1 Do not fear, for I [God] have *r'ed* you [Israel]

Isa. 50:2 Is My [God's] hand shortened...that it cannot *r*

Isa. 52:9 the LORD...has *r'ed* Jerusalem

Luke 1:68 the Lord...has visited and *r'ed* His people

Gal. 3:13 Christ has *r'ed* us from the curse of the law

Gal. 4:5 to *r* those who were under the law

Eph. 5:16 r'ing the time because the days are evil

Col. 4:5 Walk in wisdom...*r'ing* the time

Titus 2:14 He [Jesus] might *r* us from all iniquity

REDEEMER. A name for both God the Father and God the Son. In the OT, the name reflects the concept of the kinsman-redeemer. In the close-knit families and clans of Bible times, the nearest relative of a family member in trouble was expected to come to that person's rescue. The prophet Isaiah also referred to the coming Messiah as a Redeemer (Isa. 59:20). But Jesus would be a rescuer of a different type. He would free God's people from their bondage to sin through His atoning death.

REDEMPTION

Ps. 130:7 for with the LORD there is...abundant *r*

Rom. 3:24 justified...through the *r* that is in Christ Jesus

Eph. 1:7 we have *r* through His [Jesus'] blood

Heb. 9:12 by His [Jesus'] own blood He...obtained eternal *r*

RED HEIFER. An unblemished cow or ox that had never been yoked. In OT times, It was used as a sacrificial offering (Num. 19:1–9).

RED SEA. The traditional name of a body of water between Egypt and Arabia that the Israelites crossed when fleeing from the Egyptian army. The story of the Israelites' escape in Exodus 14 refers to it simply as "the sea," though Moses' song of celebration in the following chapter specifies "the Red Sea" (Exod. 15:4). Several theories about the identity of this body of water have been suggested. These range from the Gulf of Suez to the Gulf of Aqaba to one of the shallow lakes in the marshlands south of the Gulf of Aqaba. No matter its location, the crossing of the was clearly a miracle that God provided to deliver His people (Exod. 14:16–29; 15:4, 22). It is also mentioned in Exod. 10:19 • Num. 33:10–11.

REED. A grass used to make papyrus, an ancient writing material (Isa. 19:7). The word also symbolizes weakness and fragility (Matt. 11:7).

REFINE. To separate impurities from metal by heating the ore (see Jer. 6:29). This process symbolizes God's purification of His people through hardship and affliction (Isa. 48:10). The prophet Malachi compared the Lord to a "refiner's fire" (Mal. 3:2), emphasizing His role as the ultimate judge over humankind.

REFUGE. A name of God that emphasizes His role as a dependable source of protection for His people. Moses referred to God by this name as the Israelites prepared to enter Canaan (Deut. 33:27). They faced a formidable enemy in the Canaanite inhabitants. God alone could provide safety and security as they struggled for possession of the land.

REGENERATION. A process that occurs when the Holy Spirit changes a person's inner spiritual nature. The apostle Paul explained the need for regeneration when he told the believers at Ephesus, "You...were dead in trespasses and sins" (Eph. 2:1). In their natural sinful state, they were unable to respond to the Lord. But God, Paul went on to say, made them "alive together with Christ" (Eph. 2:5). This rebirth made them capable of responding to God's offer of salvation (Eph. 2:5–6).

REGENERATION

Matt. 19:28 in the *r*...you who...followed Me [Jesus] shall...sit on...thrones

Titus 3:5 He [Jesus] saved us, by the washing of *r*

REHOB. A city near the source of the Jordan River scouted by the spies who investigated the land of Canaan (Num. 13:21).

REHOBOAM. The son and successor of Solomon as king of Judah. Rather than relaxing Solomon's oppressive policies as some of his subjects requested, Rehoboam vowed to make them even worse (1 Kings 12:1–24). This drove the ten northern tribes of Solomon's kingdom to rebel and establish their own country. So from the time of Rehoboam's rule, the Israelites were divided into two factions: the Southern Kingdom known as Judah and the Northern Kingdom that was called Israel. Like his father Solomon had done, Rehoboam also built up a huge harem. Many of these wives were foreigners whom he catered to by setting up shrines for their worship of false gods. The Lord punished this sin by sending the pharaoh of Egypt to plunder the temple and Rehoboam's royal palace (1 Kings 14:21–31). Rehoboam is also mentioned in 1 Kings 11:43; 15:6 • 1 Chron. 3:10 • 2 Chron. 9:31; 10:1–18; 11:1–22; 12:1–16; 13:7 • Matt. 1:7.

REHOBOTH. A well dug by Isaac in the valley of Gerar south of Beer-Sheba (Gen. 26:17–22).

REHUM. (1) A Persian official who opposed the rebuilding project in Jerusalem after the Exile (Ezra 4:8–9, 17, 23).

(2) A man who helped rebuild the walls of Jerusalem after the Exile (Neh. 3:17).

REI. A man who supported Solomon as David's successor when David's son Adonijah tried to become the new king (1 Kings 1:8).

REIGN [ED, S]

Gen. 37:8 Shall you [Joseph] indeed *r* over us?

Judg. 9:8 The trees...said to the olive tree, *R* over us!

2 Sam. 5:4 David was thirty years old when he began to *r*

1 Chron. 29:26 David the son of Jesse *r'ed* over all Israel

Ps. 47:8 God *r's* over the nations

Ps. 93:1 The Lord *r's*; He is clothed with majesty

Ps. 146:10 The Lord shall *r* for ever

Jer. 23:5 a King shall *r* and prosper...carry out judgment

Luke 1:33 He [Jesus] shall *r* over the house of Jacob forever

Rom. 5:14 death *r'ed* from Adam to Moses

Rom. 6:12 do not let sin *r* in your mortal body

1 Cor. 15:25 He [Jesus] must *r* until...all enemies under His feet

Rev. 11:15 Christ...shall *r* forever and ever

Rev. 19:6 Alleluia. For the Lord God omnipotent *r's*

REJECT [ED]

1 Sam. 15:26 you [Saul] have *r'ed* the word of the Lord

Isa. 53:3 He [God's servant] was despised and *r'ed* by men

Mark 7:9 you [Pharisees] *r* the commandment of God

Mark 12:10 The stone that the builders *r'ed*... head of the corner

Luke 17:25 He [Jesus] must suffer...and be *r'ed* by this generation

REJOICE [D, ING, S]

Deut. 30:9 for the Lord will again *r* over you [Israel] for good

1 Sam. 2:1 My [Hannah's] heart *r's* in the Lord

1 Chron. 16:10 let the hearts of those who seek the Lord *r*

Job 8:21 Until He [God] fills...your lips with *r'ing*

Ps. 5:11 let all those who put their trust in You [God] *r*

Ps. 19:8 statutes of the Lord are right, *r'ing* the heart

Ps. 32:11 Be glad in the Lord, and *r*, you righteous

Ps. 40:16 Let all those who seek You [God] *r* and be glad in You

Ps. 63:7 in the shadow of Your [God's] wings I will *r*

Ps. 97:1 The LORD reigns; let the earth *r*

Ps. 108:7 God has spoken in His holiness: I will *r*

Ps. 118:24 day that the LORD has made; we will *r* and be glad

Ps. 119:14 I have *r'd* in the way of Your [God's] testimonies

Ps. 126:6 shall doubtless return with *r'ing*, bringing his sheaves

Prov. 5:18 and *r* with the wife of your youth

Prov. 15:30 The light of the eyes *r's* the heart

Eccles. 11:9 R, O young man, in your youth

Isa. 29:19 poor...shall *r* in the Holy One of Israel

Joel 2:21 be glad and *r*, for the LORD will do great things

Hab. 3:18 I will *r* in the God of my salvation

Matt. 2:10 they [the wise men] *r'd* with exceedingly great joy

Matt. 5:12 R...for great is your reward in heaven

Luke 15:6 R with me, for I have found my sheep

John 8:56 Abraham *r'd* to see My [Jesus'] day

Rom. 12:12 R'ing in hope, patient in tribulation

Rom. 12:15 R with those who *r*...weep with those who weep

Phil. 1:18 Christ is preached, and in it I [Paul] do *r*

REJOICE IN THE LORD

Ps. 33:1 R-i-t-L, O you righteous

Ps. 97:12 R-i-t-L...and give thanks at the remembrance of His holiness

Hab. 3:18 I will *r-i-t-L*. I will rejoice in the God of my salvation

Phil. 3:1 Finally, my brothers, *r-i-t-L*

Phil. 4:4 R-i-t-L always, and again I say, rejoice

REKEM. A Midianite king killed by the Israelites in the time of Moses (Num. 31:8).

REMAIN [S]

Eccles. 1:4 another generation comes...earth *r's* for ever

John 3:36 does not believe the Son...wrath of God *r's* on him

1 Cor. 3:14 any man's work that he has built on it *r's*

1 Cor. 13:13 faith, hope, love *r*...greatest of these is love

Phil. 1:25 I [Paul] shall *r*...with you all for your... joy

REMEMBER [ED, ING, S]

Gen. 8:1 God *r'ed* Noah and every living thing... in the ark

Gen. 9:16 that I [God] may *r* the everlasting covenant

Exod. 2:24 God heard their [Israel's] groaning, and God *r'ed* His covenant

Exod. 20:8 R the sabbath day, to keep it holy

Deut. 8:18 you shall *r* the LORD your God

Deut. 15:15 *r* that you [Israel] were a bondman in...Egypt

Ps. 20:7 we will *r* the name of the LORD our God

Ps. 25:7 Do not *r* the sins of my youth or my transgressions

Ps. 45:17 make Your [God's] name to be *r'ed*

Ps. 77:10 I will *r* the years of the right hand of the Most High

Ps. 78:39 He [God] *r'ed* that they were but flesh

Ps. 98:3 He [God] has *r'ed* His mercy...toward... Israel

Ps. 103:14 He [God] knows our form; He *r's* that we are dust

Ps. 137:1 we [Israelites] wept, when we *r'ed* Zion

Ps. 137:7 R, O LORD, the children of Edom

Eccles. 12:1 R now your Creator in the days of your youth

Jer. 31:34 I [God] will *r* their sin no more

Jon. 2:7 my [Jonah's] soul fainted...I *r'ed* the LORD

Matt. 5:23 there [at the altar] *r* that your brother has anything against you

Luke 22:61 And Peter *r'ed* the word of the Lord

Luke 23:42 Lord, *r* me [thief] when You come into Your kingdom

Luke 24:8 they [the disciples] *r'ed* His [Jesus'] words

John 16:21 as soon as she has delivered the child, she does not *r* the anguish

1 Thes. 1:3 *r'ing* without ceasing your work of faith

2 Tim. 2:8 R that Jesus Christ...was raised from the dead

Heb. 10:17 I [God] will *r* their sins and iniquities no more

REMEMBRANCE

Ps. 30:4 give thanks at the *r* of His [God's] holiness

Ps. 102:12 You, O LORD, shall endure forever... Your *r* to all generations

Luke 22:19 This is My [Jesus'] body... Do this in *r* of Me

John 14:26 the Comforter...shall...bring to your *r* all things

REMISSION. God's forgiveness of sin. The Greek term behind this English word suggests that God's forgiveness is active rather than passive. He has actually taken the initiative through the death of His Son to set people free from sin's bondage (Acts 2:38).

REMISSION

Heb. 9:22 without the shedding of blood is no *r*

Heb. 10:18 where there is *r*...there is no more offering for sin

REMISSION OF SINS

Matt. 26:28 My [Jesus'] blood...is shed for many for the *r-o-s*

Mark 1:4 John...preached the baptism of repentance for the *r-o-s*

Luke 24:47 repentance and *r-o-s* should be preached...among all nations

Acts 2:38 be baptized in the name of Jesus Christ for the *r-o-s*

Acts 10:43 whoever believes in Him [Jesus] shall receive *r-o-s*

REMNANT. A small group of God's people who remain loyal to Him in spite of the sin and idolatry of the surrounding culture. This theme of the faithful few occurs throughout the Bible, beginning with Moses. He predicted that the Israelites would eventually be scattered among the nations, but a portion of them would survive and reclaim their territory (Deut. 28:62–68). The prophet Micah declared that God would make a new beginning with "the remnant of Israel"

(Mic. 2:12). In the NT, the apostle Paul declared that the new faithful remnant was the church founded by Jesus when the nation of Israel failed to bring other nations to the Lord. God continues to work in the world today through the church (Rom. 11:5).

REMPHAN. KJV: see *Rephan*

RENDER [ED, ING]

Ps. 38:20 Those...who *r* evil for good are my adversaries

Prov. 12:14 the recompence of a man's hands shall be *r'ed* to him

Luke 20:25 r to Caesar the things that are Caesar's

Rom. 2:6 who [God] will *r* to every man according to his deeds

1 Cor. 7:3 husband *r* due benevolence to the wife

1 Thes. 5:15 See that no one *r's* evil for evil to any man

1 Pet. 3:9 not *r'ing* evil for evil or reviling for reviling

RENEW [ED, ING]

Ps. 51:10 clean heart, O God...*r* a right spirit within me

Ps. 104:30 You [God] *r* the face of the earth

Isa. 40:31 those who wait on the LORD shall *r* their strength

Rom. 12:2 be transformed by the *r'ing* of your mind

2 Cor. 4:16 yet the inner man is being *r'ed* day by day

REPAY

Gen. 50:15 Joseph...will certainly *r* us for all the evil that we did

Deut. 32:6 Do you thus *r* the Lord, O foolish... people

Job 41:11 Who has gone before Me [God], that I should *r* him?

Ps. 37:21 The wicked borrows and does not *r*

Ps. 54:5 He [God] shall *r* evil to my enemies

Ps. 116:12 r to the LORD for all His benefits toward me

Prov. 20:22 Do not say, I will *r* evil, but wait on the LORD

Jer. 51:56 the LORD God of recompense shall surely *r*

Luke 11:35 when I [Good Samaritan] come again, I will *r* you [innkeeper]

Rom. 12:17 Do not *r* evil for evil to any man

Heb. 10:30 Vengeance belongs to Me; I will *r*, says the Lord

REPENT [ED, S]

Job 42:6 I [Job] hate myself and *r* in dust and ashes

Matt. 4:17 Jesus began to preach and to say, *R*

Luke 11:32 The men of Nineveh...*r'ed* at the preaching of Jonah

Luke 15:7 more joy in heaven over one sinner who *r's*

Luke 17:3 if he [your brother] *r's*, forgive him

Acts 2:38 Peter said... *R*, and every one of you be baptized

2 Cor 12:21 I [Paul] shall mourn many who have...not *r'ed*

Rev. 3:19 I [Jesus] rebuke and chasten...be zealous and *r*

REPENTANCE. The act of turning from sin and changing one's orientation from rebellion against God to acceptance of His will and lordship (Acts 2:38). Repentance is a gift of God's love and grace that brings sinners into fellowship with Him. But repentance is not just for unbelievers. It is also essential for Christians who yield to temptation and fall into sin. The apostle John expressed this truth by writing, "If we confess our sins, He is faithful and just to forgive us our sins and to cleanse us from all unrighteousness" (1 John 1:9).

REPENTANCE

Matt. 9:13 I [Jesus] have come to call...sinners to *r*

Luke 24:47 *r*...should be preached...among all nations

2 Cor. 7:10 godly sorrow produces *r* to salvation

2 Pet. 3:9 any should perish, but that all should come to *r*

REPHAIAH. A man who helped rebuild the walls of Jerusalem after the Exile (Neh. 3:9).

REPHAIM. (1) A race of giants who lived in Canaan before Abraham's time (Gen. 14:5). *Rephaims*: KJV.

(2) A fertile valley near Jerusalem where David defeated the Philistines (2 Sam. 5:18–25; 23:13 • 1 Chron. 11:15; 14:9 • Isa. 17:5).

REPHAN. A star god of the Babylonians worshipped secretly by the Israelites—an act for which they were taken into exile by the Babylonians (Acts 7:41–43). *Remphan*: KJV.

REPROACH [ED, ES]. See also *Taunt*

Ps. 31:11 I was a *r* among all my enemies

Ps. 55:12 it was not an enemy who *r'ed* me

Ps. 102:8 My enemies *r* me all day long

Prov. 14:34 but sin is a *r* to any people

Heb. 11:26 esteeming the *r* of Christ greater riches than...treasures in Egypt

Heb. 13:13 go forth to Him [Jesus]...bearing His *r*

1 Pet. 4:14 you are *r'ed* for the name of Christ, happy are you

REPROBATE. A word meaning "depraved" or "corrupt," The apostle Paul used the term for those who reject God (Rom. 1:28).

REPROOF. A sharp rebuke or criticism. John the Baptist reproved Herod Antipas for his incestuous marriage (Luke 3:19–20).

REPROVE [D]. See also *Convict; Rebuke*

Ps. 105:14 He [God] *r'd* kings for their [Israel's] sakes

Eph. 5:13 all things that are *r'ed* are revealed by the light

2 Tim. 4:2 *R*, rebuke, exhort with all longsuffering

REPUTATION

Eccles. 10:1 a little foolishness to him who has a *r* for wisdom

Dan. 4:35 inhabitants of the earth have no *r*

Acts 6:3 choose from among you seven men of good *r*

Phil. 2:7 made Himself [Jesus] of no *r* and took... form of a servant

RESCUE. See also *Deliver, Save*

Gen. 37:22 Reuben said...that he might *r* him [Joseph]

Ps. 37:17 R my soul from their destruction, my dear life from the lions

Ps. 144:7 Send Your [God's] hand from above; *r* me and deliver me

Jer. 1:8 I am with you to *r* you, says the LORD

2 Tim. 2:26 they may *r* themselves out of the snare of the devil

RESH. Twentieth letter of the Hebrew alphabet, used as a heading over Psalm 119:153–160. In the Hebrew language, the first line of each of these eight verses begins with this letter.

RESIST [ED, S]

Matt. 5:39 I [Jesus] say to you, Do not *r* evil

Acts 7:51 You always *r* the Holy Spirit

Heb. 12:4 You have not yet *r'ed* to bloodshed

Jas. 4:6 God *r's* the proud but gives grace to the humble

Jas. 4:7 R the devil and he will flee from you

RESPECT

Gen. 4:4 the LORD had *r* for Abel and for his offering

Exod. 2:25 God saw the children of Israel, and... had *r* for them

Ps. 40:4 Blessed is that man who...does not *r* the proud

Ps. 74:20 Have *r* for the covenant

RESPECT OF PERSONS. KJV: see *Partiality*

REST. To relax or stop working. But in the biblical sense, the concept of rest refers to the Lord's promise of heavenly peace for His people. God promised His people, the Israelites, a land of rest that they could call their own (Deut. 12:10–11). This eventually happened, although their failure to trust the Lord led to a forty-year period of aimless wandering in the wilderness (Num. 14:33–35). The author of Hebrews cautioned Christian believers against making this same mistake (Heb. 4:1–11). Jesus told His followers, "Take My yoke on you and learn from Me, for I am meek and lowly in heart, and you shall find rest for your souls" (Matt.11:29).

RESTITUTION. To restore to the rightful owner something that has been wrongfully taken away. Restitution for injuries and losses of property was required by the Mosaic Law (Exod. 22:1). Zacchaeus the tax collector promised to make four-fold restitution of what he had taken from people unlawfully (Luke 19:8).

RESTORE [S]

Ps. 23:3 He [God] *r's* my soul

Ps. 51:12 R to me the joy of Your [God's] salvation

Luke 19:8 Behold, Lord...I [Zacchaeus] *r* him fourfold

Acts 1:6 Lord, will You...*r* again the kingdom to Israel

Gal. 6:1 r such a one in the spirit of meekness

RESURRECTION

Matt. 27:53 [the saints] came out of the graves after His [Jesus'] *r*

Luke 20:33 Therefore, in the *r*, whose wife is she?

John 11:25 I [Jesus] am the *r* and the life

Acts 4:33 the apostles gave witness of the *r* of...Jesus

Acts 17:32 when they [philosophers] heard of the *r*...some mocked

1 Cor. 15:13 no *r* of the dead, then Christ has not been raised

Phil. 3:10 I [Paul] may know Him [Jesus]...power of His *r*

1 Pet. 1:3 a living hope through the *r* of Jesus Christ

Rev. 20:6 Blessed...is he who has part in the first *r*

RESURRECTION AND THE LIFE, JESUS AS. See *"I Am" Statements of Jesus*

RESURRECTION OF JESUS. The return of Jesus to physical life following His death and burial. His resurrection was foretold in the Psalms (Ps. 16:10–11) and by the prophets (Isa. 53:10–12), predicted by Jesus Himself (Mark 9:9–10), and proclaimed by the apostles (Acts 2:32). It assures believers of their own bodily resurrection (1 Cor. 15:18–20), emphasizes their final victory over sin and death (1 Cor. 15:17, 26, 54, 57), and inspires faithfulness in service to Jesus (1 Cor. 15:58). He spent forty days among His followers after He was resurrected and before His ascension to the Father. Jesus used this time to show proofs that He was alive and to give them further instructions about the witness they were to bear through the church (Acts 1:1–8).

REUBEN. (1) The oldest son of Jacob who lost his birthright by committing adultery with his father's concubine (Gen. 35:22; 49:3–4). Reuben saved his brother Joseph's life by convincing his other brothers not to kill their younger sibling. When a caravan of traders happened by, they sold Joseph to them as a slave (Gen. 37:19–29). Later, Reuben and his brothers dealt with Joseph face-to-face when they came to Egypt to buy grain. When Joseph insisted that one of them be held as a hostage, Reuben reminded his siblings that they were being repaid for the way they had treated Joseph years before (Gen. 42:21–22). He is also mentioned in Gen. 29:32; 42:37; 46:8–9; 48:5.

(2) Reuben's descendants who developed into one of the twelve tribes of the nation of Israel. This tribe settled east of the Jordan River, along with Gad and Manasseh (Num. 32:1–25).

REUEL. See *Jethro*

REVEAL [ED, S]
Job 20:27 The heavens shall *r* his [man's] guilt
Isa. 40:5 glory of the LORD shall be *r'ed*
Dan. 2:28 there is a God in heaven who *r's* secrets
Matt. 16:17 flesh and blood has not *r'ed* it to you [Peter]
Luke 8:17 nothing is secret that shall not be *r'ed*
Luke 10:21 hidden these things from the wise...*r'ed* them to infants
Luke 10:22 no man knows...who the Father is...to whom the Son will *r* Him
John 9:3 that the works of God should be *r'ed* in him
Rom. 1:17 righteousness of God is *r'ed* from faith to faith
1 Cor. 3:13 it [man's work] shall be *r'ed* by fire
Phil. 3:15 God shall *r* even this to you
1 Tim. 3:16 God was *r'ed* in the flesh, justified in the Spirit

1 Pet. 1:5 kept by the power of God...ready to be *r'ed* in the last time
1 Pet. 4:13 when His [Jesus'] glory shall be *r'ed*
1 John 4:9 In this [Jesus' death] the love of God was clearly *r'ed*
Rev. 15:4 Your [God's] judgments are *r'ed*

REVELATION
Gal. 1:12 nor was I [Paul] taught it—but by the *r* of Jesus Christ
Eph. 3:3 by *r* He [God] made known to me the mystery
Rev. 1:1 The *R* of Jesus Christ, which God gave

REVELATION, BOOK OF. The last book of the NT which is known for its dramatic depiction of the end-time. It was written about AD 95 by the apostle John, one of the twelve disciples of Jesus. At this time he was imprisoned by the Roman authorities on Patmos (Rev. 1:9), a rocky island off the coast of Asia Minor. John wrote during a time of intense persecution of the Christian movement. He probably used symbols such as numbers, beasts, and angels to hide the meaning of his message from these enemies of the church. Believers understood these images, but the Roman persecutors did not have the "key" that enabled them to decode John's message.

The book of Revelation came to John under divine inspiration through a series of seven visions. These visions serve as a convenient outline of the book: (1) Christ encouraging His church against attacks (Rev. 1:9–3:22); (2) Christ the Lamb with a sealed scroll (Rev. 4:1–7:17); (3) seven angels blowing trumpets (Rev. 8:1–11:19); (4) Satan and the beast persecuting the church (Rev. 12:1–14:20); (5) seven bowls pouring out the wrath of God (Rev. 15:1–16:21); (6) divine judgment against Babylon, or Rome (Rev. 17:1–19:20); and (7) the final victory of God and His final judgment (Rev. 19:11–21). In spite of the persecution that believers were experiencing, John affirmed that the all-powerful Lord would fulfill His promises and accomplish His purpose in history. Jesus Christ would be victorious over the forces of Satan, and He would reign forever as King of kings and Lord of Lords (Rev. 19:16).

REVELATION OF GOD. The process by which the Lord makes Himself and His truth known to people. This occurs through general revelation, or His appearance in the physical world (Rom. 1:20), as well as by special revelation—His interaction with His people and His written Word, the Bible. God's initiative to reveal Himself is the only way earth-bound humans can come to know Him, since He is beyond human understanding (Ps. 139:5–6). The ultimate revelation of God and His nature came through the life and actions of His Son, Jesus (Heb. 1:1–2).

REVENGE. Retaliation against people, or "getting even" for their wrongful actions. This was a common practice in OT times (Exod. 21:23–25). But Jesus rebuked His disciples for such behavior (Luke 9:54–56) and taught them to forgive others (Matt. 5:38–44). Vengeance should be left to God, who alone is impartial in His judgment and fair in His treatment of all people (Prov. 20:22).

REVERENCE

Lev. 26:2 keep My [God's] sabbaths and *r* My sanctuary

Esther 3:2 Mordecai did not bow or show him [Haman] *r*

Luke 20:13 Perhaps they will *r* him [vineyard owner's son]

Eph. 5:33 and the wife see that she *r* her husband

Heb. 12:28 we may serve God acceptably with *r* and godly fear

REVERENCE FOR GOD. A feeling of deep respect and awe. This is often referred to as "fear of the LORD" (Psalm 19:9). The opposite of reverence for the Lord is blasphemy—or disrespect and contempt for His name and the denial that He exists (Ps. 14:1).

REVILE [D]

Matt. 5:11 Blessed are you when men *r* you

Mark 15:32 those who were crucified with Him [Jesus] *r'd* Him

1 Cor. 4:12 Being *r'd*, we bless

1 Pet. 2:23 who [Jesus], when He was *r'd*, did not *r* in return

REVIVE [ING, S]

1 Kings 17:22 the soul of the child came into him again, and he *r*

Ps. 80:18 *r* us, and we will call on Your [God's] name

Ps. 85:6 Will You [God] not *r* us again, that Your people may rejoice

Ps. 119:88 *R* me according to Your [God's] loving-kindness

Ps. 143:11 *R* me, O LORD, for Your name's sake

Isa. 57:15 I [God] dwell in the high and holy place...to *r* the spirit of the humble

Hab. 3:2 O LORD, *r* Your work in the midst of the years

Rom. 4:17 in whom he [Abraham] believed, even God, who *r's* the dead

1 Cor. 15:45 the last Adam was made a *r'ing* spirit

1 Tim. 6:13 give you charge in the sight of God, who *r* all things

REVIVING SPIRIT. A title of Jesus cited in connection with His identification as the "last Adam" (1 Cor. 15:45). Adam's act of rebellion against God brought sin and death into the world. But Jesus' perfect obedience nullified the divine curse against Adam and brought the possibility of eternal life to humankind. As the "reviving spirit," Jesus offers eternal life to all who accept Him as Savior and Lord. *Quickening spirit*: KJV.

REWARD [ED, S]

Gen. 15:1 I [God] am your [Abraham's]...exceedingly great *r*

Ps. 18:20 LORD *r'ed* me according to my righteousness

Ps. 31:23 the LORD...plentifully *r's* the proud doer

Ps. 58:11 Truly there is a *r* for the righteous

Ps. 103:10 He [God] has not...*r'ed* us according to our iniquities

Ps. 127:3 the fruit of the womb is His [God's] *r*

Prov. 17:13 Whoever *r's* evil for good, evil shall not depart from his house

Matt. 5:12 great is your *r* in heaven, for so they persecuted the prophets

Matt. 5:46 love those who love you, what *r* do you have

Luke 23:41 we [two thieves] receive the due *r* of our deeds

1 Cor. 3:8 every man shall receive his own *r*

Col. 3:24 you shall receive the *r* of the inheritance

1 Tim. 5:18 The laborer is worthy of his *r*

REZIN. A king of Syria who was killed when the army of Tiglath-pileser of Assyria invaded the region (2 **Kings** 15:37; 16:5–9 • Isa. 7:4, 8; 8:6; 9:11).

REZON. A Syrian ruler who opposed the Israelites in King Solomon's time (1 Kings 11:23–25).

RHODA. A servant girl in the home of Mary, mother of John Mark, who was shocked to see the apostle Peter standing at the door after his miraculous release from prison (Acts 12:13–16).

RHODES. A large island in the Aegean Sea where the apostle Paul stopped briefly on his way to Jerusalem (Acts 21:1). Rhodes was the site of a huge statue known as the Colossus of Rhodes, one of the seven wonders of the ancient world.

RIDDLE. A puzzling question presented as a problem to be solved. The answer to the judge Samson's riddle was revealed to the Philistines by his wife (Judg. 14:12–19).

RIGHT

Gen. 18:25 Shall not the Judge of all the earth do *r*?

Exod. 15:6 Your *r* hand, O LORD, has become glorious in power

Lev. 8:23 Moses took...blood and put it on the tip of Aaron's *r* ear

Deut. 6:18 you [Israel] shall do what is *r* and good in the sight of the LORD

Judg. 17:6 but every man did what was *r* in his own eyes

2 Sam. 19:43 we [men of Israel]...have more *r* to David than you [men of Judah]

1 Kings 15:5 David did what was *r* in the eyes of the LORD

2 Kings 18:3 he [Hezekiah] did what was *r* in the sight of the LORD

Job 6:25 How forcible are *r* words

Ps. 9:4 You [God] have maintained my *r* and my cause

Ps. 16:11 at Your [God's] *r* hand there are pleasures forevermore

Ps. 51:10 Create in me [David] a clean heart... renew a *r* spirit within me

Prov. 16:25 way that seems *r* to a man...its end are the ways of death

Eccles. 4:4 for...every *r* work a man is envied by his neighbor.

Song of Sol. 8:3 His left hand should be under my head...*r* hand should embrace me

Isa. 30:10 Do not prophesy *r* things to us. Speak smooth things to us

Isa. 41:10 I will uphold you with My righteous *r* hand

Ezek. 19:27 when the wicked man...does what is...*r*, he shall save his soul

Matt. 5:29 if your *r* eye causes you to stumble, pluck it out

Matt. 25:33 He [Jesus] shall set the sheep on His *r* hand...goats on the left

John 13:13 You [disciples] call Me [Jesus] Master and Lord, and you are *r*

Acts 6:2 not *r* that we [the apostles] should leave...word of God...serve tables

1 Cor. 9:4 Do we [apostles] not have the *r* to eat and to drink?

Gal. 2:9 they [James, Peter, and John] gave to me [Paul]...*r* hand of fellowship

Rev. 22:14 those who do His commandments... have the *r* to the tree of life

RIGHTEOUS [LY, NESS]

Gen. 15:6 the LORD...counted it to him [Abram] for *r'ness*

Gen. 18:23 Will You [God]...destroy the *r* with the wicked

Job 15:14 What is man...that he should be *r*

Job 32:1 because he [Job] was *r* in his own eyes

Ps. 1:6 For the LORD knows the way of the *r*

Ps. 9:8 And He [God] shall judge the world in *r'ness*

Ps. 19:9 judgments of the LORD are true and *r* altogether

Ps. 23:3 He [God] leads me in the paths of *r'ness*

Ps. 35:28 my tongue shall speak of Your [God's] *r'ness*

Ps. 37:16 A little that a *r* man has is better than... riches

Ps. 37:29 The *r* shall inherit the land...dwell in it forever

Ps. 45:7 You [God] love *r'ness* and hate wickedness

Ps. 97:6 The heavens declare His [God's] *r'ness*

Ps. 119:137 *R* You are, O LORD, and upright are Your judgments

Ps. 129:4 LORD is *r*; he has cut apart the cords of the wicked

Ps. 145:17 The LORD is *r* in all His ways...holy in all His works

Prov. 10:11 The mouth of a *r* man is a well of life

Prov. 14:34 *R'ness* exalts a nation

Prov. 15:29 The LORD...hears the prayer of the *r*

Prov. 16:8 Better is a little with *r'ness* than great revenues

Prov. 31:9 judge *r'ly*, and plead the cause of the poor

Isa. 62:2 the Gentiles shall see Your [God's] *r'ness*

Jer. 23:5 I [God] will raise to David a *r* Branch

Amos 5:24 let judgment run down as waters... *r'ness* like a mighty stream

Mal. 4:2 Sun of *r'ness* shall arise with healing in His wings

Matt. 5:6 Blessed are those who...thirst after *r'ness*

Matt. 5:20 unless your *r'ness* exceeds...*r'ness* of the scribes

Matt. 6:33 But seek first the kingdom of God and His *r'ness*

Luke 5:32 I [Jesus] came to call not the *r* but sinner to repentance

Luke 23:47 Certainly this [Jesus] was a *r* man

Rom. 1:17 *r'ness* of God is revealed from faith to faith

Rom. 3:10 As it is written: There is no one *r*, no, not one

Rom. 4:3 Abraham believed God, and it was counted...*r'ness*

Rom. 5:19 through the obedience of One [Jesus] many...made *r*

Rom. 10:10 with the heart man believes to *r'ness*

2 Cor. 5:21 might be made the *r'ness* of God in Him [Jesus]

2 Cor. 6:14 what fellowship does *r'ness* have with unrighteousness

Eph. 6:14 having on the breastplate of *r'ness*

2 Tim. 4:8 laid up for me [Paul] a crown of *r'ness*

Jas. 5:16 fervent prayer of a *r* man avails much

1 Pet. 3:12 For the eyes of the Lord are on the *r*

1 Pet. 3:14 if you suffer for *r'ness'* sake, happy are you

RIGHTEOUSNESS. An attribute or characteristic of God that signifies His holiness, moral purity, justice, and acts of goodness. The term comes from a root word that means "straightness." The psalmist declared that only the Lord is perfectly straight or upright in "all His ways" (Ps. 145:17). The sinful nature of humans prevents them from reaching God's standard of righteous living. But through faith in Jesus, God's righteousness is imputed or granted to believers (Titus 3:5).

RIGHTEOUS SERVANT. A name or title for the coming Messiah that occurs in the Servant Songs of the prophet Isaiah (Isa. 53:11). This divine Servant would undergo great suffering while carrying out His mission of redemption for the entire world. Jesus identified Himself specifically as the Suffering Servant from God the Father whom Isaiah predicted. At the beginning of His public ministry, He quoted Isaiah's first Servant Song (Isa. 42:1–4 • Matt. 12:18–21). The implication of His words was that the mission of this divine agent from the Lord was being fulfilled through Jesus' teaching and healing ministry. On one occasion His disciples began to argue over who would occupy the places of honor at His side in His future glory. He gently reminded them: "Whoever of you wants to be first must be servant of all. For even the Son of Man did not come to be ministered to, but to minister, and to give his life as a ransom for many" (Mark 10:44–45).

RIGHT HAND. A symbol of power and strength (Ps. 77:10). Jesus is exalted in power at God's right hand (Eph. 1:20).

RIGHT HAND OF GOD

Mark 16:19 He [Jesus] was received into heaven...sat on the *r-h-o-G*

Acts 7:55 he [Stephen]...saw...Jesus standing at the *r-h-o-G*

Col. 3:1 seek those things...above, where Christ sits on the *r-h-o-G*

Heb. 10:12 this Man [Jesus]...sat down at the *r-h-o-G*

1 Pet. 3:22 who [Jesus] has gone into heaven... at the *r-h-o-G*

RIMMON. A Syrian god of rain and storm worshipped by Naaman the leper (2 Kings 5:18).

RISE

Exod. 8:20 the Lord said to Moses, *R* up early in the morning

Lev. 19:32 You shall *r* up before the white head and honor...the old man

Num. 10:35 Moses said, *R* up, Lord, and let Your enemies be scattered

Num. 24:17 a Star out of Jacob, and a Scepter shall *r* out of Israel

Deut. 6:7 you shall teach them [God's words]... when you *r* up

1 Sam. 24:7 David stopped his servants...and did not allow them to *r* against Saul

Job 9:7 He [God] commands the sun, and it does not *r*

Ps. 3:1 Many are those who *r* up against me

Ps. 119:62 At midnight I will *r* to give thanks to You [God]

Prov. 31:28 Her children *r* up and call her blessed

Isa. 33:10 Now I will *r*, says the LORD. Now I will be exalted

Mark 8:31 the Son of Man must...be killed, and after three days *r* again

John 20:9 as yet they [the disciples] did not know...that He [Jesus] must *r* again

Acts 10:13 a voice came to him, *R*, Peter; kill and eat

1 Thes. 4:16 the Lord Himself shall descend... And the dead in Christ shall *r* first

RIZPAH. The concubine of King Saul whose two sons were hanged by the Gibeonites during David's reign. David arranged for them to be given a decent burial, along with the bodies of Saul and Jonathan (2 Sam. 21:5–14).

ROBE. A long, one-piece garment worn as the outer covering for the body. The soldiers mocked Jesus at His crucifixion by dressing Him in a scarlet robe (Matt. 27:28).

ROBOAM. KJV: see *Rehoboam*

ROCK OF ISRAEL. A title of God that refers to His protection and dependability. King David used this name in the poem identified as his final words (2 Sam. 23:3). The Hebrew word behind *rock* refers to massive outcroppings such as those on a mountainside. These formations remain fixed in place from one generation to the next, just as God is fixed and dependable, not subject to the ravages of time. David had found the Lord to be the eternal, unmovable God on whom he had depended throughout his life. Other names of God that use this imagery are "rock of my refuge" (Ps. 94:22), "rock of my salvation" (2 Sam. 22:47), and "rock of my strength" (Ps. 62:7).

ROMAN EMPIRE. The powerful pagan empire that dominated the ancient world during NT times (Rom. 1:7). Founded in 753 BC, the nation was governed by kings until it became a republic. Rome extended her borders greatly during the republic period, eventually annexing the territory of Israel and Syria and dominating the vast land mass that bordered the Mediterranean Sea. Caesar Augustus became emperor in 27 BC and was reigning when Jesus was born (Luke 2:1–7). Jesus was crucified by Roman soldiers under sentence from Pilate, the Roman governor of Judea (Matt. 27:24–26).

ROMANS, EPISTLE TO THE. An epistle of the NT on the themes of righteousness and salvation, written by the apostle Paul to Christians at Rome. It is considered his most important letter because it expounds on the concept of justification by faith alone. According to Paul, every person stands in need of God's grace. This was certainly true in the case of Gentiles, or non-Jews, because they worshipped created things rather than God the Creator (Rom. 1:24–25). But the Jewish people were in the same situation, although they claimed to be superior to the Gentiles because they knew God's revealed will through His law. The Jews were condemned by this very law because of their failure to keep it. Thus, Paul pointed out, there was no difference between Jews and Gentiles because "all have sinned and come short of the glory of God" (Rom. 3:23). The good news is that God reaches out to sinners. He expressed His love in the most dramatic way through the death of His righteous Son, Jesus, who died on behalf of the unrighteous. Sinners can receive this grace through committing themselves to Him in faith.

Throughout Christian history, Paul's epistle to the Romans has served as a catalyst for reform within the church. Martin Luther was transformed when he rediscovered the principle of salvation by grace through faith alone while studying Romans. This truth led to the greatest reform the church has ever experienced—the Protestant Reformation of the 1600s.

ROME, CITY OF. Capital city of the Roman Empire (Rom. 1:7) and the place where the apostle Paul was imprisoned during his final days. This is probably where he died as a martyr (2 Tim. 4:6–8). Rome was a prosperous city of more than one million people in Paul's time. It contained scores of temples dedicated to the worship of many different gods. Its ornate public buildings gave it the appearance of a city of modern times. The massive Coliseum, similar to a football stadium, drew thousands to watch the sporting events sponsored by the Roman government. Paul was shipwrecked on his way to Rome to appeal his case to the Roman court (Acts 27:40–44). When he finally reached the city, Christianity had already been planted here (Acts 28:14–16). Upon his arrival in Rome, Paul was placed under house arrest and allowed to continue his witnessing efforts (Acts 28:30–31). The apostle was probably released, then imprisoned a second time and eventually executed at Rome during the reign of the cruel emperor Nero. While imprisoned he wrote letters to three of the churches he had founded: Ephesians, Philippians, and Colossians. Rome is also mentioned in Acts 2:10; 18:2; 19:21; 23:11 • Rom. 1:15 • 2 Tim. 1:17.

ROOSTER

Matt. 26:34 before the *r* crows, you [Peter] shall deny Me [Jesus] three times

Mark 14:68 he [Peter] went out...and the *r* crowed

Luke 22:61 Peter remembered... Before the *r* crows, you shall deny Me [Jesus]

ROOT AND THE OFFSPRING OF DAVID, THE. A name that Jesus used for Himself that emphasizes His unique existence as the God-man, the one who is both fully human and fully divine (Rev. 22:16). Since Jesus is the divine Son who served as the agent of creation (John 1:3), He is David's creator, or root. But because He came to earth in human form, He is also David's descendant, or offspring—the Messiah from the line of David who reigns over the spiritual kingdom that He came to establish. Thus Jesus is both superior to David and the rightful heir to his throne.

ROPE. A heavy cord. To put ropes on the head or neck signified distress (1 Kings 20:31–32) and perhaps submission, since cords were used to bind prisoners.

RUBY. A precious stone to which the writer of Proverbs compared a virtuous woman (Prov. 31:10).

RUDDY. Having a vigorous, healthy appearance; a characteristic feature of the boy David (1 Sam. 16:11–12).

RUE. An herb used as a medicine and to flavor foods. Jesus criticized the Pharisees for tithing this insignificant plant while neglecting more important matters such as justice and divine love (Luke 11:42).

RUFUS. A fellow believer at Rome greeted and commended by the apostle Paul (Rom. 16:13).

RUHAMAH. A symbolic name for God's people, meaning "having obtained favor." It was given by the prophet Hosea to his daughter to show that the Israelites would be forgiven after they repented of their wrongdoing (Hos. 2:1).

RULE [ING, S]

Gen. 1:16 God made two great lights: the greater light to *r* the day

2 Sam. 23:3 He who *r's* over men must be just

Matt. 2:6 a Governor who shall *r* My people Israel

Col. 3:15 let the peace of God *r* in your hearts

1 Tim. 3:5 if a man does not know how to *r* his own house

1 Tim. 3:12 deacons...*r'ing* their children and their own houses well

RUN [NING, S]

Ps. 23:5 My cup *r's* over

Eccles. 1:7 All the rivers *r* into the sea, yet the sea is not full

Isa. 40:31 they shall *r* and not be weary

Jer. 5:1 *R* back and forth through the streets of Jerusalem

Amos 5:24 let judgment *r* down like waters

Hab. 2:2 Write the vision...that he who reads it may *r*

Luke 6:38 pressed down, and shaken together, and *r'ning* over

1 Cor. 9:24 in a race all *r*, but one receives the prize

Heb. 12:1 let us *r* with patience the race that is set before us

RUST. Corrosion of metal. Jesus used this word to warn against over-dependence on material possessions (Matt. 6:19–20).

RUTH. A Moabite woman who remained loyal to her Jewish mother-in-law Naomi after the death of their husbands. Ruth moved with Naomi to Bethlehem (Ruth 1:16–19), where she gleaned grain in the fields of Boaz. She eventually married Boaz and gave birth to Obed, the grandfather of King David (Ruth 4:13–22). Ruth, a Gentile, is included in the earthly genealogy of Jesus (Matt. 1:5). This shows that Jesus came into the world as a Savior for all people, Gentiles as well as Jews.

RUTH, BOOK OF. A short book of the OT which reads almost like a short story on the power of love in trying circumstances. It takes its name from a Gentile woman, a native of Moab, who married into an Israelite family. When all the men of the family died, Ruth remained steadfastly loyal to her mother-in-law Naomi (Ruth 1:16). Her name means "friendship," and she modeled love and friendship at its best. The events of the book happened during "the days when the judges ruled" (Ruth 1:1). This was a dark period in Israel's history. Ruth shows that even in the worst of times, God is at work in His world.

S

SABAOTH. See *Lord of Hosts*

SABBATH. The Jewish day of worship and rest, established when God rested after the six days of creation (Gen. 2:1–3). The name comes from the Hebrew term which means "cessation."

The fourth of the Ten Commandments called for the Sabbath to be observed and kept holy, which involved doing no work on that day (Exod. 20:8). The Pharisees placed restrictions on Sabbath observance that prohibited acts of mercy or necessity (Mark 2:23–24). But Jesus declared that "the Sabbath was made for man, and not man for the Sabbath" (Mark 2:27). The OT Sabbath fell on the seventh day of the week, or the modern Saturday. Most Christian groups today observe Sunday as the day of worship because of Christ's resurrection on the first day of the week (1 Cor. 16:2). See also *Lord's Day*.

SABBATH DAY'S JOURNEY. The distance a person was permitted to travel on the Sabbath. After Jesus ascended into heaven from the Mount of Olives, His disciples walked back to Jerusalem, which was "a sabbath day's journey" away (Acts 1:12).

SABBATICAL YEAR. A sacred year of rest and redemption that came around every seven years. During this time some of the land went uncultivated (Lev. 25:4–5), debtors were released from their obligations, and the people of Israel granted freedom to any of their countrymen who had been enslaved because of indebtedness (Deut. 15:1–5).

SACKCLOTH. A coarse fabric worn to express extreme grief or sorrow (Esther 4:1). The prophets of the OT often wore sackcloth to express their distress over the messages of divine judgment they delivered (Joel 1:8, 13). Jacob wore sackcloth in anguish when he thought his son Joseph had been killed (Gen. 37:34).

SACKCLOTH AND ASHES

Esther 4:3 wailing among the Jews, and many lay in *s-a-a*

Dan. 9:3 seek [God] by prayer...with fasting and *s-a-a*

Matt. 11:21 they [Tyre and Sidon] would have repented long ago in *s-a-a*

SACRIFICE [S]

1 Sam. 15:22 Behold, to obey is better than *s*

Ps. 4:5 Offer the *s's* of righteousness...trust in the LORD

Ps. 51:17 The *s's* of God are a broken spirit

Ps. 116:17 offer to You [God] the *s* of thanksgiving

Prov. 15:8 The *s* of the wicked is an abomination

Prov. 17:1 Better is a dry morsel...than...*s's* with strife

Hos. 6:6 For I [God] desired mercy and not *s*

Jon. 2:9 I will *s* to You [God] with...thanksgiving

Rom. 12:1 present your bodies as a living *s*

Heb. 7:27 who [Jesus] does not need...to offer up daily *s's*

Heb. 11:4 Abel offered...a more excellent *s* than Cain

Heb. 13:15 continually offer the *s* of praise to God

1 Pet. 2:5 offer up spiritual *s's* acceptable to God

SACRIFICIAL OFFERINGS. In OT times, sacrifices presented to God in the belief that they atoned for human sin and restored fellowship with the Lord. Most of these offerings were animals whose blood was placed on the altar by a presiding priest (Lev. 4:5–6). But offerings of wine (Num. 29:11–18) and the first of the crops to be harvested were also given (Exod. 23:19). With the coming of Jesus Christ, and His atoning death, the need for these OT sacrifices no longer exists. The author of the book of Hebrews declared: "[Not] by the blood of goats and calves, but by His own blood He entered in once into the Most Holy Place, having obtained eternal redemption for us" (Heb. 9:12).

SADDUCEES. An aristocratic party of NT times which rejected the oral traditions that had grown up around the Mosaic law. On this point they disagreed with the Pharisees, who considered these traditions almost as important as the law itself. To the Sadducees, only the original teachings of the Pentateuch (the first five books of the OT) were authoritative. Many of the Sadducees were wealthy and enjoyed a privileged position in society. They considered any challenge to the establishment as a threat to their security, and urged the people to support the Roman authorities who controlled Israel. They often opposed Jesus and His teachings (Mark 12:18–19). He urged His disciples to avoid their teachings (Matt. 16:1–12). The Sadducees are also mentioned in Matt. 3:7; 22:23–34 • **Luke 20:27 • Acts 4:1–3; 5:17–18; 23:6–8.**

SAINTS. A word for believers—those who have accepted Jesus as Savior and committed their lives to Him. The apostle Paul spoke of the wonders of the gospel of grace that had been "revealed to His saints" (Col. 1:26).

SAINTS

2 Chron. 6:41 let Your [God's] *s* rejoice in goodness

Ps. 30:4 Sing to the LORD, O you *s* of His

Ps. 89:7 God is greatly to be feared in...assembly of the *s*

Ps. 116:15 Precious in the sight of the LORD... death of His *s*

Matt. 27:52 many bodies of the *s* who slept arose

Rom. 12:13 distributing to the needs of the *s*

1 Cor. 1:2 those who are sanctified in Christ Jesus, called to be *s*

Eph. 3:8 To me [Paul], who am less than the least of all *s*

Eph. 4:12 perfecting of the *s*, for the work of the ministry

Rev. 17:6 the woman, drunk with the blood of the *s*

SAKE [S]

Ps. 23:3 paths of righteousness for His [God's] name's *s*

Matt. 5:10 Blessed are those who are persecuted for righteousness' *s*

Mark 8:35 lose his life for My [Jesus'] *s* and the gospel's

Luke 21:17 you shall be hated...for My [Jesus'] name's *s*

Acts 9:16 he [Paul] must suffer for My [Jesus'] name's *s*

Rom. 8:36 For Your [God's] *s* we are killed all day long

1 Cor. 4:10 We are fools for Christ's *s*

2 Cor. 8:9 yet for your *s* He [Jesus] became poor

1 Tim. 5:23 use a little wine for your [Timothy's] stomach's *s*

1 Pet. 3:14 suffer for righteousness' *s*, happy are you

SALAMIS. A port city on the island of Cyprus where Saul (also called Paul) and Barnabas preached during the first missionary journey (Acts 13:4–5).

SALEM. See *Jerusalem*

SALIM. A place near the Jordan River where John the Baptist baptized people who responded to his message of repentance (John 3:23).

SALMON. Father of Boaz who is listed as an ancestor of Jesus in Matthew's genealogy (Matt. 1:4–5).

SALOME. A follower of Jesus who witnessed His crucifixion and later brought spices to the tomb to anoint His body (Mark 15:40; 16:1). She may be the same woman identified as "the mother of Zebedee's children" (Matt. 27:56). Jesus' disciples James and John were the sons of a man named Zebedee (Matt. 4:21–22). If this is the same Salome, she asked Jesus to grant special favors to her sons in His coming kingdom (Matt. 20:20–23).

SALT. A mineral used to season and preserve food (Lev. 2:13). Salt was a valuable commodity in a society without refrigeration and cold storage. Jesus referred to His followers as the "salt of the earth" (Matt. 5:13) to emphasize their positive influence in a sinful world.

SALT

Job 6:6 Can what is unsavory be eaten without *s*

Matt. 5:13 You are the *s* of the earth

Col. 4:6 Let your speech always be...seasoned with *s*

SALT SEA. A name for the Dead Sea, a body of water into which the Jordan River empties at the lowest point on earth in southern Israel (Gen. 14:3 • Josh. 3:16). The water evaporates quickly in the hot, dry climate, leaving a high concentration of salt and other minerals. In recent decades the Dead Sea has declined dramatically due to diversion of irrigation water from the Jordan River. *East Sea*: Joel 2:20. *Sea of the Plain*: Deut. 3:17.

SALT, COVENANT OF. A symbolic expression for the eternal nature of the covenant between God and His people (Num. 18:19).

SALVATION. The total work of God in delivering believers from sin and reconciling them to Himself. In the OT, the word *salvation* often referred to deliverance from physical danger (Exod. 14:13). But by NT times, the term was used for spiritual release from the bondage of sin. Genuine salvation has three dimensions: past, present, and future. Believers have been saved because of their faith in Christ and His atoning death (Acts 16:31). They are in the process of being saved from sin's power day by day as they live out their comment to Jesus (Phil. 2:12). They will be saved in the end-time from the very presence of sin (Rom. 13:11).

SAMARIA, CITY OF. A major city of Israel (the Northern Kingdom) built by King Omri from the ground up as the new capital of the nation. The name is derived from Shemer, owner of the hill on which the city was built (1 Kings 16:24–29). This hilltop location offered good protection from enemy attacks, but it eventually fell to the Assyrian army after a prolonged siege of about three years (2 Kings 17:5–6). The Assyrians repopulated the city with foreigners who worshiped pagan gods (2 Kings 17:24–33). Over the centuries, intermarriage with these Gentiles produced a half-breed race that pure-blooded Jews despised. In excavations at the site of ancient Samaria, archaeologists have discovered pieces of ivory apparently used as furniture inlays and as decorative wall panels. These may have been used in the infamous "ivory house" built here by King Ahab, Omri's son and successor (1 Kings 22:39). The city of Samaria is also mentioned in 1 Kings 20:1–22 • 2 Kings 17:3–24 • Amos 3:11–12.

SAMARIA, REGION OF. One of three territories into which the land of Israel was divided in NT times. Samaria was situated between Judea in the south and Galilee in the north. On one of His trips through this territory, Jesus offered "living water" to a Samaritan woman who came to draw water from a public well (John 4:10).

SAMARITANS. Israelites who had corrupted their bloodline by intermarriage with pagans and foreigners. Most full-blooded Jews despised the Samaritans, even refusing to travel through the region where they lived. But Jesus harbored no such prejudice toward the Samaritans. In one of His parables, he told about a kind Samaritan traveler who came to the aid of a wounded man, even when the victim's fellow Jewish citizens refused to get involved (Luke 10:25–37). The Samaritans are also mentioned in 2 Kings 17:29 • Matt. 10:5 • Luke 9:52; 17:16 • John 4:9–40; 8:48 • Acts 8:25.

SAMECH. Fifteenth letter of the Hebrew alphabet, used as a heading over Psalm 119:113–120. In the Hebrew language, the first line of each of these eight verses begins with this letter.

SAMGAR-NEBO. A Babylonian official under King Nebuchadnezzar who participated in the siege and capture of Jerusalem (Jer. 39:3).

SAMOS. An island of Greece visited by the apostle Paul on his return to Jerusalem at the end of his third missionary journey (Acts 20:15).

SAMOTHRACE. An island in the Aegean Sea visited by the apostle Paul (Acts 16:11).

SAMOTHRACIA. KJV: see *Samothrace*

SAMSON. A judge, or military hero, who delivered Israel from the Philistines through his great physical strength. Set apart as a Nazarite before his birth, Samson burned Philistine crops (Judg. 15:4–5), killed a thousand warriors with nothing but a bone as a weapon (Judg. 15:15), and ripped the gate from one of their walled cities (Judg. 16:3). But his physical strength was offset by his weak moral character. His lust led him to several encounters with pagan Philistine women, including Delilah, who betrayed him to his enemies. While imprisoned, Samson's strength returned. He performed one final heroic act by toppling a pagan Philistine temple, killing many of his enemies. He was also killed by the falling stones (Judges 16:28–30). Samson is listed as a hero of the faith in the book of Hebrews (Heb. 11:32).

SAMUEL. A prophet and the last judge of Israel who anointed the first two kings of Israel—Saul (1 Sam. 10:1–25) and David (1 Sam. 16:1–13). Samuel was born in answer to the prayer of his mother Hannah. In gratitude to the Lord, she dedicated Samuel to God's service and placed him in the custody of Eli, the high priest of Israel (1 Sam. 1:24–28). Samuel followed the Lord and spoke God's message to others. Even as a boy, he predicted God's judgment against Eli and his family (1 Sam. 3:1–21). Samuel also served in a priestly role by offering sacrifices on behalf of the people and leading them to commit themselves to the Lord (1 Sam. 7:3–17). He is listed as one of the OT heroes of faith (Heb. 11:32). Samuel is also mentioned in **1 Sam.** 1:20; 2:18–26; 4:1; 8:1–22; **9:14–27**; 11:7–14; 12:1–25; 13: 8–15; 15:1–35; 25:1; 28:3, 11–20 • 1 Chron. 6:28, 33; 9:22; 11:3; 26:28; 29:29 • 2 Chron. 35:18 • Ps. 99:6 • Jer. 15:1 • Acts 3:24; 13:20.

SAMUEL, FIRST. A historical book of the OT that marks an important shift in the organization and government of the nation of Israel. Until Samuel's time about 1000 BC, the nation had no centralized form of government. It existed as a loose confederation, with each of the twelve tribes governing its own affairs. This changed when Saul was anointed the first king of Israel by the prophet Samuel (1 Sam. 10:1). For the rest of their history during OT times, God's people were ruled by an earthly king. The book is named for the prophet Samuel, the apparent author and one of its central personalities. As the last of the judges and the first of the prophets, he served as the moral conscience of the nation during this critical period. First Samuel covers the kingship of Saul, his vain attempts to remove David as a claimant to the throne, and Saul's death at the hand of the Philistines.

SAMUEL, SECOND. A historical book of the OT that picks up where 1 Samuel leaves off—with the death of King Saul and the succession of David to the kingship. At first David

was recognized by the people as king over only a part of Israel. But he eventually won out over other challengers and reigned over all the tribes (2 Sam. 5:3). The book traces the events of David's administration across a period of about forty years. As king, he followed the Lord and set a good example for his people. God rewarded David by giving him victory over all of Israel's enemies and expanding the borders of his kingdom. God even promised the king that one of his descendants would always occupy the throne of Israel (2 Sam. 7:1–17).

SANBALLAT. An influential Samaritan who plotted to kill Nehemiah to stop his rebuilding and reform projects in Jerusalem (Neh. 2:10, 19; 4:1, 7; 6:1–14; 13:28).

SANCTIFICATION. The process of setting something apart for a holy purpose. In OT times, priests, Levites, and firstborn children were consecrated to the Lord. In the NT, sanctification is regarded as a work of grace following conversion (Phil. 1:6). God calls all believers to holiness and sanctification (1 Thes. 4:3, 7). Those sanctified are committed to God's truth and serve as witnesses to His power and grace in the world (Rom. 6:11–13). The process of sanctification continues throughout the life of believers (Heb. 10:14). It will be completed only when they are "made perfect" in the presence of the Lord in heaven (Heb. 12:23).

SANCTIFICATION
1 Thes. 4:3 this is the will of God, even your *s*
2 Thes. 2:13 God has...chosen you to salvation
   through *s* of the Spirit
1 Pet. 1:2 elect...through *s* of the Spirit

SANCTIFY [IED]
Gen. 2:3 God blessed the seventh day and *s'ied* it
Lev. 20:7 *S* yourselves, therefore, and be holy
Deut. 5:12 Keep the Sabbath day to *s* it
Josh. 3:5 Joshua said to the people, *S* yourselves
1 Chron. 15:14 priests...*s'ied* themselves to bring
   up the ark
Joel 1:14 *S* a fast. Call a solemn assembly
John 17:17 *S* them [the disciples] through Your
   [God's] truth. Your word is truth

1 Cor. 6:11 you are washed...you were *s'ied*...
you were justified

1 Tim. 4:5 it is *s'ied* by the word of God and
prayer

1 Pet. 3:15 but *s* the Lord God in your hearts

SAND. Fine, granular soil. The word is used figuratively for countless numbers or multitudes, as in God's promise to Jacob that his offspring would be as numerous as the sand (Gen. 32:12).

SANHEDRIN. The high court of the nation of Israel that arrested Jesus (Matt. 26:59). This judicial body consisted of seventy-one priests, scribes, and elders, with the high priest as presiding officer. The Roman government allowed the Sanhedrin to bring Jewish citizens to trial for certain minor offenses, but it could not pronounce the death penalty. So the Sanhedrin took Jesus to Pilate, the local Roman official, after it declared Him guilty of blasphemy (Matt. 27:1–2). It would be satisfied with nothing less than Jesus' execution. This group is referred to in both the KJV and the Simplified KJV as "the council" (Mark 14:55).

SAPPHIRA. An early believer at Jerusalem who was struck dead for lying and withholding money she had pledged to the church's common treasury (Acts 5:1–11).

SAPPHIRE. A precious stone used in the breastplate of the high priest (Exod. 28:18) and in the foundation of New Jerusalem (Rev. 21:19).

SARAH. A wife of Abraham who gave birth to a son when she was ninety years old (Gen. 21:1–12). This followed a period of many years when she was unable to conceive. The couple named the child Isaac, meaning "laughter," because Sarah had laughed when the Lord told her she would bear a son in her old age (Gen. 18:6–15). She is included in the roll call of the faithful in the book of Hebrews (Heb. 11:11; *Sara*: KJV). Sarah is also mentioned in Gen. 17:15–21; 20:2–18; 23:1–19; 24:36; 25:10; 49:31 • Isa. 51:2 • Rom. 9:9 • 1 Pet. 3:6. *Sarai*: Gen. 11:29–30; 12:5.

SARDIS. Site of one of the seven churches of Asia Minor. This church was characterized as "dead." If the believers here did not recover their enthusiasm for the Lord, Jesus promised to exercise appropriate judgment (Rev. 3:1–6).

SARDIUS. A precious stone in the high priest's breastplate (Exod. 28:17) and in the foundation of New Jerusalem (Rev. 21:20).

SARDONYX. A precious stone in the foundation of New Jerusalem (Rev. 21:20).

SAREPTA. KJV: see *Zarephath*

SARGON. A king of Assyria who captured Samaria and carried the Northern Kingdom into exile (Isa. 20:1).

SARON. KJV: see *Sharon*

SATAN. An evil being who works tirelessly to oppose God and His work in the world. Satan's first appearance in the Bible was in in the form of a snake. He persuaded Adam and Eve to eat the fruit that God had declared off-limits. The couple's disobedience of the Lord's command brought sin into the world (Gen. 3:6). Satan also tempted Jesus at the beginning of His public ministry. But Jesus overcame the seductions and stayed true to His divine mission (Luke 4:5–8).

Various names and descriptions of Satan in the Bible underline his corrupt character:

- accuser of our brothers (Rev. 12:10)
- Beelzebub (Matt. 12:24)
- Belial (2 Cor. 6:15)
- devil (Rev. 20:10)
- liar (John 8:44)
- man of sin (2 Thes. 2:3)
- murderer (John 8:44)
- prince of the power of the air (Eph. 2:2)
- prince of this world (John 16:11)
- son of perdition (John 17:12)
- tempter (Matt. 4:3)
- wicked one (Matt. 13:19)

Satan is also mentioned in 1 Chron. 21:1 • Job 1:6–12; 2:1–7 • Ps. 109:6 • Zech. 3:1–2 • Matt. 4:10; 12:26; 16:23 • Mark 1:13; 3:23, 26; 4:15; 8:33 • Luke 4:8; 10:18; 11:18; 13:16; 22:3, 31 • John 13:27 • Acts 5:3; 26:18 • Rom. 16:20 • 1 Cor. 5:5;

7:5 • 2 Cor. 2:11; 11:14; 12:7 • 1 Thes. 2:18 • 2 Thes. 2:9 • 1 Tim. 1:20; 5:15 • Rev. 2:9, 13, 24; 3:9; 12:9; 20:2, 7). *Belial*: 2 Cor. 6:15. *Lucifer*: Isa. 14:12.

SAUL. (1) The first king of Israel who started well but was eventually rejected by the Lord because of his acts of disobedience. The downward spiral started when he performed a ritual sacrifice, a duty reserved for priests (1 Sam. 13:9–14). Then he disobeyed the Lord by keeping some of the spoils of war after defeating the Amalekites (1 Sam. 15:9). Because of these misdeeds, the Lord rejected Saul as king, and had David anointed as his replacement (1 Sam. 16:11–14). In a fit of jealousy, Saul tried to kill David. He even slaughtered eighty-five priests whom he suspected of aiding and befriending David (1 Sam. 22:13–18). Finally, Saul was seriously wounded in a crucial battle with the Philistines. He committed suicide by falling on his sword to keep from being captured by his enemies (1 Sam. 31:1–4).

(2) The original name of Paul the apostle (Acts 13:9). See *Paul*.

SAVE [D, ING, S]

Exod. 14:30 LORD *s'd* Israel...out of the hand of the Egyptians

Judg. 10:13 you have...served other gods...I will no longer *s*

Ps. 7:1 S me from all those who persecute me

Ps. 7:10 My defense is from God, who *s's* the upright

Ps. 44:6 not trust in my bow, nor shall my sword *s* me

Ps. 55:16 I will call on God, and the LORD shall *s* me

Ps. 67:2 Your [God's] *s'ing* health among all nations

Ps. 80:19 Cause Your [God's] face to shine, and we shall be *s'd*

Ps. 107:13 He [God] *s'd* them out of their distresses

Prov. 20:22 wait on the LORD, and He shall *s* you

Isa. 45:22 Look to Me [God] and be *s'd*, all the ends of the earth

Isa. 59:1 LORD's hand is not shortened, that it cannot *s*

Jer. 8:20 the summer is ended, and we are not *s'd*

Zeph. 1:18 silver nor their gold shall be able to *s* them...the LORD's wrath

Matt. 1:21 He [Jesus] shall *s* His people from their sins

Matt. 10:22 he who endures to the end shall be *s'd*

Mark 8:35 whoever wants to *s* his life shall lose it

Mark 10:26 Then who can be *s'd*

Luke 19:10 Son of Man has come to seek and to *s* what was lost

Luke 23:35 He [Jesus] *s'd* others; let Him save Himself

John 3:17 the world might be *s'd* through Him [Jesus]

John 12:47 I [Jesus] came not to judge...but to *s* the world

Acts 2:21 whoever calls on the name of the Lord shall be *s'd*

Acts 4:12 no other name...in which we must be *s'd*

Rom. 5:10 we shall be *s'd* by His [Jesus'] life

Rom. 10:13 whoever calls on the name of the Lord shall be *s'd*

1 Cor. 1:21 pleased God by the foolishness of preaching to *s* those who believe

1 Cor. 9:22 I [Paul] have become all things to all men, that...I might *s* some

Eph. 2:8 by grace you are *s'd* through faith

1 Tim. 1:15 Christ Jesus came into the world to *s* sinners

2 Tim. 1:9 who [Jesus] has *s'd* us...called us with a holy calling

Heb. 7:25 He [Jesus] is also able to *s* to the uttermost

Jas. 2:14 a man...has not works? Can faith *s* him

SAVIOR. A title for Christ which emphasizes His work of salvation (Matt. 1:20–21)—a ministry foretold by the prophet Isaiah (Isa. 61:1–3). The name that Mary and Joseph gave their firstborn Son expresses this saving work. *Jesus*

means "God Is Salvation." It was clear from the day He was born that His purpose was to do for sinful people what they could not do for ourselves—deliver them from bondage to sin and death.

SAVIOR

2 Sam. 22:3 God of my rock, in Him I will trust... My *S*

Isa. 43:11 besides Me [God] there is no *s*

Luke 2:11 to you is born...in the city of David a *S*

1 John 4:14 Father sent the Son to be the *S* of the world

SAVIOR OF THE BODY. A name of Jesus that expresses His close relationship to the church (Eph. 5:23). Christ is the head of the church, and the agency He founded is so closely related to Him that it is referred to as His body several times in the NT (1 Cor. 12:27 • Eph. 1:22–23 • Col. 1:18). Thus, the church is not a building or a lifeless institution but a living organism, dedicated to advancing the cause of the kingdom of God in the world. Jesus not only died for individual believers, but He also sacrificed Himself for His church. His followers bring honor and glory to Him when they work through His church to serve as witnesses of His love and grace to others.

SCAPEGOAT. A live goat which symbolized the removal of the sins of the people of Israel. It was part of a ritual performed by the high priest on the day of atonement. Of two goats, one was offered as a blood sacrifice. The other animal, known as the scapegoat, was kept alive so it could be carried away into the wilderness. This symbolized the forgiveness or carrying away of the sins of the nation (Lev. 16:8–22).

SCARLET. A color that represented wealth and privilege (2 Sam. 1:24). Its brilliance symbolized the severity of Israel's sin against God (Isa. 1:18).

SCEPTER. A staff or baton carried by a king or other high official as a symbol of authority and power (Esther 4:11).

SCEPTER OUT OF ISRAEL. A name for the coming Messiah spoken as a prediction by a pagan magician named Balaam. He was hired by the king of Moab to pronounce a curse against the Israelites. But Balaam was led by the Lord to bless the Israelites instead. He even prophesied that a strong leader would rise up to crush the Moabites: "A Scepter shall rise out of Israel," he declared, "and shall strike the corners of Moab" (Num. 24:17). His words are considered a prophecy of the Savior-Messiah whom God would send to deliver His people.

SCEVA. A Jewish priest at Ephesus whose seven sons tried to cast out evil spirits in imitation of a miracle performed by the apostle Paul. Their attempt failed (Acts 19:11–16).

SCHIN. Twenty-first letter of the Hebrew alphabet, used as a heading over Psalm 119:161–168. In the Hebrew language, the first line of each of these eight verses begins with this letter.

SCOURGING. A severe beating with a leather whip. It contained bits of sharp metal which cut into human flesh. Jesus was subjected to this cruel procedure by Roman soldiers before He was crucified (Matt. 27:26).

SCRIBES. Members of a learned class who specialized in copying, studying, and teaching the scriptures. The office developed in OT times when scribes were charged with the responsibility of copying the scriptures. Laboriously reproducing a document by hand was the only way to pass it on in written form. By NT times, scribes had taken on the task of interpreting and teaching God's law as well. They are mentioned often with Pharisees as those who opposed Jesus (Matt. 9:2–3). Both were committed to preserving the traditions that had grown up around the written law. Jesus criticized them for making these additions more important than God's commands in their original form (Mark 7:1–9).

SCRIPTURE [S]

Luke 4:21 Today this *s* is fulfilled in your ears

Luke 24:45 they [the disciples] might understand the *s's*

John 5:39 Search the *s's*, for in them...you have eternal life

John 20:9 they [the disciples] did not know the *s*, that He [Jesus] must rise again

Acts 17:11 These [the Bereans]...searched the *s's* daily

Rom. 4:3 what does the *s* say? Abraham believed God

1 Cor. 15:3 Christ died for our sins according to the *s's*

2 Tim. 3:16 All *s* is given by inspiration of God

2 Pet. 1:20 knowing this...no prophecy of *s* is of any private interpretation

SCROLL. A roll of parchment or papyrus on which ancient documents were written. Jeremiah's prophecies were written on a scroll by his secretary Baruch (Jer. 36:1–2).

SEA OF GLASS. A clear sea or lake that appeared to the apostle John in a vision. It symbolized God's purity and holiness and the victory of His redeemed people (Rev. 4:6).

SEA OF JOPPA. See *Mediterranean Sea*

SEA OF THE PHILISTINES. See *Mediterranean Sea*

SEA OF THE PLAIN. See *Salt Sea*

SEA OF TIBERIAS. See *Galilee, Sea of*

SEBAT. See *Shebat*

SECOND COMING. The return of Jesus to earth at the end of the present age to render judgment and bring His redemptive plan to conclusion. During His earthly ministry, Jesus promised that after His death, resurrection, and ascension to the Father, He would return to take His followers to the place He had prepared for them (John 14:3). But He also indicated that the time of His second coming was uncertain (Matt. 25:13). This called for Christians to live in a state of watchful readiness. Jesus could return at any time, perhaps when they least expected it (Luke 21:34–36). His return will be in accord with God's plan, just as He originally

came to earth in the "fullness of the time" (Gal. 4:4). The second coming is also referenced in Matt. 25:32–46 • Luke 12:35–48 • 1 Thes. 4:13–18.

SECOND DEATH. A phrase that refers to spiritual death, final death, or eternal separation from God—the fate of those who refuse to accept Christ as Savior and Lord. The apostle John declared that the lake of fire was the second death (Rev. 20:14). Thus, "second death" and "lake of fire" appear to be figurative ways of referring to hell, or the eternal punishment of unbelievers.

SECRET [S]

Deut. 29:29 s things belong to the LORD our God

Ps. 44:21 God...knows the *s's* of the heart

Ps. 91:1 dwells in the *s* place of the Most High

Ezek. 28:3 no *s* that they can hide from you [prince of Tyre]

Dan. 2:28 there is a God in heaven who reveals *s's*

Matt. 6:6 pray to your Father who is in *s*

Rom. 2:16 God shall judge the *s's* of men by Jesus Christ

SECUNDUS. A believer who traveled with Paul from Greece to Asia Minor as the apostle returned from his third missionary journey (Acts 20:4).

SEEK [ING, S]

2 Chron. 7:14 If My [God's] people...pray and *s* My face

Ps. 40:16 those who *s* You [God] rejoice and be glad

Ps. 63:1 You are my God; I will *s* You early

Ps. 105:4 S the LORD and His strength: seek His face

Ps. 119:2 Blessed are those...who *s* Him [God] with the whole heart

Isa. 55:6 S the LORD while He may be found

Lam. 3:25 LORD is good...to the soul who *s's* Him

Matt. 7:7 S, and you shall find

Matt. 7:8 he who *s's* finds

Mark 8:12 Why does this generation *s* after a sign?

Luke 12:31 But rather *s* the kingdom of God

Luke 17:33 Whoever *s's* to save his life shall lose it

Luke 19:10 Son of Man has come to *s* and to save what was lost

John 5:30 because I [Jesus] *s*...the will of the Father

Rom. 3:11 there is no one who *s's* after God

1 Cor. 1:22 and the Greeks *s* after wisdom

1 Cor. 13:5 [love] does not *s* its own

Col. 3:1 *s* those things that are above

1 Pet. 5:8 devil walks...like a roaring lion, *s'ing* whom he may devour

SEEK THE LORD

1 Chron. 16:11 *S-t-L* and His strength...His face continually

Ps. 34:10 those who *s-t-L* shall not lack any good thing

Prov. 28:5 those who *s-t-L* understand all things

Amos 5:6 *S-t-L*, and you shall live

Zech. 8:22 nations shall come to *s-t-L* of hosts

SELAH. A musical term that appears several times in the book of Psalms, possibly calling for a pause in the singing (Ps. 44:8).

SELEUCIA. A seaport near Antioch of Syria where Paul and Barnabas caught a ship at the beginning of the first missionary journey (Acts 13:4).

SELF-CONTROL. Mastery over one's emotions and personal desires. The apostle Paul listed self-control as a work of the Holy Spirit in the lives of believers (Gal. 5:22–23). *Temperance*: KJV.

SELF-CONTROL

1 Cor. 7:9 if they cannot exercise *s-c*, let them marry

Gal. 5:23 meekness, *s-c*. Against such there is no law

1 Tim. 2:9 women adorn themselves...with propriety and *s-c*

2 Pet. 1:6 and to knowledge *s-c*; and to *s-c*, patience

SEM. KJV: see *Shem*

SENIR. See *Hermon, Mount*

SENNACHERIB. A king of Assyria who captured several cities of Judah (the Southern Kingdom) but failed to take Jerusalem. While camped outside the city, his army was devastated by "the angel of the Lord" who killed tens of thousands (2 Kings 19:32–35). Sennacherib was forced to withdraw in humiliation and defeat. Later, he was assassinated by two of his own sons while worshipping at a pagan temple in his capital city (2 Kings 19:36–37). He is also mentioned in **2 Kings 18:13–16** • 2 Chron. 32:1–22 • Isa. 36:1; 37:17, 21, 37.

SEPARATE [D]

Prov. 19:4 Wealth makes many friends...the poor is *s'd* from his neighbor

Isa. 59:2 your iniquities have *s'd* you from your God

Matt. 25:32 He [Jesus] shall *s* them from one another

Acts 13:2 *S* Barnabas and Saul for Me [God] for the work

Rom. 8:39 nor any...creature shall be able to *s* us from the love of God

2 Cor. 6:17 come out from among them and be *s*, says the Lord

SEPHARVAIM. A city whose residents were sent to colonize Israel (the Northern Kingdom) after Samaria was captured by the Assyrians (2 Kings 17:24–31).

SERAIAH. A leader who carried Jeremiah's prophecy of doom for Judah to the city of Babylon (Jer. 51:59–61).

SERAPHIM. Angelic beings associated with the prophet Isaiah's divine call in his stirring vision in the temple. They sang God's praises and touched the prophet's lips to consecrate his words (Isa. 6:1–7).

SERMON ON THE MOUNT. Jesus' most famous sermon, a long speech in which He instructed His disciples on how to live as citizens of the kingdom of God. It is called the Sermon on the Mount because He taught these principles to His disciples from a mountainside (Matt. 5:1). It contains ten major principles:

- the Beatitudes, or rewards for those who live as citizens of God's kingdom (Matt. 5:3–12)
- Christian influence in a wicked world (Matt. 5:13–16)
- living by the deeper meaning of God's law (Matt. 5:17–48)
- giving, praying, and fasting should issue from the right motives (Matt. 6:1–18)
- putting God's kingdom first (Matt. 6:19–34)
- not judging others for sins we also commit (Matt. 7:1–6)
- asking God for good things (Matt. 7:7–12)
- pursuing the less-traveled way that leads to life (Matt. 7:13–14)
- bearing good fruit (Matt. 7:15–20)
- action matters more than idle talk (Matt. 7:21–29)

SERPENT. A crawling reptile often associated with sin, temptation, and disobedience. Satan in the form of a serpent tempted Adam and Eve to disobey the Lord's clear command (Gen. 3:1–5). Later, during the wilderness wandering years, Moses raised the image of a serpent on a pole to heal the people who had been bitten by poisonous snakes (Num. 21:9). Jesus cited this event to show that His future sacrificial death would deliver people from sin (John 3:14–15).

SERVANT. A person who served the needs of others. Jesus described Himself as one who filled this role in a spiritual sense. When His disciples quarreled about who would occupy the places of honor in His future glory, He told them: "Whoever of you wants to be the first shall be servant of all. For even the Son of Man did not come to be ministered to, but to minister, and to give His life as a ransom for many" (Mark 10:44–45). See also *Righteous Servant*.

SERVANT [S]
Gen. 9:25 a *s* of *s's* he [Canaan] shall be
Job 1:8 Have you [Satan] considered My [God's] *s* Job
Ps. 31:16 Make Your [God's] face to shine on Your *s*

Ps. 34:22 The LORD redeems the soul of His *s's*
Ps. 113:1 Praise, O you *s's* of the LORD
Ps. 116:16 I am Your [God's] *s*...the son of Your handmaiden
Ps. 119:125 I am Your [God's] *s*; give me understanding
Prov. 14:35 The king's favor is toward a wise *s*
Isa. 42:1 Behold, My [God's] *s* whom I uphold
Isa. 52:13 My [God's] *s* shall deal prudently
Dan. 9:17 hear the prayer of Your [God's] *s*
Mal. 1:6 A son honors his father, and a *s* his master
Matt. 10:24 disciple is not above his master, nor the *s* above his lord
Matt. 23:11 he who is greatest...shall be your *s*
Matt. 25:21 Well done, good and faithful *s*
Mark 9:35 the same shall be last of all and *s* of all
Luke 12:37 Blessed are those *s's* whom the master...shall find watching
Luke 15:19 Make me [the prodigal son] as one of your hired *s's*
John 8:34 whoever commits sin is the *s* of sin
Rom. 6:18 you became the *s's* of righteousness
1 Cor. 9:19 I [Paul] made myself *s* to all
Gal. 4:7 Therefore, you are no more a *s* but a son
Phil. 2:7 took on Himself [Jesus] the form of a *s*

SERVANT SONGS OF ISAIAH. Isa. 42:1–4; 49:1–6; 50:4–9; 52:13–53:12

SERVE [D, ING, S]
Gen. 27:29 Let people *s* you [Jacob] and nations bow down
Gen. 29:20 Jacob *s'd* seven years for Rachel
Deut. 6:13 You shall fear the LORD your God and *s* Him
Ps. 72:11 Yes...all nations shall *s* Him [God]
Dan. 3:17 our [Daniel's three friends'] God whom we *s* is able to deliver us
Dan. 6:16 God whom you [Daniel] *s*...He will deliver you
Matt. 4:10 worship the Lord your God, and Him only shall you *s*
Luke 16:13 No servant can *s* two masters
John 12:26 If any man *s's* Me [Jesus], let him follow Me

John 16:2 whoever kills you will think that he is *s'ing* God

Acts 6:2 not right that we [the apostles] should...*s* tables

Rom. 1:25 who...worshipped and *s'd* the creature more than the Creator

Rom. 12:11 fervent in spirit, *s'ing* the Lord

Gal. 5:13 by love *s* one another

SERVE THE LORD

Josh. 24:15 as for me [Joshua] and my house, we will *s-t-L*

Ps. 100:2 *S-t-L* with gladness

Jer. 30:9 they [Israel and Judah] shall *s-t-L*...and David their king

SERVICE

Exod. 39:1 they made cloths of *s*, to do *s* in the Holy Place

Rom. 12:1 present your bodies a living sacrifice... your reasonable *s*

Eph. 6:6 not with eye-*s*, as men pleasers, but... doing the will of God

Rev. 2:19 I know your works, and love and *s*, and faith

SETHUR. One of the twelve spies or scouts sent by Moses to investigate the land of Canaan. He represented the tribe of Asher (Num. 13:13).

SETTLE [D]

1 Kings 8:13 I [Solomon] have...built You [God]...a *s'd* place

Ps. 119:89 Forever, O LORD, Your word is *s'd* in heaven

Prov. 8:25 Before the mountains were *s'd*...I [wisdom] was brought forth

Matt. 25:19 the lord of those servants...*s'd* accounts with them

Col. 1:23 continue in the faith grounded and *s'd*

1 Pet. 5:10 God...make you perfect and establish, strengthen, and *s* you

SEVEN. A number often used symbolically because it was considered a round or perfect number. Seven is used many times in this way in the visions of the apostle John in the book of Revelation (Rev. 5:1; 15:1).

SEVEN CHURCHES OF ASIA. The seven congregations in Asia Minor to which the apostle John addressed specific messages in the book of Revelation (Rev. 1:11):

1. Ephesus (Rev. 2:1–7)
2. Smyrna (Rev. 2:8–11)
3. Pergamum (Rev. 2:12–17)
4. Thyatira (Rev. 2:18–29)
5. Sardis (Rev. 3:1–6)
6. Philadelphia (Rev. 3:7–13)
7. Laodicea (Rev. 3:14–22)

SEVEN SAYINGS FROM THE CROSS. The seven separate utterances which Jesus made from the cross shortly before He died:

1. "Father, forgive them, for they do not know what they do" (Luke 23:34)
2. "Today you shall be with Me in paradise" (Luke 23:43)
3. "Woman, behold your son" (John 19:26)
4. "My God, My God, why have You forsaken me?" (Matt. 27:46)
5. "I thirst" (John 19:28)
6. "It is finished" (John 19:30)
7. "Father, into Your hands I commend My spirit" (Luke 23:46)

SEVEN SIGNS OF JESUS IN JOHN'S GOSPEL

1. Turning of water into wine (John 2:1–11)
2. Healing of a nobleman's son (John 4:46–54)
3. Healing of a paralyzed man (John 5:1–9)
4. Feeding of the five thousand (John 6:5–14)
5. Walking on the water (John 6:15–21)
6. Healing of a man born blind (John 9:1–7)
7. Raising of Lazarus from the dead (John 11:38–44)

SEVENTY, THE. A group of Jesus' followers that He sent out to heal and preach the good news of the kingdom of God (Luke 10:1–17). Jesus also sent His twelve disciples on a similar mission (Matt. 10:5–8).

SEVENTY WEEKS PROPHECY. See *Daniel, Book of*

SHABBETHAI. A Levite after the Exile who explained the law as Ezra read it to the people (Neh. 8:7).

SHADRACH. One of three young Israelites delivered miraculously from the flaming furnace of King Nebuchadnezzar of Babylon (**Dan.** 1:7; 2:49; **3:1–28**).

SHALLUM. (1). A man who assassinated Zechariah, king of Israel (the Northern Kingdom) and took the throne, only to be killed and succeeded a month later by Menahem (2 Kings 15:10–15).

(2) A leader who helped Nehemiah rebuild Jerusalem's wall after the Exile (Neh. 3:12).

(3) Alternative name for Jehoahaz. See *Jehoahaz*, No. 2.

SHALMANESER. An Assyrian king who defeated Israel (the Northern Kingdom) and carried its leading citizens into captivity (**2 Kings 17:3–6; 18:9**).

SHAME [D]

Ps. 4:2 how long will you turn my [David's] glory into *s*

Ps. 14:6 You have *s'd* the counsel of the poor

Ps. 35:4 Let those who seek after my soul be confounded and put to *s*

Ps. 83:16 Fill their faces with *s* that they may seek Your [God's] name

Ps. 119:31 O LORD, do not put me to *s*

Prov. 3:35 *s* shall be the promotion of fools

Prov. 13:18 *s* shall come to him who refuses instruction

Prov. 29:15 a child left to himself brings his mother to *s*

1 Cor. 14:35 it is a *s* for women to speak in the church

Phil. 3:19 whose glory is in their *s*, who mind earthly things

Heb. 12:2 Jesus...endured the cross, despising the *s*

SHAMEFULLY

Hos. 2:5 She who conceived them has done *s*

Mark 12:4 they [farmers]...sent him [servant] away *s* handled

SHAMGAR. A judge of Israel who delivered the nation from oppression by killing six hundred Philistines with an ox goad (**Judg.** 3:31; 5:6).

SHAMHUTH. An officer in David's army who commanded a unit of 24,000 warriors (1 Chron. 27:8).

SHAMMAH. The name of two of David's "mighty men," an elite group of warriors known for their bravery in battle (2 Sam. 23:25, 33).

SHAMMUA. One of the twelve spies or scouts sent by Moses to investigate the land of Canaan. He represented the tribe of Reuben (Num. 13:4).

SHAMMOTH. One of David's "mighty men," an elite group of warriors known for their bravery in battle (1 Chron. 11:27).

SHAPHAT. One of the twelve spies or scouts sent by Moses to investigate the land of Canaan. He represented the tribe of Simeon (Num. 13:5).

SHARON. A fertile coastal plain in Israel that runs about forty miles along the Mediterranean Sea from Joppa to Mount Carmel. It is mentioned in 1 Chron. 27:29 • Song of Sol. 2:1 • Isa. 33:9; 35:2; 65:10 • Acts 9:35.

SHEAR-JASHUB. A symbolic name, meaning "a remnant shall return." The prophet Isaiah gave this name to his son to show God's promise to His people after their period of exile came to an end (Isa. 7:3–4).

SHEBA. A man who led a brief rebellion against King David after the revolt of Absalom ended in failure (2 Sam. 20:1–22).

SHEBAT. Eleventh month of the Hebrew year, the month when the prophet Zechariah received a stirring vision from the Lord (Zech. 1:7–10). *Sebat*: KJV.

SHEBNA. A treasurer under King Hezekiah of Judah (the Southern Kingdom) who made a tomb for himself. The prophet Isaiah predicted that he would die in exile (Isa. 22:15–19).

SHECHEM. (1) A tribal prince who was killed by Jacob's sons Simeon and Levi for seducing their sister, Dinah (Gen. 34:1–29).

(2) A camping spot where Abram built an altar after arriving in Canaan (Gen. 12:6–7; *Sichem*: KJV). This site eventually grew into a village, then a town, and finally a city. Here is where Joshua gave his farewell address to the tribes of Israel after they conquered the Canaanites (Josh. 24:1–15). Shechem is also mentioned in Josh. 20:7 • Judg. 9:1–57 • 1 Kings 12:1, 25 • Acts 7:16.

SHEEP. An animal often presented as a sacrificial offering (Lev. 12:6). Large flocks of sheep signified prosperity (Job 1:3). Jesus spoke of straying sheep as a symbol of helpless sinners (Luke 15:4–6).

SHEEP

1 Sam. 15:14 What then is the meaning of this bleating of the *s*

2 Sam. 7:8 I [God] took you [David] from the sheepfold...following the *s*

Ps. 44:22 we are counted as *s* for the slaughter

Ps. 74:1 Why does Your [God's] anger smoke against the *s* of Your pasture?

Ps. 95:7 people of His [God's] pasture and the *s* of His hand

Ps. 119:176 I have gone astray like a lost *s*

Isa. 53:6 We all like *s* have gone astray

Matt. 10:16 send you forth as *s* in the midst of wolves

Matt. 15:24 I [Jesus] was sent only to the lost *s* of the house of Israel

Mark 6:34 Jesus...saw many people...as *s* not having a shepherd

Luke 15:6 I have found my *s* that was lost

John 10:7 I [Jesus] am the door of the *s*

John 10:11 good shepherd [Jesus] gives His life for the *s*

John 21:16 He [Jesus] said to him [Peter], Feed my *s*

1 Pet. 2:25 For you were as *s* going astray

SHEM. The oldest of Noah's three sons who survived the great flood (Gen. 5:32). Shem was the father of several sons whose descendants gave rise to several peoples of the ancient world. He is also mentioned in **Gen.** 6:10; 7:13; 9:18–27; 10:1–31; 11:10–11 • 1 Chron. 1:4, 17, 24 • Luke 3:36.

SHEMA, THE. A statement quoted by Israelites of OT times as a confession of faith. It includes the words, "Hear, O Israel: The LORD our God is one LORD" (Deut. 6:4).

SHEMAIAH. (1) A prophet who warned King Rehoboam of Judah (the Southern Kingdom) not to attack Israel (the Northern Kingdom) (**1 Kings 12:22–24** • 2 Chron. 11:2).

(2) A man who helped rebuild the walls of Jerusalem after the Exile (Neh. 3:29).

SHEMER. The man from whom King Omri of Israel (the Northern Kingdom) bought a hill on which he built the capital city of Samaria (1 Kings 16:24).

SHEMINITH. A musical term in the titles of Psalms 6 and 12 and in 1 Chronicles 15:21. It may signal the instrument to be used.

SHEMUEL. A leader of the tribe of Simeon who was appointed by Moses to help divide the land of Canaan after its occupation by the Israelites (Num. 34:20).

SHENIR. See *Hermon, Mount*

SHEOL. A Hebrew word that refers to a gloomy region where the spirits of people went after they died. The word is translated as "hell" (2 Sam. 22:6) or "grave" (Ps. 49:15). Some passages in the OT describe sheol as a place inhabited by both the righteous and unrighteous (Isa. 38:10). But other passages indicate that the righteous will avoid sheol because of their commitment to the Lord (Ps. 49:15). These discrepancies show that the Israelites of OT times did not have a fully developed concept of the afterlife. This awaited the coming of Jesus and His teachings on eternal life for believers and eternal punishment for unbelievers.

SHEPHATIAH. A son of David, born at Hebron to his wife Abital (2 Sam. 3:4).

SHEPHERD. A person who took care of sheep (Gen. 31:38–40). The word is also used of Jesus, who called Himself the "Good Shepherd" (John

10:11, 14). David also referred to God as his shepherd and constant guide (Ps. 23:1).

SHEPHERD [S]
Gen. 47:3 Your servants [the Hebrews] are *s's*
Ps. 23:1 The LORD is my *s*. I shall not want
Isa. 40:11 Like a *s*, He [God] shall feed His flock
Jer. 3:15 I [God] will give you *s's* according to My heart
Jer. 17:16 I [Jeremiah] have not hurried away from being a *s*
Jer. 23:1 Woe to the *s's* who...scatter the sheep
Ezek. 34:2 Son of man, prophesy against the *s's* of Israel
Matt. 9:36 and were scattered, as sheep having no *s*
Luke 2:8 in the same country there were *s's* abiding in the field
John 10:11 I [Jesus] am the good *s*...gives His life for the sheep
Heb. 13:20 that great *S* [Jesus] of the sheep
1 Pet. 5:4 when the Chief *S* [Jesus] appears

SHEREBIAH. A Levite after the Exile who explained the law as Ezra read it to the people (Neh. 8:7).

SHESHAK. See *Babylon*

SHESHBAZZAR. See *Zerubbabel*

SHEWBREAD. See *Showbread*

SHIELD. A piece of armor that protected warriors in hand-to-hand combat (1 Sam. 17:7). The psalmist also used the word symbolically of the Lord as his protection (Ps. 5:12).

SHIELD
Gen. 15:1 Do not fear, Abram. I [God] am your *s*
2 Sam. 22:3 in Him [God] I will trust. He is my *s*
Ps. 5:12 with favor You [God] will surround him as with a *s*
Ps. 33:20 the LORD. He is our help and our *s*
Ps. 84:11 For the LORD God is a sun and *s*
Ps. 115:11 trust in the LORD: He is their help and their *s*
Prov. 30:5 He [God] is a *s* to those who put their trust in Him
Eph. 6:16 above all, taking the *s* of faith

SHIGGAION. A musical term in the title of Psalm 7, possibly referring to an increased tempo for singing.

SHILOAH. See *Siloam*

SHILOH. (1) A place of worship near Jerusalem where the Israelites set up the tabernacle soon after entering the land of Canaan (Josh. 18:1). After displacing the Canaanites, the people gathered at Shiloh to receive their share of the land (Josh. 18:10). Later, the Philistines captured the ark here (1 Sam. 4:3–11). Shiloh is also mentioned in Judg. 21:12–23 • Jer. 7:12, 14.

(2) A title of the coming Messiah which identified Him as a descendant of Judah (Gen. 49:10).

SHIMEA. A son of David, born in Jerusalem to his wife Bathsheba (1 Chron. 3:5).

SHIMEI. A man who insulted David when the king was fleeing from his son Absalom's attempt to take the throne (2 Sam. 16:5–13). Shimei was pardoned by David but later executed by Solomon (1 Kings 2:36–46).

SHINAR. See *Babylon*

SHINE [ING, S]
Num. 6:25 The LORD make His face *s* on you
Ps. 31:16 Make Your [God's] face to *s* on Your servant
Ps. 67:1 God...bless us and cause His face to *s* on us
Prov. 4:18 But the path of the just is like the *s'ing* light
Eccles. 8:1 A man's wisdom makes his face *s*
Isa. 60:1 Arise! *S*! For your light has come
Matt. 5:16 Let your light so *s* before men
John 1:5 the light *s's* in darkness
John 5:35 He [Jesus] was a burning and a *s'ing* light
Rev. 21:23 the city had no need of the sun... to *s* in it

SHIPHRAH. An Israelite midwife who, along with Puah, refused to carry out the Egyptian pharaoh's orders to kill all male Israelite babies (Exod. 1:15–17).

SHISHAK. See *Pharaoh*, No. 2

SHOBAB. A son of David and Bathsheba, born in Jerusalem after David became king over all Israel (1 Chron. 3:5).

SHOBI. A friend of David who brought provisions to the king and his aides when they fled from Absalom's rebellion (2 Sam. 17:27–29).

SHOCO. See *Soco*

SHONE

Isa. 9:2 in the land of the shadow of death, the light has *s* on them.

Matt. 17:2 And His [Jesus'] face *s* like the sun

Acts 9:3 suddenly a light from heaven *s* all around him [Paul]

2 Cor. 4:6 For God...has *s* in our hearts

SHOSHANNIM. A musical term, meaning "lilies," in the titles of Psalms 45, 69, and 80, possibly indicating the pitch or tune to which these psalms were to be sung.

SHOWBREAD. Unleavened bread kept in the temple or tabernacle for ceremonial purposes. Its name indicated it was exhibited in the presence of the Lord (Num. 4:7). *Shewbread*: KJV.

SHULAMMITE. A native of Shulam and the woman praised by King Solomon in the Song of Solomon (Song of Sol. 6:13). *Shulamite*: KJV.

SHUSHAN. KJV: see *Susa*

SHUTTLE. A rapidly moving device used in weaving thread into cloth.. The word is used as a symbol of fleeting time and the brevity of life (Job 7:6).

SIBBECAI. One of David's "mighty men," an elite group of warriors noted for their bravery in battle (1 Chron. 11:29).

SICHEM. KJV: see *Shechem*, No. 2

SICKNESS [ES]

Prov 18:14 The spirit of a man will sustain his *s*

Matt. 4:23 Jesus went about...healing all manner of *s*

Matt. 8:17 spoken by Isaiah...He Himself [Jesus]...bore our *s'es*

John 11:4 When Jesus heard that, He said, This *s* is not to death

SIDON. (1) The oldest son of Canaan (Gen. 10:15).

(2) A Canaanite city about twenty miles north of Tyre and founded by Sidon, the oldest son of Canaan (Gen. 10:15). Sidon's pagan culture infected Israel (the Northern Kingdom) when Jezebel, wife of King Ahab, promoted the worship of pagan gods throughout the nation (1 Kings 16:31). Several OT prophets predicted the destruction of Sidon because of its idolatry (Isa. 23:4 • Ezek. 28:21; *Zidon*: KJV). It is also mentioned in **Gen. 10:19** • Josh. 11:8 • Matt. 11:21–22; 15:21 • Mark 3:8; 7:24, 31 • Luke 4:26; 6:17; 10:13–14 • Acts 12:20; 27:3.

SIEGE. An assault against a fortified city to force it to surrender. The city of Samaria of the Northern Kingdom fell to the Assyrian army after a prolonged siege of about three years (2 Kings 17:5–6).

SIGHT

Exod. 3:3 I [Moses] will now turn aside and see this great *s*

Num. 13:33 we were like grasshoppers in our own *s*

Judg. 2:11 children of Israel did evil in the *s* of the LORD

1 Chron. 29:25 LORD magnified Solomon exceedingly in the *s* of all Israel

Ps. 9:19 Let the nations be judged in Your [God's] *s*

Ps. 19:14 Let the words of my mouth...be acceptable in Your [God's] *s*

Ps. 78:12 Marvelous things He [God] did in the *s* of their fathers, in...Egypt

Ps. 90:4 a thousand years in Your [God's] *s* are but as yesterday

Ps. 116:15 Precious in the *s* of the LORD is the death of His saints

Eccles. 6:9 The *s* of the eyes is better than the wandering of the desire

Matt. 11:5 the blind receive their *s* and the lame walk

Luke 1:15 he [John the Baptist] shall be great in the *s* of the Lord

Luke 15:21 I [prodigal son] have sinned...in your *s*

Acts 9:9 for three days he [Saul] was without *s*

Jas. 4:10 Humble yourselves in the *s* of the Lord

SIGN [S]

Gen. 1:14 let them [lights] be for *s's* and for seasons

Deut. 6:8 bind them [scriptures] as a *s* on your hand

Isa. 7:14 the Lord Himself shall give you a *s*

Dan. 4:3 How great are His [God's] *s's*

Matt. 12:39 An evil...generation seeks after a *s*

Matt. 24:3 what shall be the *s* of Your [Jesus'] coming

Luke 2:12 this shall be a *s* to you...baby wrapped in swaddling cloths

1 Cor. 1:22 the Jews require a *s*...Greeks seek after wisdom

Rev. 15:1 I [John] saw another *s* in heaven, great and marvelous

SIGNET. A royal seal used like a signature to authenticate documents (Jer. 22:24). Pharaoh entrusted his signet ring to Joseph to show his authority as a royal official (Gen. 41:42).

SIGNS AND WONDERS

Deut. 6:22 LORD showed great and severe *s-a-w*...on Egypt

Mark 13:22 false prophets shall arise and... show *s-a-w*

John 4:48 Unless you see *s-a-w*, you will not believe

Acts 5:12 many *s-a-w* were worked by the hands f the apostles

SIHON. An Amorite king who refused to allow Moses to pass through his territory on the way to Canaan. He was killed when he attacked the Israelites (Num. 21:21–30).

SILAS. A leader in the Jerusalem church who accompanied the apostle Paul on the second missionary journey (Acts 15:40–41). He and Paul were beaten and imprisoned in the city of Philippi for causing a disturbance. While they were praying and singing to the Lord, an earthquake shook the building, setting them

free. This led to the conversion of the jailer and his family (Acts 16:25–33). Silas was with Paul at Corinth and Thessalonica, as well (2 Cor. 1:19; *Silvanus*: KJV). He is also mentioned in 2 Thes. 1:1 • 1 Pet. 5:5.

SILENCE

Ps. 31:18 Let the lying lips be put to *s*

Ps. 39:2 I was mute with *s*. I held my peace

Isa. 65:6 I [God] will not keep *s*, but will repay

Hab. 2:20 Let all the earth keep *s* before Him [God]

1 Tim. 2:11 Let the woman learn in *s* with all submission

Rev. 8:1 opened the seventh seal, there was *s* in heaven

SILENT

Exod. 14:14 LORD shall fight for you, and you shall remain *s*

1 Sam. 2:9 the wicked shall be *s* in darkness

Job 13:5 O that you [Job's friends] would altogether remain *s*

Ps. 22:2 my God, I cry...in the nighttime, and am not *s*

Ps. 32:3 When I kept *s*, my [David's] bones grew old through my groaning

Ps. 50:3 Our God shall come and shall not keep *s*

Prov. 17:28 a fool, when he remains *s*, is counted wise

Eccles. 3:7 time to tear and a time to sew... time to keep *s* and a time to speak

Isa. 62:6 watchmen on your walls, O Jerusalem, who shall never remain *s*

Zech. 2:13 Be *s*, O all flesh, before the LORD

Mark 14:61 He [Jesus] remained *s*... Again the high priest asked Him

Acts 8:32 lamb before its shearer is *s*, so He [Jesus] did not open His mouth

Acts 18:9 Lord spoke to Paul... Do not be afraid...do not remain *s*

1 Cor. 14:26 if there is no interpreter, let him [speaker in tongues] keep *s* in the church

1 Cor. 14:34 Let your women keep *s* in the churches

SILOAM, POOL OF. A water reservoir in Jerusalem in which Jesus commanded a blind man to wash for healing (John 9:6–7). This pool and its connecting tunnel still exist today in Jerusalem's Old City. It was constructed by King Hezekiah of Judah (the Southern Kingdom) to provide water for the city in case of a siege by the Assyrian army. The tunnel connected to a spring outside the city wall (2 Kings 20:20). This pool is also mentioned in Luke 13:4. *Shiloah*: Isa. 8:6. *Shelah*: Neh. 3:15.

SILVANUS. KJV: see *Silas*

SILVER. A precious metal used in many objects, including jewelry (Exod. 3:22), containers (Num. 7:13), and items in the tabernacle (Num. 10:2). Silver was used as a medium of exchange and was valued by weight (Ezek. 27:12).

SIMEON. (1) A son of Jacob by Leah (Gen. 29:33). Simeon was held hostage by Joseph to assure the safe arrival of his brother Benjamin in Egypt. He is also mentioned in Gen. 29:33; 34:25, 30; 35:23; 42:24, 36; 43:23; 46:10; 48:5; 49:5 • Exod. 1:2; 6:15.

(2) Simeon's descendants who developed into one of the twelve tribes of Israel. After the conquest of Canaan, this tribe settled in the southern section of Israel (Josh. 19:1–9).

(3) A righteous man who blessed the child Jesus in the temple at Jerusalem (Luke 2:25–35).

SIMON. (1) Simon Peter, one of the twelve disciples of Jesus (Matt. 4:18–20).

(2) Another disciple of Jesus, called Simon the Zealot (Matt. 10:4 • Mark 3:18 • Luke 6:15 • Acts 1:13) to distinguish him from Simon Peter. Simon the Zealot may have been a member of a group that was fanatically opposed to Roman rule.

(3) A Pharisee to whom Jesus addressed His parable of the two debtors (Luke 7:36–47).

(4) A resident of Cyrene who was pressed into service by Romans soldiers to carry Jesus' cross (Mark 15:21).

(5) A magician condemned by the apostle Peter because he tried to buy the power of the Holy Spirit (Acts 8:18–21).

SIMPLE
Ps. 19:7 testimony of the Lord is sure, making wise the *s*
Prov. 8:5 O you *s*, understand wisdom
Prov. 22:3 but the *s* pass on, and are punished
Rom. 16:19 I[Paul] would have you...*s* concerning evil

SIN. A characteristic of humankind that leads to rebellion against God, willful rejection of His commands, and surrender to the power of evil rather than the divine will (Rom. 3:9). Sin was introduced into the human race when Adam and Eve disobeyed God in the garden of Eden (Genesis 3:6). This tendency to flaunt God and His authority has infected the human race ever since. As the apostle Paul declared, "All have sinned and come short of the glory of God" (Rom. 3:23). Sin causes people to fall short of the divine purpose for which they were created. The consequence of sin is spiritual death, but God's gift is forgiveness of human wrongdoing and eternal life through Jesus Christ (Rom. 6:23).

SIN [NED, S]
Gen. 4:7 if you [Cain] do not do well, *s* lies at the door
Lev. 16:34 make an atonement...once a year for all their *s's*
1 Sam. 15:24 Saul said to Samuel, I have *s'ned*
2 Chron. 7:14 then I [God] will hear...and will forgive their *s*
Job 1:22 In all this Job did not *s* or charge God foolishly
Job 13:23 How many are my iniquities and *s's*?
Ps. 32:1 Blessed is he...whose *s* is covered
Ps. 41:4 Heal my soul, for I have *s'ned* against You [God]
Ps. 51:2 Wash me...cleanse me from my *s*
Ps. 51:3 my *s* is ever before me
Ps. 51:4 Against You [God], You only, have I *s'ned*
Ps. 51:9 Hide Your [God's] face from my *s's*
Ps. 103:10 He [God] has not dealt with us according to our *s's*
Ps. 119:11 Your [God's] word have I hidden in my heart, that I might not *s*
Prov. 14:34 but *s* is a reproach to any people

Eccles. 7:20 not a just man on earth who...does not *s*

Isa. 1:18 though your *s's* are as scarlet, they shall be as white as snow

Isa. 6:7 your [Isaiah's] guilt is taken away, and your *s* purged

Isa. 40:2 she [Jerusalem] has received double... for all her *s's*

Jer. 14:20 we have *s'ned* against You [God]

Jer. 31:34 I [God] will remember their *s* no more

Ezek. 18:20 The soul that *s's*, it shall die

Mic. 7:19 You [God] will cast all their *s's* into the...sea

Matt. 1:21 He [Jesus] shall save His people from their *s's*

Matt. 18:21 how often shall my brother *s* against me and I forgive him

Matt. 26:28 My [Jesus'] blood...is shed for many for the remission of *s's*

Luke 15:21 I [the prodigal son] have *s'ned* against heaven and in your [his father's] sight

Luke 24:47 remission of *s's*...preached in His [Jesus'] name

John 1:29 Behold the Lamb of God who takes away the *s* of the world

John 8:7 He who is without *s*...let him first cast a stone

John 9:2 who *s'ned*, this man, or his parents, that he was born blind

John 16:8 He [Holy Spirit] will convict the world of *s*

Rom. 3:9 both Jews and Gentiles are all under *s*

Rom. 3:23 all have *s'ned* and come short of the glory of God

Rom. 4:7 Blessed are those...whose *s's* are covered

Rom. 5:12 through one man [Adam] *s* entered into the world

Rom. 6:1 continue in *s* that grace may abound

Rom. 6:12 do not let *s* reign in your mortal body

Rom. 6:23 the wages of *s* is death

Rom. 7:17 no longer I [Paul] who do it, but *s* that dwells in me

1 Cor. 6:18 he who commits fornication *s's* against his own body

1 Cor. 15:17 if Christ has not been raised...you are still in your *s's*

2 Cor. 5:21 He [God] has made Him [Jesus]... to be *s* for us

Heb. 9:28 Christ was offered once to bear the *s's* of many

Heb. 10:4 not possible that the blood of bulls... should take away *s's*

Heb. 12:1 lay aside...the *s* that so easily besets us

Jas. 4:17 knows to do good and does not do it, to him it is *s*

1 John 1:7 blood of Jesus...cleanses us from all *s*

1 John 1:8 say that we have no *s*, we deceive ourselves

1 John 1:9 He [God] is faithful...to forgive us our *s's*

1 John 1:10 If we say that we have not *s'ned*, we make Him [God] a liar

1 John 2:1 I write these things to you, that you may not *s*

1 John 2:2 He [Jesus] is the propitiation for our *s's*

1 John 4:10 He [God]...sent His Son [Jesus] to be the propitiation for our *s's*

SINAI, MOUNT. A mountain peak in the wilderness where God delivered the Ten Commandments to Moses. Here the Lord also ordered the people to keep the covenant He had established with their ancestor Abraham. God showed His power at Sinai by causing the mountain to shake and covering it with smoke (Exod. 19:16–18). This is probably the same mountain where Moses at an earlier time had seen a burning bush and heard God's call to deliver His people (called *Horeb*; Exod. 3:1–6). The mountain most widely accepted as Mount Sinai is known today by its Arabic name, Jebel Musa ("mountain of Moses"). It rises above the surrounding plain to an elevation of more than seven thousand feet above sea level. At the foot of this mountain sits the monastery of Saint Catherine, which memorializes God's encounter with Moses and the Israelites at this sacred site. Mount Sinai is also mentioned in **Exod. 19–23**; 24:16; 31:18; 34:2–32 • Lev. 7:38; 25:1; 26:46 • Num. 1:1, 19; 3:1–14; 9:1, 5; 10:12;

26:64; 28:6; 33:15–16 • Deut. 33:2 • Judg. 5:5 •
Neh. 9:13 • Ps. 68:8, 17 • Acts 7:30 • Gal. 4:24–25.

SINCERITY

Josh. 24:14 serve Him [God] in *s* and in truth

1 Cor. 5:8 keep the feast...with the unleavened bread of *s* and truth

2 Cor. 8:8 I [Paul] speak...to prove the *s* of your love

SING [ING]

Ps. 59:17 To You [God]...will I *s*, for God is my defense

Ps. 67:4 let the nations be glad and *s* for joy

Ps. 81:1 *S* aloud to God our strength; make a joyful noise

Ps. 92:1 It is a good thing...to *s* praises to Your [God's] name

Ps. 100:2 come before His [God's] presence with *s'ing*

Ps. 137:4 How shall we *s* the LORD's song in a foreign land?

Song of Sol. 2:12 The time of the *s'ing* of birds has come

Isa. 49:13 break out into *s'ing*, O mountains

Isa. 52:9 *s* together, you desolate places of Jerusalem

Col. 3:16 *s'ing* with grace in your hearts to the Lord

Jas. 5:13 Is anyone merry? Let him *s* psalms

SING TO THE LORD

Exod. 15:21 *S-t-t-L*, for He has triumphed

1 Chron. 16:23 *S-t-t-L*, all the earth

Ps. 13:6 I will *s-t-t-L*...He has dealt bountifully with me

Ps. 95:1 let us *s-t-t-L*...the rock of our salvation

Ps. 96:1 *s-t-t-L* a new song; *s-t-t-L*, all the earth

Ps. 98:5 *S-t-t-L* with the harp

Ps. 104:33 I will *s-t-t-L* as long as I live

Isa. 12:5 *S-t-t-L* for He has done excellent things

SINNED AGAINST THE LORD

Exod. 10:16 I [Pharaoh] have *s-a-t-L* your God

Josh. 7:20 I [Achan] have *s-a-t-L* God of Israel

2 Sam. 12:13 I [David] have *s-a-t-L*

Jer. 3:25 we [people of Judah] have *s-a-t-L* our God

SINNER [S]

Ps. 1:1 Blessed is the man who does not...stand in the way of *s's*

Eccles. 9:18 but one *s* destroys much good

Mark 2:17 I [Jesus] came to call...*s's* to repentance

Luke 5:30 Why do You [Jesus] eat and drink with...*s's*

Luke 15:7 more joy in heaven over one *s* who repents

Luke 18:13 God be merciful to me [publican], a *s*

Rom. 5:8 while we were still *s's*, Christ died for us

1 Tim. 1:15 Christ Jesus came into the world to save *s's*

Jas. 4:8 Cleanse your hands, you *s's*, and purify your hearts

SIN OFFERING. An offering of a sacrificial animal presented to God to gain forgiveness for sins, particularly those committed unintentionally or in ignorance (Lev. 4:2–3). A sin offering for all the people was made once a year by the high priest on the day of atonement (Lev. 16:6, 15).

SIN, WILDERNESS OF. A barren region where food was miraculously provided for the Israelites during the early years of the Exodus from Egypt (Exod. 16:1–8).

SION. See *Zion*

SIRION. See *Hermon, Mount*

SISERA. A Canaanite military officer killed by a woman named Jael, who drove a tent peg into his head while he slept (Judg. 4:2–22).

SKULL, THE. See *Calvary*

SLAVE. A person owned by another and forced to work on the owner's behalf. The apostle Paul appealed to Philemon to receive his runaway slave Onesimus as a fellow believer (Philem. 15–18).

SLEEP [ING, S]

Ps. 13:3 Lighten my eyes, lest I *s* the *s* of death

Ps. 44:23 Awake! Why do You sleep, O Lord?

Prov. 6:9 How long will you *s*, O sluggard?

Prov. 20:13 Do not love *s*, lest you come to poverty

Matt. 9:24 the maid is not dead, but *s'ing*

Mark 13:36 coming suddenly, he [master of the house] finds you *s'ing*

Mark 14:41 *S* on now and take your [the disciples'] rest

John 11:11 He [Jesus] said to them, Our friend Lazarus *s's*

1 Cor. 15:51 We shall not all *s*, but we shall all be changed

SLEPT

Gen. 2:21 God caused a deep sleep to fall on Adam, and he *s*

Gen. 41:5 And he [Pharaoh] *s* and dreamed a second time

1 Kings 2:10 So David *s* with his fathers and was buried

Ps. 3:5 I laid me down and *s*

Matt. 28:13 Say, His [Jesus'] disciples...stole Him away while we *s*

SLING. A simple weapon used to throw stones (Judg. 20:16). The shepherd boy David felled the giant Goliath with his sling (1 Sam. 17:50).

SMYRNA. A prosperous city where one of the seven churches of Asia Minor was located. The church was being persecuted, apparently by radical Jews. Jesus encouraged these believers to remain faithful to Him in spite of these difficulties They were privileged to belong to Jesus, the first and the last—the one who transcended time and eternity (Rev. 2:8).

SO. See *Pharaoh*, No. 3

SOBER [LY, NESS]

Acts 26:25 I [Paul]...am speaking...words of truth and *s'ness*

1 Thes. 5:6 let us not sleep... But let us watch and be *s*

1 Tim. 3:2 bishop then must be blameless... vigilant, *s*

Titus 2:12 we should live *s'ly*, righteously, and godly

1 Pet. 5:8 Be *s* and vigilant...the devil walks about

SOCO. A defense city built by King Rehoboam of Judah (the Southern Kingdom), Solomon's son and successor (2 Chron. 11:7). *Shoco*: KJV.

SODOM. One of five cities destroyed by God because of its great wickedness (Gen. 19:1–28). God promised Abraham that He would not destroy Sodom if it contained just ten righteous people. But He proceeded with His plan when only Lot and his wife and two daughters met this qualification (Gen. 18:23–33; 19:14–15). The city is cited often as a symbol of evil and as a warning to sinners (Isa. 1:9 • Rev. 11:8). Sodom is also mentioned in Jer. 49:18 • Ezek. 16:46–49 • Amos 4:11 • Zeph. 2:9 • Matt. 11:23–24 • Rom. 9:29 • 2 Pet. 2:6 • Jude 7.

SODOMA. KJV: see *Sodom*

SOJOURNER. A person who lived temporarily in a foreign country (Heb. 11:9). Abraham sojourned in Egypt (Gen. 12:10) as did the Israelites during the Exile (Ezra 1:4). The word is also used symbolically of Christians in the world (1 Pet. 1:17).

SOLEMN ASSEMBLY. A religious gathering, usually occurring during a major Jewish festival, which was devoted to repentance, confession, and prayer (Lev. 23:36 • Deut. 16:8).

SOLOMON. David's son and successor as king of Israel who was known for his wisdom and riches. He began his reign by asking the Lord to grant him wisdom to govern the nation (1 Kings 3:4–15). He went on to complete many building projects, including the temple in Jerusalem (1 Kings 6:1–38). Solomon's trade with surrounding nations also brought unprecedented wealth to the nation as well as himself (1 Kings 9:26–28; 10:26–29). The king also wrote many proverbs and other wise sayings (1 Kings 4:32). The wisdom books of Proverbs, Ecclesiastes, and Song of Solomon in the OT are attributed to him.

In spite of his wisdom, Solomon's judgment was flawed. He built a harem of hundreds of wives and concubines. Many of these marriages were political unions to seal alliances with foreign nations. He allowed these wives to worship their national deities and eventually fell under the influence of these pagan gods himself (1 Kings 11:1–5). His expensive projects and lavish lifestyle resulted in high taxes levied on the people. When Solomon died, the disgruntled ten northern tribes of the nation rebelled and formed their own nation still known as Israel (the Northern Kingdom). The two tribes that remained loyal to Solomon and his successors continued as the nation of Judah (the Southern Kingdom) (1 Kings 12:16–17).

See 1 Kings 1–11 • 2 Chron. 1–9 for a complete view of Solomon's life.

SON OF DAVID. A name of Jesus that ties together the two major sections of the Bible— the OT and the NT. His genealogies in the Gospels of Matthew and Luke emphasize that Jesus in His human lineage was descended from David (Matt. 1:6 • Luke 3:31). Thus, in a spiritual sense Jesus fulfilled His Father's promise to David that one of David's descendants would always reign over God's people (2 Sam. 7:1–16 • Ps. 132:11).

SON OF GOD. A title of Jesus that emphasizes His close relationship to God the Father. An angel revealed to Mary that she would give birth to a child who would be called the "Son of God" (Luke 1:35). After Jesus was baptized, a voice from heaven declared, "This is My beloved Son" (Matt. 3:17). Jesus as God's Son was perfectly obedient to the Father. He refused to be sidetracked from the mission on which He was sent into the world. His last words from the cross were "It is finished" (John 19:30)——a declaration of victory over the forces of sin and death. He had accomplished the work His Father had commissioned Him to do.

SON OF GOD

Matt. 27:40 If You [Jesus] are the *S-o-G*, come down from the cross

Matt. 27:54 Truly this [Jesus] was the *S-o-G*

Luke 1:35 the Holy One...shall be called the *S-o-G*

Luke 4:3 If you are the *S-o-G*, command this stone to be made bread

John 1:34 I [John the Baptist]...bore record that this [Jesus] is the *S-o-G*

John 20:31 believe that Jesus is the Christ, the *S-o-G*

1 John 4:15 Whoever confesses that Jesus is the *S-o-G*, God dwells in him

1 John 5:12 he who does not have the *S-o-G* does not have life

SON OF MAN. A name or title that Jesus used often when referring to Himself (Luke 9:58). In the OT, God addressed the prophet Ezekiel by using this name (Ezek. 2:1; 34:2). The basic meaning of the phrase is "mortal" or "human being." Jesus may have called Himself the Son of Man to emphasize His role as a bold spokesman for God in the prophetic tradition of Ezekiel. Or perhaps the name called attention to His humanity and identification with normal people. He came to earth as a brother and fellow sufferer to deliver humankind from bondage to sin.

SON OF MAN

Ps. 8:4 what is...the *s-o-m*, that You [God] care about him

Ezek. 2:1 *S-o-m* [Ezekiel], stand on your feet

Matt. 12:8 the *S-o-m* [Jesus] is Lord even of the Sabbath day

Matt. 16:13 Who do men say that I [Jesus], the *S-o-m*, am?

Matt. 24:44 the *S-o-m* [Jesus] is coming at such an hour as you do not think

Mark 10:45 *S-o-m* [Jesus] did not come to be ministered to, but to minister

Luke 9:58 *S-o-m* [Jesus] does not have anywhere to lay His head

Luke 22:48 Jesus said... Judas, will you betray the *S-o-m* with a kiss?

John 3:14 even so the *S-o-m* [Jesus] must be lifted up

John 12:23 The hour has come that the *S-o-m* [Jesus] should be glorified

SONG OF DEBORAH. Judg. 5:1–31

SONG OF MARY. Luke 1:46–55

SONG OF MIRIAM. Exod. 15:20–21

SONG OF MOSES. Deut. 32:1–44

SONG OF SOLOMON. A short book of the OT, also called the "song of songs" because the author, King Solomon, claimed it was his favorite among all the songs he wrote (Song of Sol. 1:1). This is significant, because he is reported to have written 1,005 songs (1 Kings 4:32). The book is filled with expressions of affection between two lovers (Song of Sol. 1:13; 4:1–11; 7:2–10). These words have been interpreted both symbolically and literally. Some insist the song symbolizes God's love for His people Israel, while others believe the book is a healthy affirmation of the joys of physical love between husband and wife.

SONG OF ZECHARIAH. Luke 1:67–79

SOPATER. A believer from Berea who accompanied the apostle Paul on the third missionary journey (Acts 20:4). This may be the same person as Sosipater (Rom. 16:21).

SOREK. A valley between Jerusalem and Ashdod; site of the home of Delilah, the Philistine woman who betrayed the judge Samson (Judg. 16:4).

SORROW [FUL, S]
Ps. 18:5 The *s's* of hell surrounded me
Ps. 38:17 my *s* is continually before me
Eccles. 1:18 he who increases knowledge increases *s*
Isa. 53:3 a man of *s's* and acquainted with grief
Jer. 45:3 for the LORD has added grief to my *s*
Matt. 19:22 he [rich young ruler] went away *s'ful*
Matt. 24:8 All these are the beginning of *s's*
Matt. 26:38 My [Jesus'] soul is exceeding *s'ful*
John 16:20 your *s* shall be turned into joy
2 Cor. 7:10 godly *s* produces repentance to salvation
Rev. 21:4 no more death or *s* or crying

SOSIPATER. A kinsman of Paul whose greetings were sent to the church at Rome (Rom. 16:21). See also *Sopater*.

SOSTHENES. A ruler of the synagogue at Corinth who was beaten by a mob (Acts 18:17).

SOUL. A word with several different meanings in the Bible. It refers to one's essence as a person created in God's image (Gen. 2:7); sometimes to people in general (Gen. 12:5); and in the NT to life in general, as in Jesus' famous statement, "What will it profit a man if he gains the whole world and loses his own soul?" (Matt. 16:26). In modern usage, *soul* usually refers to a person's inner or spiritual nature that lives on after physical death.

SOUL [S]
Gen. 2:7 and man became a living *s*
Deut. 6:5 you shall love the LORD your God... with all your *s*
1 Sam. 18:1 *s* of Jonathan was knit to the *s* of David
Job 19:2 How long will you afflict my [Job's] *s*
Ps. 19:7 law of the LORD is perfect, converting the *s*
Ps. 23:3 He [God] restores my *s*
Ps. 25:1 To You, O LORD, I lift up my *s*
Ps. 33:20 Our *s* waits for the LORD. He is our help
Ps. 35:9 And my *s* shall be joyful in the LORD
Ps. 42:2 My *s* thirsts for God
Ps. 42:5 Why are you cast down, O my *s*?
Ps. 56:13 You [God] have delivered my *s* from death
Ps. 72:13 He [God]...shall save the *s's* of the needy
Ps. 84:2 My *s*...faints for the courts of the LORD
Ps. 103:1 Bless the LORD, O my *s*...bless His holy name
Ps. 142:4 Refuge has failed me; no man cared for my *s*
Prov. 11:30 and he who wins *s's* is wise
Prov. 18:7 A fool's...lips are the snare of his *s*
Lam. 3:24 The LORD is my portion, says my *s*
Ezek. 18:20 The *s* that sins, it shall die
Mic. 6:7 Shall I give...fruit of my body for the sin of my *s*
Matt. 10:28 rather fear Him who is able to destroy both *s* and body
Matt. 11:29 you shall find rest for your *s's*
Matt. 16:26 what shall a man give in exchange for his *s*

Mark 14:34 My [Jesus'] *s* is exceedingly sorrowful, to death

John 12:27 Now My [Jesus'] *s* is troubled

Rom. 13:1 every *s* be subject to the governing authorities

1 Pet. 2:11 abstain from fleshly lusts that war against the *s*

1 Pet. 2:25 are now returned to the...Bishop of your *s's*

SOUND [ING]

John 3:8 The wind blows...you hear the *s* of it

Acts 2:2 came from heaven a *s* like a mighty rushing wind

1 Cor. 13:1 I [Paul] have become as *s'ing* brass

1 Cor. 14:8 if the trumpet gives an uncertain *s*

1 Cor. 15:52 trumpet shall *s*, and the dead shall be raised

2 Tim. 4:3 when they will not endure *s* doctrine

SOUTHERN KINGDOM (JUDAH) FALLS TO BABYLON. 2 Kings 25

SOVEREIGNTY OF GOD. A theological
phrase that expresses the truth that God is the all-powerful ruler of the universe. His creation of humankind and the world implies His continuing rule and sovereignty (Gen. 1:1 • Ps. 8:1–5). God's supreme authority is also expressed by several divine names, including "Almighty God" (Gen. 17:1) and "LORD of hosts" (Ps. 24:10).

SOW [ED, S]

Ps. 126:5 Those who *s* in tears shall reap in joy

Prov. 22:8 He who *s's* iniquity shall reap vanity

Matt. 13:24 kingdom...is similar to a man who *s'ed* good seed

Luke 8:5 as he [a sower] *s'ed*, some fell by the wayside

Luke 12:24 Consider the ravens, for they neither *s* nor reap

John 4:37 One *s's* and another reaps

2 Cor. 9:6 he who *s's* bountifully shall reap also bountifully

Gal. 6:7 whatever a man *s's*, that he shall also reap

SOWN

Hos. 8:7 they have *s* the wind, and they shall reap the whirlwind

Hag. 1:6 You have *s* much and bring in little

Mark 4:18 these are those that were *s* among thorns

1 Cor. 15:42 It [the body] is *s* in corruption; it is raised in incorruption

SPAIN. A country in southwestern Europe
which the apostle Paul wanted to visit (Rom. 15:24). Jonah's ship was headed for the city of Tarshish in Spain when he was thrown overboard and swallowed by a great fish (Jon. 1:3, 15).

SPAN. A measure of length; the distanced
between the thumb and little finger on an outstretched adult hand. It was equal to about nine inches (Exod. 28:16).

SPARE [D, S]

Gen. 18:26 If I [God] find in Sodom fifty righteous...then I will *s* all

1 Sam. 15:9 But Saul...*s'd* Agag and the best of the sheep and of the oxen

Neh. 13:22 God...*s* me [Nehemiah] according to the greatness of Your mercy

Job 2:6 he [Job] is in your [Satan's] hand. But *s* his life

Prov. 13:24 He who *s's* his rod hates his son

Jonah 4:11 should not I [God] *s* Nineveh, that great city

Rom. 8:32 He [God] who did not *s* His own Son [Jesus]

2 Pet. 2:4 God did not *s* the angels who sinned

SPEAR. A weapon of war, consisting of a
long shaft with a metal point (1 Sam. 13:22). The psalmist also used the word as a symbol of oppression from his enemies (Ps. 57:4).

SPECIAL PEOPLE

Deut. 14:2 LORD has chosen you [Israel] to be a *s-p*

Titus 2:14 He [Jesus] might...purify to Himself a *s-p*

1 Pet. 2:9 you [Christians] are...a holy nation, a *s-p*

SPEECH

Gen. 11:1 whole earth was of one language and of one *s*

Exod. 4:10 I [Moses] am slow of *s*

Prov. 17:7 Excellent *s* does not become a fool

Isa. 28:23 Give ear...listen and hear My [God's] *s*

Mark 14:70 you [Peter] are a Galilean, and your *s* agrees to it

1 Cor. 2:1 I [Paul] did not come with excellency of *s*

Col. 4:6 Let your *s* always be...seasoned with salt

SPICE. A pleasant-smelling substance used in perfumes and ointments (Exod. 30:23–36). Women followers of Jesus took spices to the tomb to anoint His body (Mark 16:1).

SPIES SENT INTO CANAAN. Num. 13:1–33

SPINNING. See *Weaving*

SPIRIT [S]

1 Sam. 28:8 divine to me [Saul] by the familiar *s*

2 Kings 2:9 let a double portion of your [Elijah's] *s* be upon me [Elisha]

Job 32:8 But there is a *s* in man

Ps. 31:5 Into Your [God's] hand I commit my *s*

Ps. 51:10 O God...renew a right *s* within me

Prov. 16:18 Pride goes before destruction... haughty *s* before a fall

Prov. 25:28 He who has no rule over his own *s*

Isa. 32:15 until the *S* is poured out on us from on high

Isa. 42:1 I [God] have put my *S* upon Him [God's servant]

Ezek. 3:24 Then the *S* entered into me [Ezekiel]

Ezek. 11:19 I [God] will put a new *s* within them

Dan. 6:3 because an excellent *s* was in him [Daniel]

Joel 2:28 I [God] will pour out my *S* on all flesh

Zech. 4:6 Not by might, no by power, but by My [God's] *S*

Matt. 5:3 Blessed are the poor in *s*

Matt. 26:41 The *s*...is willing, but the flesh is weak

Mark 6:7 He [Jesus]...gave them [disciples] power over unclean *s's*

Luke 23:46 Father, into Your hands I [Jesus] commend My *s*

John 3:5 unless a man is born of water and of the *S*

John 4:23 worship the Father in *s* and in truth

John 16:13 *S* of truth [Holy Spirit], has come, He will guide

Acts 17:16 his [Paul's] *s* was stirred in him

Rom. 8:16 The *S* Himself bears witness with our *s*

1 Cor. 12:4 diversities of gifts, but the same *S*

1 Cor. 12:10 to another discerning of *s's*

2 Cor. 3:6 letter kills, but the *S* gives life

Gal. 5:16 walk in the *S*...not fulfill the lust of the flesh

Gal. 5:22 fruit of the *S* is love, joy, peace, long-suffering

Eph. 4:3 unity of the *S* in the bond of peace

Eph. 6:17 sword of the *S*, which is the word of God

2 Tim. 1:7 God has not given us the *s* of fear

1 John 4:1 test the *s's* whether they are of God

Rev. 2:7 hear what the *S* says to the churches

SPIRIT, FILLING OF, AT PENTECOST.

Acts 2:1–21

SPIRIT OF GOD

Gen. 1:2 *S-o-G* moved on the face of the waters

1 Sam. 11:6 And the *S-o-G* came on Saul

Job 33:4 The *S-o-G* has made me [Elihu]

Matt. 3:16 Jesus...saw the *S-o-G* descending like a dove

Rom. 8:14 led by the *S-o-G*, they are the sons of God

1 Cor. 3:16 Do you not know...that the *S-o-G* dwells in you

Eph. 4:30 do not grieve the Holy *S-o-G*

SPIRIT OF THE LORD

Judg. 6:34 the *S-o-t-L* came on Gideon

1 Sam. 16:13 the *S-o-t-L* came on David

Isa. 11:2 the *S-o-t-L* shall rest upon Him [God's servant]

Isa. 61:1 The *S-o-t-L* GOD is upon Me [God's servant]

Luke 4:18 The *S-o-t-L* is upon Me [Jesus]

Acts 8:39 the *S-o-t-L* took Philip away

2 Cor. 3:17 where the *S-o-t-L* is, there is liberty

SPIRITUAL [LY]

Rom. 8:6 to be *s'ly* minded is life and peace

1 Cor. 14:1 Follow after love, and desire *s* gifts

1 Cor. 15:44 It is sown a natural body; it is raised a *s* body

Eph. 6:12 we wrestle...against *s* wickedness in high places

1 Pet. 2:5 you also, as living stones, are built up as a *s* house

SPIRITUAL GIFTS. Talents and abilities given by the Holy Spirit to believers for the growth and edification of fellow believers and the church. The apostle Paul identified several of these gifts in his letters to the believers at Rome (Rom. 12:6–8) and Corinth (1 Cor. 12:8–11). He went on to declare in 1 Corinthians that love for others is the supreme spiritual gift (1 Cor. 13:1–15).

SPIRITUAL WARFARE. The struggle that Christians face in trying to live out their faith in a sinful world. The concept comes from the apostle Paul, who compared this conflict to a wrestling match in which believers battle with the temptations of Satan. The devil's allies are invisible demonic forces that wield great power. Their goal is to wreck the work of Christ and put a halt to the positive influence of His followers (Eph. 6:12). Believers need an arsenal of spiritual weapons to overcome Satan's power. Paul referred to these as the "whole armor of God"—truth, righteousness, the assurance of the gospel, faith, salvation, the word of God, and prayer (Eph. 6:13–17). Equipped with these weapons and guided by the Holy Spirit, believers are assured of victory in this struggle.

STACHYS. A believer at Rome greeted and commended by the apostle Paul (Rom. 16:9).

STAFF. A stick or rod used in several different ways. The boy David had a staff, probably used to guide sheep or protect them from predators (1 Sam. 17:40). A staff also symbolized a person's authority (2 Kings 4:29) as well as the Lord's protection of His people (Ps. 23:4).

STAND [ING, S]

Exod. 3:5 the place on which you [Moses] *s* is holy ground

Exod. 14:13 *s* still, and see the salvation of the LORD

Job 19:25 my [Job's] redeemer...shall *s* at the latter day

Ps. 1:1 does not walk...or *s* in the way of sinners

Ps. 24:3 who shall *s* in His [God's] holy place

Prov. 12:7 the house of the righteous shall *s*

Isa. 40:8 but the word of our God shall *s* forever

Mal. 3:2 who shall *s* when He [God] appears

Matt. 12:25 house divided against itself shall not *s*

Acts 7:55 he [Stephen]...saw...Jesus *s'ing* at the right hand of God

Rom. 14:10 all *s* before the judgment seat of Christ

1 Cor. 10:12 let him who thinks he *s's* be careful lest he fall

1 Cor. 16:13 Watch, *s* fast in the faith, act like men, be strong

Gal. 5:1 *S* fast...in the liberty by which Christ has made us free

Eph. 6:11 able to *s* against the schemes of the devil

2 Thes. 2:15 brothers, *s* fast, and hold the traditions

Rev. 3:20 Behold, I [Jesus] *s* at the door and knock

STANDARD. A banner or flag that identified groups of warriors or members of a tribe. During the Exodus from Egypt, each tribe of Israel marched under its own distinctive standard (Num. 2:2, 34).

STAR. A heavenly body visible in the night sky. The stars were considered a mark of God's creative power (Job 9:7). The most famous star in the Bible signaled the birth of Jesus. Wise men from the east saw this star and came to pay homage to the newborn Jesus in Bethlehem (Matt. 2:1–2).

STAR OUT OF JACOB. A name for the coming Messiah spoken by Balaam, a pagan magician (Num. 24:17). The name suggested that the Messiah would rule over His people with great power and unlimited authority.

STATUTE. An official pronouncement or decree from a person in authority (Exod. 18:16). God issues His statutes for the benefit of His people (Ps. 19:8).

STATUTE [S]

Exod. 27:21 It shall be a *s* forever to their generations

Lev. 10:11 teach...Israel all the *s's* that the LORD has spoken

Lev. 16:34 this shall be an everlasting *s* to you

Deut. 5:31 I [God] will speak to you [Moses] all... the *s's* and the judgments

1 Kings 3:3 Solomon loved the LORD, walking in the *s's* of his father, David

Ps. 19:8 The *s's* of the LORD are right, rejoicing the heart

Ps. 119:12 Blessed are You, O LORD. Teach me Your *s's*

Ezek. 20:19 walk in My [God's] *s's* and keep My judgments

STAY

Ps. 119:148 My eyes *s* awake during the night watches

Jer. 3:12 I am merciful, says the LORD, and I will not *s* angry forever

Hab. 1:13 Why do You [God] look on those who act treacherously and *s* silent

Luke 19:5 Zacchaeus...today I [Jesus] must *s* at your house

Luke 24:29 they [Emmaus road travelers] urged Him [Jesus], saying, *S* with us

STEADFAST [LY, NESS]

Luke 9:51 He [Jesus] *s'ly* set His face to go to Jerusalem

1 Cor. 15:58 Therefore, my beloved brothers, be *s*, immovable

Col. 2:5 and the *s'ness* of your faith in Christ

Heb. 3:14 hold the beginning of our confidence *s* to the end

STEPHANAS. A Christian from Corinth who, along with two other believers, visited Paul at Ephesus (1 Cor. 16:17). They may have informed

the apostle of the problems in the Corinthian church.

STEPHEN. A zealous believer of Greek background who became the first martyr of the Christian faith. He was one of the seven men chosen to provide relief for Greek-speaking widows who were being neglected in the church's ministry of food distribution (Acts 6:5–8). In a long speech, he claimed the system of Old Testament laws was no longer needed because it had been replaced by the teachings of Jesus. This brought him into conflict with Jewish leaders, and they stoned him to death on a charge of blasphemy (Acts 7:55–60). Stephen's calm and resolute faith in the face of death may have been a factor in the apostle Paul's later conversion to Christianity (Acts 22:20). He is also mentioned in Acts 8:2; 11:19.

STEWARD [S]

Matt. 20:8 lord of the vineyard said to his *s*, Call the laborers...give them their wages

Luke 16:8 the master commended the unjust *s*

1 Cor. 4:2 required of *s's* that a man be found faithful

Titus 1:7 a bishop must be blameless as the *s* of God

1 Pet. 4:10 good *s's* of the manifold grace of God

STEWARDSHIP. Wise management of resources given by the Lord. Christian stewardship is based on God's ownership of all things (Gen. 1:1 • Ps. 24:1–2) and humankind's assigned task to take care of His creation (Gen. 1:26; 2:15). The message of Jesus' parable of the talents (Matt. 25:14–30) is that believers will be held accountable for how they manage the responsibility they are given as stewards of the Lord (see 1 Cor. 4:2).

STEWARDSHIP

Luke 16:2 Give an account of your *s*, for you may no longer be steward

Luke 16:3 My master is taking away the *s* from me

STONE [D, S]

Gen. 31:45 Jacob took a *s* and set it up for a pillar

Exod. 17:4 these people...are almost ready to *s* me [Moses]

Exod. 31:18 two...tablets of *s*, written with the finger of God

Lev. 26:1 Nor shall you set up any image of *s*

Josh. 4:6 What do you mean by these *s's*?

1 Sam. 17:50 David prevailed...with a sling and with a *s*

Ps. 118:22 *s* that the builders rejected has become the head cornerstone

Eccles. 3:5 and a time to gather *s's* together

Isa. 28:16 I [God] lay in Zion a *s* for a foundation, a tested *s*

Matt. 4:3 command that these *s's* be made bread

Matt. 21:42 The *s* that the builders rejected

Matt. 24:2 there shall not be one *s* left here on another

Matt. 27:66 they [soldiers]...made the sepulchre sure, sealing the *s*

Mark 16:4 they [the women] saw that the *s* had been rolled away

Luke 13:34 Jerusalem...who kills the prophets, and *s's* those who are sent

John 1:42 called Cephas (which is by interpretation, A *S*)

Acts 4:11 the *s* that was despised by you builders

Acts 7:59 they *s'd* Stephen as he was calling on God

1 Pet. 2:8 a *s* of stumbling and a rock of offence

Rev. 21:19 foundations...garnished with all manner of precious *s's*

STONING. A method of capital punishment specified in the Mosaic law for certain offenses, including breaking the Sabbath (Num. 15:32–36), idolatry (Deut. 17:2–7), and adultery (Deut. 22:23–24). A group of scribes and Pharisees brought a woman accused of adultery to Jesus. They tested Him by asking whether she should be stoned, as specified by the law. They walked away in silence when Jesus challenged them, "He who is without sin among you, let him first cast a stone at her" (John 8:7).

STRAIGHT

Isa. 40:3 Make *s* in the desert a highway for our God

Luke 3:4 Prepare the way of the Lord; make His paths *s*

Acts 9:11 Arise and go to the street that is called *S*

STRANGER [S]

Ps. 54:3 For *s's* have risen up against me

Ps. 69:8 I have become a *s* to my brothers

Matt. 25:35 I was a *s* and you took Me [Jesus] in

Eph. 2:19 therefore you are no longer *s's* and foreigners

Heb. 13:2 Do not forget to entertain *s's*...angels unawares

STRENGTH

Exod. 13:14 By *s* of hand the Lord brought us [Israel] out from Egypt

Exod. 15:2 The Lord is my [Moses'] *s* and song

Deut. 34:7 his [Moses'] *s* was not weakened

Judg. 6:14 Go in this *s* of yours, and you shall save Israel

Job 12:13 Wisdom and *s* are with Him [God]

Ps. 18:2 my God, my *s*, in whom I will trust

Ps. 19:14 words of my mouth...be acceptable... O Lord, my *s*

Ps. 27:1 The Lord is the *s* of my life

Ps. 43:2 For You are the God of my *s*

Ps. 46:1 God is our refuge and *s*, a...help in trouble

Ps. 71:9 do not forsake me when my *s* fails

Ps. 84:5 Blessed is the man whose *s* is in You [God]

Ps. 90:10 because of *s* they [days of our years] are eighty years

Ps. 118:14 The Lord is my *s* and song...my salvation

Isa. 12:2 Lord Jehovah is my *s* and my song

Isa. 30:15 In quietness and in confidence shall be your *s*

Isa. 40:31 those who wait on the Lord shall renew their *s*

Hab. 3:19 The Lord God is my *s*

Mark 12:30 love the Lord your God...with all your *s*

2 Cor. 12:9 My [God's] *s* is made perfect in weakness

STRENGTHEN [ED, ING, S]

Ps. 27:14 He [God] shall *s* your heart. Wait, I say, on the LORD

Luke 22:43 there appeared to Him [Jesus] an angel...*s'ing* Him

Phil. 4:13 do all things through Christ who *s's* me [Paul]

2 Tim. 4:17 the Lord stood with me [Paul] and *s'ed* me

STRIPES. See *Lashes*

STRIVE [D, ING, S]. See also *Quarrel*

Luke 13:24 S to enter in at the narrow gate

Rom. 15:20 I [Paul] have so *s'd* to preach the gospel

1 Cor. 9:25 every man who *s's* for victory is temperate in all things

Phil. 1:27 one mind *s'ing* together for the faith of the gospel

STRONG [ER]

Deut. 31:6 Be *s* and of good courage. Do not fear

Ps. 24:8 The LORD *s* and mighty, the LORD mighty in battle

Ps. 71:7 but You [God] are my *s* refuge

Ps. 89:8 who is a *s* LORD like You

Prov. 18:10 The name of the LORD is a *s* tower

Eccles. 9:11 the race is not to the swift, nor the battle to the *s*

Luke 2:40 the Child [Jesus] grew and became *s* in spirit

Rom. 15:1 *s* ought to bear the weaknesses of the weak

1 Cor. 1:25 the weakness of God is *s'er* than men

2 Cor. 12:10 when I [Paul] am weak, then I am *s*

Eph. 6:10 Finally, my brothers, be *s* in the Lord

STUBBLE. Stalks left in the ground after grain was harvested (Exod. 5:12). To the prophet Isaiah, stubble symbolized the Lord's approaching judgment against sinful Judah (the Southern Kingdom) (Isa. 33:11).

STUMBLING BLOCK. A hindrance to belief or understanding; a concept cited by the apostle Paul (1 Cor. 1:23). Jesus was not the military deliverer that the Israelites expected. Instead He was a spiritual leader who died on a Roman cross. This was a stumbling block that kept many Jews of Paul's time from accepting Jesus as the Messiah.

STUMBLING BLOCK [S]

Jer. 6:21 I [God] will lay *s-b's* before this people

Matt. 16:23 Get behind Me [Jesus], Satan. You are a *s-b* to Me

Rom. 14:13 no man should put a *s-b*...in his brother's way

1 Cor. 1:23 Christ crucified, a *s-b* to the Jews

1 Cor. 8:9 liberty...becomes a *s-b* to those who are weak

SUBMISSION TO OTHERS IN THE LORD.
1 Pet. 3:1–12

SUBMIT [TING]

Eph. 5:21 *s'ting* yourselves to one another in the fear of God

Eph. 5:22 Wives, *s* yourselves to your own husbands

Jas. 4:7 S yourselves, therefore, to God. Resist the devil

1 Pet. 5:5 you who are younger, *s* yourselves to the elders

SUCCOTH-BENOTH. An idol set up in Samaria by the people who colonized the area after the Northern Kingdom fell to the Assyrians (2 Kings 17:29–30).

SUFFER [ED, INGS, S]. See also *Allow, Endure*

Matt. 16:21 Jesus...must go to Jerusalem, and *s* many things

Luke 24:26 Ought not Christ to have *s'ed* these things

Luke 24:46 it was necessary for Christ to *s* and to rise

Acts 9:16 he [Paul] must *s* for My [Jesus'] name's sake

Rom. 8:18 *s'ings*...not worthy to be compared with the glory...revealed

Phil. 3:10 the fellowship of His [Jesus'] *s'ings*

2 Tim. 2:12 If we *s*, we shall also reign with Him [Jesus]

Heb. 5:8 He [Jesus] learned obedience by the things that He *s'ed*

1 Pet. 4:13 you are partakers of Christ's *s'ings*

SUFFERING SERVANT. See *Righteous Servant*

SUKKIIM. An African or Ethiopian tribe allied with Pharaoh Shishak of Egypt when he invaded Judah (2 Chron. 12:3).

SUN. The heavenly body created by the Lord that brings life-giving heat and light to the earth (Ps. 74:16). Some civilizations of the ancient world, including Egypt, worshipped the sun. But this form of idolatry was strictly forbidden by the Lord (Deut. 4:14–19).

SUNDIAL. An instrument that measures the hour of the day by the position of the sun. The Lord miraculously reversed the shadow on a sundial to assure King Hezekiah of Judah (the Southern Kingdom) that he would be healed (2 Kings 20:1–11).

SUN STANDS STILL AT AJALON. Josh. 10:12–14

SUPPLICATION. An earnest prayer for God to meet a personal need (Jer. 38:26). This type of prayer is similar to petition. See also *Petition*.

SUSA. A wealthy and powerful city of Persia where Queen Esther interceded for her people (Esther 1:2). It was the site of the palace of King Ahasuerus, also known as Xerxes I, who selected the Jewish girl Esther as his new queen. It is also mentioned in Neh. 1:1 • Esther 1:5; 2:3–8; 3:15; 4:8, 16; 8:14–15; 9:6–19 • Dan. 8:2. *Shushan:* KJV.

SUSANCHITES. Foreign colonists who settled in Samaria after the Northern Kingdom fell to Assyria (Ezra 4:9).

SUSANNA. A female follower of Jesus who apparently provided food and lodging for Him and His disciples (Luke 8:2–3).

SWADDLING CLOTHS. Narrow strips of cloth wrapped around a newborn baby, a practice followed with the infant Jesus (Luke 2:7–12). *Swaddling clothes:* KJV.

SWEAR

Lev. 19:12 you shall not *s* falsely by My [God's] name

Matt. 5:34 I [Jesus] say to you, do not *s* at all

Mark 14:71 he [Peter] began to curse and to *s*

SWORD. A long sharp blade used as a weapon of war. The word is also used symbolically of God's judgment (Isa. 27:1) and of God's Word, the Bible (Eph. 6:17).

SYCHAR. A city of Samaria where Jesus offered "living water" to the woman at Jacob's well (John 4:5–40). She was so impressed with Him that she urged her villagers, "Come, see a man who told me all things that I ever did. Is this not the Christ?" (John 4:29).

SYCHEM. KJV: see *Shechem*, No. 2

SYNAGOGUE. A house of worship for the Israelites which developed during their exile in Babylon and Persia. The apostle Paul preached in many synagogues on his missionary journeys (Acts 18:4).

SYNAGOGUE [S]

Matt. 4:23 Jesus went about all Galilee, teaching in their *s's*

Mark 5:22 one of the rulers of the *s*, Jairus by name

Mark 13:9 you shall be beaten in the *s's*

Luke 4:16 He [Jesus] went into the *s*...and stood up to read

SYNOPTIC GOSPELS. A phrase that refers to the Gospels of Matthew, Mark, and Luke as documents with many similarities. The term comes from a Greek word that means "to see together." These three Gospels report many of the same events from the life of Jesus, using a similar chronology. Sometimes their accounts of an event follow one another almost word-for-word. Scholars believe the Gospel of Mark was written first, and that Matthew and Luke followed Mark's pattern, even including some material from Mark almost verbatim. But both Matthew and Luke do contain information not found in Mark, or any other Gospel. For example, only Luke records the birth of Jesus in Bethlehem (Luke 2:1–7). And Matthew alone reports Jesus' parable of the unforgiving servant (Matt. 18:23–35).

The Gospel of John is not considered a synoptic Gospel because it is so different from Matthew, Mark, and Luke in how it treats the life and ministry of Jesus. For example, it does not contain a single major parable of Jesus. Many of the miracles of Jesus reported by the three synoptic Gospels do not appear in John. Instead of focusing exclusively on the major events in Jesus' life, John goes behind the scenes to give the theological meaning of many of these happenings (John 20:30–31).

SYNTYCHE. A female believer in the church at Philippi who apparently had a problem with another woman in the church named Euodia. The apostle Paul called on them to settle their differences (Phil. 4:2).

SYRACUSE. A city on the island of Sicily where the apostle Paul spent three days during his voyage to Rome (Acts 28:12).

SYRIA. A nation that often battled the Israelites for control of the territory along its northern border in OT times (2 Sam. 10:9). Syria should not be confused with Assyria, the pagan nation much farther to the north in the region known as Mesopotamia. The Syrians were particularly hostile toward the Israelites during the time of the prophets Elijah and Elisha. At God's instruction, Elijah anointed Hazael as king of Syria (1 Kings 19:15). Hazael was apparently selected as an instrument of judgment against Israel (the Northern Kingdom) because of its idolatry (2 Kings 10:32). On one occasion Elisha healed a Syrian military officer of leprosy in an act of compassion (2 Kings 5:9–14). Later, Syria was a province under Roman control when Jesus was born (Luke 2:2). It is also mentioned in Judg. 10:6 • 2 Sam. 8:11–13 • 1 Kings 20:1–34 • 2 Kings 13:3–24 • Isa. 17:1–3 • Acts 15:23, 41. *Aram*: Num. 23:7.

SYRIA OF DAMASCUS. See *Damascus*

T

TAANACH. An ancient Canaanite city conquered by Joshua (Josh. 12:21).

TABERNACLE. A tent or portable sanctuary set up in the wilderness at God's command as a place of worship (Exod. 40:2–8). The Lord told the Israelites exactly how to build the tabernacle to emphasize that it would be a place devoted exclusively to worship of Him (Exod. 25:1–27:21). It was built of the finest materials but constructed in such a way that it could be dismantled and moved from place to place. When the Israelites settled in their own land, the tabernacle was eventually replaced by the temple, an ornate, permanent worship center in Jerusalem.

TABERNACLES, FEAST OF. A festival observed annually during the harvest season (Lev. 23:34). It commemorated Israel's wilderness wandering experience. The people lived in tents or booths in remembrance of their days as nomadic wanderers before they settled permanently in Canaan (Lev. 23:43)

TABITHA. A Christian widow from the city of Joppa known for kindness to the poor. She was restored to life by the apostle Peter (Acts 9:36–41). Her Greek name was Dorcas.

TABOR, MOUNT. A mountain about ten miles southwest of the Sea of Galilee where the judges Deborah and Barak summoned Israelite warriors to attack an army of the Canaanites. (Judg. 4:6–14). This mountain may have been the place where Jesus was transfigured before three of His disciples (Mark 9:2). But another claimant to this honor is Mount Hermon, north of the Sea of Galilee. Mount Tabor is also mentioned in Josh. 19:22 • Judg. 8:18 • Ps. 89:12 • Jer. 46:18 • Hos. 5:1.

TADMOR. A city built by King Solomon along Israel's northern border, perhaps as a defensive outpost in this region (2 Chron. 8:4).

TAHPANHES. An Egyptian city on the Nile River to which citizens of Judah (the Southern Kingdom) fled after a rebellion against Babylonian control of Jerusalem (Jer. 43:7–10).

TAKE CARE OF

Gen. 2:15 God...put him [Adam] into the garden of Eden...to *t-c-o* it

Gen. 28:15 I [God] am with you [Jacob] and will *t-c-o* you

Num. 1:53 the Levites shall *t-c-o* the needs of the tabernacle of testimony

1 Tim. 3:5 how shall he *t-c-o* the church of God

TALENT. A term used by Jesus in His parable of the talents (Matt. 25:14–30). It probably referred to a sum of money. The exact equivalent in modern currency is unknown.

TAMAR. A daughter of David and sister of David's son Absalom. Tamar was sexually assaulted by her half-brother Amnon. Absalom avenged this crime by killing Amnon (**2 Sam. 13:1–32** • 1 Chron. 3:9).

TARPELITES. Foreign colonists who settled in Samaria after Israel (the Northern Kingdom) fell to Assyria (Ezra 4:9–10).

TARSHISH. A city in the western reaches of the Mediterranean Sea, several hundred miles from Israel. This is where the ship boarded by the prophet Jonah was headed when he attempted to avoid God's call to preach to the citizens of Nineveh, Assyria (Jon. 1:3).

TARSUS. A major city of the Roman province of Silicia in Asia Minor and birthplace of the apostle Paul (Acts 9:11). His trade of tent-making (Acts 18:1–3) may have been influenced by one of the products for which Tarsus was famous—a rough fabric woven from the hair of goats. When and why Paul left Tarsus is unknown. But he showed up in Jerusalem as a persecutor of the church before his conversion to Christianity. When Paul began to preach the gospel in Jerusalem, zealous Jews threatened to kill him. His fellow believers sent him off to Tarsus for his own protection (Acts 9:26–30). Tarsus is also mentioned in Acts 11:25; 21:39; 22:3.

TARTAK. A pagan god worshipped by the Avvites, a people who colonized Samaria after Israel (the Northern Kingdom) fell to the Assyrians (2 Kings 17:31).

TARTAN. Title of the chief commander of the Assyrian army who demanded the surrender of Jerusalem from King Hezekiah of Judah (the Southern Kingdom) (2 Kings 18:17).

TATNAI. KJV: see *Tattenai*

TATTENAI. A Persian official who appealed to King Darius of Persia to stop the returned Jewish exiles from rebuilding the temple in Jerusalem (Ezra 5:3–9). *Tatnai*: KJV.

TAU. Twenty-second letter of the Hebrew alphabet, used as a heading over Psalm 119:169–176. In the Hebrew language, the first line of each of these eight verses begins with this letter.

TAUGHT

Ps. 119:102 not departed from Your [God's] judgments, for You have *t* me

Isa. 54:13 all your children shall be *t* by the LORD

Mark 1:22 He [Jesus] *t* them as one who had authority

Mark 4:2 He [Jesus] *t* them many things by parables

John 8:28 But as My [Jesus'] Father has *t* Me, I speak these things

2 Thes. 2:15 hold the traditions that you have been *t*

TAUNT [ING, S]

2 Kings 19:4 his master the king of Assyria has sent to *t* the living God

Prov. 14:31 He who oppresses the poor *t's* his Maker

Jer. 24:9 I [God] will deliver them [Judah]...to be a reproach and...a *t*

Zeph. 2:8 I [God] have heard the *t'ing* of Moab

TAX [ES]

Ezra 7:24 it shall not be lawful to impose toll, tribute, or *t* on them

Dan. 11:20 a raiser of *t'es* shall stand up in his place in the glory of the kingdom

Matt. 9:9 He [Jesus] saw...Matthew...at the place where *t* was collected

Matt. 22:17 Is it lawful to give *t* to Caesar or not?

Mark 2:16 How is it that He [Jesus] eats and drinks with *t* collectors and sinners?

Luke 18:10 Two men went up...to pray, the one a Pharisee and the other a *t* collector

Rom. 13:7 render to all their due: *t'es* to whom *t'es* are due

TAX COLLECTOR.

A Jewish citizen who purchased the right to collect taxes in his homeland for the Roman government. They were hated and looked upon as traitors by their fellow citizens (Matt. 5:46). The best known tax collector in the Bible is Matthew, whom Jesus called to become one of His disciples (Matt. 9:9). *Publican*: KJV.

TEACH [ES, ING]

Deut. 6:7 you shall *t* them [God's commands] diligently to your children

Job 21:22 Shall anyone *t* God knowledge

Job 36:22 God exalts by His power. Who *t'es* like Him?

Ps. 25:4 Show me Your ways, O LORD. *T* me Your paths

Ps. 51:13 Then I will *t* transgressors Your [God's] ways

Ps. 86:11 *T* me Your way, O LORD. I will walk in Your truth

Ps. 90:12 So *t* us to number our days

Prov. 16:23 The heart of the wise *t'es* his mouth

Jer. 31:34 no longer shall every man *t* his neighbor...saying, Know the LORD

Matt. 21:23 elders...came to Him [Jesus] as He was *t'ing*

Matt. 28:19 Therefore go and *t* all nations

Matt. 28:20 *t'ing* them to observe all the things...I [Jesus] have commanded

Mark 8:31 He [Jesus] began to *t* them that the Son of Man must suffer

Luke 11:1 Lord, *t* us [the disciples] to pray

Luke 12:12 Holy Spirit shall *t* you...what you ought to say

John 14:26 the Comforter...He shall *t* you all things

Rom. 2:21 You therefore, who *t* another, do you not *t* yourself?

Col. 3:16 *t'ing*...one another in psalms and hymns

1 Tim. 3:2 A bishop...given to hospitality, able to *t*

TEACHER.

A learned person who instructed others in religious matters. Nicodemus called Jesus "a teacher come from God" (John 3:2). This title implied that Jesus had received revelation about the truths He taught directly from God the Father. Jesus was an effective teacher because of His teaching style. He focused on down-to-earth truths that the common people could understand. He used familiar objects from everyday life—birds, flowers, sheep, salt, bread, water, light—to connect with the life experiences of His audience (Matt. 13:3). He told stories, or parables, to illustrate divine principles He wanted people to understand and act upon (Mark 4:11). All the truths He taught were stamped with divine authority. This amazed the people, because "His word was with power" (Luke 4:32).

TEACHER [S]

Ps. 119:99 I have more understanding than all my *t's*

John 3:2 we know that You [Jesus] are a *t* come from God

1 Cor. 12:29 Are all prophets? Are all *t's*?

Eph. 4:11 He [God] gave some apostles...and some pastors and *t's*

TEARS

Ps. 6:6 I [David[water my couch with my *t*

Ps. 126:5 Those who sow in *t* shall reap in joy

Jer. 9:1 Oh that my [Jeremiah's] head were waters...my eyes a fountain of *t*

Luke 7:38 wash His [Jesus'] feet with *t*...wiped them with the hair of her head

Rev. 21:4 God shall wipe away all *t* from their eyes

TEKOA. A fortress city on a mountain that served as a lookout post for the city of Jerusalem. The word means "trumpet blast." The city's unique role was to warn officials at the Holy City about an enemy attack (2 Chron. 11:6 • Jer. 6:1). Tekoa was the birthplace of the prophet Amos (Amos 1:1).

TEKOAH. KJV: see *Tekoa*

TEL-ABIB. A site in Babylon where the prophet Ezekiel lived with other exiles from Judah (the Southern Kingdom) (Ezek. 3:15). The modern city of Tel Aviv in Israel derives its name from this place.

TEMPERANCE. KJV: see *Self-Control*

TEMPERATE

1 Cor. 9:25 every man who strives for victory is *t* in all things
Titus 1:8 a lover of good men, sober, just, holy, *t*
Titus 2:2 that the aged men be sober, grave, *t*, sound in faith

TEMPLE. The ornate shrine which served as the central place of worship for the Israelite people. Three separate temples were built on the same site in Jerusalem.

(1) The first was the original structure known as Solomon's temple, built about 961–954 BC (1 Kings 6:37–38). This temple was destroyed by the Babylonians when they overran Jerusalem.

(2) The second structure was Zerubbabel's temple, completed about 515 BC by residents of Jerusalem who returned to their homeland after the Exile among the Babylonians and Persian (Ezra 3:8–10).

(3) About 10 BC the Roman ruler Herod the Great began reconstruction of Zerubbabel's temple. This building was more ornate and larger than its predecessors, with outer courts added. The infant Jesus was brought to this temple for dedication, and here Jesus taught and drove out the moneychangers (Mark 11:15 • John 2:14–15). This temple was destroyed by the Roman army in AD 70, and has never been rebuilt. The only part of Herod's temple that remains is the foundation, known as the Temple

Mount or the Western Wall. This is the sacred spot where people gather today for prayer and meditation, often stuffing written prayers into the crevices in this massive wall.

The Israelites believed that God's presence inhabited the temple. Even Jesus referred to it as "the house of God" (Matt. 12:4). But the church that He established is a new type of temple. As His body, the church includes people of all nations and races, not just one select group. It is the new temple of God in which the spirit of God dwells (1 Cor. 3:16).

TEMPT [ED, ING]

Deut. 6:16 You shall not *t* the LORD your God
Ps. 78:41 Yes, they turned back and *t'ed* God
Matt. 4:1 Jesus was led...into the wilderness to be *t'ed*
Matt. 4:7 You shall not *t* the Lord your God
John 8:6 They said this, *t'ing* Him [Jesus]...to accuse Him
1 Cor. 7:5 that Satan will not *t* you for your lack of self-control
1 Cor. 10:13 God...will not allow you to be *t'ed* above what you are able
Heb. 4:15 high priest [Jesus]...was in all points *t'ed* as we are
Jas. 1:13 Let no man say... I am *t'ed* by God

TEMPTATION. Enticement to disobey God and give in to sin. The first recorded temptation in the Bible was Satan's suggestion to Eve that she eat the forbidden fruit in the garden of Eden (Gen. 3:1). She fell for Satan's trickery, an act that plunged humankind into a state of sin. The subtle lure of temptation demonstrates the power of human thoughts. If kept in the mind long enough, they can result in sinful actions. For this reason, believers should monitor their minds constantly and replace tempting thoughts with reflections that are pure and uplifting (Phil. 4:8). God promises a means of escape for every temptation (1 Cor. 10:13).

TEMPTATION [S]

Matt. 6:13 do not lead us into *t*, but deliver us from evil

Luke 4:13 when the devil had ended all the *t*, he departed from Him [Jesus]

1 Cor. 10:13 No *t* has taken you but such as is common to man

Jas. 1:2 count it all joy when you fall into various *t's*

Jas. 1:12 Blessed is the man who endures *t*

2 Pet. 2:9 Lord knows how to deliver the godly out of *t's*

TEMPTATIONS OF JESUS. The forty-day period at the beginning of Jesus' public ministry when He was tempted by Satan in the wilderness. While He was alone and hungry, Satan tempted Him to turn stones into bread to meet His physical needs (Matt. 4:2–3). Then Satan tried to convince Him to prove His divine power by jumping off the highest point of the temple to impress the crowds (Matt. 4:5–7). Another temptation was to pay allegiance to Satan and seek the kingdoms of the world for His own glory (Matt. 4:8–9). But Jesus resisted all of Satan's tricks. He would not be turned aside from His spiritual mission as God's Son to become an atoning sacrifice for sin.

TEN COMMANDMENTS. The ethical commands issued by the Lord to Moses on Mount Sinai (Exod. 20:2–17). Also called the Decalogue, the Ten Commandments summarize the basic moral laws of the OT that are still considered authoritative today. Four of these commandments deal with the individual's responsibilities to God:

1. recognize the Lord alone as God,
2. have nothing to do with pagan gods,
3. do not misuse the Lord's name, and
4. sanctify the Sabbath day (Exod. 20:1–11)

The last six commandments deal with personal obligations to other people:

5. honor one's father and mother,
6. do not murder,
7. do not commit adultery,
8. do not steal,
9. do not bear false witness against others, and
10. do not desire anything that belongs to others (Exod. 20:12–17)

The Ten Commandments are repeated in Deut. 5:7–21.

Jesus summed up these commandments in two great principles—supreme love for God and loving one's neighbors as oneself (Matt. 22:37–40).

TERAH. Father of Abraham and a native of the city of Ur of the Chaldeans, or ancient Babylon. Terah migrated with part of his family, including Abraham, to Haran, a city in Mesopotamia (**Gen. 11:24–32** • Josh. 24:2 • 1 Chron. 1:26 • Luke 3:34).

TERAPHIM. Miniature images of false gods which were venerated in households as guardians of good fortune (Judg. 17:5).

TERTIUS. The scribe or secretary to whom the apostle Paul dictated his epistle to the Romans (Rom. 16:22).

TERTULLUS. An orator who accused the apostle Paul of desecrating the temple in Jerusalem. Tertullus spoke against Paul in a hearing before the Roman governor Felix at Caesarea (Acts 24:1–8).

TEST [ED, ING]

Deut. 13:3 God is *t'ing* you...whether you love the LORD

Ps. 26:2 Examine me, O LORD, and *t* me. *T* my mind and my heart

Mal. 3:10 and *t* me now in this, says the LORD of hosts

Mark 8:11 seeking from Him [Jesus] a sign from heaven, *t'ing* Him

1 Thes. 5:21 *T* all things. Hold fast what is good

1 Tim. 3:10 first be *t'ed*. Then...let them serve in the office of a deacon

TESTIFY [IED, IES, ING]

Num. 35:30 one witness shall not *t* against any person to cause him to die

Isa. 59:12 our transgressions have multiplied... our sins *t* against us

John 4:44 Jesus Himself *t'ied*...prophet has no honor in his own country

Acts 20:21 *t'ing* both to the Jews and also to the Greeks of repentance

Acts 23:11 as you [Paul] have *t'ied* of Me [Jesus] in Jerusalem

Heb. 7:17 He [God] *t'ies*, You [Jesus] are a priest forever

1 John 4:14 we have seen and *t* that the Father sent the Son

1 John 5:9 the witness of God...has *t'ied* of His Son

Rev. 22:20 He [Jesus] who *t'ies* these things says, Surely, I come quickly

TESTIMONY. See *Witness*

TESTIMONY [IES]

Deut. 6:20 What do the *t'ies*...mean that...God has commanded you

Ps. 19:7 The *t* of the LORD is sure, making wise the simple

Ps. 119:24 Your [God's] *t'ies* also are my delight

Mark 6:11 shake off the dust...for a *t* against them

John 21:24 and we know that his [John's] *t* is true

2 Tim. 1:8 do not be ashamed of the *t* of our Lord

TETH. Ninth letter of the Hebrew alphabet, used as a heading over Psalm 119:65–72. In the Hebrew language, the first line of each of these eight verses begins with this letter.

TETRAGRAMMATON. A Greek term that means "four letters," or YHWH. It refers to the form in which the divine name Yahweh was written in the original Hebrew language of the OT. The Israelites believed this name for God was too sacred to be pronounced or read aloud. So they cloaked the name by putting it in a form that could not be spoken. The only way to pronounce it in English is to add vowels to the four consonants, like this: YaHWeH. See also *Yahweh.*

TETRARCH. Title for a governor or ruler of part of a country in the Roman Empire (Luke 3:1).

THADDAEUS. See *Judas*, No. 1

THANK

Matt. 11:25 I [Jesus] *t* You, O Father, Lord of heaven and earth

Luke 18:11 Pharisee...prayed this: God, I *t* You that I am not as other men

Phil. 1:3 I [Paul] *t* my God on every remembrance of you [Philippians]

THANKS

1 Chron. 16:34 give *t* to the LORD, for He is good

Ps. 92:1 It is a good thing to give *t* to the LORD

Ps. 107:1 give *t* to the LORD, for He is good

Luke 22:19 And He [Jesus] took bread, and gave *t*

1 Cor. 11:24 when He [Jesus] had given *t*, he broke it [bread]

1 Cor. 15:57 *t* be to God, who gives us the victory

2 Cor. 9:15 *T* be to God for His unspeakable gift

1 Thes. 5:18 Give *t* in everything, for this is the will of God

THANKSGIVING. Enthusiastic praise of God for His blessings. The psalmist praised the Lord for His goodness and mercy (Ps. 116:12–19). The apostle Paul encouraged believers to live each day in a spirit of thanksgiving (Eph. 5:19–20).

THARA. KJV: see *Terah*

THEBES. A city on the Nile River which served as the capital of Egypt in OT times (Nah. 3:8). The city was destroyed in 81 BC, as predicted by the prophet Jeremiah (Jer. 46:25). *No*: KJV.

THEBEZ. A fortified city attacked by Abimelech in his campaign to become ruler over all Israel in the time of the judges. He died when a stone was dropped on his head from a defense tower (**Judg. 9:50–55 • 2 Sam. 11:21**).

THEOPHILUS. A friend of Luke to whom he addressed his Gospel and the book of Acts (Luke 1:3 • Acts 1:1). The name means "friend of God." Luke could have used the name to imply that his writings were meant for anyone who was a "friend of God." Or, Theophilus may have been a Roman official of high rank.

THESSALONIANS, FIRST EPISTLE TO. One of the apostle Paul's earliest epistles, known for its emphasis on the second coming of Christ. Every chapter contains some reference to this future event (1 Thes.1:10; 2:19; 3:13; 4:13–18; 5:1–11, 23). Paul mentioned Silas and Timothy in the greeting of the letter (1 Thess. 1:1). This suggests that these two missionary associates worked with Paul to encourage and strengthen this young congregation at Thessalonica.

THESSALONIANS, SECOND EPISTLE TO. A short letter of only three chapters closely related to Paul's first letter to the believers at Thessalonica. It was probably written within a few months of the first epistle. Paul encouraged the believers in this church to remain faithful to the Lord in the midst of persecution (2 Thes. 2:15). He also exhorted those who were idly waiting for the return of the Lord to get back to work (2 Thes. 3:6–12).

THESSALONICA. A port city of Macedonia where the apostle Paul founded a church during the second missionary journey. It was also the scene of a riot incited by Jews who opposed the apostle and his missionary associate, Silas (Acts 17:1–9). In later years, two believers from Thessalonica—Aristarchus and Secundus—traveled with Paul on his missionary tours (Acts 20:4). Paul would write two letters—1 and 2 Thessalonians—to Christians in this city.

THIEF [VES]

Matt. 6:20 treasures in heaven...where *t'ves* do not break in or steal

Mark 14:48 Have you come out, as against a *t*

Mark 15:27 they crucified two *t'ves* with Him [Jesus]

Luke 10:30 A certain man...fell among *t'ves*

Luke 19:46 you have made it [God's house] a den of *t'ves*

John 10:10 The *t* does not come except to steal

John 12:6 He [Judas Iscariot] said this...because he was a *t*

1 Thes. 5:2 the day of the Lord comes as a *t* in the night

2 Pet. 3:10 the day of the Lord will come as a *t* in the night

THINK [S]

Prov. 23:7 as he *t's* in his heart, so is he

Jer. 29:11 I [God] know the thoughts that I *t* toward you

Matt. 6:7 heathen...*t* that they shall be heard for their many words

Matt. 24:44 the Son of man is coming at such an hour as you do not *t*

Luke 10:36 which of these three do you *t* was neighbor

John 16:2 whoever kills you will *t* that he is serving God

Rom. 12:3 not to *t* of himself more highly than he ought to *t*

1 Cor. 10:12 let him who *t's* he stands be careful lest he fall

1 Cor. 13:5 [Love] is not easily provoked, does not *t* evil

Gal. 6:3 if a man *t's* himself to be something when he is nothing

Eph. 3:20 to Him [Jesus] who is able to do... above all that we ask or *t*

Phil. 4:8 if there is any praise, *t* on these things

THINK ABOUT

Rom. 8:5 those...according to the flesh *t-a* the things of the flesh

Rom. 12:14 Do not *t-a* haughty things

THOMAS. One of the twelve apostles or disciples of Jesus, also called Didymus or "twin" (Luke 6:15 • John 11:16). Thomas is known for his refusal to believe that Jesus was alive until he could actually see and feel the wounds on the Lord's resurrected body. When Jesus encouraged Thomas to do so, he cried, "My Lord and my God" (John 20:28). On an earlier occasion, Jesus told His disciples He was going away to prepare a place for them. Thomas wondered how they would find their way to Him. Jesus responded with His famous answer, "I am the way the truth, and the life. No man comes to the Father except through Me" (John 14:6). Thomas is also mentioned in Matt. 10:3 • Mark 3:18 • John 14:5; 20:24–29; 21:2 • Acts 1:13.

THORN IN THE FLESH. An unknown affliction, perhaps a physical infirmity, from which the apostle Paul prayed to be delivered (2 Cor. 12:7–8). It may have been a problem with his eyesight (Gal. 6:11). Rather than remove the problem, the Lord assured Paul that He would give him grace and strength to endure the difficulty.

THOUGHT [S]

Gen. 50:20 you *t* evil against me [Joseph], but God meant it for good

Job 42:2 no *t* can be withheld from You [God]

Ps. 92:5 O LORD...Your *t's* are very deep

Prov. 16:3 Commit your works to the LORD... your *t's* shall be established

Isa. 55:8 For My [God's] *t's* are not your *t's*

Jer. 29:11 I [God] know the *t's* that I think toward you

Mark 7:21 out of the heart of men, proceed evil *t's*

1 Cor. 3:20 The Lord knows the *t's* of the wise

1 Cor. 13:11 I [Paul] understood as a child, I *t* as a child

Phil. 2:6 who [Jesus]...*t* it not robbery to be equal with God

Heb. 4:12 the word of God...is a discerner of the *t's* and intentions

THREE TAVERNS. A station on the road known as the Appian Way where believers met the apostle Paul when he arrived in Rome (Acts 28:15).

THRESHING FLOOR. A flat surface where grain was separated from the stalk (2 Sam. 6:6). King David bought a threshing floor on which to build an altar to stop a plague among the people (2 Sam. 24:21–24).

THRONE. An ornate chair on which kings sat to symbolize their authority. The image of God on His throne signifies His unlimited power and authority (Isa. 6:1). The prophet Isaiah declared that heaven was God's throne and earth was His footstool (Isa. 66:1). This showed clearly that God ruled over every part of the universe. In the NT, Jesus is said to be sitting "at the right hand of the throne of God" (Heb. 12:2), serving side by side with the Father as judge and ruler of the world. In the apostle John's vision of heaven, he saw the Lord sitting on a throne (Rev. 4:2–3). From this throne He will preside in the end-time over the defeat of the forces of evil (Rev. 20:9–10).

THRONE

Ps. 45:6 Your *t*, O God, is forever and ever

Ps. 97:2 righteousness and judgment are the habitation of His [God's] *t*

Prov. 20:28 preserve the kind...his *t* is upheld by mercy

Isa. 6:1 I [Isaiah] also saw the Lord sitting on a *t*

Isa. 66:1 This is what the LORD says: The heaven is My *t*

Jer. 33:17 David shall never lack a man to sit on the *t*...of Israel

Lam. 5:19 Your [God's] *t* from generation to generation

Matt. 19:28 when the Son of Man sits on the *t* of His glory

Matt. 25:31 then He [Jesus] shall sit on the *t* of His glory

Luke 1:32 God shall give to Him [Jesus] the *t* of His father David

Heb. 4:16 let us come boldly to the *t* of grace

Rev. 4:2 and One [Jesus] sat on the *t*

THRONE OF GOD

Heb. 12:2 Jesus...is seated at the right hand of the *t-o-G*

Rev. 7:15 before the *t-o-G*, and serve Him day and night

Rev. 22:1 water of life...proceeding out of the *t-o-G*

THYATIRA. A city of Asia Minor where one of the seven churches addressed in the book of Revelation was located. Jesus commended this church for its faith, love, service, and patient endurance. But it had permitted a false prophetess named Jezebel to lead some of its members astray. She was encouraging them to engage in illicit sexual acts and to "eat things sacrificed to idols" (Rev. 2:20). Thyatira was the home of Lydia, a seller of purple cloth, who was converted during the apostle Paul's ministry at Philippi (Acts 16:14). She may have been one of the believers who formed the nucleus of the church at Thyatira.

TIBERIAS. (1) A city on the western shore of the Sea of Galilee (John 6:23) built by Herod

Antipas and named for the Roman emperor Tiberius.

(2) The body of water known as the Sea of Tiberias, another name for the Sea of Galilee (John 6:1; 21:1). See *Galilee, Sea of.*

TIBERIUS. See *Caesar*, No. 2

TIBNI. A king of Israel (the Northern Kingdom) who ruled as a rival to Omri for three years. When Tibni died, Omri became the undisputed king (1 Kings 16:21–22).

TIGLATH-PILESER. An Assyrian king who defeated the Northern Kingdom and carried Jewish captives to Assyria (2 Kings 15:29; 16:1–10 • 2 Chron. 28:20). *Pul*: 1 Chron. 5:26.

TIGRIS RIVER. A major river of Mesopotamia which is possibly the same as the Hiddekel cited in the account of the garden of Eden (Gen. 2:14). It rises in the Taurus mountains and flows for more than a thousand miles before joining the Euphrates River.

TIMNATH-SERAH. A town in the mountains north of Jerusalem where the warrior Joshua was buried (Josh. 24:29–30). This town had been allotted to him as his inheritance when the land of Canaan was conquered and divided among the tribes. Also called Timnath-heres (Judg. 2:9).

TIMON. One of the seven persons of Greek background who were appointed by the church at Jerusalem to coordinate the distribution of food to needy widows (Acts 6:1–7).

TIMOTHEUS. KJV: see *Timothy*

TIMOTHY. A young missionary associate of Paul (Rom. 16:21), who accompanied the apostle on some of his travels and briefly shared his imprisonment at Rome (Philem. 1). Born to a Greek father and a Jewish mother (Acts 16:1–3), Timothy was reared by his mother Eunice and grandmother Lois in a godly home (2 Tim. 1:5). He was converted during Paul's first visit to Lystra (Acts 16:1) and served for a time as leader of the church at Ephesus (1 Tim. 1:3; 4:12). Timothy was apparently associated with Paul in his work at churches in several other cities, including Corinth, Philippi, Colosse, and Thessalonica. The apostle referred to him as his "beloved and faithful son" (1 Cor. 4:17) and his "son in the faith" (1 Tim. 1:2). Several of the apostle's letters to these congregations—as well as his epistle to Philemon—open with greetings from Paul as well as Timothy. Paul addressed two of his letters to Timothy. He is also mentioned in Acts 17:14–15; 18:1–5; 19:22; 20:4 • 1 Cor. 16:10 • 2 Cor. 1:1, 19 • **Phil. 1:1; 2:19, 23** • Col. 1:1 • 1 Thes. 1:1; 3:2, 6 • 2 Thes. 1:1 • 1 Tim. 1:18; 6:20 • 2 Tim. 1:2 • Heb. 13:23.

TIMOTHY, FIRST EPISTLE TO. A letter of the apostle Paul to his missionary associate Timothy on the theme of church leadership. He instructed Timothy to teach sound doctrine (1 Tim. 1:1–20), organize the church appropriately (1 Tim. 2:1–3:16), beware of false teachers (1 Tim. 4:1–16), administer church discipline (1 Tim. 5:1–25), and exercise his pastoral gifts with love and restraint (1 Tim.6:1–21).

TIMOTHY, SECOND EPISTLE TO. A second letter of Paul to Timothy, probably written about two years after 1 Timothy. This is perhaps Paul's most personal letter, in which he expressed tender affection for the young minister (2 Tim. 1:1–2:20) and warned of approaching days of persecution for the church (2 Tim. 3:1–4:5) as well as the possibility of his own execution (2 Tim. 4:6–22). He looked back with no regrets over his life that had been poured out for the gospel of Jesus Christ (2 Tim. 4:6–8).

TIRZAH. A Canaanite town captured by Joshua (Josh. 12:1, 24). In later years it served as the capital of Israel (the Northern Kingdom) until the city of Samaria was built by King Omri (1 Kings 15:33). Tirzah is also mentioned in 1 Kings 14:17; 15:21; 16:6–23 • 2 Kings 15:14–16 • Song of Sol. 6:4.

TITHE. One-tenth of a person's income presented as an offering to God. The practice began with Abraham, who gave Melchizedek tithes of the spoils he had taken from several Canaanite kings (Gen. 14:18–20). The Mosaic law specified that the Israelites were to present a portion of their crops and livestock as a special offering to God (2 Chron. 31:5). Jesus encouraged believers to give generously and promised to bless sacrificial giving (Luke 6:38).

TITHE [S]

Lev. 27:30 all the *t* of the land...is the LORD's

Deut. 14:22 You shall truly *t* all the increase of your seed

Neh. 13:12 Then all Judah brought the *t* of grain

Mal. 3:8 How have we robbed You [God]? In *t's* and offerings

Mal. 3:10 Bring all your *t's* into the storehouse

Luke 11:42 you [Pharisees] *t* mint and rue and... herbs

Heb. 7:6 he [Melchisedec]...received *t's* from Abraham

TITTLE. A small mark over an individual letter of the Hebrew alphabet. Jesus used the word to show the importance of the most minute requirement of the law of Moses (Matt. 5:18).

TITUS. A Greek Christian who was one of Paul's most dedicated and dependable missionary associates. The apostle sent messages to the Corinthian church by Titus (2 Cor. 7:5–16). Paul also assigned Titus the task of collecting an offering for the impoverished believers of Jerusalem (2 Cor. 8:6, 16–24; 12:18). Titus served as a church leader on the island of Crete (Titus 1:5–3:11). He is also mentioned in 2 Cor. 2:13 • Gal. 2:1–3 • 2 Tim. 4:10.

TITUS, EPISTLE TO. A short epistle written by the apostle Paul to Titus, who apparently was serving as a leader of the church on the island of Crete (Titus 1:5). Paul dealt with several practical church matters, including the qualifications of elders (Titus 1:6–9), dealing with false teachers (Titus 1:10–16), and the behavior of Christians in an immoral world (Titus 3:1–11).

TOBIAH. An Ammonite official who opposed the rebuilding of Jerusalem's defensive wall by Nehemiah (Neh. 2:10, 19; 4:3, 7; 6:1–19; 13:4, 7–8).

TOLA. A minor judge of Israel who ruled for twenty-three years (Judg. 10:1–2).

TOMB. A burial place for the dead, consisting of a natural cave or a space dug out of solid rock. Abraham and his family were buried in the cave of Machpelah (Gen. 49:30). Jesus' body was laid in an excavated burial site, the tomb of Joseph of Arimathea (Matt. 27:57–60).

TONGUE. The organ of the body associated with speech. The tongue may be used for good or evil (James 3:5–10). Jesus declared that the tongue symbolizes a person's spirit, revealing what is in the heart (Matt. 12:34–37).

TONGUE, POWER OF. Jas. 3:1–12

TONGUES, GIFT OF. Ecstatic utterances; a spiritual gift exercised by some believers in the NT church. This phenomenon apparently first occurred on the day of Pentecost with the outpouring of God's spirit on believers (Acts 2:1–13). The apostle Paul mentioned tongues (1 Cor. 14:2–28), but also made it clear that love was superior to this spiritual gift (1 Cor. 13:1).

TOOTH FOR A TOOTH

Matt. 5:38 An eye for an eye, and a *t-f-a-t*

TOPAZ. A precious stone used in the breastplate of the high priest (Exod. 28:17) and in the foundation of New Jerusalem (Rev. 21:20).

TOPHET. KJV: see *Topheth*

TOPHETH. A place of human sacrifice in the Valley of Hinnom near Jerusalem (Jer. 7:31–32).

TOWER. A heavily fortified point on a city wall (2 Chron. 26:9) or a tall structure used as a observation point (Isa. 21:8). The word is also used figuratively of God's protection of His people (2 Sam. 22:3).

TOWER OF BABEL. Gen. 11:1–9

TRADITION. An interpretation of the law which the Pharisees considered as binding as the written law itself (Matt. 15:2).

TRADITION [S]

Matt. 15:6 commandment of God of no effect by your [Pharisees'] *t*

Mark 7:5 Why do Your [Jesus'] disciples not walk according to the *t* of the elders

2 Thes. 2:15 hold the *t's* that you have been taught

1 Pet. 1:18 empty conduct received by *t* from your fathers

TRANSFIGURATION OF JESUS. The radical change in Jesus' appearance as He prayed before three of His disciples: Peter, James, and John. Moses and Elijah appeared and discussed Jesus' death, emphasizing Jesus as the fulfillment of the law and the prophets. Jesus was overshadowed by a cloud as God the Father declared, "This is My beloved Son, in whom I am well pleased. Hear Him" (Matt. 17:5). This experience glorified God, attested to Jesus' oneness with the Father, and helped prepare Him and His disciples for the events leading to His death.

TRANSGRESS [ED, ES]

Deut. 26:13 I have not *t'ed* Your [God's] commandments

1 Sam. 15:24 I [Saul] have *t'ed* the commandment of the LORD

Jer. 2:29 You all [Judah] have *t'ed* against Me [God]

Matt. 15:2 Why do Your [Jesus'] disciples *t* the tradition...do not wash their hands

1 John 3:4 Whosoever commits sin also *t'es* the law

TRANSGRESSION [S]

1 Chron. 10:13 Saul died for his *t*...against the LORD

Job 13:23 Make me [Job] know my *t* and my sin

Ps. 32:1 Blessed is he whose *t* is forgiven

Ps. 32:5 I will confess my *t's* to the LORD

Ps. 51:1 according to...Your tender mercies, blot out my *t's*

Prov. 12:13 The wicked is snared by the *t* of his lips

Prov. 29:6 In the *t* of an evil man there is a snare

Isa. 53:5 He [God's servant] was wounded for our *t's*

Amos 1:3 For three *t's* of Damascus, and for four

TRANSGRESSOR [S]

Ps. 51:13 Then will I teach *t's* Your [God's] ways

Prov. 22:12 He [God] overthrows the words of the *t*

Mark 15:28 He [Jesus] was numbered with the *t's*

James 2:11 yet you kill, you have become a *t* of the law

TRANSJORDAN. A large mountainous plateau east of the Jordan River, generally referred to in the Simplified KJV as the land "beyond the Jordan" (Matt. 4:15). This is the area from which Moses viewed the promised land (Deut. 34:1–4).

TREASURE [S]

Exod. 19:5 you [Israel] shall be a special *t* to Me [God]

Ps. 135:4 LORD has chosen...Israel for His peculiar *t*

Prov. 10:2 *T's* of wickedness profit nothing

Prov. 15:16 Better is little with...fear of the LORD than great *t* with trouble

Matt. 2:11 when they [the wise men] had opened their *t's*

Matt. 6:20 lay up for yourselves *t's* in heaven

Matt. 13:44 kingdom of heaven is similar to *t* hidden in a field

Luke 12:34 where your *t* is, there your heart will be also

2 Cor. 4:7 we have this *t* in earthen vessels

Col. 2:3 in whom [Jesus] are hidden all the *t's* of wisdom

TREE OF KNOWLEDGE OF GOOD AND EVIL. A tree in the garden of Eden whose fruit was declared off-limits by the Lord (Gen. 2:9–17). The tree symbolized the sovereignty of God—His right as the ruler of creation to set limits on human behavior. After Adam and Eve disobeyed God and ate the forbidden fruit, they were banished from the garden and became subject to hard labor and death (Gen. 3:3–24).

TREE OF LIFE. A tree in the garden of Eden with fruit which would bring eternal life if eaten (Gen. 3:22). In the heavenly Jerusalem, there will also be a tree of life. This symbolizes eternal life that is available to all who place their faith in Jesus Christ (Rev. 22:2).

TRESPASS [ED, ES]

Ezek. 15:8 I [God] will make the land desolate...
they have committed a *t*

Ezek. 39:23 Israel went into captivity...because
they *t'ed* against Me [God]

Matt. 6:14 if you forgive men their *t'es*, your...
Father will also forgive you

Mark 11:25 your Father...may also forgive you
for your *t'es*

Luke 17:3 If your brother *t's* against you, rebuke
him

2 Cor. 5:19 God was...not imputing their *t'es*
to them

Eph. 2:1 He [Jesus] has made alive you who
were dead in *t'es*

TRIALS OF JESUS. A series of trials or
appearances of Jesus before Jewish and Roman
authorities which ended with His death. Jesus
appeared before Annas, the former high priest
(John 18:12–23); Caiphas, the current high
priest, and the full Jewish Sanhedrin (Matt.
26:57–68); Pilate, the Roman governor (John
18:28–38); and Herod Antipas, ruler of Galilee
(Luke 23:6–12), before finally being sentenced
to death by Pilate (Mark 15:6–15).

TRIBES OF ISRAEL. The tribes that
descended from the sons of Jacob—Asher,
Benjamin, Dan, Gad, Issachar, Judah, Levi,
Naphtali, Reuben, Simeon, and Zebulon (Gen.
49:1–28)—plus the two sons of Joseph (Ephraim
and Manasseh; Gen. 48:5). After the conquest of
Canaan, these tribes were assigned specific territories in the land, with the exception of Levi,
the priestly tribe. The Levites were assigned to
forty-eight different towns and villages scattered among all the other tribal territories to
perform ceremonial duties.

TRIBULATION. Affliction endured by believers because of their commitment to the Lord
(1 Thes. 3:4). Jesus warned that His followers
should expect such treatment (John 16:33). The
apostle Paul encouraged believers to endure
such troubles through prayer and by cultivating
a joyful spirit (Rom. 12:12).

TRIBULATION [S]

Matt. 24:21 shall be great *t*...not been since the
beginning of the world

John 16:33 In the world you shall have *t*

Rom. 5:3 glory in *t's*, knowing that *t* works
patience

Rom. 8:35 shall separate us from the love of
Christ? Shall *t*

2 Cor. 1:4 who [Jesus] comforts us in all our *t*

Eph. 3:13 I [Paul] desire that you not lose hope
by my *t's* for you

TRINITY, THE. The Christian doctrine that
God makes Himself known in three separate
but related realities—God the Father, God the
Son, and God the Holy Spirit. At the creation,
God's Spirit hovered over the formless mass
that He shaped into the orderly universe (Gen.
1:2). The Gospel of John declares that Jesus the
Son was active with God the Father in the creation process (John 1:1–3). All three persons of
the Trinity were also present at Jesus' baptism
when He launched His public ministry. As Jesus
came out of the water, "He saw the Spirit of God
descending like a dove and lighting on Him.
And behold, a voice from heaven said, 'This is
My beloved Son, in whom I am well pleased' "
(Matt. 3:16–17). The experience of believers as
recipients of salvation also confirms the reality
of the Trinity. God's love for sinful humankind
motivated Him to send His Son, Jesus, as an
atoning sacrifice. Jesus was obedient to His
Father's will and died on the cross to redeem
humankind from bondage to sin. Through the
work of God's Spirit, people are convicted of
their sin and moved to repent and accept God's
generous gift.

TRIUMPHAL ENTRY OF JESUS. Jesus'
entry into Jerusalem on the Sunday before
His crucifixion the following Friday. He was
greeted with shouts of joy from the crowds,
who were looking for an earthly king. With this
entry, Jesus acknowledged He was the promised
Messiah—but a spiritual deliverer rather than
a conquering military hero (Matt. 21:1–11). This

event is observed by believers every year on Palm Sunday, the Sunday before Easter.

TROAS. A city in Asia Minor where the apostle Paul received a vision during his second missionary journey. He saw a man across from Troas in Macedonia who pleaded, "Come over into Macedonia and help us" (Acts 16:9). His obedience to the vision resulted in the entry of the gospel into the region now known as Europe. Troas is also mentioned in **Acts 16:8–11; 20:5–6** • 2 Cor. 2:12 • 2 Tim. 4:13.

TROPHIMUS. A Christian who accompanied the apostle Paul on the third missionary journey (Acts 20:4; 21:29 • 2 Tim. 4:20).

TROUBLE [D, S]

1 Sam. 16:14 an evil spirit from the LORD *t'd* him [Saul]

1 Kings 18:17 Are you [Elijah] he who *t's* Israel?

Job 14:1 Man...is of few days and full of *t*

Ps. 9:9 The LORD also will be a refuge...in times of *t*

Ps. 31:9 Have mercy on me, O LORD, for I am in *t*

Ps. 38:6 I am *t'd*; I am bowed down greatly

Ps. 46:1 God is...a very present help in *t*

Ps. 77:2 In the day of my *t* I sought the Lord

Ps. 90:7 by Your [God's] wrath we are *t'd*

Ps. 108:12 Give us help from *t*

Prov. 15:27 He who is greedy of gain *t's* his own house

Jer. 8:15 We looked for peace...for a time of health, and behold, *t*

Matt. 2:3 he [Herod] was *t'd*, and all Jerusalem with him

Luke 1:29 she [Mary] was *t'd* at his [the angel's] saying

John 12:27 Now My [Jesus'] soul is *t'd*, and what shall I say?

John 14:1 Do not let your hearts be *t'd*; you believe in God

2 Cor. 4:8 We are *t'd* on every side, yet not distressed

Gal. 1:7 there are some who *t* you and would pervert the gospel

2 Thes. 1:6 repay tribulation to those who *t* you

TRUE

Ps. 19:9 judgments of the LORD are *t* and righteous

Zech. 7:9 Carry out *t* judgment, and show mercy

John 1:9 the *t* Light [Jesus] that gives light to every man

John 6:32 My [Jesus'] Father gives you the *t* bread from heaven

John 15:1 I [Jesus] am the *t* vine...My Father is the vinedresser

John 21:24 we know that his [John's] testimony is *t*

Rom. 3:4 let God be *t* but every man a liar

TRUE VINE. A name that Jesus called Himself to emphasize the strength and support that He provides for His followers (John 15:1). He was referring to a grapevine. This domestic plant had one main stem with several smaller shoots or runners branching off in all directions. These smaller branches owed their lives to this main stem. Jesus was emphasizing that His disciples should stay attached to Him as their Lord and Savior. He would sustain and nourish them so they would bear witness of Him in the days ahead. In the OT, the nation of Israel was often referred to as a vine (Ps. 80:8 • Isa. 5:2). But the people fell into sin and idolatry, becoming an empty vine that bore no fruit for the Lord (Hos. 10:1). Jesus became the "true vine" whom God sent to bring salvation to His people.

TRUST. To put one's confidence in a person or thing. In OT times, the prophets often criticized the Israelites because they put their trust in military might rather than in the power of the Lord (Isa. 36:9). Believers may place ultimate trust and confidence in Jesus as Savior and Lord (John 6:35–37).

TRUST [ED, ING, S]

Deut. 32:37 Where are their gods...in whom they *t'ed*

2 Sam. 22:3 The God of my rock; in Him I will *t*

Job 13:15 Though He [God] slay me [Job], I will still *t* in Him

Ps. 13:5 I have *t'ed* in Your [God's] mercy

Ps. 16:1 Preserve me, O God, for in You I put my *t*

Ps. 26:1 I have *t'ed* also in the LORD...I shall not slide

Ps. 34:8 Blessed is the man who *t's* in Him [God]

Ps. 37:5 *T* also in Him [God], and He shall bring it to pass

Ps. 56:3 When I am afraid, I will *t* in You [God]

Ps. 112:7 His heart is steadfast, *t'ing* in the LORD

Ps. 118:8 better to *t* in the LORD than to put confidence in man

Prov. 3:5 *T* in the LORD with all your heart

Prov. 11:28 He who *t's* in his riches shall fall

Mark 10:24 how hard is it for those who *t* in riches to enter...the kingdom

1 Tim. 1:11 the glorious gospel...which was committed to my [Paul's] *t*

TRUTH. That which is reliable and consistent with God's revelation. Truth is established by God's Law (Ps. 119:142–144) and personified by Jesus Christ (John 14:6). Believers are purified by obeying the truth (1 Pet. 1:22) and by worshipping God in spirit and truth (John 4:23–24).

TRUTH

1 Sam. 12:24 serve Him [God] in *t* with all your heart

Ps. 25:5 Lead me in Your [God's] *t*, and teach me

Ps. 33:4 all His [God's] works are done in *t*

Ps. 86:11 Teach me Your way, O LORD; I will walk in Your *t*

Ps. 100:5 His [God's] *t* endures to all generations

Ps. 119:30 I have chosen the way of *t*

John 1:17 grace and *t* came by Jesus Christ

John 4:24 must worship Him [God] in spirit and in *t*

John 8:32 know the *t*, and the *t* shall make you free

John 14:6 I [Jesus] am the way, the *t*, and the life

John 16:13 the Spirit of *t*...will guide you into all *t*

John 18:38 Pilate said to Him [Jesus], What is *t*?"

1 Cor. 13:6 [Love] rejoices in the *t*

Gal. 4:16 Am I [Paul]...your enemy, because I tell you the *t*

Eph. 4:15 speaking the *t* in love

1 Tim. 2:4 who [God] wants all men...to come to the knowledge of the *t*

1 Tim. 3:15 the church...the pillar and ground of the *t*

2 Tim. 2:15 does not need to be ashamed, rightly dividing the word of *t*

1 John 1:8 If we say that we have no sin...the *t* is not in us

3 John 4 no greater joy than...that my [John's] children walk in *t*

TUMORS. A mysterious disease which broke out among the Philistines when they placed the stolen ark of the covenant next to their false god Dagon (1 Sam. 5:6). *Emerods:* KJV.

TWELVE, THE. The twelve apostles or disciples chosen by Jesus. See *Disciples of Jesus.*

TYCHICUS. A Christian who accompanied the apostle Paul on his third missionary journey (Acts 20:4).

TYRANNUS. A citizen of Ephesus who allowed Paul to use his lecture hall (Acts 19:8–10).

TYRE. An ancient coastal city of Phoenicia north of Israel. The king of Tyre helped David and Solomon with their building projects (1 Kings 5:1–12). In the prophet Ezekiel's day, the city was a thriving trade center. He predicted Tyre's destruction because of its sin and idolatry (Ezek. 28:6–10). Jesus visited the city, where He healed a woman's daughter who was possessed by a demon (Mark 7:24–29). Tyre is also mentioned in Josh. 19:29 • Ezek. 26:1–21; 27:1–36 • Joel 3:4–6 • Amos 1:10 • Matt. 15:21–28.

TYRUS. KJV: see *Tyre*

TZADDI. Eighteenth letter of the Hebrew alphabet, used as a heading over Ps. 119:137–144. In the Hebrew language, the first line of each of these eight verses begins with this letter.

UCAL. An unknown person to whom Agur addressed his comments in the book of Proverbs. The other person mentioned with Ucal was Ithiel (Prov. 30:1).

ULAI. A Persian stream, perhaps an irrigation canal, by which the prophet Daniel was standing when he received his vision of a ram and a goat (Dan. 8:2–16).

UNBELIEF. Refusal to believe in God and to acknowledge His works (John 16:8–9). Jesus encountered unbelief in His own hometown. The people of Nazareth had known Him as a boy, so they assumed He was nobody special. He left them with their skeptical attitudes and went to other places where people were more open to His message (Matt. 13:54–58). Unbelief is caused by Satan (John 8:43–44) and an evil heart (Heb. 3:12). See also *Belief.*

UNBELIEF

Mark 9:24 Lord, I believe; help my *u*

Heb. 3:12 lest there be in any of you an evil heart of *u*

Heb. 4:11 lest any man fall according to the same example of *u*

UNBELIEVERS

1 Cor. 6:6 brother goes to law with brother... before the *u*

2 Cor. 6:14 Do not be unequally yoked together with *u*

UNBELIEVING

Acts 14:2 But the *u* Jews stirred up the Gentiles

1 Cor. 7:14 the *u* husband is sanctified by the wife

Titus 1:15 to those who are defiled and *u* nothing is pure

UNCIRCUMCISED. A term used by Israelites for Gentiles, or non-Jews (1 Sam. 17:26). It also symbolized impurity and unrighteousness (Isa. 52:1). See also *Circumcision.*

UNCIRCUMCISED

1 Sam. 17:26 this *u* Philistine [Goliath], that he should defy...the living God

Ezek. 44:9 No foreigner, *u* in heart...shall enter into My [God's] sanctuary

Acts 7:51 stiff-necked people, and *u* in heart and ears

UNCIRCUMCISION

1 Cor. 7:19 Circumcision is nothing and *u* is nothing

Gal. 5:6 neither circumcision nor *u* avails anything

Col. 3:11 neither Greek nor Jew, circumcision nor *u*

UNCLEAN. A term for physical, spiritual, or ritual impurity—a condition for which purification rituals were prescribed by the Mosaic law (Lev. 11–15). Certain animals were declared unclean to the Israelites and not suitable for eating (Lev. 11:4-8). See also *Ceremonial Washing.*

UNCLEAN [NESS]

Num. 19:11 He who touches the dead body... be *u* seven days

Isa. 6:5 because I [Isaiah] am a man of *u* lips

Isa. 64:6 But we are all as an *u* thing

Mark 6:7 He [Jesus]...gave them [the disciples] power over *u* spirits

Acts 10:14 I [Peter] have never eaten anything that is...*u*

Rom. 1:24 God also gave them up to *u'ness*

Rom. 14:14 am persuaded...that there is nothing *u* by itself

Gal. 5:19 works of the flesh are evident...adultery, fornication, *u'ness*

1 Thes. 4:7 God called us not to *u'ness* but to holiness

UNDEFILED

Ps. 119:1 Blessed are the *u*...walk in the law of the LORD

Heb. 7:26 high priest [Jesus]...who is holy, harmless, *u*

Jas. 1:27 Pure and *u* religion before God and the Father

UNDERSTAND [ING, S]

1 Kings 4:29 God gave Solomon...great wisdom and *u'ing*

Job 26:12 by His [God's] *u'ing* He strikes...the proud

Job 28:28 to depart from evil is *u'ing*

Job 32:9 Nor do the aged *u* judgment

Job 42:3 I [Job] have uttered what I do not *u*; things too wonderful

Ps. 119:27 Make me to *u* the way of Your [God's] precepts

Ps. 119:34 Give me *u'ing*, and I shall keep Your [God's] law

Ps. 147:5 Great is our Lord...His *u'ing* is infinite

Prov. 2:2 and apply your heart to *u'ing*

Prov. 2:5 then you shall *u* the fear of the LORD

Prov. 3:5 do not lean on your own *u'ing*

Prov. 4:7 and with all your getting, get *u'ing*

Prov. 10:13 a rod is for...him who is void of *u'ing*

Prov. 14:6 knowledge is easy for him who *u's*

Prov. 17:28 he who shuts his lips is...a man of *u'ing*

Isa. 40:28 There is no searching of His [God's] *u'ing*

Isa. 44:18 He [God] has shut...their hearts, that they cannot *u*

Dan. 9:22 come now to give you [Daniel] skill and *u'ing*

Dan. 10:14 make you [Daniel] *u* what shall happen to your people

Matt. 15:16 Are you [the disciples] also still without *u'ing*?

Mark 8:21 How is it that you [the disciples] do not *u*?

Luke 24:45 He [Jesus] opened their [Emmaus travelers'] *u'ing..u* the scriptures

John 12:16 His [Jesus'] disciples did not *u* these things at first

Acts 8:30 Philip...said, Do you [Ethiopian eunuch] *u* what you are reading?

Rom. 3:11 no one who *u's*...no one who seeks after God

1 Cor. 13:2 though I [Paul]...*u* all mysteries

1 Cor. 14:19 would rather speak five words with my *u'ing*...than...unknown tongue

Phil. 4:7 peace of God, which passes all *u'ing*

Heb. 11:3 we *u* that the worlds were formed by the word of God

UNDERSTOOD

Job 13:1 My [Job's] ear has heard and *u* it

Isa. 40:21 Have you not *u* from the foundations of the earth?

1 Cor. 13:11 When I [Paul] was a child...I *u* as a child

UNGODLY [INESS]

Ps. 1:1 man who does not walk in the counsel of the *u*

Prov. 16:27 An *u* man digs up evil

Rom. 1:18 wrath of God is revealed...against all *u'iness*

Rom. 5:6 in due time Christ died for the *u*

Titus 2:12 denying *u'iness*...we should live soberly

Jude 18 mockers...would walk after their own *u* lusts

UNIVERSALISM. A belief that all people are covered by the salvation of Christ, even those who never make a personal profession of faith in Him as Lord and Savior. Universalists emphasize the love of God and deny that there will be a final judgment or an eternal punishment for unbelievers.

UNJUST

Matt. 5:45 He [God]...sends rain on the just and on the *u*

Luke 16:8 the master commended the *u* steward

1 Pet. 3:18 Christ...suffered for sins, the just for the *u*

UNKNOWN

Acts 17:23 altar with this inscription: To THE U GOD

1 Cor. 14:4 He who speaks in an *u* tongue edifies himself

1 Cor. 14:19 with my understanding...than ten thousand words in an *u* tongue

UNLEAVENED BREAD. See *Passover and Feast of Unleavened Bread*

UNPARDONABLE SIN. Blasphemy against the Holy Spirit, or attributing the work of Christ to Satan, as the critics of Jesus did. They accused Him of casting demons out of people "by the prince of the demons" (Mark 3:22). Many interpreters believe this sin consists of decisively and finally rejecting the testimony of the Holy Spirit about Jesus Christ and the invitation to confess Him as Savior and Lord.

UNRIGHTEOUS [NESS]

Ps. 92:15 and there is no *u'ness* in Him [God]
Isa. 55:7 Let the wicked abandon his way...the *u* man his thoughts
Rom. 1:18 wrath of God is revealed from heaven against all...*u'ness* of men
1 Cor. 6:9 the *u* shall not inherit the kingdom of God
2 Cor. 6:14 what fellowship does righteousness have with *u'ness*
1 John 1:9 He [Jesus] is faithful...to cleanse us from all *u'ness*

UNSEARCHABLE

Ps. 145:3 Great is the LORD...His greatness is *u*
Rom. 11:33 How *u* are His [God's] judgments
Eph. 3:8 I [Paul] should preach...the *u* riches of Christ

UNTILLED GROUND. Farm land left idle for a time to restore its fertility (Jer. 4:3). *Fallow ground*: KJV.

UPHAZ. A place in Arabia where gold was obtained, perhaps the same place as Ophir (Jer. 10:9).

URBANUS. A fellow believer greeted and commended by the apostle Paul (Rom. 16:9). *Urbane*: KJV.

URIAH. (1) A warrior in David's army whose death was arranged by the king to cover up his adulterous relationship with Uriah's wife, Bathsheba. The affair resulted in her pregnancy with David's child. After several desperate attempts to hide the crime, David finally ordered Uriah sent to the front lines of the battlefield, where he was killed (2 Sam.

11:1–26). Uriah was one of David's valiant warriors known as "mighty men" (2 Sam. 23:39). He is also mentioned in 2 Sam. 12:9–10 • 1 Kings 15:5 • 1 Chron. 11:41 • Matt. 1:6.

(2) A faithful prophet in Jeremiah's time who was killed by King Jehoiakim for predicting God's judgment on Judah (the Southern Kingdom) (Jer. 26:20–23; *Urijah*: KJV).

URIAS. KJV: see *Uriah*

URIM AND THUMMIM. Two objects, perhaps colored stones, used by the high priest to determine God's will in certain matters. These stones were apparently carried in the breastplate of the high priest (Exod. 28:30). The Urim and Thummim are also mentioned in Lev. 8:8 • Num. 27:21 • Deut. 33:8 • Ezra 2:63 • Neh. 7:65.

UR OF THE CHALDEANS. An ancient city between the Tigris and Euphrates rivers where Abraham grew up (Gen. 11:31). Excavations on this site have revealed that Ur was a center for worship of the pagan moon god known as Sin. Yet Abraham emerged from this pagan culture as a worshipper of the one true God. The Babylonians, also known as Chaldeans, occupied this territory for a time. It is also mentioned in **Gen. 11:28**; 15:7 • Neh. 9:7. *Ur of the Chaldees*: KJV.

USELESS

1 Sam. 12:21 then you should go after *u* things that cannot profit
Ps. 60:11 *u* is the help of man
Isa. 44:9 Those who make a carved image, all of them are *u*
1 Cor. 3:20 Lord knows the thoughts of the wise, that they are *u*
1 Cor. 15:14 if Christ has not been raised, then our preaching is *u*

USURY. Interest levied on borrowed money. Under the Mosaic law, Jews could exact interest only from non-Jews, not from their own countrymen (Lev. 25:35–37). Nehemiah denounced Israelites who were breaking this law (Neh. 5:7, 10).

UZ. An unknown place where Job lived (Job 1:1). Uz is mentioned in only two other places in the Bible (Jer. 25:20 • Lam. 4:21).

UZZAH. A man struck dead for reaching out to steady the ark of the covenant while it was being carried on a cart to Jerusalem (2 Sam. 6:1–8 • 1 Chron. 13:7–11). Apparently, only Levites were authorized to care for the ark, and it was to be carried on poles inserted through rings in each corner (Exod. 25:14).

UZZIAH. An initially godly king of Judah (the Southern Kingdom) who obeyed God and governed wisely during a time of great prosperity for his country. A good military strategist, he defeated the Philistines and the Ammonites,

fortified key cities, and built up his army to protect Judah from enemy attacks (2 Chron. 26:1–15). But Uzziah's pride led him to offer a sacrifice in the temple—a role reserved for priests. He was struck with leprosy that sidelined him for the rest of his life (2 Chron. 26:16–21). Uzziah's reign of fifty-two years was one of the longest in Judah's history. Isaiah was called to the prophetic ministry through a stirring vision of God "in the year that King Uzziah died" (Isa. 6:1). He is also mentioned in 2 Kings 15:13–34 • 2 Chron. 27:2 • Isa. 1:1; 7:1 • Hos. 1:1 • Amos 1:1 • Zech. 14:5 • Matt. 1:8. *Azariah*: 2 Kings 14:21.

UZZIEL. A man who helped rebuild the walls of Jerusalem after the Exile (Neh. 3:8).

V

VAGABOND. A fugitive or wanderer. Life as a fugitive was part of the curse against Cain for murdering his brother Abel (Gen. 4:10–12). The "vagabond Jews" of Acts 19:13 were professional exorcists.

VAIN. See also *Useless*
Exod. 20:7 shall not take the name of the LORD your God in *v*
Ps. 2:1 Why do...the people plot a *v* thing
Ps. 127:1 Unless the LORD builds the house, those who build it labor in *v*
Prov. 31:30 Favor is deceitful and beauty is *v*
Matt. 6:7 when you pray, do not use *v* repetitions
2 Tim. 2:16 But shun profane and *v* babblings

VAIZATHA. A son of Haman who was executed, along with his father, when Haman's plot to destroy the Jews was exposed by Esther (Esther 9:7–10). *Vajezatha*: KJV.

VALLEY OF DRY BONES. A site seen in a vision by the prophet Ezekiel. The bones represented Israel's exile in a foreign land, When Ezekiel addressed the bones, they came to life by God's Spirit. This was God's assurance that His people would return one day to their native land (Ezek. 37:1–14).

VANITY. Emptiness and futility; a word that appears throughout the book of Ecclesiastes written by King Solomon (Eccles. 1:2). Vanity or emptiness characterized life as he had experienced it. He looked for meaning in work, wisdom, knowledge, pleasure, money, and power. But he concluded that none of these things brought happiness or joy when pursued as ends in themselves. Solomon ended his book with a declaration about the one thing that infuses life with purpose: "Fear God and keep His commandments," he concluded. "for this is the whole duty of man" (Eccles. 12:13).

VANITY [IES]. See also *Breath*; *Nothing*
Job 35:13 God will not hear *v*, nor...regard it
Ps. 31:6 I have hated those who regard lying *v'ies*
Ps. 39:5 every man at his best condition is altogether *v*
Eccles. 1:2 v of *v'ies*; all is *v*
Acts 14:15 Sirs [people of Lystra]...turn from these *v'ies*
Eph. 4:17 do not walk...in the *v* of their mind

VASHTI. The queen of King Ahasuerus of Persia who refused the king's command to display her beauty to his guests (Esther 1:10–12). She was eventually replaced as queen by Esther (Esther 2:2, 15–17).

VAU. Sixth letter of the Hebrew alphabet, used as a heading over Psalm 119:41-48. In the Hebrew language, the first line of each of these eight verses begins with this letter.

VEIL OF THE TEMPLE. A curtain or drape that divided the Jewish temple in Jerusalem into two separate sections—one for Jews and the other for Gentiles, or non-Jews. Gentiles were not allowed to go beyond this curtain into the Jewish section. When Jesus died on the cross, this barrier was "torn in two from the top to the bottom" (Matt. 27:51). This showed that Jesus' atoning death brought reconciliation and peace to people of all races and nationalities. The apostle Paul recognized this truth when he declared that Jesus had "broken down the middle wall of partition between us" (Eph. 2:14).

VENGEANCE. See also *Revenge*
Ps. 94:1 God, to whom *v* belongs, show Yourself
Isa. 61:2 to proclaim...the day of *v* of our God
Luke 21:22 these are the days of *v*, that all things...may be fulfilled
Rom. 12:19 V is Mine. I will repay, says the Lord

VIA DOLOROSA. A Latin phrase, meaning "way of sorrow," for the route that Jesus walked on the way to His crucifixion. A total of fourteen "stations of the cross" have been identified along this route in the streets of Jerusalem's Old City. But it is impossible to determine the precise location He walked, since Jerusalem was destroyed by the Romans in AD 70 and then rebuilt. This phrase does not appear in the Bible.

VICTORY
Isa. 25:8 He [God] will swallow up death in *v*
1 Cor. 15:55 O grave, where is your *v*
1 Cor. 15:57 God, who gives us the *v* through... Jesus Christ
1 John 5:4 this is the *v* that overcomes the world

VINE. A plant which bore grapes (1 Kings 4:25). The word is also used figuratively of the nation

of Israel (Hos. 10:1). Jesus referred to Himself as the "true vine" (John 15:1).

VINE [S]
Judg. 9:12 the trees said to the *v*, Come and reign over us
Song of Sol. 2:15 the little foxes that ruin the *v's*
Mic. 4:4 every man shall sit under his *v* and under his fig tree
Luke 22:18 I [Jesus] will not drink of the fruit of the *v*
John 15:5 I [Jesus] am the *v*; you are the branches

VINEGAR. Wine that was fermented until it turned sour. This drink was offered to Jesus on the cross (Matt. 27:34, 48).

VINE OF SODOM. A symbolic reference to the wickedness of the city of Sodom which led to its destruction by the Lord (Deut. 32:32).

VINEYARD. A field or orchard where grapevines grew (Deut. 20:6). The word is used symbolically for the nation of Israel (Isa. 5:4-5).

VIRGIN BIRTH OF JESUS. The miraculous conception of Jesus by the Holy Spirit and His birth to the virgin Mary. This event was foretold by the prophet Isaiah (Isa. 7:14) and revealed to Mary by an angel (Luke 1:26–33). This miracle was just as puzzling for Mary as it is for most people today. But the angel explained that in some strange and mysterious way God would "overshadow" Mary by His Spirit to bring about a miraculous conception. Once formed in Mary's womb, Jesus was born through the natural biological process that brings children into the world. Thus, Jesus existed as God's Son as well as a man in the flesh—fully human and fully divine.

VIRTUE. See also *Power*
Phil. 4:8 if there is any *v*...think on these things
2 Pet. 1:5 add to your faith *v*; and to *v* knowledge

VIRTUOUS
Ruth 3:11 all the city...know that you are a *v* woman
Prov. 12:4 A *v* woman is a crown to her husband

VISION

Prov. 31:10 Who can find a *v* woman...price is far above rubies

VISION [S]

Prov. 29:18 Where there is no *v*, the people perish

Ezek. 1:1 heavens were opened and I [Ezekiel] saw *v's*

Ezek. 11:24 the Spirit...brought me [Ezekiel] in a *v*...into Chaldea

Dan. 2:19 Then was the secret revealed to Daniel in a night *v*

Joel 2:28 your young men shall see *v's*

Hab. 2:2 Write the *v* down, and make it plain on tablets

Luke 1:22 he [Zechariah] had seen a *v* in the temple

Acts 16:9 a *v* appeared to Paul in the night

Acts 26:19 I [Paul] was not disobedient to the heavenly *v*

VISIONS. See *Dreams and Visions*

VOICE [S]

Gen. 22:18 you [Abraham] have obeyed My [God's] *v*

Exod. 5:2 Who is the LORD, that I [Pharaoh] should obey His *v*

Josh. 24:24 serve the LORD our God, and we will obey His *v*

1 Kings 19:12 And after the fire a still small *v*

Job 40:9 can you thunder with a *v* like Him [God]

Ps. 27:7 Hear, O LORD, when I cry with my *v*

Ps. 66:8 make the *v* of His [God's] praise to be heard

Ps. 116:1 He [God] has heard my *v* and my supplications

Isa. 40:3 The *v* of him who cries in the wilderness

Jon. 2:2 and You [God] heard my [Jonah's] *v*

Matt. 3:3 The *v* of one crying in the wilderness

Matt. 3:17 a *v* from heaven said, This is My [God's] beloved Son

Mark 9:7 a *v* came...saying, This is My [God's] beloved Son

Luke 23:46 when Jesus had cried with a loud *v*

John 10:27 My [Jesus'] sheep hear My *v*, and I know them

Acts 9:4 a *v* saying... Saul, why are you persecuting Me [Jesus]

1 Cor. 14:10 There are...so many kinds of *v's* in the world

Heb. 3:15 Today, if you will hear His [God's] *v*

Rev. 1:10 I [John]...heard behind me a great *v*

Rev. 3:20 any man hears My [Jesus'] *v* and opens the door

VOICE OF THE LORD

Gen. 3:8 they [Adam and Eve] heard the *v-o-t-L*

Deut. 13:18 when you listen to the *v-o-t-L* your God

1 Sam. 15:22 Has the LORD as great delight in... sacrifices as in obeying the *v-o-t-L*

Ps. 29:4 The *v-o-t-L* is powerful...full of majesty

Isa. 6:8 I [Isaiah] heard the *v-o-t-L*, saying, Whom shall I send

VOID. A word for desolation and emptiness. The earth was formless and void before God shaped it and filled it with life through His creative power (Gen. 1:2).

VOW. A voluntary pledge or agreement to perform a service for God (Gen. 28:20–22). Once a vow was made, it was considered binding (Deut. 23:21). Vows were to be made only after careful deliberation (Eccles. 5:5). See also *Oath*.

VOW [ED, S]

Judg. 11:30 Jephthah made a *v* to the LORD

Ps. 50:14 and pay your *v's* to the Most High

Ps. 116:14 I will pay my *v's* to the LORD

Eccles. 5:4 When you make a *v* to God, do not put off paying it

Jon. 1:16 the men...offered a sacrifice...and made *v's*

Jon. 2:9 I will pay what I have *v'ed*

WADI. A dry stream bed which fills with water during the rainy season. This word does not appear in the Bible, but many of these geographical features appear in Israel's dry landscape.

WAGES. Payment for work done by common laborers. The Mosaic law specified that wages were to be paid daily, at the end of the workday (Lev. 19:13). The word is also used to symbolize the consequences of a person's deeds, as in the apostle Paul's declaration, "The wages of sin is death" (Rom. 6:23).

WAGES
Lev. 19:13 *w* of him...shall not remain with you all night
Hag. 1:6 earns *w* to put it into a bag with holes
Rom. 6:23 the *w* of sin is death

WAIT ON THE LORD
Ps. 27:14 *W-o-t-L*. Be of good courage... strengthen your heart
Ps. 37:34 *W-o-t-L* and keep His way...He shall exalt you
Prov. 20:22 *w-o-t-L*, and He shall save you

WALK. A word often used figuratively to describe a person's lifestyle or daily behavior. To "walk" with God was to be committed to Him and obedient to His commands (Gen. 5:24).

WALL OF FIRE. A name of God used by the prophet Zechariah that described God's protection of the city of Jerusalem after the Exile (Zech. 2:5). The city's defensive walls had been destroyed by the Babylonians several decades before. This meant the Jewish exiles who returned to Jerusalem were in danger of being overrun by their enemies. But God promised to protect them by becoming a "wall of fire" around the city. Fire is often associated with God's protection of His people (Exod. 13:21).

WALLS OF JERUSALEM REBUILT AFTER THE EXILE. Neh. 6:15

WANDERING IN THE WILDERNESS BY ISRAEL. Num. 14:20–35

WAR. Armed conflict between nations. Israel often went to battle with more powerful foes, but God often gave them victory by intervening on their behalf (Josh. 10:11). The prophet Isaiah warned about the danger of relying on military power rather than depending on the Lord (Isa. 31:1).

WASHING. See *Ceremonial Washing*

WATCH [ED, ES, FUL, ING]
Job 14:16 Do you [God] not *w* over my sin?
Ps. 90:4 a thousand years in Your [God's] sight are...as a *w* in the night
Ps. 141:3 Set a *w*, O LORD...*w* over the door of my lips
Matt. 24:42 *W* therefore, for you do not know what hour
Mark 14:37 could you [Peter] not *w* with Me [Jesus] one hour
Luke 2:8 shepherds...keeping *w* over their flock
Luke 12:37 Blessed are those servants...the master...shall find *w'ing*
Luke 12:39 had known what hour the thief would come, he would have *w'ed*
1 Pet. 4:7 be sober, and *w'ful* in prayer
Rev. 16:15 I [Jesus] come as a thief. Blessed is he who *w'es*

WATCHFULNESS. An attitude of expectant readiness for the return of Christ that should characterize believers. Jesus told a parable about ten members of a bridal party, half of whom failed to prepare for the delay that occurred in the wedding festivities (Matt. 25:1–13). His message was clear: Be prepared. The second coming of Christ can happen at any moment, and believers should be ready at all times.

WATCHMAN. A guard stationed at a city gate (2 Sam. 18:24). His job was to patrol the streets and call out the hours of the night. The Lord appointed the prophet Ezekiel as a watchman to warn the Jewish exiles in Babylon about the consequences of their sin (Ezek. 3:17–18).

WATCHTOWER. A tall guard station or lookout post that provided early warning of approaching danger. The prophet Isaiah described a watchtower from which a sentinel foresaw the destruction of Babylon (Isa. 21:5–11).

WATER. Vital liquid essential for sustaining life and growing crops. In Israel's dry climate, water was a precious commodity (Ps. 63:1). People depended on wells or cisterns for their water. At a public well, Jesus promised "living water" to a sinful Samaritan woman (John 4:10–14).

WATER[S]

Gen. 1:2 the *w's* moved on the face of the *w's*

Gen. 7:24 the *w's* prevailed on the earth

Gen. 9:11 neither shall all flesh be cut off anymore by the *w's* of a flood

Exod. 7:18 Egyptians shall loathe to drink of the *w* of the river

Exod. 14:22 the *w's* were a wall to them [the Israelites]

Num. 20:11 Moses...struck the rock... And the *w* came out

Josh. 9:27 Joshua made them [Gibeonites]... drawers of *w*

1 Kings 18:38 fire of the LORD fell...and licked up the *w*

Job 5:10 who [God]...sends *w's* on the fields

Ps. 1:3 like a tree planted by the rivers of *w*

Ps. 22:14 I am poured out like *w*...all my bones are out of joint

Ps. 23:2 He [God] leads me beside the still *w's*

Ps. 63:1 flesh longs for You [God] in a...thirsty land where there is no *w*

Ps. 65:9 You [God] visit the earth and *w* it

Ps. 69:14 let me be delivered...out of the deep *w's*

Ps. 119:136 Rivers of *w's* run down my eyes

Prov. 5:15 Drink *w* out of your own cistern

Prov. 25:21 if he [one's enemy] is thirsty, give him *w* to drink

Eccles. 11:1 Throw your bread on the *w's*

Song of Sol. 8:7 Many *w's* cannot quench love

Isa. 11:9 full of the knowledge of the LORD, as the *w's* cover the sea

Isa. 40:12 Who [God] has measured the *w's* in...His hand

Isa. 55:1 Everyone who thirsts, come to the *w's*

Jer. 2:13 abandoned Me [God] the fountain of living *w's*

Jer. 9:1 Oh that my [Jeremiah's] head were *w's*

Ezek. 7:17 all knees shall be weak as *w*

Ezek. 12:18 drink your [Ezekiel's] *w* with trembling

Amos 5:24 let judgment run down like *w's*

Hab. 2:14 filled with...the glory of the Lord, as the *w's* cover the sea

Mark 1:8 I [John the Baptist]...have baptized you with *w*

Luke 8:24 He [Jesus]...rebuked...the raging of the *w*

John 3:5 unless a man is born of *w* and of the Spirit

John 4:14 drinks of the *w* that I [Jesus] shall give him

Acts 1:5 John baptized with *w*, but you shall be baptized with the Holy Spirit

Acts 8:36 here is *w*! What hinders me [Ethiopian eunuch] from being baptized?

1 Cor. 3:7 neither he who...*w's* is anything, but God who gives the increase

Rev. 22:17 whoever desires, let him take the *w* of life freely

WATERS OF MEROM. A body of water in northern Canaan where Joshua and the Israelites fought one of the last battles in their campaign to claim the land of promise (Josh. 11:7). Several Canaanite kings combined their forces into a large army under the command of Jabin. But Joshua seized the initiative and attacked first, and the Israelites were victorious.

WAVE OFFERING. A sacrificial animal presented to God to celebrate restoration of a right relationship with the Lord. The sacrifice was "waved" before the Lord to gain acceptance (Exod. 29:24).

WAX. A substance secreted by bees when making honey. The word is also used figuratively for God's punishment of the wicked (Ps. 68:2).

WAY [S] OF THE LORD
2 Sam. 22:22 I have kept the *w's-o-t-L*

2 Kings 21:22 he [Amon]...did not walk in the *w-o-t-L*

Ps. 18:21 For I have kept the *w's-o-t-L*

Ps. 138:5 they shall sing in the *w's-o-t-L*

Isa. 40:3 voice of him who cries... Prepare the *w-o-t-L*

Jer. 5:4 They are foolish. For they do not know the *w-o-t-L*

Ezek. 33:17 your people say, The *w-o-t-L* is not equal

Hos. 14:9 the *w's-o-t-L* are right...just shall walk in them

Mark 1:3 Prepare the *w-o-t-L*; make His paths straight

Acts 13:10 will you [Elymas] not cease perverting the right *w's-o-t-L*

WAY OF THE SEA. A road which ran from Phoenicia in the north to Egypt in the south, passing through the territory of Israel (Isa. 9:1).

WAYS
Deut. 10:12 what does...God require...to walk in all His *w*

1 Sam. 18:14 David behaved...wisely in all his *w*

2 Chron. 7:14 if my [God's] people...turn from their wicked *w*, then I will hear

Job 34:21 His [God's] eyes are upon the *w* of man

Ps. 25:4 Show me Your *w*, O LORD. Teach me Your paths

Ps. 128:1 Blessed is everyone...who walks in His [God's] *w*

Prov. 3:6 In all your *w* acknowledge Him [God]

Prov. 14:12 but its end are the *w* of death

Prov. 28:18 he who is perverse in his *w* shall fall

Isa. 55:8 nor are your *w* My *w*, says the LORD

Lam. 3:40 Let us search and test our *w*, and return to the LORD

Rom. 11:33 How unsearchable are His [God's] judgments...*w* past finding out

Jas. 1:8 A double-minded man is unstable in all his *w*

WAY, THE. (1) A name that Jesus used for Himself, emphasizing that He was the key to finding God the Father. He was responding to the disciple Thomas, who wanted to know how he and the other disciples could find their way to Jesus after His ascension. Jesus replied: "I am the way, the truth, and the life. No man comes to the Father except through Me" (John 14:6).

(2) A phrase for the Christian movement in its early years. Intended as a criticism, it was embraced with pride by believers (Acts 24:14, 22).

WEAK [ENED]
Deut. 34:7 his [Moses'] eyes were not dim and his strength was not *w'ened*

Ps. 6:2 Have mercy on me, O LORD, for I am *w*

Ps. 102:23 He [God] *w'ened* my strength in the way

Matt. 26:41 the spirit indeed is willing, but the flesh is *w*

Acts 20:35 laboring in this way you ought to support the *w*

1 Cor. 1:27 God has chosen the *w* things of the world to confound the...mighty

1 Cor. 9:22 I [Paul] became *w*, that I might gain the *w*

WEAKNESS [ES]
Ps 77:10 This is my *w*: but I will remember... the Most High

Rom 15:1 We...who are strong ought to bear the *w'es* of the weak

1 Cor. 1:25 the *w* of God is stronger than men

1 Cor. 15:43 It [the body] is sown in *w*; it is raised in power

2 Cor. 12:9 My [Jesus'] strength is made perfect in *w*

2 Cor 12:9 I [Paul] will boast...in my *w'es*

Heb 4:15 high priest [Jesus] who cannot be concerned with...our *w'es*

WEAVING. The skill of making cloth from several raw materials, including wool, camel hair, and flax (Exod. 35:35 • Lev. 13:47). The people of Egypt were highly skilled at weaving, and the Israelites may have perfected this craft while living in that country.

WEDDING. A ceremony in which a man and woman are united in marriage. In Bible times, this was a festive occasion that lasted for several days, with the entire community participating (Matt. 25:6–10 • Luke 12:36; 14:8).

WEDDING

Song of Sol. 3:11 behold King Solomon with the crown...on the day of his *w*

Matt. 22:8 The *w* is ready, but those who were invited were not worthy

John 2:1 there was a *w* in Cana of Galilee

WELL. A source of water reached by a deep hole dug in the ground. Some wells had steps that extended all the way down to the water (Gen. 24:16), while others were furnished with a rope to draw the water to the surface. The prophet Jeremiah spoke of the "great waters that are in Gibeon" (Jer. 41:12). This may refer to a huge well that archaeologists have uncovered at this site. It was 36 feet in diameter and extended 30 feet deep through solid rock. The word is also used figuratively of salvation (Isa. 12:3) and wisdom (Prov. 16:22).

WHEAT. A grain which was ground and baked into bread (1 Kings 5:11). The wheat harvest was observed as a festival and time of celebration (Exod. 34:22).

WHIRLWIND. A destructive wind or violent storm (Job 37:9). The Lord transported the prophet Elijah to heaven by a whirlwind (2 Kings 2:1, 11). A whirlwind often symbolizes sudden destruction (Isa. 17:13) and God's punishment of the wicked (Nah. 1:3).

WICKED [LY, NESS]

Gen. 6:5 GOD saw that the *w'ness* of man was great

Gen. 18:23 Will You [God] also destroy the righteous with the *w*?

Job 4:8 those who...sow *w'ness* reap the same

Job 18:5 Yes, the light of the *w* shall be put out

Job 27:4 my [Job's] lips shall not speak *w'ness*

Ps. 10:2 The *w* in his pride persecutes the poor

Ps. 34:21 Evil shall slay the *w*

Ps. 58:3 The *w* are estranged from the womb

Ps. 71:4 Deliver me, O my God, out from the hand of the *w*

Ps. 84:10 rather be a doorkeeper...than dwell in the tents of *w'ness*

Ps. 94:3 LORD...how long shall the *w* triumph

Ps. 106:6 we have committed iniquity; we have done *w'ly*

Ps. 129:4 He [God] has cut apart the cords of the *w*

Prov. 4:17 they [evil men] eat the bread of *w'ness*

Prov. 15:29 The LORD is far from the *w*

Isa. 53:9 He [God's servant] made His grave with the *w*

Jer. 4:14 O Jerusalem, wash *w'ness* from your heart

Jer. 17:9 The heart is...desperately *w*. Who can know it?

Hos. 10:13 You have plowed *w'ness*...have reaped iniquity

Jon. 1:2 their [Ninevites'] *w'ness* has come up before Me [God]

Matt. 16:4 A *w* and adulterous generation seeks after a sign

Eph. 6:12 we wrestle...against spiritual *w'ness* in high places

Eph. 6:16 able to quench all the fiery darts of the *w*

WICKED ONE. See *Satan*

WICKED ONE

Matt. 13:19 the *w-o* comes and snatches away what was sown

Matt. 13:38 the weeds are the children of the *w-o*

1 John 2:13 because you have overcome the *w-o*

1 John 3:12 Cain...was of that *w-o* and slayed his brother

1 John 5:18 born of God...that *w-o* does not touch him

WIDOW. A woman whose husband had died. In Bible times, widows did not have public assistance or life insurance to fall back on. In the OT, kind treatment of widows was prescribed by Mosaic law (Exod. 22:22). The early church provided support for widows within its fellowship (Acts 6:1–7).

WILDERNESS. A dry, desolate, uncultivated region where little vegetation grew. John the Baptist preached in the Judean wilderness (Matt. 3:1). Jesus was probably in the same region at the beginning of His public ministry when He was tempted by Satan (Luke 4:2).

WILDERNESS WANDERINGS. The aimless course taken by the Israelites in the barren region between Egypt and Canaan after they left Egypt. Lasting forty years, these wanderings were God's punishment for their sin of disobedience (Josh. 5:6). God provided food and guidance through Moses until the people arrived at the edge of Canaan (Exod. 16:35).

WILLING [LY]

Exod. 35:5 Whoever is of a *w* heart, let him bring it as an offering

1 Chron. 28:9 Solomon...serve Him [God] with a perfect heart and with a *w* mind

Neh. 11:2 people blessed all the men who *w'ly* offered...to dwell in Jerusalem

Prov. 31:13 She [virtuous woman]...works *w'ly* with her hands

Lam. 3:33 He [God] does not *w'ly* afflict or grieve the children of men

Mark 2:41 Jesus...said to him [a leper], I am *w*. Be clean

Mark 14:38 The spirit truly is *w*, but the body is weak

Luke 22:28 Father, if You are *w*, remove this cup from Me [Jesus]

Rom. 8:2 the creation was made subject to vanity, not *w'ly*

2 Cor. 5:8 more *w* to be absent from the body and to be present with the Lord

1 Tim. 6:18 be rich in good works, ready to distribute, *w* to share

WILL OF GOD. What the Lord desires for His people. In Jesus' prayer in the garden of Gethsemane, He asked for God's will to be done as He faced the agony of the cross (Luke 22:42). The disciples of Jesus were taught to pray for

God's will to be done on earth as it is in heaven (Matt. 6:10).

WILL OF GOD

Mark 3:35 does the *w-o-G*, the same is My [Jesus'] brother

Rom. 12:2 what is that good and acceptable and perfect *w-o-G*

1 Thes. 4:3 this is the *w-o-G*...abstain from fornication

1 Thes. 5:18 give thanks...this is the *w-o-G* in Christ Jesus

1 John 2:17 he who does the *w-o-G* abides forever

WIND. Movement of the air. The Holy Spirit is often compared to the wind. Jesus told Nicodemus that no one sees the wind, yet everyone feels its effects (John 3:8). This shows how the Holy Spirit works. God's Spirit is not visible, but believers know He works in their hearts to convict them of sin and bring them closer to the Lord. When the Holy Spirit empowered believers on the day of Pentecost, this mysterious, invisible force made a sound "like a mighty rushing wind" (Acts 2:2).

WINE. The fermented juice of grapes (Num. 28:7). Wine was prohibited to Nazarites (Num. 6:3) as well as to priests before they officiated at the altar (Lev. 10:9). Excessive consumption of wine could lead to inappropriate behavior (Prov. 20:1). Used as a medicine, wine apparently could also relieve stress (Prov. 31:6) and ease suffering (Luke 10:34).

WINE

Job 32:19 my [Elihu's] belly is like *w* that has no vent

Prov. 4:17 they [the wicked]...drink the *w* of violence

Prov. 20:1 W is a mocker; strong drink is raging

Isa. 5:22 Woe to those who are mighty to drink *w*

Mark 2:22 no man puts new *w* into old bottles

John 2:3 mother of Jesus said to Him, They have no *w*

Acts 2:13 These men [believers at Pentecost] are full of new *w*

Eph. 5:18 do not be drunk with *w*

1 Tim. 3:8 deacons be grave...not given to much *w*

1 Tim. 5:23 use a little *w* for your [Timothy's] stomach's sake

WINEPRESS. A site where juice was squeezed from grapes in the process of making wine. Usually hewn out of rock, the winepress had an upper vat where the grapes were crushed and a lower vat that received the juice (Judg. 6:11 • Isa. 63:2–3). Crushing grapes in a winepress symbolized God's judgment (Joel 3:13).

WINESKIN. See *Bottle*

WINGS OF GOD. A symbolic expression for God's protection (Ps. 17:8). He is depicted as delivering His people on the wings of eagles (Exod. 19:4). See also *Anthropomorphism.*

WISDOM. The ability to apply knowledge or facts to practical situations (James 3:17). Wisdom is an attribute or characteristic of God's nature. This divine quality is often cited in accounts of the creation of the universe, as in the proverb, "The LORD, by wisdom, has founded the earth; by understanding He has established the heavens" (Prov. 3:19). He not only knew how to create the various parts of the universe; He was also wise enough to fit them all together into a harmonious whole for the benefit of earth's creatures. Wisdom is not something that God hoards for Himself. He wants to share it with humankind, as He did with the prophet Daniel. This wisdom enabled Daniel to interpret a dream of one king of Babylon (Dan. 4:18–27) and the strange writing that appeared on the palace wall of another (Daniel 5:1–28). Even this pagan ruler recognized that the prophet had "understanding and excellent wisdom" (Dan. 5:14). Godly wisdom is a positive witness in an ungodly world.

WISDOM

1 Kings 4:29 God gave Solomon exceedingly great *w*

Job 28:28 Behold, the fear of the Lord—that is *w*

Job 34:35 his [Job's] words were without *w*

Ps. 90:12 number our days...apply our hearts to *w*

Ps. 111:10 fear of the LORD is the beginning of *w*

Prov. 2:2 so that you incline your ear to *w*

Prov. 4:7 *W* is the principal thing. Therefore get *w*

Prov. 10:13 *W* is found on the lips of him who has understanding

Prov. 23:4 Do not labor to be rich; cease from your own *w*

Eccles. 1:18 For in much *w* is much grief

Isa. 11:2 the Spirit of *w* and understanding

Jer. 9:23 Let the wise man not boast in his *w*

Luke 2:52 And Jesus increased in *w* and stature

Acts 6:3 seven men...full of the Holy Spirit and *w*

1 Cor. 1:20 Has not God made foolish the *w* of this world?

1 Cor. 1:22 Jews require a sign, and the Greeks seek after *w*

1 Cor. 3:19 the *w* of this world is foolishness with God

Col. 3:16 Let the word of Christ dwell in you richly in all *w*

Jas. 1:5 If any of you lacks *w*, let him ask of God

WISDOM LITERATURE. A category of literature in the Bible, including Job, Proverbs, Ecclesiastes, and some of the psalms. They are called "wisdom writings" because they deal with some of the most important ethical and philosophical issues of life—the meaning of suffering, the nature and purpose of God, and how to live in harmony with others.

WISE

Ps. 19:7 testimony of the LORD is sure, making *w* the simple

Prov. 3:7 Do not be *w* in your own eyes; fear the LORD

Prov. 6:6 Consider her [the ant's] ways and be *w*

Eccles. 4:13 Better is a poor and a *w* child than an old and foolish king

Isa. 5:21 Woe to those who are *w* in their own eyes

Jer. 9:23 Let the *w* man not boast in his wisdom

Matt. 2:1 when Jesus was born...there came *w* men from the east

Matt. 7:24 a *w* man who built his house on a rock

Matt. 10:16 be *w* as serpents and harmless as doves

Matt. 11:25 You [God] have hidden these things from the *w*

Matt. 25:8 the foolish said to the *w*, Give us some of your oil

Rom. 12:16 Do not be *w* in your own opinions

1 Cor. 1:20 Where is the *w*? Where is the scribe?

1 Cor. 1:26 not many *w* men according to the flesh...are called

WISE MEN. Astrologers from the region of Mesopotamia, often referred to as "magi," who brought gifts to the young child Jesus in Bethlehem (Matt. 2:10–11). Their visit shows that Jesus' birth had worldwide implications. Although born a Jew in Jewish territory, He was worshipped from the very beginning by other nations—represented by these pagan magicians—as one who was destined to become a universal king.

WITCHCRAFT. The practice of sorcery or black magic by witches and wizards—an activity forbidden by God (Deut. 18:10 • Mic. 5:12). King Saul displeased God by asking the witch of Endor to summon the spirit of Samuel from the dead (1 Sam. 28:3–25). See also *Magic*.

WITNESS. A person who testifies about something he has personally seen or experienced. Under Mosaic law, the testimony of at least two persons was required to convict a person of a capital offense (Deut. 17:6). Giving false testimony was strictly prohibited by the Ten Commandments (Exod. 20:16). Believers are empowered to serve as witnesses for Christ (Acts 1:8).

WITNESS [ES]

Exod. 20:16 not bear false *w* against your neighbor

Ps. 35:11 False *w's* rose up

Prov. 19:9 A false *w* shall not be unpunished

Matt. 24:14 gospel...be preached...as a *w* to all nations

Mark 14:56 many bore false *w* against Him [Jesus]

John 1:8 He [John the Baptist]...was sent to bear *w* of that Light [Jesus]

Acts 1:8 and you shall be *w's* to Me [Jesus]

Acts 22:15 you [Paul] shall be His [Jesus'] *w* to all men

Rom. 8:16 The Spirit Himself bears *w* with our spirit

Heb. 12:1 surrounded by such a great cloud of *w's*

WIVES

Matt. 19:8 Moses...allowed you to divorce your *w*

Eph. 5:22 *W*, submit yourselves to your own husbands

Eph. 5:25 Husbands, love your *w* even as Christ... loved the church

Col. 3:18 *W*, submit yourselves to your own husbands

Col. 3:19 Husbands, love your *w* and do not be bitter

1 Tim. 4:7 But refuse profane and old *w'* fables

1 Pet. 3:1 *w*, be in submission to your own husbands

WIZARD. See *Magic*; *Witchcraft*

WOE. An expression of extreme grief or distress (Matt. 24:19). The prophets often used this word to express their dismay over the sins of the nations of Judah (the Southern Kingdom) and Israel (the Northern Kingdom) (Isa. 3:9 • Jer. 10:19).

WOLF. A wild animal that posed a threat to sheep (John 10:12). Jesus used the word figuratively of false prophets who pretended to be sheep but were actually "ravenous wolves" (Matt. 7:15; *ravening wolves*: KJV).

WOMAN AT THE WELL TALKS WITH JESUS. John 4:5–42

WOMB. A bodily cavity in which a woman nurtures a child before birth. Children were called figuratively the "fruit of the womb" and were considered a blessing from the Lord (Ps. 127:3–5).

WONDERS

Ps. 77:14 You are the God who does *w*

WORD

Ps. 96:3 Declare His [God's]...*w* among all people

John 4:48 Unless you see signs and *w*, you will not believe

Acts 2:43 many *w* and signs were done by the apostles

Acts 6:8 Stephen, full of faith and power, did great *w*

WORD [S]

Job 8:2 *w*'s of your [Job's] mouth be like a strong wind

Ps. 12:6 The *w*'s of the LORD are pure *w*'s: as silver tried

Ps. 19:14 Let the *w*'s of my mouth...be acceptable in Your [God's] sight

Ps. 119:11 Your [God's] *w* have I hidden in my heart

Ps. 119:81 I hope in Your [God's] *w*

Ps. 119:105 Your [God's] *w* is a lamp to my feet

Prov. 15:1 but harsh *w*'s stir up anger

Prov. 15:23 a *w* spoken in due season—how good is it

Isa. 40:8 the *w* of our God shall stand forever

Jer. 1:9 I [God] have put My *w*'s in your [Jeremiah's] mouth

Dan. 12:9 Go on your way, Daniel, for the *w*'s are closed up

Mal. 2:17 You have exhausted the LORD with your *w*'s

Matt. 12:36 every idle *w* that men speak, they shall give account of it

Matt. 24:35 My [Jesus'] *w*'s shall not pass away

Luke 1:38 Mary said... May it be to me according to your [Gabriel's] *w*

Luke 4:32 His [Jesus'] *w* was with power

Luke 5:5 at Your [Jesus'] *w* I [Peter] will let down the net

John 1:1 In the beginning was the *W*...the *W* was God

John 6:68 You [Jesus] have the *w*'s of eternal life

John 17:17 Sanctify them...Your [God's] *w* is truth

Acts 8:4 those who were scattered went everywhere preaching the *w*

1 Cor. 2:4 speech and my [Paul's] preaching were not with enticing *w*'s

2 Cor. 5:19 God...committed to us the *w* of reconciliation

Col. 3:17 whatever you do in *w* or deed...all in the name of the Lord Jesus

2 Tim. 2:15 a workman...rightly dividing the *w* of truth

Jas. 1:22 you be doers of the *w* and not hearers only

1 John 3:18 let us not love in *w* or tongue but in deed

WORD OF GOD. God's revelation of Himself to humankind, especially through Jesus and the Bible (Heb. 4:12). The written scriptures, which believers accept as the Word of God, testify to Jesus as the eternal and living Word of God (John 1:1). God's Word has the power to separate truth from falsehood and to discern "the thoughts and intentions of the heart" (Heb. 4:12).

WORD OF GOD

Prov. 30:5 Every *w-o-G* is pure

Luke 4:4 not live by bread alone, but by every *w-o-G*

Luke 5:1 people pressed upon Him [Jesus] to hear the *w-o-G*

Luke 8:21 My [Jesus'] brothers are these who hear the *w-o-G* and do it

Acts 4:31 they were all filled with the Holy Spirit...spoke the *w-o-G*

Rom. 10:17 faith comes by hearing...hearing by the *w-o-G*

Eph. 6:17 the sword of the Spirit, which is the *w-o-G*

Heb. 4:12 the *w-o-G* is living and powerful

Heb. 11:3 the worlds were formed by the *w-o-G*

WORD [S] OF THE LORD

Ps. 33:6 By the *w-o-t-L* the heavens were made

Amos 8:11 not a famine of bread...but of hearing the *w*'s-o-t-L

Acts 19:10 those who dwelled in Asia heard the *w-o-t-L*

1 Pet. 1:25 the *w-o-t-L* endures forever

WORD, THE. A name for Jesus that emphasizes His eternity and His role as co-creator of the universe with God the Father (John 1:1). John's description of Jesus as the Word is an obvious reference to the first words of the book of Genesis in the OT. Just as God was "in the beginning" (Gen. 1:1), so Jesus existed "in the beginning" (John 1:1) as the eternal Word. This Word assumed human form to make His dwelling among people on earth (John 1:14). He is comparable to the words that God used to speak the universe into being (Gen. 1:3).

WORK. Physical or mental activity in a worthwhile cause. Meaningful work was a part of God's plan for humankind from the very beginning. He gave Adam the responsibility of taking care of the garden of Eden and by implication, the physical world (Gen. 2:15). A believer's work should be performed as service to the Lord (Eph. 6:6–8).

WORK [ING, S]

Gen. 2:2 on the seventh day God ended His *w*
Exod. 23:12 Six days you shall do your *w*
Neh. 4:6 For the people had a mind to *w*
Ps. 8:3 consider Your [God's] heavens, the *w* of Your fingers
Ps. 77:12 I will also meditate on all Your [God's] *w*
Ps. 90:17 Yes, establish the *w* of our hands
Ps. 115:4 Their idols are...the *w* of men's hands
Eccles. 12:14 God shall bring every *w* into judgment
John 4:34 My [Jesus'] food is...to finish His [God's] *w*
John 5:17 My [Jesus'] Father is *w'ing*...and I *w*
John 6:29 This is the *w* of God, that you believe on Him [Jesus]
John 9:4 The night comes when no man can *w*
John 17:4 I [Jesus] have finished the *w* that You [God] gave Me
Acts 13:2 Separate Barnabas and Saul for Me for the *w*
Rom. 8:28 we know that all things *w* together for good
Rom. 13:10 Love *w's* no ill to his neighbor
1 Cor. 3:14 If any man's *w*...remains, he shall receive a reward
1 Cor. 12:10 to another the *w'ing* of miracles
Eph. 4:12 perfecting of the saints, for the *w* of the ministry

Phil. 1:6 He [God] who has begun a good *w* in you
Phil. 2:13 God...*w's* in you...to do of His good pleasure
1 Tim. 3:1 office of a bishop, he desires a good *w*
Heb. 13:21 *w'ing* in you what is well pleasing in His [God's] sight

WORKERS

Ps. 6:8 Depart from me, all you *w* of iniquity
1 Cor. 12:29 Are all teachers? Are all *w* of miracles?
Phil. 3:2 Beware of dogs, beware of evil *w*

WORKS OF BELIEVERS. See *Good Works*

WORKS OF GOD. God's mighty acts on behalf of His people (Deut. 3:24). Throughout the Bible, believers are encouraged to praise the Lord for all his awesome deeds. Praise should be offered particularly for the wonders of the natural world (Ps. 104:24–25), His provision for human needs (Ps. 107:8–9), His teachings (Ps. 119:27), His mercy (Ps. 5:7), and His redemptive acts (Ps. 31:5).

WORK [S] OF GOD

Exod. 32:16 And the tablets were the *w-o-G*
Ps. 64:9 all men...shall declare the *w-o-G*
Ps. 66:5 Come and see the *w's-o-G*
Ps. 78:7 not forget the *w's-o-G*, but keep His commandments
Eccles. 7:13 Consider the *w-o-G*
Eccles. 8:17 then I beheld all the *w-o-G*
John 6:28 that we might work the *w's-o-G*
Acts 2:11 hear them speaking...the wonderful *w's-o-G*

WORK [S] OF THE LORD

Ps. 77:11 I will remember the *w's-o-t-L*...Your wonders
Ps. 118:17 I shall...declare the *w's-o-t-L*
Jer. 48:10 Cursed is he who does the *w-o-t-L* deceitfully
Jer. 51:10 declare in Zion the *w-o-t-L* our God
1 Cor. 15:58 be steadfast, immovable, always abounding in the *w-o-t-L*

WORKS

1 Chron. 16:9 tell of all His [God's] wondrous *w*

WORMWOOD

1 Chron. 16:24 Declare His [God's] glory...marvelous *w* among all nations

Job 37:14 Stand still and consider the wondrous *w* of God

Ps. 33:4 all His [God's] *w* are done in truth

Ps. 40:5 Many, O LORD my God, are Your wonderful *w*

Ps. 92:5 O LORD, how great are Your *w*

Ps. 143:5 I meditate on all Your [God's] *w*

Ps. 145:9 His [God's] tender mercies are over all His *w*

Matt. 5:16 see your good *w*, and glorify your Father

Matt. 13:58 He [Jesus] did not many mighty *w* there [Nazareth]

John 6:28 that we might work the *w* of God

John 9:3 the *w* of God should be revealed in Him [Jesus]

John 14:12 greater *w* than these shall he do

Gal. 2:16 a man is justified not by the *w* of the law

Eph. 2:9 Not of *w*, lest any man should boast

2 Tim. 3:17 That the man of God may be perfect... furnished for all good *w*

Titus 3:5 Not by *w* of righteousness that we have done

Jas. 2:17 faith, if it does not have *w*, is dead, being alone

Rev. 3:8 I [Jesus] know your [church at Philadelphia's] *w*

WORMWOOD. A plant noted for its bitter taste. The prophet Jeremiah cited this plant as a symbol of God's approaching judgment against the nation of Judah (the Southern Kingdom) (Jer. 9:15).

WORRY [ING]

Matt. 6:27 Which of you by *w'ing* can add one cubit to his stature?

Matt. 6:34 don't *w* about tomorrow, for tomorrow shall *w* about its own

Matt. 10:19 they deliver you [disciples] up, do not *w*...what you shall speak

WORSHIP. Praise and adoration of God expressed both publicly and privately (1 Chron. 16:29). The term comes from an old English

word *worthship*, referring to someone or something that deserves devotion or commitment. Only the one supreme God of the universe is worthy of worship. The elements of authentic worship include praise (Ps 113:3), thanksgiving (Phil. 4:6), and confession of sin (1 John 1:9).

WORSHIP [PED, S]

Ps. 95:6 *w* and bow down...before the LORD our Maker

Ps. 99:5 *w* at His [God's] footstool; for He is holy

Jer. 25:6 do not go after other gods...to *w* them

Dan. 3:6 whoever does not fall down and *w* shall be cast...into...fiery furnace

Dan. 3:18 we [Daniel's three friends] will not...*w* the golden statue

Matt. 2:2 we [the wise men]...have come to *w* Him [Jesus]

John 4:24 those who worship...must *w* Him [God] in spirit and in truth

Acts 17:23 whom you *w* ignorantly, I [Paul] declare Him [God] to you

Acts 17:25 Nor is He [God] *w'ped* with men's hands

Rom. 1:25 who [ungodly people]...*w'ped*...the creature more than the Creator

Rev. 7:11 all the angels...fell before the throne on their faces and *w'ped* God

WORSHIP THE LORD

1 Chron. 16:29 *W-t-L* in the beauty of holiness

Ps. 29:2 *W-t-L* in the beauty of holiness

Ps. 96:9 O *w-t-L* in the beauty of holiness

Luke 4:8 *w-t-L* your God, and you shall serve Him only

WRATH

Exod. 32:11 why does Your [God's] *w* grow hot

Job 5:2 For *w* kills the foolish man

Ps. 21:9 The LORD shall swallow them up in His *w*

Ps. 90:7 by Your [God's] *w* we are troubled

Prov. 14:29 He who is slow to *w* has great understanding

Matt. 3:7 Who has warned you [Pharisee] to flee from the *w*

Rom. 5:9 we shall be saved from *w* through Him [Jesus]

Eph. 4:26 Don't let the sun go down on your *w*

Eph. 6:4 fathers, do not provoke your children to *w*

Rev. 6:17 the great day of His [God's] *w* has come

WRATH OF GOD. God's reaction against sin that is designed to lead people to repent and renew their commitment to Him. In the OT, His indignation was often directed against the Israelites when they slipped into worship of false gods (Jer. 44:8). In the NT, the wrath of God is often connected with His future judgment. For example, the apostle Paul spoke of a day of wrath to come that would condemn unbelievers. But believers would be delivered from this judgment of the Lord (Eph. 2:2–5).

The Bible is clear that all people are sinners, and thus fully deserving of God's judgment against sin (Rom. 3:23). But the gospel's good news is that believers are delivered from His wrath through faith in Jesus and His atoning death (Rom. 3:24–25).

WRATH OF GOD

Ps. 78:31 the *w-o-G*...slew the fattest of them

John 3:36 does not believe the Son...*w-o-G* remains on him

Rom. 1:18 w-o-G is revealed...against all ungodliness

Rev. 16:1 pour out the vials of the *w-o-G* on the earth

XERXES. See *Ahasuerus*

YAHWEH. The rendering in the Hebrew language of one of the major names for God in the OT. A form of the Hebrew verb "to be," it emphasizes God's eternity. This word is translated as "Lord" in most English Bibles, and printed in what is called capital and small capital letters: Lord.

YEAR OF JUBILEE. See *Jubilee*

YEAST. See *Leaven*

YIELD [ED, ING]

Gen. 1:11 earth bring forth grass, the herb *y'ing* seed

Num. 17:8 rod of Aaron...had budded...*y'ed* almonds

Ps. 67:6 Then shall the earth *y* her increase

Rom. 6:13 but *y* yourselves to God

Rev. 22:2 the tree of life...*y'ed* its fruit every month

YOKE. A wooden harness worn by draft animals and attached to agricultural tools (Jer. 31:18). The word was also used to indicate

oppression or servitude (1 Kings 12:4–14). To Jesus, a yoke symbolized commitment to Him, but He declared that it was not heavy or burdensome (Matt. 11:29–30).

YOKE

Lev. 26:13 I [God] have broken the bands of your [Israel's] *y* and made you walk upright

Deut. 28:48 He [God] shall put a *y* of iron on your neck

1 Kings 19:19 Elisha...was plowing with twelve *y* of oxen

2 Chron. 10:14 My [Rehoboam's] father made your *y* heavy

Jer. 28:2 I [God] have broken the *y* of the king of Babylon

Matt. 11:30 My [Jesus'] *y* is easy and My burden is light

Gal. 5:1 do not be entangled again with the *y* of bondage

YOUTH

1 Sam. 17:33 you [David] are only a *y*, and he [Goliath]...a man of war

Ps. 25:7 Do not remember the sins of my *y*

Ps. 71:17 O God, You have taught me from my *y*

Prov. 5:18 rejoice with the wife of your *y*

Eccles. 12:1 Remember now your Creator in the days of your *y*

Matt. 19:20 All these things I have kept from my *y*

1 Tim. 4:12 Do not let any man despise your *y*

ZABAD. One of David's "mighty men," an elite group of warriors noted for their bravery in battle (1 Chron. 11:41).

ZABULON. KJV: see *Zebulun*

ZACCHAEUS. A chief tax collector from the city of Jericho who is known for his life-changing encounter with Jesus. Zacchaeus promised to repay the people he had cheated four times more than what he had taken. He also vowed to give half of what he owned to the poor. Jesus welcomed Zacchaeus into God's kingdom (Luke 19:1–10).

ZACCUR. A man who helped rebuild the walls of Jerusalem after the Exile (Neh. 3:2).

ZACHARIAH. KJV: see *Zechariah*, No. 1

ZACHARIAS. KJV: see *Zechariah*, No. 3

ZADOK. (1) A high priest during King David's administration. He fled from Jerusalem with the king when David's son Absalom tried to seize the throne (2 Sam. 15:23–25). Later, during the king's final days, David instructed Zadok and the prophet Nathan to anoint his son Solomon as his successor (1 Kings 1:7–8, 32–45).

(2) A man who helped rebuild the walls of Jerusalem after the Exile (Neh. 3:4).

ZAIN. Seventh letter of the Hebrew alphabet, used as a heading over Psalm 119:49–56. In the Hebrew language, the first line of each of these eight verses begins with this letter.

ZALMON. One of David's "mighty men," an elite group of warriors known for their bravery in battle (2 Sam. 23:28).

ZAMZUMMIM. A race of giants who lived in the region later occupied by the Ammonites (Deut. 2:20–21). *Zamzummims*: KJV.

ZAPHNATH-PAANEAH. The Hebrew form of the Egyptian name given to Joseph when he was promoted to a high position in the pharaoh's court (Gen. 41:45).

ZAREPHATH. A city in Phoenicia where the prophet Elijah lodged with a widow (1 Kings 17:9–10). When Elijah came to her house, she and her son were on the verge of starvation. But she fed the prophet from the meager ingredients she had left. God blessed her generosity by replenishing this supply so that it never ran out (1 Kings 17:16). Zarephath is also mentioned in Obad. 20 • Luke 4:26 (*Sarepta*: KJV).

ZEAL. Fervent desire and determination (Phil. 3:6). The prophet Isaiah predicted the "zeal of the LORD" would establish the Messiah's kingdom (Isa. 9:7).

ZEAL

Ps. 69:9 the *z* of Your house has eaten Me up

John 2:17 was written, The *z* for Your house has eaten Me up

Phil. 3:6 Concerning *z*, persecuting the church

ZEALOT, THE. A nickname for Simon, one of Jesus' twelve disciples—a different Simon than the better-known Simon Peter. A zealot was a member of a political-religious party whose aim was to overthrow Roman rule and put the Israelites back in power. Simon may have been a member of this party or sympathetic with its views (Luke 6:15; *Zelotes*: KJV).

ZEALOUS

Acts 21:20 Jews...who believe...are all *z* of the law

Acts 22:3 I [Paul]...was *z* toward God, as you all are

Titus 2:14 purify to Himself [God] a special people, *z* of good works

ZEBADIAH. An officer in David's army who commanded a large unit of warriors (1 Chron. 27:7).

ZEBAH. A Midianite king killed by Gideon's army (Judg. 8:4–21).

ZEBEDEE. A Galilean fisherman and father of James and John, two of Jesus' disciples (Matt. 4:21–22). He is also mentioned in Matt. 10:2; 20:20; 26:37; 27:56 • Mark 1:19–20; 3:17; 10:35 • Luke 5:10 • John 21:2.

ZEBOIIM. A city destroyed along with Sodom and Gomorrah because of its sin (Gen. 10:19; 14:2, 8 • **Deut.** 29:23 • Hos. 11:8). See also *Cities of the Plain.*

ZEBULUN. (1) A son of Jacob and Leah (Gen. 30:19–20). He is also mentioned in Gen. 35:23; 46:14; 49:13 • Exod. 1:3 • 1 Chron. 2:1.

(2) Descendants of Zebulun's three sons who developed into one of the twelve tribes of Israel (Gen. 46:14; Num. 26:26–27). This tribe settled in the fertile hill country of Galilee (Josh. 19:10–16). It is also mentioned in Matt. 4:13.

ZECHARIAH. (1) Son and successor of Jeroboam II as king of Israel (the Northern Kingdom). Zechariah ruled only a few months before being assassinated and succeeded by Shallum (2 Kings 14:29; 15:8–12; *Zachariah*: KJV).

(2) A prophet who delivered his messages to the people of Judah (the Southern Kingdom) after they returned from the Exile. His prophecies appear in the OT book that bears his name (Zech. 1:1).

(3) A godly priest and the father of John the Baptist. Zechariah was stricken speechless for his reluctance to believe a son would be born to him in his old age (Luke 1:5–22). After John was born, his speech of returned. In a beautiful song known as the Benedictus, he praised the Lord for sending this son who would prepare the way for the coming Messiah (Luke 1:67–79). *Zacharias*: KJV

ZECHARIAH, BOOK OF. A prophetic book of the OT written to encourage the people of Judah (the Southern Kingdom) during the difficult years back in their homeland following the Exile. Zechariah encouraged the people to complete the task of rebuilding the temple in Jerusalem. He also presented God's promises for the future, including the coming of the Messiah (Zech. 9:9–10:12), the restoration of the Jewish nation (Zech. 10:1–12), and the universal reign of God (Zech. 14:1–14). Perhaps the most famous passage from the book is Zechariah's prediction that the future Messiah would enter the city of Jerusalem "riding on a donkey, and on a colt, the foal of a donkey" (Zech. 9:9). Matthew quoted this verse in his Gospel to show that Jesus fulfilled Zechariah's prophecy in His triumphal entry into the Holy City (Matt. 21:5).

ZEDEKIAH. (1) A false prophet condemned by the prophet Jeremiah (Jer. 29:21).

(2) The last king of Judah who was renamed and placed on the throne as a puppet ruler by King Nebuchadnezzar of Babylon (2 Kings 24:15–20). His original name was Mattaniah (2 Kings 24:17). Ignoring the prophet Jeremiah's advice, Zedekiah rebelled against the Babylonians. When the Babylonian army attacked Jerusalem, he fled the city, only to be blinded and taken away in chains after seeing his sons put to death (2 Kings 25:6–7). Zedekiah is also mentioned in 2 Kings 25:2–7 • 1 Chron. 3:15 • 2 Chron. 36:10–11 • **Jer.** 21–52.

ZEEB. A Midianite prince killed by the Israelites under the judge Gideon (Judg. 7:25).

ZELA. A town not far from Jerusalem where King Saul and his son Jonathan were buried in the territory of Benjamin, Saul's ancestral home (2 Sam. 21:14). *Zelah*: KJV.

ZELEK. One of David's "mighty men," an elite group of warriors known for their bravery in battle (2 Sam. 23:37).

ZELOPHEHAD. A member of the tribe of Manasseh who died in the wilderness during the Exodus from Egypt. Since he had no male heirs, his five daughters petitioned Moses for the right to inherit his future property in the land of Canaan. Their request was granted on the condition that they not marry outside their ancestral tribe (Num. 26:33; 27:1–8).

ZELOTES. KJV: see *Zealot, The*

ZENAS. A Christian missionary whom Paul asked Titus to bring while the apostle was spending the winter at Nicopolis (Titus 3:12–13).

ZEPHANIAH. A priest and friend of the prophet Jeremiah and author of the OT book which bears his name. Zephaniah often served as a messenger between Jeremiah and King Zedekiah of Judah (the Southern Kingdom) (Jer. 21:1–2). After Jerusalem fell, Zephaniah was killed by the Babylonians (Jer. 52:24–27). He is also mentioned in 2 Kings 25:18 • Jer. 29:25, 29; 37:3.

ZEPHANIAH, BOOK OF. A short prophetic book of the OT known for its vivid portrayal of the certainty of God's judgment against the nation of Judah (the Southern Kingdom) for its sin and idolatry. Zephaniah's prophecies were fulfilled when the nation was overrun by the Babylonian army several years after he issued his warning. Even as the Lord was punishing His people and sending them into exile, the prophet declared, God would preserve a remnant that would remain faithful to Him (Zeph. 3:17–20). These would eventually inherit the promise God made to Abraham hundreds of years before (Gen. 12:1–5). People of all nations would gather in Jerusalem to worship the Lord when the remnant of Judah returned to their homeland. The King of kings, the Messiah would rule among them (Zeph. 3:14–20).

ZERUBBABEL. Leader of a group of returned exiles who faced the difficult task of rebuilding the temple in Jerusalem (Ezra 2:1–2). This building had been in ruins since its destruction by the Babylonians several decades before. Enemies of the Israelites opposed the rebuilding effort and even succeeded in getting it stopped for several years (Ezra 4:1–24). With prodding from two OT prophets (Hag. 2:1–3; Zech. 4:6–10), Zerubbabel finally completed the task (Ezra 6:14–15). This building is often referred to as "Zerubbabel's Temple." It was not as ornate as the original structure built by King Solomon several centuries before. Zerubbabel also helped

restore religious practices among his people (Ezra 6:14–22). He apparently was appointed governor of Judah (Hag. 2:21) by King Cyrus of Persia. Also called *Sheshbazzar* (Ezra 5:14).

ZIBA. A former servant of King Saul who helped David locate Jonathan's son Mephibosheth. He became Mephibosheth's servant on the land restored by the king (2 Sam. 9:2–11).

ZIDON. KJV: see *Sidon*

ZIGGURAT. A tall tower built in successive stages like a pyramid with a shrine for pagan worship on the top level. This type of structure was common among the ancient Babylonians and Assyrians. The tower of Babel was probably a ziggurat (Gen. 11:1–9). See also *Babel, Tower of.*

ZIKLAG. A city in southern Israel where David hid from King Saul and began to pull together a unit of brave warriors and other supporters (1 Chron. 12:1). These loyal soldiers and friends helped him transition to the kingship after Saul passed from the scene. At Ziklag, David showed that he was a person of godly character as well as an effective leader. When a party of Amalekites raided Ziklag and carried off all the women and children, David sought the Lord's will before he acted. After the captives were rescued, David insisted that the spoils of war should be shared with everyone—even those who couldn't finish the campaign because they were exhausted (1 Sam. 30:22–25). This reflected David's solid character and generous spirit.

ZILPAH. A servant of Jacob's wife Leah who became his concubine and bore two of his twelve sons, Gad and Asher (Gen. 30:9–13).

ZIMRI. A chariot commander under King Elah of Israel (the Northern Kingdom) who killed the king and seized the throne. After reigning only seven days, he committed suicide when threatened with retaliation from Omri, commander of Elah's army (1 Kings 16:8–18).

ZIN. A desert near the Dead Sea through which the Israelites passed during the Exodus from Egypt. Moses' sister Miriam died and was buried here (Num. 20:1). Zin is also mentioned in Num. 13:21; 27:14; 33:36; 34:3–4 • Deut. 32:51 • Josh. 15:1–3.

ZION. (1) One of the hills on which the city of Jerusalem was built. This hill was the site of an ancient fortified city of the Jebusites before it was captured by King David (2 Sam. 5:6–9). In Solomon's time this section of Jerusalem was extended to include the temple area. Sometimes all of Jerusalem is referred to as "Zion" (Ps. 132:13). It is also mentioned in Pss. 48:2, 11–12; 102:13–21; 137:1, 3; 149:2 • Lam. 2:1–18 • Rev. 14:1.

(2) A word used figuratively of the nation of Israel as the people of God (Heb. 12:22).

ZIPH. A wilderness region in southern Israel where David hid from King Saul (1 Sam. 23:14–18).

ZIPPORAH. A Midianite woman who became the wife of Moses and mother of his sons Gershom and Eliezer (Exod. 2:21–22; 4:25; 18:2).

ZOAR. A city near the Dead Sea to which Lot and his family fled when other cities of the area, including Sodom and Gomorrah, were destroyed (Gen. 19:22–23, 30). It is also mentioned in Deut. 34:3 • Isa. 15:5 • Jer. 48:34. *Bela*: Gen. 14:2.

ZOBA. KJV: see *Zobah*

ZOBAH. A Syrian kingdom that warred against King Saul (1 Sam. 14:47 • 2 Sam. 10:6, 8. *Hamath-zobah*: 2 Chron. 8:3).

ZOPHAR. One of Job's friends or "comforters" (Job 2:11). His speeches appear in Job 11:1–20; 20:1–29.

ZORAH. A defense city built by King Rehoboam of Judah (the Southern Kingdom), Solomon's son and successor (2 Chron. 11:5, 10).

ZOROBABEL. KJV: see *Zerubbabel*

ZUPH. A district near Jerusalem where Saul, the future king of Israel, first met the prophet Samuel (1 Sam. 9:5–14).

NOTES

NOTES

NOTES

NOTES

NOTES

NOTES

NOTES

NOTES

NOTES